IARIA

SECURWARE 2017

The Eleventh International Conference on Emerging Security Information, Systems and Technologies

September 10 - 14, 2017

Rome, Italy

SECURWARE 2017 Editors

Carla Merkle Westphall, Federal University of Santa Catarina, Brazil
Hans-Joachim Hof, Technical University of Ingolstadt, Germany
Aspen Olmsted, College of Charleston, USA
Stefan Schauer, Scientist, Austrian Institute of Technology, Center of Digital Safety and Security, Vienna, Austria
Martin Latzenhofer, Scientist, Austrian Institute of Technology, Center of Digital Safety and Security, Vienna, Austria
Aysajan Abidin, KU Leuven, Belgium
George Yee, Carleton University & Aptusinnova Inc., Ottawa, Canada

Printed from e-media with permission by:

Curran Associates, Inc.
57 Morehouse Lane
Red Hook, NY 12571

Some format issues inherent in the e-media version may also appear in this print version.

Printed by Curran Associates, Inc. (2017)

International Academy, Research, and Industry Association (IARIA)
412 Derby Way
Wilmington, DE 19810

Phone: (408) 893-6407
Fax: (408) 527-6351

petre@iaria.org

Additional copies of this publication are available from:

Curran Associates, Inc.
57 Morehouse Lane
Red Hook, NY 12571 USA
Phone: 845-758-0400
Fax: 845-758-2633
Email: curran@proceedings.com
Web: www.proceedings.com

Table of Contents

SECURWARE 2017

Forward

The Eleventh International Conference on Emerging Security Information, Systems and Technologies (SECURWARE 2017), held between September 10-14, 2017 in Rome, Italy, was an event covering related topics on theory and practice on security, cryptography, secure protocols, trust, privacy, confidentiality, vulnerability, intrusion detection and other areas related to low enforcement, security data mining, malware models, etc.

Security, defined for ensuring protected communication among terminals and user applications across public and private networks, is the core for guaranteeing confidentiality, privacy, and data protection. Security affects business and individuals, raises the business risk, and requires a corporate and individual culture. In the open business space offered by Internet, it is a need to improve defenses against hackers, disgruntled employees, and commercial rivals. There is a required balance between the effort and resources spent on security versus security achievements. Some vulnerability can be addressed using the rule of 80:20, meaning 80% of the vulnerabilities can be addressed for 20% of the costs. Other technical aspects are related to the communication speed versus complex and time consuming cryptography/security mechanisms and protocols.

Digital Ecosystem is defined as an open decentralized information infrastructure where different networked agents, such as enterprises (especially SMEs), intermediate actors, public bodies and end users, cooperate and compete enabling the creation of new complex structures. In digital ecosystems, the actors, their products and services can be seen as different organisms and species that are able to evolve and adapt dynamically to changing market conditions.

Digital Ecosystems lie at the intersection between different disciplines and fields: industry, business, social sciences, biology, and cutting edge ICT and its application driven research. They are supported by several underlying technologies such as semantic web and ontology-based knowledge sharing, self-organizing intelligent agents, peer-to-peer overlay networks, web services-based information platforms, and recommender systems.

To enable safe digital ecosystem functioning, security and trust mechanisms become essential components across all the technological layers. The aim was to bring together multidisciplinary research that ranges from technical aspects to socio-economic models.

The conference had the following tracks:

- Information security
- Advances and challenges
- Security management
- Secure software development
- Security frameworks, architectures and protocols
- Critical Infrastructure Protection – Novel Concepts and Technologies
- Risk and security

- Security for Automotive Cyber Systems
- Security-as-a-Service
- Malware and Anti-malware
- Emerging Solutions for Continuous Authentication
- Smart home security

We take here the opportunity to warmly thank all the members of the SECURWARE 2017 technical program committee, as well as all the reviewers. The creation of such a high quality conference program would not have been possible without their involvement. We also kindly thank all the authors that dedicated much of their time and effort to contribute to SECURWARE 2017. We truly believe that, thanks to all these efforts, the final conference program consisted of top quality contributions.

We also gratefully thank the members of the SECURWARE 2017 organizing committee for their help in handling the logistics and for their work that made this professional meeting a success.

We hope that SECURWARE 2017 was a successful international forum for the exchange of ideas and results between academia and industry and to promote further progress in the field of emerging security information, systems and technologies. We also hope that Rome, Italy provided a pleasant environment during the conference and everyone found some time to enjoy the historic charm of the city.

SECURWARE 2017 Chairs

SECURWARE Steering Committee

Yuichi Sei, The University of Electro-Communications, Japan
Carla Merkle Westphall, Federal University of Santa Catarina, Brazil
Hans-Joachim Hof, Technical University of Ingolstadt, Germany
Eric Renault, Institut Mines-Télécom - Télécom SudParis, France
Steffen Wendzel, Worms University of Applied Sciences, Germany
Aspen Olmsted, College of Charleston, USA
Calin Vladeanu, University Politehnica of Bucharest, Romania
Geir M. Køien, University of Agder, Norway
George Yee, Carleton University & Aptusinnova Inc., Ottawa, Canada
Sokratis K. Katsikas, Norwegian University of Science & Technology (NTNU), Norway
Hector Marco Gisbert, University of the West of Scotland, United Kingdom

SECURWARE Research/Industry Chairs

Rainer Falk, Siemens AG, Germany
Mariusz Jakubowski, Microsoft Research, USA
Malek ben Salem, Accenture Labs, USA
Jiqiang Lu, Institute for Infocomm Research, Singapore
Heiko Roßnagel, Fraunhofer IAO, Germany

Scott Trent, Tokyo Software Development Laboratory - IBM, Japan
Robert Forster, Edgemount Solutions S.à r.l., Luxembourg
Peter Kieseberg, SBA Research, Austria
Tzachy Reinman, Cisco, Israel

SECURWARE 2017
Committee

SECURWARE Steering Committee

Yuichi Sei, The University of Electro-Communications, Japan
Carla Merkle Westphall, Federal University of Santa Catarina, Brazil
Hans-Joachim Hof, Technical University of Ingolstadt, Germany
Eric Renault, Institut Mines-Télécom - Télécom SudParis, France
Steffen Wendzel, Worms University of Applied Sciences, Germany
Aspen Olmsted, College of Charleston, USA
Calin Vladeanu, University Politehnica of Bucharest, Romania
Geir M. Køien, University of Agder, Norway
George Yee, Carleton University & Aptusinnova Inc., Ottawa, Canada
Sokratis K. Katsikas, Norwegian University of Science & Technology (NTNU), Norway
Hector Marco Gisbert, University of the West of Scotland, United Kingdom

SECURWARE Research/Industry Chairs

Rainer Falk, Siemens AG, Germany
Mariusz Jakubowski, Microsoft Research, USA
Malek ben Salem, Accenture Labs, USA
Jiqiang Lu, Institute for Infocomm Research, Singapore
Heiko Roßnagel, Fraunhofer IAO, Germany
Scott Trent, Tokyo Software Development Laboratory - IBM, Japan
Robert Forster, Edgemount Solutions S.à r.l., Luxembourg
Peter Kieseberg, SBA Research, Austria
Tzachy Reinman, Cisco, Israel

SECURWARE 2017 Technical Program Committee

Nabil Abdoun, Université de Nantes, France
Aysajan Abidin, KU Leuven | COSIC and imec, Belgium
Habtamu Abie, Norwegian Computing Centre, Norway
Afrand Agah, West Chester University of Pennsylvania, USA
Yatharth Agarwal, Phillips Academy, Andover, USA
Rose-Mharie Åhlfeldt, University of Skövde, Sweden
Jose M. Alcaraz Calero, University of the West of Scotland, UK
Firkhan Ali Bin Hamid Ali, Universiti Tun Hussein Onn Malaysia, Malaysia
Basel Alomair, University of Washington-Seattle, USA / King Abdulaziz City for Science and Technology (KACST), Saudi Arabia
Louise Axon, University of Oxford, UK
Ilija Basicevic, University of Novi Sad, Serbia

Julian Murguia, Omega Krypto, Uruguay
Syed Naqvi, Birmingham City University, UK
Mehrdad Nojoumian, Florida Atlantic University, USA
David Nuñez, University of Malaga, Spain
Jason R. C. Nurse, University of Oxford, UK
Aspen Olmsted, College of Charleston, USA
Carlos Enrique Palau Salvador, Universidad Politecnica de Valencia, Spain
Brajendra Panda, University of Arkansas, USA
Zeeshan Pervez, University of the West of Scotland, UK
Nikolaos Pitropakis, University of Piraeus, Greece
Mila Dalla Preda, University of Verona, Italy
Walter Priesnitz Filho, Federal University of Santa Maria, Rio Grande do Sul, Brazil
Khandaker A. Rahman, Saginaw Valley State University, USA
Silvio Ranise, Fondazione Bruno Kessler, Trento, Italy
Kasper Rasmussen, University of Oxford, UK
Danda B. Rawat, Howard University, USA
Tzachy Reinman, Cisco, Israel
Eric Renault, Institut Mines-Télécom - Télécom SudParis, France
Leon Reznik, Rochester Institute of Technology, USA
Martin Ring, University of Applied Sciences Karlsruhe, Germany
Ricardo J. Rodríguez, University of Zaragoza, Spain
Juha Röning, University of Oulu, Finland
Heiko Roßnagel, Fraunhofer IAO, Germany
Antonio Ruiz Martínez, University of Murcia, Spain
Abdel-Badeeh M. Salem, Ain Shams University, Cairo, Egypt
Simona Samardjiska, Faculty of Computer Science and Engineering, Skopje, Macedonia
Rodrigo Sanches Miani, Universidade Federal de Uberlândia, Brazil
Luis Enrique Sánchez Crespo, University of Castilla-la Mancha & Sicaman Nuevas Tecnologias, Spain
Anderson Santana de Oliveira, SAP Labs, France
Vito Santarcangelo, University of Catania, Italy
Stefan Schauer, AIT Austrian Institute of Technology GmbH - Vienna, Austria
Sebastian Schinzel, Münster University of Applied Sciences, Germany
Yuichi Sei, The University of Electro-Communications, Japan
Kun Sun, George Mason University, USA
Chamseddine Talhi, École de technologie supérieure, Montréal, Canada
Li Tan, Washington State University, USA
Enrico Thomae, Operational Services GmbH, Germany
Tony Thomas, Indian Institute of Information Technology and Management - Kerala, India
Scott Trent, Tokyo Software Development Laboratory - IBM, Japan
Alberto Tuzzi, iInformatica S.r.l.s., Trapani, Italy
Luis Unzueta, Vicomtech-IK4, Spain
Alastair Janse van Rensburg, University of Oxford, UK
Emmanouil Vasilomanolakis, Technische Universität Darmstadt, Germany

Copyright Information

A Novel Central Arbiter to Mitigate Denial of Service Attacks on Duplicate Address Detection in IPv6 Networks

Shailendra S.Tomar, Anil Rawat
Computer Division
Raja Ramanna Centre for Advanced Technology
Indore, Madhya Pradesh, India
e-mail: tomar@rrcat.gov.in, rawat@rrcat.gov.in

Prakash D. Vyavahare
Dept. of Electronics & Telecommunication Eng.
Shri G.S.Institute of Technology & Science
Indore, Madhya Pradesh, India
e-mail:prakash.vyavahare@gmail.com

Sanjiv Tokekar
Department of Electronics & Telecommunication Engineering, Institute of Engineering & Technology,
Devi AhilyaVishwa Vidyalaya
Indore, Madhya Pradesh, India
email: stokekar@ietdavv.edu.in

***Abstract*—A node joining any Internet Protocol version 6 (IPv6) network is susceptible to Denial of Service (DoS) attack in the Duplicate Address Detection (DAD) phase of the IP address assignment process. A lot of research work is being carried out to mitigate this form of DoS attack. However, available approaches require changes in the Neighbor Discovery Protocol (NDP) and/or lead to increased computational and configuration overheads/complexity on each client. In this paper, we present a central arbiter approach to detect and mitigate DoS attacks on DAD in Software Defined Network (SDN) controlled wired IPv6 networks. Advantages of this approach over other approaches are its simplicity and zero modification requirements to the NDP. The proposed approach has been simulated on a Mininet emulator configured for SDN using RYU controller and is observed to achieve the desired results. The effectiveness of the proposed scheme in handling DAD DoS attacks is also presented in the paper. The results show that this scheme introduces a delay of the order of 0.34 seconds in the DAD process which is a good trade-off for providing DoS attack protection.**

Keywords - IPv6; DAD; DoS Attack; Central Arbiter Approach; SDN; NDP.

I. INTRODUCTION

IPv6 [1] networks use NDP [2] with State-Less Address Auto-Configuration (SLAAC) [3] feature for zero configuration. NDP has many known vulnerabilities [4], which may be exploited to perform DoS attacks on network nodes. One of them is the DAD vulnerability, which can be exploited to perform DoS attacks during the address initialization phase of a node. The Hackers Choice (THC) toolkit [5] provides simple tools to perform such attacks. Various solutions to mitigate this problem have been proposed by researchers. The best known and accepted approach to mitigate NDP related attacks is provided by the Secure Neighbor Discovery (SeND) protocol [6] [7]. However, the lack of mature implementations of the SeND protocol, and the computational and configuration complexities involved in the approach makes it less practical in the real world. Other approaches like Simple Secure Addressing Scheme (SSAS) [8], Trust-ND [9], and Secure-DAD [10] have also been proposed in the literature, but all of them have the same drawbacks. All of these approaches require modifications in the NDP messages. Hence, they require changes in the NDP implementation in various Operating Systems (OS). Network access control (IEEE 802.1x) based solutions have also evolved for mitigating layer-2 related attacks. But the complexity involved in configurations of intermediate switches and end nodes, have led researchers to think of alternate solutions.

SDN [11] [12] technology has matured in recent years. The programmable controller in SDN can be utilized to view and control the flow of NDP packets in a network. The controller can, thus, become an arbiter settling DAD disputes without requiring changes in the NDP messages and hence, no changes and complex configurations are needed in the client OS. This is the basis for the motivation of the present work.

In this paper, a central arbiter approach to mitigate DoS attacks on DAD is proposed. The central arbiter acts as a big brother and NDP related Internet Control Message Protocol version 6 (ICMPv6) messages flow controller. It sends DAD replies on behalf of genuine nodes only, thus blocking the replies of rogue nodes. The proposed solution has been tested using the Mininet network emulation software configured for SDN using RYU [13] controller. The results show that DAD attacks can be mitigated without making modifications to the NDP. This approach has an added advantage of zero computation and configuration overheads on the client side, which is a major drawback in other approaches.

The rest of this paper is organized as follows. Section II is the study of literature and the technology background section. Section III presents the review of already reported approaches. Section IV presents the hypothesis for the research work. Section V describes the methodology of the proposed approach in detail. Section VI describes the methods, tools and techniques used to implement and test the proposed approach. Section VII is the results section. The conclusions and future works section is at the end of the article in Section VIII.

II. STUDY OF LITERATURE

IPv6 security issues have been studied by a number of researchers [14][15]. One Hop Security or First Hop Security are common terms used to refer to NDP related security in IPv6 networks. NDP vulnerabilities are well known and many researchers demonstrated it to be easily exploitable [16]-[19]. DAD implementation in NDP is also vulnerable to DoS attacks and is easily exploitable [20]-[22] .

DAD ensures uniqueness of the IPv6 address in the network. According to the specification, DAD in IPv6 networks works during the IP address assignment phase only, if the following two conditions are satisfied:

- A node which is the genuine owner of an IP address must also listen to the Solicited Node Multicast Address (FF02::1:FFXX:YYZZ) of its corresponding unicast IP address and respond to queries, whenever requested, for DAD. Here, XXYYZZ are the last 24 bits of the unicast IPv6 address.
- The DAD reply, in the form of Neighbor Advertisement (NA) packet, to the all node multicast group (FF02::1) must be sent by the node in possession of the duplicate IP address.

IP address assignment of a node in an IPv6 network is complete after the following steps are successfully completed:

- IP Address Generation: A node generates an IP address for itself by using any one of the following techniques: Static random, Extended Unique Identifier (EUI) formatted, Cryptographically Generated Address (CGA) and Hashed.
- DAD: The node attempting to connect to the network, sends a DAD request in the form of Neighbor Solicitation (NS) request to the solicited node multicast address of the corresponding unicast address and if no reply (NA) is received within a specified timeout period, then it assigns that address to itself.

DoS attack on the DAD vulnerability works as follows: Rogue nodes in the network falsely claim to possess any IP address requested by any new node, which is attempting to join the network or may claim all IP addresses of the network prefix. This causes DoS attack on all new nodes that are attempting to connect to the network. Thereafter, no new node can connect to the network, if this situation persists. The characteristics of possible forms of DoS attacks on the DAD can be categorized as follows:

a) **Reactive:** In a reactive attack, the attacker listens to the DAD requests and gets to know the target IP address being assigned to the new node. It then reacts to such requests and sends DAD replies, thereby forcing DAD failure.

b) **Guessing:** In this case, the attacker does not know the target IP address. It only guesses the target address as to be in a particular pattern as predicted from IP addresses of other nodes. It then sends DAD replies for next in pattern target IP addresses.

c) **Flooding:** In this type of attack, the attacker floods the network with DAD replies claiming all IPv6 addresses related to a network prefix.

Research work has been carried out to mitigate all types of NDP attacks. The root cause of the problem has been identified as lack of adequate security measures in NDP message exchanges in the IPv6 network. Hence, the entire research work focuses on a) incorporating some authentication mechanism in message exchanges and b) securing the exchange of NDP messages by encrypting them. All this adds to computational and configuration complexity to the client nodes and requires changes in the NDP. Computational complexity in the client nodes is introduced in the form of additional computation required for encrypting and decrypting NDP packets. Configuration complexity is introduced in the client nodes in the form of loading of additional OS patches and their configuration for the network.

Network access control based approaches for one hop security solutions in intelligent network switches, like the 802.1x [23] and IP-MAC binding, address the DAD related DoS attack problem by registering, rate limiting and blocking rogue nodes. The configuration complexity, in the form of additional configurations of (Internet Protocol – Media Access Control) IP-MAC binding, setting rate limits at the switch level and loading and configuring necessary software agent at the client level involved in the process, makes these approaches less popular and are rarely used. Hence, there is a need for an alternative and simpler solution.

SDN is emerging as a promising network architecture. It is worthwhile to explore the possibility of detecting and mitigating NDP related attacks in SDN. SDN controller can be programmed to become a central arbiter for NDP traffic flow. In this paper, we are focusing on making the SDN controller to act as a central arbiter for only the DAD related NDP traffic.

III. ONE HOP SECURITY IN IPv6

One hop security in IPv6 networks can be divided into two main categories. In the first category, researchers secure NDP messages by using cryptographic techniques. In the second category, researchers try to control the access to the network and thereby, minimize/check the flow of NDP messages from rogue devices into the network. This section describes the features and limitations of these mechanisms in brief.

SeND uses CGA and certificate distribution framework to securely transmit NDP messages. Although SeND is able to prevent DAD related attacks, it is observed that [8] [9]

SeND has a drawback like high computation to generate the options, especially the CGA option and Rivest, Shamir, and Adelman (RSA) signature. Thus, it requires higher computation time. SeND mechanism adds significant processing time, of the order of 300-400 milliseconds, to perform the message verification [9]. Hence, the usage of SeND adds to delay and increased complexity during the DAD process, as highlighted by researchers [7]. These delays are unacceptable for some real-time mobile applications. Further, DoS attacks can also be performed on SeND [7].

SSAS [8] was proposed as an improved version of the SeND mechanism. SSAS introduces alternative addressing scheme by employing Elliptic Curve Cryptography (ECC) algorithm as compared to RSA which is used by SeND mechanism for address configuration. Although SSAS has reduced complexity and decreased message processing time as compared to SeND mechanism, this method depends on signature and key exchanges. Hence, the time complexity issue still exists [9]. Based on research conducted by Praptodiyono et al. in 2015 [9], SSAS mechanism takes 223.1 milliseconds to generate an interface identifier, which is still a substantial amount of processing time.

Another research work, proposed as Trust-ND [9], is a lightweight mechanism for the DAD process. The main approach of this mechanism is to reduce the processing time of ND messages during the DAD process, as compared to the SeND and SSAS. In Trust-ND message, authentication is done by employing Secure Hash Algorithm 1 (SHA-1) operation as message integrity check. Researchers [24] [25] have shown that SHA-1 and Message Digest 5 (MD5) hash functions are susceptible to hash collision attacks.

Yet another research work proposed as Secure-DAD [10] states to use Message Authentication Code using Universal hashing (UMAC) for hashing and authentication of the messages. It is argued that UMAC is a more efficient algorithm and more secure algorithm than SHA-1/MD5 [26] [27]. Their work is similar to that of Trust-ND but with a different hashing algorithm. This approach also suggests to make changes to the original NDP message exchanges.

Another research work [28] proposes a novel duplicate address detection with a hash function. It exchanges hash values of the IPv6 addresses between all the nodes. Only the node owning the real IPv6 address can generate the equivalent hash and thus, claim to be the real owner of the address. This work also requires modification to the NDP protocol.

An SDN based authentication mechanism for securing neighbor discovery protocol in IPv6 is proposed in [29]. It basically provides a solution to counter IP spoofing attacks in IPv6 networks using the SDN architecture. It utilizes a table on the controller to learn MAC addresses and binds them to ports, thus ensuring MAC spoofing protection from other network ports.

Recent research work [30] proposes to address the one hop security concerns from ground up, by using the Trusted Platform Module (TPM) for ensuring trusted endpoints on the network. The required restrictions on clients, to be TPM enabled for ensuring one hop security, makes this solution less practical in real world.

IV. Hypothesis

In this section, we state the hypothesis on which our approach is based. We also discuss the mechanism which we have used to prove our hypothesis.

Assume a central arbiter which acts as a gateway for all IPv6 related NDP traffic, especially DAD requests (NS) and DAD replies (NA). We know that every DAD process is initiated by a DAD request in the form of a NS packet from a new node. If all DAD requests are blocked by the central arbiter then no other node will get DAD requests, from which it can extract the target IP address to attack. Thus, rogue nodes cannot generate DAD replies. The central arbiter can selectively generate DAD replies on behalf of the genuine target node which is definitely present in the network. Thus, the DAD process can be completed securely without changing the NDP message formats and without configuration of the intermediate devices, if some alternate mechanism to search "already in use IP addresses" for the network is present.

Thus, our hypothesis states that "*using a central arbiter approach, the security of the DAD process can be successfully accomplished without:*

a) change in the NDP message structures,
b) change in client configurations,
c) additional computational overheads at clients,
d) additions in network access control configurations in intermediate switches".

This hypothesis can be tested using the emerging SDN technology. The SDN managed network must be configured with a modified controller as per our approach. The hypothesis for providing a solution to the DoS attack on DAD process can be tested if the following conditions are met:

1) SDN controller must have a global view of all nodes connected to the network. It should also be able to intercept all NDP traffic related to the network.

2) The controller must be enabled as a central arbiter for analyzing all DAD requests (NS).

3) The controller should be able to fabricate DAD replies for duplicate requests and dispatch them to the node from where DAD request was received.

4) The SDN controller should be able to distinguish between genuine nodes and rogue nodes with respect to DAD processing based on the following:

- Searching a persistent table called "IP_MAC_Port_Time" table which contains the list of all nodes and the IP addresses presently assigned on the network.

The management of the IP_MAC_Port_Time table is done as follows:

- The table gets populated on the attachment of every node to the network followed by its subsequent IP address assignment.
- The table entries are pruned after the expiry of the configured IP address lifetime for the network or if a reply to heartbeat packet is not received within a specified time.
- Static IP address assignments can be manually inserted into the table with an infinite lifetime. These can be manually pruned by the administrator to reflect topology changes.
- Limits on the number of entries on per port basis should be implemented to counter table flooding attacks.

V. PROPOSED SOLUTION

This section describes the proposed mechanism. It describes the workflow and explains the design of various modules of the proposed solution.

A. *Workflow*

Figure 1 depicts the workflow of the proposed approach. All NDP related ICMPv6 packets are fed into the SDN controller which is configured with central arbiter module. This allows the controller to learn all IP MAC Data Path Identifier (DPID) Port associations that are existing in the network. The Collector sub-module is responsible for populating the IP_MAC_PORT_Time table which is a table with IP, MAC address, DPID, Port Number and timestamp fields, as shown in Table I. DPID is the identifier of the switch connected in the network. Other fields are self-explanatory. Only DAD request packets are fed into the Verification sub-module.

The Verification sub-module extracts the target IP from the NDP packet and searches for the target IP. If the target IP is found in the IP_MAC_Port_Time table, then the DADReplyGenerator sub-module is invoked. The DADReplyGenerator sub-module fabricates a DAD reply based on the DAD Request packet and then dispatches the DAD reply to the corresponding switch port of node from where the DAD request has originated. If the target IP search fails, then no DAD reply packet is sent by the controller and DAD request packet is blocked at the controller level itself. A node, thus, completes the IP address assignment process.

TABLE I. IP_MAC_PORT_TIME TABLE FIELDS

IP	MAC	DPID	Port	Time stamp

Figure 2 depicts the logic for deleting entries from the table used in the central arbiter. The Prune_IP_MAC_PORT_TIME sub-module extracts the target IP from a new DAD request, and checks whether the IP address exists. If so, it generates an ICMPv6 ECHO REQUEST packet and dispatches it to the switch port with which the IP is associated. If the ECHO REPLY is not received within a time period, then the associated IP entry is deleted from the table. The entries in the table are also deleted on expiry of the IP lifetime for the network, which can be defined by the administrator.

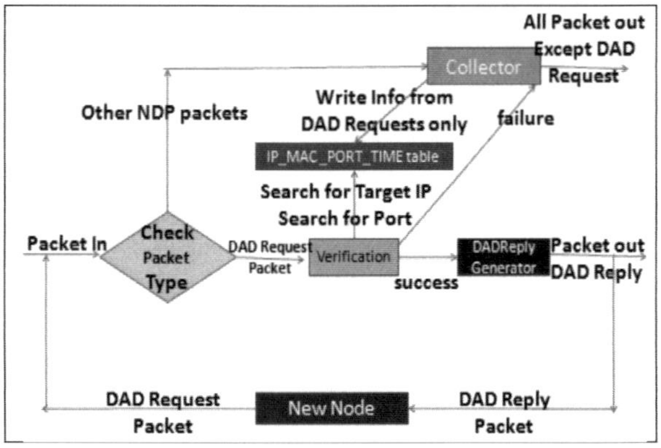

Figure 1. Workflow inside the Central Arbiter enabled SDN controller

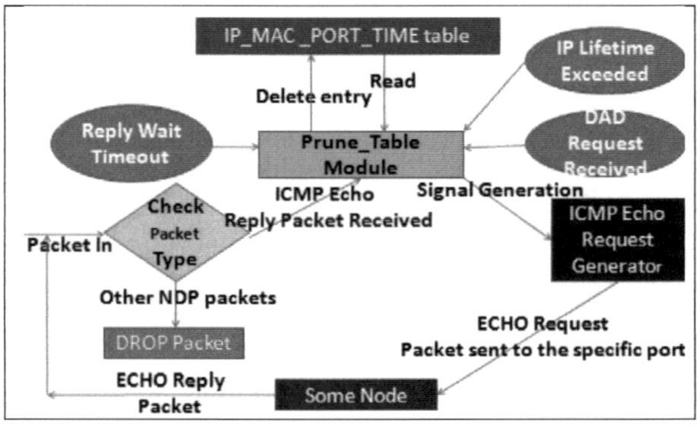

Figure 2. Pruning logic for the IP_MAC_PORT_TIME table

B. *Modules*

The proposed solution consists of four modules, which are as follows:

i) Collector Module

The collector module is designed to read all ICMPv6 packets. It populates the IP_MAC_PORT_TIME table on new DAD requests only. A limit is also imposed on the number of MAC addresses and IP addresses that can be associated with one switch port. Every new IP address to the port association, which does not exceed the allowed per port level MAC and IP limits is inserted in this table. The input to the module is the DAD request packet. The module connects to a database and inserts new entries into the table. The table will be populated just after a DAD request is received and it is verified that no such IP address is present in the network, as well as the switch port, and it does not exceed the maximum IP/MAC address associations. The module can also make permanent entries with value zero (0) in the timestamp field. This is required for static IP addresses. This table is made persistent across reboots.

ii) Verification Module

The verification module receives all DAD request packets. It then parses the packet and extracts the target IP of the packet. Then, it searches for that IP in the IP_MAC_PORT_TIME table. If an entry for the target IP is present in the table, then success is reported by the module, otherwise failure is reported. In the case of success, the packet is passed on to the DADReplyGenerator module for further action. In the case of failure, the packet is passed on to the collector module.

iii) DAD Reply Generator Module

This module is responsible for fabricating a DAD reply packet. The input to the module is the DAD request packet. The target IP and the switch DPID, along with the port number, are extracted from the packet by the module. The controller fabricates a Neighbor Advertisement (NA) packet on behalf of the node which owns the target IP. This fabricated DAD reply is then dispatched to the node on the switch port from where the DAD request was received.

iv) Prune_IP_MAC_PORT_TIME table module

This module is responsible for pruning the table entries after a configured time (one day as per RFC 4941) has elapsed and/or the node with an IP-MAC-PORT association in the table is no longer active. The state of a node is confirmed at the time when a new DAD REQUEST packet is received for an existing IP address in the table. The state is confirmed by sending a heartbeat packet to the port on which the IP address was last associated and upon reception of ICMP ECHO REPLY packet. The timestamps of the entries for IPv6 addresses from which a reply is received within a specified period are updated. If the entry is older than a configured time, then it is pruned. The table can also be pruned manually by the administrator.

VI. TEST SETUP

A laptop with a single Intel core i5-4200U processor (1.6 GHz), 8 GB RAM and 200 GB free hard disk space has been used as the physical machine for the simulation setup. Oracle Virtualbox version 5.1.22 has been used as virtual machine manager to load two Virtual Machines (VM) on the laptop. The test setup is based on Mininet emulator version 2.2.1, SDN RYU controller version 4.13, THC toolkit version 3.2 and Wireshark version 1.10.6. The freely available "simple_switch_13.py" python application of the RYU controller has been extended with the proposed central arbiter module.

The Mininet emulator and SDN RYU controller are run on two different virtual machines. Both the virtual machines use one core of the processor (1.6 GHz), 1 GB RAM and 16GB of storage. The Mininet emulator VM and the RYU controller VM are on the same network.

The network topology is as depicted in Figure 3. The Mininet topology consists of two OpenFlow version 1.3 compatible Openvswitch virtual switches. Each switch is further connected to three nodes. The topology is a flat network with no routing node since we want to test DAD behavior only. One of the hosts, h3, is configured to act as a rogue node generating DAD DoS traffic. This node is capable of performing all three types of DAD DoS attacks, as mentioned in Section II. The response of the central arbiter configured SDN controller, to all three types of attacks was observed separately in three different test cases. In the first test case, this rogue node is used for generating DAD NA replies for every DAD NS request that is generated by new nodes joining the network, thus performing reactive attacks. In the second test case, the node h3 was programmed to perform guessing attacks by generating DAD NA replies for random IPv6 addresses. The guess is done using the information about earlier assigned addresses on the network. In the third test case, h3 was programmed to generate DAD DoS flooding attack by claiming all IPv6 addresses for the network prefix.

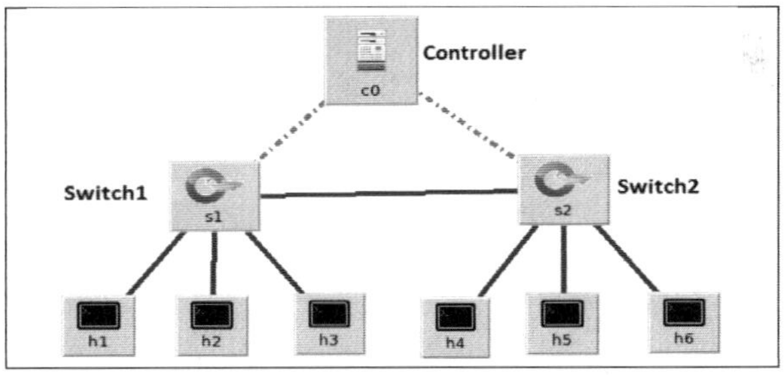

Figure 3. Topology of the test setup with 6 nodes

VII. RESULTS

A) Effectiveness of central arbiter approach in handling DAD DoS attacks:

In the test setup, firstly, we performed a test by disabling the central arbiter module in the SDN RYU controller, for which the RYU controller with the unmodified "*simple_switch_13.py*" script was invoked. For achieving this "*ryu-manager ryu/ryu/app/simple_switch_13.py*" command is executed on the VM configured as controller. On the attacker host, named h3, the command "*dos-new-ip6 h3-eth0*" which is available in the THC toolkit is executed. The output of the command is as shown in Figure 4.

Figure 4: Screenshot of launch of DAD Denial of Service attack in h3

This command configures host h3 to generate DAD NA (ICMPv6 Type 136) reply packets for every DAD NS (ICMPv6 Type 135) request packet received on the network. Next, the addition of a new node is simulated by manual assignment of a new IPv6 address to the host named h6, using the "*ifconfig h6-eth0 inet6 add fec0::6/64*" command. It was observed that the host named h3 which is configured as the attacker, received the multicasted DAD NS packet and responded by spoofing the DAD NA reply packet, claiming to be the owner of requested IPv6 address. The screenshot of the output, as generated on the attacker host h3, is shown in Figure 5.

```
root@mininet-vm:~/thc-ipv6-master# ./dos-new-ip6 h3-eth0
Started ICMP6 DAD Denial-of-Service (Press Control-C to end) ...
Spoofed packet for existing ip6 as fec0::6
```

Figure 5: Screenshot showing the spoofed packet log on h3

This was further confirmed by executing the "ip addr sh" command on host h6. The output containing the highlighted "tentative dadfailed" line on host h6 is shown in Figure 6.

```
root@mininet-vm:~/mininet/examples# ifconfig h6-eth0 inet6 add fec0::6/64
root@mininet-vm:~/mininet/examples# ip addr sh
1: lo: <LOOPBACK,UP,LOWER_UP> mtu 65536 qdisc noqueue state UNKNOWN group defaul
t
    link/loopback 00:00:00:00:00:00 brd 00:00:00:00:00:00
    inet 127.0.0.1/8 scope host lo
       valid_lft forever preferred_lft forever
    inet6 ::1/128 scope host
       valid_lft forever preferred_lft forever
2: h6-eth0: <BROADCAST,MULTICAST,UP,LOWER_UP> mtu 1500 qdisc pfifo_fast state UP
 group default qlen 1000
    link/ether 0a:67:6a:da:93:a6 brd ff:ff:ff:ff:ff:ff
    inet 10.0.0.6/8 brd 10.255.255.255 scope global h6-eth0
       valid_lft forever preferred_lft forever
    inet6 fec0::6/64 scope site tentative dadfailed
       valid_lft forever preferred_lft forever
    inet6 fe80::867:6aff:feda:93a6/64 scope link
       valid_lft forever preferred_lft forever
root@mininet-vm:~/mininet/examples#
```

Figure 6. Screenshot of commands and output generated in h6 while testing non duplicate IPv6 address assignment with central arbiter module disabled on the controller and attacker active in h3

Next, we performed the IP address assignment by disconnecting the attacker node. In case of an unused IPv6 address assignment and in the absence of the attacker host named h3, the host named h6 could complete the IPv6 address assignment process and get connected to the network as expected. It is shown in Figure 7.

```
root@mininet-vm:~/mininet/examples# ifconfig h6-eth0 inet6 add fec0::6/64
root@mininet-vm:~/mininet/examples# ip addr sh
1: lo: <LOOPBACK,UP,LOWER_UP> mtu 65536 qdisc noqueue state UNKNOWN group defaul
t
    link/loopback 00:00:00:00:00:00 brd 00:00:00:00:00:00
    inet 127.0.0.1/8 scope host lo
       valid_lft forever preferred_lft forever
    inet6 ::1/128 scope host
       valid_lft forever preferred_lft forever
2: h6-eth0: <BROADCAST,MULTICAST,UP,LOWER_UP> mtu 1500 qdisc pfifo_fast state UP
 group default qlen 1000
    link/ether a2:f2:c1:00:89:76 brd ff:ff:ff:ff:ff:ff
    inet 10.0.0.6/8 brd 10.255.255.255 scope global h6-eth0
       valid_lft forever preferred_lft forever
    inet6 fec0::6/64 scope site
       valid_lft forever preferred_lft forever
    inet6 fe80::a0f2:c1ff:fe00:8976/64 scope link
       valid_lft forever preferred_lft forever
root@mininet-vm:~/mininet/examples#
```

Figure 7. Screenshot of commands and output generated in h6 while testing non duplicate IPv6 address assignment with central arbiter module disabled on the controller and in the absence of the attacker

After this, we enabled the attacker host h3 and the central arbiter module in the controller. Then, we assigned an IPv6 address to the host named h6 using the "*ifconfig h6-eth0 inet6 add fec0::6/64*" command. This time the attacker host h3 did not receive the DAD NS request packet and hence could not perform DAD DoS attack. Thus, this address assignment was successful. The combined screenshots of host h3 showing active attacker in h3 and results of the IP address assignment and displaying commands in host h6 are shown in Figure 8. This shows that the central arbiter module in the controller effectively blocked the DAD related NS packets from reaching other hosts of the network. This is further confirmed by checking the log messages on the controller enabled with central arbiter module. The screenshot on the controller is as shown in Figure 9.

```
root@mininet-vm:~/thc-ipv6-master# ./dos-new-ip6 h3-eth0
Started ICMP6 DAD Denial-of-Service (Press Control-C to end) ...

"Host: h6"
root@mininet-vm:~/mininet/examples# ifconfig h6-eth0 inet6 add fec0::6/64
root@mininet-vm:~/mininet/examples# ip addr sh
1: lo: <LOOPBACK,UP,LOWER_UP> mtu 65536 qdisc noqueue state UNKNOWN group defaul
t
    link/loopback 00:00:00:00:00:00 brd 00:00:00:00:00:00
    inet 127.0.0.1/8 scope host lo
       valid_lft forever preferred_lft forever
    inet6 ::1/128 scope host
       valid_lft forever preferred_lft forever
2: h6-eth0: <BROADCAST,MULTICAST,UP,LOWER_UP> mtu 1500 qdisc pfifo_fast state UP
 group default qlen 1000
    link/ether 6e:02:a8:95:52:b5 brd ff:ff:ff:ff:ff:ff
    inet 10.0.0.6/8 brd 10.255.255.255 scope global h6-eth0
       valid_lft forever preferred_lft forever
    inet6 fec0::6/64 scope site
       valid_lft forever preferred_lft forever
```

Figure 8. Screenshot of commands and output generated in h3 and h6 while testing non duplicate IPv6 address assignment with central arbiter module enabled on the controller and attacker active in h3

```
DAD Request to Solicited Node Multicast address
Src IP ::
Dst IP ff02::1:ff00:6
In Port 3
Target fec0::6
nd_neighbor(dst='fec0::6',option=None,res=0)
fec0::6
Opened database successfully
4098 3
Opened database successfully
Count of IP matches = 0
Entry Count for Port = 1
```

Figure 9. Screenshot displaying log information on the controller while testing non duplicate IPv6 address assignment with central arbiter module enabled on the controller and attacker active in h3

Finally, to check whether the central arbiter correctly sends DAD replies in case of true duplicate addresses on the network, the IPv6 address of host h6 was duplicated by manually assigning the address to host named h1 using the "*ifconfig h1-eth0 inet6 add fec0::6/64*" command.

Figure 10. Screenshot displaying dadfailed message on h1 while testing duplicate IPv6 address assignment with central arbiter module enabled on the controller and attacker active in h3

It was observed that in this case, the central arbiter module correctly identified the duplicate IPv6 address and sent the NDP DAD NA reply to host h1, as shown in Figure 11. This caused the IP address assignment process to end without permanent IP address assignment on node h1, as shown in Figure 10.

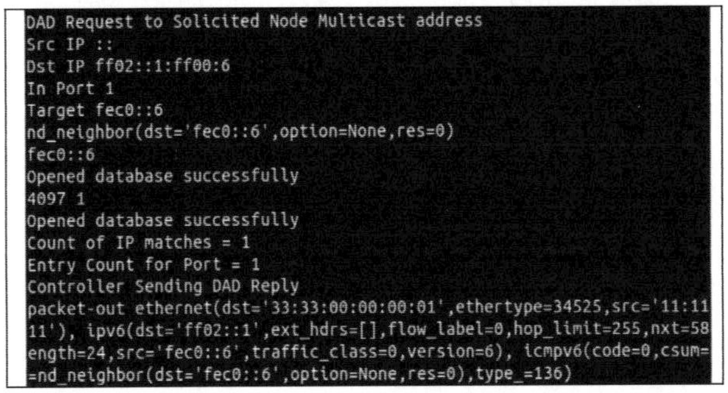

Figure 11. Screenshot displaying log information on the controller while testing duplicate IPv6 address assignment with central arbiter module enabled on the controller and attacker active in h3

It is verified that the Central Arbiter approach presented in the paper is able to effectively detect and mitigate DoS attacks on DAD in IPv6 networks. The design goals of not introducing any change in NDP, and not increasing client configuration and computation complexity in the proposed solution, are fully met as explained in Table II.

TABLE II. CENTRAL ARBITER EFFECTIVENESS

Type of DoS Attack on DAD	Additional Client Configuration Complexity for protection	Additional Client Computation Complexity for protection	Results with Logic in Central Arbiter providing protection
Reactive	None	None	**PROTECTED** All DAD Requests were blocked by central arbiter from reaching other nodes and DAD replies were sent by central arbiter only for already in use IPv6 address.
Guessing	None	None	**PROTECTED** The maximum limits defined on Per Switch Port IP and MAC address associations did not permit more than the allowed number of IPv6 address requests from a node attached to a switch port.
Flooding	None	None	**PROTECTED** The maximum limits defined on Per Switch Port IP and MAC address associations did not permit more than the allowed number of IPv6 address requests from a node attached to a switch port.

B) *DAD process timing comparison with and without central arbiter module:*

DAD timing tests were performed in the network with the topology as shown in Figure 3. The time taken to complete DAD process was observed in 5 cases that are mentioned in Table III.

TABLE III. DAD PROCESS TIMING COMPARISON

S.No.	Time taken in DAD process With Central Arbiter (sec)	Time taken in DAD process Without Central Arbiter (sec)	Delay introduced by central arbiter scheme (sec)
1.	0.888826	0.14075	0.748076
2.	0.939575	0.593365	0.34621
3.	1.018122	0.67268	0.345442
4.	0.474215	0.311938	0.1662277
5.	0.655199	0.54579	0.109409

The results indicate that, on an average, a delay of about 0.34 seconds is introduced in the central arbiter scheme. This is because data processing and searching on sqlite database (used for persistent storage of all IPv6 addresses currently in use on the network) is involved in the process.

VIII. CONCLUSIONS & FUTURE WORK

In any IP network, IP address assignment is the first step that needs to be completed before a node can start communicating with other nodes. Duplicate Address Detection phase in IPv6 address assignment step needs to be completed for successful assignment of an IPv6 address. IPv6 uses NDP control messages for updating and checking the status of the network. NDP security vulnerabilities lead to security loopholes in the network. All existing mechanisms are complex to implement.

IPv6 networks can be controlled efficiently by central arbitration of NDP messages. The central arbiter approach to mitigate DoS attacks on DAD in IPv6 networks is proposed in this paper. It achieves the desired goal by intelligently filtering DAD requests and corresponding replies. The simulation results have shown that the DAD process can be completed with additional delay of the order of 0.34 seconds, using the approach presented in this paper. This approach has been demonstrated to work in Software Defined Networks.

The management (purging/updating of stale entries) of IP_MAC_PORT_TIME table, introduced in the presented approach is critical for the functioning of the central arbiter.

The central arbiter approach presented in the paper may seem to introduce single point of failure by having dependency on a SDN controller for controlling the DoS attacks. With Active-Active failover mode of operation of SDN controllers becoming popular, this concern can be addressed effectively. Further, since no changes in the NDP messages are suggested in this approach, the failure of a SDN controller will only lead to a network without DAD DoS protection and the network will continue to work under the usual threat of DAD DoS attacks.

The scalability of the proposed approach depends on the maximum permissible size of the IP_MAC_PORT_TIME table in the SDN controller, which in turn will be governed by the amount of the primary memory availability in the controller. With the usage of fast data insertion and search algorithms, the proposed solution can scale to work in the largest of the IPv6 networks with 2^64 nodes. Since, practically such large networks are not foreseen in near future, it can safely be assumed that the proposed approach will scale to work in all practical IPv6 networks.

Further, the work presented here programs SDN controller as a central arbiter in such a way that it can emphatically and proactively confirm whether an IP address is already in use in that network without completing the DAD process, which involves timeout. This concept can be further extended to achieve fast IP address assignments by making minor changes in the NDP. The reduction of DAD timeout is a major requirement of fast handovers in mobile networks. Further, the heartbeat mechanism presented in the paper for the management of this table can be improved.

REFERENCES

[1] S. Deering, and R. Hinden, "Internet Protocol, Version 6 (IPv6) Specification", RFC 2460, DOI 10.17487/RFC2460, December 1998, [retrieved: July, 2017].

[2] T. Narten, E. Nordmark, E, W. Simpson, and H. Soliman, "Neighbor Discovery for IP version 6 (IPv6)", RFC 4861, DOI 10.17487/RFC4861, September 2007, [retrieved: July, 2017].

[3] S. Thomson, T. Narten, and T. Jinmei, "IPv6 Stateless Address Autoconfiguration", RFC 4862, DOI 10.17487/RFC4862, September 2007, [retrieved: July, 2017].

[4] P. Nikander, J. Kempf, and E. Nordmark, "IPv6 Neighbor Discovery (ND) Trust Models and Threats," Internet rfc 3756 edn. 2004, [retrieved: July, 2017].

[5] THC-IPv6, https://www.thc.org/thc-ipv6/, [retrieved: July, 2017]

[6] J. Arkko, J. Kempf, B. Zill, and P. Nikander, "Secure Neighbor Discover (SEND)," Internet rfc 3971 edn. 2005, [retrieved: July, 2017].

[7] A. AlSa'deh, and C. Meinel, "Secure neighbor discovery: Review, challenges, perspectives, and recommendations". Security & Privacy, IEEE, 10(4), 26-34, 2012.

[8] H. Rafiee and C. Meinel, "SSAS: A simple secure addressing scheme for IPv6 autoconfiguration," 2013 Eleventh Annual Conference on Privacy, Security and Trust, Tarragona, 2013, pp. 275-282.doi: 10.1109/PST.2013.6596063.

[9] S. Praptodiyono, R. K. Murugesan, I. H. Hasbullah, C. Y. Wey, M. M. Kadhum and A. Osman, "Security mechanism for IPv6 stateless address autoconfiguration," 2015 International Conference on Automation, Cognitive Science, Optics, Micro Electro-Mechanical System, and Information Technology (ICACOMIT), Bandung, 2015, pp. 31-36.

[10] S. U. Rehman and S. Manickam, "Improved Mechanism to Prevent Denial of Service Attack in IPv6 Duplicate Address Detection Process" International Journal of Advanced Computer Science and Applications(IJACSA), 8(2), 2017.

[11] E. Haleplidis, K. Pentikousis, S. Denazis, H. Salim, J. Meyer, and O. Koufopavlou, "Software-Defined Networking (SDN): Layers and Architecture Terminology", RFC 7426, DOI 10.17487/RFC7426, January 2015, [retrieved: July, 2017].

[12] M. Jammal, T. Singh, A. Shami, R. Asal, and Y. Li, "Software defined networking: state of the art and research challenges," Computer Networks, vol. 72, pp. 74–98, 2014.

[13] RYU, https://osrg.github.io/ryu/, [retrieved: July, 2017].

[14] V. Nicolls, N. A. Le-Khac, L. Chen and M. Scanlon, "IPv6 security and forensics," *2016 Sixth International Conference on Innovative Computing Technology (INTECH)*, Dublin, 2016, pp. 743-748.

[15] R. Radhakrishnan, M. Jamil, S. Mehfuz and M. Moinuddin, "Security issues in IPv6," *Networking and Services, 2007. ICNS. Third International Conference on*, Athens, 2007, pp. 110-110.

[16] A. S. Ahmed, R. Hassan and N. E. Othman, "Improving security for IPv6 neighbor discovery," 2015 International Conference on Electrical Engineering and Informatics (ICEEI), Denpasar, pp. 271-274, 2015.

[17] R. Hassan, A. S. Ahmed, and N. E. Osman, "Enhancing security for ipv6 neighbor discovery protocol using cryptography". American Journal of Applied Sciences, 11(9), 1472-1479, 2014.

[18] F. Xiaorong, L. Jun, and J. Shizhun, "Security analysis for IPv6 neighbor discovery protocol," in Proceedings of the 2nd International Symposium on Instrumentation and Measurement (IMSNA '13), pp. 303–307, Toronto, Canada, December 2013.

[19] A. S. Ahmed, R. Hassan and N. E. Othman, "Improving security for IPv6 neighbor discovery," 2015 International Conference on Electrical Engineering and Informatics (ICEEI), Denpasar, pp. 271-274, 2015.

[20] S. U. Rehman and S. Manickam, "Significance of Duplicate Address Detection Mechanism in Ipv6 and its Security Issues:A Survey," Indian Journal of Science and Technology, vol. 8(30), 2015.

[21] S. Praptodiyono, I. H. Hasbullah, M. M. Kadhum, R. K. Murugesan, C. Y. Wey and A. Osman, "Improving Security of Duplicate Address Detection on IPv6 Local Network in Public Area," 2015 9th Asia Modelling Symposium (AMS), Kuala Lumpur, pp. 123-128, 2015.

[22] C. Zhang, J. Xiong and Q. Wu, "An efficient CGA algorithm against DoS attack on duplicate address detection process," 2016 IEEE Wireless Communications and Networking Conference, Doha, pp. 1-6, 2016.

[23] IEEE 802.1x, http://www.ieee802.org/1/pages/802.1x.html, [retrieved: July, 2017].

[24] E. Andreeva, B. Mennink, B. Preneel, "Open problems in hash function security. Designs, Codes and Cryptography," vol. 77, pp. 611-631, 2015.

[25] K. Bhargavan, and G. Leurent "Transcript collision attacks: Breaking authentication in TLS, IKE, and SSH," NDSS, 2016.

[26] V. Shoup, "Fast and provably secure message authentication based on universal hashing". In Advances in Cryptology—CRYPTO'96, pp. 313-328, 1996.

[27] T. Krovetz, "UMAC: Message authentication code using universal hashing," Internet RFC 4418, 2006, [retrieved: July, 2017].

[28] G. Song, and Z. Ji, "Novel Duplicate Address Detection with Hash Function," PLoS ONE 11(3): e0151612, 2014, https://doi.org/10.1371/journal.pone.0151612.

[29] Y. Lu, M. Wang, and P. Huang, "An SDN-Based Authentication Mechanism for Securing Neighbor Discovery Protocol in IPv6," Security and Communication Networks, vol. 2017, Article ID 5838657, 9 pages, 2017. doi:10.1155/2017/5838657.

[30] Tian, K. Butler, J. I. Choi, P. D. McDaniel, P. Krishnaswamy, "Securing ARP/NDP From the Ground Up," in IEEE Transactions on Information Forensics and Security , vol.PP, no.99, pp.1-1doi: 10.1109/TIFS.2017.269598.

A Context-Aware Malware Detection Based on Low-Level Hardware Indicators as a Last Line of Defense

Alireza Sadighian*, Jean-Marc Robert*, Saeed Sarencheh† and Souradeep Basu‡
*Département de génie logiciel et des TI
École de technologie supérieure, Montréal, Canada
Email: alireza.sadighian.1@ens.etsmtl.ca, jean-marc.robert@etsmtl.ca
†Concordia Institute for Information Systems Engineering (CIISE)
Concordia University, Montréal, Canada
Email: s_saren@encs.concordia.ca
‡School of Computer Science, McGill University, Montréal, Canada
Email: souradeep.basu@mail.mcgill.ca

***Abstract*—Malware detection is a very challenging task. Over the years, numerous approaches have been proposed: signature-based, anomaly-based, application-based, host-based and network-based solutions. One avenue that has been less considered is detecting malware by monitoring of low-level resources consumption (e.g., CPU, memory, network bandwidth, etc.). This can be considered as a last-line of defense. When everything else has failed, the monitoring of resources consumption may detect abnormal behaviors in realtime. This paper presents a context-aware malware detection approach that use semi-supervised machine learning and time-series analysis techniques in order to inspect the impact of ongoing events on the low-level indicators. In order to improve the systems automation and adaptability with various contexts, we have designed a context ontology that facilitates information representation, storage and retrieval. The proposed malware detection approach is complementary to the current malware detectors.**

Keywords*–*Malware Detection; Low-level Indicators; Context-Aware; Machine Learning; Time-Series Analysis; Ontologies.

I. INTRODUCTION

Today, the emergence of complex heterogeneous infrastructures has led to the evolution of various applications, services, and systems within these computer networks. At the same time, there is an increasing trend of malware exploiting the vulnerabilities of these infrastructures. Hence, technologies and defensive systems aiming to support the efforts of Information Technology (IT) personnel to improve the reliability of their organizations IT assets (i.e., network infrastructure and computer systems) continue to be paramount.

Anomaly-based and signature-based malware detection systems are among the most popular front line tools to protect network infrastructures against malicious attackers. Various approaches have been proposed in the past two decades and commercial off-the-shelf (COTS) malware detection products have found their way into Security Operations Centers (SOC) of most organizations. Nonetheless, the usefulness of these solutions has remained relatively limited due to two main factors: their inability to detect new types of malware (for which new detection rules or training data are unavailable) or simply their high rate of false negative detection and their often very high rate of false positive detection. Due to the increasing prevalence of complex multi-pronged malware, the necessity for organizations to deploy reliable defense systems is undeniable. This is especially important with respect to targeted malware that tries to avoid detection by conventional security products.

One of the essential shortcomings of existing malware detection approaches is that they mostly inspect events on the higher layers of multilayered software or network architectures. Due to the increasing use of metamorphic and polymorphic malware [1], dynamic anomaly-based detection techniques that concentrate on the execution layer or hardware layer are needed more than ever before. The main reason is that attackers do not have control over low-level hardware indicators as they have over higher level features. For example, it is easier for attackers to modify system calls or access control rules than the cache hit rate or the CPU usage rate. As shown in some of the recent works [2], malware events can be differentiated from normal events via their impacts on the low-level feature spaces, such as hardware events collected by performance counters on modern CPUs. Such features have been called sub-semantic because they do not rely on a semantic model of the monitored programs. We believe that sub-semantic features or hardware low-level indicators, such as CPU usage, CPU temperature, memory usage, etc., can be very useful to identify anomalous events in a real-time mode.

Malware detection systems mostly perform offline event analysis. Usually, a dataset of captured events is prepared as an input for these systems to be analyzed. Moreover, they are not easily adaptable with various contexts because a time-consuming configuration process is required. One solution is to propose a real-time, dynamic and highly adaptable malware detection system using ontologies and ontological engineering tools to represent the relevant information [3]. Ontologies provide powerful knowledge representations of the information structure in an unified format [4].

The work presented in this paper strives to address the problems described above, and provide a comprehensive solution to improve the effectiveness of malware detection approaches in real environments. For this purpose, we present a context-aware real-time malware detection approach that relies on ontologies and ontology description logic to accomplish its goals:

1) Analyze impacts on several heterogeneous low-level hardware indicators
2) Identify anomalies using semi-supervised machine learning and time-series analysis techniques

Such a system can be seen as the last line of defense. Whenever the higher level detection mechanisms fail to detect abnormal behaviors, our proposed hardware level system may have the last chance to catch them.

The paper is organized as follows. In Section 2, we discuss the related work. In Section 3, we present our proposed anomaly detection approach in detail. We demonstrate in Section 4 the effectiveness of our proposed approach by describing a reference implementation and applying it to the analysis of two different case studies. We conclude in Section 5 with some insights for future research.

II. Related Work

Anomaly detection, and more specifically, malware detection is one of the main challenges in computer security. A summary of recent studies in anomaly and malware detection is presented in this section.

Khasawneh *et al.* [2] proposed a dynamic malware detection approach based on low-level features, mainly opcodes, to improve the work of Ozsoy *et al.* [5]. In this work, they use a learning approach to perform an online detection and improve detection accuracy. In a way, signatures of the opcodes and similarity graphs of opcode sequences can be considered as low-level features [6] [7] [8]. Abbasi *et al.* [9] considered processor temperature and power consumption as low-level indicators to detect malicious activities in embedded systems. They use a K-means technique to cluster sequences of actions done by processes. Tang *et al.* [10] proposed an unsupervised anomaly-based malware detection using low-level architectural and micro-architectural features available from hardware performance counters.

Detecting anomalies with time-series and temporal sequences has been studied by several researchers [11] [12] [13]. Laptev *et al.* [11] proposed Extendable Generic Anomaly Detection System (EGADS), an automated anomaly detection system based on time-series. They try to detect three classes of anomalies: outliers, change points and anomalous time-series. Chandola *et al.* [12] studied sequence anomaly detection from different perspectives. The authors believe that sequence anomaly detection can be useful for various purposes, such as OS system call analysis, biological sequences analysis (e.g., DNA sequences), and analyzing navigational click sequences from web sites. Lane and Brodley [13] proposed an anomaly detection approach based on Instance-Based Learning (IBL) techniques wherein they transform temporal sequences of discrete, unordered observations into a metric space via a similarity measure that encodes intra-attribute dependencies.

Machine learning techniques, including supervised, semi-supervised and unsupervised techniques, have been widely employed within various anomaly and intrusion detection approaches [14]. Farid *et al.* [15], proposed a learning algorithm for adaptive Network Intrusion Detection Systems (NIDS) based on Naive Bayes and decision trees. Wang *et al.* [16], using feed forward Backward Propagation (BP) neural networks, proposed an intrusion detection approach based on workflow feature definition. Workflows allow to define new attack sequences to assist BP neural networks in order to detect new attack types. Teng *et al.* [17], proposed a cooperative intrusion detection approach using fuzzy Support Vector Machines (SVM), which consists of three detection agents for the Transmission Control Protocol (TCP), User Datagram Protocol (UDP), and Internet Control Message Protocol (ICMP) connections.

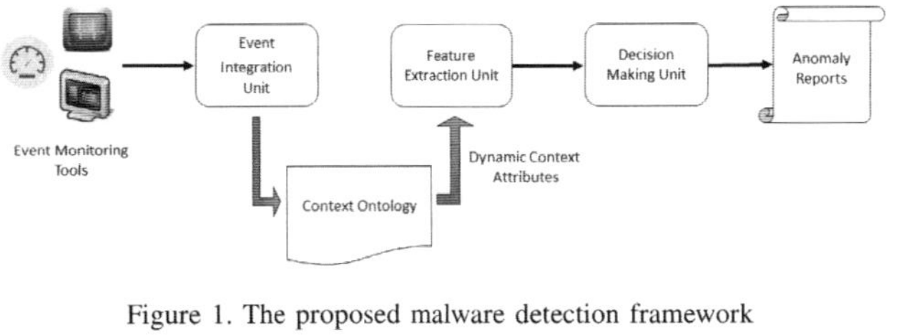

Figure 1. The proposed malware detection framework

In summary, most of these works concentrate on limited aspects of a comprehensive malware detection procedure, such as high-level behavior analysis, a very limited hardware-level low-level indicator analysis, or offline event analysis. However, none of them intends to provide a generic solution dynamically analyzing malware impacts on the normal behavior of the underlying system or network. Motivated by these shortcomings, we propose a context-aware anomaly-based malware detection approach that analyzes dynamically the impact of any event on the hardware-level of the underlying system.

III. The Proposed Malware Detection Approach

In this section, we give a high-level overview of our context-aware malware detection framework as illustrated in Figure 1, which takes full advantage of dynamic events happening within a specific environment. In the first step, the event-integration unit gathers and normalizes the information provided by the different monitoring tools. These tools installed in different architectural layers of the underlying environment provide a wide range of contextual information which can be used to significantly improve the accuracy of the final decisions of the detection framework.

In the second step, the context ontology is populated with the information collected by the monitoring tools. This ontology facilitates traversing (drilling down and rolling up) various levels of the underlying environment to extract very generic or very specific information. It provides dynamic information on the underlying environment for real-time analysis. This information is *normalized* in some way to ease the analysis.

In the third step, the feature extraction unit queries the context ontology to retrieve useful information required for its analysis. It retrieves top meaningful features that provide useful data for a sophisticated malware detection system.

The last step consists of detecting anomalous events happening in the underlying environment. For this purpose, semi-supervised machine learning and time-series analysis techniques are employed in this phase.

A. Event Monitoring Tools

In order to track the impact of any event happening within a network, we need monitoring tools to oversee the behavior of the main components based on various low-level indicators, such as CPU usages, memory usage, disk usage, incoming/outgoing traffic rates, etc. Some of the main components that attackers usually try to bypass or compromise are: network firewall, web server, email server, Intrusion Detection System (IDS), etc. Hence, monitoring the behavior of low-level

TABLE I. AN EXAMPLE LIST OF LOW-LEVEL INDICATORS

CPU	Utilization Time	IOWaits
		Nice
		Softirq
		User
		System
		Steal
		Idle
	Load	
	Number of interrupts	
	Context switches/second	
Memory	Physical Memory	Available
		Total
	Swap	Available
		Total
OS	Max number of opened files	
	Number of processes	
	Max number of processes	
	Host reachability using ICMP	
	Server configured domain	
	Check name resolution	

Network	Incoming	traffic on each interface
		dropped packets
		errors on each interface
		Packet Loss
	Outgoing	traffic on each interface
		dropped packets
		errors on each interface
		Packet Loss
Disk	Free space for each filesystem	
	Used space for each filesystem	
	Total space for each filesystem	
	Free inodes for each filesystem	
System	Up-time	
	Local time	
	Boot-time	
	Number of logged in users	
	Host location	

TABLE II. THE LIST OF ATTRIBUTES OF THE CONTEXT ONTOLOGY CLASSES

Organization	Network	Host	User	OS	Application
ID Product Client Location Network	Topology Protocol Address Range Firewall Switch Host User #hosts #subnets #switches	Name IP/MAC Address Role Location User Service OS Application CPU / Memory #user / #OS	ID Role Location Access rights	Platform Type SPVersion Version	Name Version
	Traffic Type	Memory/CPU Usage Disc Usage Open ports Started Apps Current Users Connections Status Application CPU/Memory Sent/Received Bytes	Per User Per Host Per Net	Syscall Table Process	Started State

indicators in these components provides useful information to detect various malware.

Table I lists the low-level indicators that we monitor. Thus, anomaly-based monitoring tools should take advantage to monitor the behavior of such indicators. They would look for any significant changes, such as an abrupt increase or decrease over a short period of time (a burst).

B. Event Integration Unit

In general, monitoring tools provide reports in various formats that might not be natively interpretable by the context ontology and the malware detection engines. Hence, it is necessary to preprocess these reports and export them in a format that is understandable by both engines. In production environments, this would be done by specific drivers that would match monitoring fields with class attributes at the appropriate abstraction level. In the proposed framework, the event integration unit converts the collected events from monitoring tools to a unified format which can be understood by the next units. The other major tasks of the event integration unit are as follows:

- The monitoring tools may generate attributes in different types (string, integer, etc.). The event integration unit transforms all the received information (attribute values) to a unified type for the ontology engine.
- Some of the monitoring tools may not support particular class attributes. The event integration unit completes the missing data and attributes.
- The event integration unit removes noises and meaningless values in the collected data from monitoring tools.

Once the integration process has been completed by the event integration unit, the context ontology is populated using the normalized information.

C. Context Ontology

Ontologies provide a powerful knowledge representation in a unified format which is understandable by both machines and humans [4]. Ontologies allow the use of reasoning logic formalisms that can be used to retrieve information in a generic structure-agnostic fashion. We use these formalisms to design our real-time malware detection algorithms. Our main objective is to detect complex and challenging malware that bypasses current security solutions. The use of ontologies and ontology description logic enables us to fully automate the dynamic contextual information retrieval that is typically done manually by the analysts.

In our malware detection framework, we have designed a context ontology easily adaptable to various environments, indicating its flexibility and power of abstraction. Additionally, it is highly extensible to include more contextual classes and attributes depending on the level of abstraction.

The context ontology is populated using the information integrated by the event integration unit. Figure 2 illustrates our designed context ontology, which has been implemented using the popular open-source ontology editor Protégé (as shown in Figure 11 of Appendix C). The context ontology includes a Context base class and User, Host, Network and Service associated classes with their corresponding attributes. Each of these classes has both static (above the line) and dynamic (below the line) attributes (as listed in Table II). These attributes are provided either by network fingerprinting tools or network administrators.

In order to navigate among various levels of class hierarchies within the context ontology, we use the following two operators in the form of a set of logic rules expressed in Semantic Query-Enhanced Web Rule Language (SQWRL) [18]:

- **Drill-Down** allows to navigate among levels of data ranging from the most summarized to the most detailed concepts.
- **Roll-Up** allows to navigate among levels of data ranging from the most detailed to the most summarized concepts.

D. Feature Selection Unit

Once the context ontology has been populated with the dynamic events of the underlying monitored system, this information can be used to detect potential anomalous events.

The first step is therefore to query the context ontology to extract dynamic information on the environment and to prepare them for analysis. We use a set of logic rules expressed in

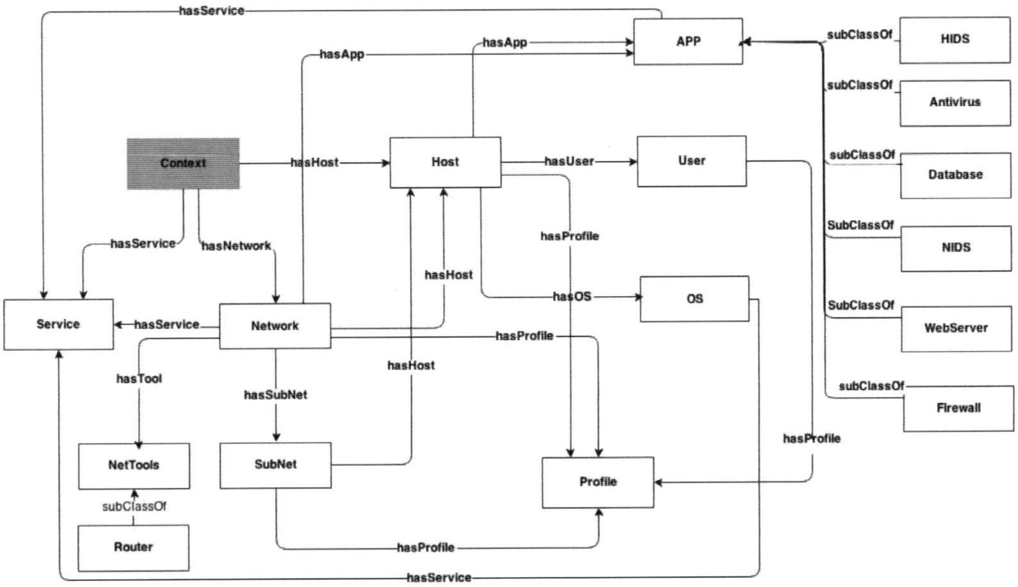

Figure 2. Class diagram relationship of the context ontology

SQWRL to query the context ontology. These rules facilitate the traversing of the ontology class hierarchy to retrieve the important attributes for the anomaly detection algorithms. Some examples are given in the appendix. These queries extract events, which are represented as follows: e_i is a feature vector $x_i = (x_{i,1}, x_{i,2}, \cdots, x_{i,m})$.

Several attributes of the context ontology can be used as input features for machine learning techniques to detect anomalous events. Using various feature analysis algorithms [19], the most useful features can be selected for the analysis by the decision-making unit. Principal Component Analysis (PCA) [19] and parallel coordinates [20] have been used for this paper. PCA is a statistical procedure that transforms a set of observations of possibly correlated variables into a set of values of linearly uncorrelated variables called principal components. On the other hand, parallel coordinates is a way of visualizing high-dimensional geometry and analyzing multivariate data. It eases feature selections by analysts.

In order to have a real-time malware detection system, the feature selection unit consists of a number of pre-defined triggers for the most critical features (e.g., CPU usage, memory usage). When one of these triggers is activated, it starts extracting contextual information from the context ontology as machine learning features, and selects those features providing meaningful information.

E. Decision Making Unit

In this section, we provide a detailed picture of the proposed malware detection approach. Two different approaches are used: machine learning techniques and time-series analysis. Semi-supervised machine learning techniques [21] (e.g., One-Class Support Vector Machine (OC-SVM)) have been chosen because the cost associated with the event labeling process in supervised machine learning techniques is significantly high, whereas acquisition of unlabeled or partly labeled data is significantly inexpensive. Time-series analysis techniques [22] (e.g., Cumulative Sum (CUSUM) [23]) try to extract meaningful statistics and internal structure of the input data. These two techniques complement each other considering that OC-SVM does not take into account internal correlation of events, while time-series analysis accounts for the fact that data points taken over time may have an internal structure, such as autocorrelation, trend or seasonal variation. Time series reflect also the stochastic nature of events over time. Hence, data may be skewed, with fluctuating mean and variation, non-normally distributed, and not randomly sampled. The pseudocode for the proposed malware detection approach is presented in Figure 10 (Appendix A).

1) Detecting Anomalous Events Using OC-SVM: The One-Class Support Vector Machine (OC-SVM) has been used since it can be trained with only normal events. OC-SVM can be viewed as a regular two-class SVM where all the training data lies in the first class, and the origin is taken as the only member of the second class. Then, in the testing phase, any abnormal event is considered as an outlier in theory. This removes the need to gather attacks or abnormal traffic. Hence, the main idea is to classify the training data as positive, and classify testing data as negative only if it is sufficiently different from the training data.

A One-Class SVM is a linear classifier in a multi-dimensional feature space [21]. It maps a hyper-sphere to the input data in order to separate normal events from the origin. These points lying inside the hyper-sphere are classified as outliers. This can be formulated as an optimization problem as follows:

$$\begin{gathered}\min_{R,b,\xi} R^2 + \frac{1}{vn}\sum_{i=1}^{n}\xi_i \\ \text{subject to} : \left(\|\phi(x_i) - b\|^2 \leq R^2 - \xi_i \quad \text{and} \quad \xi_i \geq 0\right)\end{gathered} \tag{1}$$

where, b and R are the center and radius of the hyper-sphere, and ξ is the slack variable. When v is small, we try to put more data into the ball. On the other hand, when v is larger, we try to squeeze the size of the ball. This optimization can be solved by Lagrangian multipliers.

2) Malware Detection Based on Time-Series Analysis: Detecting anomalous event sequences is one of the most important requirements of any malware detection system to prevent potential disasters. Sometimes, a single event does not sound anomalous, whereas, a sequence of such events can represent malicious behavior. Sending a few emails per hour sounds normal for a trusted computer system. However, sending thousands of emails per hour may demonstrate that the system has been compromised by spammers.

A time-series consists of a sequence of events obtained over repeated measurements of time [24]. An anomalous time-series is defined as a time-series whose average deviation from the other time-series is significant. In order to detect anomalous time-series, we use the CUSUM technique.

CUSUM is a standard sequential analysis technique used for online changepoint detection [23]. In the following, we describe the procedure of calculating CUSUM for a sequence of events $(x_0 ... x_n)$. For each event, a probability density function (PDF) $p(x_i, \theta)$ depending on a deterministic parameter θ is defined. In the case of a changepoint at time t_c, we define $\theta = \theta_0$ before t_c and $\theta = \theta_1$ after t_c. CUSUM uses a likelihood ratio test as its changepoint detection theory. Thus, the $instantaneous \quad log - likelihood \quad ratio$ at time i is defined as follows:

$$s[i] = L_x[i, i] = \ln\left(\frac{p(x_i, \theta_1)}{p(x_i, \theta_0)}\right) \tag{2}$$

and CUSUM from 0 to k: $S[k] = \sum_{i=0}^{k} s[i]$. Accordingly, the decision function $G_x[k]$ and change time estimate $\widehat{i}$ will be defined as follows:

$$G_x[k] = S[k] - \min_{1 \leq i \leq k} S[i-1] \tag{3}$$

$$\widehat{i} = arg \min_{1 \leq i \leq k} S[i-1] \tag{4}$$

Equation (4) shows that the change time estimate is the time following the current minimum of the cumulative sum. The value of decision function $G_x[k]$ is zero before the changepoint and increasing afterwards. When the value of $G_x[k]$ exceeds a certain threshold, an anomalous event or event sequence is detected.

Thus, our approach to detect anomalous event sequences consists of the following phases:

1) Concentrate on the training dataset to find the thresholds describing the normal behaviors of the system, such as the decision interval and the shift decision. We first calculate CUSUM of the training dataset. As a result, we find the threshold interval of the CUSUM approach for the training dataset.
2) Analyze the testing dataset to list potential anomalies. For this purpose, first, the CUSUM of the testing dataset is calculated. Next, all the events or event sequences having CUSUM greater than the highest threshold or less than the lowest threshold will be reported as anomalous event sequences.

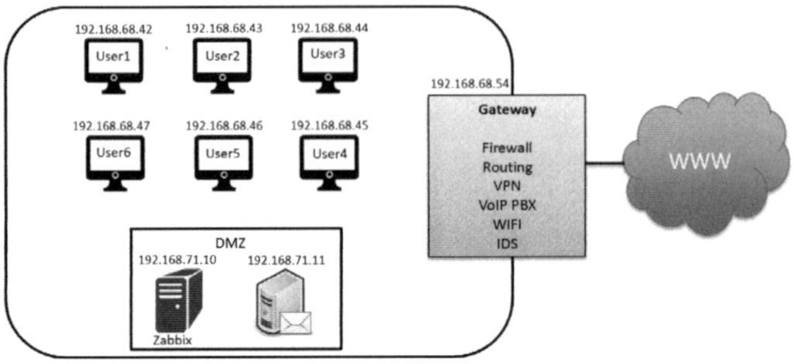

Figure 3. The experiments test-bed

IV. Implementation and Evaluation

In order to illustrate and validate our approach, we have developed a reference implementation using a collection of tools including network monitoring tools, ontology representation and reasoning tools, as well as machine learning and time-series platforms.

We used this collection of tools to conduct two experiments in a real network as our field test-bed. Figure 3 illustrates our test-bed for the experiments. The normal users of this network are mostly programmers and researchers. A Zabbix server is used to monitor the behavior of the low-level indicators (CPU usage, memory usage, CPU temperature, network traffic, etc.) of the critical components, such as the network gateway and the email server, during the experiments. The network gateway (192.168.68.54) provides several services, such as network firewall, routing, Virtual Private Network (VPN), Voice over IP Private Branch Exchange (VoIP PBX), WIFI and NIDS.

In this section, we describe the reference implementation of our malware detection framework and present two case studies to demonstrate how it can detect various types of anomalous events happening in a real computer network.

A. Reference Implementation

Our event monitoring solution relies on the open source monitoring software Zabbix [25], and our event integration tool relies on the agent-less universal Security Information Management System (SIEM) Prelude [26].

As mentioned earlier, the Protégé ontology editor and knowledge acquisition system [27] has been used to design and implement our context ontology using the Ontology Web Language Description Logic (OWL-DL). The context ontology is instantiated with the normalized information coming from Prelude. Furthermore, the Pellet plug-in [28] is used as a reasoner for OWL-DL, and SQWRL to query the ontologies for various purposes.

For feature selection and machine learning-based decision making, we use scikit-learn [29], pyplot NumPy [30] and SciPy [31] Python libraries. Finally, we use CUSUM (a library in R) for time series-based decision making.

B. Case Study 1: Detecting TorrentLocker Ransomware

Our first case study is to detect TorrentLocker ransomware. TorrentLocker is a ransomware that encrypts private data of infected computer systems, and asks users to pay a ransom (usually, in Bitcoins) to re-gain access to their data. Once TorrentLocker infects a system, it encrypts the first two megabytes

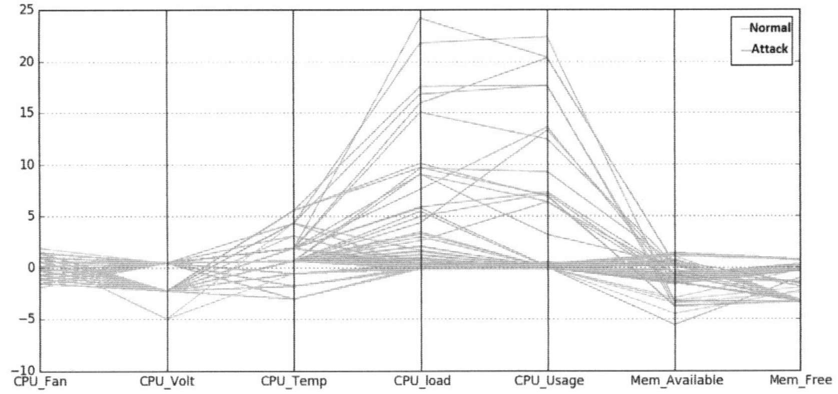

Figure 4. Low-level indicators during the ransomware detection experiment

of all the existing files found on that system. Encrypting partially the files is sufficient to conceal the information and is more efficient for the malware. Unfortunately, currently, antiviruses and intrusion detection systems have difficulties to detect such polymorphic malware.

In this case study, we simulate TorrentLocker behavior wherein once the ransomware infects the network gateway (Figure 3), it starts encrypting all the existing files. For this purpose, in a similar way as TorrentLocker, we launch multiple suspicious processes (multi-threaded Python scripts) accessing a large number of structured files, encrypting them using the AES-256 encryption algorithm in CBC mode, and overwriting them with encrypted files. Our dataset includes 6000 JPEG files (1MB each).

We conducted a one-week (work-days from 10:00 to 17:00) experiment in a real network. During the first five days of the experiment, we captured the normal behavior of the network gateway and prepared the training dataset. The training dataset includes low-level hardware indicators (e.g., CPU usage, memory usage, disk usage, etc.) of the normal events. The last two days was used to test our solution. To simulate TorrentLocker ransomware behavior, we ran the ransomware in several steps (Table III). In each step, we ran the ransomware with different number of threads and files. To discover which low-level indicators have been affected during the experiment, we queried the context ontology (Rule 2 in Appendix B) and visualized them using parallel coordinates. Figure 4 illustrates the extracted features. Each feature has been shown by a separate coordinate. Different colors have been used to visualize normal and abnormal events. Horizontal lines indicates how each event affects the extracted features. As shown, the main features affected during the simulated attack are: CPU Temperature, CPU Usage, CPU Load and Memory Free. As Figure 5 illustrates, CPU Usage is the key feature targeted by the attack.

In order to start analyzing this suspicious event using our proposed approach, we applied PCA algorithm to the extracted feature list to reduce data dimension. As Table IV shows, features like CPU Temp, CPU Load, Memory Available and CPU Usage have been mainly affected during this experiment. In the rest of this section, we explain how the decision-making unit of our malware detection framework employs the final feature list to detect the anomalous activities.

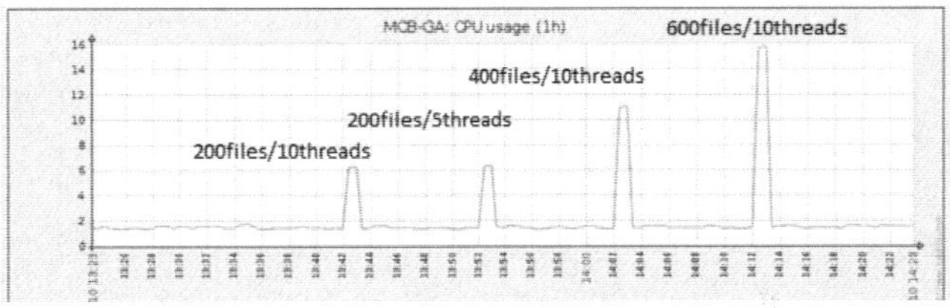

Figure 5. CPU usage during the test-day

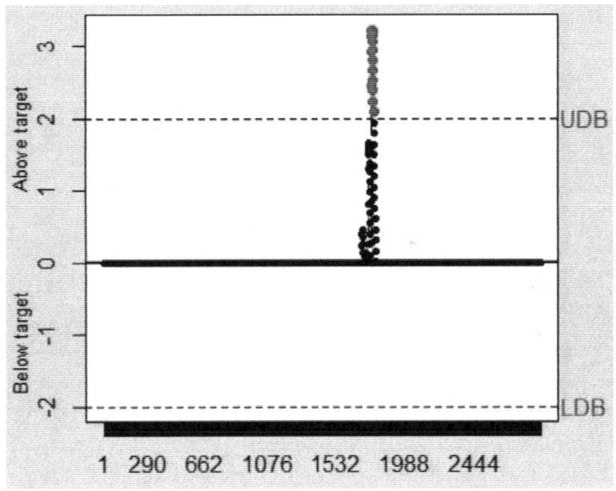

Figure 6. Time-series analysis of test data in Case Study 1

The decision-making unit has been developed based on two main techniques: OC-SVM and time-series analysis. First, OC-SVM was trained using the training dataset. Next, OC-SVM was applied to the test dataset that contains the anomalous event sequences. Table V shows the results. The amount of False Positive (FP), True Positive (TP), False Negative (FN) and True Negative (TN) are given. These statistics can be used to compute the $accuracy = \frac{(TP+TN)}{(TP+TN+FN+FP)}$. Except for Step 6, all the anomalous steps were detected by OC-SVM. Step 6 was not detected because its impact on the low-level indicators is significantly low.

In the second phase, we used the time-series analysis technique to detect anomalous event sequences. Thus, the time-series analysis module was trained using event sequences to learn normal thresholds, such as the decision interval and the

TABLE III. RANSOMWARE EXPERIMENT STEPS

Steps	1	2	3	4	5	6	7	8	9	10
Day-time	F-13:42	F-13:52	F-14:02	F-14:12	F-14:42	F-14:52	S-14:14	S-14:24	S-14:34	S-14:44
File #	200	200	400	600	100	50	2000	2000	4000	6000
Thread #	10	5	10	10	10	10	50	100	100	100

TABLE IV. THE RESULT OF APPLYING PCA TO THE EXTRACTED FEATURES

Attribute	PC 1	PC 2	PC 3
CPU_Fan		-0.258	0.652
CPU_Volt		0.375	-0.342
CPU_Temp	-0.226	-0.207	-0.555
CPU_Load	-0.555	0.231	0.18
CPU_Usage	-0.538	0.21	0.197
Mem_availability	0.158	0.651	
Mem_Free	0.307	0.449	0.28

TABLE V. RESULTS FOR CASE STUDY 1

Alarms	OC-SVM	Time-Series
FP	21	146
TP	46	9
FN	19	56
TN	1474	1349
Accuracy	0.97	0.87

shift. Next, the time-series analysis module was applied to the test dataset. The results (Table V) show that using time-series analysis, we were able to detect only step 10. The main reason is that the number of events generated during the first 9 steps is less than the considered time-series window size. Figure 6 illustrates how time-series analysis processes the data to detect anomalous event sequences.

Consequently, overall, our proposed anomaly detection approach succeeded to detect all the abnormal activities of this experiment except the abnormal activity of Step 6 that very lightly affected the system low-level indicators. This means, our proposed approach was able to detect TorrentLocker ransomware by sacrificing only 100 files of the infected system.

C. Case Study 2: Spamming Bot

We evaluate here our malware detection approach using a spamming bot scenario wherein a compromised machine (192.168.68.45). inside the network sends a massive number of spam emails that significantly affects incoming and outgoing traffic rate within the network gateway. For this purpose, we conducted a three day (work-days from 10:00 to 17:00) experiment in our network. During the first two days, we captured the normal behaviors of the network gateway and prepared the training dataset, which includes low-level hardware indicators (e.g., CPU, memory and disk usage, incoming and outgoing traffic, etc.).

The last day was dedicated to prepare the testing dataset. A bot machine started to send a massive number of spam emails at time periods 14:41-15:11 (100 kb/s), 15:22-15:52 (400 kb/s), 16:03-16:33 (800 kb/s) and 16:43-17:13 (1.1 mb/s). This produced a very large traffic rate on the network gateway which affects a number of low-level indicators.

TABLE VI. RESULTS FOR CASE STUDY 2

Alarms	OC-SVM	Time-Series
FP	19	0
TP	35	186
FN	205	34
TN	1301	1340
Accuracy	0.87	0.98

In order to discover which low-level indicators have been significantly affected during the experiment, we queried the context ontology for a number of features and visualized them using parallel coordinates (Figure 7). As we see, CPU Temperature/Usage/Load and Free Memory are the main features affected during this scenario. Figure 8 illustrates CPU Load and CPU Temperature behaviors during the test-day. Next, we applied the PCA algorithm to the extracted feature list to reduce data dimension. In the following paragraphs, we explain how the decision-making unit of our malware detection framework is able to detect such abnormal activities.

We applied the two phases of the decision making process (same as Case Study 1) to the training and test dataset. Table VI shows the obtained results. Figure 9 illustrates how time-series analysis processes the input data to detect anomalous event sequences. The results indicate that both OC-SVM and time-series analysis module ware able to detect the anomalous events. Consequently, the proposed malware detection approach successfully detected the abnormal activities of this experiment.

As the first phase of the decision making process, first, OC-SVM was trained using the training dataset. The maximum CPU load in the training dataset were 2.19. Next, it was applied to the test dataset that contains four abnormal activities. Table 5 shows the results. The results indicate that OC-SVM detected only one of the abnormal activities (the highest traffic) as its CPU load was higher than maximum CPU load in the training dataset.

In the second phase, first, we trained the time-series analysis module using event sequences of training dataset to learn normal thresholds. The time-series analysis module was applied to the test dataset. The obtained results (Table VI) show that using time-series analysis, we were able to detect three of the anomalous abnormal activities. The first abnormal activity was not detected as its impact on low-level indicators was mostly similar to normal activities. Consequently, the proposed anomaly detection approach successfully detected three abnormal activities of this experiment.

V. CONCLUSIONS

In this paper, we discussed the shortcomings of malware detection systems (e.g., inability to detect new types of attacks and the often very high rate of false positives), and proposed a new context-aware anomaly-based malware detection approach

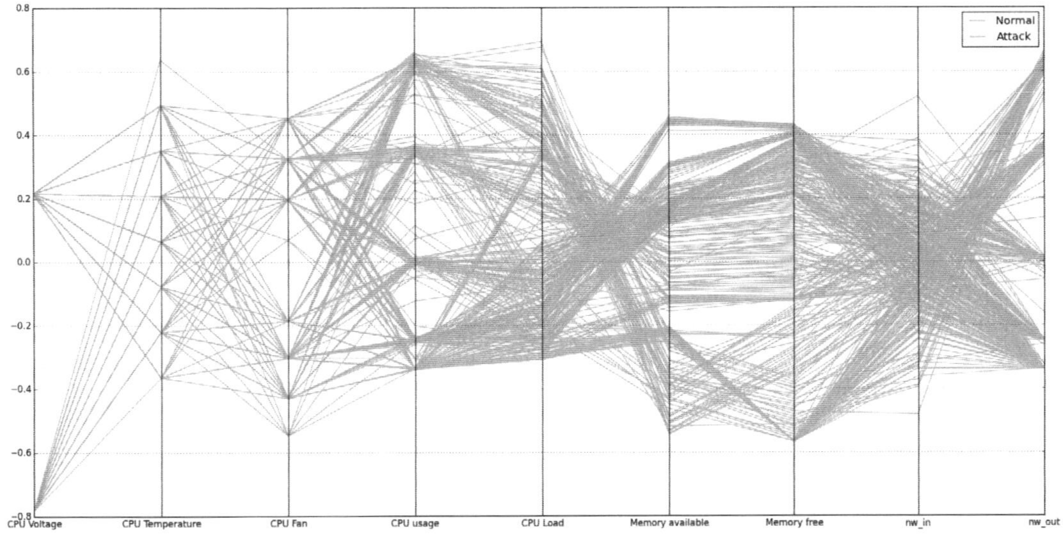

Figure 7. Low-level indicators behavior during the spamming bot experiment

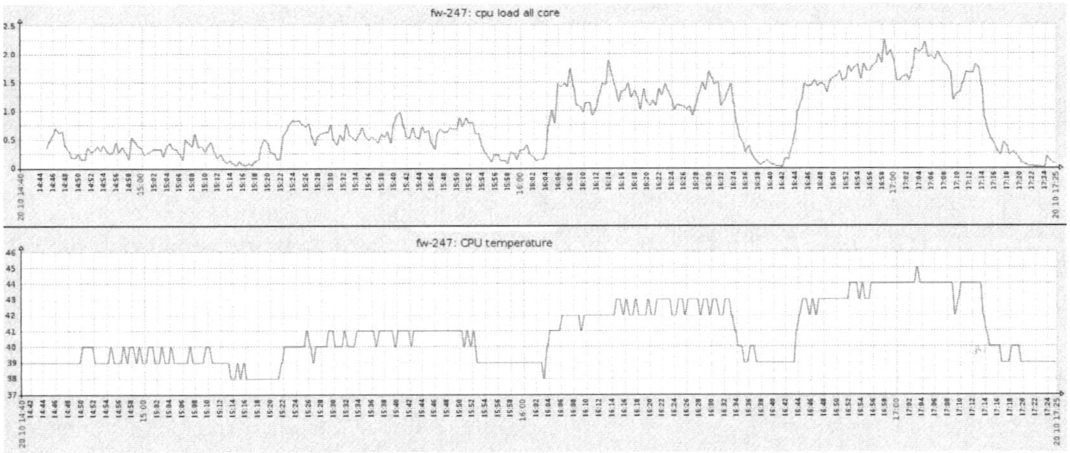

Figure 8. CPU load and CPU temperature during the test-day

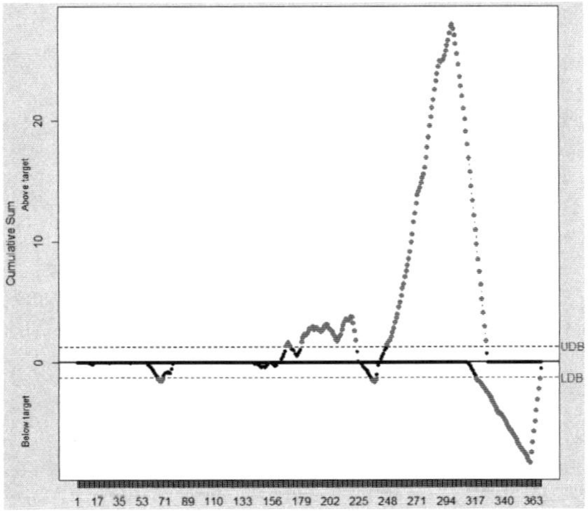

Figure 9. Time-series analysis of test data in Case Study 2

based on low level sensors as a last-line of defense to overcome these shortcomings. If malicious attackers may be able to deactivate firewall or IDS, they cannot alter the low level sensors.

The main idea of our approach is to detect any anomaly at the hardware layer by verifying legitimacy or maliciousness of an event or an event sequence based on the impacts that it enforces to the underlying monitoring low-level indicators (e.g., CPU/memory usage, network traffic rate, etc.). For this purpose, several monitoring tools are employed to collect and analyze low-level indicators behavior in a real-time mode. To do so in a manner that can be automated, but that yet can be easily extended to new concepts (richer concepts of context), we used ontologies and ontological engineering tools to represent knowledge and information about contextual information using the Ontology Web Language (OWL). We proposed the ontology for contextual information accordingly, considering the capability to import both explicit contextual information from Configuration Management Systems (CMS) or implicit contextual information obtained from users and system profiling techniques. In order to verify legitimacy or maliciousness of ongoing events, we used semi-supervised machine learning and time-series analysis techniques that complement each other to identify both anomalous events and sequences.

To illustrate our approach, we implemented our new approach on two distinct case studies (i.e., remote code execution attack scenario and spamming bot scenario) designed based on current challenging malware and attack scenarios, we successfully evaluated the proposed anomaly detection approach in a real network environment. The results show that our proposed approach can successfully detect abnormal behaviors at a very low system level.

By 1) collecting more and more normal events from the underlying context in order to appropriately train and adjust the OC-SVM and time-series analysis module, and 2) adding more low-level indicators of the underlying context to the context ontology, both false positive and false negative rates will be significantly reduced. Hence, the reliability of the proposed malware detection approach will be improved. Consequently, our approach can appropriately complement existing malware detection approaches that mostly inspect events on the higher layers of multilayered software or network architectures without taking into account the execution layer or hardware layer.

As our future work, we intend to populate the context ontology with more sophisticated context models, populated with network fingerprinting and profiling tools. We also plan to evaluate our proposed anomaly detection approach against other complex attacks in order to reliably gauge its performance and effectiveness in real-life situations.

ACKNOWLEDGMENT

We would like to thank Groupe Access which allows us to develop our low-level sensors in their network. This research was sponsored in part by Mitacs Canada and Groupe Access Inc.

REFERENCES

[1] I. You and K. Yim, "Malware obfuscation techniques: A brief survey," in 2010 International conference on broadband, wireless computing, communication and applications. IEEE, 2010, pp. 297–300.

[2] K. N. Khasawneh, M. Ozsoy, C. Donovick, N. Abu-Ghazaleh, and D. Ponomarev, "Ensemble learning for low-level hardware-supported malware detection," in Research in Attacks, Intrusions, and Defenses. Springer, 2015, pp. 3–25.

[3] A. Sadighian, J. M. Fernandez, A. Lemay, and S. T. Zargar, "Ontids: A highly flexible context-aware and ontology-based alert correlation framework," in Foundations and Practice of Security. Springer, 2014, pp. 161–177.

[4] A. Gomez-Perez, M. Fernández-López, and O. Corcho, Ontological Engineering: with examples from the areas of Knowledge Management, e-Commerce and the Semantic Web. Springer Science & Business Media, 2006.

[5] M. Ozsoy, C. Donovick, I. Gorelik, N. Abu-Ghazaleh, and D. Ponomarev, "Malware-aware processors: A framework for efficient online malware detection," in High Performance Computer Architecture (HPCA), 2015 IEEE 21st International Symposium on. IEEE, 2015, pp. 651–661.

[6] N. Runwal, R. M. Low, and M. Stamp, "Opcode graph similarity and metamorphic detection," Journal in Computer Virology, vol. 8, no. 1-2, 2012, pp. 37–52.

[7] I. Santos et al., "Idea: Opcode-sequence-based malware detection," in Engineering Secure Software and Systems. Springer, 2010, pp. 35–43.

[8] G. Yan, N. Brown, and D. Kong, "Exploring discriminatory features for automated malware classification," in Detection of Intrusions and Malware, and Vulnerability Assessment. Springer, 2013, pp. 41–61.

[9] Z. Abbasi, M. Kargahi, and M. Mohaqeqi, "Anomaly detection in embedded systems using simultaneous power and temperature monitoring," in Information Security and Cryptology (ISCISC), 2014 11th International ISC Conference on. IEEE, 2014, pp. 115–119.

[10] A. Tang, S. Sethumadhavan, and S. J. Stolfo, "Unsupervised anomaly-based malware detection using hardware features," in Research in Attacks, Intrusions and Defenses. Springer, 2014, pp. 109–129.

[11] N. Laptev, S. Amizadeh, and I. Flint, "Generic and scalable framework for automated time-series anomaly detection," in Proceedings of the 21th ACM SIGKDD International Conference on Knowledge Discovery and Data Mining. ACM, 2015, pp. 1939–1947.

[12] V. Chandola, A. Banerjee, and V. Kumar, "Anomaly detection for discrete sequences: A survey," Knowledge and Data Engineering, IEEE Transactions on, vol. 24, no. 5, 2012, pp. 823–839.

[13] T. Lane and C. E. Brodley, "Temporal sequence learning and data reduction for anomaly detection," ACM Transactions on Information and System Security (TISSEC), vol. 2, no. 3, 1999, pp. 295–331.

[14] V. Chandola, A. Banerjee, and V. Kumar, "Anomaly detection: A survey," ACM computing surveys (CSUR), vol. 41, no. 3, 2009, pp. 1–58.

[15] D. M. Farid, N. Harbi, and M. Z. Rahman, "Combining naive bayes and decision tree for adaptive intrusion detection," arXiv preprint arXiv:1005.4496, 2010.

[16] Y. Wang, D. Gu, W. Li, H. Li, and J. Li, "Network intrusion detection with workflow feature definition using bp neural network," in Advances in Neural Networks–ISNN 2009. Springer, 2009, pp. 60–67.

[17] S. Teng, H. Du, N. Wu, W. Zhang, and J. Su, "A cooperative network intrusion detection based on fuzzy svms," Journal of Networks, vol. 5, no. 4, 2010, pp. 475–483.

[18] M. J. O'Connor and A. K. Das, "Sqwrl: A query language for owl." in OWLED, vol. 529, 2009.

[19] I. Jolliffe, Principal component analysis. Wiley Online Library, 2002.

[20] A. Inselberg, Parallel coordinates. Springer, 2009.

[21] Y. Chen, X. S. Zhou, and T. S. Huang, "One-class svm for learning in image retrieval," in Image Processing, 2001. Proceedings. 2001 International Conference on, vol. 1. IEEE, 2001, pp. 34–37.

[22] G. E. Box, G. M. Jenkins, G. C. Reinsel, and G. M. Ljung, Time series analysis: forecasting and control. John Wiley & Sons, 2015.

[23] P. Granjon, "The cusum algorithm-a small review," 2014.

[24] H. Madsen, Time series analysis. CRC Press, 2007.

[25] L. Zabbix, "Zabbix," The Enterprise-class Monitoring Solution for Everyone2016, Available from http://www. zabbix. com, 2015.

[26] K. Zaraska, "Prelude ids: current state and development perspectives," URL http://www. prelude-ids. org/download/misc/pingwinaria/2003/paper. pdf, 2003.

[27] M. A. Musen, "Protégé ontology editor," Encyclopedia of Systems Biology, 2013, pp. 1763–1765.

[28] E. Sirin, B. Parsia, B. C. Grau, A. Kalyanpur, and Y. Katz, "Pellet: A practical owl-dl reasoner," Web Semantics: science, services and agents on the World Wide Web, vol. 5, no. 2, 2007, pp. 51–53.

[29] F. Pedregosa et al., "Scikit-learn: Machine learning in python," The Journal of Machine Learning Research, vol. 12, 2011, pp. 2825–2830.

[30] W. McKinney, Python for data analysis: Data wrangling with Pandas, NumPy, and IPython. " O'Reilly Media, Inc.", 2012.

[31] E. Jones, T. Oliphant, and P. Peterson, "{SciPy}: open source scientific tools for {Python}," 2014.

APPENDIX

A. Malware Detection Pseudocode

```
INPUT: Train-Event-List, Test-Event-List.
OUTPUT: Malware-Report
BEGIN

{Training}
for all e ∈ Train − Event − List do
    OC − SVM(e)
end for

while ( Train-Event-List is not empty) do
    w ← createwind(Train − Event − List)
    CUSUMList ← CUSUM(w)
    h ← max(CUSUMList)
end while

{Testing}
for all e ∈ Test − Event − List do
    EventClass ← OC − SVM(e)
    if EvenetClass is attack then
        attack − list1 ← e
    end if
end for

while ( Test-Event-List is not empty) do
    w ← createwind(Test − Event − List)
    if CUSUM(w) > h then
        attack − list2 ← w
    end if
end while

Malware − Report ← attack − list1 ⋁ attack − list2

END
```

Figure 10. The Proposed Malware Detection Pseudocode

B. Rule Examples

Rule 1 extracts all the events in the Web Server (192.168.71.247) having CPU usage higher than 60%. The outcome event list can be analyzed in order to discover any potential cause of abnormal CPU usage.

Rule 1:

$$\text{Event}(?e_1) \wedge \text{Host}(?h_1) \wedge \text{hasAddress}(?h_1, \text{"192.168.71.247"}) \wedge \text{hasSource}(?e_1, ?h_1) \wedge \text{hasCPUUsage}(?e_1, ?\text{cpuusage}) \wedge \text{greaterThanOrEqual}(?\text{cpuusage}, \text{"60\%"}) \longrightarrow \text{sqwrl:select}(?e_1)$$

Rule 2 extracts values of a set of low-level hardware indicators (i.e. Timestamp, CPU Usage, CPU Voltage, CPU Temperature, CPU Fan, CPU Load, Network Input, Network Output, Available Memory and Free Memory) in the Network Gateway (192.168.68.54) to be analyzed in order to discover major affected features.

Rule 2

$$\text{Host}(?h) \wedge \text{hasAddress}(?h, \text{"192.168.68.54"}) \wedge \text{hasTimeStamp}(?h, ?\text{timestamp}) \wedge \text{hasCPUUsage}(?h, ?\text{cpuusage}) \wedge \text{hasCPUVoltage}(?h, ?\text{cpuvoltage}) \wedge \text{hasCPUTemperature}(?h, ?\text{cputemperature}) \wedge \text{hasCPUFan}(?h, ?\text{cpufan}) \wedge \text{hasCPULoad}(?h, ?\text{cpuload}) \wedge \text{hasNetworkInput}(?h, ?\text{networkinput}) \wedge \text{hasNetworkOutput}(?h, ?\text{networkoutput}) \wedge \text{hasMemoryAvailable}(?h, ?\text{memoryavailable}) \wedge \text{hasMemoryFree}(?h, ?\text{memoryfree}) \longrightarrow \text{sqwrl:select}(?\text{timestamp}, ?\text{cpuusage}, ?\text{cpuvoltage}, ?\text{cputemperature}, ?\text{cpufan}, ?\text{cpuload}, ?\text{networkinput}, ?\text{networkoutput}, ?\text{memoryavailable}, ?\text{memoryfree})$$

C. Ontology Implementation

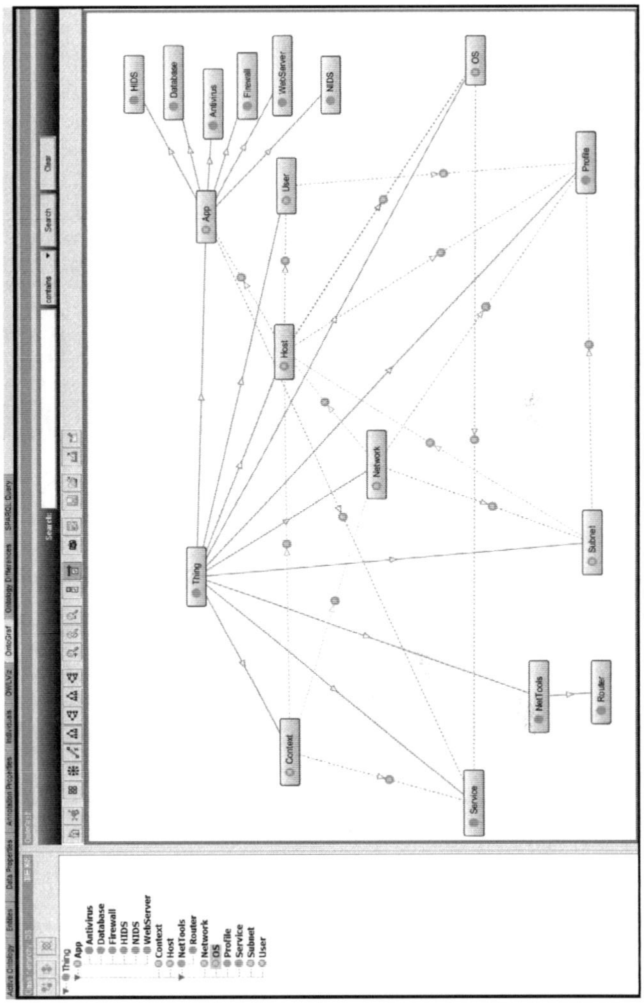

Figure 11. Implementation of the context ontology using Protégé

Clustering based Evolving Neural Network Intrusion Detection for MCPS Traffic Security

Nishat I Mowla
Dept. of Computer Science and Engineering
Ewha Womans University
Seoul, Korea
e-mail: nishat.i.mowla@gmail.com

Inshil Doh
Dept. of Cyber Security
Ewha Womans University
Seoul, Korea
e-mail: isdoh1@ewha.ac.kr

Kijoon Chae*
Dept. of Computer Science and Engineering
Ewha Womans University
Seoul, Korea
e-mail: kjchae@ewha.ac.kr

***Abstract*— In the era of Internet, exploits and vulnerabilities of our systems can be used by attackers to violate confidentiality, integrity, and availability. These attacks pose even more serious consequences when we consider medical networks such as Medical Cyber Physical Systems (MCPS). Therefore, the design of an efficient intrusion detection system is vital. However, the success of most of these systems is linked to custom statistical signature based solutions. It becomes a limiting constraint when there are myriad possible attacks emerging every day. To solve the above issues, several machine learning techniques have been developed to form robust detection systems. Nevertheless, these systems are not efficient with low-frequency attacks and are often considered as outliers, even though the consequences of missing upon such attacks can be dangerous. Therefore, this paper proposes an evolving machine learning technique, based on clustering and neural network classification to improve the detection accuracy of all forms of network intrusion traffic. Our experimental results on the standardized Knowledge Discovery and Data Mining (KDD) Cup 99 public dataset show that the proposed mechanism can outperform the well-established boosted decision tree algorithm under different selected features environments.**

Keywords-Intrusion Detection; Machine Intelligence; Clustering; Neural Networks; Medical Cyber Physical Systems.

I. INTRODUCTION

Network security lies at the heart of the future Internet, as various intrusions in the technological systems can cause fatal damage. Various forms of body worn devices that record multiple physiological signals, such as ECG (Electrocardiogram) and heart rate, or even more sophisticated devices that measure physiological markers such as body temperature, skin resistance, gait, posture, and EMG (Electromyography) are well-connected to the Internet. Medical Cyber Physical Systems (MCPS) combining such sensors aim at providing remote healthcare to patients. Malicious attackers can exploit the vulnerabilities in these networks to breach confidentiality, integrity, and availability. MCPS require assurance of health information privacy during transmission from the sensory network to cloud and from the cloud to the doctor's mobile devices. Therefore, a malicious traffic detection system is vital in such scenarios [1].

The success of most intrusion detection systems is linked to custom signature based solutions. However, it becomes unfeasible when we consider time-critical networks, such as Medical Cyber Physical Systems. Intrusion Detection Systems have been developed over time. They can be divided into two main categories, namely, misuse detection and anomaly detection. Misuse detection systems are based on a signature database of already known attacks. These techniques fail in detecting new forms of attacks. With the emergence of new technologies, such as Cyber Physical Systems and Internet of Things, we are also experiencing new forms of network attacks. On the other hand, anomaly detection works by defining a profile for 'normal behavior' where attacks are detected as deviations from this profile. One of the drawbacks of this technique is that it can incur more false positives and slight deviations of normal instances can affect the detection as they depend greatly on this normal profile [2]. Various data mining approaches have also been proposed over time to detect intrusion. Nonetheless, data combined with machine intelligence has seen a higher success rate. Since networks such as Medical Cyber Physical System can monitor the traffic features over long periods of time, machine learning based intrusion detection systems can form a symbiotic relationship with these networks for creating high performance detection tools.

Following to the stream, we propose a clustering based evolving neural network intrusion detection system leveraging machine intelligence. The idea combines supervised and unsupervised machine learning to work with an evolved pairwise learning approach, which highly enhances the classification borderline. Hence, the technique is used to detect the four major forms of network attacks in different feature selected environments.

We discuss some of the related works in Section II. In Section III, we discuss our proposed mechanism and evaluation results followed by the conclusion in Section IV.

II. RELATED WORKS

A. Intrusion Detection Systems (IDS)

The Intrusion Detection Expert System was first proposed by Dorothy E. Denning in 1986[3]. It was an expert system to detect known types of intrusions with a statistical anomaly detection component leveraging profiles of users, host systems and the target systems. Subsequently, a new version called Next-Generation Intrusion Detection Expert System was developed [4]. Anomaly detection came into mainstream with DARPA (Defense Advanced Research Projects Agency) Intrusion Detection Evaluation in information security [5]. Later on, it appeared that the DARPA datasets are not appropriate to simulate real network systems. This initiated the need for development of new datasets with a view to developing IDS [6].

B. *Machine Learning techniques for IDS*

Machine Intelligence has achieved high detection accuracy in developing IDS. The literatures from [7] and [8] discuss a survey of these techniques. One of the most promising techniques among them is the neural network. It consists of a collection of actions to transform a set of inputs to a set of searched outputs through a set of simple processing units, or nodes and connections between them. Both supervised and unsupervised neural network techniques have been developed such as Multi-Layer Perceptron (MLP) [9] and Self-Organizing Maps (SOM) [10] respectively. Neural networks are found to be ideal when we consider all various forms of network attack traffic that we can encounter [11].

Network traffic can sometimes be better represented by clustering techniques where traffic data are clustered and are often unsupervised. There are commonly two main clustering algorithms namely k-means clustering and c-means clustering. Clustering also allows subsampling. Therefore, it can reduce the complexity when fed into a classifier machine. The authors of [12] investigated multiple centroid-based unsupervised clustering algorithms for intrusion detection and proposed a self-labeling heuristic for detecting attacks and normal clusters of network traffic. Clustering techniques are also useful in identifying unseen types of attacks. However, clustering techniques alone are not sufficient to create an effective decision boundary which can achieve promising accuracy rate. Due to these reasons, various hybrid approaches have been developed overtime. The authors of [2] proposed an intrusion detection system using Support Vector Machine and hierarchical clustering where the clustering techniques mainly aided in enhancing the training time of the Support Vector Machine by subsampling of the problem space. Support Vector Machine is an efficient classification technique but it requires higher training time. [13] proposed an intrusion detection technique using ANN (Artificial Neural Network) and fuzzy clustering. In this system, fuzzy clustering technique is used to generate different training subsets which are then trained to formulate different ANN based models. Thereafter, it determines membership grades of these subsets and combines them via a new ANN to get final results. The goal of this mechanism is to increase the detection accuracy of less frequent attacks by evaluating subsets. However, the accuracy of this mechanism increases when the number of clusters is increased, which recurrently incurs computational cost. [14] proposed the use of genetic fuzzy systems and pairwise learning for improving detection rates of low frequency attacks. The pairwise learning approach is used to create m*(m-1)/2 two-class problems for an original m-class problem which is then classified with Genetic Fuzzy Systems (GFS) based on evolutionary algorithm. The pairwise learning approach was helpful to simplify the decision boundary by making the problem space smaller to a two-class problem. Even so, the binarization technique is subject to high computational complexity as the number of total classes will exponentially increase for their proposed two-class problem forming formula.

Neural networks alone perform worse than Support Vector Machine (SVMs), which are outperformed by efficient techniques, such as Decision Tree. Multi-Layer Perceptron (MLP) is one of the simplest Deep Learning Neural Network architectures. In this paper, we have used a fully connected Multi-Layer Perceptron Neural Network with one hidden layer. To reduce the classification complexity provided to the MLP, we have utilized the clustering technique to simplify the decision boundary of our learner tool. Notably, the Clustered Neural Network is applied on an evolved two class problem to leverage the benefits of pair-wise learning approach while the computation complexity of the approach is not subject to increases with an increasing number of class as was identified in [14]. The computational complexity is kept at minimum by maintaining only one two-class problem always. It will be discussed in more detail in the next section. Our proposed mechanism is simple and efficient. It achieves a promising performance in terms of accuracy for all the different attack types including low frequency attacks used in the experiment.

III. PROPOSED MECHANISM

Our proposed mechanism is built on top of a clustering based Neural Network, which essentially clusters an evolved two class problem, which is then trained by a Neural Network model. Therefore, we first discuss our used algorithms before moving on to our proposed model.

A. *K-means Clustering and Neural Network*

K-means clustering is the widely-adopted technique of clustering input vectors to k number of clusters and can be represented by a summation function as shown in (1),

$$\sum_{i=1}^{n} \sum_{j=1}^{k} u_{ij}^{m} d(\vec{x_i}, \vec{c_j}) \qquad (1)$$

where n in is the number of objects with k clusters where u_{ij}^{m} is the degree of membership and $d(\vec{x_i}, \vec{c_j})$ is the Euclidean distance of vector $\vec{x_i}$ from cluster centre $\vec{c_j}$ which can, in turn, be represented as the weighted average of all objects, as shown in (2),

$$c_j = \frac{\sum_{i=1}^{n} u_{ij}^{m} x}{\sum_{i=1}^{n} u_{ij}^{m}} \qquad (2)$$

The relationship between u_{ij}^{m} and $d(\vec{x_i}, \vec{c_j})$ can be considered as:

$$u_{ij}^{m} \propto \frac{1}{d(\vec{x_i},\vec{c_j})} \quad (3)$$

Thus, (3) shows that as the distance between vector $\vec{x_i}$ and cluster centre $\vec{c_j}$ increases, the degree of membership u_{ij}^{m} decreases.

On the contrary, Neural Networks classify by training feature inputs through a number of hidden layers to derive higher level features. It can be classified by a non-linear activation function. As shown in Fig 1, x_i are the feature vectors input to the ANN system. In our case, we used 41 features provided by the KDD'99 dataset [15]. KDD'99 is one of the few public datasets that are recognized as standard datasets specifically for intrusion detection [16]. As shown in the figure, u_j and u_k are the hidden layers which are also called the intermediary output layers. u_l is the final output layer which helps us to identify the classes. In this figure, we show two possible output classes by the red and blue circle. w_{ij}, w_{jk} and w_{kl} are the weight from x_i to u_j, u_j to u_k and u_k to u_l respectively which are fine-tuned by Back-propagation algorithm to reduce error in calculating the output.

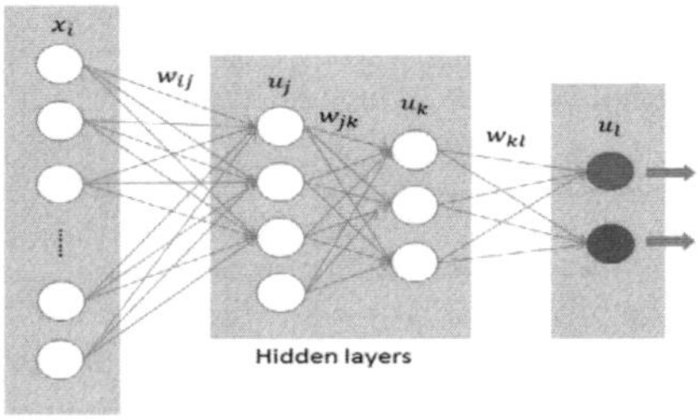

Figure 1. Neural Network classification

B. *Clustering based Evolving Neural Network*

In literature, it has been observed that when a certain classifier is faced with a multi-class problem, it often shows poor results for low-frequency classes. It often happens in case of low-frequency attacks such as U2R (User-to-Root) and R2L (Remote-to-Local) though they are equally fatal to bring a major system down by malicious root access or remote machine access. Hence, we propose an evolving pair of classes to perform a pairwise learning by a Clustered Neural Network. Thus, a single pair of equal size of classes is formed from the standard KDD'99 dataset in order to avoid bias created by low-frequency input vectors. The data is then pre-processed with feature selection. The evolved pairs of classes are then clustered by k-means clustering before classifying them with fully connected neural networks. Fig 2 shows the basic workflow of our evolved pair wise learning with clustered Neural Network.

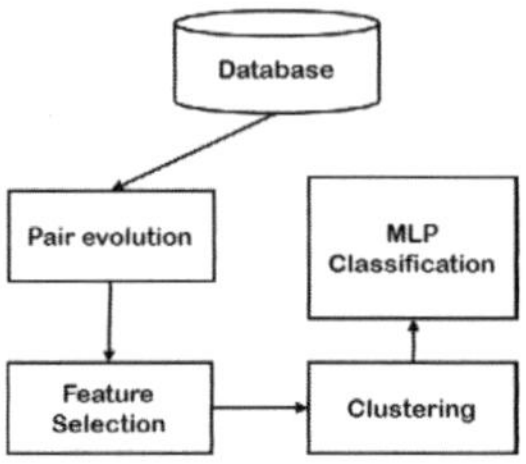

Figure 2. Workflow of pair evolution and training Clustered Neural Network

There are four major types of network attack traffic namely DoS (Denial-of-Service), Probe, R2L and U2R. Among them, DoS refers to all the network traffic flooding attack types. Probe attacks are the attacks conducted by sending meaningless packets in order to gain knowledge about the network. R2L refers to remote access attacks, where the attacker tries to gain access to a remote system. U2R is the type of attack in which the attacker tries to log-in to a normal account and then gain root administrator access [17]. We created our clustered evolving neural network architecture by evolving these four main modalities into a single evolved pair of classes similar to pair evolution algorithm in [18]. Therefore, our first pair of evolved two classes are 'normal' and 'attack'. Here the attack class contains all the four network attacks: DoS, Probe, R2L and U2R. If the tested instance is found not to fall under normal class then the normal class is eliminated from the problem space and a new two class problem is formed from the 'attack' class. Based on prioritization of the attacks, the new two classes are formed. For a certain scenario, let us consider the DoS class to be the most prioritized class. Therefore, the new evolved pair will be 'DoS' and 'other attacks' where the other attacks class contains the other three network attacks: Probe, R2L and U2R. In the next step, if the tested instance is not DoS, we can take the evolved two pair as 'Probe' and 'other attacks' where the other attacks class contains: R2L and U2R. If it is not Probe then we take the network evolved pair as 'R2L' and 'U2R'. In this way, we can make the problem space smaller, which can be better evaluated by our clustered neural network.

IV. Analysis And Simulation

For experimentation, KDD99 dataset with 41 features [17] was used to create a clustered evolving neural network. A total of 10,000 data instances were used.

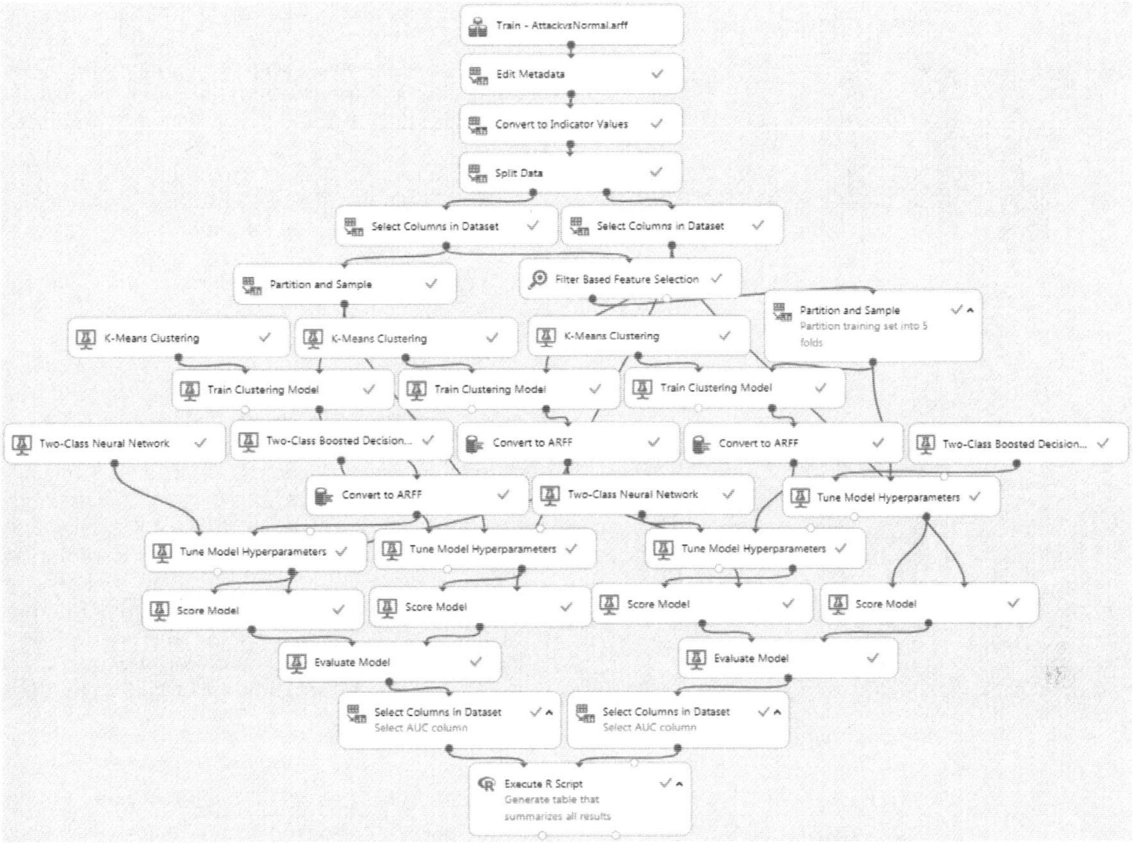

Figure 3. Implementation of Clustered Evoloving Neural Network Intrusion Detection

The data set is split between training and validation set. Therefore, 10% of the data set is used for training and 90% of the dataset is used for validation purpose. Samples from all the subclasses of the 4 major types of network attack traffic were used as shown, in Table 1 [17].

TABLE I. NETWORK ATTACK TRAFFIC

Attack class	Attack Types
DoS	Back, Land, Neptune, Pod, Smurf, Teardrop
Probe	Satan, Ipsweep, Nmap, Portsweep
R2L	Guess_Password, Ftp_write, Imap, Phf, Warezmaster
U2R	Loadmodule

A. *Performance Evaluation*

We compared our clustered evolving neural network intrusion detection performance with Boosted Decision Tree in two different modes of experiment. In the first experiment, we tested the KDD'99 dataset without feature selection in our proposed environment and in the boosted decision tree environment. In the second experiment, we performed a feature selection method on the dataset to leave it with less number of features. We again compared our proposed model to boosted decision tree. Fig. 4, Fig. 5, Fig. 6 and Fig. 7 show the performance gain in terms of accuracy with clustered neural network in multiple filter based feature selection with Pearson's correlation, i.e., 5 features selection, 10 features selection, 20 features selection and 30 features selection and all features selection. The performances are shown according to the four cases, normal vs attack, DoS vs other attacks, Probe vs other attacks, R2L vs U2R respectively.

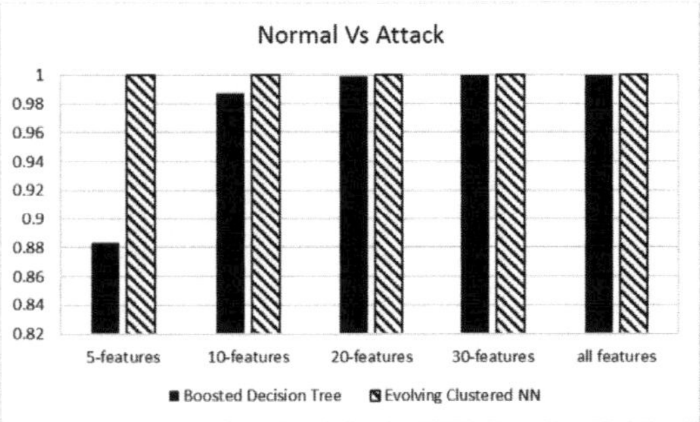

Figure 4. Comparison between Clustered NN and Boosted Decision Tree for Normal Versus Attack

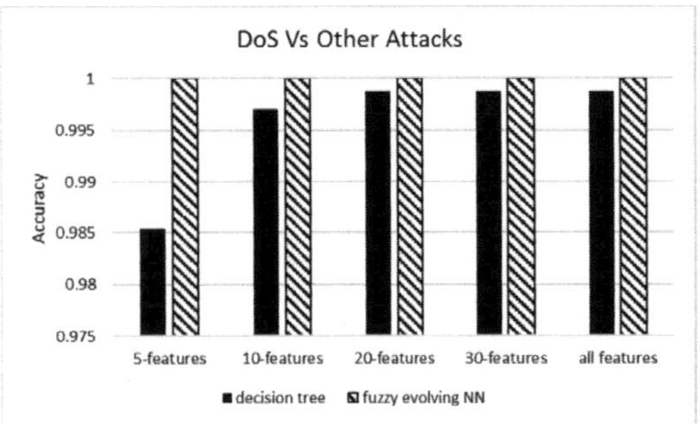

Figure 5. Comparison between Clustered NN and Boosted Decision Tree for DoS Versus Other Attacks

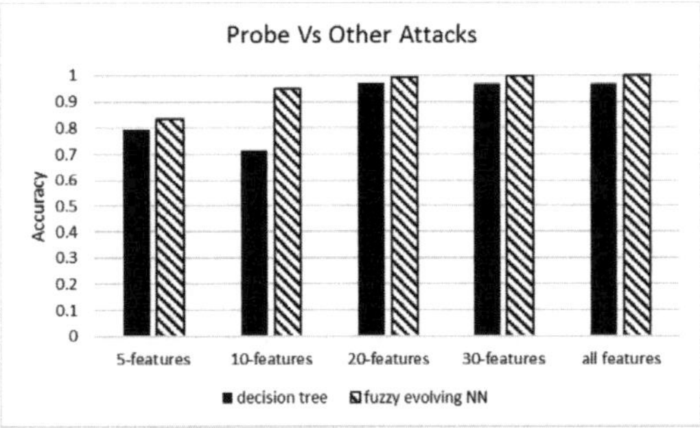

Figure 6. Comparison between Clustered NN and Boosted Decision Tree for Probe Vs Other Attacks

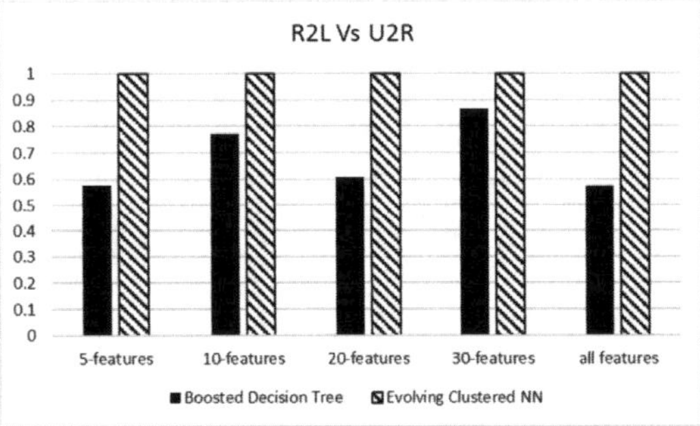

Figure 7. Comparison between Clustered NN and Boosted Decision Tree for R2L Vs U2R

As it can be seen from the above figures, our model has a higher correct classification in all test cases. In Fig. 6, Probe versus other attacks with 5 and 10 features in clustered neural network was found to have slightly lower performance, which we believe could be due to reduced feature size, an essential factor for separation of certain attack categories. However, our proposed mechanism has a higher correct classification when compared to Decision Tree in all the separate experiments of the 4 cases of network attack traffic analysis. This also depicts that if we are limited with the number of features our proposed model may outperform well-known architectures such as Decision Tree. There were no false positives in all the experiments for our proposed model except in the case of Probe Vs Other Attack in 5 and 10 feature cases with 46 cases and 45 cases respectively. The performance gain was exceptionally high for most of our experiment, which could be due to the smaller size of our dataset. Initially, we used 10,000 data instances and it was subject to reduction based on elimination of classes that were not considered to belong to our test instances. To minimize the effect of the size of the dataset, we used 10% of the dataset for training and about 90% of the dataset for validation. Therefore, if we use 1000 instances for training, we used 9000 instances for testing in order to validate the classification methodology in a more constrained environment. Besides, we also tested in different feature selected environments and as can be seen in all cases the performance of our methodology is higher than Decision Tree.

V. DISCUSSION

The performance gain of the method described in this paper is credited to the fact that we decrease the number of concerned classes, thus making the classification simpler. Accordingly, the classifier's complexity is reduced which can be evolved every time to create a two-class problem and solved pairwise to find the specific class of interest. The reduction in complexity is also contributing to the time efficiency of our mechanism. Besides, the elimination process to create a new two-class problem allows us to make the problem space smaller and thus to save more space.

The paper also embraces the idea of combining unsupervised learning with supervised learning by unsupervised clustering of the data before feeding it to the supervised neural network. The prior clustering technique works by creating two subsets where one class is the pure class of concern and the other class is the other class combination. This clustering aids the decision process in neural network by enhancing the classification borderline further and thus achieving higher accuracy.

Finally, the combination of evolved pairwise learning with clustered neural network creates an ultimate leap of performance while reducing the complexity. In this way, it makes the problem space simpler and smaller. The idea, thus, achieves a unique combination of high performance, speed with less space consumption.

Our proposed mechanism, however, does not have any standardized method to prioritize the attack classes which will be given to the evolved two-class pair. Therefore, in future work, we will consider dynamic techniques to prioritize network attack classes for different network scenarios. We will also consider other emerging attack classes and evaluate our proposed mechanism in such scenarios. Correspondingly, as it was discussed in the performance evaluation section, we will consider bigger initial data instance size for both testing and training for validating our proposed mechanism.

VI. CONCLUSION

In this paper, we have proposed an Intrusion Detection System inspired by evolving a clustered neural network classification technique in order to detect the four key categories of attack traffic that can occur in a Medical Cyber Physical System network. We have presented an enhanced version of the traditional supervised Multi-Layer Perceptron Neural Network developed further when combined with unsupervised clustering. The performance gain has been compared with Boosted Decision Tree in different feature selected environments. To the best of our knowledge, this is the first work done on developing an intelligent intrusion detection system combining evolving pairwise learning with supervised and unsupervised machine intelligence for the Medical Cyber Physical System.

ACKNOWLEDGMENT

This work was supported by the National Research Foundation of Korea (NRF) grant funded by the Korea government(MSIP) (No. 2016R1A2B4015899). Kijoon Chae is the corresponding author.

REFERENCES

[1] O. Kocabas, T. Soyata, and M. K. Aktas, “Emerging Security Mechanisms for Medical Cyber Physical Systems”, IEEE/ACM Transactions on Computational Biology and Bioinformatics, Vo. 13, No. 3, June 2016.

[2] L. Khan, M. Awad, and B. Thuraisingham, “A new intrusion detection system using support vector machines and hierarchical clustering” The VLDB Journal—The International Journal on Very Large Data Bases, Vol. 16, No. 4, pp. 507-521, October 2007.

[3] D. E. Denning, “An Intrusion-Detection Model,” in IEEE Symposium on Security and Privacy, pp. 118–131, February 1986.

[4] D. Anderson, T. Frivold, and A. Valdes, “Next generation Intrusion Detection Expert System (NIDES): A summary,” SRI Int., pp. 47, May 1995.

[5] M. Lincoln Laboratory, “DARPA Intrusion Detection Data Sets.” [Online]. Available: https://www.ll.mit.edu/ideval/data/. [Accessed: 07- Apr-2016].

[6] J. McHugh, “Testing Intrusion detection systems: a critique of the 1998 and 1999 DARPA intrusion detection system evaluations as performed by Lincoln Laboratory,” ACM Trans. Inf. Syst. Security., Vol. 3, No. 4, pp. 262–294, November 2000.

[7] J. Singh and M. J. Nene, “A Survey on Machine Learning Techniques for Intrusion Detection Systems,” International Journal of Advanced Research in Computer and Communication Engineering, Vol. 2, No. 11, pp. 4349–4355, November 2013.

[8] S. K. Wagh, “Survey on Intrusion Detection System using Machine Learning Techniques,” International Journal of Computer Applications, Vol. 78, No. 16, pp. 30–37, September 2013.

[9] C. Qiu, J. Shan, B. Polytechnic, and B. Shandong, “Research on Intrusion Detection Algorithm Based on BP Neural Network,” International Journal of Security and Its Applications Vol. 9, No. 4, pp. 247–258, 2015.

[10] L. Vokorokos, A. Baláž, and M. Chovanec, “Intrusion detection system using self-organizing map,” Informatica, Vol. 6, No. 1, pp. 1–6, 2006.

[11] J.-P. Planquart, “Application of Neural Networks to Intrusion Detection,” Sans Institute, 2001.

[12] S. Zhong, T. M. Khoshgoftaar, and N. Seliya, “Clustering-based network intrusion detection”, International Journal of reliability, Quality and safety Engineering, Vol. 14 No. 02, pp. 169-187, April 2007.

[13] G. Wang, J. Hao, J. Ma, and L. Huang, “A new approach to intrusion detection using Artificial Neural Networks and fuzzy clustering”, Expert systems with applications, Vol. 37, No. 9, pp-6225-6232, September 2010.

[14] S. Elhag, A. Fernández, A. Bawakid, S. Alshomrani, and F. Herrera, “On the combination of genetic fuzzy systems and pairwise learning for improving detection rates on Intrusion Detection Systems”, Expert Systems with Applications, Vol. 42, No. 1, pp. 193-202, August 2015.

[15] TunedIT, “KDD Cup 1999 dataset” [Online]. Available: http://tunedit.org/repo/KDD_Cup/KDDCup99.arff [Accessed: 01- January-2017].

[16] C. F. Tsai, Y. F. Hsu, C. Y. Lin, and W. Y. Lin, “Intrusion detection by machine learning: A review”, Expert Systems with Applications, Vol. 36 No. 10, pp. 11994-12000, 2009.

[17] S. Potluri, C. Diedrich, “Accelerated deep neural networks for enhanced Intrusion Detection System”, 2016 IEEE 21st International Conference on Emerging Technologies and Factory Automation (ETFA), pp. 1-8, September 2016

[18] N. Mowla, I. Doh, and K. Chae, "Evolving neural network intrusion detection system for MCPS," IEEE International Conference on. Advanced Communication Technology (ICACT), pp. 183-187, February 2017.

An Empirical Study of Root-Cause Analysis in Information Security Management

Gaute Wangen, Niclas Hellesen, Henrik Torres, and Erlend Brækken
NTNU Gjøvik
Teknologiveien 22,
2802 Gjøvik, Norway
Email: gaute.wangen@ntnu.no, niclashellesenl@gmail.com,
henrik.torres@gmail.com, erlendlbr@gmail.com

***Abstract*—This paper studies the application of Root-cause analysis (RCA) methodology to a complex socio-technical information security (InfoSec) management problem. InfoSec risk assessment (ISRA) is the common approach for dealing with problems is InfoSec, where the main purpose is to manage risk and maintain an acceptable risk level. In comparison, the RCA tools are designed to identify and eliminate the root-cause of a reoccurring problem. Our case study is a complex issue regarding multiple breaches of the security policy primarily through access control violations. By running a full-scale RCA, this study finds that the benefits of the RCA tools are a better understanding of the social aspects of the risk; RCA highlighted previously unknown social and administrative causes for the problem which in turn provided an improved decision-basis. The problem treatments recommended by the ISRA and the RCA differed in that the ISRA results recommended technical controls, while the RCA suggested more administrative treatments. Furthermore, we found that the ISRA and RCA can complement each other in administrative and technical issues. The main drawback was that our cost-benefit analysis regarding hours spent on RCA was on the borderline of being justifiable. As future work, we propose to develop a leaner version of the RCA scoped for information security problems.**

Keywords*—*Information Security; Root cause analysis; Risk Management; Case study.

I. Introduction

Judging by the available literature on standards and methods, the common approach to dealing with problems in information security (InfoSec) is risk assessments. Risk assessment aims to estimate the probability and consequence of an identified scenario or for reoccurring incidents, and propose risk treatments based on the results. By estimating the expected risk of repeating incidents or an identified scenario, risk assessment aims at proposing risk treatments based on the estimated results. The InfoSec risk assessment (ISRA) has been developed to analyze risks that occur when applying technology to information, and revolve around securing the confidentiality, integrity, and availability of information or other assets [1]. By focusing on assets and vulnerabilities, these assessments tend to have a technical scope [2] [3] with estimates of consequences and respective probabilities of events as key outputs. Although the InfoSec risk management (ISRM) approach is useful for maintaining acceptable risk levels, they are not developed to solve complex socio-technical problems. In comparison, the Root Cause Analysis (RCA) is *"a structured investigation that aims to identify the real cause of a problem and the actions necessary to eliminate it."* [4] RCA incorporates a broad range of approaches, tools, and techniques to uncover causes of problems, ranging from standard problem-solving paradigms, business process improvement, benchmarking, and continuous improvement [4]. The ISRA and RCA approaches are different in that RCA investigates incidents that have occurred with some frequency aiming to understand and eliminate the problem from a socio-technical perspective. While ISRA attempts to estimate the risk and propose and implement risk treatments based on the results to achieve acceptable risk.

The case study presented in this paper extends the ISRA of a complex socio-technical problem with RCA and discusses the cost/benefit of the results. The objective of ISRM is to reduce risk to an acceptable level. A typical ISRA would be to estimate annual incident cost, compare it to risk appetite, and if found unacceptable: implement a treatment to address either probability, consequence, or both, to maintain the risk within acceptable levels, while RCA aims to remove the problem in its entirety. However, both approaches seek to treat the problem at hand, which makes the output comparable. The application of formal RCA tools is an area that has remained largely unexplored in InfoSec literature. Therefore, the problem we are addressing in this study is to determine the utility of RCA for InfoSec and if it provides useful input to the decision-making process beyond the ISRA. The problem is investigated using a case study, qualitative assessment of results, and cost-benefit analysis.

The case is of breaches to the access control (AC) security policy (SecPol), such as access card and Personal Identification Number (PIN) exchange between employees. This complex problem is located at the intersection of the social and technological aspects that many organizations may face. The Scandinavian organization in our case study had logged multiple occurrences of policy violations together with costly incidents as a consequence. This study investigates if RCA can be applied as a useful extension to the ISRM process for the AC SecPol problem. To investigate this issue, we qualitatively assess the results of a RCA conducted as an extension to a high-level ISRA of the problem. Further, we discuss if RCA can be justified for complex InfoSec problems through cost-benefit analysis. This paper applies the seven-step process RCA methodology [4] for comparison of results. The data collected for this study was primarily from historical observations and data in the target institution together with qualitative interviews of thirty-six representatives from six relevant stakeholder groups.

The remainder of the paper is structured as follows: The following section addresses previous work on RCA in InfoSec. Section III provides a description of the applied

ISRA method and the RCA tools methods including statistical analysis. Further, we present the results from the ISRA and the RCA. Lastly, we discuss the qualitative differences and discuss cost-benefit. Finally, we discuss the limitations, propose future work, and conclude the results.

II. Related Work

RCA was developed to solve practical problems in traditional safety, quality assurance, and production environments [4]. However, RCA has also been adopted in selected areas of InfoSec: Julisch [5] studied the effect of the RCA, by considering RCA for improvement of decision-making for handling alarms from intrusion detection systems. The study provides evidence towards the positive contribution of RCA, but it does not apply the RCA tools as they are proposed in the recent literature [4], [6], [7]. Julisch builds on the notion that there are root causes accounting for a percentage of the alarms, but proposes his tools for detecting and eliminating root causes outside of the problem-solving process, Fig. 1. A more recent study conducted by Collmann and Cooper [8] applied RCA for an InfoSec breach of confidentiality and integrity in the healthcare industry. Based on a qualitative approach, the authors find the root cause of an incident and propose remediation. Their results also show a clear benefit from applying RCA, although their RCA approach seems non-standardized, being primarily based on previously published complex problem-solving research articles. Wangen [9] utilizes RCA to analyze a peer review ring incident, where an author managed to game the peer review process and review his papers. This incident is analyzed by combining RCA tools and the Conflicting Incentives Risk Analysis (CIRA) to understand the underlying incentives and to choose countermeasures. Further, Abubakar et.al. [10] applied RCA as a preliminary tool to investigate the high-level causes identity theft. The study applies a structured RCA approach [7] and identifies multiple causes and effects for setbacks to the investigation of identity theft. The Abubakar et.al. study shows the utility of RCA for InfoSec by providing an insight into a complex problem such as identity theft. Hyunen and Lenzini [11] discuss RCA application in InfoSec by contrasting the traditional approaches to Safety and Security to highlight shortcomings of the latter. Furthermore, the authors propose an RCA-based tool for InfoSec management to address said shortcomings and demonstrate the tool on a use case. The tool is designed to reveal vulnerable socio-technical factors.

Some of the tools applied in an RCA are also recognizable in the risk assessment literature, for example, instruments such as Flowcharts and Tree diagrams model processes and events visually. Typical comparable examples from risk assessment are Event-tree and Fault-tree analysis, where the risk is modeled as a set of conditional events, however, these approaches are not specifically developed for InfoSec risk analysis. Schneier adapted the Fault-tree analysis mindset and created *Attack Trees* [12]. These tools resemble those of RCA. However, the frame for applying them is different in the sense that attack trees focus on the technical threat and vulnerability modeling, while RCA tools focus on problem-solving.

Although there are a couple of published studies on the application and utility of formal RCA methodologies, the previous work on RCA in InfoSec is scarce, and there is a research gap in experimenting with the RCA tools for solving re-occurring InfoSec problems. The studies we found provided positive results and motivation for further experiments with RCA for InfoSec problems.

III. Method

The primary research approach was a case study which was conducted in a Scandinavian R&D institution to investigate the complex problem of internal AC policy violations. The ISRA was conducted as a high-level risk assessment for the institution which revealed the need for deeper analysis of the problem. Three independent researchers conducted the RCA and gathered data from 36 scientific interviews and applied historical data on incidents caused by unauthorized access.

Further, we qualitatively compare the results where we analyze the differences in approaches, findings, and treatment recommendation. Additionally, we applied a cost-benefit analysis to measure resources regarding time spent on conducting RCA and benefits concerning additional knowledge about the problem.

The following section briefly describes the ISRA approach applied in this study, while the second section describes the RCA approach. The latter contains a description of the seven-step RCA process, the tools used, data collection method, and a brief overview of the statistical methods used for data analysis.

A. ISRA Method

The ISRA method applied for the case study is based on the standard ISO/IEC 27000-series [1]. Further substantiated with the Wangen et.al. [13] [14] approaches which centers on estimations of asset value, vulnerability, threat, and control efficiency, these are combined with available historical data to obtain both quantitative and qualitative risk estimations. The applied method identifies events together with adverse outcomes and uses conditional probability to estimate the risk of each identified outcome. The results section provides a summary of the initial ISRA results.

B. Approach to Root cause analysis

In choosing a RCA framework, we looked at comprehensiveness, academic citations, and availability. Based on the criteria, our study chose to follow the seven-step RCA process proposed by Andersen and Fagerhaug [4], as shown in Fig. 1. Each step consists of a set of tools to produce the results needed to complete the subsequent steps, whereas step 7 is out of scope. Each step consists of different tools to solve problems where one or more are required to complete the RCA and conclude the root cause(s). As recommended in the methodology, we chose tools per step based on our judgment of suitability. The RCA in this study was conducted by a three-person team supported by a mentor. We have anonymized information according to the employer's requests. The following subsections describe each step in the RCA process and our selected tools (see [4] for further description).

Step 1 - Problem understanding, Performance Matrices. The goal of this step is to understand the problem and rank the issues. Performance Matrices are used to illustrate the target system's current performance and importance. The performance matrix contributes towards establishing priority of the different problems, factors, or problems in the system [4]

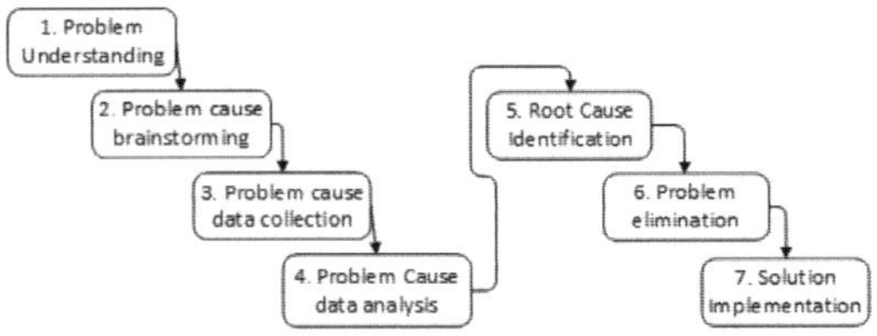

Fig. 1: Seven step process for RCA [4].

(P.36-41): (i) which part of the problem is the most important to address, and (ii) which problem will reduce the highest amount of symptoms. The problems are qualitatively identified and ranked on a scale from 1 to 9, on performance (x-axis) and importance (y-axis).

Step 2 - Problem cause brainstorming. The main idea of this step is to cover other possible issues that may be causing the problem, not thought of in Step 1. For this purpose, we applied unstructured *Brainstorming*, which is a technique where the participants verbally suggested all possible causes they could think of, which was immediately noted on a whiteboard and summarized together at the end.

Step 3 - Problem Cause Data Collection - Interviews. RCA recommends several data collection techniques [4], this study chose scientific interviews as the main data collection approach as the study required an in-depth understanding of the motivations for AC SecPol violation problem. The interviews were conducted in a face-to-face setting, and was designed using category, ordinal, and continuous type questions together with open-ended interview questions for sharing knowledge about the problem. The interview subjects were primarily categorized as representatives of key stakeholder groups within the organization and one group of external contractors. Each interview had twenty-six questions with follow-up questions if deemed necessary to clarify the opinion or to extract valuable knowledge from particularly knowledgeable individuals.

Step 4 - Problem Cause Data Analysis - Statistics & Affinity diagram. We applied a variety of statistical data analysis methods specified in the results, and the IBM SPSS software for the statistical analysis. A summary of the statistical tests used in this research is as follows.

For *Descriptive analysis* on continuous type questions, we applied the median as the primary measure of central tendency. We also conducted *Univariate* analysis of individual issues and *Bivariate* analysis for pairs of questions, such as a group belonging and a continuous question, to see how they compare and interact. As the Likert-scale seldom will satisfy the requirements of normality and not have a defined scale of measurement between the alternatives, we restricted the use of mean and standard deviation. We analyzed the median together with an analysis of range, minimum and maximum values, and variance. This study also analyses the distributions of the answers, for example, if they are normal, uniform, bimodal, or similar. We used Pearson two-tailed *Correlation test* to reveal relationships between pairs of variables as this test does not assume normality in the sample.

The questionnaire had several open-ended questions which we treated by listing and categorizing the responses. Further, we counted the occurrence of each theme and summarized the responses. We also applied the *Affinity diagram* for analyzing our qualitative data, which is a RCA tool for grouping data and discovering underlying relationships.

Step 5 - Root Cause Identification - Cause-and-Effect Charts. The goal of this step is to identify the root cause(s) of the problem. For this task, we applied the Cause-and-Effect chart (Fishbone diagram) which is a tool for identifying the major causes of a problem, together with the secondary causes/factors influencing the problem. The results from this process should map to the undesired effect, the problem.

Step 6 - Problem elimination - Systematic Inventive Thinking (SIT). The goal of this step is to propose solutions to deal with the root causes of the problem, Andersen and Fagerhaug [4] describe primarily two types of tools for drafting treatments; one is designed to stimulate creativity for new solutions, while the other is designed for developing solutions.

IV. CASE STUDY: ACCESS CONTROL POLICY VIOLATIONS

In this section, we first present a summary of the results from the ISRA, in terms of risk estimation and proposed treatment. Further, we present the results from our RCA for comparison.

The case data was collected from an institution whose IT-operations delivers services to about 3000 users. The organization is a high-availability academic organization providing a range of services to the users, mainly in research, development, and education. The IT Operations are the internal owners of the AC regimes and most of the lab equipment; they represent the principal in this study. The objectives of the IT-operations is to deliver reliable services with minimal downtime, together with information security solutions.

During the last years, the Institution has experienced multiple incidents of unauthorized access to its facilities. The recurring events primarily lead to theft and vandalism of equipment in a range of cost that is deemed unacceptable. Thus, the hypothesis is that this has partially been caused by employees and students being negligent of the SecPol regarding AC, providing unauthorized access to the facilities. While the SecPol explicitly states that both the token and the PIN are personal and shall not be shared, there has been registered multiple incidents of this occurring.

A. *The Risk of Access control policy violations*

The goal of the ISRA was to derive the annual risk of the incidents. This section summarizes the asset identification and evaluation, vulnerabilities assessment, threat assessment, control efficiency, and outcomes.

The Institution had two key asset groups: (i) hardware and (ii) physical sensitive information, both stored in access controlled facilities. The hardware's primary protection attribute was availability, and the value was estimated in the range of moderate according to the budget, with a low to medium importance in the day-to-day business processes.

The two controls in place are primarily (i) AC mechanisms - physical control in place to prevent unauthorized accesses and mitigate the risk of theft. (ii) The SecPol - administrative control, which is a written statement concerning the proper use of AC mechanisms.

For the vulnerability assessment, experience showed that illegitimate users were accessing the facilities on a daily basis. We identified two primary vulnerabilities; (i) lack of security training and awareness, whereas the stakeholders do not understand the risk exposure of the organization. (ii) Insufficient organizational security policies, whereas the SecPol itself lacks clear consequences for breaches, leaving the personnel complacent. The main attack for exploiting these two vulnerabilities was social engineering, where the attacker either manages to get a hold of a security token and PIN. Alternatively, the attacker manages to gain unauthorized access to the facilities by entering with others who have legitimate access (tailgating). With the number of stakeholders having access, both attacks are easy for a motivated threat actor. The exposure is summarized in Table I.

TABLE I. SUMMARY OF VULNERABILITY ASSESSMENT.

Scenario	Vulnerability Description	Attack description	Attack Difficulty	Vulnerability Severity	Exposure Assessment
A1	Lack of Security Training and Awareness, Insufficient InfoSec Policies	Social Engineering - Employee or Student Gives away Token and PIN (Likely)	Medium	Very High	High
A2	Lack of security training and awareness, Insufficient InfoSec Policies	Social Engineering-Employee or Student leaves doors opened for convenience	Easy	Medium	Medium

For the threat assessment, the experts identified one threat group motivated by a financial incentive with the intent of stealing either physical equipment or sensitive information, with two actors; (i) Actors who frequently steals small items, representing high frequency - low impact risk. (ii) Actors who conduct a few significant thefts, representing the low frequency - high impact risk.

B. Risk Analysis Results.

The ISRA results showed that the most severe risk facing the organization is theft of sensitive information, while physical theft of equipment is also a grave risk. According to past observations, the risk is greatest during holidays with few people on campus. The two primary risks were major equipment thefts during the holiday season and several minor equipment thefts that aggregated into an unacceptable amount.

C. Implemented Treatment - Camera Surveillance

As a result of the ISRA, the treatment implemented to reduce the two risks was camera surveillance of the main entry points of buildings. Firstly, this treatment has a preventive effect in the sense that it will heighten the attack threshold for threat actors. Besides, it will provide audit trails that will be useful in future investigations. Camera surveillance had also been proven to reduce the number of incidents as well as increasing the amount of solved crimes in similar institutions. This data indicates a high control efficiency; however, the measure also comes with some drawbacks, such as equipment cost together with the required resources to operate the system. Due to the data collection on employees surveillance brings, this

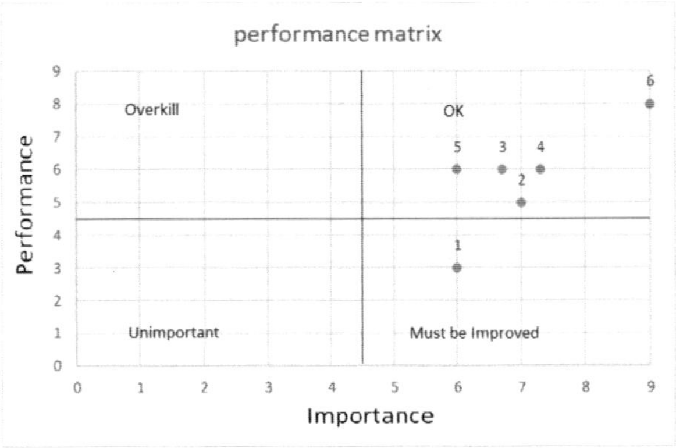

Fig. 2: Performance matrix.

risk treatment also subjects the organization to requirements from data privacy protection laws. Neither did it address the socio-technical problem with the SecPol, card swapping, and card lending.

V. Root Cause Analysis Results for a Socio-Technical problem

In this section, we present the results from conducting the RCA according to the method described in Section III-B. The results are derived from conducting RCA on the previously outlined problem and risk; we outline the hypothesized root causes and proposed treatments.

A. RCA Process, Step 1 & 2 - Problem Understanding and Cause Brainstorming

The goal of these steps is to scope the RCA and center on the preliminarily identified problem causes. The performance matrix, Fig. 2, is used to rank the identified causes on their *Importance* and *Performance*. With the help of resource persons, the team derived six topics from the preliminary *RCA steps 1 & 2*, Fig. 1): (i) Theoretical knowledge of the SecPol for AC, (ii) Practical implementation of the SecPol for AC, (iii) Consequences for policy breaches, (iv) Security Culture, (v) Backup solutions for forgotten and misplaced cards, and (vi) Card hand out for new employees. The RCA team and the expert ranked the issues and prioritized the data collection step accordingly, illustrated in Fig. 2.

B. RCA Process Step 3 - Data Collection

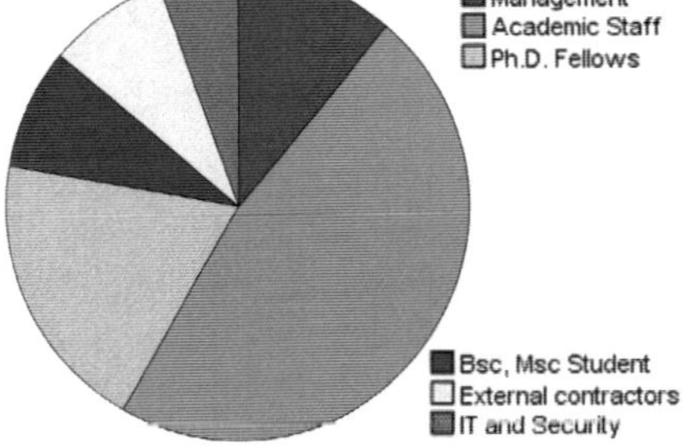

Fig. 3: Stakeholder groups included in the study

TABLE II. DEMOGRAPHICS INCLUDING AGE AND SEX DISTRIBUTIONS

	Age				Sex		
	Group	Freq.	Percent		Group	Freq.	Percent
Valid	20-29	8	22,2	Valid	Women	10	27,8
	30-39	7	19,4		Men	26	72,2
	40-49	10	27,8		Total	36	100,0
	50-59	8	22,2				
	60-69	3	8,3				
	Total	36	100,0				

For the categorical analysis, the team used age, gender, and stakeholder group as the primary categories, with the emphasis on the latter as our hypothesis was that parts of the root cause are found in conflicting interests between internal groups. The team interviewed thirty-six people located at the site, Fig. 3 displays age and gender distributions, with the six primary stakeholder groups. The interview subjects for the academic staff, Ph.D. Fellows, B.Sc. and M.Sc. students were chosen at random. The representatives of management and IT and security were key stakeholders in the organization, such as decision-makers and policy writers.

C. RCA Step 4 - Problem Cause data analysis

The Descriptive analysis showed that about half of the respondents had read the SecPol. All but two reported that it is was not allowed to lend away cards, whereas the remaining two did not know, indicating a high level of security awareness for the issue. Also, the study uncovered uncertainty among the respondents when we asked them about what the potential consequences for breaching the SecPol would bring for the employees. Whereas most of them assumed no consequence, and none perceived any severe consequences. We also uncovered that most people would be reluctant to admit to sharing cards. Further, we asked them *"How often do you think access cards are shared at the Institution?"* on a scale from 1 - 5 (1- Never, Yearly, Monthly, Weekly, 5 -Daily), to which the respondents thought that this is an issue that occurs on at least a weekly basis (Median 4). Using the same scale, the team asked how often the respondents had the need to borrow cards from others. Over half reported to not ever had the need, while twelve reported having had to lend cards on an annual basis, only two reported having the problem more than that. However, half of the respondents said to have been asked by others to borrow cards, which documented the frequency of the problem.

TABLE III. NOTABLE DIFFERENCES BETWEEN GROUPS ON "HOW LONG DID IT TAKE FOR YOU TO GET ACCESS TO THE FACILITIES YOU NEEDED?" (BETWEEN 1 VERY LONG - 6 IMMEDIATE ACCESS)

Category	N	Range	Median	Minimum	Maximum	Variance
Management	3	0	6,00	6	6	0,000
Senior Academic Staff	17	4	6,00	2	6	1,654
Ph.D. Students	7	5	5,00	1	6	3,238
BSc. and MSc. Students	3	4	3,00	1	5	4,000
External Contractors	3	3	4,00	1	4	3,000
Total	33	5	5,00	1	6	2,729

1) Summary of categorical analysis: The statistical analysis showed differences between the responses of men and women; where the latter viewed incidents involving card borrowing among employees more severely than men. The women in our sample also believe that it is more likely that employees admit to borrowing cards. Another visible difference between the stakeholder groups was who had read the policy, where all the representatives of the Management and IT and Security groups had read it. The Ph.D. Fellows and the student groups scored the lowest on having read the policy. Another observable finding was that the waiting time varied between the groups, whereas the permanent employees perceived the shortest waiting times, Table III.

2) Qualitative analysis of differences between groups: **IT and Security.** The IT operations owned much of the hardware in the facilities and was in charge of both designing, implementing, and operating the AC policy. Both representatives had read the policy and considered it important that staff and students also know the policy. The IT operations believed that card lending is an increasing problem within the institution, especially in the modern facilities where AC mechanisms are more frequent. One also answered that since he had been involved in developing the policy, he felt more ownership of it and, therefore, experienced a greater responsibility to follow it than other departments. They also felt the legal responsibility not to break the policy due to owning the AC system.

Management. This group consists of middle and upper management, which had all read the SecPol. Half believed it was important to have those who will be subject to the policy involved in the policy development process. When we asked this group about what they saw as the worst scenario, this group had similar opinions: their main concerns was loss and compromise of information together with relevant legal aspects. Two members of this group reported that they did not get the service they expected from IT regarding forgotten cards. Three out of four said that they believed the security culture to be good, while the last one reported the security controls to be cumbersome.

Senior academic staff. Consists of different types of professors, researchers, and lecturers, and represents the majority of employees in the case. This group was the largest with the most widespread opinions. Regarding the SecPol, several expressed discontent and said that it was neither security department or IT service that should be responsible for it. The organization should provide the content of the policy to ensure that it was not an obstacle in the day to day work. Further, delivering on the aims and goals of the organizational assignment should be compared to the potential harm from card swapping incidents, meaning that the policy should be designed with a better understanding of risk. An example of this was that employees must have access to rooms to do their job where a too-strict policy would stand in the way. Regarding this, several mentioned that if the cards were not lent to other employees, it would be very problematic due to the lack of backup solutions. They missed good fallback solution if one had forgotten access card.

Ph.D. Fellows. Out of this group, only one had read the SecPol. Most assumed it was not allowed to lend out their access cards, but two said they did not know. One expressed discontent from not receiving his access card quick enough, which he hypothesized as one of the reasons for borrowing other people's cards. Longer times to hand out access cards may force them to lend cards internally in an office. Another issue was that Ph.D. Fellows occasionally worked with students and that they often needed access to restricted facilities to be able to work. This issue required the Ph.D. fellow either to open the door physically for the students or to loan them their card. When we asked about the security culture, the responses were split: Two did not know, one thought that security was good, another one said that people trust each other, one said it was wrong, while one said that people knew that they should not lend it to others. The last one said that others could borrow it for practical reasons.

Students. Represents the main bulk of people with access to the main facilities, but with limited access to offices and employee areas. Only one of the students had read the policy, and none of the students who participated knew of any instances of card lending, although two out of three had been asked by someone if they could lend them their cards.

External contractors. Represents the contractors in charge of running the physical facilities, such as cleaning personnel and physical maintenance. In the External group, only one had read the policy. All believed that it was not allowed to borrow cards and that the school saw this as a serious offense. Only one of them reported having had the need to borrow a card.

D. RCA Step 5 - Identified Root causes

The interviews with the groups provided an insight into the many views on this problem and the complexity it entails, visualized with the Fishbone diagram in Fig. 4. Based on our RCA we found five possible root causes:

1. Uncertainty regarding fallback solutions. We found that there was uncertainty surrounding available backup solutions among all the stakeholder groups. Where 14 of the 31 respondents were undecided if there existed any fallback solution, and suggested to create better backup solutions. 17 said there existed backup solutions, but we uncovered different opinions regarding what these were and who was responsible for them. For example, six respondents thought they could summon the IT department, three thought the student help desk, while the remainder thought either management could help or ask a colleague to lend them access cards. Even from the two key stakeholders in IT the replies were contradictory.

2. Discomfort when using fallback solutions. Two of our respondents reported to have forgotten their cards and had contacted the on-campus card distributor to use the fallback solution. The respondents meant they had not been well-received and had not gotten the help they needed. Overall, they reported the situation to be discomforting, which was unfortunate, as this may lead to the employees using different methods for solving the problem.

3. Misaligned SecPol regarding authorization. Our interviews highlighted that being able to do their work is the most important goal for every employee. Thus, the SecPol should aim to facilitate this aim. Too strict AC will in some cases lead to obstruction in day-to-day tasks and lead to employees finding workarounds which may compromise security, such as asking trusted co-workers to borrow cards. Some of the respondents reported not having been included in the development of the SecPol and felt that it was misaligned.

4. Too much security. In especially one of the most modern buildings, there is a very strict AC regime in place, where low-level security rooms and facilities are regulated. Several of the respondents highlighted this as the main reason for card lending. These low-security rooms only required the card and not the PIN code, so the respondents did not consider this a serious breach of policy. Several of our respondents said that this was too much security and could not understand the reasoning underlying this decision.

5. Lack of risk awareness and consequences. 33 out of 36 defined possible negative consequences for the institution, so, the awareness around possible risks for the institution was high. However, we found that less than half of the respondents had read the overarching SecPol and that the respondents were unaware and uncertain about the organization's and their personal risk if their cards went astray. Everybody agreed that it was a bad thing, but nobody could say with certainty what the consequences would be, if any at all.

E. RCA Step 6 - Proposed root cause treatments

Based on our findings we conducted *Systematic Inventive Thinking* and came up with following root cause treatments:

Improve fallback solutions. Regarding root cause 1 and 2, the RCA team proposed to develop a solution for reserve access cards with adequate and tailored room access. The solution should provide basic access to low-security level facilities, with tailored room access according to stakeholder needs. This suggestion should be a public and low threshold offer for those who have forgotten or misplaced their cards.

Align SecPol with objectives. Regarding root causes 3 and 4, the RCA team proposed to risk assess the need for physical security and AC for the facilities based on the organizational goals, employee needs, and the assets stored in the room. Include key stakeholders in the process and focus on balancing productivity and security to revise the security baseline.

Improve the overarching SecPol. Regarding cause 5, the RCA team proposed to improve the overarching SecPol, the suggestions were: (i) clarify consequences for breaches of policy, (ii) assigning a responsible for sanctions per department, (iii) including the employees in the shaping of policy, and (iv) increase the accessibility of the policy.

Improving risk awareness. Regarding root cause 5, we also propose to improve risk awareness among the stakeholders, by running awareness campaigns including both the risks the organization and employees are facing. As a part of this, we proposed to create an information bank regarding risks, fallback solutions, and how to make use of them.

VI. Discussion

This section discusses the additional insight gained from the RCA; first qualitatively, and then through cost/benefit analysis.

A. Additional insight gained from RCA

Upon completing the RCA, we see that the results from the ISRA and RCA provide different models of the same problem. The information gathered from the ISRA process was scoped towards technical risks with solutions for reducing probability and consequence. Furthermore, we found the RCA

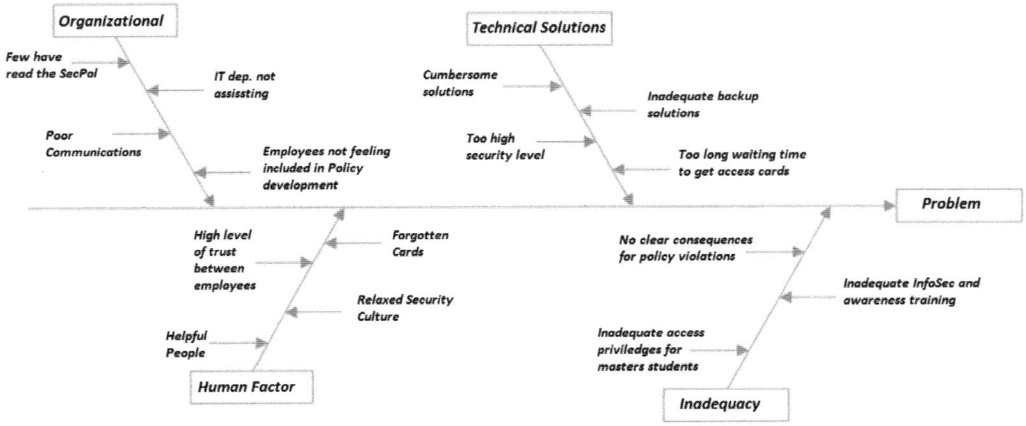

Fig. 4: Fishbone diagram illustrating contributing causes to the main problem.

to work better to visualize complexity and providing insight into the human aspects of the problem. However, the RCA process was resource intensive and required extra training to complete. The RCA process also required the inclusion of more stakeholders than the ISRA.

The results show that the benefits of the RCA are a better understanding of the social dimensions of the problem, such as conflicts between users and the security organization. This insight provides an improved decision basis and an opportunity for reaching a compromise with the risk treatment. The risk assessment team were aware of two (cause 3. and 5.) out of the five identified root causes of the problem. Thus, in our case study, the RCA did provide a valuable extension to the risk assessment for solving the problem. The RCA results showed all root causes to be on the administrative and human side of the problem. Thus, the treatments produced from the two approaches were different; ISRA produced a technical treatment in camera surveillance, while RCA produced multiple administrative treatments, each for addressing separate root causes.

Although the ISRA did highlight the vulnerabilities related to the human factor and risk perception as one of the risk factors, in this case, the decision-makers did not opt for revision of the AC policy. To summarize, the ISRA findings viewed card lending as a technical security problem, while RCA extended the knowledge into the administrative problem.

B. *Cost-benefit analysis*

For cost-benefit analysis, we consider time spent on tasks and usefulness of the task. Table IV shows that the process of achieving desired results was time and resource consuming for our team. The reported hours are the total amount from start to end without having a budget constraint. The reported hours does contain resources spent beyond the three-man team, e.g. from interview attendance and supervision.
The most time consuming and crucial tasks were the steps 3 and 4, data collection and analysis. Further, the table shows that the resource demand for the Root cause identification and elimination phases as low, this is because the team primarily identified the root causes during the data analysis. While

TABLE IV. TOTAL HOURS SPENT CONDUCTING RCA FOR AN UNTRAINED THREE MAN TEAM (APPROXIMATELY 220 HOURS PER TEAM MEMBER)

Step	Phase	Tasks	Time spent
Preliminary	Preparations	Collecting available data	100 hours
Preliminary	Preparations	Testing and choosing tools	72 hours
1	Problem Understanding	Performance Matrix	3 hours
2	Problem cause brainstorming	Brainstorming	1 hours
3	Problem cause Data Collection	Planning interviews	150 hours
3	Problem cause Data collection	Conducting interviews	100 hours
4	Data analysis	Qualitative & Statistical	220 hours
5	Root cause identification	Fishbone	7 hours
6	Root cause elimination	SIT	7 hours
			Total 660 h.
		Only RCA Process	Total 488 h.

the main task of the root cause identification phase was to formalize the causes and effects, and the elimination was used to propose treatments.

As the team gain experience with using RCA on cases, the time estimate should be significantly be reduced. For example, our study spent 172 hours in the preparation phases gathering data on the problem and testing tools. With more experience, the preliminary steps will be significantly shortened. Our team also estimated that the whole process itself would become leaner with practice.

To summarize, we derived the primary benefit from the problem cause data collection and analysis phases, which enabled the root cause identification. Furthermore, the group benefited from working on the performance matrix, which set the direction for the remainder of the project. Regarding the remaining tools, the benefits the problem cause brainstorming was that it helped to provide an overview of the problem space and invited creative thinking. The advantage of the Fishbone tool was to group and visualize the identified problems in the context. Further, the process step contributed to determine and analyze causes. The SIT tool has a series of five principles that attempts to discover how to solve the components of the root cause. This tool offers a well-structured way to traverse a problem situation but could be resource intensive when handling many problems with all their components.

Issues of minor importance should not be subject to such an extensive effort as RCA requires. During the preparations for this study, we ran RCA for minor issues and found it not worthwhile as it was unproductive to use a complicated problem-solving process to less costly problems. However, future projects should consider RCA when they perceive the issue as important and do not know its nature or cause. The problem should be expensive, complicated, and cannot be addressed sufficiently with less comprehensive methods. These properties make conducting an RCA on the project justifiable and a valuable addition to the decision-making process.

C. Limitations & Future Work

The case study presented in this article is specific to the organization and culture; thus our results have limited generalizability, but the RCA method and results provide an insight into what to expect from the process. Another aspect is that our RCA team was inexperienced and other more experienced teams will run the process more efficiently with a better cost-benefit. Another issue is if a similar insight could have been gained if we delegated a similar amount of resources into the ISRA to investigate the problem. It is possible that the results of the ISRA would have overlapped more with the RCA with more time and resources spent on the former. However, the ISRA process does not argue for such a deep dive into the problem as the RCA process and does not provide tools for doing so. It is therefore unlikely that a more thorough ISRA process would have produced a similar result. However, the incentive for such an investigation was not there, and we perceive the ISRA methodologies as immature in this area [14]. Instead of considering the RCA as an extension of the ISRA, a possible path for future work is to conduct case studies where the researchers invest a similar amount of resources into both the RCA and ISRA and then compare results.

An additional direction for future work is to apply RCA to more and diverse case studies to get a better understanding of the contributions and limitations of the approach for InfoSec. Recent work has also proposed a novel approach for conducting socio-technical security analysis [11], and a path for future work is to adapt, develop, and improve RCA tools for InfoSec. Furthermore, the future efforts could research RCA efficiency through automation of tasks and build knowledge repositories. Regarding the latter, a repository of tools for data collection would help streamline step 3 in the RCA process.

VII. Conclusion

This study has applied RCA tools to propose a solution to a complex socio-technical InfoSec problem and found the RCA method a valid but costly extension to the ISRA. Running a full-scale RCA requires a lot of time and resources and the problem should be expensive enough to justify the RCA. The results from the RCA overlapped slightly with the initial ISRA. The main differences were that the RCA team proposed administrative treatments aimed at solving problems in the social domain, while the ISRA produced a more technical analysis and treatment for the problem. We conclude that practitioners should look at these two approaches as complimentary for dealing with complex socio-technical risks and problems. The combination of the ISRA and RCA will also have utility when planning for defense-in-depth, where administrative and technical risk controls can work in coherence to mitigate threats. The main drawback was that our cost-benefit analysis of the time and resources invested in the project is on the borderline of being justifiable, and the cost of the problem should be considered before launching a RCA. Thus, the RCA provides a viable option when dealing with complex and costly InfoSec problems and should be a part of the InfoSec management toolbox.

Acknowledgements

The authors acknowledge the help and support from Professor Einar Snekkenes, Christoffer Hallstensen and Stian Husemoen. We also extend our gratitude to all the participants in our study and to the anonymous reviewers.

References

[1] *Information technology, Security techniques, Information Security Risk Management*, International Organization for Standardization Std., ISO/IEC 27005:2011.

[2] G. Wangen and E. Snekkenes, "A taxonomy of challenges in information security risk management," in *Proceeding of Norwegian Information Security Conference - NISK 2013 - Stavanger*, vol. 2013. Akademika forlag, 2013, pp. 76–87.

[3] P. Shedden, W. Smith, and A. Ahmad, "Information security risk assessment: towards a business practice perspective," in *Australian Information Security Management Conference*. School of Computer and Information Science, Edith Cowan University, Perth, Western Australia, 2010, pp. 119–130.

[4] B. Andersen and T. Fagerhaug, *Root cause analysis: simplified tools and techniques*. ASQ Quality Press, 2006.

[5] K. Julisch, "Clustering intrusion detection alarms to support root cause analysis," *ACM transactions on information and system security (TISSEC)*, vol. 6, no. 4, pp. 443–471, 2003.

[6] P. F. Wilson, *Root cause analysis: A tool for total quality management*. ASQ Quality Press, 1993.

[7] A. M. Doggett, "Root cause analysis: a framework for tool selection," *The Quality Management Journal*, vol. 12, no. 4, p. 34, 2005.

[8] J. Collmann and T. Cooper, "Breaching the security of the kaiser permanente internet patient portal: the organizational foundations of information security," *Journal of the American Medical Informatics Association*, vol. 14, no. 2, pp. 239–243, 2007.

[9] G. Wangen, "Conflicting incentives risk analysis: A case study of the normative peer review process," *Administrative Sciences*, vol. 5, no. 3, p. 125, 2015. [Online]. Available: http://www.mdpi.com/2076-3387/5/3/125

[10] A. Abubakar, P. B. Zadeh, H. Janicke, and R. Howley, "Root cause analysis (rca) as a preliminary tool into the investigation of identity theft," in *Cyber Security And Protection Of Digital Services (Cyber Security), 2016 International Conference On*. IEEE, 2016, pp. 1–5.

[11] J.-L. Huynen and G. Lenzini, "From situation awareness to action: An information security management toolkit for socio-technical security retrospective and prospective analysis," in *Proceedings of the 3rd International Conference on Information Systems Security and Privacy*, 2017, pp. 213 – 224.

[12] B. Schneier, "Attack trees," *Dr. Dobbs journal*, vol. 24, no. 12, pp. 21–29, 1999.

[13] G. Wangen, A. Shalaginov, and C. Hallstensen, "Cyber security risk assessment of a ddos attack," in *International Conference on Information Security*. Springer, 2016, pp. 183–202.

[14] G. Wangen, C. Hallstensen, and E. Snekkenes, "A framework for estimating information security risk assessment method completeness," *International Journal of Information Security*, Jun 2017. [Online]. Available: http://dx.doi.org/10.1007/s10207-017-0382-0

Library-Level Policy Enforcement

Marinos Tsantekidis
Vassilis Prevelakis
TU Braunschweig
Institute of Computer and Network Engineering
Email: {tsantekidis, prevelakis}@ida.ing.tu-bs.de

***Abstract*—We propose a system that allows policy to be implemented at the library call level. Under our scheme, calls to libraries are monitored and their arguments examined to ensure that they comply with the security policy associated with the running program. Our system automatically creates wrappers for libraries so that calls to external functions in the library are vectored to a policy enforcement engine. In this paper, we describe our system, which screens calls to protected functions, while allowing the implementation of a high level form of control flow integrity based on library calls. It is a transparent approach that can protect applications in many different domains and real-life environments.**

Keywords*—*policies; library calls; argument examination; wrapper functions

I. Introduction

Access control, in a narrow sense, is the ability of a system to grant or reject access to a protected resource. This way, in the context of software security, the system can keep track of who has access to what code, who can call what function in a library and under which conditions this is possible. These restrictions are imposed by a set of mandatory controls that are enforced by the system in the form of policies. Policies may represent the structure of an organization or the sensitivity of a resource and the clearance of a user trying to access it. A mechanism maps a user's access request to a collection of rules that need to be implemented in order for the system to function in a secure manner.

An access control system can be implemented in many places and at different levels in an infrastructure (e.g., operating system, database management system, etc.) and must be configured in a way that provides the assurance that no permissions will be leaked to an unintended actor, which may give her the ability to circumvent any defenses in place.

In this paper, we propose a novel mechanism that aims to allow access control policies for library calls to be enforced at the user-code level in order to restrict access to functions held in a protected library, in addition to identifying the complete execution path regarding the functions in question. At runtime, the policy system may be used for policy enforcement. It can coexist with existing defense techniques, boosting the security of the protected system.

The remainder of this paper is organized in the following manner: Section 2 describes related work done to address relevant issues. In Section 3, we present the architecture of our framework. In Section 4, we describe the implementation details, along with possible applications. In Section 5, we present a simple use-case scenario. Section 6 concludes this paper.

II. Related work

This work revisits our earlier work on Access Controls For Libraries and Modules (SecModule) [1]. This framework forces the user-level code to perform library calls only via a library policy enforcement engine providing mandatory policy checks over not just system calls, as in the case of Systrace [2], but calls to user level libraries as well. This results in a system which can be used to systematically formulate and formalize rights management for software. The access rights in question would be whether a process (which may be malicious) is allowed to execute some function held securely in a library module. Initially, the mechanism retrofitted functions in order to be included in a secure "enclosure" (SecModule). The kernel has a list of all the SecModules and when a process asks for access to a secured function, the kernel verifies that the requested SecModule is registered and that the process is valid with respect to its policy. Then, it allows that and only that process to use only the specific function.

This means that access to a specific function or procedure is controlled by the kernel. While this is particularly suited to SecModule-enabled applications, the overhead of two context switches per function invocation (once to transfer control to the kernel and – when it reaches a decision – once more to transfer control back to the caller) makes the technique quite expensive for more general use.

One of the issues identified by the authors of the SecModule paper was the difficulty in encapsulating library modules. This manual process was error prone and extremely labor intensive, since most of the applications compiled within the framework required patching. Another issue was the inability to evaluate call arguments. Although they were contained in a known structure pointed to by a stack pointer, their examination required lots of casting in the C++ functions, which in turn needed additional information for these functions held in the module.

Relevant to our work is the Systrace [2] system which supports fine-grained policy generation. It guards the calls to the operating system at the lowest level, enforcing policies that restrict the actions an attacker can take to compromise a system. In the process, although, it makes higher level actions indistinguishable. As an example, we can look at `libancillary` [3], a tiny library that provides an interface to operations that can be done on Unix domain sockets.

Programs that use this library can send/receive one or more file descriptors to/from a socket, actions particularly useful when the primary process lacks the rights required to open a file or a device. In this case, another – privileged – process opens the resource and sends a corresponding file descriptor to the requesting process for further processing. To control this exchange and prevent arbitrary usage of this library, the system calls (`open(2)`, `send(2)`, `recv(2)`) would need to be examined and policies enforced under Systrace. However, these calls result in a number of lower level calls to the operating system all of which Systrace would need to check. Since only the high-level calls are of importance in this case, the examination of underlying calls would be not only unnecessary, but unwanted too. The fine-grain control offered by the framework while checking calls required by system or user level libraries when implementing complex operations, is overly verbose. Additionally, it may leave a library in an inconsistent state if the sequence of these calls is interrupted in the middle of execution by a misconfiguration [1]. Furthermore, for applications that use high-level abstractions away from low-level system calls, there may be difficulties generating precise policies. Later research [4] showed that concurrency vulnerabilities were discovered that gave an attacker the ability to construct a race between the engine and a malicious processes to bypass protections. More specifically, in a multiprocessor environment the arguments of a system call were stored by a process in shared memory. After Systrace performed the check and permitted the call, another malicious process had a time window to replace the cleared arguments in shared memory, effectively negating the presence of Systrace and evading its restrictions. In a uniprocessor environment, this could be achieved by forcing a page fault or in-kernel blocking so the kernel would yield to the attacking user process.

Multics [5] operating system uses multiple rings of protection [6] – [7] that isolate the most-privileged code from other processes, forming a hierarchical layering. Each process is associated with multiple rings – domains – so it is necessary to change the domain of execution of a process. This way the process can access specific domains only when particular programs are executed. To prevent arbitrary usage, specific "gates" between rings are provided to allow passing from an outer (less-privileged) to an inner (more-privileged) ring, restricting access to resources of one layer from programs of another layer. The change of domain occurs only after the control is transferred to a gate of another domain. Switching to a lower ring requires more access rights as opposed to a higher ring where reduced rights suffice. Downward switching requires a control transfer to a gate of an inner ring, if the transfer is to be allowed, whereas an upward domain switch is an unrestricted transfer that can be performed by any process. Nevertheless, the need-to-know principle cannot be enforced, because if a resource needs to be accessible by a ring `a` but not from another `b`, then `a` needs to be lower than `b`. But, in this case every resource in `b` is accessible in `a`.

Similar to our mechanism, `ltrace` [8] [9] is a utility that runs a specified command until it exits. It intercepts the calls made to shared libraries by an application and displays the parameters used and the values returned by the calls. Moreover, it can trace system calls executed by the application. However, because it uses the dynamic library hooking mechanism, it cannot trace statically linked executables/libraries, as well as libraries that are loaded automatically using `dlopen(3)`. This mechanism gives the programmer the ability to inject symbols in the dynamic library, but these symbols need to be unresolved in the main executable or be exported in its dynamic symbol table. When the linker tries to resolve them, it will find the injected symbols and not the original ones. A statically linked application has neither unresolved symbols nor a dynamic symbol table. Additionally, `ltrace` can only display the parameters used and values returned by the calls. It offers no ability to manipulate them.

Abadi et al. proposed CFI [10] which enforces the execution of a program to adhere to a control flow graph (CFG), which is statically computed at compile time. If the flow of execution does not follow the predetermined CFG, an attack is detected. This approach, however, suffers from two main disadvantages. First, the implementation is coarse-grained. Computing a complete and accurate CFG is difficult since there are many indirect control flow transfers (jumps, returns, etc.) or libraries dynamically linked at run-time. Furthermore, the interception and checking of all the control transfers incur substantial performance overhead.

In our work, we also implement access control similar to the work presented above. Under our scheme, each call to an external function of a library is intercepted and checked to ensure that it complies with the security policy associated with the running program. Every time a call to such a function is made, its arguments are examined and it is vetted by policy evaluation code to determine whether the control flow transfer is warranted. This allows high-level policy checks to be carried out in a similar fashion to the Systrace engine [2] – which, however operates at the system call level – and SecModule [1] that introduced a form of authentication when calling functions from a library.

III. DESIGN

Our system aims to automate the process of encapsulating library modules and allow entire libraries to be instrumented, checking the arguments of the calls to functions within a library along the way, before reaching a policy decision. The flow of execution inside the protected library can also be detailed, revealing the sequence of calls to its functions. Figure 1 depicts a high level overview of the steps taken when an untrusted app calls a protected function.

In step (1), the application calls a function secured in our custom library (in this case SHA1). In step (2), instead of the intended function, the secure wrapper version of it is executed. Instrumented inside the wrapper, there is argument and policy evaluation code, which is first run before any other steps are taken (step 3). If the evaluation is successful, the originally

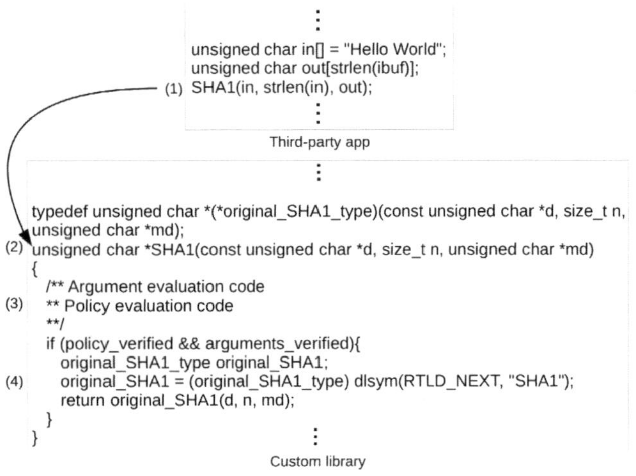

Figure 1. Overview of the call sequence

intended function is called (step 4) and the execution continues normally.

Due to the fact that we interject our evaluation code between the original call and the intended function, our approach is transparent. It requires no code modifications on the library's code, which makes it suitable for legacy applications. Also, it can be used on binary programs, since there is no need to have access to or recompile the source code of the application.

The product of the customization of a library – which is a shared custom library – can be easily adopted by security experts and used in real-life environments, since it only needs to be preloaded before running an application.

No context switch is necessary, using our custom library, since the kernel is not invoked in anyway whatsoever. Contrary to SecModule, our technique is inexpensive that way. Furthermore, the encapsulation of the library functions is straightforward using just a python script to automate the procedure, requiring only minimal manual intervention. Past experience of the writers and simplicity in producing the code, as well as major support from the community, lead to the decision of using Python as the means to create the shared library.

Under our scheme, the parameters of the intercepted calls can not only be observed, but also manipulated in order to be sanitized if necessary. Unlike `ltrace`, our mechanism relies on `dlsym(3)` and `dlopen(3)` to find the address of a symbol in memory, but because it also relies on dynamic library hooking, it is unsuitable for tracing statically linked applications.

Based on our current approach, the size of the code is increased because extra code needs to be added for every function. Before making the intended call, an extra wrapper is executed in order to decide whether to redirect the flow to the initial call or not.

Additionally, our framework depends on the programming language used to develop the protecting application, since – currently – it can only protect applications written in C/C++.

Furthermore, if an attacker knows of the presence of the protection mechanism, he might be able to bypass the policy evaluation step and call the intended function directly. Nevertheless, we believe that randomization techniques, such as ASLR [11], will make direct calls to libraries untenable.

IV. Implementation

Our technique aims to monitor calls to external functions inside a protected library. We investigated two ways of doing this: (a) individual wrappers or (b) one overall wrapper

- In the first approach, we install separate wrapper functions. Each function in the library that has an interface to the outside world is enclosed in a wrapper. When the wrapper is called, first it executes policy evaluation code to determine if the caller is permitted to call the function and then redirects the flow to the originally intended function or not.
- In the second case, the wrapper stands at the entry point of the library. A policy enforcement engine inside the wrapper monitors the incoming requests and when a call is made to a function, it determines whether that call is warranted (i.e., in accordance to the system policies). It then diverts the flow of execution to the called function.

In both approaches, the policy evaluation code examines the arguments of the call to ensure that they comply with the security policy associated with the running program.

In this first version of our prototype, we decided to follow the first path, due to the simplicity of the implementation. As an example, we created a wrapper for the OpenSSL library. The header files of the library can be included in any C/C++ program by the developers and contain all the functions that they can call. First, we extracted from the header files all the relative functions and their signatures. The extraction was done using a custom Python script that identifies each function that is within the scope of our work and analyzes its arguments. This way we are able to manipulate each of the arguments in any way necessary. Before calling the originally intended function we added code that verifies that the module, indeed, captured the call and that we operate from within the custom library. After implementing the security features (i.e., argument examination, policy enforcement, etc.) and if the continuation of the execution is permitted, the flow progresses to the original path. The result is a C file that is compiled to a shared library which is preloaded when running a program.

Automatic generation of policy (learning phase) will also be supported in future versions, while at run-time the policy system will be used for policy enforcement and/or for ensuring that the program behaves in a similar manner as in the learning phase. During this phase, as many as possible execution paths will need to be discovered, that correspond to actions taken from a benign application, aiming to implement a CFI [10] scheme that uses library calls to extract execution paths, instead of intercepting or instrumenting or emulating the control flow instructions. This will form a basis on top of which more complete policies will be built.

Applications

Wrapped functions can be accessed in a controlled manner via mandatory policy checks prior to the execution of the original flow. When an attacker tries to manipulate the protected library, the malicious efforts will be thwarted since they do not conform with the policies enforced. Nevertheless, our code can be bypassed if the attacker knows of its existence and calls the original library function directly. However, within the SHARCS project [12], we are working on hardware primitives that will force the user code to go through our wrapper.

Digital Rights Management (DRM) is another domain that our framework can be used for. In this context, it can provide access control in order to restrict usage of a piece of software the owner of which retains the right to distribute on his own conditions (e.g., after getting some form of payment or even just recognition for his efforts) or prevent the theft of it.

In the case of a library that requires heavy resources from the host system, the administrator may wish to control access to the rights to invoke the code in such a way that the system does not hang by over-use or is not affected by a DDoS attack. Access restrictions can be imposed according to certain criteria or security policies enforced by an organization.

The misuse of a critical component in a secure infrastructure can result in unforeseen consequences for the system. Our framework can make sure that only authorized personnel can have access to the secure part. Even in the case of deliberate actions that lead to an attack that jeopardizes the system, our framework can be used as a logging mechanism. The inner workings of a protected library will be traced, which will follow the flow of execution of functions held within the library. Forensic actions (after the fact) can, then, be taken to analyze in a more detailed view the events that led to the compromise and identify the culprits responsible.

V. USE-CASE STUDY

In this section, we present a scenario where a vulnerability of an application is exploited to affect the availability of the system. In our use-case, we use a vulnerable version of OpenSSL library, where a buffer overflow is triggered under specific circumstances to launch a DoS attack, in order to crash the application. By using our instrumented library to observe calls to the OpenSSL functions, we can better understand the behavior of the attack and characterize the vulnerability.

A. ChaCha20-Poly1305 heap buffer overflow

CVE-2016-7054 [13] [14] is a recent heap-based buffer overflow vulnerability related to TLS connections using *-CHACHA20-POLY1305 cipher suites. It was discovered on September 2016 and characterized as highly severe. Servers implementing versions 1.1.0a or 1.1.0b of OpenSSL, can crash when using the ChaCha20-Poly1305 cipher suite to decrypt large payloads of application data, making them vulnerable to DoS attacks. It is triggered by an error during the verification of the MAC. If it fails, the buffer on which the decrypted ciphertext is stored, is cleared by zeroing out its content via the `memset` function. However, the pointer to the buffer that is passed to the function points to the end of the buffer instead of the beginning. If the payload to be cleared is large enough, the contents of the heap will be erased, resulting in a crash when OpenSSL frees the buffer.

B. Custom library implementation

Although the vulnerability described in the previous section was addressed in versions later than 1.1.0b, we can use our prototype to examine the chain of events inside the OpenSSL library that result in a crash when the vulnerability is exploited.

When we first start an OpenSSL server (e.g., `LD_PRELOAD=/home/user/Desktop/custom_lib.so ./bin/openssl s_server -cipher 'DHE-RSA-CHACHA20-POLY1305' -key cert.key -cert cert.crt -accept 4433 -www -tls1_2 -msg`), an initialization phase takes place, where we can see that memory is allocated for the `s_server` app. Excerpt from our framework:

....

Intercepted call to function CRYPTO_strdup
String parameter: apps/s_server.c".

....

Then, the private key and certificate files are read. Excerpt:

....

Intercepted call to function BIO_new_file
String parameter 1: cert.key
String parameter 2: r

....

Intercepted call to function BIO_new_file
String parameter 1: cert.crt
String parameter 2: r

....

After that, a pointer to every cipher supported by TLS v1.2 is pushed on the cipher stack, if it is not already there. Excerpt:

....

Intercepted call to function EVP_add_cipher
Intercepted call to function EVP_aes_256_ccm
Intercepted call to function EVP_add_cipher
Intercepted call to function EVP_aes_128_cbc_hmac_sha1

....

Continuing in a similar manner, a pointer to every message digest supported by TLS v1.2 is pushed on the digest stack, if it is not already there. In addition, aliases are mapped to ciphers/digests. Excerpt:

....

Intercepted call to function EVP_md5
Intercepted call to function EVP_add_digest
Intercepted call to function OBJ_NAME_add
String parameter 1: ssl3-md5
String parameter 2: MD5
Intercepted call to function EVP_add_digest
Intercepted call to function EVP_sha1

....

Intercepted call to function OBJ_nid2sn
Intercepted call to function EVP_get_cipherbyname
String parameter: DES-EDE3-CBC

....

Then, memory is allocated based on the compiled-in ciphers and aliases. Excerpt:

....

Intercepted call to function CRYPTO_malloc
String parameter: ssl/ssl_ciph.c
Intercepted call to function FIPS_mode

....

At the end of this initialization process, an "ACCEPT" message is displayed, notifying the user that the server is up and running and awaits incoming connections. Excerpt:

....

Intercepted call to function BIO_printf
String parameter: ACCEPT

....

To automate our efforts we used an open-source, python, TLS test suite and fuzzer named tlsfuzzer [15] which includes a script to exploit CVE-2016-7054.

When the script is executed, we see a number of calls to `BIO_printf` function which display the messages exchanged between client and server (ClientHello, ServerHello, ServerKeyExchange, etc.). Then, at some point during execution, we see a call to `ERR_put_error` which signals that an error occurred and adds the error code to the thread's error queue. Excerpt:

....

Intercepted call to function ERR_put_error
String parameter 1: ssl/record/ssl3_record.c

....

Continuing, the program gets the error's code from the queue via `ERR_peek_error`. Then `ERR_print_errors` is called to print the error string. At this point, memory is freed via calls to functions like `CRYPTO_free`, `BIO_free_all`, `CRYPTO_free_ex_data`, `OPENSSL_cleanse`, `EVP_CIPHER_CTX_free` etc. Under normal circumstances, the server would reset the connection awaiting new incoming messages, but due to the CVE-2016-7054 bug the heap is nullified and the sever crashes, potentially indicating a DoS attack.

During the exploitation of this vulnerability, our library shows all the system calls made from the phase of the initialization of the server, to the handshake between it and the client, to the crash after the attack. This can provide a forensic trail to identify the functions executed in the OpenSSL session, in order to pinpoint where the vulnerability is triggered – in this case, when the memory is freed.

VI. CONCLUSION

In this paper, we presented an access control scheme that produces custom libraries and examines calls to functions within them along with their arguments, to ascertain if they adhere to specific security policies. Our framework improves important aspects of SecModule in which it can be incorporated, simplifying and automating the generation of libraries and providing a seamless way of evaluating the arguments of each call.

Our approach is transparent and can be used on binary/legacy applications and existing environments, as well as serve as a complimentary measure of defense alongside already implemented mechanisms.

ACKNOWLEDGEMENT

This work is supported by the European Commission through project H2020 ICT-32-2014 "SHARCS" under Grant Agreement No. 644571. Additionally, it is supported by the DFG Research Unit, Controlling Concurrent Change (CCC) project, funding number FOR 1800.

REFERENCES

[1] J. W. Kim and V. Prevelakis, "Base line performance measurements of access controls for libraries and modules," in *Proceedings of the 20th International Conference on Parallel and Distributed Processing*, ser. IPDPS'06. Washington, DC, USA: IEEE Computer Society, 2006, pp. 356–356. [Online]. Available: http://dl.acm.org/citation.cfm?id=1898699.1898911 [accessed: 2017-07-26]

[2] N. Provos, "Improving host security with system call policies," in *Proceedings of the 12th Conference on USENIX Security Symposium - Volume 12*, ser. SSYM'03. Berkeley, CA, USA: USENIX Association, 2003, pp. 18–18. [Online]. Available: http://dl.acm.org/citation.cfm?id=1251353.1251371 [accessed: 2017-07-26]

[3] N. George, "Ancillary library." [Online]. Available: http://www.normalesup.org/ george/comp/libancillary/ [accessed: 2017-07-26]

[4] R. N. M. Watson, "Exploiting concurrency vulnerabilities in system call wrappers," in *Proceedings of the First USENIX Workshop on Offensive Technologies*, ser. WOOT '07. Berkeley, CA, USA: USENIX Association, 2007, pp. 2:1–2:8. [Online]. Available: http://dl.acm.org/citation.cfm?id=1323276.1323278 [accessed: 2017-07-26]

[5] "Multics." [Online]. Available: http://www.cse.psu.edu/~trj1/cse443-s12/docs/ch3.pdf [accessed: 2017-07-26]

[6] "Multics rings," 1996. [Online]. Available: http://www.cs.unc.edu/ dewan/242/f96/notes/prot/node11.html [accessed: 2017-07-26]

[7] M. D. Schroeder and J. H. Saltzer, "A hardware architecture for implementing protection rings," 1972. [Online]. Available: ftp://ftp.stratus.com/vos/multics/tvv/protection.html [accessed: 2017-07-26]

[8] J. Cespedes, "ltrace." [Online]. Available: https://linux.die.net/man/1/ltrace [accessed: 2017-07-26]

[9] "ltrace." [Online]. Available: http://www.ltrace.org/ [accessed: 2017-07-26]

[10] M. Abadi, M. Budiu, U. Erlingsson, and J. Ligatti, "Control-flow integrity," in *Proceedings of the 12th ACM Conference on Computer and Communications Security*, ser. CCS '05. New York, NY, USA: ACM, 2005, pp. 340–353. [Online]. Available: http://doi.acm.org/10.1145/1102120.1102165 [accessed: 2017-07-26]

[11] T. PaX, "Address space layout randomization," 2001. [Online]. Available: https://pax.grsecurity.net/docs/aslr.txt [accessed: 2017-07-26]

[12] SHARCS, "Secure hardware-software architectures for robust computing systems," 2015. [Online]. Available: http://www.sharcs-project.eu/ [accessed: 2017-07-26]

[13] CVE_2016_7054, "Chacha20/poly1305 heap-buffer-overflow," 2016. [Online]. Available: https://cve.mitre.org/cgi-bin/cvename.cgi?name=CVE-2016-7054 [accessed: 2017-07-26]

[14] CVE-2016-7054, "Chacha20/poly1305 heap-buffer-overflow," 2016. [Online]. Available: https://www.openssl.org/news/secadv/20161110.txt [accessed: 2017-07-26]

[15] H. Kario, "Tls test suite and fuzzer," 2015. [Online]. Available: https://github.com/tomato42/tlsfuzzer [accessed: 2017-07-26]

Netflow Based HTTP Get Flooding Attack Analysis

Jungtae Kim, Jong-Hyun Kim and Ikkyun Kim
Information Security Research Division
Electronics & Telecommunications Research Institute
Daejeon, Republic of Korea
e-mail: {jungtae_kim, jhk, ikkim21}@etri.re.kr

Koohong Kang
[2]Dept. of Information and Communications Engineering
Seowon University
Cheongju, Republic of Korea
e-mail: khkang@seowon.ac.kr

Abstract— The paper proposes a security analysis method using the netflow information to analyze the HyperText Transfer Protocol (HTTP) get flooding attacks. As it is hard to distinguish from the normal Web accesses and further severely disturb the normal Web user accesses, the attack is considered as one of the most effective Distributed Denial-of-Service (DDoS) attacks. In this paper, we propose an analysis method of the HTTP Get flooding attacks based on the netflow information. In particular, the byte over packet per flow ratio helps to achieve the attack detection without the individual packet processing overheads.

***Keywords-HTTP Get Flooding; Netflow; DDoS Attack;*.**

I. INTRODUCTION

Netflow is a feature that was introduced on Cisco routers that provides the ability to collect IP network traffic as it enters or exits an interface [1]. The major advantage of utilizing the flow data is that it helps to analyze the network traffic usage and further enables network security enhancement. The flow is generally defined by the 7 unique key fields including the following information: source and destination IP address, source and destination port, layer 3 protocol type, type of service byte, and the input logical interface [2]. In order to utilize the netflow information to analyze the DDOS traffic, a system requires to have the following components: flow exporter, which processes packets to produce flow data, the preconfigured flow collectors and storages. Consequently, the flow collectors store and index the collected flows for search purposes. Later, an analysis application then analyzes the stored flow data for the network traffic or security analysis purposes. Based on the above systems components with the netflow information, we propose a network anomaly detection method based on the detailed analysis on the HTTP Get Flooding Attacks.

II. LITERATURE REVIEW

The HTTP Get flooding attacks are being exploited in the most efficient way among Denial-of-Service (DoS) type attacks aimed at the Web server application layer [3]. The attack is specially designed to send a large volume of the HTTP-Get requests to the targeted Web applications and servers. The attacks are initiated by virus infected zombie PCs under the control of Command and Control (C&C) server. Consequently, the victim's Web server is unable to reply to the normal user requests due to the processing overheads. Since these attack packets contain the normal HTTP requests, Web servers cannot easily distinguish between normal user's HTTP-Get request messages and the malicious requests [4]. The advantage of the approach presented in this paper is that the netflow helps the network administrator to identify network anomalies by monitoring the detailed traffic flows information rather than the conventional network security devices including the firewall, Intrusion Detection System (IDS) or Intrusion Prevention System (IPS), which obviously involve an extra cost of deploying the devices, as well as a change of network settings to capture the traffic information for signature based analysis. Although the default setting for the netflow information exports is set depending on the switch or router manufacturers, such as the inactive timer set at 15 sec and the active timer set at 1800 sec, the flow analysis is helpful in case of the HTTP Get Flooding attack, which has a unique characteristic with the repeated short TCP 3-Way Handshake periods. The paper introduces an experimental setting with system and network configurations in Section III. Details of the attack analysis technique using netflow information with the analysis results are described in Section IV. Finally, Section V concludes the paper with future works.

III. EXPERIMENTAL SETTINGS

Figure 1 shows 2 minute attacks to conduct the HTTP Get flooding attacks. The Command and Control server, with the Netbot Attacker [5], was installed in a separate external network from the attack target network. The target network was configured with 3 zombie PCs with 2 Web servers hyperlinked unidirectional.

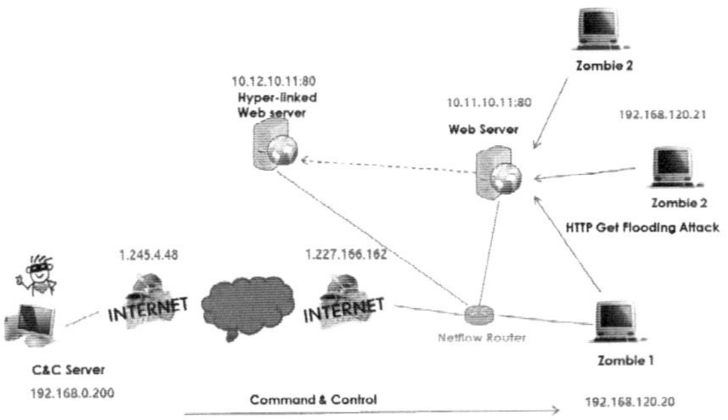

Figure 1. Network Configuration of the HTTP Get flooding attack using Netbot Attacker.

IV. ATTACK ANALYSIS TECHNIQUE USING NETFLOW

Although conventional HTTP Get flooding attack detection adopts a method that specifically analyzes the contents of the packet, especially installed and operated in the input of particular Website or Web server [4], our approach proposes an analysis method of the HTTP Get flooding attacks based on the netflow information rather than the detailed network traffic statistics. Figures 2-4 show the flow information for the attack caused by using the Netbot Attacker by flow duration, number of packet, and byte size, respectively. The attack flow is generated for 2 minutes (Figure 2), and the number of packets (Figure 3) within the flow is fixed in its size. The flow analysis experiment was conducted considering a 2 minutes attack from 3 zombie PCs with a break. The total number of flows measured were approximately 22,985 at each zombie PC which includes the recursive HTTP Get request and reply messages with the TCP 3-way Handshake packets (48 Byte SYN & SYN ACK and 40 byte ACK, FIN & RST ACK).

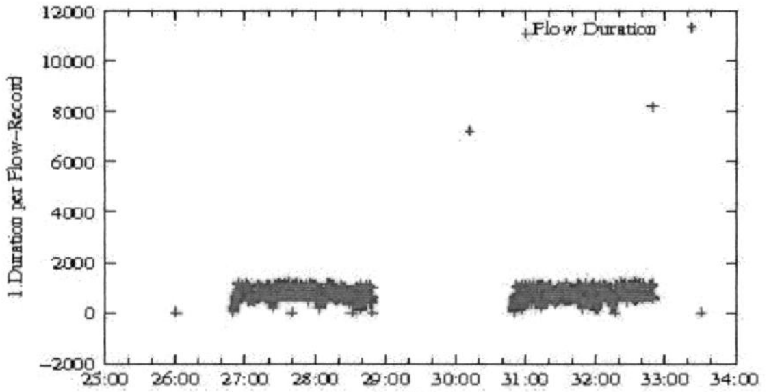

Figure 2. Flow Duration for HTTP Get flooding attack patterns.

The results, as depicted in Figure 2, show that most of the attack related flow duration fell into within the 2000 ms (2 secs) boundary with short TCP sessions. Figures 3 and 4 show the total number of packets and bytes per flow record of the attack. The machine generated attack by zombie PCs was fixed in its packet size of 6 with 285 byte size and additional 5 & 7 packets with 245 and 333 byte size, respectively, due to the reset (RST) packet. Figure 5 provides a Byte over Packet Ratio (BPR) per flow record for the HTTP Get flooding attack and the results are listed in Table I. The proposed analysis result shows that, the BPR is 47~49 for the HTTP Get flooding attack.

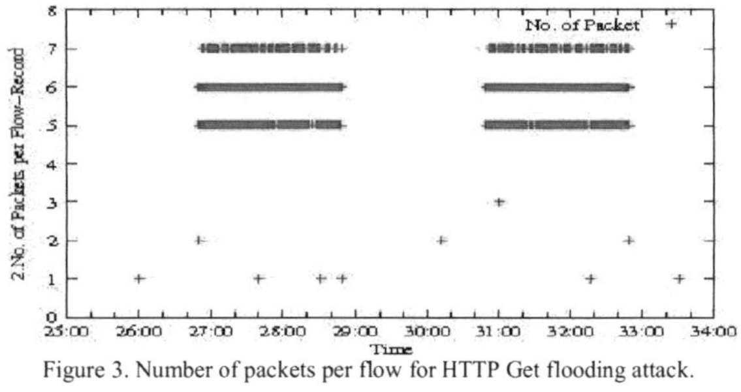

Figure 3. Number of packets per flow for HTTP Get flooding attack.

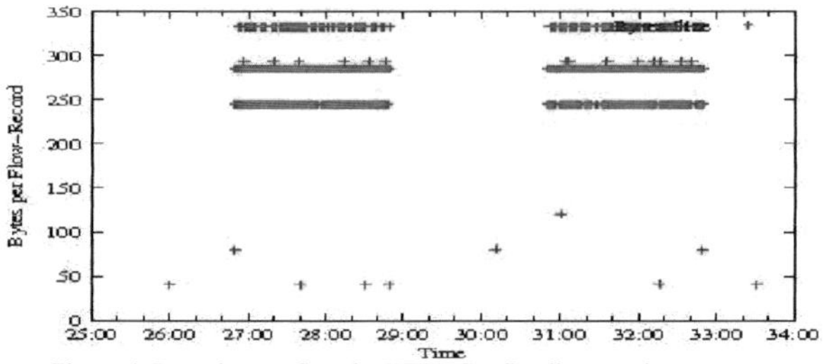

Figure 4. Byte size per flow for HTTP Get flooding attack patterns.

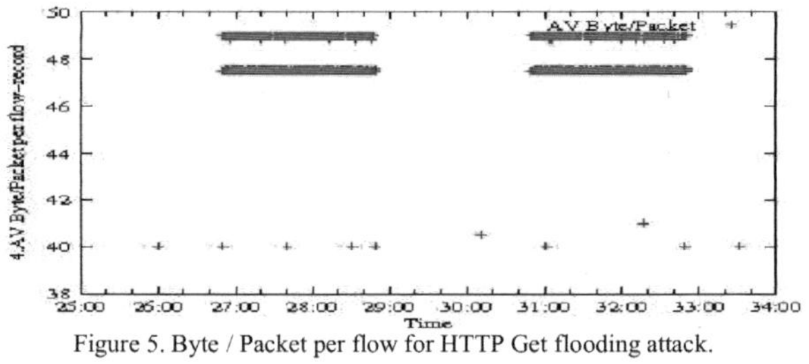

Figure 5. Byte / Packet per flow for HTTP Get flooding attack.

TABLE I. HTTP GET FLOODING ATTACK PATTERNS.

No. PACKET	*BYTE SIZE*	*BYTE/PACKET*
5	245	49.00000
6	285	47.50000
7	333	47.57143

V. CONCLUSION AND FUTURE WORK

We propose an analysis method of the HTTP Get flooding attacks based on the netflow information rather than the detailed network traffic statistics, such as the packer per second (pps) and total byte size. In particular, machine generated attack patterns show that a specific BPR can be applied to detect the DDoS attack.

ACKNOWLEDGMENT

This work was supported by Institute for Information & communications Technology Promotion(IITP) grant funded by the Korea government(MSIP) (No.R-20160222-002755, Cloud based Security Intelligence Technology Development for the Customized Security Service Provisioning).

REFERENCES

[1] Cisco IOS NetFlow, Cisco Systems, Inc. https://www.cisco.com/c/en/us/products/ios-nx-os-software/ios-netflow/index.html [accessed July 2017]

[2] NetFlow Export Datagram Format, Cisco Systems, Inc. http://www.cisco.com/c/en/us/td/docs/net_mgmt/netflow_collection_engine/3-6/user/guide/format.html [accessed July 2017]

[3] Y. Choi and et. al, "AIGG Threshold Based HTTP GET Flooding Attack Detection," in Proc. of WISA 2012, pp 270-284, 2012. [accessed July 2017]

[4] Y. Kim and et. al, "HTTP Get Flooding Detection Technique based on Netflow Information," in Proc. Of Internet 2016, pp 26, 2016. [accessed July 2017]

[5] Netbot Attacker VIP 4.7 Version. http://cfs13.tistory.com/image/5/tistory/2009/02/19/18/02/499d203101657 [accessed July 2017]

Secure Software Development – Models, Tools, Architectures and Algorithms

Aspen Olmsted
College of Charleston
Department of Computer Science, Charleston, SC 29401
e-mail: olmsteda@cofc.edu

Abstract— **Secure software development is a process which integrates people and practices to ensure application Confidentiality, Integrity, Availability, Non-Repudiation, and Authentication (CIANA). Secure software is the result of a security- aware software development process in which CIANA is established when an application is first developed. Current secure software development lifecycles are simply old software development lifecycles with security training prepended to the traditional development steps and an incident response process appended to the lifecycle. To solve our application cyber-security issues, we need to develop the models, tools, architectures, and algorithms that support CIANA on the first day of a development project.**

Keywords-Cyber-security; Software Engineering; CRM

I. INTRODUCTION

In this work, we investigate the problem of developing software that is built to provide the security required in our modern, connected world. Secure software development is the process involving people and practices that ensure application Confidentiality, Integrity, Availability, Non-Repudiation, and Authentication (CIANA). Secure software is the result of a security aware software development processes where CIANA is established when an application is first developed.

Current secure software development lifecycles (SSDLC) are just old software development lifecycles (SDLC) with a security training prepended before the traditional development steps and an incident response process append to the end of the lifecycle. To solve our application cyber-security issues, we need to develop the models, tools, architectures, and algorithms that support CIANA on the first day of a development project.

The organization of the paper is as follows. Section II describes the related work and the limitations of current methods. In Section III, we document student work from our lab in the creation of algorithms and architectures that provide consistency, availability, and partition tolerance for distributed systems. Section IV looks at algorithms the lab has developed to provide correctness guarantees for the integration of heterogeneous systems. Section V explores our solutions for authenticating autonomous processes and securing the communication between them. Section VI analyzes the lab's solutions for securing code and data in an operating system. In Section VII, we share our additions to UML modeling to move the awareness of potential system vulnerabilities to an earlier point in the software development life-cycle. Finally, in Section VIII, we look at ways to reduce the software development cost through the use of cloud architectures. We conclude and discuss future work that needs to be done to advance our algorithms, architectures, tools, and modeling in Section IX.

II. RELATED WORK

For many years, software engineering firms followed an SDLC that consisted of five steps: requirements gathering, solution design, implementation, testing, and maintenance. Many new SSDLCs have evolved with the goal of helping software developers write software with fewer vulnerabilities. Microsoft created the Security Development Lifecycle [1] as a recommended solution to a more SDLC. In the Microsoft recommendations, a preliminary training phase is introduced to teach users to not only distrust data from external sources but also to understand typical vulnerabilities found in software applications. In the testing phase, they recommend using penetration testing software to ensure typical secure programming mistakes are caught. At the end of the development lifecycle, they recommend implementing a response system to address the software once a vulnerability has been found. Our work attempts to be more proactive in developing the models, tools architectures, and algorithms the developers need to guarantee vulnerabilities are discovered and addressed earlier in the development lifecycle.

Over the last decade, many books have been written to help developers understand the technical programming solutions to two standard problems:

1. SQL Injection – A vulnerability in an application through which a malicious user can execute malicious SQL statements against the application's back end data store.
2. Cross Site Scripting – A vulnerability in an application through which a malicious user can execute client side JavaScript inside a page of the application.

One such book is Edmund's recent book *Securing PHP Applications* [2]. In each of these books, algorithms which sanitize user input that may be coming from user forms, cookies, or even the back-end database are explained in detail. The basic premise these books espouse is trust no-one. We attempt to give the developer some trust in addition to their programming repertoire already consisting of the models, tools, architectures, and algorithms to guarantee security in the development process.

Walden, Doyle, Lenhof and Murray [3] studied whether the variation in vulnerability density is greater between languages or between different applications written in a single language by comparing eleven open source web applications written in Java with fourteen such applications written in PHP. To compare the languages, they created a Common Vulnerability Metric (CVM) which represents the count of four vulnerability categories common to both languages. Our work

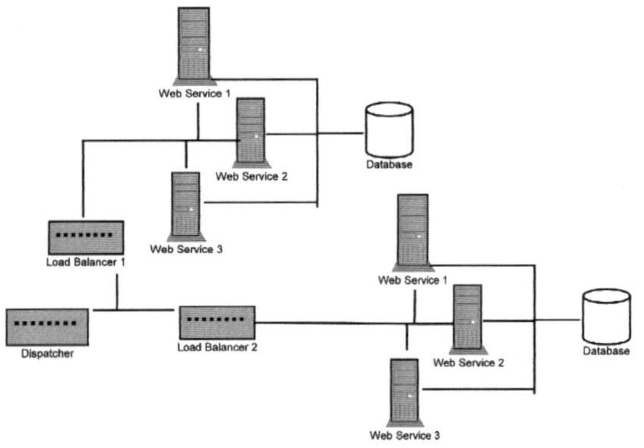

Figure 1. WS Farm with Buddy System.

here looks to find common vulnerabilities in enterprise applications and provide solutions to those vulnerabilities.

III. DISTRIBUTED CONSISTENCY, AVAILABILITY AND PARTITION TOLERANCE

Modern web-based transaction systems need to support many concurrent clients consuming a limited quantity of resources. These applications are often developed using a Service Oriented Architecture (SOA). SOA supports the composition of multiple web services (WSs) to perform complex business processes. SOA applications provide a high-level of concurrency; we can think of the measure of concurrency as the availability of the service to all clients requesting services. Replication of these services and their corresponding resources increases availability. Unfortunately, designers sacrifice consistency and durability to achieve this availability. The CAP theory [4] [5] states that distributed database designers can achieve at most two of the following properties: consistency (C), availability (A), and partition tolerance (P). Distributed database designers often relax the consistency requirements under its influence.

Our proposed system [6] has three benefits: it decreases the risk of losing committed transactional data in the event of a site failure, increases consistency of transactions, and increases the availability of "read" requests. The three main components of our proposed system are 1) Synchronous Transactional Buddy System, 2) Version Master-Slave Lazy Replication, and 3) Serializable Snapshot Isolation Schedule.

Our solution [6] adopts the WS-Farm (WSF) architecture (Figure 1) to allow the system to provide the features iterated above. Transactions arrive at the dispatcher at the TCP/IP level 7 allowing the dispatcher to use application specific data for transaction distribution and buddy selection. The dispatcher also receives the requests from clients and distributes them to the WS clusters which each contain a load balancer, a single database, and replicated services. The load balancer receives the service requests from the dispatcher and distributes them among the service replicas. Within a WS cluster, each service shares the same database, and database updates among the clusters are propagated using lazy replication propagation [6].

This method of propagation is vulnerable to a loss of updates in the event of a database server failure, though [6]. If a server failure occurs after the transaction has committed, but before the replica updates are initiated, the updates are lost. To guarantee data persistence even in the presence of hardware failures, we propose to form strict replication between pairs of replica clusters "buddies." In this method of replication, at least one replica in addition to the primary replica is updated and, therefore, preserves the updates.

After receiving a transaction, the dispatcher picks the two clusters, chosen by versioning history, to form the buddy-system. The primary buddy (b1) receives the transaction along with its buddy's (b2) IP address. The primary buddy (b1) becomes the coordinator in a simplified commit protocol between the two buddies. Both then buddies perform the transaction and commit or abort together. The dispatcher maintains metadata about the freshness of data items in the different clusters in addition to incrementing the version number for each data item after it has been modified. Any two service providers in two different clusters with the latest version of the requested data items can be selected as a buddy. Note, that the databases (DBR) maintained by the two clusters must have the same version of the requested data items but may not for the other data items.

IV. HETEROGENEOUS SYSTEM INTEGRATION

Enterprise transaction processing systems support several different use cases to fulfill the entire set of requirements of an organization. An organization will partition an enterprise system at the department level for several different reasons. Two of these reasons are to simplify the functional model and to enable geographic proximity to the users entering the transactional data.

The result of the departmental partitioning is a duplication of data across departmental systems, and the management of this duplication is a difficult problem. Often, an organization will enter this data manually in each local system. The organization is then forced to tolerate the data inconsistencies that come from the difference not only in human interpretation of the source data but also transcription differences.

In our previous work [7], we investigated the problem of providing guarantees for heterogeneous system integration. We proposed a set of strong properties: Fresh, Atomic, Consistent and Durable (FACD), which will deliver correct results when held in the integration transaction. The strong properties support an integration technique called Continuous, Consistent, Extract, Translate, and Load (CCETL). CCETL consumes UML class diagrams to identify transactional membership of the data elements that make up the integration. CCETL transforms the hierarchical relationships using a version of the topological sort that maintains a navigation path from the original UML classes.

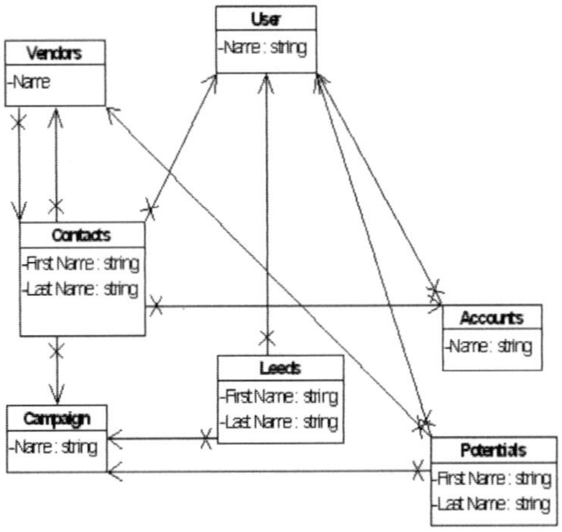

Figure 2. Cyclical UML Class Diagram.

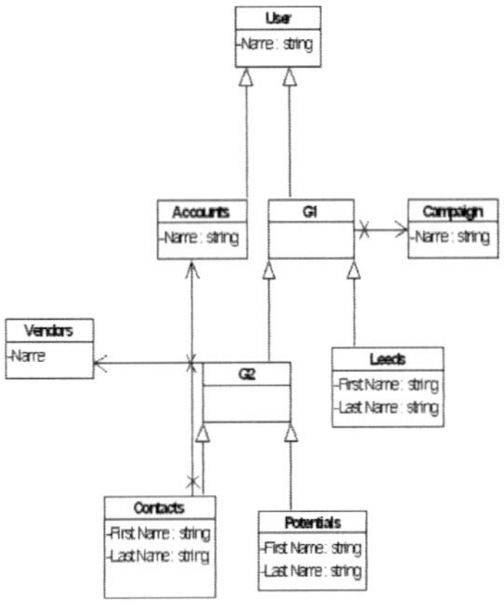

Figure 3. Acyclic Sorted UML Class Diagram.

The CCETL approach guarantees ACID properties up to the level of snapshot isolation between systems supporting a continuous integration.

The example application for CCETL used a collection of Zoho web-service and a back-office ERP solution for Cultural Arts Organizations named Tessitura [8]. Tessitura transactions include patron donations and ticket purchases. The Zoho web services [9] provide a timestamp on every entity record modification. This timestamp is used to identify all records changed since the last execution of the integration.

For this project, we choose to use a sub-model of the Zoho CRM service. Zoho CRM is a software-as-a-service product for managing customer data such as biographical data, emails, phone calls, etc. We choose Zoho for the project because the Zoho CRM product provides web services that allow user-defined data queries against all the available entity objects. Figure 2 shows a UML diagram of a subset of the web-services provided by Zoho. Each web service represents a coarse-grained entity object. The diagram shows the navigation knowledge of each web-service with respect to other web services. The associations form a directed cyclical-graph.

There are two ways to identify transactional data: intercept original transactions synchronously or reform transactions asynchronously from the original transaction. To intercept the original transaction synchronously, we need an application hook to inform the integration when a transaction is taking place. An example of this application hook is available in Oracle Forms [10]. Synchronous integration increases the latency of the original transaction.
To reform a transaction asynchronously from the original transaction, we need to identify what data changed in the original transaction. To identify which records make-up a transaction, CCETL includes all associated records modified along with the parent record. This identification requires an ordering of the original UML diagram Figure 2. In our previous work [7] we provide an algorithm that de-cycles and sorts the original graph.

Figure 3 shows a version of the original UML diagram from Figure 2 with cycles removed and sorted. The algorithm inserts mock objects when there are identical inbound edges into a node. The addition of the mock objects reduces the branches in the path of the UML graph.

We ran the integration two ways: integrate on a record by record change (Record Integration) and use CCETL. (Snapshot Integration). We ran the two integration techniques with transaction sizes in blocks of 100 up to 1000. The snapshot isolation method provided much higher throughput and provided isolation guarantees at snapshot isolation. The record integration method was slower and only provided isolation at the read committed isolation level. The higher latency and lower consistency stems from dealing with a single record at a time.

V. PROCESS AUTHENTICATION AND COMMUNICATION

Authentication is used to verify that a specific user or process is who they say they are and is one of the major domains in cyber security research. Unfortunately, autonomous process authentication is a neglected segment of this domain. The autonomous processes are often native operating system services, but sometimes the autonomous process is a part of a larger enterprise application where the process needs access to different resources unavailable to the user who is operating the application. In this case, the process needs different credentials. The resources protected fall into three categories: operating system files, data and process execution. Operating system files are traditionally secured based on the user logged into the operating system. Permissions can be discreetly assigned to the user or inherited from a user's group membership. Data permissions are normally managed by a relational database system. In the database system, access is granted to tables, columns and tuples in the database based on the user's credentials or the user's group membership. The permission to launch processes is often guarded by the operating system based on the logged in user and the user's group membership.

There are four standard ways we authenticate users:

- Something you know – In this form of authentication, a user or process must know a secret. The typical secret used in authentication is a combination of a user and a password.
- Something you have – In this form of authentication, a user or process must have access to a physical entity. The typical example is a token that is sent to an SMS number. If the user has their registered phone and can receive SMS messages then only they can enter back the one time generated token. This form of authentication is not typically used with autonomous processes on servers because an operator with a mobile device is not typically on the server's console. Autonomous processes on mobile devices with SMS service can use this technique to validate that a user has the phone, but a server process does not typically have SMS support. If they do have SMS support, then the process is typically using a virtual SMS service which would no longer be something to which the process has access.
- Something about you - In this form of authentication, a unique characteristic is used to validate access. Examples include retina scans, fingerprint readers, and facial recognition. This form of authentication when dealing with a human operator tends to be the strongest form of authentication, but it is not used with process authentication as processes do not have these characteristics.
- Someplace you are – In this form of authentication, the address where the user or process is located controls access to the resources. Examples in this category include a range of IP addresses or the geographic longitude and latitude points where a machine may be operating.

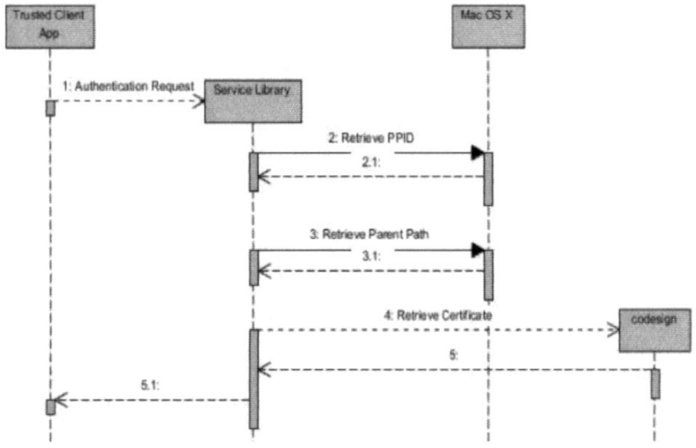

Figure 4. Sequence Diagram of Application Authentication Process.

In our previous work [11], we add autonomous process authentication in a limited environment. To add "something about you" security for an autonomous process, we investigated verifiable properties of an application. These properties need to validate the process is not a malicious user or a different process posing as the valid process. In this work, our solution uses the security certificate used to code-sign an application that is listed in the Mac Apple Store [12]. This certificate is not applied to the application for the validation purpose we propose, but it works quite nicely. The certificate is signed by Apple to ensure that no malicious user has changed the application code. Unlike in PKI, where a certificate can be signed by many different trusted third parties, the Mac Apple Store certificates are only signed by Apple, Inc. Algorithm 1 shows the algorithm we use to extract the certificate and validate the application. The current application requires a native Mac OS X application signed by the Apple Mac Store. Our service is a database service written as a native Mac OS X application. When the 3rd party application forks to our service app, we can retrieve the process id of the external application. With the process id, we can determine the operating system path of the application that is calling our service. From this path, we can validate the certificate. The Mac OS X operating system includes a utility called code-sign [13] that allows you to retrieve and verify the signature on an application. Our algorithm uses this utility in the final step to verify the process is the process it says it is. Figure 4 shows the flow of the algorithm in a UML sequence diagram. Our current work looks to leverage this work for inter-process communication.

VI. SECURE DATASTORE AND CODESTORE

In [11], we provide a secure data store that offers operations to an authorized client application. We also provide an administration application that can call a method to add an application's credentials. This tool allows an administrator to add other applications with their certificates to the valid applications list. We sign the code for our administration application with the Mac App Store and hard code the certificate for the administration application into our service provider application. This hard coding enforces at installation time that the only application authorized to connect to the data store provider is the administration tool itself. Using the administration tool, we can grant access to the service for other applications. One of the services provided is the ability to add human user credentials that can

Algorithm 1. Process Authentication Algorithm.

3rd Party App Forks to Service App
Service gets parent pid
Service uses parent pid to get parent path
Service gest parent cert
Cert validated against valid apps

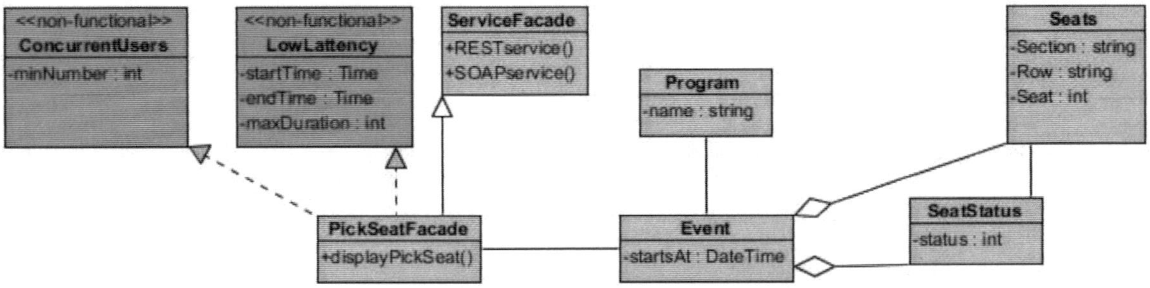

Figure 5. UML with Multi-Inheritance.

authenticate to the application. The addition of these application credentials allows data to be secured so only a specific application can get access or so a specific human user can gain access or by the combination of both the application and a user authenticated in the application.

VII. SECURE MODELING

The focus of our previous research work in secure modeling is to investigate the problem of modeling vulnerable partitions of a software application in the design and analysis phase of the software development lifecycle. We focus on two key areas: providing partition tolerance in cloud-based applications while maintaining application data integrity [14] and modeling non-functional requirements using standard UML design tools. Our contribution in this research field is to experiment with not only modeling application domain specific NFRs that are used in enterprise application architectures but also mapping the mode to application code that will enforce the requirement. Our hypothesis was that we could use standard modeling tools, traditionally used to model functional requirements, and extend them to allow modeling and code generation of NFRs. We modeled the NFRs using the extensibility mechanisms built into the standard modeling notations of UML and OCL to specify those NFRs. The models are exported to the XML standard XMI to enable our tooling to read the model. Java code is then generated to enforce each NFR by parsing the XMI of the model, matching the stereotype or OCL constraint to a Java fragment and producing the code.

In the first iteration of our work, different scalar values were represented by different stereotypes. For example, to represent different quantities of concurrent users, we had to create different stereotypes to represent each specific quantity, such as "1000 concurrent users" and "500 concurrent users". Though this method allowed us the granular control to specify specific NFR requirements, there are two flaws. First, there is no way to group stereotypes into categories in standard UML notation. The stereotype only method does not allow any semantic relationship between the two stereotypes that both represent quantities of concurrent users. A developer would need to know the relationship to avoid making an error when switching between values, thus causing the semantics of the NFR to change completely. Second, on a large enterprise development project, the number of stereotypes required to represent all the different combinations of NFRs and scalar measurements would become unwieldy.

The solution we developed to solve both of these two challenges combines OCL and mock objects in the UML class diagrams. Specifically, we insert mock objects that provide new attributes to represent the scalar values measured in the enforcement of the NFR into the UML class diagram inheritance tree. The mock objects are generalizations that specify attributes that are inherited by the real façade objects. Once the new attributes are added through inheritance, we can specify standard OCL constraints to express the NFR and the appropriate measurement. Figure 5 shows a design using the mock multi-inheritance to enforce two non-functional requirements ("Low Latency" and "Concurrent Users"). Java code is generated from the mock objects using the single inheritance the programming language supports.

VIII. PLATFORM, EFFORT, AND SECURITY

With the advent of cloud computing, Platform-As-A-Service (PAAS) has become a way that a developer can leverage pre-built components to reduce the time to market. The goal of PAAS is to allow the developer to focus on the development of a solution for the business functions and not software functions that span many application domains. A good example of PAAS is force.com where the developer is provided many of the essential parts of an application out of the box. In [15], we evaluate the programming effort savings from leveraging different PAAS providers. In [16] we investigate the technical debt arising from software engineers ignoring the security vulnerabilities while developing software. In both works, we leverage COCOMO II [17] to estimate the development costs to track code leverage and technical debt accrued.

The 21st century has been dominated by bytecode compiled languages that have runtime engines that execute the code on different hardware platforms. The Java Runtime Engine (JRE) and the Microsoft .NET Runtime Engine (.NET) are the most dominant examples of the bytecode engines that free the developer from thinking about the underlying hardware. PAAS is the next evolution in freeing up the developer's time so they can focus on the problem they are trying to solve instead of the technical plumbing required for the solution.

A hypervisor is computer software, firmware, or hardware, which executes virtual machines. A computer on which a hypervisor is called a host machine and each virtual machine is called a guest machine. Type 1 hypervisors run directly on top of hardware. Type 2 is a hypervisor that operates as an application on top of an existing operating system. If you were deploying an application to a Java PAAS today, it would be in a JRE running on a Type 1 hypervisor. OSv [18] is a JRE that can execute directly on a Type 2 hypervisor. Not having an extra operating system layer removes all the security vulnerabilities found in the OS layer below the JRE. Developing a solution that executes in OSv will be naturally more secure than other PAAS providers due to the fewer layers of potential exploits.

IX. Conclusion and Future Work

In this paper, we described the work done in our lab to provide the missing modeling components, development tools, application architectures, and algorithms to increase the security guaranteed in software and improve the estimation of the effort in the SDL. Our current solutions are examples which prove that robust commercial solutions can be developed. Our future work includes developing a model-driven development solution that can be deployed on a secure bytecode runtime engine. The runtime engine should be capable of running directly on a hypervisor without the insecure extra layer of a traditional operating system.

References

[1] Microsoft, Inc., "What is the Security Development Lifecycle ?," 2017. [Online]. Available: https://www.microsoft.com/en-us/sdl/. [Accessed 26 March 2017].

[2] B. Edmunds, Securing PHP Applications, New York: Apress, 2016.

[3] J. Walden, M. Doyle, R. Lenhof and J. Murray, "Java vs. PHP: Security Implications of Language Choice for Web Applications," in *Conference: Engineering Secure Software and Systems, Second International Symposium*, Pisa, Italy, 2010.

[4] S. Gilbert and N. Lynch, "Brewer's conjecture and the feasibility of consistent, available, partition-tolerant web services," *SIGACT News*, vol. 33, pp. 51-59, 2002.

[5] D. Abadi, "Consistency tradeoffs in modern distributed database system design: Cap is only part of the story," *Computer*, vol. 45, pp. 37-42, 2012.

[6] A. Olmsted and C. Farkas, "Buddy System: Available, Consistent, Durable Web Service Transactions.," *Journal of Internet Technology and Secured Transactions (JITST)*, vol. 2, no. 1/2, pp. 131-140, 2013.

[7] A. Olmsted, "Heterogeneous System Integration Data Integration Guarantees," *Journal of Computational Methods in Science and Engineering (JCMSE)*, vol. 17, no. 51, pp. S85-S94, 2017.

[8] Tessitura Network. Inc, "Tessitura Software," 2017. [Online]. Available: http://www.tessituranetwork.com/en/Products/Software.aspx. [Accessed 13 August 2017].

[9] Zoho Corporation Pvt. Ltd., "Zoho CRM API," 2017. [Online]. Available: https://www.zoho.com/crm/help/api/. [Accessed 13 August 2017].

[10] S. C. Corp., Oracle9iDS Forms II: Customize Internet Apps Vol B, Sideris Courseware Corp., 2003.

[11] A. Olmsted, "Native Autonomous Process Authentication," in *Proceedings of World Congress on Internet Security 2016 (World-CIS 2016)*, London, UK, 2016.

[12] Apple Inc, "The Mac App Store," Apple Inc, [Online]. Available: http://www.apple.com/osx/apps/app-store/. [Accessed 01 June 2016].

[13] OS X Daily, "How to Show & Verify Code Signatures for Apps in Mac OS X," OS X Daily, [Online]. Available: http://osxdaily.com/2016/03/14/verify-code-sign-apps-mac-os-x/. [Accessed 01 June 2016].

[14] A. Olmsted, "Modeling Cloud Applications for Partition Contingency," in *Proceedings of the 11th International Conference for Internet Technology and Secured Transactions (ICITST-2016)*, Barcelona, Spain, 2016.

[15] A. Olmsted and K. Fulford, "Platform-As-A-Service Application Effort Estimation," in *Proceedings of The Eighth International Conference on Cloud Computing, GRIDs, and Virtualization (Cloud Computing 2017)*, Athens, GR, 2017.

[16] C. Brill and A. Olmsted, "Security and Software Engineering: Analyzing Effort and Cost," in *Proceedings of the The Third International Conference on Advances and Trends in Software Engineering* , Venice, IT, 2017.

[17] R. Madachy, "COCOMO II - Constructive Cost Model," [Online]. Available: http://csse.usc.edu/tools/COCOMOII.php. [Accessed 10 02 2017].

[18] Cloudius Systems, "OSv Designed for the Cloud," 2016. [Online]. Available: http://osv.io/. [Accessed 25 March 2017].

Security Vulnerabilities in Hotpatching Mobile Applications

Sarah Ford, Aspen Olmsted
Department of Computer Science
College of Charleston
Charleston, SC
fordsr@g.cofc.edu, olmsteda@cofc.edu

***Abstract*— The need for developers to be able to update mobile apps immediately on discovery of a critical bug is something the Apple iOS software patching system does not allow through their traditional app patching lifecycle. Two tools have been developed to solve this problem, one commercial and one open-source. Both employ JavaScript and dynamic code downloads and provide a method for users to receive immediate updates, but both have the potential to be abused and open the user to multiple security vulnerabilities. This paper will discuss how the tools JSPatch and Rollout.io, open-source and commercial respectively, enable quick updates but also expose users to multiple security vulnerabilities and argue for why Apple should not allow them; it proposes a better solution using the same technology that preserves security.**

Keywords- Javascript; iOS; patching; mobile computing; open-source tools; Apple; security

I. INTRODUCTION

There is a strong business need for developers to be able to quickly and safely patch their iOS Apps. In the past, the only option for developers was to submit their updated app to the Apple store, who reviewed the changes and then allowed the app to be included in the 'Updates' section of a user's phone for the user to download.

Though most apps still employ this method to update their source code, some developers, wanting to patch apps immediately, have begun to employ commercial and open source tools, which allow developers to include a small amount of code in the source code of their app upon its initial submission to Apple's App Store, which makes a call to a remote server that returns executable JavaScript code. The tool then converts the JavaScript to Objective-C or Swift and adds it to the original source at runtime.

These tools provide a much-needed solution to developers who find critical bugs or security vulnerabilities in their apps after they have been deployed on the app store, but they also create security vulnerabilities and allow malicious developers to evade Apple's strict app review process, which has previously kept the iOS app environment relatively safe for users and their information.

This paper examines how JavaScript hot patching works and documents the vulnerabilities associated with both the commercial and the open-source tool. We demonstrate the dangers and conclude that Apple has an urgent need to change its security policy but also a great opportunity to adopt this technology into its app review process with its full security measures.

The organization of the paper is as follows. Section II describes the related work and the limitations of current methods. In Section III, we document three example use cases as a motivating example. Section IV explains how the hotpatching works technically. Section V explores the commercial tool available for hotpatching. Section VI takes a look at the open source tool available for hotpatching. In Section VII, we explain our test implementation. Section VIII looks at the policy of the Apple, the owner of the phone operating system. Section IX looks at the core problem that led to the situation we find ourselves in. In Section X, we propose a solution. We conclude and discuss future work in Section XI.

II. RELATED WORK

The need to enable users to have access to an app update quickly is not just a need in iOS. More research, in fact, has been done in the other chief mobile operating system, Android. Previous work has formulated various solutions to the need to patch apps quickly and prevent crashes.

Bissyandé et. al. [1] formulated a solution to the need for app users to quickly have access to app updates through a peer-to-peer, network-based update propagation system using a middleware. They were able to demonstrate its effectiveness at a large conference.

In a different approach to the update problem, Azim, Meamtiu, and Marvel [2] propose a solution to allow smartphone apps to "self-heal" by detecting when an app is crashing and altering the byte code to prevent it from interacting with the crashing part of the app and allow the user to continue using other parts of the app.

Both solutions provide options to the need to update quickly to preserve application functionality, but neither allows for the developer to immediately patch their own code as soon as the user opens the broken app.

III. MOTIVATING EXAMPLE

For our motivating example, we propose three variations of the following scenario: a student developer develops a simple game, which is accepted by Apple's App Store.

In the first scenario, our developer is well meaning: she simply wants to update her app if there are bugs quickly. She includes the open-source hot patching tool: JSPatch. JSPatch makes a call to a remote server every time the app runs and downloads executable JavaScript code. Though her intentions are good, she exposes her users to the danger of the well-known Man-in-the-Middle attack (MitM) [3]. If her user is using her app on an unencrypted or dangerous network, an attacker could intercept and modify the JavaScript and maliciously attack the game user's phone or our developer's app functionality.

In our second scenario, our developer is also well-intentioned, and also in need of income, because she is, after all, a university student; therefore, she includes an advertising software developer kit (SDK) in her app in order to make some money from her app. The advertising SDK, however, is from a malicious developer and includes JSPatch. When a user runs the app, the advertising SDK may employ some private iOS APIs, which make us of private APIs to steal personal information from the user's device [3] .

In our third scenario, our developer is malicious. She wants to steal her user's information to sell to interested third parties. She includes JSPatch in her app with no malicious code downloading at first, but once her app is already in the app store, she modifies the JavaScript to include an iOS private API, which accesses the user's personal information and stores it on her remote server to sell to third parties.

IV. How JavaScript Hotpatching works

JavaScript injection at runtime is possible in the iOS operating system because of the JavaScriptCore framework and a technique called method swizzling [4].

The JavaScriptCore Framework "allows you to evaluated JavaScript programs from within an Objective-C or C-based program. It also lets you insert custom objects into the JavaScript environment" [5].

The code to be excuted by the JavaScriptCore framweork gets into the app through a call to a remote server, which downloads the Javascript and then executes it with a technique known as method swizzling. Method swizzling "is the process of changing the implementation of an existing selector. It's a technique made possible by the fact that method invocations in Objective-C can be changed at runtime, by changing how selectors are mapped to underlying functions in a class's dispatch table" [6].

Both the use of the JavaScriptCore and method swizzling are compliant with Apple's development guidelines because the JavaScriptCore is a public API and method swizzling does not alter the binary of the app [7]. See Figure 1 for a visual representation of the process.

V. The Commercial Tool: Rollout.io

Rollout.io is an Israeli startup company, which offers a tool to implement all phases of hot patching [8]. They provide not only the code to be put in the source code of the app but also an interface and server from, which to push these code updates to your app. Because they have direct control over the server pushing the code, they also have fewer security vulnerabilities than the open-source tool (described below).

The most major vulnerability in Rollout.io is the ability to load an "arbitrary public framework" and use the associated APIs with malicious intent [9]. For example, to access sensitive user data and export it without the user's knowledge. Though many apps access sensitive user data (photos, contacts, etc.) with a clear purpose, Apple's review

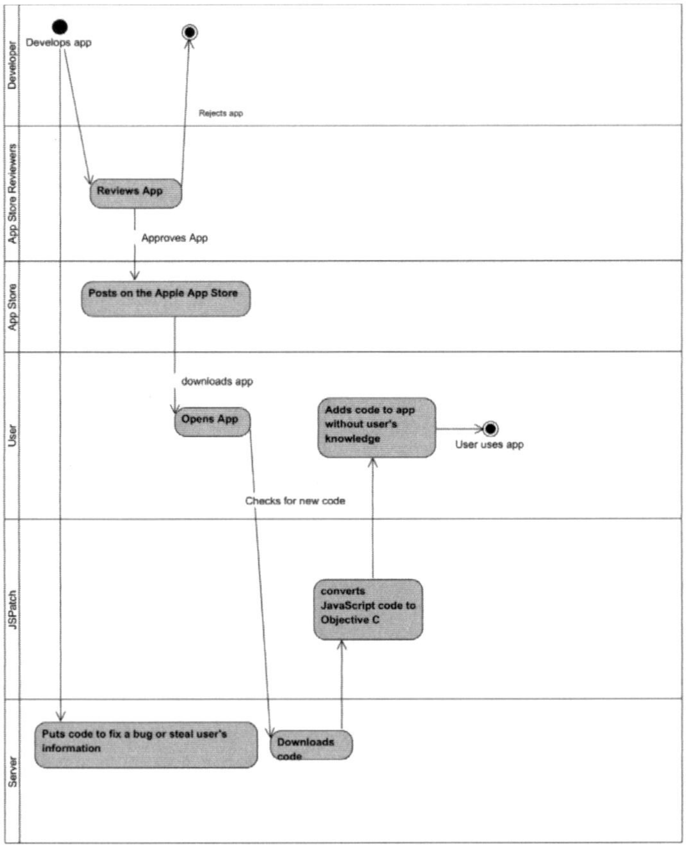

Figure 1. How JSPatch works.

ensures that these apps do not export private user data or access user data without a legitimate reason [7].

After security researchers at Fire Eye [9] identified that Rollout.io could be used maliciously through the use of private APIs, Rollout.io responded that they would be preventing users from accessing private APIs when submitting patches through their system article. Developers do not need to use private APIs to gain access to sensitive user information and abuse it, however, so this is not a perfect solution.

VI. The open-source Tool: JSPatch

JSPatch is an open source project created by a Chinese developer in 2014 [10]. It is regularly updated and has more than 30 contributors. It is similar in functionality to its commercial equivalent (discussed above). However, it has two additional security vulnerabilities, which Rollout.io does not.

The first major problem occurs when the developer is malicious. The developer can invoke a private Apple API in the JSPatch code without Apple's knowledge [3]. Apple does not allow for private APIs to be invoked in any app that is on the app store, but they only check for it in the app review process [3].

A non-malicious developer could still be put at risk by using JSPatch if they do not "protect the communication from client to the server for JavaScript content" and thus open themselves up to a man-in-the-middle attack (MITM) [3]. The attacker could then modify the JavaScript and attack the host app and the user's device in a variety of different ways.

VII. IMPLEMENTATION

To test the usability of these tools, JSPatch was chosen to test the ease of implementation, since, because it is open-source, it is more accessible to the normal developer, and more widely used in the App Store. We found it relatively easy to implement JSPatch using its documentation (though it should be noted that the Chinese documentation is more detailed, so it would probably be easier for a native Chinese speaker).

The exploit we chose to replicate was adopted from researchers at FireEye [3] who provided multiple compelling examples of the dangers of JSPatch. The exploit chosen was trivial one but emblematic of the problems, which can occur in JSPatch. We were able to load an arbitrary public framework which, once loaded, grants the script access to any private APIs which the framework has access to. Thus, without going through any review by Apple, privacy violations or bad practices, which would be grounds for an application to be rejected by official Apple reviwers, can be carried out without their knowledge.

VIII. APPLE'S POLICY

Rollout.io and JSPatch claim their tool is being accepted by Apple. JSPatch does not make an explicit legal claim, but in a GitHub issue thread, one user complains their app was rejected based on its inclusion of JSPatch, they include text from their rejection notification: "app contains an SDK designed to update the app outside of the App Store process. It would be appropriate to remove this SDK before resubmitting for review" [11]. In the same thread, user bang590, creator of JSPatch, claims Apple has been accepting apps, which include JSPatch, so there is no reason for it to be rejected and makes some suggestions for things to change, so the user will be accepted [11].

User bang590 is correct, according to FireEye's analysis as of January 2016, 1,200 apps in the app store contained JSPatch [3]. Rollout.io claims to be used on over 370 apps with a total device count of over 50 million [12].

Rollout.io, as a company, must have some sort of legal precedent to sell their product. They claim that according to Apple's developer guidelines 3.3.2 and 3.3.3 [7], they are not in violation of the rules because " 1. The code is run by Apple's built-in WebKit framework and JavascriptCore. The code does not provide, unlock or enable additional features or functionality" [13]. The author also claims that no app has ever been rejected for containing Rollout.io.

Rollout.io is correct that its product is not designed to add new feature or functionality. However, that does not prevent it or JSPatch from being used to do just that: to use it for the addition of functionality without the user's knowledge, which violates the user's privacy or puts them at risk.

Since this is not a discussion of the legality but the security of this policy, regardless of whether or not this exploit is within Apple's developer guidelines, Apple has been allowing apps with both JSPatch and Rollout.io on its app store for several years now.

Clearly, both Rollout.io and JSPatch pose major problems to Apple's supposedly stringent security policies. Apple's security is often praised as superior to Google's Android because of their strict review process and single, proprietary app store. However, tools like JSPatch and Rollout.io directly undermine the review process, which is supposedly keeping apps secure.

IX. PROBLEM THAT LEADS TO CURRENT STATE

The problem, which these tools are trying to address, though, is not creating a way to undermine the app review process, but creating a way to avoid the time delay, which Apple's review process creates for developers who are anxious to keep users if their app is crashing and users who are irritated by apps they want to use but are crashing. Apple [14] provides a way for developers to request an expedited review for fixing a critical bug, but, of course, it is not guaranteed that your request will be granted.

Comparably, the Google [15] play store, implemented a similar app review process. However, the times dramatically differ. In fact, Google rolled out the app review process in 2015 without notifying developers, and there was no noticeable change in rollout time because review times remained, on average, under an hour. They automate part of the process before submitting it to app reviewers. Therefore, they can do it much more quickly.

Apple [16] has significantly improved its review time since the invention of JSPatch and Rollout.io, shrinking it from an average of 8.8 days in 2015 to 1.95 days in May 2016. However, this is still significantly longer than Google's, their main competitor. Since Apple does not publicize information about their review process, it is unknown what is taking so long compared to Google.

X. TOWARDS A BETTER SOLUTION

Apple has an urgent need to change their review process to make it comparable to Google's, perhaps automating parts of it to speed up a review, to eliminate the need for tools like JSPatch and Rollout.io. Though they have decreased the review time (see above) since the invention of these tools, they have not decreased it to an acceptable level for developers who want to patch immediately.

With this lag time and their allowance of JSPatch and Rollout.io, they have undermined their entire security process, and these tools should be banned from use but not without a quicker patching solution.

The technology of Rollout.io and JSPatch represent a creative and easy solution to this problem, which should not be disregarded, however. To secure the process, Apple could

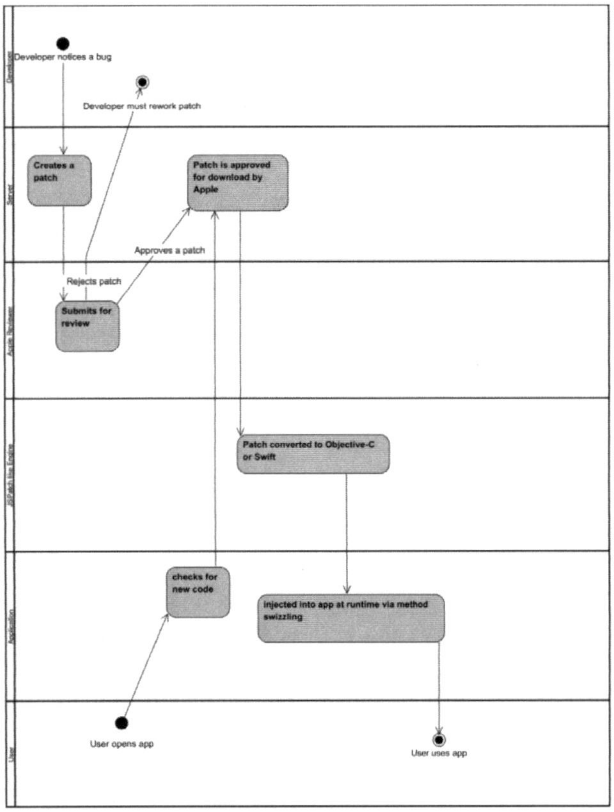

Figure 2. A better solution.

require submission of these patches to undergo review before they are actually downloaded to the app. These patches are not designed to be large scale changes to the entire app, but small hotfixes to bugs. The code being added when the tool is used correctly, should be relatively few lines and thus easy for an Apple app reviewer to approve within minutes. To protect against MITM attacks, developers who submit with this technology could be required to add code to ensure that the JavaScript being downloaded was protected and Apple could reject apps, which did not protect the network communication between the app and the server.

If developers began making their small patches through this technology and not resubmitting their entire app for even the smallest of bug patches, it would, in theory, free up the time of the Apple app reviewers to review initial app submissions and large updates more quickly. Therefore, this solution solves the problem of secure hot-patching and the problem of long submission wait times while maintaining the clean iOS app environment; see Figure 2 for a visual representation of the suggested process.

XI. Conclusion and Further Research

The need to be able to patch apps immediately is vital to developers and has driven them to create tools that expose loopholes in Apple's otherwise strict development guidelines and inconsistencies in its review process. Rollout.io and JSPatch provide significant benefits to developers and users when they are used safely and responsibly, but when they are in the hands of a malicious developer or if JSPatch is used without proper encryption, malicious code can enter the otherwise clean iOS environment.

On March 7, 2017, Apple began sending emails to developers using both Rollout.io and JSPatch to warn them that apps containing these tools will no longer be accepted on the app store. However, there has been no change in Apple's official development guidelines with regards to the language used [17]. It seems like Apple is moving in the right direction in terms of securing their ecosystem. However, there remains no good solution for quickly patching iOS apps. It is also worth noting that Apple has taken an alarmingly long time to recognize the problem with these tools, despite extensive reporting on it from security researchers. Apple's review system is slow and inefficient and also seems to lack efficacy and consistency.

Despite these concerns, Apple has an opportunity to make developers and users happy while maintaining security through the solution proposed here. It would allow them to review apps more quickly by relegating small changes to the hotpatching fixes, which would require much less time to review than the whole app code base that is resubmitted through the current Apple app update process.

REFFERENCES

[1] T. F. Bissyandé, L. Réveillère, J.-R. Falleri and Y.-D. Bromberg, "Typhoon: a middleware for epidemic propagation of Software Updates," in *Proceedings of the Third International Workshop on Middleware for Pervasive Mobile and Embedded Computing*, Lisbon, 2011.

[2] M. T. Azim, I. Neamtiu and L. M. Marvel, "Towards self-healing smartphone software via automated patching," in *Proceedings of the 29th ACM/IEEE international conference on Automated software engineering*, New York, 2014.

[3] J. Xie, Z. Chen and J. Su, "Hot or Not? The Benefits and Risks of IOS Remote Hot Patching," 2016 January 2016. [Online]. Available: https://www.fireeye.com/blog/threat-research/2016/01/hot_or_not_the_bene.html. [Accessed 11 December 2016].

[4] Rollout.io, "Rollout Under The Hood – 2016 Update," 22 March 2016. [Online]. Available: https://blog.rollout.io/under-the-hood-2016-update/. [Accessed 1 December 2016].

[5] Apple, "JavaScriptCore," [Online]. Available: https://developer.apple.com/reference/javascriptcore. [Accessed 11 December 2016].

[6] M. Thompson, "Method Swizzling," 17 February 2014. [Online]. Available: http://nshipster.com/method-swizzling/. [Accessed 13 December 2016].

[7] Appe, "iOS Developer Program Information," 3 4 2015. [Online]. Available: https://developer.apple.com/programs/ios/information/iOS_Program_Information_4_3_15.pdf. [Accessed 11 December 2016].

[8] Rollout.io, "About Rollout," [Online]. Available: https://rollout.io/about/. [Accessed 17 December 2016].

[9] J. Xie and J. Su, "Rollout or Not: The Benefits and Risks of IOS Remote Hot Patching," 4 April 2016. [Online]. Available: https://www.fireeye.com/blog/threat-research/2016/04/rollout_or_not_the.html. [Accessed 30 November 2016].

[10] bang590, "JSPatch," 7 August 2016. [Online]. Available: https://github.com/bang590/JSPatch. [Accessed 13 December 2016].

[11] xnth97, "Rejected by App Store," 15 September 2015. [Online]. Available: https://github.com/bang590/JSPatch/issues/111. [Accessed 2017 April 2017].

[12] Rollout.io, "Our Customers Fix Things Faster and Get More 5 Star Reviews," 2016. [Online]. Available: https://rollout.io/success-stories/. [Accessed 17 April 2017].

[13] O. Prusak, "Update Native iOS Apps without the App Store. How is this Legit?," 27 January 2016. [Online]. Available: https://rollout.io/blog/updating-apps-without-app-store/. [Accessed 17 April 2017].

[14] Apple, "App Review Support," [Online]. Available: https://developer.apple.com/support/app-review/. [Accessed 17 April 2017].

[15] S. Perez, "App Submissions On Google Play Now Reviewed By Staff, Will Include Age-Based Ratings," 17 March 2015. [Online]. Available: https://techcrunch.com/2015/03/17/app-submissions-on-google-play-now-reviewed-by-staff-will-include-age-based-ratings/. [Accessed 17 April 2017].

[16] O. Raymuldo, "Apple is approving apps for the iOS App Store much faster now," 12 May 2016. [Online]. Available: http://www.macworld.com/article/3070012/ios/apple-is-approving-apps-for-the-ios-app-store-much-faster-now.html. [Accessed 17 April 2017].

[17] E. Rusovsky, "Rollout's Statement on Apple Guidelines," 13 March 2017. [Online]. Available: https://rollout.io/blog/rollout-statement-on-apple-guidelines/. [Accessed 19 April 2017].

Secure Development of Healthcare Medical Billing Software

Paige Peck
Department of Computer Science
College of Charleston
Charleston, SC, United States of America
e-mail: paigepeck@hotmail.com

Aspen Olmsted
Department of Computer Science
College of Charleston
Charleston, SC, United States of America
e-mail: olmsteda@cofc.edu

Abstract— **Healthcare medical billing has been progressing into the digital era for several years, but it has been a slow and expensive process that has left many parts of the industry behind. One of the many things that have been overlooked in the progression is security, especially now that medical records are worth far more than credit card numbers on the black market. Another issue the healthcare industry has been dealing with is the lack of systems being incorporated. Currently, there are companies that are using printed out spreadsheets to find rules for coverage of a procedure based on any insurance company's policies. Using business rules engines and rule validations, we make it easier for a doctor or office to type in lab results and see whether a procedure will be covered by a patient's insurance company. We chose to create these using the Salesforce Cloud development service.**

Keywords- Healthcare billing software; Current Procedural Terminology; CPT codes; Healthcare Common Procedure Coding System; HCPCS codes; Salesforce Cloud development

I. Introduction

Healthcare has been transitioning to digital for years now, but up until recently, it has been a slow process. As Ballas [1] discussed back in 2001, the Internet would help to reduce the ever-rising costs of healthcare and would give the patient more power by allowing them to become more educated about specific medical procedures. He goes on to suggest that the internet will be able to help medical record keeping by giving access to these files on the web. While some of these have been implemented using Cloud development such as CureMD, Practice Fusion, and Athenahealth [2], healthcare is still behind where it should be. Payor rules are still being viewed on printed excel spreadsheets to find the information needed, and doctors do not have easy access to them electronically in a simple application. Having this could prevent doctors from prescribing drugs or procedures that should not be due to the patient's needs.

Now over fifteen years later, the conversion of healthcare to the Cloud is advancing, according to Ratchinsky [3]. While $3.73 billion was spent on Cloud services for healthcare in 2015, that number is expected to rise to $9.5 billion by 2020 [3]. Healthcare is moving towards the Cloud Technology more because Cloud applications are so flexible with scaling, are highly accessible, and are cost effective. Within a few years, it is expected that there will be less direct face-to-face interaction between patients and their providers [3]. Not only will the patient have more access and control of their medical records, but the use of business rules engines will help ensure that someone cannot be automatically prescribed a drug or procedure they cannot have without their knowledge. Business rules engines can be set up by healthcare providers and administrators using near English formats for non-software developers to easily set conditions on anything that a patient could automatically access. Having a system where admins could set these rules would save countless amounts of dollars. It would also prevent errors from occurring that could lead to a patient having a treatment they should not be able to have due to health conditions.

But is the Cloud secure enough for the many different laws concerning healthcare privacy? Guccione [4] discusses this very question along with a recent break into an Indiana-based medical software company. According to the company, patient names, email addresses, Social Security numbers (SSNs), and medical records were possibly stolen. The criminals also managed to break in the company's Cloud service, a system which allowed the patients to gain access to their medical records remotely. Healthcare is being targeted more with medical records having an increased value on the black market, far exceeding credit card numbers by tenfold. However, with all these break-ins and loss of data, at the time of the article's writing there had not been an update to the Health Insurance Portability and Accountability Act (HIPAA) rules on Cloud services in over three years [4]. With Cloud computing on the rise and healthcare using it now more than ever, the security regulations will need to be updated far more frequently. Those creating the applications will also need to consider potential outside threats.

To ensure that a system is secure, we put an effort into Confidentiality, Integrity, and Availability (CIA). Most research about healthcare security focuses on the Confidentiality of the system due to the nature of the data that is being stored and used. As the system will be interacting with personal health information, it is important for the system to keep the records confidential and secure. We are also working on the Integrity of the billing required by the clients. Most physicians have said that Integrity is the most important aspect of their job in the medical field. Integrity is also in the HIPAA Security Rules by stating that one must "implement policies and procedures to protect electronic Protected Health Information (ePHI) from improper alterations or destruction" [5]. Because the application is designed in Salesforce, availability is based mostly on their platform. Salesforce has several data centers spread across the United States in case of power failure, network connection issues, or hardware failure. Because of these centers, the loss of data is very minimal, measuring at mere seconds of lost data while the other centers take the traffic from the failing center.

The organization of the paper is as follows: Section II describes the related work and how others have attempted to tackle the mentioned issues. In Section III, we give a motivating example and describe a rule, why it is enforced, and why it is important. In Section IV, we go over the implementation of what we are building, why we chose a building in the Cloud, and show how we got to the point we are at. Section V discusses the results of our work such as what was good, bad, and difficult. We finish off the paper with Section VI that goes over the conclusion and future research.

II. RELATED WORK

There are several ways to ensure the correctness in healthcare medical billing software. One of these ways is by using a business rule engine. These are functions that can be used to create business rules without the need of a programmer. Olmsted and Stalvey [6] discussed these business rule engines and how they have been designed to allow users and non-programmers to change the business rules without changing the application code. According to their research, ninety percent of people completing a survey from International Data Corporation in 2007 said they change their business rules at least annually, if not more frequently. Of those that change, thirty-four percent change the rules monthly. There are several methods on how to develop these rules based engines, such as Drools [7]. Drools is a business rules management system. Drools facilitates the definition and enforcement of business rules engines. Another process was created and implemented by Abdullah, Sawar, and Ahmed [8] using Structured Query Language (SQL) specifically for applying billing compliance rules on medical claims. Medical billing is very complex and ever changing. Many times claims are rejected initially causing payments for services rendered to take a long time. Using the MTBC Rule Based System makes it easy for a user to edit rules in near English format, which is then translated into SQL statements. This system is currently being used by billing executives to enter medical claims into the database. The system is being continually updated. One of these newer updates is an "Auto Rule Generator" based on machine learning techniques [8].

Due to privacy laws dealing with medical information, security is an imperative component when designing medical billing software. Löhr, Sadeghi, and Winandy [9] discuss the lack of security in current online healthcare software and possible solutions to these security flaws. Throughout their paper, they describe the different types of electronic healthcare options giving several examples as to why it is not secure and how the systems can be breached. From there, they discuss the solution by separating medical data from billing and accounting data using a working prototype called Trusted Virtual Domains. They are also creating a user interface for this prototype. Though they have solutions to several of the issues they bring up, there are still a few security concerns involving these solutions. They discuss some of these such as the use of USB sticks that could be carrying malware and viruses.

Another solution to the risks of healthcare systems online is discussed by Kobayashi [10] by using Open Source Software (OSS). The use of open source software is also a solution to the rising costs of healthcare software. OSS is developed by volunteers and is provided 'as is' usually, which makes people skeptical about the security of the product. However, evaluations have been done on proprietary software that shows OSS has often been more reliable and has fewer bugs in the source code. OSS has also been shown to release patches more often that fix identified vulnerabilities.

Vanitha, Narasimha, and Chaitra [11] discuss using Electronic Health Records (EHR) and electronic billing systems on the Cloud with the platform MedBook. MedBook uses open source Cloud computing to help fight rising costs and detect fraudulent activities in the healthcare system. They continue to discuss how Cloud computing allows for costs being reduced when using this infrastructure. Reliability is improved when redundant sites are used, and security is improved because of the centralization of data and resources that focus on security. MedBook is a Software-as-a-Service (SaaS) application [11]. This is like our application since it is utilizing Salesforce, which is considered both a SaaS and a Platform-as-a-Service (PaaS). Software-as-a-Service is software that is hosted in the Cloud, which allows users to access the application through a web browser or an application on PCs or mobile devices.

Begum, Bhargavi, and Rani [12] wrote a review on how healthcare was utilizing the Cloud. This article discussed how organizations are still using paper records and handwritten notes to pass around data and come to conclusions. The authors go on to discuss possible solutions to potential problems when using the Cloud for medical data and the benefits that would be seen such as preventing any Protected Health Info (PHI) from being stored on hospital computers. This would prevent the current PHI violations that have been occurring due to the theft of computers.

As stated earlier, Salesforce is considered a PaaS Cloud-based system, which allows the developer of the software to not worry about the operating system the platform runs on [13]. Olmsted and Fulford [14] discuss the problems with the costs of development with PaaS Cloud systems. They continue to discuss PaaS systems and group them into two categories, each of which is used in our system. The first one is the previously mentioned rule engine to check business rules that are often changing and should not be coded directly into the system. The other being an importing feature using Comma Separated Values (CSV) formats and state that this should be validated to ensure that the database is secure.

III. MOTIVATING EXAMPLE

We are contributing to this industry by creating an application for a healthcare consultant agency. This application is being developed using the Cloud development tool Salesforce. The focus of the application is on the lookup field for rules set for drugs, Current Procedural Terminology (CPT) codes, and Healthcare Common Procedure Coding System (HCPCS) codes. CPT codes are medical codes that are used to describe any medical procedure done by a healthcare provider. They are created and maintained by the American Medical Association. There are thousands of these codes split up into categories for medical coders to enter so the healthcare providers will be reimbursed from the insurance companies. Some of these CPT codes are variations of other procedures. These codes need to be entered properly, with the more specific variation chosen when possible, or a claim can be rejected due to the procedure not being covered. HCPCS codes were created by the Centers for Medicare and Medicaid. HCPCS codes are very similar to CPT codes, often the exact same, but they are used to represent Medicare, Medicaid, and other third-party payors. HCPCS codes are also used more as a specific drug where CPT codes are procedures done on a patient. The level II category HCPCS codes vary from the CPT codes in that they begin with an alphanumeric letter. The codes we use as an example fall under this category and begin with the letter 'J.' J-codes are the most common codes, and they are codes for non-oral medication and chemotherapy drugs that cannot be self-administered. HCPCS codes have more specificity than CPT codes, which includes many variations of equipment and drugs, so it is far more important for medical coders to put in the claims [15].

The drug we will use as an example is PROCRIT (HCPCS: J0885). According to the company that sells PROCRIT, "PROCRIT (epoetin alfa) [16] is used to treat a lower than a normal number of red blood cells (anemia) caused by chronic kidney disease in patients on dialysis and not on dialysis. Chemotherapy that will be used for at least 2 months after starting PROCRIT. A medicine called zidovudine (AZT) used to treat HIV infection" [16]. Every one of these drugs and procedures has requirements based on the patient's lab results. The requirements placed on the drugs and procedures are laid out by the insurance companies, or "payors." Because of this, a drug can have requirements from one payor that are not listed from a different payor. As an example, Medicaid might list a requirement for a patient's hemoglobin (Hgb) level to be below 10 to allow administration of PROCRIT. In contrast, BlueCross BlueShield might have a requirement for the patient's Hgb levels to be below 12 or not even have a requirement for the Hgb levels to allow administration of PROCRIT.

The rules placed on these drugs and procedures are what can cause a patient's claim to be rejected by the payor if the rules are not followed. With all these details placed upon a drug/procedure, claims are often rejected at first. Currently, the client is traveling and passing out laminated cards of these rules for the drugs. By doing this, they have cut down claim rejections by nearly 50%. By creating this application, we will be cutting down far more claim rejections by making the rules a validation step when entering the values into the system in addition to displaying the rules of each drug/procedure based on the payor. This will save the healthcare industry thousands of dollars by ensuring the billers will get paid by performing the correct procedure on a patient. Table I shows the requirements for the drug PROCRIT. Hgb levels and hematocrit (HCT) are considered "OR" statements provided in the table. As an example, for "Anemia: Chemo Induced – Encounter for chemotherapy" the Hgb levels must be below 10 OR HCT must be below 30 for PROCRIT to be administered and covered. A disclaimer is also included on these laminated cards based on the drug. These disclaimers are a non-payable list of diagnoses that are not covered. An example of one of these non-payable diagnoses is "any anemia in cancer or cancer treatment due to iron deficiency." For the

TABLE I. PROCRIT J0885 REQUIREMENTS CHECK LIST

Rules	Anemia: Chemo Induced – Encounter for chemotherapy	Anemia: Chemo Induced – Encounter for chemotherapy	Myelodysplastic Syndrome (MDS) – No Secondary Requirements	MDS – Anemia in other chronic diseases classified elsewhere	Chronic Kidney Disease (CKD) – Anemia in CKD
Hgb for initiation	< 10		< 10		< 10
HCT for initiation	< 30		< 30		< 30
Hgb for continuation of Therapy		< 10		< 11	< 11
HCT for continuation of Therapy		< 30		< 33	< 33
TSAT	> 20%			> 20%	> 20%
Ferritin	> 80 ng/mL			> 80 ng/mL	> 80 ng/mL
Timing of Labs	Within 7 days Prior to Initiation of Therapy	Every 4 weeks for continued Therapy	48 Hours Prior to Initiation of Therapy	Every 4 weeks for continued Therapy	Within 7 days prior to Initiation of Therapy Every 4 weeks for continued Therapy

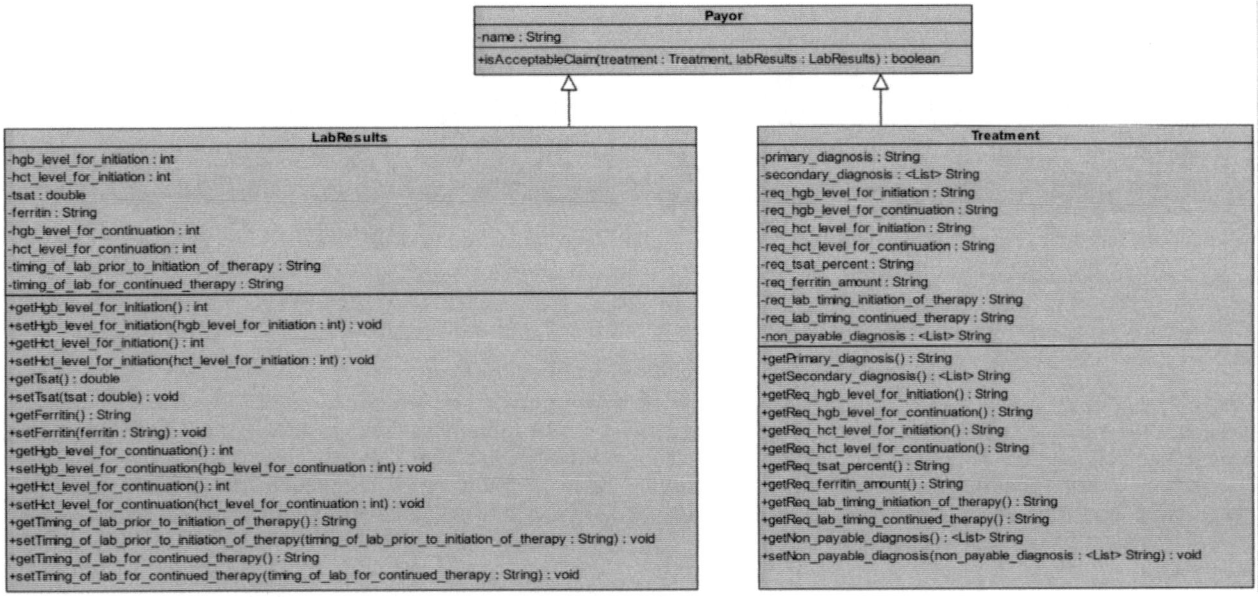

Figure 1. UML Class Diagram

application, the client requested that these disclaimers merely be displayed at the bottom of each drug. Figure 1 is a UML class diagram showing how the lab results and treatment requirements relate to the payor. In the system, a payor will accept a claim if the lab results are within range of the treatment requirements. The treatment variables are set as string variables due to the fact most of them include a comparison operator to check with the lab result variable.

To keep these requirements checked and ensure there is no error on the user's side, we are using the business rules engines mentioned previously. Salesforce has its own form of a business rules engine called "Validation Rules." These validation rules can be set on each object in Salesforce. The rules have functions such as "AND', "OR," "CONTAINS," and much more that can be used to validate a field or multiple fields of an object. After assigning the fields, operators, and functions, we can hit the "check syntax" button to make sure we typed everything in correctly. After assigning this rule, we can set the error message that will be shown when an error condition occurs. For the example drug PROCRIT, we can have an object called "Drug" with the above fields stored into the object's fields based on a lookup field for another object called "Payor." For one validation rule, we can read the lab results and parse through the text using "CONTAINS" to find Hgb or HTC levels. If we have found them, we ensure the level of the patient is below the values listed in Table I using the less than or greater than operators. If they are, the system continues down the list of validation rules set. Otherwise, it throws an error showing the user that PROCRIT is not covered under the selected payor.

IV. Implementation

The client first brought their idea for this application to our attention by stating that current insurance companies and healthcare organizations are searching through printed out Excel spreadsheets and finding the rules laid out by each payor for a specific treatment. These rules are not laid out in any easily trackable system. These rules need to allow for a transfer of information from the administrators who create and edit the rules to the doctors' offices. The offices need to be able to explain why a claim was not covered or a specific drug cannot be administered. As Begum, Bhargavi and Rani [12] discussed, the lack of proper healthcare applications on the Cloud, or even in general, is costing the industry millions of dollars. Figure 2 shows a model they created for a PaaS system where users can have a local electronic medical record and not have to manage the system framework. The application we are building is utilizing one of the PaaS development models, Salesforce.

The choice to use Salesforce for this application was simple as the client wanted the application to be created quickly and with a service that can be used on more than just a computer, such as use on a tablet or mobile device. Salesforce excels in both. It is also reliable and has very good support. Salesforce was also good because it is not too costly for the client's planned model. When it comes to security, Salesforce stays on top of current malware, phishing, and intrusion attempts and is constantly updating their system to reflect these. They have event monitoring, which gives a client detailed information about any action that is taking place on the system. They also use the most up-to-date authentication and encryption methods and hosts its data on a secure server environment [14].

To fix the clients first problem, they asked for an administration toolkit where those who used it could import and export rules based on Comma Separated Values (CSV) files. In these import and export pages, they requested an easy way to edit the rules and add new ones when needed. When

Figure 2. Platform-as-a-Service Healthcare Model

designing the system, we decided that two separate pages were called for, one for importing and adding rules, and another for exporting and editing the rules. We were given an excel spreadsheet from an insurance company as a template, and we modeled the system around this. For the importing function, if the file is a CSV and follows along with a given template that a user can download, they can easily import new rules after setting an effective date. Exporting works about the same way, where a user selects the fields they want to export to CSV, and the system then downloads a file with the rules selected under the fields that were searched.

The client was happy with the admin toolkit design and wanted us to move on to their next step before they planned to present the product as an early prototype to the insurance companies that they are consultants for. They wanted the next part of the application to focus on the doctors and offices that will use it, focusing on the specific rules of the drugs laid out by the payors. These rules are what we will be using to ensure the correctness of the software. The final product for this part of the application will allow a doctor to traverse through it on a tablet and enter the procedure with the constraints given, and the application will inform the doctor whether the drug can be administered or not.

V. RESULTS AND DISCUSSION

Throughout the process of creating this application, we discussed several options on how to handle validating the requirements for the drugs. At first, we discussed writing a parser and regular expressions to ensure the requirements were met. As this could potentially take some time to write and improve, we looked elsewhere to see if there was a better and faster way of doing it. We debated using business rules engines such as Drools, which was less complicated than parsing and using regular expressions but still not exactly what we were looking for. Creating a tool for a user to create these rules themselves was another option that has been done before, but this can create problems overall if a user mistakenly writes an incorrect validation. Then we came across the out-of-the-box rules validation that Salesforce controls for each object type. This built-in feature was already designed into a system we had been working on for over a year as well. If we write the validation rules properly, then this feature will do the work for us.

The difficulty lies in writing these validation rules properly to ensure they do the work correctly. As stated before, several of the drug requirements can have an "OR" associated with them, for example, HCT and Hgb levels each have their own requirement levels, but only one is needed to meet this. An example of a properly written validation rule based on Table I would say: "(Hgb for initiation < 10) OR (HCT for initiation) < 30". If one of these are true for an attempt of administering PROCRIT for anemia due to Chronic Kidney Disease or Chemo Induced, then the system will allow the user to continue. There are requirements for initiation of taking the drug and separate requirements for continuation of taking the drug that can be misunderstood or improperly set. As this is the main function we want doctors and users to trust, it will have to be very carefully checked that the validation rules entered are correct.

The next phase will be working closely with the client to build these validation rules ourselves, so the user will not be writing them. As each drug and payor combination has their own set of requirements, this will take some time to get all of them working. For now, we will be building out the rules that the client deems worthy for showing off a prototype to potential buyers. As they pass along the laminated cards, they will be showing off the application as an easier and all around better way for checking these requirements. Because it will be checking the data entered from the lab results, it will be easier for them to see when a drug or procedure will not be covered. administered or not.

VI. CONCLUSION AND FURTHER RESEARCH

In this work, we discuss ways to guarantee medical billing software to be secure on the Cloud and accurate. As healthcare makes the transition more to the Cloud, accurate and secure data is pertinent for the application if we want the clients to trust using it. There are several options one can use to ensure the correctness of the data entered, and the choice that is easiest to implement and follow is the one that is built in for us already using Salesforce validation rules. Salesforce is constantly monitoring new attempts at malware and phishing to give us one of the most secure Cloud development tools on the market. Future work will help us broaden the application for more users to access it and be able to easily add the ever changing and new requirements from the healthcare industry.

REFERENCES

[1] M. S. Ballas, "The Impact of the Internet on the Healthcare Industry: A Close Look at the Doctor-Patient Relationship, the Electronic Medical Record, and the Medical Billing Process," *Einstein Quarterly Journal of Biology and Medicine,* vol. 18, no. 2, pp. 79-83, 2001.

[2] R. Lowes, "Medscape," 15 May 2012. [Online]. Available: http://www.medscape.com/viewarticle/763894. [Accessed 14 August 2017].

[3] K. Ratchinsky, "Why the healthcare industry's move to cloud computing is accelerating," 27 June 2016. [Online]. Available: https://www.cloudcomputing-news.net/news/2016/jun/27/why-healthcare-industrys-move-cloud-computing-accelerating/. [Accessed 3 June 2017].

[4] D. Guccione, "Healthcare Informatics Institute," 20 July 2015. [Online]. Available: https://www.healthcare-informatics.com/article/cloud-safe-healthcare. [Accessed 05 June 2017].

[5] H. C. Pros, "Integrity: More than Just a Piece of the Healthcare Compliance Puzzle," 17 June 2014. [Online]. Available: http://www.healthcarecompliancepros.com/blog/integrity-more-than-just-a-piece-of-the-healthcare-compliance-puzzle-2/. [Accessed 28 June 2017].

[6] A. Olmsted and R. Stalvey, "Highly available, consistent, business rule filters," *The 9th International Conference for Internet Technology and Secured Transactions (ICITST-2014),* 2014.

[7] "Drools," Red Hat, Inc., [Online]. Available: https://www.drools.org/. [Accessed 14 August 2017].

[8] U. Abdullah, M. J. Sawar and A. Ahmed, "Design of a rule based system using Structured Query Language," *2009 Eighth IEEE International Conference on Dependable, Autonomic and Secure Computing,* pp. 223-228, 2009.

[9] H. Löhr, A.-R. Sadeghi and M. Winandy, "Securing the e-Health Cloud," *Proceedings of the ACM international conference on Health informatics - IHI '10,* 2010.

[10] S. Kobayashi, "Open Source Software Development on Medical Domain," InTech, 2012.

[11] T. N. Vanitha, M. Narasimha Murthy and B. Chaitra, "E-Healthcare Billing and Record Management Information System using Android with Cloud," *IOSR Journal of Computer Engineering (IOSR-JCE,* vol. 11, no. 4, pp. 13-19, 2013.

[12] F. Begum, K. Bhargavi and T. Suneetha Rani, "A Review on Healthcare in Cloud," *IJSTE - International Journal of Science Technology & Engineering,* vol. 2, no. 06, pp. 124-129, 2015.

[13] "Salesforce," Salesforce.com, Inc., [Online]. Available: https://www.salesforce.com/ap/. [Accessed 14 August 2017].

[14] A. Olmsted and K. Fulford, "Platform As A Service Effort Reduction," *CLOUD COMPUTING 2017, The Eighth International Conference on Cloud Computing, GRIDs, and Virtualization,* pp. 60 - 65, 2017.

[15] "Medical Billing & Coding Certification," [Online]. Available: http://www.medicalbillingandcoding.org. [Accessed 08 June 2017].

[16] Janssen Products, "Procrit epoetin alfa," Janssen Products, 24 July 2015. [Online]. Available: https://www.procrit.com/. [Accessed 09 June 2017].

Attack Maze for Network Vulnerability Analysis

Computing the Maximum Possible Incursion and Intuitive Metrics

Stanley Chow
STHC Creative Technologies
Ottawa, Canada
e-mail: stanley.chow@pobox.com

***Abstract*— Even a well administered computer network will be vulnerable to attacks. There have been many proposals in the literature to address the problem of Network-Vulnerability Analysis. One approach is to generate an attack graph (a logical graph representation of all possible sequences of vulnerabilities) using some formal model. Attack graphs suffer from scalability issues as the size of the network or the number of services and vulnerabilities increase. This paper presents a new approach that treats the network as a *maze*, which the attacker has to solve. We then use the classical way to solve mazes in computer games – remembering where we have been by dropping things at each node. We present a graph-based algorithm to solve this maze and compute the Maximum Possible Incursion (MPI) for a given set of attackers or compromises. The developed simple breadth-first algorithm provides performance improvements over previous approaches (less than a minute to analyze a network with over 10,000 nodes). We also present a methodology to capture mission dependency, which represents how a mission relies on the underlying network. Finally, we compute an extensible set of security metrics that identify the current network status in multiple dimensions (e.g. Confidentiality, Integrity, and Availability). We also discuss future work to enumerate the specific attack paths that could be used to generate corrective recommendations.**

Keywords- Network security; vulnerability analysis; scalable; vulnerability; exploit; maximum incursion; cyber security; metric; security metric; mission dependency.

I. INTRODUCTION

Cyber security has become more complex – the early generations of malware exploited a single vulnerability in a single computer system. Subsequently, worms and other malware propagate through a whole network. Recently, we have seen Stuxnet [1] and other sophisticated malware that use multiple vulnerabilities. Not only are malware getting more sophisticated, in many incidents, the attackers are known to have used a chain of vulnerabilities to gain access. There are many examples of such chains documented in various security advisories and so on.

Before we can analyze the possible chains of vulnerabilities, it is necessary to identify all the vulnerabilities present on each node. More generally, we need to identify the total attack surface of each node. Since there are many vulnerability scanners [2], and many agencies maintain databases of vulnerabilities, this paper assumes that all vulnerabilities are already known. It can also be difficult to capture the necessary network information, but this paper deals only with the analysis problem.

The problem of analyzing the many possible chains of vulnerabilities has attracted much attention. Most approaches ask: Can this node attack that node? One major approach is the *attack graph* introduced in 1998 [3]. Attack graphs are logical representations of all the ways an attacker could reach any target node in a given network. Although useful, attack graphs suffer from scalability in memory and performance issues as the network grows in number of nodes, services, vulnerabilities, etc. There are techniques in the literature that attempt to address the scalability of attack graphs in order to perform well for realistic-sized networks [4, 5]. This scalability problem is due to capturing all possible attack paths in the attack graph, so CPU time and memory usage grow rapidly with the size of the network. Another approach constructs an *access graph* of nodes in the network, where each directed edge in the graph represents a possible access along the edge [6].

We analyze the vulnerabilities for a different goal. Instead of calculating attack paths between specific nodes, we want to know exactly what privileges the attacker can possibly achieve – the *Maximum Possible Incursion* on each node. Clearly, this computation is specific to the particular class of attackers and must be recomputed for each class. Our approach, the *Attack Maze*, is similar to an access graph, but computes the MPI (Maximum Possible Incursion) directly. This means we do not record all possible Attack Paths, only the resultant incursion at each node – this is enough to achieve good scalability even for large networks.

Formal methods rely on accurately capturing all the intricacies of all the data – any missing data cannot be part of the inference chain. Some data are difficult to handle in formal systems, examples include: the privilege of a userid may be already in an LDAP (Lightweight Directory Access Protocol) directory and may change frequently – the difficulty is due to the unpredictable changes to the LDAP entry; the firewall may have rules that are dependent on time/data or even user – the difficulty is due to the sheer number of combinations that are possible and some dynamic rules that may include factors/variables not captured in the formal model, many transactions will depend on business logic (be it decision tree, decision tables, database look up or complex programmatic logic) - the difficulty is that many factors/variables may not be captured and that logic may be ill suited for the formal system. Since our approach is not based on a formal model, there is no need to precisely capture all details into the model; instead, the conditions can be embedded in code that is able to query LDAP, etc. (we do not allow arbitrary code - we require the code to respect monotonicity, see Step 5.d of the algorithm.)

The proposed approach also takes into account *mission dependency*. That is, given a mission that depends on some nodes of the network and given the current network status, what are the potential impacts on this mission? Some examples of mission dependency work in the cyber arena include [7, 8] and in the civil infrastructure area [9, 10].

We use the concept of *capabilities* to encapsulate what functions are exported by the network. Each mission can then use these capabilities without knowing the details of how they are implemented (e.g. which nodes provide email service).

We also present a suite of metrics that can be easily computed from the MPI. These metrics can be calculated at the levels of node, capability and mission, and have intuitive meaning to the owners of the node, capability or mission.

These ideas are implemented in a prototype using Python3 scripts. Our experiments show that even the simple algorithms perform very well – a well maintained network with few vulnerable nodes can be analyzed very quickly and even a network with many vulnerable nodes takes only minutes.

II. Attack Maze

A. Approach

Our approach is quite close to how an attacker tries to penetrate a network – find initial points of entry, then launch attacks from the compromised nodes to access more nodes and gain more privileges, repeat until no new privilege is possible. Along the way, the attacker keeps track of what access has already been achieved on each node, and only "better" accesses are of real interest. Eventually, all possible compromises on all nodes will be found. We define a *node* to be anything that is addressable (possibly with multiple addresses), so network printers, desktops, laptops, servers, proxies, are all nodes. We also generalize *firewalls* that control which nodes can access across *zone* boundaries.

B. Status

The key idea of the proposed algorithm is that we attach multiple *statuses* to each node. Each *status-type* records one particular type of privilege that the attacker can achieve at the node. The exact details of the statuses are expected to change with different applications (this paper presents some common statuses). Note that this algorithm does not rely on any specific status.

Each status-type should be at least a partial order – that is, the different levels of privilege should form a tree or hierarchy (as opposed to a complete order where the privilege forms a linear chain). We define *levels(s)* to be the number of levels in the hierarchy. The partial ordering of each status-type will induce a partial order on the whole node, that is, for nodes n_1 and n_2:

$n_1 > n_2$ iff $s(n_1) > s(n_2)$ for all status-types s

Note that there are two kinds of status-types:

- Status types that document increasing privilege,
  - None, anonymous shell, chroot jail, full user shell, root shell
  - None, write on /tmp only, write on ~/ only, write on anywhere
  - None, write file as anonymous, write file as user, write file as root
- Status types that document decreasing capability:
  - None (or Normal), 50% capacity, Non-functional (for example, measuring the capacity of a Domain Name Server)
  - Normal, some transaction over 100 millisecond, all transactions over 1 second (for example, measuring the throughput of a Web server)

C. Attack Step

We start by looking at the following attack step:

Node *A* uses exploit *E* to attack node *T*

We will refer to node *A* as the *attacker,* exploit *E* as the *exploit vector,* and node *T* as the *target* or the *victim* (a target is the intended victim of the attack, whereas a victim is after the attack succeeds). Each attack step will have *pre-conditions* and *post-conditions*. In this design, we explicitly limit pre-conditions to be dependent only on the combination {*A*, *E*, *T*} and the post-conditions are limited to status-fields of the victim. In other words, the pre-conditions for a particular vector *E* may be dependent on the statuses of *A*, and the statuses of *T*; whereas the post-conditions can only be statuses of *T*. Intuitively, when node *A* launches an attack, the attack may use all the privileges already gained at *A* as well as the privledges already gained at *T*. After the attack succeeds, the privilege gained **must** be at *T*. Note that no other nodes may be a part of the pre-conditions nor the post-conditions.

For example, we allow pre-conditions such as status-type "UserAccount" must be at least "user shell account" and status-type "UserpPiv" must be at least "can execute arbitrary program" – as long as the requirement is only on *A* or *T*. This is inherent in the definiton of status-type.

Most formal models do not restrict free variable like "user has FTP access on **some** server" (e.g., MulVAL [11] uses Datalog/Prolog logic rules so there is no problem with using another variable that will bind to another node). We explicitly disallow them in the pre-conditions, but allow them in the programatic code with some restrictions. As will be seen in Section E, this ensures the efficiency of the algorithm.

The restriction on pre-conditions does limit the kinds of attack steps that can be modeled; but we allow the programatic code to check for the same conditions – although this check must be consistent, repeatable and respects the monotonicity (a node can only increase its possible attacks when its statuses go up). This monotonicity ensures that we never have to backtrack. With this relaxation, we can easily handle attack vectors that require multiple intermediate nodes to cooperate. This means the resultant lost of expressive power is only nominal and the vast majority of real attacks can be modeled exactly and easily.

D. Solving the Attack Maze

To solve the maze, we start with the attacker(s) and try all possible victims (by recursively trying all possible attack steps on all possible targets). This ensures that we will traverse all possible attack paths from all attackers; along the way, we track only the maximum incursion at each victim. We use the naïve breadth-first algorithm described as follows:

Step 1. Start with just the nodes, initializing each node to have *None* (the lowest state) for each status-type. Intuitively, this is a sea of islands that any attacker has to hop to get anywhere, and the attacker starts with no access to anything.

Step 2. Initialize *newWorkList* to be the set of nodes that the attacker is assumed to have compromised - all their own machines (in their own domains) plus our machines that has been compromised.) This is an input to the Attack Maze computation. The statuses for the attacker(s) are set to the maximum privileges achieved. Intuitively, this represents the initial set of accesses that the attacker has.

Step 3. Check *newWorkList*, if it is empty, then we are done. If it is not-empty, copy *newWorkList* to *workList*, set *newWorkList* to empty.

Step 4. Removing an attacker Node *A* from *workList*. (If *workList* is empty, got to Step 3.) Intuitively, we will attempt to launch attacks from this node.

Step 5. Go through every node *T* in the system as a possible target from attacker *A*. (After running through every node, go to Step 4 for the next attacker.) Check if node *A* can attack node *T*:

a. Node *T* has a vulnerability *V*

b. The vulnerability *V* must have an exploit *E*

c. Node *A* can reach the address/port on node *T* needed to exploit *E*

d. Node *A* meets the pre-conditions of exploit *E* (note, this is the place for the non-local checks that must respect node monotonicity)

Step 6. If all the conditions (in Step 5)

a. are not met, this attack step is not possible. Go to Step 4 for the next target.

b. are met, then this attack step succeeds. The post-conditions of exploit *E* are merged into the statuses of node *T*. That is, we record the maximum of each status-type (since each status-type must be a partial order, there will be a maximum). If any status is increased as a result, add node *T* to *newWorkList*.

E. Analysis of performance

For analysis of performance, we will use:

- n – number of nodes
- $s - \sum_0^n levels(s_i)$
- v – number of actual vulnerabilities or exploits

Since each node can only be added to the *workList* with an increase in status, and since the statuses are monotonic, each node can only be on the *workList* s times. Each time a node is on the *workList*, the algorithm will examine all possible attacks from that node, so the total work will be $O(s*n*n*v)$ and since s and v are independent of the network, they can be subsumed into the coefficients, so the total work is $O(n^2)$. Note that this is for the algorithm, but we allow (in step Step 5.d) the pre-condition check to do arbitrary computation. In our prototype, we did not rely on this.

We make several observations on aspects that are often difficult:

- Exactness – within the accuracy of our status-fields (and extended pre-condition checks), we compute the exact MPI (Maximal Possible Incursion). This is true even if the pre-conditions are not completely formalized (i.e. embedded in code).
- Multiples paths getting to a node – we handle each possible step, but the effects of the steps are merged at the node. This means we compute the MPI without enumerating all possible paths, we only enumerate all possible steps.
- Cycles in attack paths – each complete cycle is handled; no extra processing is caused by multiple cycles. This is all implicit in the merging of status at nodes.

F. Practical performance

In the preceding analysis, the number of times a node can be put onto the WorkList is bound by s, the number of steps in the statuses. In practice, the loop (Step 4) iterates in lockstep with each link in an attack chain; that is, we start at the attacker(s) and follow all attack paths/chains simultaneously, one link per iteration. Therefore, the number of iterations is usually equal to the length of the longest attack path (counting in nodes, which is 1 more than the length in links). Even though this is only changing the constants and does not affect big-O, it does mean we can freely add more status-types without significantly affecting run-time.

Some optimizations that do not change the big-O, but can save significant time, are possible. For example, in step Step 5.c, instead of trying every node, we could try just the reachable nodes (either grouped by subnets or by nodes). It is also possible to precompute the attack surface of each node so that step Step 5.b becomes trivial. With these types of optimizations, the algorithm can hope to get close to O(n) on average, although O(n^2) is still the worst case. Note that, as we show later, n (the total number of nodes) is a poor predictor of performance; different types of node can have different impact – by factor of thousands.

G. Prototype

Our Python3 prototype is intended as a light weight, flexible, easy to use experimental test bed. The system is controlled by a control file (usually filetype ".maze") that controls every aspect of operation – the input data, the processing, the options, the output, the debugging. The control files processing (around 1K lines of Python) implements many facilities: nested includes, comments, timing, conditional jumps, setting of variables (such as the debug level), printing out data, sequencing operations.

We implemented a *Data Model* that includes *firewalls, zone, nodes, vulnerability,* etc. The Data Model is also around 1K lines of Python. The Attack Maze and the metrics total another 1K lines of Python.

The Attack Maze code has several parts:

- Status – code to handle definition of status-type
- Maze – algorithm to solve the maze
- Rules – the specific attack steps implemented as Python functions.

The rules are just individual attack steps. For example, this rule from MulVAL [11]:

accessFile(P, H, Access, Path) :-
    execCode(P, H, Owner), filePath(H, Owner, Path).

says "if an attacker P can access machine H with Owner's privilege, then he can have arbitrary access to files owned by Owner". Our equivalent Python code is show below in Figure 1:

```
have_priv=lookup_status(dfd_node.statuses, "Privilege")
if (have_priv > 1): ## have root priv
    ## is there any desired data on this machine?
    dfd_data = lookup_host_properties(dfd_node.host,
                                        "Data_Bind")
    if (0 < len(dfd_data)):
        ## yes, so this succeeds
        updated=updateStatus(1,"GotData",
                             dfd_node.statuses)
```

Figure 1. Python code example

In Figure 1, *dfd_node* is the target. We first lookup it's status of Privilege into *have_priv*, then check whether root privilege has been achieved. If it has, then, we lookup whether it has any *data binding* (MulVAL [11] term for data that the attacker wants). If both conditions are met, then the post-condition of *GotData* is set to record that this node will leak that data.

H. Examples

For our sample network , we start with the example from [11] and add the watering-hole attack from [12]. The network is the usual 2-firewall with DMZ. (DeMilitarized Zone.) Connectivity is shown in blue. For simplicity, each zone is assumed to be flat – any node can talk to any other node. The attack, which is from the Internet, takes 3 steps and is shown in red.

While running the algorithm, the *workList* will be: on iteration 1 {Attacker}, on iteration 2 {WebServer}, on iteration 3 {FileServer}, and, finally, on iteration 4 {Workstation}. So, a chain of 3 steps needs 4 iterations, as expected. We also include a node WorkSafe that is like WorkStation but without the vulnerabilities. In a well maintained network, most of the node will be of the WorkSafe variety (in a primitive way, the proportion of WorkSafe nodes serves as a measure of the security of the network.)

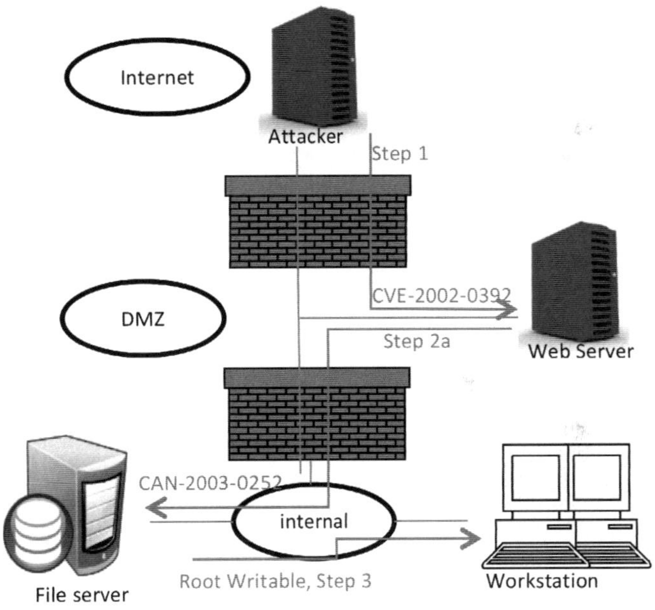

Figure 2. Test network

I. Timings

Our prototype implemented a "clone" directive to clone many copies of a node to test the scalability. Since we expect different behaviours for different types of nodes, we set up a number of scenarios listed in Table 1:

- Victim – vary the number of victims (cloning WorkStation up to 9K times)
- Innocent – vary the number of innocent bystanders (clone WorkSafe)
- Intermediate – vary the number of attack path intermediate nodes (clone WebServer)
- 3 X 1K – a fix 1K of each Victim/WorkStation, Innocent/WorkSafe, Intermediate/WebServer

Table 1. SCALABILITY CASES

Scenrio	WorkStation	WorkSafe	WebServer
Victim	1...9K	10	1
Innocent	10	1...9K	1
Intermediate	5	10	1...9K
3 X 1K	1K	1K	1K

The timings are done on an Dell XPS laptop with Intel i5-4210U CPU at 1.7GHz, 8GiB memory, Ubuntu 14.04 LTS, Python version 3.4.3a and times are reported in seconds of CPU time. Note that the memory usage for all cases was under 0.5 GiB and entirely in main memory, the script is single threaded, so multi-process is irrelevant. The data points are average of several runs.

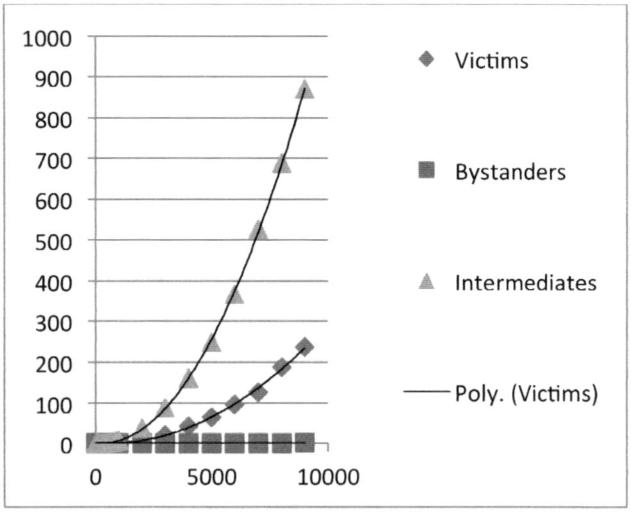

Figure 3. Scalability timing

In Figure 3, the green triangles are the number of vulnerable Web Servers (the intermediate stop in the attack path), the red squares are "safe" work stations (not in any attack path), and the blue diamonds are the WorkStations (victims). Not surprisingly, the timings all fit O(n^2) very well with R^2 values well above 0.99. On the other hand, the coefficients are quite different – 1e-5, 3e-6, 3e-9 respectively, or in ratio 3K:1K:1; this means "safe" nodes take practically no time, so a large well maintained network can be analysed in seconds. The victim nodes take more time, but even 10K victims take only a few minutes. The intermediate nodes are the most time consuming – 10K intermediates take around 20 minutes.

We also ran a case of 1K intermediates, 1K victims, 1K safes, for a total of 3K nodes (to be exact, we make that many clones of each type, but the network includes firewalls and other house keeping nodes, so the actual number of nodes is 3,026). It took around 40 seconds. This shows that even without any optimizations, it is entirely feasible for a network of realistic size.

III. Mission Dependency

To quote from [13] "It is critical that the [Department of Defense] develop better cognizance of Cyber Network Mission Dependencies". Some proposals, such as [14] are elaborate and somewhat difficult to construct. For example, a mission commander may know a particular mission needs email, but unlikely (may be even not allowed) to know which nodes are actually involving in provding email.

Our contribution is to define the concept of a *capability* which can be *exported* and *used*. The exporter is responsible to define how the capability is *implemented*, for example, in terms of nodes that are required. The *user* merely has to use the capability without knowing which nodes are involved.

This fits the real world situation quite nicely. For example, corporate IT may provide email, File Server, Print Server etc. while different groups may provide Sales Data, Inventory Data. A branch office IT can simply make use of these capabilities, and the system can resolve the dependencies. If the nodes that implement email are replaced or renamed, the users do not need to know (and probably will not know)!

This concept can extend to physical infrastructure like cables, buildings. It is also possible to capture redundancy requirements into the implementation of each capability. For example, the email capability requires just one of two nodes to be working (along with DNS capability).

IV. Metrics

There are different kinds of metrics for Situation Awareness: the patch status of each node, the attack surface of each node, where are the critical assets, active attacks in progress, etc., see [15] for a survey. Eigenvalues have been proposed as a mechanism for computing metrics, but they generally are not intuitive – a localized change can affect the metrics of nodes far away, for no clear reason. Even the sign of the change may be unpredictable.

We are interested in quantitative measures that are intuitive for questions like:

- How much damage can an attacker do? (For different classes of attackers)
- Which particular assets are vulnerable (to that class of attackers)?
- Is my particular mission safe – according to my requirements of the nodes and Confidentiality, Integrity, and Availability?
- Why did this metric go up? Because this particular attack path has been prevented by this particular patch.
- Assuming a new exploit, what will happen to the different missions?

To answer our kinds of questions, we start by solving the Attack Maze (for that class of attacker), so we know the MPI (Maximum Possible Incursion) at each node. Note that the status-types should be defined for the metrics. For example, in Figure 1. Python code example, the metric *GotData* records whether a node can access that particular data. Presumably, this particular fact is used in the metric calculation.

We then proceed to calculate metrics. We have several kinds of metrics:

- Self-metric – these metrics describe only what has happened to a node, ignoring other nodes.
- Other-metric – these metrics consider what this node can do to other nodes (give the MPI).
- Mission-metrics – these metrics are for missions, knowing the implementations of each capability, and the self-metric and other-metric of each underlying node.

A. Metric Routine supplied by user

We rely on the users to compute metrics from the MPI. That is, the user provides a routine to compute a metric for a node given the MPI. This allows users to link metrics to resources that are monitored:

- One group may have sales data that needs to be confidential, so they define a metric Sales_Confidential that is 0 or 1.
- Another group, say HR, may have salary data that also needs to be confidential, they define Salary_Confidential that is 0.0 to 1.0 depending on the difficulty of accessing that data (the evaluation routine will need attack models and other information that is not in the prototype, but there is no limit in principle).
- Another group may want a Web site to be available to the public, so they define Site_Available that is 0.0 to 1.0 depending on the state of DDoS (Distributed Denial of Service) attacks and how many servers are still up.
- A mission may define a metric Mission_Up from 0.0 to 1.0 to mean the percentage of capabilities and nodes are up. Of course, it does not need to be linear – the routine can set it arbitrarily.

B. Self-metric

Self-metrics are easily calculated – just invoke the associated user routine for each node. The meaning is explicitly narrow – the metric *Sale_Confidential* on a node means only whether attacker **on the node itself** can access the sales data.

The key is that the self-metrics form a "summary" for what a node can do, and we use self-metrics as the basis of mission-metrics.

C. Mission-metric

Mission-metrics are also computed by routines supplied by the user. These routines start with the self-metric for each node (that is needed for the mission), and produces metric for the mission. In our prototype, we favor the use of the "max" function. That is, the metric *Sale_Confidential* for the mission is just the max of the metric for each node. That is, the sales data is confidential in the mission if and only if it is confidential for each node.

D. Example

```
metric Confidentiality: max
    GotData,          No_Data=0.0, Got_Data=1.0
end metric Confidentiality

posture WorstC: max, "itemgetter('Confidentiality')"
```

Figure 4. Sample Metrics

This defines a metric *Confidentiality* that is 0.0 if the data is not compromised, or 1.0 if it is. Recall that this metric is computed for each node.

The posture (or mission-metric) *WorstC* is computed by taking each node, using Python itemgetter to get the *Confidentiality* metric, then take the *max* over all the nodes. In other words, this posture is indicative of whether a data leak is possible.

V. CONCLUSION AND FUTURE WORK

When solving the attack maze, it is relative simple to remember each (successful) attack step; that makes it possible to enumerate each possible attack path. The attack paths can be used to generate recommendations for securing the network. For example, it may be that there are many paths, but all the paths share a single link, in which case, patching a single machine may block all the paths. Essentially, we are trying to partition the network so that the attackers cannot get to the assets.

The attack maze can also be solved backward as well – that can tell us what privileges are required to get to a particular asset.

The capabilities concept can be expaned to deal with redundancy – n out of m, 75% capacity, etc.

ACKNOWLEDGMENT

This work was initiated by the author while on contract at Defence Research and Development Canada. We are grateful to Dr. Natalie Nakhla for helpful reviews and discussions.

REFERENCES

[1] R. Langner, "Stuxnet: Dissecting a cyberwarfare weapon," *IEEE Security & Privacy*, vol. 9, no. 3, pp. 49-51, 2011.

[2] T. N. SecurityTM, "Nessus Open Source Vulnerability Scanner Project," ed, 2005.

[3] C. Phillips and L. P. Swiler, "A graph-based system for network-vulnerability analysis," in *Proceedings of the 1998 workshop on New security paradigms*, 1998, pp. 71-79: ACM.

[4] P. Ammann, D. Wijesekera, and S. Kaushik, "Scalable, graph-based network vulnerability analysis," in *Proceedings of the 9th ACM*

Conference on Computer and Communications Security, 2002, pp. 217-224: ACM.

[5] X. Ou, W. F. Boyer, and M. A. McQueen, "A scalable approach to attack graph generation," in *Proceedings of the 13th ACM conference on Computer and communications security*, 2006, pp. 336-345: ACM.

[6] P. Ammann, J. Pamula, R. Ritchey, and J. d. Street, "A host-based approach to network attack chaining analysis," in *Computer Security Applications Conference, 21st Annual*, 2005, pp. 10 pp.-84: IEEE.

[7] P. A. Porras, M. W. Fong, and A. Valdes, "A mission-impact-based approach to INFOSEC alarm correlation," in *International Workshop on Recent Advances in Intrusion Detection*, 2002, pp. 95-114: Springer.

[8] G. Jakobson, "Mission cyber security situation assessment using impact dependency graphs," in *Information Fusion (FUSION), 2011 Proceedings of the 14th International Conference on*, 2011, pp. 1-8: IEEE.

[9] A. Antelman, J. J. Dempsey, and B. Brodt, "Mission dependency index-a metric for determining infrastructure criticality," *Infrastructure Reporting and Asset Management*, pp. 141-46, 2008.

[10] P. R. Garvey and C. A. Pinto, "Introduction to functional dependency network analysis," in *The MITRE Corporation and Old Dominion, Second International Symposium on Engineering Systems, MIT, Cambridge, Massachusetts*, 2009.

[11] X. Ou, S. Govindavajhala, and A. W. Appel, "MulVAL: A Logic-based Network Security Analyzer," in *USENIX security*, 2005.

[12] D. Kindlund, "Holyday watering hole attack proves difficult to detect and defend against," *ISSA J*, vol. 11, pp. 10-12, 2013.

[13] A. Schulz, M. Kotson, and J. Zipkin, "Cyber Network Mission Dependencies," ed: MIT Lincoln Laboratory, Tech. Rep, 2015.

[14] W. Heinbockel, S. Noel, and J. Curbo, "Mission Dependency Modeling for Cyber Situational Awareness." https://ist.gmu.edu/~csis/noel/pubs/2016_NATO_IST_148.pdf

[15] U. Franke and J. Brynielsson, "Cyber situational awareness–a systematic review of the literature," *Computers & Security*, vol. 46, pp. 18-31, 2014.

A Survey on Open Automotive Forensics

Robert Altschaffel, Kevin Lamshöft, Stefan Kiltz, Jana Dittmann
Advanced Multimedia and Security Lab
Otto-von-Guericke-University
Magdeburg, Germany
email:Robert.Altschaffel|Stefan.Kiltz|Jana.Dittmann@iti.cs.uni-magdeburg; Kevin.Lamshoeft@st.ovgu.de

Abstract—**Modern cars are very complex systems incorporating an internal network of connecting an array of actuators and sensors to ECUs (Electronic Control Units), which implement basic functions and advanced driver assistance systems. Opening these networks to outside communication channels (like Car-to-X-communication) new possibilities but also new attack vectors arise, as shown by successful access to internal vehicle data from outside the vehicle. Any attack on the security of a vehicle in principle also constitutes an impact on the safety of road traffic, amongst other threats (e.g., privacy concerns). In this paper, we discuss challenges and propose a means to perform a forensic investigation based on an existing process model from desktop IT forensics and using openly available tools in order to reconstruct an attack or an error, leading to an incident. The main contribution is the identification of requirements for tools used within a forensic process in an automotive environment.**

Keywords-automotive; computer forensics; embedded systems; forensic processes; safety & security.

I. INTRODUCTION

Modern cars rely on a broad range of actuators, sensors and ECUs (electronic control units) to perform basic functions, implementing instrumentation and control circuits. Those ECUs form a decentralized network of resource-limited heterogeneous components. The ECUs are also used in driver assistance systems, some of which are directly involved in vital control functions of vehicles, such as steering (e.g., lane assist), braking and accelerating.

These components form a network inside the vehicle, which is more and more connected with interfaces to the outside (e.g., by using mobile communication technology to update traffic status reports for the navigation system). This increasing interconnection makes attacks on automotive IT easier, as was shown by [1].

Any attack on the security of a component within a vehicle carries a potential implication on the safety of road traffic (both intended and just reckless). Error and faults of individual vehicular components can lead to dangerous situations either through direct means (e.g., brake failure), interruption of an assistance function the driver relies on (e.g. ABS) or distraction (e.g. Multimedia).

When there is an attack or an error, it is necessary to reconstruct the event. This might be necessary to fix the problem, prevent further attacks or to prove guilt or innocence of the involved parties. Especially in the latter case, it is necessary that such a reconstruction follows scientific and well-proven principles. These principles are referred to as a forensic process. A forensic process requires traces used for event reconstruction to be gathered and analyzed in an authentic (originating from the subject of the investigation), with integrity (unaltered by external influences or during the course of the investigation) fashion, as well as the whole process being comprehensively documented. Since in the beginning of an investigation it is very often unclear if an incident arises from an error or an attack, an investigation should follow the same principles without regard to the starting hypothesis of the investigator.

The challenge nowadays is that there is a distinct lack of automotive forensic processes that are openly discussed and peer-reviewed within the scientific community. Nowadays typically isolated solutions are applied, often shrouded in secrecy and heavily protected by intellectual property and copyright mechanisms. The work we present aims at establishing a forensic automotive process for an incident investigation within vehicle IT. This is a supplement to the use of Event Data Recorders (EDRs), which are employed in vehicles to record data relevant to traffic accidents. The rest of this work is structured as follows. Section 2 gives an overview on the technical background of automotive Systems and forensics. Section 3 discusses the forensic process in the context of automotive systems. Currently available tools, which might support the forensic process within an automotive system and their suitability, are discussed in section 4. Section 5 discusses the requirements for tools geared towards supporting automotive forensics while section 6 concludes this paper.

II. TECHNICAL BACKGROUND

This section gives a brief overview on the topic of forensic in classical desktop IT and a basic understanding of automotive IT in order to bring these topics together in the following sections. An overview on the topic of EDR will be given in order to better understand the scope of this paper.

A. *Automotive IT*

Modern cars consist of components with fixed logic (or none at all) and components with (re-) programmable logic. The latter often include embedded systems and thus are more important for this paper, although being only useful in conjunction with electronic devices with fixed or no built-in logic. Of particular relevance for our discussion are:

- **Sensors** measure the conditions of the vehicle's systems and environment (e.g., pressure, speed, light levels, rain intensity etc.) as well as user input.
- **Actuators** are electrically operated and manipulate their environment in non-electric aspects (e.g., mechanics, temperature, pressure, etc.).
- **Electronic Control Units** (ECUs) electronically process input signals acquired via sensors and relay commands to actuators. Some units control critical systems, such as the engine or safety-critical systems like ESC (Electronic Stability Control) or SRS (Supplemental Restraint System), while others control comfort functionality (e.g., door control units). ECUs are custom-tailored compact, embedded systems. Due to high cost constraints in the automotive industry, they operate on a minimum set of resources regarding CPU computing power, mass storage and main memory. Common exceptions are ECUs that handle multimedia functionality. The number of ECUs embedded with a vehicle is still rising - while a luxury car in 1985 contained less than 10 ECUs, the numbers increased to more than 100 in 2010 [2].
- **Direct analogue cable connections** connect sensors and actuators directly to a specific ECU.
- **Shared Digital Bus Systems** are used for communication among ECUs [3]. In modern cars, several different technologies for digital automotive field bus systems are used with different capabilities, requirements and cost factors. The most common automotive field bus system, often forming the core network of vehicle systems communication, is the Controller Area Network (CAN) [4]. This CAN network is often divided into sub-networks such as powertrain/engine, diagnostics, comfort or info-tainment. ECUs are connected to the sub-network and these sub-networks interconnect using a CAN Gateway ECU, which handles the routing of messages to different sub-networks. The CAN message consists of several flags, the CAN ID and the payload. The CAN ID represents the type of a message and implies a certain sender and receiver for the message. It is assumed that a message with the corresponding ID is sent by the ECU normally responsible for this message. In addition, the CAN ID serves as priority.

The above implement essential instrumentation and control circuits for the functionality of today's vehicles.

B. Forensics in Desktop IT

The forensic process aims at finding traces that support the reconstruction of an event. In order to increase the validity of the reconstruction, these traces have to be gathered in a way to preserve authenticity (trace origin) and integrity (trace is unaltered). To ensure this, a range of models for the forensic process exist, both for classical crime scenes [5], as well as for computer forensics in Desktop IT [6]. These models are often practitioner driven and usually break down the forensic process into distinct phases. For this paper, we use the forensic process from [7], as it contains both the practitioner's and the computer scientist's view (see [8]), the latter often being omitted in an attempt to provide guidelines for practitioners only. This model includes investigation steps (practitioner's view), data types (computer scientist's view) and methods for data access (computer scientist's view). Thus, by adhering to this model, both the research aspect as well as the implementation of forensic procedures in practice is supported.

For this first survey on automotive IT forensics we rely on the investigation steps:

- **Strategic preparation** (*SP*) represents measures taken by the operator of an IT-system, prior to an incident, which support a forensic investigation.
- **Operational preparation** (*OP*) represents the preparation for a forensic investigation after a suspected incident.
- **Data gathering** (*DG*) represents measures to acquire and secure digital evidence.
- **Data investigation** (*DI*) represents measures to evaluate and extract data for further investigation.
- **Data analysis** (*DA*) represents the detailed analysis and correlation between digital evidence from various sources.
- **Documentation** (*DO*) represents the detailed documentation of the investigation.

The forensic process is furthermore also divided into live forensic and post-mortem forensics. Live forensics covers the part of the forensic examination performed while the system under investigation is active. Post-mortem forensics covers all the part of the forensic examination while the system under investigation is powered-off. Live forensics offer the possibility to find traces in highly volatile areas such as main memory but often comes with the implication of substantially altering the state of the system under investigation - either by letting it perform its current operations or by querying the system for certain information from the main memory, which actively alters the state of the system. Post-mortem forensics allows access to lesser volatile mass storage and analyze it in ways ensuring integrity of the mass storage device (typically by using read-only adapters) but cannot gain insight into the main memory contents. The consideration when to power off a system under investigation and switch from live forensics to post-mortem is to be decided on a case-by-case basis and represents a crucial decision in every forensic examination.

C. Event Data Recorders (EDR)

EDRs describe a range of various devices installed within cars to record data in case of an accident. EDRs are in general use since 1990 [9]. The implementations are generally vendor-specific and are often added functionality of the SRS ECU [10]. Data sets recorded by these devices were only recently standardized [11] and include e.g.:

- The forward and lateral crash force.
- The crash event duration.

- Indicated vehicle speed.

The forensic use of this data is well researched (see [12]). While this data gives insight into accidents, it would not be enough to investigate a malicious attack on automotive IT.

III. REVIEW OF THE FORENSIC PROCESS IN AUTOMOTIVE ENVIRONMENTS

Forensic investigations on automotive IT come with a broad range of challenges originating from the nature of automotive IT. These challenges include:

- The low storage capacity in the ECU means that there is little storage available to store fault codes and event logs. Sometimes fault codes are implemented in a ring buffer where older fault codes are frequently overwritten with newer ones. Time stamps and even a system-wide time base for fault codes are very uncommon.
- CAN Bus communication contains neither explicit senders nor receivers offering no form of sender authenticity. Any message on the CAN Bus can originate from any attached device.
- Access to memory and mass storage is managed by the respective MCUs and is typically inaccessible due to intellectual property and copyright protection measures. In Desktop IT, mass storage generally is easily separated from the system under investigation and attached to a workstation. Here, write-blockers are utilized to prevent all write-operations on the mass storage are possible and hence the integrity is guaranteed. In automotive IT, (parts of) mass storage often is part of the MCU silicone itself, rendering the access a very complex issue.
- Components are seldom standardized. This includes ECUs, mass storage, memory, the message transferred via the bus systems, etc.

These challenges have a great impact on the forensic process on automotive IT. However, with the inclusion of a strategic preparation (SP) step, the selected forensic process model allows to mitigate some of these effects at least as the strategic preparation step allows to prepare a system before an incident occurs (forensic readiness).

The starting point of a case-specific forensic investigation is the operational preparation (OP). In this step, an overview on possible traces is developed. A discussion on what traces shall be gathered and in which order is made. A careful weighting process is initiated, in which the potential gain from the traces is weighted against the structural impact (i.e. side effects on the data contained in the system) of their acquisition. This includes the consideration if live forensics shall be performed at all. To allow for a well-considered decision, in the following we present considerations on live forensics and post-mortem forensics.

A. Live forensics in Automotive IT

Live forensics is performed when IT systems inside the vehicle in question are still active and not powered off. During this state, the vehicle contains traces in the *communication* between the various ECUs, their *main memory* and their *mass storage*.

Access to *main memory* and *mass storage* in general is only possible by sending requests to the respective ECUs. This can be done during the normal operation of the car or during some specially initiated diagnosis sessions. In each case, this type of data gathering carries the same implications as in Desktop IT - sending these requests alters the state of the system under investigation (structural impact). Hence, it alters the communication on the bus system transferring the requests to (and the answer from) the ECU, the state of the gateway (usually external tools performing diagnostic requests would be directly attached to the gateway which then routes the requests to the specific bus network) and the specific ECU. While these implications seem grave, it might still be worth when the investigators take these implications into account during the discussion of the conclusiveness of the traces. Hence, the investigator should have an idea of what specific data should be requested in order to keep these implications low.

Communication concerns the data transferred on the various communication channels within the vehicle. These channels include the various CAN bus systems, which form the backbone of vehicular communication. Another technology, used for communication between ECUs, is MOST (Media Oriented Systems Transport, see [13]). From the forensic perspective, both of them have a lot in common. Both of them are broadcast, which means that any device attached to any of these networks can receive all communication on this bus. While it would be possible to set some gateway ECUs into a type of monitoring mode, akin to a monitoring port in Desktop IT routers, this would alter the state of the gateway ECU. It is however, possible to include a data tap in the various networks (as a form of SP) in order to capture communication data if necessary.

B. Post-mortem Forensics in Automotive IT

During post-Mortem forensics mass storage data is the main concern. As pointed out before access to mass storage in automotive ECUs is difficult. Mass storage (at least in part is often realized as (re-) programmable non-volatile memory on the MCU silicone. Access is often only possible using debug mechanisms such as JTAG (Joint Test Action Group, see [14]) or Background Debug Mode (BDM, see [15]) and for intellectual property protection purposes this access is often hindered (e.g., by software fuses or removal of pins on the MCU casing). A further challenge is the interpretation of the resulting data (if the acquisition was successful). Due to space limitations, often compact code with little or no documentation or other means of rendering the data intelligible (e.g., ASCII texts), is used. This severely impacts the usage of two old favorites of IT forensics, i.e. the hexadecimal editor and the string search.

On the border between live Forensics and post-Mortem Forensics stands a hardware-in-the-loop test, where a single component is removed from the automotive system, powered on again and then investigated using diagnosis requests. This often alters the state of the ECU under investigation and the nature of the hardware-in-the-loop test might also have some influence on gathered traces. With the self-diagnose routines implemented in most of the ECUs, a simulation of all the expected outside behavior from sensors, actuators and busses (e.g., with respect to impedance, capacitance etc.) is paramount to maintain the diagnostic trouble codes and status information (see also [16]) for this approach.

Another data source for forensic investigation are external maintenance logs (see [17]) or vehicle logs.

IV. SURVEY OF EXISTING TOOLS AND THEIR APPLICABILITY TO THE AUTOMOTIVE FORENSIC PROCESS

In this section we want to give an overview on how some currently available open tools, which can support forensic investigations into automotive IT hold up on the requirements of forensic investigations. These shall give some context to the considerations made in Section III on the nature of live and post-Mortem Forensics in automotive IT. Some of the tools presented in this section offer functionality used in different steps of the forensic process (for the selection of the particular forensic process see Section II-B). In these cases, only the functionality relevant to the specific step is discussed in the specific subsections.

A. Strategic Preparation (SP)

There are currently no open source tools, which are designed for the use during Strategic Preparation. However, a range of the tools presented for other steps can be used to gather 'known good' states of the vehicle IT in question. This knowledge can also help during the Operational Preparation. A list of the vehicular ECUs, extracted by the tool *UDSim EC* [18], usually used during Data Analysis, can greatly supplement OP - hence producing such a listing before an incident would be a way of SP. In Section V, we present the design process of a tool specifically for the use during SP.

B. Operational Preparation (OP)

For operational preparation, obtaining any documentation on the electronic and electrical system is paramount. Wiring schemes and electronic parts catalogues, as well as repair manuals are a vital source of information before starting any attempt at data acquisition/gathering. While in previous generations of vehicles failing to prepare properly for the acquisition 'only' resulted in a botched investigation destroying vital data, with the upcoming vehicles operating with hazardous high voltage circuits (e-mobility), the safety of the investigators is on the line.

C. Data Gathering (DG)

As mentioned before the in-vehicle communication offers some traces, which might be of interest for a forensic investigation. There are several cross-platform tools that allow the capturing of data on the CAN BUS. Three of them are now described in detail:

- *SavvyCAN* [19] is a graphical tool for capturing and visualizing CAN frames. It provides modules for logging, sniffing and injecting CAN frames as well as interpretation and dissection of signals.
- *Kayak* [20] uses TCP/IP via *SocketCANd* [21] as an additional abstraction layer, providing simultaneous bus access for several users. It comes with a rich set of possibilities to log, sniff and inject CAN frames as well identifying and interpreting CAN signals. It also comes with several options for visualization (e.g., a simulated cockpit) and replay options.
- *Octane CAN Bus Sniffer*[22] is a project of the George Mason University and provides features for sniffing and injection, cyclic keep-alive transmissions for diagnostic sessions and a transmission interface for fuzzing and flooding.

None of these tools does provide any mechanisms to ensure integrity or authenticity of the gathered data and hence external mechanisms needs to be implemented to ensure authenticity and integrity of the gathered data. However the passive reading access does not come with a structural impact.

Another source for possible traces is the gathering of diagnostic data from ECUs. One possibility to gather this data is to use the OBD2 functionality of modern cars. open-source like *Freediag* [23], *OBD2-Scantool* [24] or *O2OO Data Logger* [25] support a wide range of protocols and primarily work with ELM237 based interfaces. These tools allow querying diagnostic trouble codes and diagnosis of ECUs as specified in OBD. There is a structural impact as these tools do transmit messages while establishing, maintaining and performing diagnostic sessions. In addition there are no mechanisms to ensure integrity or authenticity of the gathered data.

D. Data Investigation (DI)

Some of the tools used during the Data Gathering can also help during the Data Investigation by handling prior captured data. This includes, for example:

- *SavvyCAN* can visualize CAN frames. It provides modules for the interpretation and dissection of signals. It supports several formats of CAN signal databases.
- *Kayak* can be used to identify and interpret CAN signals. It also comes with several options for visualization (e.g., a simulated cockpit) and replay options.
- *Octane CAN Bus Sniffer* also offers multiple filtering options and XML signal definitions.

While these tools offer no functionality to ensure integrity and authenticity of the investigation results the integrity of the data under investigation can be ensured by using copies of the original data.

E. Data Analysis (DA)

A number of different tools can be used during the DA. While all these tools can be connected directly to the CAN of an active automotive this is not advisable from a forensic point of view. Connecting these tools to a virtual CAN device, which replays a trace of CAN communication captured during DG preserves integrity of the trace under investigation. These tools include:

- *CANToolz* also referred to as *YACHT* (*Yet Another Car Hacking Tool,* see [26]) is a framework providing several modules for performing black box analyses of CAN. It can work with multiple interfaces at the same time allowing testing of gateway and firewall functionality. The suite supports UDS and ISO-TP detection and interpretation. Its modular structure allows easy implementation of customizations and extensions. In the current state, it supports integration of different I/O functionalities, such as multiple CAN hardware SocketCAN, TCP tunneling, discovery of ECUs and related services, capture and replay of frames, fuzzing, filtering, sorting, blocking of specific IDs and statistical analysis and interpretation of occurring frames, e.g., for detecting ISO-TP and UDS messages.
- *UDSim ECU Simulator* is a graphical tool for identifying ECUs connected to a bus. It offers three modes: learning, simulation and attack. In learning mode, it identifies ECUs by monitoring their responses to UDS diagnostic queries. Hence it can create a list of available ECUs
- *c0f* (*CAN of Fingers,* see [27]) is a tool for generating fingerprints of CAN busses based on statistical measurements. If fingerprints indicating a healthy system state are known prior to an incident, a following fingerprint might provide an indication of an incident modifying the system state.

As with the tools used during DI these tools offer no functionality to ensure integrity and authenticity of the investigation results. However, the integrity of the data under investigation can be ensured by using copies of the original data.

F. Documentation (DO)

The documentation (according to [7]) can be split into two sections. First, there is the process of accompanying documentation, which maintains an account for all the actions taken by the examiners. This process should ideally be highly assisted by software, recording all parameters and menu selections (see e.g., the script command [28] or the automated documentation in dedicated desktop IT forensic suites such as X-Ways forensics [29]). Within the application context of this article, a mostly manual process involving screenshots, digital photographs, etc. is very likely to be used due to the lack of dedicated forensic software packages as of today.

Using the results from the process accompanying documentation, the final examination report is compiled, which describes the examination process and the results as well the most likely chain of events according to the reconstruction from traces. No dedicated tool support apart from a word processor is typically involved.

V. DESIGN RECOMMENDATIONS FOR FUTURE AUTOMOTIVE FORENSIC TOOLS

As depicted in the prior section, there is a lack of tools geared towards the use in forensic investigation into car IT.

To support the forensic process a tool should:

- the collected/processed data should be useful for the forensic process
- ensure the integrity and authenticity of the collected/processed data
- have a minimized and well-known structural impact
- document the actions performed

An exemplary tool and its design process is described here:

The exemplary tool should be able to support DG by capturing bus traffic. This data is useful for the forensic process as it covers the communication between the various ECUs.

We developed a prototype using open source hardware and software. A Raspberry Pi 3 [30] running Raspbian [31] and PiCAN2 [32] as well as CANtact [33] boards were used to connect to the CAN bus. The Raspberry Pi is controlled via SSH and runs a WiFi Access Point, allowing easy access. We developed a CLI tool, which adapts the concepts of the Linux Forensic Transparent Bridge [34] to automotive CAN networks. In order to create a session for examination, the user has to set name and password which are later used for generating HMACs (Keyed-Hash Message Authentication Code, see [35]). SocketCAN [36] is used for both Cantact and PiCAN boards, allowing passive capturing of network traffic by candump from can-utils, as well as Wireshark/tshark, and neglecting any structural impact by only performing passive read functions. Our tool comes with an automated setup for SocketCAN and allows to set filters for specific IDs. If data is recorded by candump, it can be played back to any other CAN interface (e.g., to a virtual CAN), which then can be monitored by Wireshark as well. This can be useful for further analysis of the network data. We use the default implementation of Python 3 for the HMAC with SHA-512. The concatenation of examiner's name and password is used as key for the HMAC, ensuring integrity and authenticity for the capture.

This setup could also be used as part of Strategic Preparation, as it can be directly installed in to the car (e.g., using a smaller Raspberry Pi Zero) and capturing network traffic for a given period. These captures can be extracted after an incident occurred, providing integer and authentic data.

VI. CONCLUSION

This paper presents the challenges of forensic investigation into potential security incidents in automotive IT. It shows the current state of automotive forensic security and puts the existing isolated solutions into a bigger picture.

A survey on current tools usable for forensic investigations into automotive IT shows the need for dedicated tools geared towards forensics - or at least for the inclusion of means to ensure safety and integrity. As main contribution requirements for such tools are enumerated and the design process of such a tool is presented with the hope to spark the inclusion of forensic functionality in other tools.

ACKNOWLEDGMENT

We like to thank our students working on automotive forensic topics.

REFERENCES

[1] C. Miller and C. Valesek, "Remote Exploitation of an Unaltered Passenger Vehicle," Black Hat USA, 2015.

[2] T. Sugimura, "Junction Blocks Simplify and Decrease Networks When Matched to ECU and Wire Harness". Encyclopedia of Automotive Engineering. 1–7.

[3] A. Hillier, " Hillier's Fundamentals of Automotive Electronics Book 2 Sixth Edition," Oxford University Press, 2014.

[4] Robert Bosch GmbH, "CAN Specification 2.0, 1991" http://www.bosch-semiconductors.de/media/ubk_semiconductors/pdf_1/canliteratur/can2spec.pdf (18/10/2016).

[5] K. Inman and N. Rudin, "Principles and Practises of Criminalistics: The Profession of Forensic Science," CRC Press LLC Boca Raton Florida, USA, ISBN 0-8493-8127-4, 2001.

[6] M. Pollit, "Applying Traditional Forensic Taxonomy to Digial Forensics," IFIP International Federation for Information Processing, Volume 258; Advances in Digital Forensics IV, pp. 17-26, DOI: 10.1007/978-0-387-84927-0_2, 2008.

[7] S. Kiltz, J. Dittmann, and C. Vielhauer, "Supporting Forensic Design - a Course Profile to Teach Forensics," IMF 2015.

[8] S. Peisert, M. Bishop and K. Marzullo, "Computer forensics in forensis", In SIGOPS Operating Systems Review, Volume 42, Issue 3, pp 112-122, ACM, DOI=10.1145/1368506.1368521, 2008.

[9] NHTSA EDR Working Group, "Event Data Recorders", https://www.nhtsa.gov/sites/nhtsa.dot.gov/files/nhtsa_edrtruckbusfinal.pdf, 2002 (retrieved: 9, 2017).

[10] W. Bortles, W. Biever, N. Carter, and C. Smith, "A Compendium of Passenger Vehicle Event Data Recorder Literature and Analysis of Validation Studies," SAE Technical Paper 2016-01-1497, 2016, doi:10.4271/2016-01-1497.

[11] NHTSA, "Federal Motor Vehicle Safety Standards; Event Data Recorders", https://one.nhtsa.gov/staticfiles/rulemaking/pdf/EDR_NPRM_2012-12-07.pdf, 2014 (retrieved: 9, 2017).

[12] N. Singleton, J. Daily, G. Manes, "Automobile Event Data Recorder Forensics," 2008.

[13] MOST Cooperation, "MOST Specification Rev 3.0 E2 07/2010," 2010.

[14] R. Johnson and S. Christie, "JTAG 101 IEEE 1149.x and Software Debug, " https://www.intel.com/content/dam/www/public/us/en/documents/white-papers/jtag-101-ieee-1149x-paper.pdf, 2009, (retrieved: 9, 2017).

[15] Freescale Semiconductor Inc., "CPU 12 Reference Manual," http://www.nxp.com/docs/en/reference-manual/CPU12RM.pdf, 2006, (retrieved: 9, 2017).

[16] W. Rosenbluth and H. A. Adams, "Retrieval and Interpretation of Crash-Related Data from Nonresponsive Electronic Control Units in Land Vehicle Systems," In Journal of Testing and Evaluation, Volume 30, Issue 4, pp. 350-361, ASTM International, ISSN 0090-3973, 2002.

[17] H. Mansor, K. Markantonakis, R. N. Akram, K. Mayes, and I. Gurulian:, "Log your car: The non-invasive vehicle forensics", 2016.

[18] https://github.com/zombieCraig/UDSim (retrieved: 9, 2017).

[19] http://www.savvycan.com/ (retrieved: 9, 2017).

[20] http://kayak.2codeornot2code.org/ (retrieved: 9, 2017).

[21] https://github.com/dschanoeh/socketcand (retrieved: 9, 2017).

[22] http://octane.gmu.edu/ (retrieved: 9, 2017).

[23] http://freediag.sourceforge.net/ (retrieved: 9, 2017).

[24] https://www.scantool.net/ (retrieved: 9, 2017).

[25] https://www.vanheusden.com/O2OO/ (retrieved: 9, 2017).

[26] https://github.com/eik00d/CANToolz (retrieved: 9, 2017).

[27] https://github.com/zombieCraig/c0f (retrieved: 9, 2017).

[28] M. Kerrisk, "script(1) - Linux manual page" [Online] http://man7.org/linux/man-pages/man1/script.1.html (24/05/2017).

[29] X-Ways Software Technology AG, "X-Ways Forensics: Integrated Computer Forensics Software" [Online] http://www.x-ways.net/forensics/(24/05/2017).

[30] https://www.raspberrypi.org/ (retrieved: 9, 2017).

[31] https://raspbian.org/ (retrieved: 9, 2017).

[32] http://skpang.co.uk/catalog/pican2-canbus-board-for-raspberry-pi-2-p-1475.html (retrieved: 9, 2017)

[33] https://linklayer.github.io/cantact/ (retrieved: 9, 2017).

[34] S. Kiltz, M. Hildebrandt, and J. Dittmann, "A transparent bridge for forensic sound network traffic data acquisition", In Sicherheit 2010 - Sicherheit, Schutz und Zuverlässigkeit, 5. Jahrestagung des Fachbereichs Sicherheit der Gesellschaft für Informatik e.V. (GI) Berlin, 5-7 Oktober 2010. S. 93-104. 2010.

[35] H. Krawczyk, M. Bellare and R. Canetti, "RFC 2104, HMAC: Keyed-Hashing for Message Authentication," 1997 .

[36] https://github.com/linux-can/can-utils (retrieved: 9, 2017).

[37] https://docs.python.org/3.5/library/hashlib.html?highlight=sha256 (retrieved: 9, 2017).

A Method for Preventing Slow HTTP DoS attacks

Koichi Ozaki[1)], Astushi Kanai[2)]
Faculty of Science and Technology
Hosei University
Tokyo, Japan
[1)] koichi.ozaki.3t@stu.hosei.ac.jp, [2)]yoikana@hosei.ac.jp

Shigeaki Tanimoto
Faculty of Social Systems Science
Chiba Institute of Technology
Chiba, Japan
shigeaki.tanimoto@it-chiba.ac.jp

***Abstract*—A Slow Hypertext-Transfer-Protocol (HTTP) Denial-of-service (DoS) Attack looks like a genuine user and can block access to genuine users. Over the past few years, several studies have been performed on the defense against Slow HTTP DoS Attacks. However, little attention has been given to a Slow HTTP DoS Attack that resembles a normal DoS Attack. In this paper, the effectiveness of setting the longest session time and the longest packet interval with an appropriate threshold was evaluated by changing each threshold and comparing the results. As a result, we demonstrated the effectiveness of the proposed method. To prevent a Slow HTTP DoS attack completely, it is necessary to not only take measures for typical Slow HTTP DoS attacks but also set a threshold for anomaly detection in consideration of Slow HTTP DoS attacks that resemble a normal DoS attack.**

Keywords- Slow HTTP DoS Attack; session time; packet interval

I. INTRODUCTION

DoS attacks are mainly classified as three types of attacks [1]. The first type is an attack that sends mass requests or a huge amount of data to a leased line and thereby fills up the line's bandwidth. The second type is an attack that exhausts the system resources (processing capacity of central-processing-units (CPUs), memory, etc.) of a Web server. The third type is an attack that exploits vulnerabilities of routers and servers. The aims of these attacks are to violate the availability of services and to impose the accompanying economic burden on the server owner. If a DoS attack is considered from the viewpoint of the layers of the network system, when the DoS attacks were initially made, the network layer and the transport layer were often attacked with a large amount of data traffic. However, as DoS attacks diversified over the years, they started to attack the application layer with a small amount of data traffic. Most DoS Attacks targeting the application layer are difficult to detect because many of them follow regular processes in the network layer and the transport layer. A "Slow HTTP DoS attack" is one such attack targeting the application layer [2][3]. Unlike other DoS attacks, as shown in Figure 1, it continues Transmission-Control-Protocol (TCP) sessions for a long time with a small number of packets. A normal communication and a Slow HTTP DoS attack are shown in Figure 2.

The attack method is classified into three categories: "Slow HTTP Headers Attack," "Slow HTTP BODY Attack," and "Slow Read DoS Attack," depending on how the duration of the TCP session is extended. A Slow HTTP Headers Attack (aka "Slowloris") extends the duration of a TCP session by sending a long HTTP request header little by little with a wait time in between returning responses and sending requests. A Slow HTTP BODY Attack (aka "Slow HTTP BODY Attack" or "R.U.D.Y") extends the duration of a TCP session by sending a long HTTP request body little by little with a waiting time in between returning responses and sending requests. A Slow Read DoS Attack extends the duration of a TCP session by specifying a very small TCP window size and receiving an HTTP response from the Web server little by little. This rest of paper is organized as follows: Section II introduces related works, Section III describes the proposed method for prevent Slow HTTP DoS Attacks, Section IV describes the experimental environment under which the method was evaluated, Section V presents results of an evaluation of the effectiveness of the method, and Section VI presents the conclusions of this work.

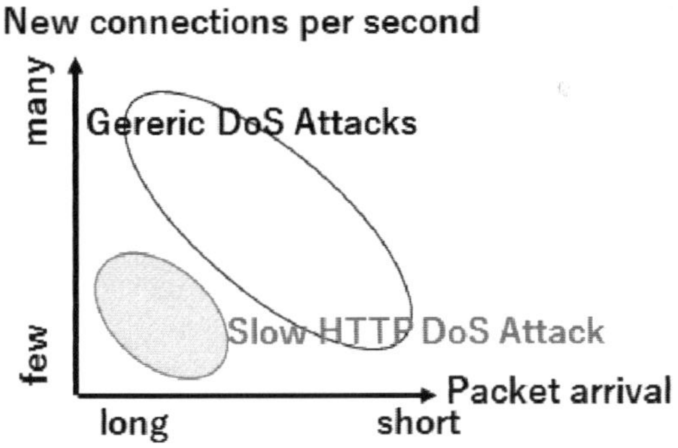

Figure 1. Conceptual diagram of the range of a Slow HTTP DoS Attack.

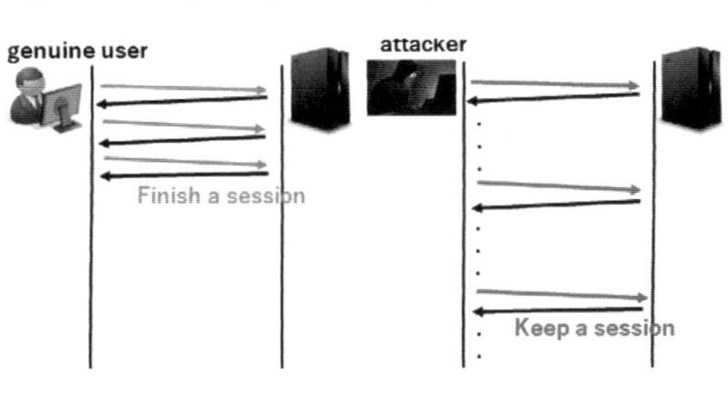

Figure 2. Normal communication and Slow HTTP DoS Attack

II. RELATED WORKS

Generic DoS attacks with large amounts of data traffic can be detected by anomaly detections and signature detections. However, a Slow HTTP DoS Attack looks like a genuine user, and it can attack the Web server (without alerting the Web server) with a small amount of traffic. Accordingly, it cannot be detected by anomaly detections; it can only be detected by signature detections. Over the past few years, how to defend against a Slow HTTP DoS Attack has been studied [3]-[7]. However, many problems remain to be solved. For example, a method of limiting the number of simultaneous sessions from the same Internet-Protocol (IP) address has been introduced [8]. However, when multiple genuine users use a common Network-Address-Translation (NAT) and simultaneously use a Web server with the same global address, the Web server may recognize genuine users as attackers and restrict their accesses. Also, if the attacker imitates an IP address, uses multiple IP addresses, or uses a Botnet, the defense method cannot defend the Web server as shown in Figure 3 [9].

Another method of defense is to limit parameters such as longest session time, minimum reception rate, and longest packet interval [10]. However, a genuine user communication via a Secure-Socket-Layer (SSL) or slow communication lines must not be misrecognized as an attacker. Also, Slow HTTP DoS Attacks have received little attention compared to that paid to normal DoS Attacks. Even though it is configured to detect only typical Slow HTTP DoS Attacks, the defense based on this method cannot defend Web servers from a Slow HTTP DoS Attack that resembles a normal DoS attack in order to sneak through the detection mechanism.

A so-called high-performance "Web-application firewall" (WAF) compares an assumed amount of data with the actual amount of data while gradually decreasing window sizes. It thereby distinguishes genuine users from attackers [11]. However, a high-performance WAF is costly, and in some cases, it cannot be introduced from the viewpoint of the balance between asset value and risk of service outage. High-performance protection with low cost and easy set-up is thus desired.

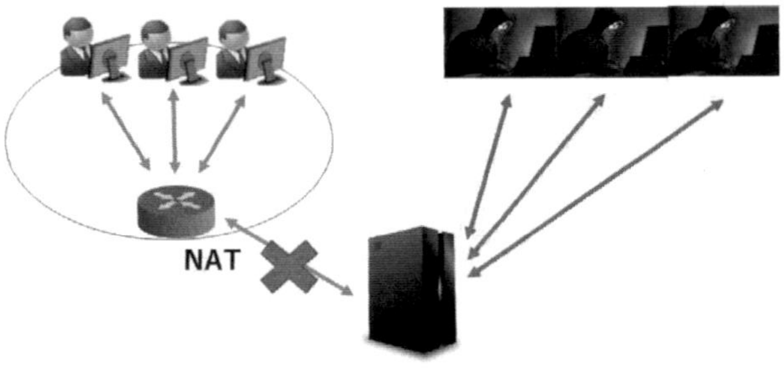

Figure 3. Problems when limiting access by IP address

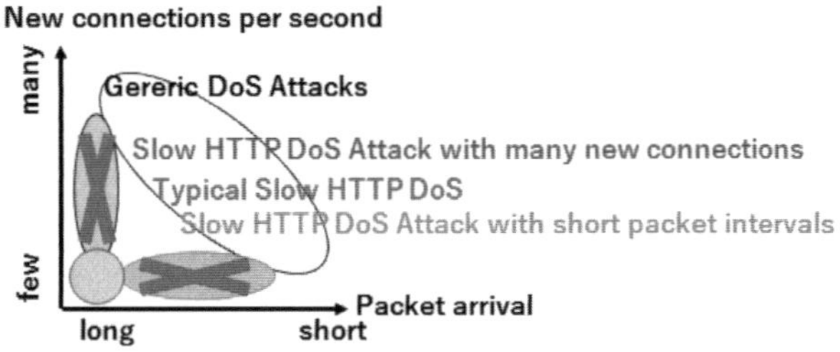

Figure 4. Position of Slow HTTP DoS Attacks in relation to generic DoS

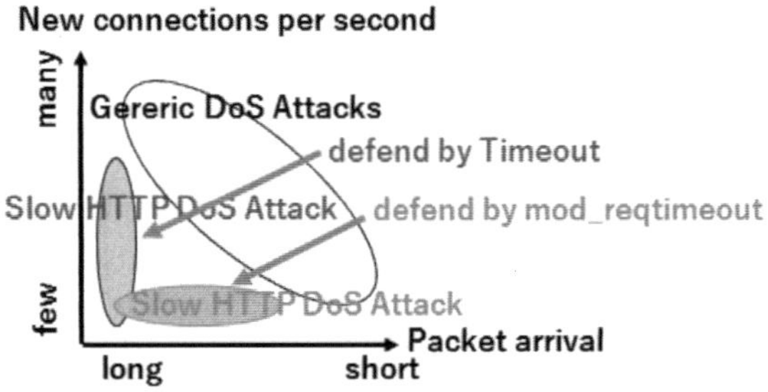

Figure 5. Conceptual diagram of the range to be defended

III. PROPOSED APPROACH

It is relatively easy to detect typical Slow HTTP DoS Attacks with long packet intervals and little conections. However, attackers may sometimes make a Slow HTTP DoS Attack like a normal DoS attack in order to sneak through a detection-and-defense mechanism. Little attention has been paid to such attacks. It is impossible to prevent such attacks if, as shown in Figure 4, the threshold length of the longest session time and the longest packet interval are not appropriate or only one defense measure is applied. A defense method proposed in this study limits session time, packet interval and average reception rate with appropriate values. As shown in Figure 5, it can thus prevent a wider range of Slow HTTP DoS Attacks.

The Web service was unavailable when the number of connections exceeds the-maximum number-of-connections-that-could-access-the-Web-server (Maxclients). In this proposed method, it is whether the packet is for an attack or a usual usage in following three steps. In step 1, when the average packet interval is longer than the threshold of packet intervals, it is judged as an attack. Thereby, if the number of connections connected within the packet interval threshold time does not exceed Maxclients, the Web service becomes available. However, even if the packet intervals are limited, attacks with short packet intervals cannot be blocked. Such attacks are prevented in step 2 and step 3. Step 2 prevents false detection of a usual usage who takes much traffic and long communication time as an attack. If the average reception rate is larger than the threshold of reception rate, it is judged as a usual usage. Otherwise, the process shifts to step 3. In step 3, when the session time is longer than the threshold of session time, it is judged to be an attack.

Thereby, if the number of connections connected within the session time threshold time does not exceed Maxclients, the Web service becomes available.

IV. EXPERIMENTAL ENVIRONMENT

An experimental environment in which a defending Web server and an attacking client are directly connected by a switch was set up as shown in Figure 6.

A. *Environment of the defending Web server*

The OS of the defending Web server used CentOS 6.5, and Apache version 2.2.27 (with mod_reqtimeout as a standard feature) [12][13]. The Apache configuration was set in the /etc/httpd/conf/httpd.conf file, and the main configuration is listed in TABLE I. The maximum number of connections that could access the Web server was 256. The longest packet interval was limited by setting the value of Timeout to 2 or 60 s. The mod_reqtimeout configuration of the defending server was described in httpd.conf. The longest session time was limited by setting the value of mod_reqtimeout to 20 or 3 s. When the average reception rate was 300 Mbps or more, the time limit was extended to 120 s.

B. *Environment of the attacking client*

The attacking client's OS used Ubuntu 14.04, and slowhttptest 1.7 was used as an attack-testing tool [14][15]. The purpose of the attacking client is usually to occupy all connections with a small amount of traffic so that the defending Web server does not notice it is being attacked. As such a typical Slow DoS HTTP Attack, the attacking client attacked with 15 new connections per second and with a packet interval of 10 s. Also, for attacks with short packet intervals, the attacking client made a Slow HTTP DoS Attack with 15 new connections per second and short packet intervals of 1 s. Moreover, for attacks with many new connections per second, the attacking client made a Slow HTTP DoS Attack with 100 new connections per second and a packet interval of 10 s. Both Slow HTTP Headers Attacks and Slow HTTP BODY Attacks were made, and the experimental results were evaluated. Both attacks were set as common configurations as shown in TABLE II. The experimental result was evaluated by the HTML generated by the attacking client's slowhttptest.

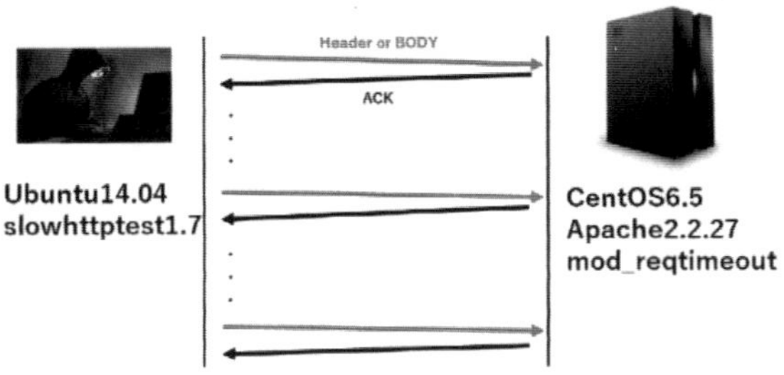

Figure 6. Experimental environment

TABLE I. APACHE CONFIGURATION

Timeout	60 or 2
KeepAlive	On
MaxKeepAliveRequests	5
KeepAliveTimeout	2
StartServers	8
MinspareSevers	5
MinspareSevers	20
ServerLimit	256
MaxClients	256
MaxRequestsPerChild	4000

TABLE II. COMMON CONFIGURATION OF SLOW HTTP HEADERS ATTACK AND SLOW HTTP BODY ATTACK

Total number of connections	300 or 2000
Number of new connections per second	15 or 100
Should results be generated in CSV and HTML format	Yes
Path and name of generated file	for example：head-test1
Response RTT to check connection status (s)	1
Attacked URL	http://centostestsrv.com
Test time (s)	20
Packet interval (s)	10 or 1

V. EVALUATION

In this paper, implementation and evaluation are not as Section III, but based on the following test model in two steps. In step 1, packet interval is longer than the threshold of packet intervals, it is judged as an attack. And the effectiveness of appropriately limiting the packet intervals was evaluated by changing the threshold of the longest packet interval and comparing the results. The inappropriate threshold was set to 60 s (which has been used by default). The appreciate threshold was set to two seconds in consideration of genuine users who are communicating via SSL or a slow communication line. In step 2, when the session time is longer than the threshold of session time, it is judged to be an attack. And the effectiveness of appropriately limiting the session time was evaluated by changing the threshold of the longest session time and comparing the results. The inappropriate threshold was set to 20 s (which has been conventionally used). The appropriate threshold was set to 3 seconds in consideration of a genuine user using communication via SSL or a slow communication line.

This paper focuses only on Slow HTTP Headers Attacks and Slow HTTP Body Attacks, not Slow HTTP Read Attacks. Effectiveness of the proposed attack-prevention method was experimentally evaluated under four conditions, namely, "Timeout," "mod_reqtimeout" setting of the defending server, "packet interval," and "number of new connections per second" of the attacking client, listed as "cases A to D" in Table III.

A. *Typical Slow HTTP DoS Attack (case A)*

Timeout of the defending Web server was set to 60 s as the default setting, and the threshold of mod_reqtimeout was set to 20 s. The attacking client made a typical Slow HTTP

DoS Attack with 15 new connections per seconds and a packet interval of 10 s. The experimental results when the Slow HTTP Headers Attack was made and those when the Slow HTTP BODY Attack was made are shown in Figures 7 and 8, respectively.

As for the graphs in the figures, the horizontal axis shows the elapsed time of the experiment, the blue line on the vertical axis indicates the number of closed connections, the red line indicates the number of waiting connections, the yellow line indicates the number of connections being made, and the green line indicates whether the Web server service is available or not.

As shown in the figures, the Web service became unavailable because the number of connections established during the longest session time exceeded MaxClients. Even the typical Slow HTTP DoS Attack could not be prevented because the longest session time was limited inappropriately.

TABLE III. VALIDATION CONTENTS

case	Timeout (s)	mod_reqtimeout (s)	packet interval (s)	number of new connections/s
A	60	20	10	15
B	60	3	1	15
C	60	3	10	100
D	2	3	10	100

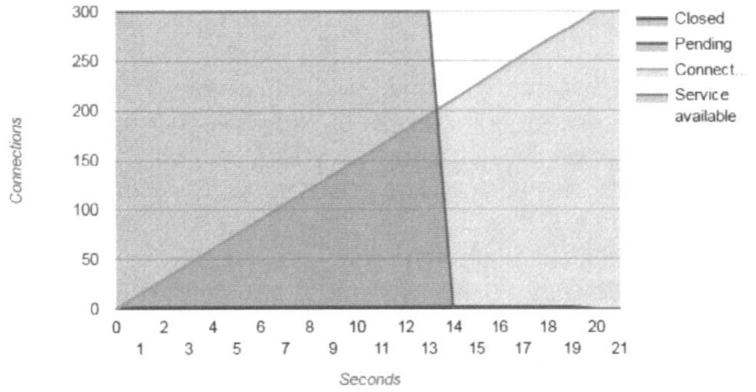

Figure 7. Typical Slow HTTP Headers Attack on Web server with incorrect mod_reqtimeout

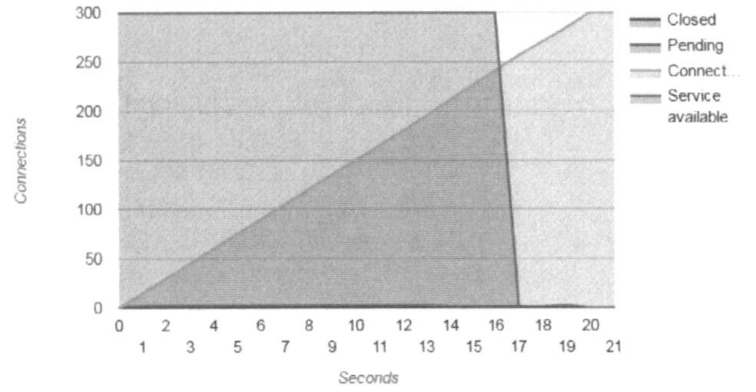

Figure 8. Typical Slow HTTP BODY Attack on Web server with incorrect mod_reqtimeout

B. Slow HTTP DoS Attack with short packet intervals (case B)

Timeout of the defending Web server was set to 60 s (as the default setting value), and the threshold of mod_reqtimeout was set to 3 s. The attacking client made a Slow HTTP DoS Attack with 15 new connections per second and a short packet interval of 1 s. The experimental results when the Slow HTTP Headers Attack was made and when the Slow HTTP BODY Attack was made are shown in Figures 9 and 10, respectively.

As shown in the figures, the Web service was available because the number of connecting connections was stable at 70 to 80, and the connections were closed steadily. The Slow HTTP DoS Attack with short packet intervals could be prevented because the longest session time was limited appropriately.

C. Slow HTTP DoS Attack with many new connections per second (case C)

Timeout of the defending Web server was set to 60 s as the default setting value, and the threshold of mod_reqtimeout was set to 3 s. The attacking client made a Slow HTTP DoS Attack with many (100) new connections per second and a packet interval of 10 s. The results when the Slow HTTP Headers Attack was made and when the Slow HTTP BODY Attack was made are shown in Figures 11 and 12, respectively.

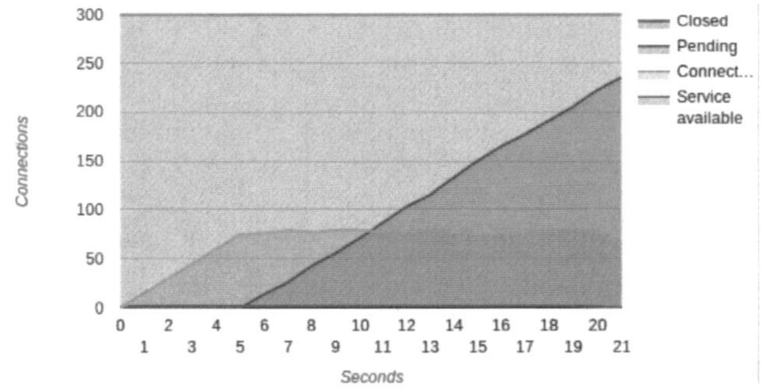

Figure 9. Slow HTTP Headers Attack with short packet intervals on Web server with appropriate mod_reqtimeout

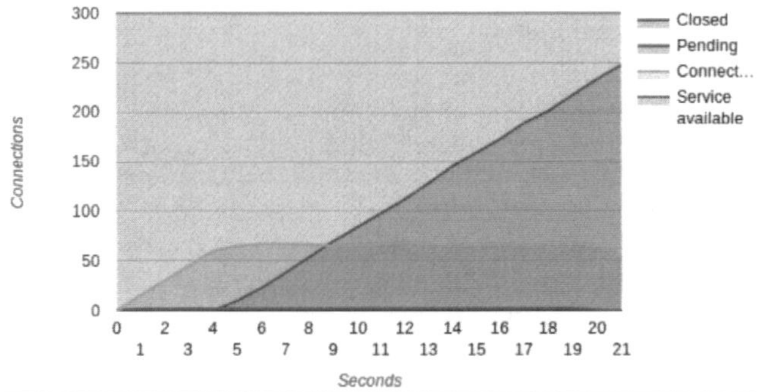

Figure 10. Slow HTTP BODY Attack with short packet interval on Web server with appropriate mod_reqtimeout

As shown in the figures, the service became unavailable because the number of new connections being made was larger than the number of connections closed. Even though the longest session time limit is appropriate, a Slow HTTP DoS Attack with many new connections could not be prevented.

D. Slow HTTP DoS attack with many new connections per second (case D)

Timeout of the defending Web server was set to 2 s, and the threshold of mod_reqtimeout was set to 3 s. The attacking client made a Slow HTTP DoS Attack with many (100) new connections per second, and a packet interval of 10 s. The results when a Slow HTTP Headers Attack was made and when a Slow HTTP BODY Attack was made are shown in Figures 13 and 14, respectively.

As shown in the figures, the Web service was available because the number of connections being made was stable (except for a short time) below MaxClients of 256. However, when it exceeded MaxClients for only the short time, the service was unavailable. This instability is considered to be due to processing delay of Apache and mod_reqtimeout. The Slow HTTP DoS attack with many new connections could be prevented because the longest packet interval was limited appropriately.

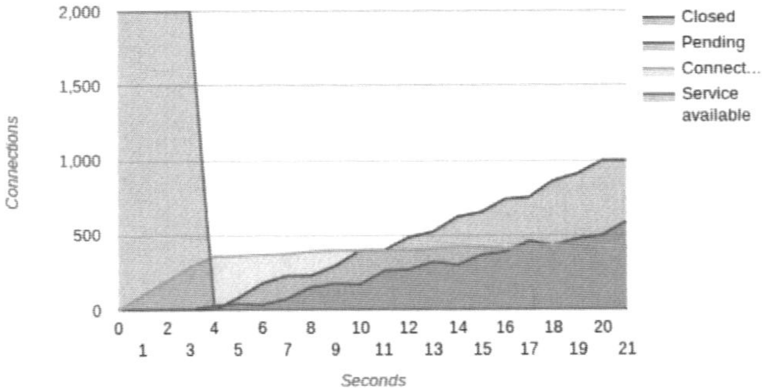

Figure 11. Slow HTTP Headers Attack with many new connections per second on Web server with appropriate mod_reqtimeout

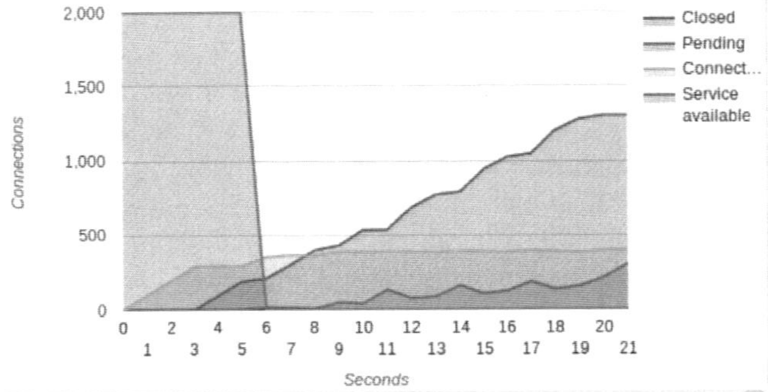

Figure 12. Slow HTTP BODY Attack with many new connections per second on Web server with appropriate mod_reqtimeout

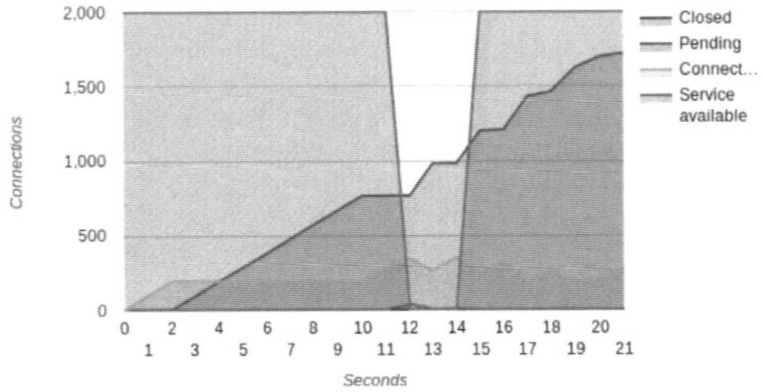

Figure 13. Slow HTTP Headers Attack with many new connections per second on Web server with appropriate Timeout

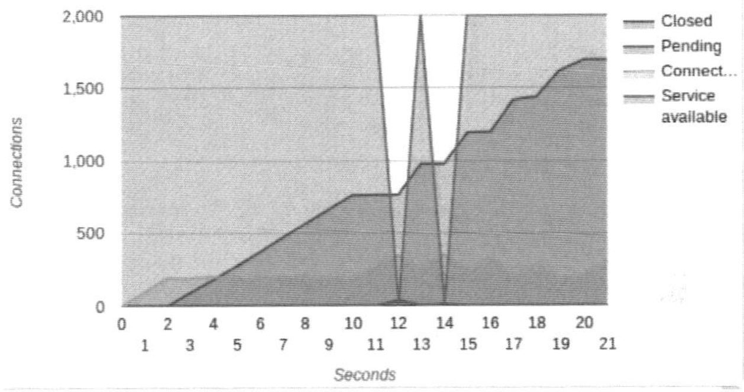

Figure 14. Slow HTTP BODY Attack with many new connections per second on Web server with appropriate Timeout

VI. CONCLUSION

In this experiment, aiming to sneak through detection by a defending Web server against a Slow HTTP DoS Attack, the attacking client made an attack with many new connections per second (with 100 new connections per seconds and a packet interval of 10 s) or an attack with short packet intervals (with 15 new connection per seconds and packet a packet interval of 1 s). These attacks could be prevented by limiting the longest packet interval and longest session time. In other words, applying multiple measures with an appropriate threshold was effective in preventing these attacks. However, this defense method cannot prevent attacks in which the number of new connections per second is further increased and "Timeout × new connections per second > MaxClient" (example: an attack with 150 new connections per seconds and second packet interval of 10 s) or an attack with many new connections per second and short packet intervals (example: an attack with 100 new connections per seconds and second packet interval of 1 s). However, increasing the number of new connections per second or shortening the interval between packets means increasing the number of packets. Such attacks with such a large number of packets are subject to anomaly detection against general DoS attacks intended to fill the line bandwidth. To prevent a Slow HTTP DoS Attack completely, it is necessary to not only take measures for typical Slow

HTTP DoS Attacks but also set a threshold for anomaly detection in consideration of Slow HTTP DoS Attacks that resemble a normal DoS Attack.

The appropriate Timeout and mod_reqtimeout thresholds will change depending on the service provided by the Web server, communication method, and so on. If a genuine user accesses the Web server with the defense method in this study via SSL or a line with low communication speed, and communication takes time due to sending of large files, they may be misrecognized as an attacker. In this evaluation, two kinds of the threshold of packet interval and session time was set and evaluated, but it was not the best threshold. Also, there was no setting of the threshold of the minimum reception rate. Accordingly, a future direction of this study will evaluate all the threshold in detail and reduce the possibility of misrecognizing a genuine user as an attacker as much as possible and expand the range that can be defended by further improving the detection accuracy and performance of the proposed method for preventing Slow HTTP DoS Attacks.

ACKNOWLEDGMENT

This work was supported by JSPS KAKENHI Grant Number 15H02783.

REFERENCES

[1] AndMen, "About DoS/DDoS Attack," [online]. Available: http://andmem.blogspot.jp/2014/02/dosattack.html. [retrieved: 7, 2017].

[2] E. Cambiaso, G. Papaleo, G. Chiola, and M. Aiello, "Slow DoS attacks: definition and categorisation," Int. J. Trust Management in Computing and Communications, Volume 1, Number 3-4, pp.300-319, 2013.

[3] @police, "Notice on Slow HTTP DoS Attack," [online]. Available: https://www.npa.go.jp/cyberpolice/detect/pdf/20151216.pdf. [retrieved: 1, 2017]

[4] Kuzmanovic and E. Knightly, "Low-Rate TCP -Targeted Denial of Service Attacks (The Shrew vs. the Mice and Elephants)," roceedings of ACM SIGCOMM 2003, Karlsruhe, Germany, August 2003, pp. 75-86.

[5] Dalia Nashat, Xiaohong Jiang, and Susumu Horiguchi, "Router based detection for Low-rate agents of DDoS attack," In 2008 International Conference on High Performance Switching and Routing, pp.177–182, May 2008.

[6] Amey Shevtekar and Nirwan Ansari, "A Proactive Test Based Differentiation Technique to Mitigate Low Rate DoS Attacks," In 2007 16th International Conference on Computer Communications and Networks, August 2007.

[7] Ian Muscat, "How To Mitigate Slow HTTP DoS Attacks in Apache HTTP Server," [online]. Available: https://www.acunetix.com/blog/articles/slow-http-dos-attacks-mitigate-apache-http-server/ [retrieved: 8, 2017].

[8] Jieren Cheng, Jianping Yin, Yun Liu, Zhiping Cai, and Min Li, "DDoS attack detection algorithm using IP address features," In Frontiers in Algorithmics, pages 207–215. Springer, 2009.

[9] Esraa Alomari, Selvakumar Manickam, B. B. Gupta, Shankar Karuppayah, and Rafeef Alfaris, "Botnet-based Distributed Denial of Service (DDoS) Attacks on Web Servers," Classification and Art. International Journal of Computer Applications, July 2012. Published by Foundation of Computer Science, New York, USA.

[10] S. Sarat and A. Terzis, "On the Effect of Router Buffer Sizes on Low-Rate Denial of Service Attacks," Proceedings of IEEE ICCCN 05, San Diego, California, October 2005, pp.281-286.

[11] @IT, "Barracuda strengthens the WAF appliance, measures to "Slow DoS Attack"," [online]. Available: http://www.atmarkit.co.jp/ait/articles/1211/09/news067.html. [retrieved: 7, 2017].

[12] CentOS, "Download CentOS," [online]. Available: https://www.centos.org/download/. [retrieved: 7, 2017].

[13] Apache, "Download - The Apache HTTP Server Project," [online]. Available:https://httpd.apache.org/download.cgi. [retrieved: 7, 2017].

[14] Ubuntu, "The leading operating system for PCs, TABLEts, phones, IoT devices, servers and the cloud | Ubuntu," [online]. Available:https://www.ubuntu.com. [retrieved: 7, 2017].

[15] slowhttptest, "GitHub - shekyan/slowhttptest: Application Layer DoS Attack simulator," [online] Available:https://github.com/shekyan/slowhttptest. [retrieved: 7, 2017]

Mutual Authentication Scheme for Lightweight IoT Devices

Seungyong Yoon, Jeongnyeo Kim
Information Security Research Division
Electronics and Telecommunications Research Institute
Daejeon, Rep. of Korea
e-mail: syyoon@etri.re.kr, jnkim@etri.re.kr

***Abstract*— Since the Internet of Things (IoT) network is a resource-limited and heterogeneous interconnection environment, lightweight security technology is required that takes into consideration various environmental features, such as computing power, memory capacity, battery power, and communication bandwidth. In this paper, we analyze the problems of the existing Datagram Transport Layer Security (DTLS) authentication protocol and simplify the handshaking procedure of this authentication process so that it is applicable to lightweight IoT devices with very limited resources.**

Keywords-IoT; security; authentication.

I. INTRODUCTION

The IoT environment is a Low power and Lossy Network (LLN) environment to which it is difficult to apply the existing IP-based security protocol considering the communicational capability. Therefore, a hardened security protocol considering computing power and limited resources is needed. It is necessary to minimize the number and size of transmitted messages and to apply a lightweight cryptographic algorithm, for example, Elliptic Curve Cryptography (ECC) [1] and Lightweight Encryption Algorithm (LEA) [2], without performance degradation. The Internet Engineering Task Force (IETF) classifies resource-constrained IoT devices into three classes [3]. Since class 0 and class 1 devices have a lot of restrictions on Random Access Memory (RAM) and Flash, it is difficult to apply cryptographic modules and messages used in security protocols such as existing DTLS. Therefore, in this paper, we analyze the requirements of DTLS authentication protocol and propose a mutual authentication scheme for lightweight IoT devices to solve it.

II. RELATED WORK

Open Mobile Alliance (OMA) has proposed the Constrained Application Protocol (CoAP) [4] based on the User Datagram Protocol (UDP) and the DTLS in IoT environments. DTLS is proposed as a security protocol that provides data confidentiality, integrity, and authentication function to application services using UDP protocol, but it has many limitations to be applied to lightweight IoT devices. This is described in detail in Section III. Therefore, various lightweight techniques have been studied to overcome the limitations of DTLS [5]-[7].

III. ANALYSIS OF DTLS AUTHENTICATION PROTOCOL

DTLS is a security protocol that provides data confidentiality, integrity, and authentication function to application services using the UDP protocol. It was presented as a protocol that can add security to IoT based on UDP protocol. However, DTLS has the following limitations:

- Due to the complexity of the handshake procedure and the large number of messages transmitted, there is a limit to use on lightweight IoT devices.
- The handshake message of DTLS has fate-sharing characteristic, so if one packet is lost, the entire message must be retransmitted. Retransmission causes increase in throughput and performance degradation.
- Fragmentation - The Maximum Transmission Unit (MTU) size of the 802.15.4 Media Access Control (MAC) layer used in the IoT environment is 127 bytes, which causes performance degradation by transmission delay and reassembly process due to fragmentation in lightweight IoT devices.

IV. THE PROPOSED MUTUAL AUTHENTICATION SCHEME

The mutual authentication scheme for the lightweight IoT devices proposed in this paper has the following characteristics. First, the mutual authentication function is performed between the security management server (shortly, server) and the lightweight IoT device, including the authentication process as well as the session key exchange process used for the encrypted communication channel. Peer-to-peer authentication is out of scope in this paper, for example, between two IoT devices. In the mutual authentication process, the gateway is included in the authentication. The proposed scheme basically begins with assuming that it has a pre-shared secret key between the server and the IoT device or between the server and the gateway. The server stores and manages the identifier (ID) of the IoT device and the gateway, and the pre-shared key in the Database (DB). After the mutual authentication process, the session key exchange used in the encrypted communication channel for data transmission is usually performed. However, the lightweight IoT device having limited computing power or resources does not participate in the session key generation process, both session key generation and key distribution functions are performed on the server. The proposed scheme reduces the amount of messages transmitted by simplifying the handshaking process for mutual authentication and session key distribution, solving the problems of the DTLS protocol. In addition, it provides an encrypted communication channel by creating and exchanging new session keys each time a new session is established through a lightweight mutual authentication scheme, thereby further enhancing the security of the lightweight IoT device. The lightweight mutual authentication scheme proposed in this paper can be roughly divided into two cases. The first case does not include a gateway. This is the case where mutual authentication is performed directly between the server and the IoT device, and there is no gateway in the IoT network environment. The second case involves a gateway, where the gateway acts as an intermediary between the server and the IoT device and participates in authentication. Table 1 defines the parameters used in the lightweight mutual authentication scheme.

TABLE I. LIGHTWEIGHT MUTUAL AUTHENTICATION PARAMETER

Parameter	Definition
Server	Security management server (Authentication server)
Gateway	IoT gateway
IoT Device	IoT Device
IDd	IoT device identifier
IDg	IoT gateway identifier
Kd	The pre-shared secret key between server and IoT device
Kg	The pre-shared secret key between server and gateway
SK	The session key between server and IoT device
eK()	Symmetric encryption function
dK()	Symmetric decryption function
Rg	Random number generated by gateway
Rd	Random number generated by IoT device
Rs	Random number generated by server
||	Concatenation operation

In this paper, in the case of mutual authentication without a gateway, the authentication procedure is relatively simple. Figure 1 shows the mutual authentication process between the server and the IoT device in this case.

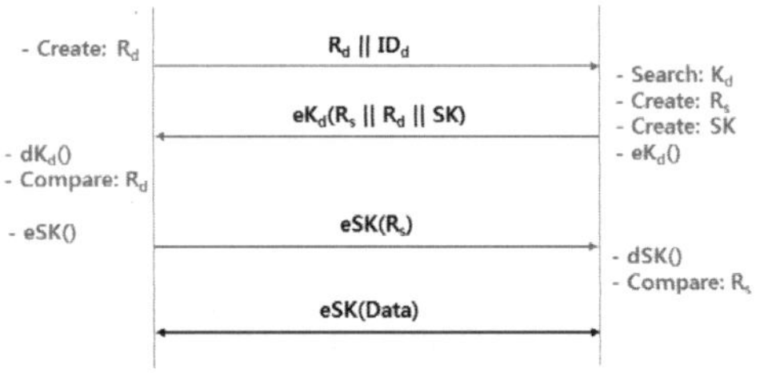

Figure 1. The case of mutual authentication without a gateway.

Figure 2 shows the mutual authentication process between the server and the IoT device including the gateway as an intermediary. When communicating via gateways in an IoT network environment, gateway impersonation attacks are possible, so a gateway authentication must be included to ensure that it is a trusted gateway. The attacker has communication information between the device and the server, and can perform a replay attack on a target after a predetermined time. This attack can be prevented because a new random number is generated and authenticated for every session for communication.

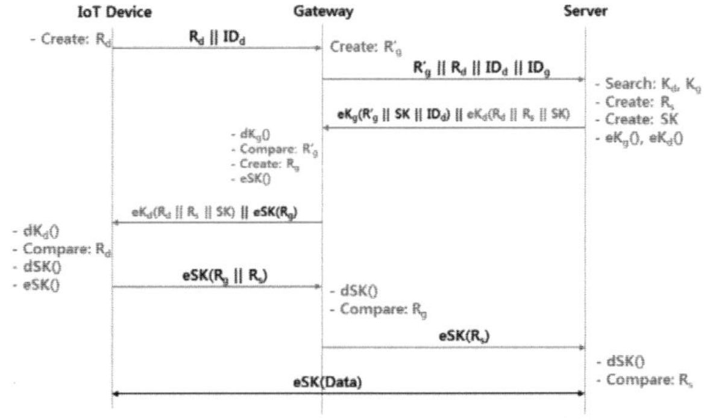

Figure 2. The case of mutual authentication with a gateway.

In addition, since the encrypted communication is performed using the exchanged session key during the authentication process, it is safe even if the attacker makes a spoofing or sniffing attack. Since it is authenticated including the gateway, it is possible to prevent gateway impersonation attack and man-in-the-middle attack.

V. CONCLUSION

In this paper, we propose a mutual authentication scheme that can be used for lightweight IoT devices with high computing power and resource constraints. It simplifies the handshaking process for mutual authentication and reduces the amount of messages transmitted, making it suitable for use in lightweight IoT devices.

ACKNOWLEDGMENT

This work was supported by Institute for Information & communications Technology Promotion (IITP) grant funded by the Korea government (MSIT) (2015-0-00508, Development of Operating System Security Core Technology for the Smart Lightweight IoT Devices).

REFERENCES

[1] V. Miller, "Use of elliptic curves in cryptography", Proc. LNCS CRYPTO, 1985, pp. 417-426.

[2] D. Hong, et al., "LEA: a 128-bit block cipher for fast encryption on common processors", Proc. LNCS WISA, Aug. 2013, pp. 3-27.

[3] C. Bormann, M. Ersue, and A. Keranen, "Terminology for Constrained-Node Networks", IETF, RFC 7228, 2015.

[4] Z. Shelby, K. Hartke, and C. Bormann, "The constrained application protocol (CoAP)", IETF, RFC 7252, 2014.

[5] R. Hummen, J. Ziegeldorf, H. Shafagh, S. Raza, and K.Wehrle, "Towards viable certificated-based authentication for the Internet of Things", Proc. ACM HotWiSec, Apr. 2013, pp. 37-42.

[6] S. Raza, D. Trabalza, and T. Voigt, "6LoWPAN compressed DTLS for CoAP", Proc. IEEE DCOSS, May 2012, pp. 287-289.

[7] S. Raza, et al., "Securing communication in 6LoWPAN with compressed IPsec", Proc. IEEE DCOSS, Jun. 2011, pp. 1-8.

Identifying and Managing Risks in Interconnected Utility Networks

The HyRiM Risk Management Process

Stefan Schauer, Sandra König, Martin Latzenhofer
Center for Digital Safety & Security
AIT Austrian Institute of Technology GmbH
Vienna, Austria
Email: {stefan.schauer, sandra.koenig, martin.latzenhofer}@ait.ac.at

Stefan Rass
Institute of Applied Informatics, System Security Group
Alpen-Adria Universität Klagenfurt
Klagenfurt, Austria
Email: stefan.rass@aau.at

Abstract— **Critical infrastructures and especially their utility networks play a crucial role in the societal and individual day-to-day life. Thus, the estimation of potential threats and security issues as well as a proper assessment of the respective risks is a core duty of utility providers. Despite the fact that utility providers operate several networks (e.g., communication, control and utility networks), most of today's risk management tools only focus on one of these networks. In this article, we will give an overview of a novel risk management process specifically designed for estimating threats and assessing risks in highly interconnected networks. Based on the international standard for risk management, ISO 31000, our risk management process integrates various methodologies and tools supporting the different steps of the process from risk identification to risk treatment. At the heart of this process, a novel game-theoretic framework for risk minimization and risk treatment is applied that is able to deal with uncertainty by using distribution-valued payoffs. This approach is specifically designed to take information generated by various tools into account and model the complex interplay between the heterogeneous networks, systems and operators within a utility provider. It operates on qualitative and semi-quantitative information as well as empirical data, including expert opinions.**

Keywords-risk management; interconnected utility networks; game theory; ISO 31000

I. INTRODUCTION

Utility networks are critical infrastructures consisting of physical and cyber-based systems. The organizations operating these networks are providing essential services for society, e.g., the electric power production and distribution, water and gas supply as well as telecommunication services. A failure within a critical infrastructure has huge societal impact, as shown for example in [1] [2].

These infrastructures are heavily relying on Information and Communication Technology (ICT) as well as Supervisory Control and Data Acquisition (SCADA) systems for providing their services. As it has been shown in recent events [3] [4], ICT and SCADA systems are potential targets of cyber-security threats and may have vulnerabilities that attackers could exploit. Therefore, protecting and assuring availability and security is of the utmost importance for normal societal and business continuity.

In this context, risk management is a core duty in critical infrastructures. Current risk management frameworks [5]–[8] are mostly a matter of best practices, often focusing on one specific topic (e.g., the ICT area, SCADA systems or the physical utility layer). In particular, the aforementioned network-centric structure within utility providers relies on a high integration and a heavy interrelation between the different networks (cf. Figure 1). Hence, an incident in one network might affect not only the network itself but might also have cascading effects on several other networks as well. Standard risk management frameworks are often not designed to identify and assess these cascading effects, thus leaving them underestimated or even undetected.

In this article, we present a novel risk management process, which is specifically tailored to work on highly interconnected networks and take the aforementioned cascading effects into account. With this process, we go beyond the classical approaches in risk management and use a game-theoretic framework to identify an optimal set of risk mitigation measures. Therefore, we extend the well-known risk management process given in the international standard ISO 31000 by special tools. These tools support risk managers obtaining a holistic view of their organization, an in-depth identification of potential threats and a thorough analysis of the propagation of incidents together with their respective impacts. By integrating the collected semi-quantitative data into probability distributions or histograms, the presented process accounts for the intrinsic randomness given in this field of application. This utilization of distribution-valued payoffs represents also an extension to standard game-theoretic frameworks.

In the following Section II, we will give a short overview on the research already done in this field. Section III then describes the HyRiM Project in which the HyRiM Risk Management Process has been developed, in further detail. The ISO 31000 standard, which represents the basis for the HyRiM Risk Management Process, is sketched in Section IV. The core contribution of this work, the detailed description of the HyRiM Risk Management Process, is provided in Section V; the respective subsections describe each sub-step of the process. Section VI concludes the work.

II. RELATED WORK

In the past decade, risk and security management have become core parts of any company's day-to-day business. This is caused by the increasing number of attacks on cyber systems over the last years, where in particular critical infrastructures have moved in the center of attacker's attention. General standards for risk management (e.g., the ISO 31000 [5], ISO/IEC 27005 [6] or the NIST SP800-30 [7]) and security management (e.g., the ISO/IEC 27001 [9] or NIST SP800-37 [10]) as well as common business frameworks (e.g., COBIT 5.0 for Risk [8] or Octave [11]) provide a good approach to prepare organizations against the current threat landscape. Nevertheless, these standards and frameworks are quite generic and need a lot of tailoring to meet the specific requirements of critical infrastructures. Moreover, they represent best practice approaches with little or no mathematical basis for the assessment of risks.

For critical infrastructures, there are more specialized guidelines available, e.g. the NIST SP800-82r2 [12] or the ISA/IEC 62443 family of standards [13], covering the field of industrial control systems. Although these frameworks focus more on cyber-physical systems and thus intend to close the gap between those two worlds, they leave other aspects like organizational and human factors aside. Hence, they take some (more technical) parts of the critical infrastructure's network architecture into consideration but don't provide a holistic view on the whole organization as such. The HyRiM Project [14] described in the following section provides a more comprehensive view of these organizations and thus further improves the overall risk management.

III. THE HYRIM PROJECT

In the course of the FP7 project HyRiM ("Hybrid Risk Management for Utility Networks") [14], we are focusing on these sensitive interconnection points between different networks operated by a utility provider. The main goal is to define a novel risk management approach for identifying, assessing and categorizing security risks and their cascading effects in interconnected utility infrastructure networks. In more detail, we are concentrating on three major networks operated by utility providers, i.e., (cf. also Figure 1)

- the utility's *physical network infrastructure*, consisting of, e.g., gas pipes, water pipes or power lines;
- the utility's *control network* including SCADA systems used to access and maintain specific nodes in the utility network;
- the *ICT network*, collecting data from the SCADA network and containing the organization's business logic.

Additionally, we also include the *human factor and the social interrelations* (i.e., the social network) between employees, wherever possible. In other words, we choose a holistic or "hybrid" view on these networks, strongly emphasizing on the interrelations between them. Hence, we refer to our approach as "Hybrid Risk Management" and to the respective risk measures as "Hybrid Risk Metrics".

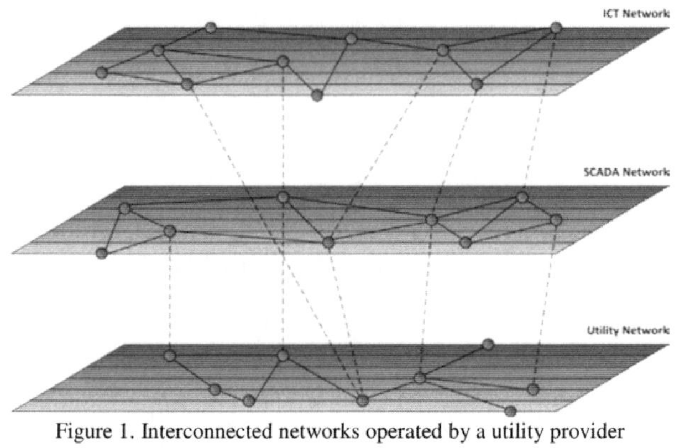

Figure 1. Interconnected networks operated by a utility provider

The risk measures developed in HyRiM are focusing on a qualitative approach to avoid the illusion of "hard facts" based on subjective numerical risk estimates provided by humans. Nevertheless, simulation tools based on well-defined mathematical frameworks like percolation and co-simulation are provided, which support the qualitative analysis with quantitative results.

Hence, our risk management process unifies the advantages of quantitative assessment with the ease and efficiency of a qualitative analysis and supports a qualitative assessment with a sound quantitative mathematical underpinning. The aim is to provide utility network operators with a risk management framework supporting qualitative risk assessment based on numerical (quantitative) techniques. In this way, the HyRiM project takes an explicit step towards considering security in the given context of utility networks based on a sound and well-understood mathematical foundation, ultimately supporting utility network operators with a specially tailored solution for the application at hand.

IV. THE ISO 31000 STANDARD

The international standard for risk management, ISO 31000 [5] describes the principles and guidelines for the implementation of risk management in organizations. It is based not only on the operational risk management process, but also on general organizational factors and their respective underlying structure. Therefore, the standard describes, to a large extent, a strategic risk management framework, which is constantly seeking to develop and improve the operational risk management process in the context of the defined principles.

A distinct characteristic of the ISO 31000 is the two-tier structure with a *risk management framework* on the one hand, and the *operative risk management process* on the other hand (cf. Figure 2). These two life cycles are linked by the framework's activity "implementing risk management". The risk management framework represents the top down approach, ensures the consistent embedding of risk management in the organization based on a quality management perspective. It follows an iterative and continuous improvement approach, i.e., the plan-do-check-act (PDCA) cycle. Furthermore, the operative risk management process supports the bottom-up approach, which puts the concrete risks in an organizational context,

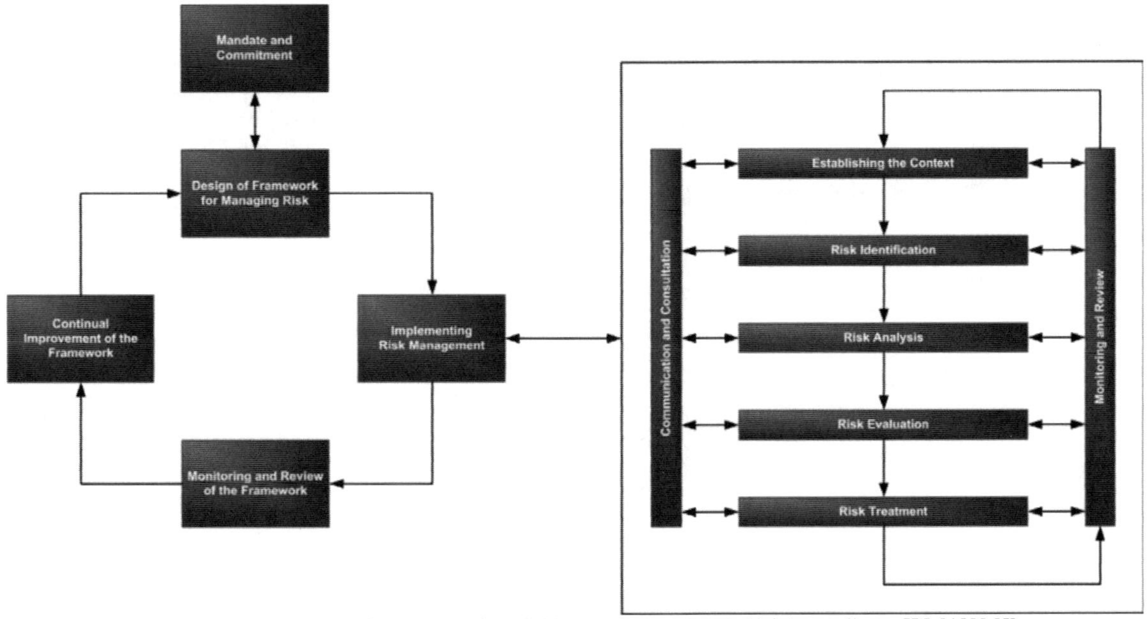

Figure 2. Risk management framework (left) and risk management process (right) according to ISO 31000 [5]

assesses and treats them. During the whole risk management process, two guiding sub-processes ensure communication and consultation as well as monitoring and review. The first one interacts with the stakeholders, the latter enables performance measure.

In order to support the PDCA-driven risk management framework, a strong and sustainable commitment of the organization's top management is required. Only with such a top-level commitment, a risk management policy is supported, objectives and strategies can be coordinated within the organization, indicators can be defined and legal and regulatory requirements can be met. Furthermore, this commitment also ensures that the necessary resources and responsibilities are allocated at all levels of the organization, the benefits are communicated to all stakeholders, and the framework for dealing with risks continues to be adequate.

The implementation of the risk management process describes the application of the risk management policy to the organizational processes including their schedule. Therefore, the following five generic steps are defined, which divide the operational risk management process into specific actions: *Establishing the Context*, *Risk Identification*, *Risk Analysis*, *Risk Evaluation* and *Risk Treatment*. In short, framework conditions for risk management in relation to the organization are specified in the beginning, followed by the identification of the potential threats together with their respective likelihood of occurrence and consequences. The resulting list of risks is assessed according to the predefined context of the organization and ranked according to its importance. This makes it possible to directly identify a procedure for risk management.

V. THE HYRIM RISK MANAGEMENT PROCESS

A. *General Setting*

The HyRiM Risk Management Process we are presenting here is tailored to organizations operating highly interconnected networks at different levels, such as utility providers or critical infrastructure operators. Therefore, the HyRiM process is compliant with the general ISO 31000 process for risk management [5] shortly introduced in the previous section and thus can also be integrated into existing risk management processes already established in the aforementioned organizations.

In detail, the operative risk management process of the ISO 31000 framework (cf. Figure 2) is adopted and each step of the process is supported with the tools developed in the HyRiM project. These tools cover different social and technical analysis techniques and simulation methodologies that facilitate the risk process. The relevant HyRiM tools have been identified and mapped onto the risk management process as shown in Figure 3. Since the ISO 31000 is a generic process and is often used as a template in other ISO standards itself (like in the ISO 27005 [6], the ISO 28001 [15] or others), the HyRiM process described here can also be integrated into these standards. This makes it possible to apply the HyRiM process to multiple fields of application.

The general framework applied in HyRiM to model the interplay between different networks is game theory. Game theory not only provides a solid mathematical foundation but can also be applied without a precise model of the adversary's intentions and goals. Therefore, a zero-sum game and a minimax approach [16] can be used, where the gain of one player is balanced with the loss of the other. This can be used to obtain a worst-case risk estimation.

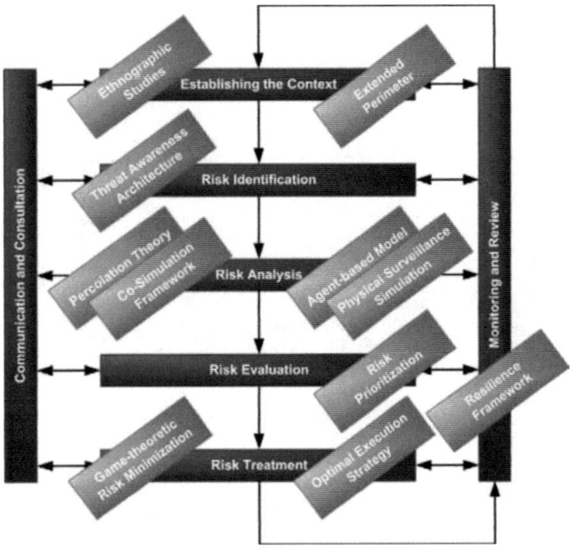

Figure 3. HyRiM Risk Management Process

The game-theoretic framework we developed in HyRiM [12] [13] also allows modeling the intrinsic randomness and uncertainty encountered in real-life scenarios. This is realized using distribution-valued payoffs for the game [19], as opposed to the standard modeling where security needs to be quantified in numeric terms; a task that is typically difficult and reasonable figures measuring security are hard to obtain. These payoffs are coming from both the percolation and the co-simulation, since those are stochastic processes and the results are described as distributions.

The output of the game-theoretic framework is threefold and includes the maximum possible damage that can be caused by an adversary, an optimal attack strategy resulting in that damage and an optimal security strategy for the defender. The optimal defense strategy is, in general, a mixture of several defensive (i.e., mitigation) activities. These activities, if implemented correctly, provide a provable optimal defense against the adversary's worst case attack strategy. The implementation can be simplified and guaranteed, for example, by the use of a job scheduling tool.

B. Establishing the Context

The HyRiM risk management process starts by defining the objectives which should be achieved and attempting to understand the external and internal factors that may influence the goal. This summarizes a description of the external and internal environment of the organization as well as detailed requirements for the risk management process itself.

The first step takes the information about SCADA and ICT communication networks (e.g., network architecture diagram), components of the utility network (e.g., architecture of the physical utility network layer), industrial control functions and information assets as input. Further, information about the social and organizational aspects as well as other necessary documentation that is relevant for the overall risk management context is also required. Whereas the technical aspects are often more or less documented within the organization, for analyzing the social aspects, we suggest using firsthand and more qualitative analysis techniques, like interviews or ethnography. This allows identifying the gap between the way policies and security measures are planned and should be implemented within the organization and how the organizational structure works in real life. In the HyRiM project, we applied such studies to obtain a holistic and in-depth view on the relevant infrastructures of the end user partners.

The main output of this step is a specification of the different networks (ICT, SCADA, social, etc.), their interdependencies among each other and a definition of the basic criteria for the risk management process as well as its scope, boundaries, and responsible parties.

C. Risk Identification

Risk identification involves the application of systematic techniques to understand a range of scenarios describing what could happen, how and why. Therefore, the infrastructure within the scope of the risk management process needs to be defined, including technical assets, organizational roles and individual personnel as well as their interdependencies. Based on that, potential vulnerabilities and threats can be identified.

As an input, this step requires a detailed specification of the organization's infrastructure relevant for the risk assessment process. This information is obtained from the previous step "Establishing the Context". The main objective of this step is to get an overview on the relevant aspects for a risk assessment. Therefore, firstly a list of assets has to be created, describing the subset of the organization's overall infrastructure under evaluation. Secondly, a list of asset-related threats needs to be extracted from the general set of potential threats in the organization's field of application. Further, specific vulnerabilities (not only from the technical area, but also from a general point of view) for these assets need to be gathered.

To avoid missing potential threats or vulnerabilities, a structured approach for risk identification has to be applied. Hence, a *Threat Awareness Architecture* [20], which is based on *Organizational, Technology and Individual* (OTI) viewpoints, was developed in the HyRiM project. This architecture comprises a three-stage process, including Situation Recognition, Situation Comprehension and Situation Projection. In this process, the OTI viewpoints serve as a basis and include not only the technical aspects but also cover policies and processes within an organization as well as how individual people behave under particular conditions. Thus, this architecture provides a holistic view on an organization's threat landscape and also specifies and collects structured information on threats and vulnerabilities. This information can be gathered and also shared with open source threat and vulnerability repositories to achieve a continuous exchange with other utility providers.

This step produces several outputs, including a structured representation (e.g., a network graph) of relevant assets and their interrelations, a list of open vulnerabilities and potential threats related to these assets.

D. Risk Analysis

Risk analysis deals with developing an understanding of each risk, its consequences and the likelihood of these consequences. In general, the level of risk is determined by taking into account the present state of the system, existing controls and their level of effectiveness. Whereas in a classical risk analysis approach both the consequences and the likelihood of an incident are aggregated into a single value, in the HyRiM process, both are described by distributions or histograms including all the relevant information coming from different sources. Hence, the more information is available to build up these distributions, the higher the quality of the results. Nevertheless, since most of the time only scarce information about potential threats and vulnerabilities is available within an organization, the HyRiM process is designed to work also with such limited information.

This step takes the list of potential threats and the list of the organization's assets together with their vulnerabilities as an input (resulting from the previous step "Risk Identification"). Based on this list, specific threat scenarios tailored to the organization's infrastructure are defined. These threat scenarios are evaluated according to their likelihood and consequences.

In general, there is a plethora of different methodologies for estimating the likelihood and consequences of a specific threat scenario. They range from simple questionnaires collecting expert opinions up to complex mathematical models. Especially in the context of utility networks, estimating the potential consequences of a threat often is quite complex due to the interconnected nature of the networks and the related cascading effects. Hence, for the HyRiM Risk Management Process, we suggest four specific simulation-based approaches, which are well-suited for utility networks: *Percolation Theory*, *Co-Simulation*, *Agent-based Modelling* and *Physical Surveillance Simulation*.

In particular, when looking at the different networks operated by a utility provider (cf. Figure 1) percolation theory [21]–[23] as well as co-simulation [24]–[26] can be used to describe the cascading effects spreading over the different networks. More precisely, percolation theory is particularly helpful when only high-level or sparse (e.g., qualitative) information is available [23]. In this case, the nodes and edges in the network graph from the previous step can be distinguished according to several characteristics. Based on these different types, a specific probability of failure is assigned to each type and the propagation of an error is modeled according to these probabilities. This model allows computing the probability that an error affects a significant number of components, i.e., it causes an epidemic or even pandemic, as well as how many nodes are indeed affected in this case.

If more details on the infrastructure and the communication between certain systems are known, a co-simulation approach can provide more accurate information about the spreading of a failure among these networks [26]. In this context, the overall network is represented in different tools, each responsible for simulating a part of the complex system. Then, the co-simulation framework models and manages the communication between these tools, e.g., by exchanging variables, data and status information. In this way, the separated simulations of the complex system are synchronized and the effects of an incident propagating over several systems in the different networks can be analyzed.

In case of threats against the physical infrastructure of a utility provider, e.g., the buildings, machinery, warehouses, tank depots, etc., a simulation framework for physical surveillance is more applicable. In this context, game theory is often used as a mathematical approach to model an intruder's behavior and to find optimal strategies to defend against specific scenarios [27]–[29]. A similar framework has been developed in the HyRiM project [14]. It takes the layout of the utility provider's premises, including the buildings and pathways connecting them and allows simulating the movements of an adversary entering the premises. In more detail, the adversary's capabilities, potential entry points and targets can be modeled. Additionally, the security measures (cameras, identity badges, etc.) together with the routes and routines of the security guards within the premises can be represented in the simulation. In this way, the framework allows reproducing and analyzing different attack scenarios together with the respective defensive actions. Using this framework, not only the potential physical damage caused by one or more intruders but also soft factors (like the effect of increased surveillance on the employees) can be estimated.

Complementary to these methodologies, agent-based modelling is much more focused on the societal impact of specific actions taken by an organization. Since utility providers are, in general, critical infrastructures, incidents happening within utility providers as well as the respective security actions can directly affect societal structures in a certain region. As shown in the HyRiM project, an agent-based model can be used to simulate such social response and provide an overview on the potential implications on society [30].

Taking the results of one or several of the simulation methodologies mentioned above, this step provides two unsorted lists as output, containing the consequences and likelihoods for each identified threat scenario. As already mentioned, the consequences as well as the likelihoods are represented as histograms to prevent the loss of important information.

E. Risk Evaluation

Risk evaluation involves making a decision about the level or priority of each risk by applying the criteria developed when the context was established (c.f. Section V.B above). In classical approaches, a cost benefit analysis can be used to determine whether specific treatment is worthwhile for each of the selected risks. In contrast, the game-theoretic model applied in the HyRiM process allows an optimization according to several tangible and intangible goals (i.e., not only costs but also soft factors like employee satisfaction or social response). Nevertheless, the result needs to be visualized in a well-known representation, i.e., a *risk matrix*, to provide a high recognition value for top level management.

This step requires the compilation of the empirical histograms or distributions (or, more general, the probability mass functions) representing the likelihood and consequences of each of the threats as evaluated in the previous step "Risk Analysis". The input is created from data obtained from the aforementioned simulation approaches, i.e., percolation, co-simulation, agent-based modelling and physical surveillance simulation.

A general approach for risk evaluation is to compute the risk as the product "*consequence × likelihood*" and to order the results according to their magnitude. Due to the fact that we are dealing with histograms or distributions instead of single values, forming this product is not possible and the ordering becomes non-trivial. Hence, we need another way of ordering the consequences and likelihoods for each threat scenario. One solution for this is given by the stochastic $\preccurlyeq$-ordering, which has been introduced in [17] [18], and allows comparing two distributions (cf. [17] [18] for technical explanation of $\preccurlyeq$-ordering). By applying this ordering to the unsorted lists of the threat scenarios' consequences and likelihoods, is it possible to identify the risks with the most severe consequences and the highest likelihood. Unlike rankings based on values (only), this form of evaluation uses all available information, rather than relying on a lossy aggregation thereof (such as the product of likelihood and damage, which corresponds to condensing a distribution into its first moment only).

The main output of this step is a two-dimensional risk matrix including all risks according to their respective likelihood and consequences (cf. Figure 4). Based on this matrix, a priority list of all risks can be compiled.

F. Risk Treatment

Risk treatment is the process in which existing controls are improved and new controls are implemented. In classical

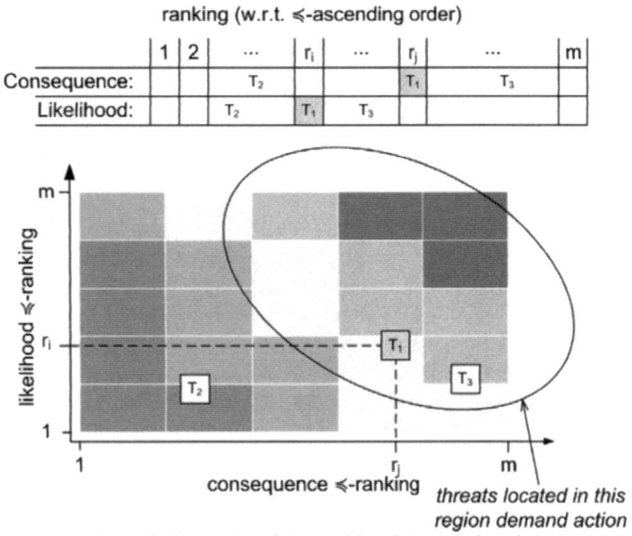

Figure 4. Illustration of the resulting risk matrix based on the two ordered lists for the consequences and likelihoods.

risk management approaches, the aim is to apply these new or improved controls to reduce either the likelihood of a specific threat to occur or the magnitude of the consequences. The decision about which controls to implement is often a subjective one, carried out by the risk manager. In the HyRiM Risk Management Process, the goal is to identify the *optimal set of controls* to reduce the maximum damage that can be caused by an attacker to a minimum. In this context, the optimality of the resulting controls is given due to the game-theoretic algorithms developed in the course of the project [17]–[19].

This step takes the list of risks resulting from the Risk Evaluation as input. The main goal is to identify an optimal treatment plan for risks with the highest priority. Therefore, the list of controls which can be implemented to counter a specific risk is evaluated according to their effect on the consequences. The game-theoretic approach applied here allows not only to identify the optimal choice of controls for a specific risk but also to cluster several risks with similar controls to identify the set of controls, which are most effective against all of the clustered risk. Additionally, the game-theoretic algorithm is capable of optimizing over different security goals, e.g., also taking the costs for implementing the controls into account.

To compute the optimal mitigation action, it has to be evaluated, how much a specific defense strategy affects a certain attack strategy. This is done by rerunning the consequence analysis for the organization's asset structure assuming that the specific defense strategy has been implemented. Therefore, the simulation approaches from Section V.D can be used again. The evaluation has to be done for all combinations of attack and defense strategies. The resulting table of the evaluated consequences (i.e., the payoff matrix) is then fed into the game-theoretic algorithm (cf. [18] for details on the computation of the game).

The output of this step is threefold: the first result is an optimal security strategy for the defender, pointing at the best choice of defense strategies. Those strategies can be pure (i.e., indicating one specific strategy) or mixed (i.e., several strategies have to be implemented with specific probabilities). The second output is an optimal attack strategy for the attacker identifying the neuralgic assets within the organization, and the third is the maximum damage that can be caused by an adversary. This information is then fed into a job scheduling tool, resulting in a well-defined sequence of mitigation activities implementing the optimal defense strategy.

G. Communication and Consultation

Concurrent to the five main steps of the risk management process (as described above), the Communication and Consultation step is performed. Therein, the main and partial results of the process are communicated to the respective stakeholders (as identified during the Establishing the Context step). This is a core part of the overall process due to the fact that the stakeholders, in particular the top level management, need to be kept well-informed about the results from the process. It is important to maintain awareness for the risk management activities, since their continued support

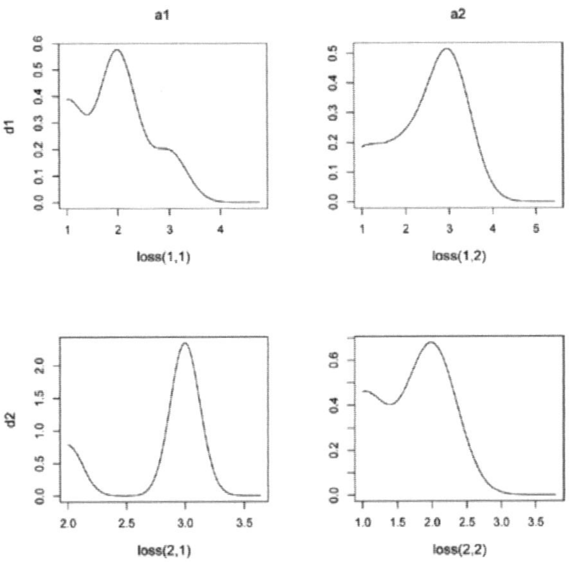

Figure 5. Example of a payoff matrix consisting of distributions (taken from [23])

for the risk management process is crucial for the overall risk management framework (cf. also Section IV about the ISO 31000).

H. *Monitoring and Review*

Besides the Communication and Consultation, a second step running in parallel to the five main steps of risk management is Monitoring and Review. This step represents a constant feedback loop, using the main and partial results from each step and evaluating their effectiveness. Although the outputs of the game-theoretic model are optimal (which can be proven mathematically), but any risk guarantee is only valid provided that the input data is accurate and the threat lists are exhaustive. Here comes another advantage of using payoff distribution models over normal numbers (as in competing approaches) into play: we can even account for rare and unexpected events, since the utilized distributions are based on input data, but by taking the tails of these distributions into account, we can capture extreme outcomes that have not been observed so far (e.g., zero-day exploits). In more detail, the inputs are based on the general organizational structure (cf. Section V.B), the list of potential threats and vulnerabilities (cf. Section V.C) as well as the estimation of the consequences and likelihood for each threat scenario (cf. Section V.D). If these inputs are not comprehensive enough or erroneous, the output of the risk treatment plan will also be incomplete. Hence, the correct implementation of the mitigation actions needs to be validated and their consequences on the organization needs to be compared to the effect estimated during the risk assessment process.

VI. Conclusion

In this paper, we presented a novel approach towards risk management for utility networks, the HyRiM Risk Management Process. This approach has been developed in the HyRiM project and extends the international risk management standard ISO 31000 by tools specifically designed to address the particular requirements of utility providers. As a main advantage over standard risk management processes like the ISO 31000, ISO/IEC27005, COBIT 5 for Risk or others, the presented risk management process accounts for the "hybrid" nature of utility networks, i.e., the strong and complex interrelations between the different networks operated by utility providers. To achieve that, several simulation techniques can be integrated into the process, for example, depending on the quality of the underlying information, to improve the analysis of the dynamics stemming from these interrelations and their resulting cascading effects. By including techniques from the field of social and human studies, not only technical but also individual, organizational and social impact of threats can be evaluated.

Further, the HyRiM Risk Management Process relies on a sound mathematical basis, building on game-theoretic concepts and algorithms, to improve mitigation actions to their optimum. This game-theoretic framework allows the estimation of the worst-case damage and the identification of the corresponding optimal mitigation strategy for a given set of potential threats. Hence, the HyRiM Risk Management Process has a clear advantage over standard frameworks, since those often rely on best practice approaches, lacking a general mathematical basis. Moreover, the notions of worst case damage and optimal defense strategy are well defined according to the game-theoretical framework.

In the course of the HyRiM project, the process' practicality and applicability have been evaluated in real-life use case scenarios. These scenarios include malware propagation in a power provider's cyber-physical network, an APT attack on a water provider's control room and a physical intrusion into an oil and gas refinery. The detailed scenarios will be described in [31].

Acknowledgment

This work was supported by the European Commission's Project No. 608090, HyRiM (Hybrid Risk Management for Utility Networks) under the 7th Framework Programme (FP7-SEC-2013-1).

References

[1] S. Fletcher, "Electric power interruptions curtail California oil and gas production," *Oil Gas J.*, 2001.

[2] M. Schmidthaler and J. Reichl, "Economic Valuation of Electricity Supply Security: Ad-hoc Cost Assessment Tool for Power Outages," *ELECTRA*, no. 276, pp. 10–15.

[3] E-ISAC, "Analysis of the Cyber Attack on the Ukrainian Power Grid," Washington, USA, 2016.

[4] J. Condliffe, "Ukraine's Power Grid Gets Hacked Again, a Worrying Sign for Infrastructure Attacks," 22-Dec-2016. [Online]. Available: https://www.technologyreview.com/s/603262/ukraines-power-grid-gets-hacked-again-a-worrying-sign-for-infrastructure-attacks/. [Accessed: 26-Jul-2017].

[5] International Standardization Organization, *ISO 31000: Risk Management – Principles and Guidelines*. Geneva, Switzerland, 2009.

[6] International Standardization Organization, *ISO/IEC 27005: Information technology - Security techniques - Information security risk management*. Geneva, Switzerland, 2011.

[7] G. Stoneburner, A. Goguen, and A. Feringa, *NIST SP800-30 Risk Management Guide for Information Technology Systems*. Gaithersburg, USA, 2002.

[8] ISACA, *COBIT 5 for Risk*. Rolling Meadows, USA, 2013.

[9] International Standardization Organization, *ISO/IEC 27001: Information technology - Security techniques - Information security management systems - Requirements*. Geneva, Switzerland, 2013.

[10] NIST, *NIST SP800-37 Rev. 1 Guide for Applying the Risk Management Framework to Federal Information Systems: a Security Life Cycle Approach*. Gaithersburg, USA, 2010.

[11] C. Richard A., S. James F., Y. Lisa R., and W. William R., "Introducing OCTAVE Allegro: Improving the Information Security Risk Assessment Process," Software Engineering Institute, Carnegie Mellon University, Pittsburgh, USA, Technical Report CMU/SEI-2007-TR-012, 2007.

[12] K. Stouffer, V. Pillitteri, S. Lightman, M. Abrams, and A. Hahn, *NIST SP800-82 Rev. 2 Guide to Industrial Control Systems (ICS) Security*. Gaithersburg, USA, 2015.

[13] International Society of Automation, "ISA/IEC 62443 Series of Standards on Industrial Automation and Control Systems (IACS) Security." [Online]. Available: http://isa99.isa.org/ISA99%20Wiki/Home.aspx. [Accessed: 26-Jul-2017].

[14] "HyRiM | Hybrid Risk Management for Utility Providers." [Online]. Available: https://www.hyrim.net//. [Accessed: 26-Jul-2017].

[15] International Standardization Organization, *ISO 28001: Security management systems for the supply chain - Best practices for implementing supply chain security, assessments and plans - Requirements and guidance*. Geneva, Switzerland, 2007.

[16] M. Maschler, E. Solan, and S. Zamir, *Game Theory*. Cambridge University Press, 2013.

[17] S. Rass, S. König, and S. Schauer, "Deliverable 1.2 - Report on Definition and Categorisation of Hybrid Risk Metrics," Vienna, Austria, HyRiM Deliverable, 2015.

[18] S. Rass, "On Game-Theoretic Risk Management (Part One) – Towards a Theory of Games with Payoffs that are Probability-Distributions," *ArXiv E-Prints*, Jun. 2015.

[19] S. Rass, S. König, and S. Schauer, "Uncertainty in Games: Using Probability-Distributions as Payoffs," in *Decision and Game Theory for Security*, London, UK: Springer, 2015, pp. 346–357.

[20] A. Gouglidis, B. Green, J. Busby, M. Rouncefield, D. Hutchison, and S. Schauer, "Threat Awareness for Critical Infrastructures Resilience," in *Resilient Networks Design and Modeling (RNDM), 2016 8th International Workshop on Resilient Networks Design and Modeling*, Halmstad, Sweden, 2016, pp. 196–202.

[21] G. R. Grimmett, *Percolation Theory*. Heidelberg, Germany: Springer, 1989.

[22] S. König, S. Rass, and S. Schauer, "A Stochastic Framework for Prediction of Malware Spreading in Heterogeneous Networks," in *Secure IT Systems. 21st Nordic Conference, NordSec 2016, Oulu, Finland, November 2-4, 2016. Proceedings*, B. Brumley and J. Röning, Eds. Cham: Springer International Publishing, 2016, pp. 67–81.

[23] S. König, S. Rass, S. Schauer, and A. Beck, "Risk Propagation Analysis and Visualization using Percolation Theory," *Int. J. Adv. Comput. Sci. Appl.*, vol. 7, no. 1, pp. 694–701, 2016.

[24] M. Faschang, F. Kupzog, R. Mosshammer, and A. Einfalt, "Rapid control prototyping platform for networked smart grid systems," in *Proceedings IECON 2013 - 39th Annual Conference of the IEEE Industrial Electronics Society*, Vienna, Austria, 2013, pp. 8172–8176.

[25] M. Faschang, "Loose Coupling Architecture for Co-Simulation of Heterogeneous Components," Vienna University of Technology, Vienna, Austria, 2015.

[26] M. Findrik, P. Smith, J. H. Kazmi, M. Faschang, and F. Kupzog, "Towards secure and resilient networked power distribution grids: Process and tool adoption," in *Smart Grid Communications (SmartGridComm), 2016 IEEE International Conference on*, Sidney, Australia, 2016, pp. 435–440.

[27] M. Aigner and M. Fromme, "A game of cops and robbers," *Discrete Appl. Math.*, vol. 8, no. 1, pp. 1–12, 1984.

[28] S. Bhattacharya, T. Başar, and M. Falcone, "Surveillance for Security as a Pursuit-Evasion Game," in *Decision and Game Theory for Security*, vol. 8840, R. Poovendran and W. Saad, Eds. Cham: Springer International Publishing, 2014, pp. 370–379.

[29] G. Hahn and G. MacGillivray, "A note on *k*-cop, *l*-robber games on graphs," *Discrete Math.*, vol. 306, no. 19–20, pp. 2492–2497, 2006.

[30] J. Busby, A. Gouglidis, S. Rass, and S. König, "Modelling security risk in critical utilities: the system at risk as a three player game and agent society," in *Systems, Man, and Cybernetics (SMC), 2016 IEEE International Conference on*, Budapest, Hungary, 2016, pp. 1758–1763.

[31] S. Rass and S. Schauer, *Game Theory for Security and Risk Management: From Theory to Practice*. Boston, USA: Birkhäuser, to appear.

Protecting Eavesdropping over Multipath TCP Communication Based on Not-Every-Not-Any Protection

Toshihiko Kato[1)2)], Shihan Cheng[1)2)], Ryo Yamamoto[1)], Satoshi Ohzahata[1)] and Nobuo Suzuki[2)]
1) University of Electro-Communications, Tokyo, Japan
2) Advanced Telecommunication Research Institute International, Kyoto, Japan
e-mail: kato@is.uec.ac.jp, chengshihan@net.is.uec.ac.jp, ryo_yamamotog@is.uec.ac.jp,
ohzahata@is.uec.ac.jp, nu-suzuki@atr.jp

Abstract—**Recent mobile terminals have multiple interfaces, such as 4G and wireless local area network (WLAN). In order to use those interfaces at the same time, multipath transmission control protocol (MPTCP) is introduced in several operating systems. However, it is possible that some interfaces are connected to untrusted networks and that data transferred over them is observed in an unauthorized way. In order to avoid this situation, we propose a new method to improve privacy against eavesdropping using the data dispersion by exploiting multipath nature of MPTCP. One feature of the proposed method is to realize that an attacker cannot observe data on any path, even if he observes traffic over only a part of paths. Another feature is to use data scrambling instead of ciphering. The results of performance evaluation show that the processing overhead of the proposed method is much smaller than cipher based methods.**

Keywords- Multipath TCP; Eavesdropping; Data Dispersion; Data Scrambling.

I. INTRODUCTION

Recently, mobile terminals with multiple interfaces have come to be widely used. For example, most smart phones are installed with interfaces for 4G Long Term Evolution (LTE) and WLAN. In the next generation (5G) network, it is studied that multiple communication paths provided multiple network operators are commonly involved [1]. In this case, mobile terminals will have more than two interfaces at the same time.

In order for applications to use multiple interfaces effectively, MPTCP [2] is being introduced in several operating systems, such as Linux, Apple OS/iOS [3] and Android [4]. MPTCP is an extension of TCP. Conventional TCP applications can use MPTCP as if they were working over traditional TCP and are provided multiple byte streams through different interfaces.

MPTCP is defined in three request for comments (RFC) documents by the Internet Engineering Task Force. RFC 6182 [5] outlines architecture guidelines for developing MPTCP protocols, by discussing the high level design decisions on selecting the protocol functions from multiple candidates. RFC 6824 [6] presents the details of extensions to the traditional TCP to support multipath operation. It defines the MPTCP control information realized as new TCP options, and the MPTCP protocol procedures for the initiation and association of subflows (TCP connections related with an MPTCP connection), the data transfer and acknowledgment over multiple subflows, and the closing MPTCP connection. RFC 6356 [7] presents a congestion control algorithm that couples the congestion control algorithms running on different subflows.

When a mobile terminal uses multiple interfaces, i.e., multiple paths, some of them may be unsafe such that an attacker is able to observe data over them in an unauthorized way. For example, a WLAN interface is connected to a public WLAN access point, data transferred over this WLAN may be disposed to other nodes connected to it. In order to prevent this eavesdropping, the transport layer security (TLS) is used to provide communication security. Although TLS can be applied various applications including web access, e-mail and ftp, however, it is widely used only with HTTP, and some applications like VoIP cannot use TLS. In this paper, we propose a new method to improve privacy against eavesdropping by exploiting multipath nature of MPTCP. Even if an unsafe WLAN path is used, another path may be safe, such as LTE supported by a trusted network operator. So, we propose a method such that if an attacker cannot observe the data on *every* path, he cannot observe the traffic on *any* path [8]. We call this scheme a *not-every-not-any* protection. Although there are several proposals on multipath data dispersion to protect eavesdropping, all of them adopt just a simple method dispatching data packets among multiple paths with or without encryption. The feature of the proposed method is to adopt the not-every-not-any protection, and to use the data scrambling instead of ciphering.

The rest of this paper is organized as follows. Section II explains the overview [9] and the security issues of MPTCP. Section III describes the design of the proposed method protecting against eavesdropping. Section IV gives the performance evaluation on the processing overhead of the proposal method and other ciphering methods. In the end, Section V concludes this paper.

II. OVERVIEW AND SECURITY ISSUES OF MPTCP

A. MPTCP connections and subflows

As described in Figure 1, the MPTCP module is located on top of TCP. As described above, MPTCP is designed so that the conventional applications do not need to care about the existence of MPTCP. MPTCP establishes an *MPTCP connection* associated with two or more regular TCP connections called *subflows*. The management and data transfer over an MPTCP connection is done by newly introduced TCP options for MPTCP operation.

Figure 2 shows an example of MPTCP connection establishment where host A with two network interfaces invokes this sequence for host B with one network interface.

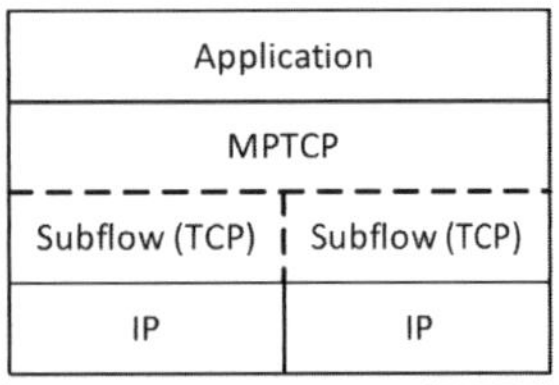

Figure 1. Layer structure of MPTCP.

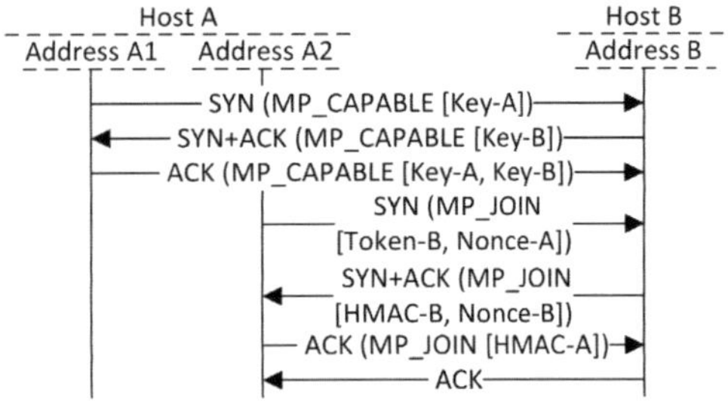

Figure 2. Example of MPTCP connection establishment.

In the beginning, host A sends a SYN segment to host B with a *Multipath Capable (MP_CAPABLE)* TCP option. This option indicates that the initiator supports the MPTCP functions and requests to use them in this TCP connection. It contains host A's *Key* (64 bits) used by this MPTCP connection. Then, host B replies a SYN+ACK segment with MP_CAPABLE option with host B's Key. This reply means that host B accepts the use of MPTCP functions. In the end, host A sends an ACK segment with MP_CAPABLE option including both A's and B's Keys. Through this three-way handshake procedure, the first subflow and the MPTCP connection are established. Here, it should be mentioned that these "Keys" are not keys in a cryptographic sense. As described below, they are used for generating the Hash-based Message Authentication Code (HMAC), but MPTCP does not provide any mechanisms to protect them from attackers' accessing while transfer.

Next, host A tries to establish the second subflow through another network interface. In the first SYN segment in this try, another TCP option called a *Join Connection (MP_JOIN)* option is used. An MP_JOIN option contains the receiver's *Token* (32 bits) and the sender's *Nonce* (random number, 32 bit). A Token is an information to identify the MPTCP connection to be joined. It is obtained by taking the most significant 32 bits from the SHA-1 hash value for the receiver's Key (host B's Key in this example). Then, host B replies a SYN+ACK segment with MP_JOIN option. In this case, MP_JOIN option contains the random number of host B and the most significant 64 bits of the HMAC value. An HMAC value is calculated for the nonces generated by hosts A and B using the Keys of A and B. In the third ACK segment, host A sends an MP_JOIN option containing host A's full HMAC value (160 bits). In the end, host B acknowledges the third ACK segment. Using these sequence, the newly established subflow is associated with the MPTCP connection.

B. Data transfer

An MPTCP implementation will take one input data stream from an application, and split it into one or more subflows, with sufficient control information to allow it to be reassembled and delivered to the receiver side application reliably and in order. The MPTCP connection maintains the *data sequence number* independent of the subflow level sequence numbers. The data and ACK segments may contain a *Data Sequence Signal (DSS)* option depicted in Figure 3.

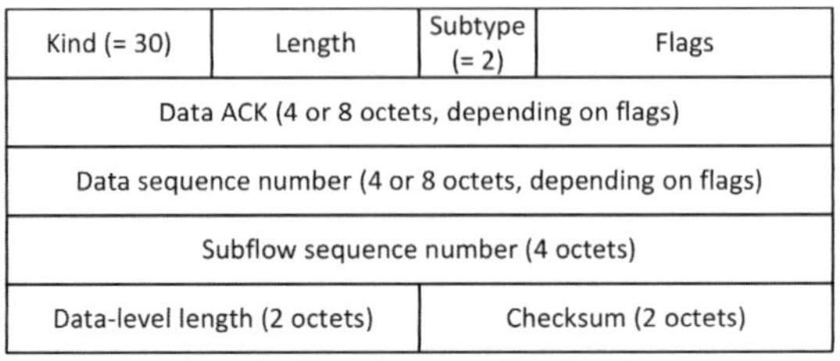

Figure 3. Data Sequence Signal option.

The data sequence number and data ACK is 4 or 8 byte long, depending on the flags in the option. The number is assigned on a byte-by-byte basis similarly with the TCP sequence number. The value of data sequence number is the number assigned to the first byte conveyed in that TCP segment. The data sequence number, subflow sequence number (relative value) and data-level length define the mapping between the MPTCP connection level and the subflow level. The data ACK is analogous to the behavior of the standard TCP cumulative ACK. It specifies the next data sequence number a receiver expects to receive.

C. Security issues on MPTCP and related work

Some new security issues emerge by the introduction of MPTCP [8]. One is a new threat that an attacker splits malicious data over multiple paths. Traditional signature-based intrusion detection systems (IDSs) suppose that they can monitor all packets of a given flow. If a target system uses MPTCP and an attacker sends signatures over different subflows, IDSs cannot detect them. Ma, et al. [10] proposed a new approach for this problem, where each IDS locally scans and processes its monitored traffic, and all IDSs share asynchronously a global state of string matching automaton.

Another issue is related to MPTCP and privacy. MPTCP has a potential to provide improved privacy against attackers who are able to observe or interfere with subflow traffic along a subset of paths. Dispersing traffic over multiple paths makes it less likely that attackers will get access to all of the data. Pearce and Zeadally [8] suggested the concept of the not-every-not-any protection and introduced some ideas including sending cryptographic signing details using multiple paths and applying cryptographic chaining, such as cipher block chaining (CBC), across multiple paths.

There have been several proposals on the data dispersion over multiple paths. Yang and Papavassiliou [11] provided a method to analyze the security performance when a virtual connection takes multiple disjoint paths to the destination, and a traffic dispersion scheme to minimize the information leakage when some of the intermediate routers are attacked. Nacher, et al. [12] tried to determine the optimal trade-off between traffic dispersion and TCP performance over mobile ad-hoc networks to reduce the chances of successful eavesdropping while maintaining acceptable throughput.

These two studies use multiple TCP connections by their own coordination methods instead of MPTCP. Gurtov and Polishchuk [13] used host identity protocol (HIP), which locates between IP and TCP to provide multiple paths, and propose how to spread traffic over them. Apiecionek, et al. [14] proposed a way to use MPTCP for more secure data transfer. After data are encrypted, they are divided into blocks, mixed in the predetermined random sequence, and then transferred through multiple MPTCP subflows. A receiver rearranges received blocks in right order and decrypts them.

All of those proposals aim at just spreading data packets over multiple paths, and do not consider the coordination over multiple paths. If the transferred data are encrypted before dispersion, it can be said that they are coordinated by the encryption procedure, but the coordination is not realized by the dispersion schemes. In contrast with them, our proposal adopts an approach to improve privacy by coordinating data over multiple paths through data scrambling not encryption.

III. PROPOSAL

A. *Requrements and possible approaches*

The followings are the requirements for designing a not-any-not-every protection method protecting eavesdropping.

- The method needs to cope with two way data exchanges within one MPTCP connection.
- The length of exchanged data should not be expanded.
- Even if there are any bytes with known values, such as fixed bytes in an application protocol header, the method provides protection from information leakage.
- The method does not introduce any new overheads into MPTCP as much as possible.
- The method does not change the behaviors of MPTCP as much as possible.

In designing the proposed method, we have considered the following possible candidates.

(1) Secret sharing method

The secret sharing method is to divide data D into n pieces in such a way that D is easily reconstructed from any k pieces, but even complete knowledge of k - 1 pieces reveals absolutely no information about D [15]. Shamir [15] gave an example method based on polynomial interpolation. It is possible to apply the idea of secret sharing to data transfer. Zhao et al. [16] proposed an efficient anonymous message submission protocol based on secret sharing and a symmetric key cryptosystem. It aggregates messages of multiple members into a message vector such that a member knows only his own position in the submission sequence.

Figure 4 shows an idea of applying secret sharing to the eavesdropping protection. It supposes the case that $n = 2$ and $k = 2$. Pieces D_1 and D_2 are generated from an original data and transferred through different paths. An attacker can access only D_2 over an untrusted path, and so he cannot obtain the original data. In this approach, however, the amount of transferred data is increased, twice in this example.

(2) Network coding

The second candidate is the network coding [17]. In this framework, the exclusive OR (XOR) is calculated among multiple packets and the result is transferred instead of packets themselves. Ahlswede, et al. [17] mentioned that by employing coding at network nodes, which they referred to as network coding, it is possible to save bandwidth in general. Li, et al. [18] proposed a network coding based multipath TCP (NC-MPTCP), which uses the mix of regular subflows, delivering original data, and network coding subflows, which deliver linear combinations of original data. NC-MPTCP achieves higher goodput compared to MPTCP in the presence of different subflow qualities.

Figure 5 shows an idea of applying network coding to the eavesdropping protection. Using data A and B, their XOR ($A \oplus B$) is calculated. Through a trusted path, an original data A is transferred, and through an untrusted path, $A \oplus B$ is transferred. Since an attacker observes only $A \oplus B$, he cannot obtain data B without knowledge of data A. This idea can be said a *packet level data scrambling*. Although it can provide the not-every-not-any protection, it introduces an additional overhead due to the variable length packets, and an additional control in MPTCP, such as sending XOR data only over an untrusted path.

(3) Mode of operation in block ciphering

The third candidate is the mode of operation, such as CBC and output feedback (OFB), used in block ciphering [19]. The block cipher defines only how to encrypt or decrypt a fixed length bits (block). A mode of operation defines how to apply this operation to data longer than a block. CBR and OFB introduce a chaining between blocks such that a block is combined with the preceding block by XOR calculation.

Figure 6 shows an idea of applying mode of operation to the eavesdropping protection. Data to be sent (data 1 and 2) are divided into blocks (A through D). The first block is XORed with the initialization vector (IV), and the following

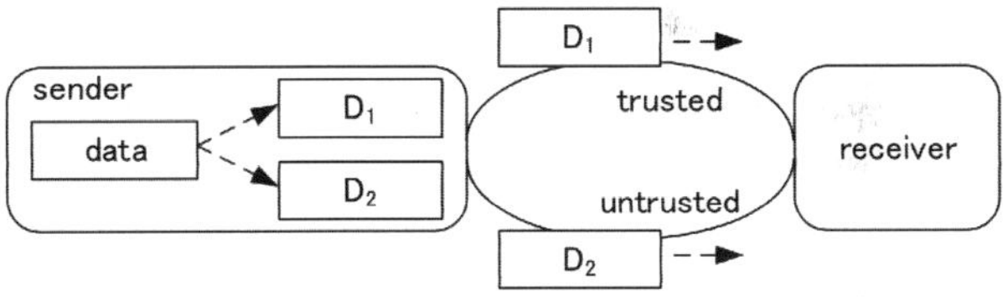

Figure 4. Secret sharing based approach.

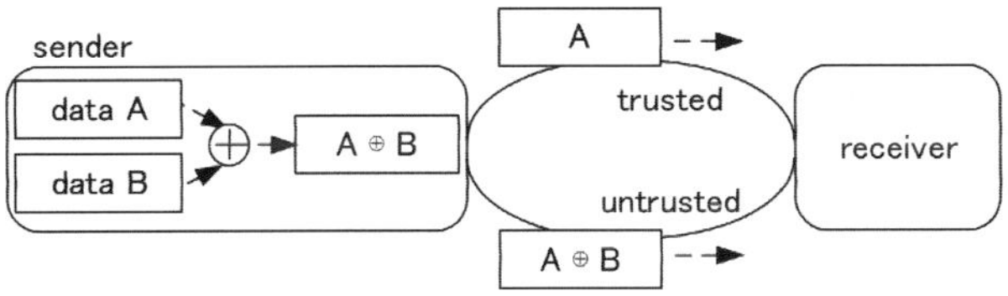

Figure 5. Network coding based approach.

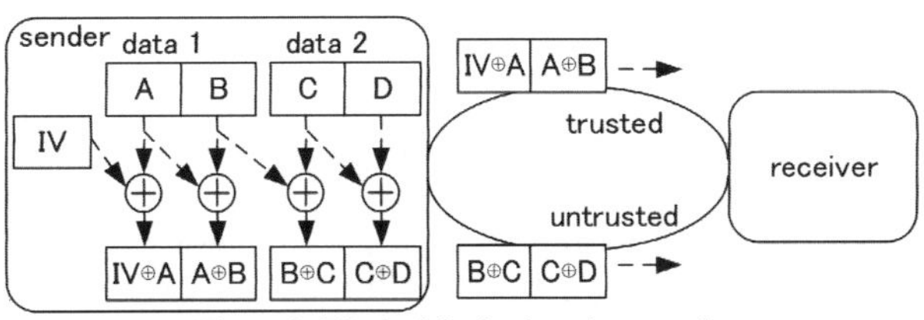

Figure 6. Block ciphering based approach.

blocks are XORed with their preceding blocks. The XORed results are transferred via different paths. In the example, an attacker can only observe B ⊕ C and C ⊕ D, and does not know block B, which is transferred through a trusted path. So, he cannot obtain C and D any more. This idea can be said a *block level data scrambling*. Although it can provide the not-every-not-any protection, it introduces an additional data overhead because the length of packets is not integral multiple of block length in general.

According to those considerations, we select a byte stream based data scrambling approach described below.

B. Detailed design of proposed method

As shown in Figure 7, we introduce a data scrambling function within MPTCP and on top of the original MPTCP. When an MPTCP communication is started, the use of data scrambling is negotiated. It may be done using a flag bit in MP_CAPABLE TCP option.

Figure 8 shows an overview of data scrambling. In the data sending side, an application sends data to MPTCP. It is stored in the send socket buffer, and the data scrambling module scrambles it in a byte-by-byte basis. The result is stored in the send socket buffer again. The data in this buffer is transferred reliably by MPTCP. While sending data, MPTCP tries to send the first packet over an MPTCP connection via a subflow that uses a trusted path. After that, the data transfer by MPTCP is performed according to its native scheduler. We suppose that the distinction of trusted or untrusted path can be done by the IP address of interfaces. In the data receiving side, data is transferred through MPTCP without any losses, transmission errors, nor duplications. The received in-sequence data is stored in the receive socket buffer. After that, the data descrambling module is invoked to restore the scrambled data to the original one.

Figure 9 shows the details of data scrambling. As described above, the scrambling is performed in a byte-by-byte basis. More specifically, one byte being sent is XORed with its preceding 64 bytes. In order to realize this scrambling, the data scrambling module maintains the *send scrambling buffer*, whose length is 64 bytes. It is a shift buffer and its initial value is HMAC of the key of this side. Since the length of HMAC is 20 bytes, the higher bytes in the send scrambling buffer is filled by zero. When a data comes from an application, each byte (b_i in the figure) is XORed with the result of XOR of all the bytes in the send scrambling buffer. The obtained byte (B_i) is the corresponding sending byte. After calculating the sending byte, the original byte (b_i) is added to the send scramble buffer, forcing out the oldest (highest) byte from the buffer. The send scrambling buffer holds recent 64 original bytes given from an application. By using 64 byte buffer, the access to the original data is protected even if there are well-known byte patterns (up to 63 bytes) in application protocol data.

Figure 10 shows the details of data descrambling, which is similar with data scrambling. The data scrambling module also maintains the receive scramble buffer whose length is 64 bytes. Its initial value is HMAC of the key of the remote side. When an in-sequence data is stored in the receive socket buffer, a byte (B_i that is scrambled) is applied to XOR calculation with the XOR result of all bytes in the receive scramble buffer. The result is the descrambled byte (b_i), which is added to the receive scramble buffer.

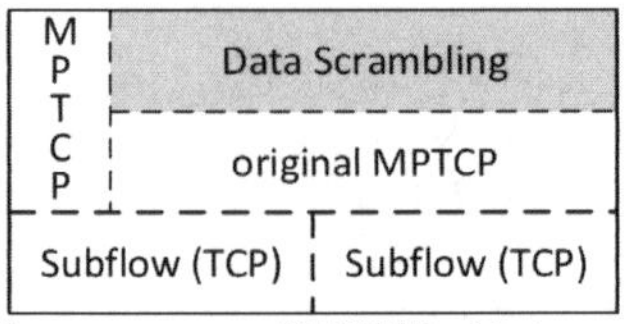

Figure 7. Layer structure of MPTCP with data scrambling.

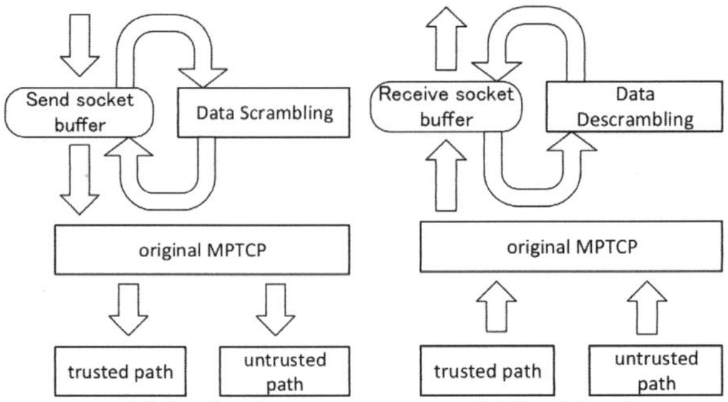

(a) Sending data (b) Receiving data

Figure 8. Overview of data scrambling processing.

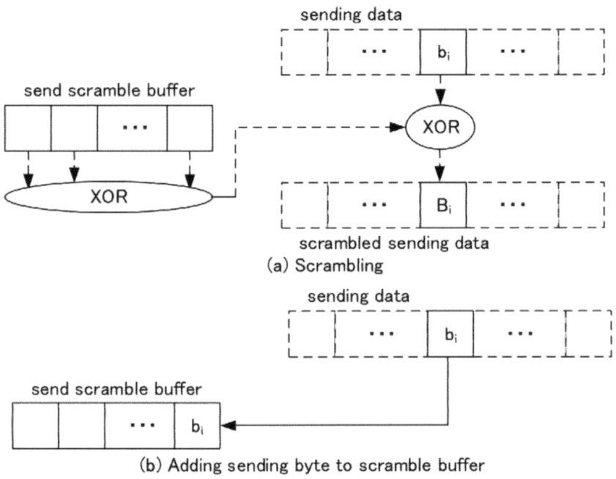

Figure 9. Processing of data scrambling.

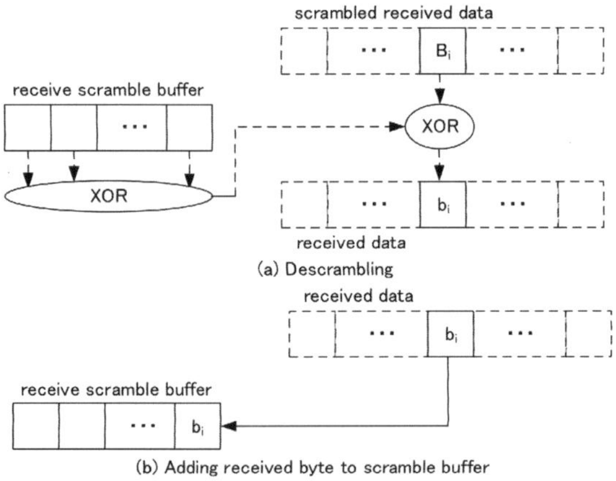

Figure 10. Processing of data descrambling.

By using the byte-wise scrambling and descrambling, the proposed method does not increase the length of exchanged data at all. The separate send and receive control enables two way data exchanges to be handled independently. Moreover the proposed method introduces only a few modification to the original MPTCP.

IV. PERFORMANCE EVALUATION

In this section, we evaluate the processing overhead of the proposed method. In addition, we evaluate the overhead of commonly used cryptographic methods for the purpose of comparison. We adopt the data encryption standard (DES) [20], the triple data encryption algorithm (TDEA) [20], and the advanced encryption standard (AES) [21].

DES is a block based ciphering algorithm standardized by the National Institute of Standards and Technology (NIST). It is designed to encipher and decipher of blocks of data consisting of 64 bits (8 bytes) under control of a 64 bit (8 byte) key. Currently, it has been withdrawn as a standard ciphering method, but the TDEA, a compound operation of DES encryption and decryption operations, can be used as one of cipher suites in TLS.

AES is another block based ciphering algorithm newly standardized by NIST in 2001. It is a symmetric block cipher that can process data blocks of 128 bits (16 bytes), using cipher keys with lengths of 128, 192, and 256 bits (16 bytes, 24 bytes, and 32 bytes, respectively).

In this paper, we used publicly available source programs for DES and AES [22] distributed by PJC, a Japanese software company. They are written in C language. As for the DES algorithm, we prepared 160 blocks ($8 \times 160 = 1280$ bytes) and performed encryption and decryption for those blocks with the electronic codebook (ECB) mode. That is, each block is just encrypted and decrypted independently from other blocks. As for the TDEA algorithm, each of 160 blocks is encrypted or decrypted three times according to the DES algorithm with independent three keys. As for the AES algorithm, we prepared 80 blocks ($16 \times 80 = 1280$ bytes) and used keys with 128, 192 and 256 bit length (AES-128, AES-192 and AES-256). We also used the ECB mode here. It should be mentioned that we suppose 1280 byte long message to be transferred.

As for the proposed method, we introduced two kinds of implementations. One is a straightforward implementation, where the proposed method described in the previous section is programmed in C language as they are. The followings are the summary of the straightforward implementation.

- The send/receive scramble buffers are realized by an array of unsigned char type.
- When a byte is scrambled or descrambled, the exclusive OR of all bytes in the scramble buffer is calculated.
- When a byte is scrambled or descrambled, it is added to the scramble buffer by shifting all bytes in the buffer.

The other is a revised implementation, where unnecessary data copying nor exclusive OR calculation are avoided. The followings are the summary of the revised implementation.

- The send/receive scramble buffers are realized by an array of unsigned char type. In order to avoid unnecessary data copying, the oldest element in the array is maintained by an index parameter.
- The exclusive OR calculation for all bytes in the scramble buffer is performed just once in the beginning. This result is maintained by a static variable *sXor* or *rXor*.
- When a byte is to be scrambled or descrambled, the static variable (*sXor* or *rXor*) is overwritten by the exclusive OR of the oldest element in the scramble buffer, *sXor* (or *rXor*) and the new byte.
- When a byte is to be scrambled or descrambled, it is added to the scramble buffer just by moving the index parameter.

By use of these two implementation, we executed the data scrambling and descrambling for a message with length of 1280 bytes.

We evaluated the performance of those seven methods (DES, TDEA, AES-128, AES-192, AES-256, the proposed method by straightforward implementation, and the proposed method by revised implementation). Table I shows the specification of personal computer used for the evaluation. It is a laptop computer manufactured by Lenovo over which the Linux operating system is installed. We measured the processing time of the encryption and decryption, or the scrambling and descrambling for a message with 1280 byte length. We used Linux *time* command for 10,000 iterations, and calculated the processing time for one operation.

Table II gives the performance results. The encryption and decryption of the DES and AES-128 algorithms require around 2.2 or 2.3 msec. The AES-192 and AES-256 algorithms requires a little more time. The TDEA algorithm requires around 6.7 msec, which is about three time of the DES algorithm. On the other hand, the straightforward implementation of the proposed method requires around 1 msec. This is smaller than the cryptographic approaches, but the improvement is not large. However, the revised implementation of the proposed method decreases the processing time largely, to around 0.04 msec. It is less than 1/60 compared with the DES and AES algorithms. Although the implementation of DES and AES algorithms is a publicly accessible software, which may be optimized adequately, the obtained results are considered to show that the proposed method is able to decrease the processing overhead of

TABLE I. SPECIFICATION OF PC USED IN EVALUATION.

model	lenovo ThinkPad E430
CPU	Intel Core i5-3230M CPU × 4
clock	2.60GHz
memory size	3.7 Gbytes
kernel	ubuntu 16.04 LTS

TABLE II. PROCESSING TIME OF 1280 BYTE MESSAGE.

DES	TDEA	AES-128	AES-192	AES-256	Proposed (straight)	Proposed (revised)
2.24 msec	6.69 msec	2.29 msec	2.80 msec	3.40 msec	0.950 msec	0.0352 msec

ciphering operations and to provide some level of security against the eavesdropping over untrusted paths in MPTCP communications.

V. Discussions and Conclusions

This paper proposes a new method to improve privacy against eavesdropping over MPTCP communications, which has become popular among recent mobile terminals. Recent mobile terminals have multiple communication interfaces, some of which are connected to trusted network operators (e.g. LTE interfaces), and some of which may be connected to untrusted network, such as public WLAN hot spots. The proposed method here is based on the not-every-not-any protection principle, where, *if an attacker cannot observe the data on every path, he cannot observe the traffic on any path.* We designed detailed procedure by following the byte oriented data scrambling in order to avoid unnecessary data length expansion.

We need to discuss here about the security scheme of the proposed method. The proposed method does not use the data ciphering, and so it does not protect eavesdropping in a strict sense. It depends on the difficulty of unauthorized data access over trusted network operators. That is, the intruder model is that an attacker can access to only untrusted networks, such as public WLAN access points. We also need to point out that the proposed method gives a small modification to MPTCP. It uses the HMAC value of sender side Key as an initial value of XORing, which means that no additional vulnerabilities are introduced for the initialization vector setting. Besides, as for the dependency between multiple paths that a byte cannot obtained only after the precedence bytes are received, it is intrinsic to MPTCP and is not a defect of the proposed method itself.

We evaluated the processing overhead of the DES, TDEA and AES encryption/decryption and that of data scrambling in the proposed method. The result showed that the optimized implementation of our method requires only less than 1/60 processing time compared with the cryptographic approaches. Although the proposed method is a practical solution, as described above, the processing capability of mobile terminals is still low, and so our proposal is considered to be useful to increase the security against eavesdropping over untrusted mobile communication networks.

We are currently implementing the proposed method on top of MPTCP software in the Linux operating system. We will continue this implementation and conduct the performance evaluation over real networks. Moreover, the proposed method can only prevent eavesdropping, and cannot ensure the integrity of transferred data. We need to improve our method in this aspect.

Acknowledgment

This research was performed under the research contract of "Research and Development on control schemes for utilizations of multiple mobile communication networks," for the Ministry of Internal Affairs and Communications, Japan.

References

[1] NGNM Alliance, "5G White Paper," https://www.ngmn.org/uploads/media/NGMN_5G_Paper_V1_0.pdf, Feb. 2015, [retrieved: May 2017].

[2] C. Paasch and O. Bonaventure, "Multipath TCP," Communications of the ACM, vol. 57, no. 4, pp. 51-57, Apr. 2014.

[3] AppleInsider Staff, "apple found to be using advanced Multipath TCP networking in iOS 7," http://appleinsider.com/articles/13/09/20/apple-found-to-be-using-advanced-multipath-tcp-networking-in-ios-7, [retrieved: May 2017].

[4] icteam, "MultiPath TCP – Linux Kernel implementation, Users:: Android," https://multipath-tcp.org/pmwiki.php/Users/Android, [retrieved: May 2017].

[5] A. Ford, C.Raiciu, M. Handley, S. Barre, and J. Iyengar, "Architectural Guidelines for Multipath TCP Development," IETF RFC 6182, Mar. 2011.

[6] A. Ford, C. Raiciu, M. Handley, and O. Bonaventure, "TCP Extensions for Multipath Operation with Multiple Addresses," IETF RFC 6824, Jan. 2013.

[7] C. Raiciu, M. Handley, and D. Wischik, "Coupled Congestion Control for Multipath Transport Protocols," IETF RFC 6356, Oct. 2011.

[8] C. Pearce and S. Zeadally, "Ancillary Impacts of Multipath TCP on Current and Future Network Security," IEEE Internet Computing, vol. 19, iss. 5, pp. 58-65, Sept.-Oct. 2015.

[9] T. Kato, M. Tenjin, R. Yamamoto, S. Ohzahata, and H. Shinbo, "Microscopic Approach for Experimental Analysis of Multipath TCP Throughput under Insufficient Send/Receive Socket Buffers," in Proc. 15th ICWI 2016, pp. 191-199, Oct. 2016.

[10] J. Ma, F. Le, A. Russo, and J. Lobo, "Detecting Distributed Signature-based Intrusion: The Case of Multi-Path Routing Attacks," in Proc. 2015 INFOCOM, pp. 558-566, Apr. 2015.

[11] J. Yang and S. Papavassiliou, "Improving Network Security by Multipath Traffic Dispersion," in Proc. MILCOM 2001, pp. 34-38, Oct. 2001.

[12] M. Nacher, C. Calafate, J. Cano, and P. Manzoni, "Evaluation of the Impact of Multipath Data Dispersion for Anonymous TCP Connections," In Proc. SecureWare 2007, pp. 24-29, Oct. 2007.

[13] A. Gurtov and T. Polishchuk, "Secure Multipath Transport For Legacy Internet Applications," In Proc. BROADNETS 2009, pp. 1-8, Sep. 2009.

[14] L. Apiecionek, W. Makowski, M. Sobczak, and T. Vince, "Multi Path Transmission Control Protocols as a security solution," in Proc. 2015 IEEE 13th International Scientific Conference on Informatics, pp. 27-31, Nov. 2015.

[15] A. Shamir, "How to share a secret," Communications of the ACM, vol. 22, no. 11, pp.612-613, Nov. 1979.

[16] X. Zhao, L. Li, G. Xue, and G. Silva, "Efficient Anonymous Message Submission," in Proc. INFOCOM 2012, pp.2228-2236, Mar. 2012.

[17] R. Ahlswede, N. Cai, S. Li, and R. Yeung, "Network Information Flow," IEEE Trans. Information Theory, vol. 46, no. 4, pp.1204-1216, Jul. 2000.

[18] M. Li, A. Lukyanenko, and Y. Cui, "Network Coding Based Multipath TCP," in Proc. Global Internet Symposium 2012, pp.25-30, Mar. 2012.

[19] ISO JTC 1/SC27, "ISO/IEC 10116: 2006 – Information technology – Security techniques – Modes of operation for an n-bit cipher," ISO Standards, 2006.

[20] Federal Information Processing Standards Publication 46-3, "Annoucing the Data Encryption Standard," Oct. 1999.

[21] Federal Information Processing Standards Publication 197, "Anouncing the Advanced Encryption Standard (AES)," Nov. 2001.

[22] PJC, "Distribution of Sample Program / Source / Software (in Japanese)," http://free.pjc.co.jp/index.html, [retrieved: May 2017].

Visual Risk Specification and Aggregation

Jasmin Wachter, Thomas Grafenauer, Stefan Rass
Institute of Applied Informatics, System Security Group
Universität Klagenfurt
email: {jasmin.wachter, thomas.grafenauer, stefan.rass}@aau.at

Abstract—**Quantitative risk assessments are commonly based on estimates of impacts and likelihoods regarding threats. Both quantities are usually uncertain, subjective and therefore difficult to estimate objectively and reliably. To ease the matter, assessments are often done in categorical terms, which avoids the issue of finding numeric figures where there is typically no accuracy, but at the same time makes an expression of uncertainty more difficult. If, for an impact or the likelihood, two categories apply (not necessarily to an equal extent) or neither of the offered options is a good match, how can an expert express this kind of uncertainty or fuzzyness? Moreover, how should we deal with multiple diverging opinions on the same risk? We propose a graphical approach to tackle both issues on a single ground, by casting a common visual risk representation form into a visual risk specification system. The proposed method aids the specification of risk parameters under uncertainty, as well as opinion pooling based on the so-obtained results.**

Keywords–uncertainty representation; expert elicitation; risk assessment; opinion pooling.

I. INTRODUCTION

The quantitative specification of risks typically involves stating beliefs about impact and likelihood of a given incident. Both such specifications strongly depend on domain expertise and can usually not be described in fixed terms. Instead, the recommended way of quantifying likelihoods and impacts is based on a few (commonly three to six) categories whose textual description is matched against the current incident or threat description. Treating impact and likelihood categories as defining a cartesian coordinate system, we arrive at the well-known risk matrices, which help prioritizing risks along the +45 degrees diagonal from lower risks (events with low impact and low likelihood) up to high priority risks with significant impact and large likelihood. An example of this technique is displayed in Figure 1.

Mostly, these pictures appear in later stages of a risk management process, at the risk evaluation stage when the relevant threats have been identified and classified in both dimensions. The specification of impacts and likelihood is done a priori, and not regulated to happen in any particular form by any standard (as ISO31000 [2], or its relatives [3] [4]). Neither are matters of consensus finding and opinion pooling subject of a deeper discussion or detailed recommendations. A suitable method for such data aggregation is the second contribution of this work.

While using an illustration like Figure 1 as an output format, why not use the same form of graphical display to *input* the same values in first place? In other words, when an expert is polled regarding its opinion about a given threat, this person will see which category describes best the threat regarding its impact and likelihood, and utter the respective categories as the risk assessment. It can hardly be expected that the ultimate choice is perfect, and there may be an almost equally good alternative category to describe the matter. The idea put forth in this work is letting the domain expert not point to a single category, but rather allow marking a whole range along both axes, to express uncertainty, or (in a different view), an "overlapping" membership to the categories at hand.

Such a flexible specification appears beneficial for several reasons:

- The expert is not forced to choose a specific category, possibly issuing a caveat regarding other alternative choices,
- The expert has an intuitive way of expressing uncertainty in the overall opinion, regarding both dimensions.

Organisation of this work: Section II puts this work in the context of selected existing risk management literature. Section III describes the visual method to specify risks, and Section IV develops an algorithm to compile several assessments (based on the previous input method) into a single risk estimate. Conclusions and an outlook to future work are given in Section V.

II. RELATED WORK

Though purely quantitative risk assessment is sometimes discouraged [5], an assessment in qualitative (categorical) terms is nevertheless standard in almost all risk management approaches (as [3] [2] [4] and many more). A typical issue with any such assessment is the specific domain [6] [7], different a priori knowledge of the involved experts as well as their risk attitudes, incentives [8] and personal history that all play a strong role in how risk is perceived (and hence assessed). Interestingly (though perhaps not too surprisingly),

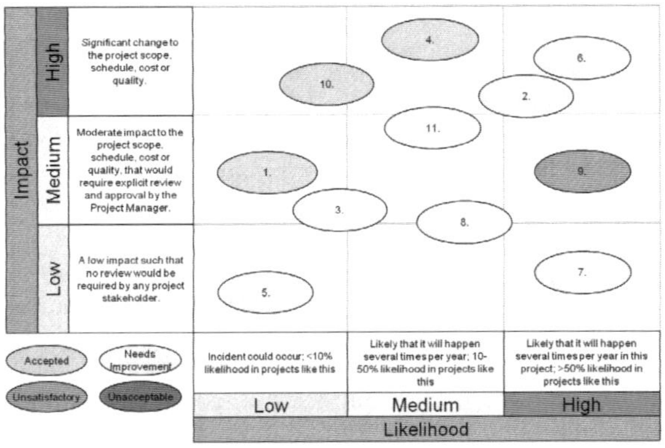

Figure 1. Example of Risk Bubble Chart [1]

the personality itself has only a relatively minor impact on how risk is assessed, as some empirical studies investigated [9]. Designing good questionnaires for empirical investigations is a challenging issue on its own, but left mostly unconstrained and without much explicit recommendations in risk management applications and standards. Likewise, the problem of consensus finding and compiling multiple opinions into a representative value received interest as an isolated problem [10] [11] [12], but should be an intrinsic part of the risk management process [13]. This is the gap that this work aims to fill, by proposing a first step towards a graphical way of risk specification as an alternative to existing textual and discussion based ways of getting these values. This step is mostly left open and a degree of freedom in the instantiation of various risk management methods [14] [15] [2]. Our work is intended as an auxiliary tool when using such standards.

III. Visual Risk Specification

To put this idea to work, we directly cast Figure 1 into an input system for risks, where the expert – upon speaking about a given threat – can simply draw a rectangle within 2D-area spanned by the categorical axes, where the projections onto the horizontal and vertical axis mark the matching categories. The extent of coverage expresses the degree of match, and the width/height of the rectangle corresponds to the uncertainty in the assessment (in both dimensions). Figure 2 shows an example of this technique.

Naturally, this process results in not only two but four values, which we denote as $impact_{\min}, impact_{\max}$ and $likelihood_{\min}, likelihood_{\max}$, and abbreviate as $i_{\min}, i_{\max}, \ell_{\min}, \ell_{\max}$. Both define ranges in which the expert considers the respective quantity to fall into. Constructing a statistical model from this information is straightforward: for analytic convenience, let us suppose that the expert's assessment and uncertainty is expressible by a Gaussian distribution, then based on these four values, the risk assessment would come to two Gaussians, denoted as X_I for the impact, and X_L for the likelihood, with distributions

$$X_I \sim \mathcal{N}\left(\frac{1}{2}(i_{\max}+i_{\min}), \frac{1}{3}(i_{\max}+i_{\min})\right), \quad (1)$$

$$X_L \sim \mathcal{N}\left(\frac{1}{2}(\ell_{\max}+\ell_{\min}), \frac{1}{3}(\ell_{\max}+\ell_{\min})\right), \quad (2)$$

where $X \sim \mathcal{N}(\mu, \sigma)$ denotes the distribution of the random variable with mean μ and standard deviation σ. Our choice makes the well-known 99.73% of probability mass of the Gaussian distribution fall into the given range, leaving a small residual inaccuracy allowance in the assessment. The overall uncertainty in the risk assessment is reflected in the area of the specified box; the larger the box, the less certain is the risk assessment.

Outlier Elimination

When compiling a risk picture, it is often useful to apply occasional corrections when risks are implausibly assessed relative to each other. Manually, this can be done by placing all boxes into the same picture to see outliers or do a fine-correction of risks in light of one another. Figure 3 shows an example.

IV. Pooling Several Expert Opinions

When considering several domain experts' opinions it can be a complex and tiresome task to agree upon a common risk quantity. Especially when data are sparse and risk assessments do not coincide, aggregating the final risk parameters can be challenging. Communicative methods, such as the Delphi technique or time-consuming meetings with discussion often do not lead to a consensus. Instead, mathematical pooling functions and formulas are employed to merge the opinions to a single value. This method called mathematical opinion pooling has a long tradition in statistics concerning forecast combination as well as decision making. There exist a large number of approaches and opinion pooling formulas, which can be found in [10] [11].

The easiest and most straight forward way of opinion pooling is done by simply averaging over all values, i.e., by computing the arithmetic mean. This approach is widespread and in practice often implemented blindly, as many decision makers are not aware there exist severe drawbacks of the arithmetic mean when dealing with expert opinions.

First of all, the arithmetic mean is very sensitive to outliers – especially when the sample size is small. A single extreme data point might cause a remarkable shift in the aggregated value and hence might distort the final result. Therefore, depending on the data, robust approaches and/or outlier detection and correction prior to risk aggregation should be considered. Secondly, when data are sparse smoothing might lead to more stable estimates and should thus not be neglected when aggregating data. Thirdly, the different levels of expertise and knowledge of the individual experts and their level of assurance or uncertainty regarding their risk quantity statements need to be taken into account. The arithmetic mean lacks all of the above points, yet they are crucial to the validity of the pooled result and thus need to be considered when aggregating individual expert opinions.

We, therefore, propose an intuitive iterative opinion pooling scheme that considers all aspects mentioned before. We remark that opinion pooling is generally a lossy form of data aggregation, in opposition to *lossless aggregation*, where the full data defines a whole distribution object. Decision theory in this generalized setting rests on stochastic orders, and comes with the appeal of inherently avoiding the aforementioned problems of consensus finding. Expanding this alternative branch of theory is, however, beyond the scope of this work (see [16] [17] for example).

A. Iterative Opinion Pooling Method

The input system for risk assessment described in Section III serves to specify the parameters of two Gaussian distributions – one for the impact X_I, and one for the likelihood X_L – with parameters $\mu_i = \frac{1}{2}(i_{\max}+i_{\min})$, $\sigma_i = \frac{1}{3}(i_{\max}+i_{\min})$, and $\mu_\ell = \frac{1}{2}(\ell_{\max}+\ell_{\min})$, $\sigma_\ell = \frac{1}{3}(\ell_{\max}+\ell_{\min})$ respectively. Thus, after all N experts contibuted with their risk assessment, four vectors of length N are obtained: $\boldsymbol{\mu}_i = (\mu_{i1}, \ldots, \mu_{iN})$, $\boldsymbol{\sigma}_i = (\sigma_{i1}, \ldots, \sigma_{iN})$ regarding the impact, and $\boldsymbol{\mu}_\ell$, $\boldsymbol{\sigma}_\ell$ for the likelihood respectively. For simplicity reasons, we will now drop the subscripts i or ℓ, as impact and likelihood will be pooled separately. The aim is to separately aggregate the impact and likelihood estimates, i.e., to obtain two Gaussian distributions representing the final risk distribution for the impact and the likelihood of a certain threat.

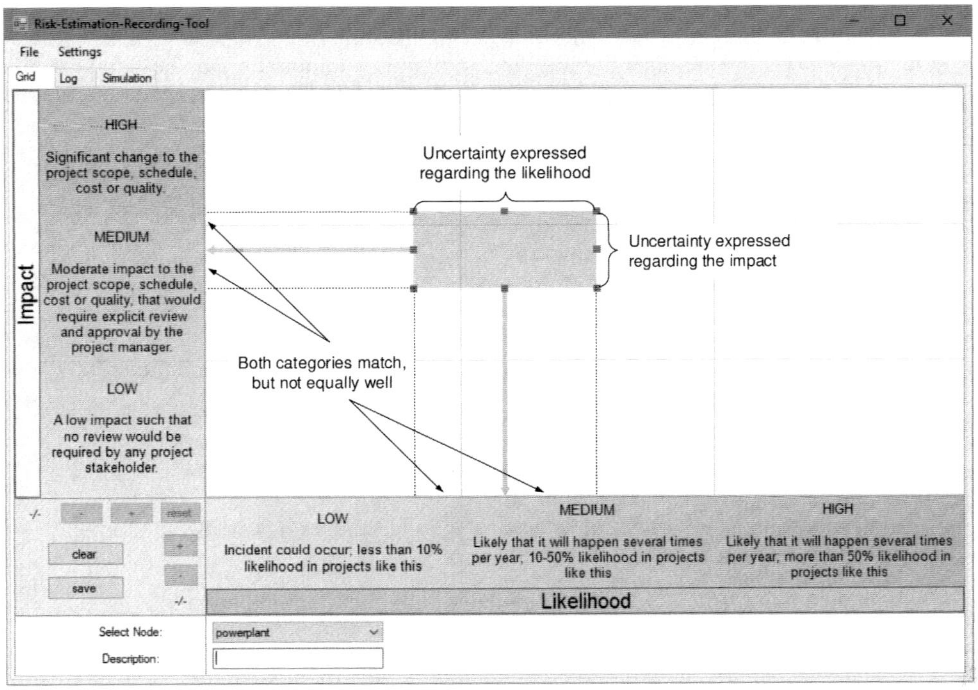

Figure 2. Graphical Risk Specification

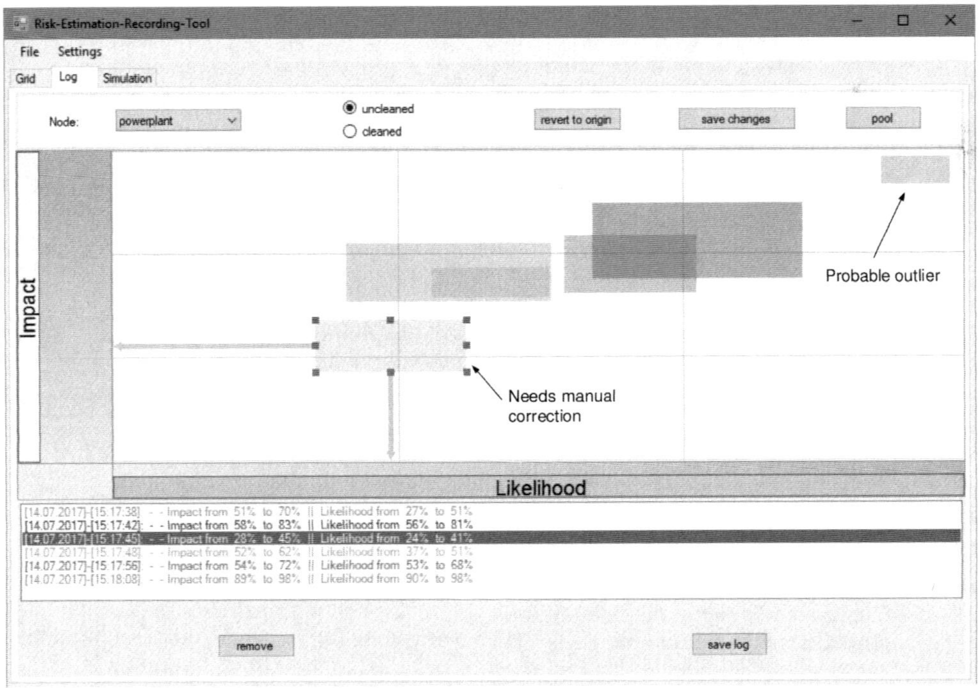

Figure 3. Manual Corrections

A possible solution to this is to consider the situation in a Bayesian framework: each expert $j \in 1, \ldots, N$ regards his estimates of the parameter of interest (e.g., impact) as prior knowledge of the parameter. Thus, the prior distribution hyperparameters are $\mu \overset{prior}{\sim} \mathcal{N}(\mu_j, \sigma_j)$. Expert j interprets the remaining experts distributions (μ_k, σ_k), $k \in \{1, \ldots, j-1, j+1, \ldots N\}$ as independent observations which make up the likelihood function. Applying Bayes rule, the posterior distribution of μ has the parameters

$$\sigma^p = \frac{1}{\sigma_j} + \sum_{k \neq j} \frac{1}{\sigma_k}, \tag{3}$$

$$\mu^p = \mu_j \cdot \frac{\sigma^p}{\sigma_j} + \sum_{k \neq j} \mu_k \cdot \frac{\sigma^p}{\sigma_k}, \tag{4}$$

and $\mu \overset{posterior}{\sim} \mathcal{N}(\mu^p, \sigma^p)$. Note that for symmetry reasons all σ^p and μ^p are the same, no matter which expert rating $j \in \{1, \ldots, N\}$ is chosen as prior distribution. Thus, the expert's posterior distribution represents the aggregated distribution for the quantity of interest. This way, each expert's (un)certainty regarding their risk assessment is incorporated in the pooling process. Hence, it is ensured that risk estimates with very high levels of assurance are given more weight than those having very low levels of assurance.

Although this method is quite intuitive and possesses many convenient mathematical properties, it does not incorporate any kind of smoothing to the data.

An alternative method, which is described as consensual opinion pooling in [12], iteratively smooths the data with a discrete inverse distance kernel until convergence to the same value. Epistemically, their procedure can be interpreted in the following way: in every iteration, each expert updates their belief about the unknown parameter by incorporating information of all experts (including themselves). Therefore, in every iteration t, each expert $j \in \{1, \ldots, N\}$ updates their belief μ_j on μ as a linear combination of all risk assessments: $\mu_j^{(t)} = \sum_{k=1}^{N} c_{kj}^{(t)} \cdot \mu_k^{(t-1)}$ with $c_{kj}^{(t)}$ inversely proportional to the distance of $\mu_k^{(t-1)}$ and $\mu_j^{(t-1)}$,

$$c_{kj}^{(t)} = \frac{\alpha_j^{(t)}}{\epsilon + d(\mu_k^{(t-1)}, \mu_j^{(t-1)})} \quad \text{with} \quad \alpha_j^{(t)} = \frac{1}{\sum_{k=1}^{N} c_{kj}^{(t)}} \tag{5}$$

and $\epsilon > 0$. This way, each expert assigns more weight to those experts, whose risk assessment are close to their own, than to experts whose risk assessments deviate strongly from their own. After a number of iterations a "consensus" among all experts is reached. While this method is very intuitive, it does not include any weighting of the experts' estimates regarding their assurance. Therefore, we suggest an adapted iterative method, which interpolates between the two above mentioned methods.

In the algorithm shown in Figure 4, in each step the risk statements are smoothed based on a discrete inverse-distance kernel and updated according to Bayes rule. This way, the data are not only smoothed, but the assurance of each expert about their risk judgement is considered too. The Bayes update ensures that risk estimates with very high levels of assurance are given more weight than those having very low certainty, while smoothing gives more weight to expert

Data: $\boldsymbol{\mu}^{(0)} = (\mu_1^{(0)}, \ldots, \mu_N^{(0)})$, $\boldsymbol{\sigma}^{(0)} = (\sigma_1^{(0)}, \ldots, \sigma_N^{(0)})$, $\epsilon > 0$, $\delta > 0$
Result: μ^p – the pooled value for μ; σ^p – the pooled value for the standard deviation; w – the vector of weights assigned to each expert.
$W \leftarrow I_N$;
while $\|\boldsymbol{\mu}\|_{\max} > \delta$ **do**
  for $j = 1$ *to* N **do**
    for $k = 1$ *to* N **do**
      $c_{kj}^{(t)} \leftarrow \frac{\alpha_j^{(t)}}{\epsilon + d(\mu_j^{(t-1)}, \mu_k^{(t-1)})}$;
    end
    $\sigma_j^{2^{(t)}} \leftarrow \left(N \cdot \sum_{k=1}^{N} \frac{c_{kj}^{(t)}}{\sigma_k^{2^{(t-1)}}}\right)^{-1}$;
    $\mu_j^{(t)} \leftarrow \sigma_j^{2^{(t)}} \cdot N \cdot \sum_{k=1}^{N} \mu_k^{(t-1)} \frac{c_{kj}^{(t)}}{\sigma_k^{2^{(t-1)}}}$;
  end
  $\tilde{W}^{(t)} \leftarrow \left(\sigma_j^{2^{(t)}} \cdot N \cdot \frac{c_{kj}^{(t)}}{\sigma_k^{2^{(t-1)}}}\right)_{j=1,\ldots N,\ k=1,\ldots,N}$;
  $W \leftarrow \tilde{W}^{(t)} \cdot W$;
  $\boldsymbol{\sigma}^{2^{(t)}} \leftarrow \frac{\boldsymbol{\sigma}^{2^{(t)}}}{\sum_{j=1}^{N} \sigma_k^{2^{(t+1)}}}$;
  $t \leftarrow t + 1$;
end
$\mu^p \leftarrow \mu_1^{(t)}$; $w \leftarrow W_1$; $\sigma^p \leftarrow \sqrt{\sum_{k=1}^{N} \sigma_k^{2^{(0)}} \cdot w_k^2}$;

Figure 4. Iterative Opinion Pooling method with weights

opinions that are located in the center than to extreme data points. This procedure is iterated until all risk statements have converged to one value, which yields the aggregated risk. Note that the pooling algorithm (Figure 4) interpolates between the two above mentioned methods: if $\epsilon \to \infty$ this method coincides with the Bayes update, whereas equal variances, i.e., $\sigma_1^2 = \cdots = \sigma_N^2$, yield the consensual opinion pooling.

Note that $\left(\sigma_j^{2^{(t)}}\right)_{t \in \mathbb{N}}$ is a monotonically decreasing null sequence for all $j = 1, \ldots, N$, which may lead to numerical instability in the computation process. To avoid this, we added the command $\boldsymbol{\sigma}^{2^{(t+1)}} \leftarrow \frac{\boldsymbol{\sigma}^{2^{(t+1)}}}{\sum_{j=1}^{N} \sigma_j^{2^{(t+1)}}}$ to normalize the sum of the variances in each step. It can be shown that the procedure converges and that $\lim_{t \to \infty} \mu_1^{(t)} = \cdots = \lim_{t \to \infty} \mu_N^{(t)}$ holds. In every iteration, the entry w_{jk} in matrix of weights W corresponds to the weights expert j has so far assigned to all experts $k = 1, \ldots, N$. Note that W converges to a matrix with equal rows. Thus, the final weights of all experts coincide. By default, we choose the first row of W, $w = W_1$ as a final weighting vector.

B. Numerical Example

Assume four experts were asked to quantify the likelihood of a certain threat. Let $\boldsymbol{\mu}^{(0)} = (0.26, 0.255, 0.43, 0.315)^T$ and $\boldsymbol{\sigma}^{(0)} = (0.03, 0.018\dot{3}, 0.0\dot{3}, 0.028\dot{3})^T$ respectively. In figure 5 the densities are depicted. By choosing $\epsilon = 1$, we then obtain $\mu^p = 0.2922$ as pooled mean value for the likelihood, $\sigma^p = 0.0127$ as standard deviation and the weight vector $w = (0.1798, 0.4804, 0.1386, 0.2012)^T$.

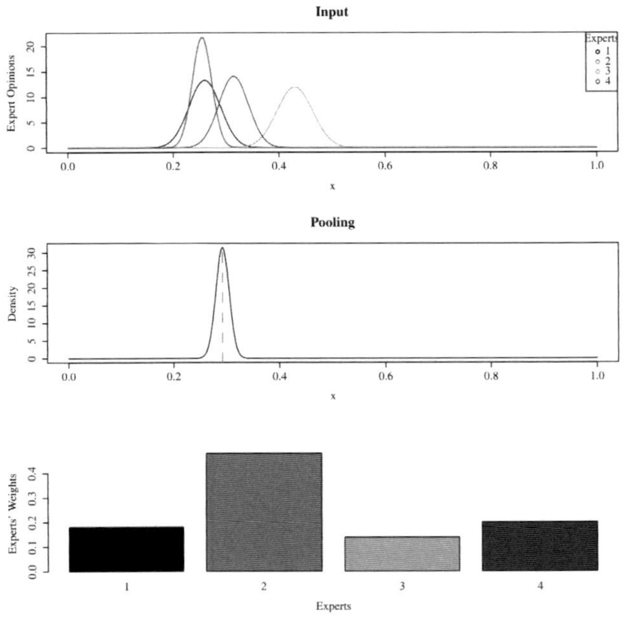

Figure 5. Numerical Example – Opinion Pooling of four Opinions

TABLE I. POOLED VALUES DEPENDING ON THE CHOICE OF THE TUNING PARAMETER

ϵ	μ^P	σ^P	w_1	w_2	w_3	w_4
0.001	0.2792	0.0130	0.211	0.564	0.083	0.142
0.01	0.2833	0.0129	0.201	0.534	0.099	0.166
0.022	0.2852	0.0128	0.195	0.519	0.106	0.179
0.1	0.2887	0.0127	0.187	0.496	0.120	0.197
1	0.2922	0.0127	0.180	0.480	0.139	0.201
5	0.2929	0.0127	0.179	0.478	0.143	0.200
10	0.2931	0.0127	0.178	0.478	0.144	0.200

Note that the choice of the tuning parameter ϵ has a strong impact on the result. Depending on the desired degree of smoothness ϵ can be increased or decreased. Table I illustrates how different values for ϵ result in different outcomes regarding the opinion pooling. We suggest, however, not to oversmooth the data, and thus keep the size of ϵ reasonable. A handy approach is to use a modified version of Silverman's rule of thumb, i.e., $\epsilon \approx 1.06 \cdot \bar{\sigma} \cdot N^{-1/5}$, where $\bar{\sigma}$ denotes the arithmetic mean of $\boldsymbol{\sigma}$. In the given numeric example Silverman's rule yields $\epsilon \approx 0.02209$.

We suggest the opinion pooling method to be implemented in the visual risk specification. This way, the whole process from data collection, data correction and smoothing, to risk aggregation is combined in a single tool. In Figure 6 it is depicted how the experts' assessments are compiled into a single value.

V. Conclusion and Future Work

Specifying risks is in any case a matter of dealing with subjectivity and uncertainty. The application of statistical methods is especially challenging in this field, since "risk" is not an observable property of some physical process (as common elsewhere when statistics or probability theory is applied). Nonetheless, the issue is one of reasoning under uncertainty, and specifying this uncertainty in first place should

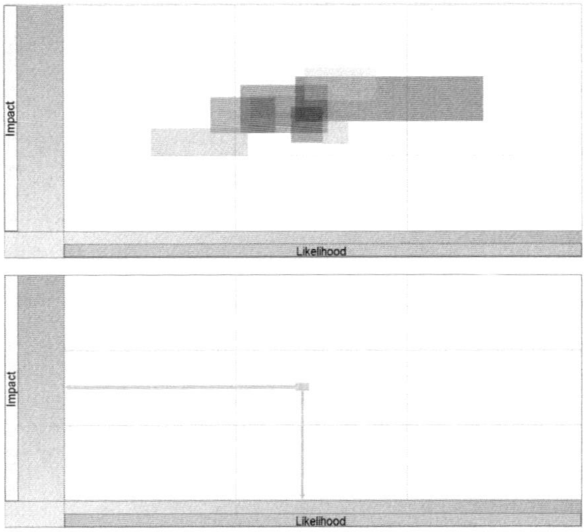

Figure 6. Graphical Risk Specification (top) and Aggregation (bottom)

be consistent with how the results are presented. This brings us to the proposed method of turning a risk presentation mechanism into an input system, and framing important tasks like data correction and opinion pooling into this approach. The techniques put forth here straightforwardly apply for one-dimensional quantities, such as when only likelihood or only impact should be elicited. Future steps mainly concern outlier analysis and way to automate outlier elimination. This entails in particular an analysis of bias and non-inferiority of the outlier-corrected risk data sets, and a more detailed stochastic model of risk estimation, where the risk is an unknown quantity, about which only correlated (independent, yet not necessarily identically distributed) random quantities can be measured (i.e., the subjective estimates).

Acknowledgment

This work was done in the context of the project "Cross Sectoral Risk Management for Object Protection of Critical Infrastructures (CERBERUS)", supported by the Austrian Research Promotion Agency under grant no. 854766.

References

[1] S. De Bock, "Effective risk management for complex it projects," https://sdb-plus.com/2012/05/15/effective-risk-management-for-complex-it-projects/, May 2012, [retrieved: July 14th, 2017].

[2] I. S. Organisation, "Iso/iec 31000: Risk management – principles and guidelines," 2009.

[3] Information Systems Audit and Control Association, "Cobit 5," 2012, [retrieved: August 11th, 2017]. [Online]. Available: http://www.isaca.org/cobit/pages/default.aspx

[4] C. J. Alberts and A. Dorofee, Managing Information Security Risks: The Octave Approach. Boston, MA, USA: Addison-Wesley Longman Publishing Co., Inc, 2002.

[5] I. Münch, "Wege zur Risikobewertung," in DACH Security 2012, P. Schartner and J. Taeger, Eds. syssec, 2012, pp. 326–337.

[6] E. U. Weber, A.-R. Blais, and N. E. Betz, "A domain-specific risk-attitude scale: Measuring risk perceptions and risk behaviors," Journal of Behavioral Decision Making, vol. 15, no. 4, 2002, pp. 263–290.

[7] C. S. Weber, "Determinants of risk tolerance," International Journal of Economics, Finance and Management Sciences, vol. 2, no. 2, 2014, p. 143.

[8] C. F. Camerer and R. M. Hogarth, "The effects of financial incentives in experiments: A review and capital-labor-production framework," Journal of Risk and Uncertainty, vol. 19, no. 1/3, 1999, pp. 7–42.

[9] J. Brenot, S. Bonnefous, and C. Marris, "Testing the cultural theory of risk in france," Risk Analysis, vol. 18, no. 6, 1998, pp. 729–739.

[10] F. Dietrich and C. List, "Probabilistic opinion pooling," October 2014, [retrieved: August 11th, 2017]. [Online]. Available: http://philsci-archive.pitt.edu/11349/

[11] A. O'Hagan and J. J. Forster, "Kendall's advanced theory of statistics, volume 2b: Bayesian inference," 2004.

[12] A. Carvalho and K. Larson, "A consensual linear opinion pool," in Proceedings of the Twenty-Third International Joint Conference on Artificial Intelligence, ser. IJCAI '13. AAAI Press, 2013, pp. 2518–2524.

[13] S. Rass, J. Wachter, S. Konig, and S. Schauer, "Subjektive Risikobewertung – Über Datenerhebung und Opinion Pooling," in DACH Security 2017, P. Schartner and J. Taeger, Eds. syssec, 2017.

[14] h. . https://www.coso.org/Pages/ermupdate.aspx. y. . . m. . D. n. . r. Committee of Sponsoring Organizations of the Treadway Commission, title = COSO Enterprise Risk Management – Integrated Framework Update.

[15] J. Chittenden, J. van Bon, and S. Polter, Risk Management: A Management Guide based on M_O_R, ser. Best Practice. Zaltbommel: Van Haren Pub, 2006.

[16] S. Rass, S. Konig, and S. Schauer, "Decisions with uncertain consequences-a total ordering on loss-distributions," PLoS ONE, vol. 11, no. 12, 2016, p. e0168583.

[17] M. Shaked and J. G. Shanthikumar, Stochastic Orders. Springer, 2006.

Addressing Complex Problem Situations in Critical Infrastructures using Soft Systems Analysis: The CS-AWARE Approach

Thomas Schaberreiter*, Chris Wills†, Gerald Quirchmayr* and Juha Röning‡
*Faculty of Computer Science
University of Vienna (Vienna, Austria)
e-mail: thomas.schaberreiter@univie.ac.at
e-mail: gerald.quirchmayr@univie.ac.at
†CARIS Research Ltd. (Fowey, United Kingdom)
e-mail: ccwills@carisresearch.co.uk
‡Faculty of Information Technology and Electrical Engineering
University of Oulu (Oulu, Finland)
e-mail: juha.roning@oulu.fi

***Abstract*—In a world in which large-scale cyber attacks are the norm rather than the exception, the need for cybersecurity gains in importance every day. Current cybersecurity solutions are often not taking the holistic approach that would be required to provide comprehensive security to their users (for example, strategic/critical infrastructure, large organizations, small and medium-sized enterprises (SMEs) or public institutions). A new way of thinking about cybersecurity is required: Cooperation and collaboration among individual actors as a way to improve the security situation for society and economy as a whole is a promising approach. In the European Union, the legal framework that is currently developing (like the network and information security (NIS) directive), recognizes the need for cooperation and collaboration among individual actors to improve cybersecurity. Information sharing is one of the key elements of the NIS directive. In this paper, we present a system and dependency analysis based on soft systems thinking that is able to capture the relations between assets and its internal and external dependencies in the complex systems of organizations like critical infrastructures or other organizations that base their operations on complex systems and interactions. The analysis is done in a socio-technological manner; the human aspect of the systems is considered as important as the technical or organizational aspects. As a use case, we present CS-AWARE, a European H2020 project which relies on the presented system and dependency analysis method as a core concept for providing a cybersecurity solution that is in line with the cooperative and collaborative efforts of the NIS directive.**

Keywords–Cybersecurity; Critical Infrastructures; System Analysis; Soft Systems Methodology; Socio-technological Analysis; Cyber Situational Awareness; Information Sharing.

I. INTRODUCTION

Cybersecurity is one of today's most challenging societal security problems, affecting both individuals and organisations, such as strategic/critical infrastructures, large commercial enterprises, SMEs, non-governmental organizations (NGOs) or governmental institutions. Deliberate or accidental threats and attacks threaten digitally administered data and digitally handled processes. Sensitive data leaks can ruin the reputation of companies and individuals, and the interruption of digital processes that organisations rely upon in their daily work flow can cause severe economic disadvantages. Reaching beyond the technology-focused boundaries of classical information technology (IT) security, cybersecurity strongly interrelates with organisational and behavioural aspects of IT operations, and the need to comply with the current and actively developing legal and regulatory framework for cybersecurity. For example, the European Union (EU) recently passed the NIS directive that obliges member states to get in line with the EU cybersecurity efforts. Most EU member states and the EU itself have a cybersecurity strategy in place which will eventually lead to the introduction of laws and regulations that fulfil cybersecurity requirements. One of the main aspects of the NIS directive, as well as the European cybersecurity strategies is cooperation and collaboration among relevant actors in cybersecurity. Enabling technologies for coordination and cooperation efforts are situational awareness and information sharing. Situational awareness in this context is a runtime mechanism to gather cybersecurity relevant data from an IT infrastructure and visualise the current situation for a user or operator. Information sharing refers to the ability to share this information with cybersecurity information sharing communities, like the NIS relevant authorities. In the long term, information sharing will improve cybersecurity sustainably and benefit society and economy as a whole.

One of the major aspects of information sharing to facilitate collaboration and cooperation, is a proper understanding of the cybersecurity relevant aspects within an organization's systems. This is a complex and often neglected task that will, as we argue in this paper, greatly improve the cybersecurity of organizations in the context of cybersecurity situational awareness and cooperative/collaborative strategies towards cybersecurity. We propose a system and dependency analysis methodology to analyse the environment and: (a) Identify the assets and dependencies within the system and how to monitor them; (b) capture not only technological aspects, but the socio-technical relations within the organisation; (c) identify external information sources that could either be provided by official and cybersecurity specific sources (for example, legal/regulatory framework, standardisation, cybersecurity information sharing communities), or more general publicly available information relating to cybersecurity (for example, social networks or twitter); (d) provide the results in a form that can be utilized by support tools. We base our work around established and well proven methods related to systems thinking, the soft systems methodology (SSM) and PROTOS-MATINE/GraphingWiki.

The paper is organized as follows: Section II discusses background and related work, Section III details our system and dependency analysis approach. In Section IV, an application example in the context of CS-AWARE, a European H2020 project which uses the presented system and dependency analysis as a core part of its cybersecurity solution, is given. Section V discusses the approach in a wider context and Section VI concludes the paper.

II. Related Work

In December 2015, The European Parliament, the European Council and the European Commission agreed on the European NIS directive as the first EU wide legislation on cybersecurity [1]. The directive lays down the obligations of member states concerning NIS. Most notably for this work, it requires the implementation of proper national mechanisms for incident prevention and response, in addition to information sharing and cooperation mechanisms. The NIS directive is the main action stemming from the EU cybersecurity strategy [2], which emphasises the need for a decentralized prevention and response to cyber incidents and attacks. By now, most EU countries have put a national cybersecurity strategy in place [3] that is in line with many actions proposed by the NIS directive. Coordination and information sharing are key elements of the strategy, with the requirement for national NIS authorities, national law enforcement and defence authorities to interact with each other, as well as their EU counterparts. International cooperation and coordination is envisioned at the EU level. On the standardisation front, the ISO/IEC 27000 [4] standard is the first in a series of standards on information security management that have provided organisations with a best practice framework for assessing security risks and implementing security controls as countermeasures. Similarly, the privacy focused ISO/IEC 29100 [5] standard provides a framework to help organisations to manage and protect personally identifiable information. In 2011 the European standardisation organisations CEN, CENELEC and ETSI have formed the cybersecurity coordination group (CSCG), which was converted to the focus group on cybersecurity in 2016 [6], in order to undertake the strategic evaluation of IT security, cybersecurity and NIS standardisation.

A systems analysis methodology that will be used in this work is the Soft Systems Methodology developed by Peter Checkland [7][8]. The key thought behind the soft systems methodology is that it is hard to completely analyse and describe a complex system, especially if human interaction plays a key role. The SSM represents an analysis methodology that aims to achieve an holistic understanding of the system while at the same time only focusing on the actual problems at hand. Soft Systems Methodology has been used in an extraordinarily wide variety of problem domains as diverse as knowledge management in the building industry [9], to evaluating government policy to promote technological innovation in the electricity sector [10]. In the case of the building industry example, the tacit knowledge held by staff involved in the tendering process was made explicit by the application of SSM. In the case of the electricity supply industry, SSM was used understand how better to to promote and foster technological innovation in the sector.

The PROTOS-MATINE methodology [11] is another approach that relates to systems thinking. While the SSM focuses on understanding complex systems and processes by interviewing its users, PROTOS-MATINE takes the standpoint that a truly holistic view on complex situations can only be achieved if as many relevant information sources as possible (e.g., technical, organisational, human on all organizational levels as well as external and publicly available information), are combined to create a complete picture and eliminate discrepancies between information from different sources. The key to PROTOS-MATINE is that collected information from different sources is set in context to each other and graphically processed and visualized to make it simple for domain experts to identify discrepancies in information coming from different sources. For this purpose, GraphingWiki [12], a graphical extension to the MoinMoin Wiki, was developed to visualize dependencies between semantic data collected in Wiki pages in the context of PROTOS-MATINE. The methodology was used in many case studies, for example for highlighting vulnerabilities in anti-virus software [13] and for a socio-technological analysis of a VoIP (voice over IP) provider [14]. In [15], the methodology was extended for analysing complex systems in the critical infrastructure context, where the analysis goal is to achieve a dependency graph of critical infrastructure assets, dependencies between the assets and measures to observe those assets (base measurements).

III. Soft Systems Analysis in the Context of Cybersecurity for Complex Systems

The system and dependency analysis proposed in this paper is seen as the basis for the automatic incident detection and cybersecurity situational awareness efforts of future cybersecurity initiatives, as discussed in the related work. The objective is to identify in the specific organizational context what needs cybersecurity protection and what are the main threats it needs protection from. More specifically, this means that the challenge for system and dependency analysis is to identify the assets within an organisation and their internal and external dependencies in order to be able to protect them from cybersecurity threats. Observable information sources that can be used to determine the on-line state of those assets need to be identified to allow for monitoring and detecting abnormal behaviour, thus describing the security state. Furthermore, the goal of the system and dependency analysis is to identify external information sources that can provide information to help detect and classify security threats correctly. Those information sources can be dedicated cybersecurity information providers like, for example, computer emergency response teams (CERTs) or other threat and vulnerability databases, or they can be publicly available information sources via, for example, platforms like Twitter, Facebook or Google+. The usage of open source intelligence (OSINT) has been proved to be valuable before in other contexts like disaster management. Sail Labs Media Mining System is an example of a system which makes use of freely available information. It aims to allow accurate situational analysis of crisis locations by analysing different relevant data feeds. It gathers information from multiple sources including television, radio and various Internet sources and uses data mining techniques to extract information about the content [16].

Since technology is only one factor in cybersecurity, the system and dependency analysis is designed to capture and monitor the socio-technical nature of an IT infrastructure, taking into account the human, organisational and technological factors, as well as other legal/regulatory and business related factors that may contribute to the cybersecurity in a specific context. As can be seen in Figure 1, systems thinking is a way of looking at some part of the world, by choosing to regard it as a system, using a framework of perspectives to understand its complexity and undertake some process of change. The key concepts are holism - looking at things as a whole and not as isolated components and systemic - treating things as systems, using systems ideas and adopting a systems perspective.

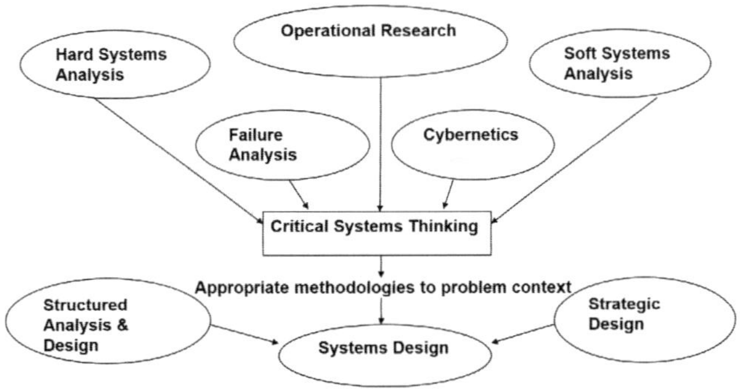

Figure 1. Systems thinking - The systems approach

Two concepts of systems thinking are hard systems thinking and soft systems thinking. Hard systems design is based on systems analysis and systems engineering. It assumes that the world is comprised of systems that we can describe and that these systems can be understood through rational analysis. It is based on the assumption that it is possible to identify a "technically optimal" engineering solution for any system and that we can then write software to create the "solution". Hard systems design assumes that there is a clear consensus as to the nature of the problem that is to be solved. It is unable to depict, understand or make provisions for "soft" variables such as people, culture, politics or aesthetics. It is based on the assumption that it is possible to identify a "technically optimal" engineering solution for any system. It assumes that those commissioning the system have the ability and power to implement the system. While hard systems design is highly appropriate for domains involving engineering systems structures that require little input from people, the complex systems and interactions in critical infrastructures or other organizations - especially with cybersecurity in mind - usually do not allow this type of analysis. Hard systems design is inappropriate and unsuitable for analysing human activity systems that require constant interaction with, and intervention from people. Such systems are complicated, fuzzy, messy and ill defined and are typified by unclear situations, differing viewpoints and unclear objectives, containing politics, emotion and social drama. This is the type of system domain for which a SSM design approach is highly appropriate and to which it should be applied. That is not to say that the SSM approach cannot or should not be used in the design of engineering systems and structures, indeed one of the authors has used this approach very successfully in many complex and diverse problem domains. For example, SSM has been used by one of the authors in the design of naval command and control systems for the British Navy and in the design of system architectures for automated fare collection in very large light railway and mass transit operations.

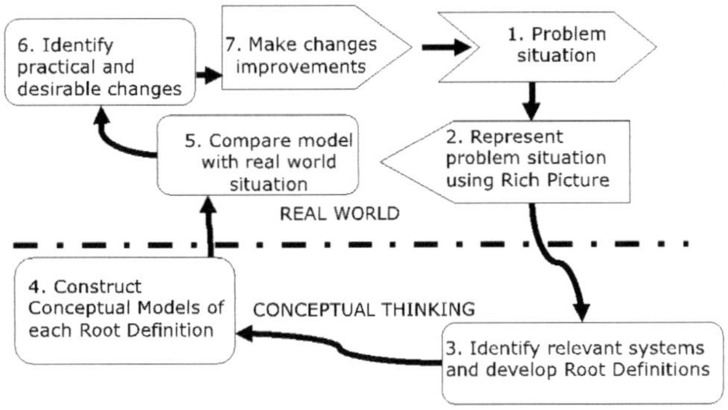

Figure 2. Soft systems design

An overview of the stages of SSM is set out in Figure 2. The SSM methodology has 7 steps: (1) Enter the problem situation; (2) Express the problem situation; (3) Formulate root definitions of systems behaviour; (4) Build conceptual models of systems in root definitions; (5) Compare models with real-world situations; (6) Define possible and feasible changes; (7) Take action to improve the problem situation. A detailed description of the approach is beyond the scope of this paper, however, reader may wish to refer to Checkland's work [7][8]. In this work, we will focus on the earlier steps of the SSM that deal with the system analysis and problem definition (specifically, steps 1-4). One key element of this phase is that systems stakeholders (users, managers, administrators, etc.) are engaged in workshops to define the problems they are facing, since those who are using systems on a daily basis are the ones that have the most information about it. Since this is not explicit knowledge, but tacit knowledge, it is important to create an environment that facilitates information sharing. The SSM utilizes rich pictures for this purpose, and depicting the problem in a rich picture is a key stage early in the process. Rich pictures are a representation of the problem domain. They utilize "cartoon-style" techniques to portray a complex situation and concentrate on:

- Structure - Key individuals, organisations etc.
- Process - What could be or is happening?
- Climate - Pressures, attitudes, cultures, threats etc.

An example of a Rick Picture depicting a malfunctioning airline passenger check-in system appears in Figure 3, outlining different viewpoints in case the system goes off-line.

Rich pictures are a tool for understanding where we are and are a mix of drawings, pictures, symbols and text. They represent a particular situation or issue and they are depicted from viewpoint(s) of the person or people who drew them. They can both record and evoke insight into a situation. Rich pictures are pictorial 'summaries' of a situation, embracing both the physical, conceptual and emotional aspects of a problem situation. They can depict complicated situations or issues, and relevant systems are identified from the rich picture. These systems are described in Root Definitions, which are then used in conjunction with the rich pictures to develop Conceptual Models. These are formed from the actions stated or implied in the Root Definition(s). Of course, each rich picture may be interpreted from quite differing 'world view

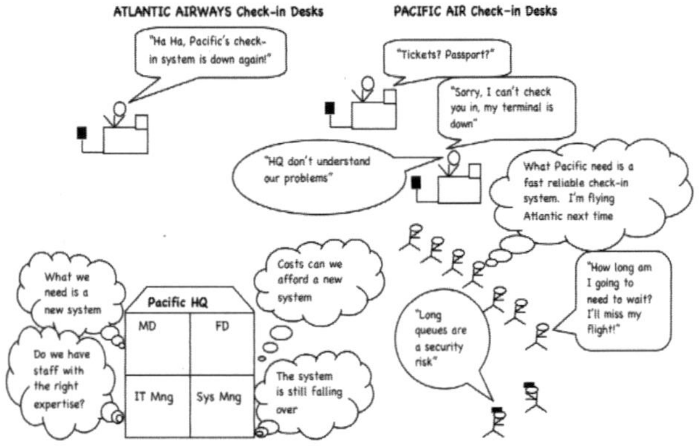

Figure 3. Rich picture of an airline check-in system

points'. A Conceptual Model is like an activity sequence diagram, but is aimed at representing a conceptual system as defined by the logic of the Root Definition and not just a set of activities.

The role of PROTOS-MATINE and GraphingWiki in this proposed analysis method is to complement the information gathering effort in the user workshops with information from other sources, and provide a solid base for discussion in those workshops through visualization. The main additional sources are expected to be legal requirements and regulatory efforts like the NIS directive; cybersecurity relevant standardization like the ISO/IEC 27000 family of standards and information about relevant and current risks and threats via official sources like CERTs, or more dynamic information sources like social media. Where relevant, the information received via rich pictures from the workshop participants can easily be complemented by more detailed information available such as, for example, technical manuals, business continuity plans or disaster recovery plans. One of the capabilities of GraphingWiki is to instantly link gathered information to other relevant information and thus allowing to update the graphical representation of the analysed system as soon as new information arrives. We hope to utilize this feature in the user workshops to create more dynamic discussions and give even more incentive to the participants to create a system model that is as close to reality as possible.

The expected result of the proposed system and dependency analysis will be a dependency graph containing an organizations security relevant or critical assets and the dependencies among them. Furthermore, observable measurements that are able to determine the security state of those assets are identified and associated to them. Though GraphingWiki this dependency graph is in digital form and can be further utilized as the basis for advanced cybersecurity situational awareness and monitoring services. One example of such a service will be given in the next section.

IV. The CS-AWARE Approach

CS-AWARE is a European H2020 project that was funded by the European Union under the project number 740723. The aim of the project is to improve the cybersecurity situation in local public administrations (LPAs). While the project is focused on LPAs, the ideas and methods developed in this project are applicable to any organizations that rely on complex systems, interactions and procedures (like strategic/critical infrastructures, large organizations or SMEs).

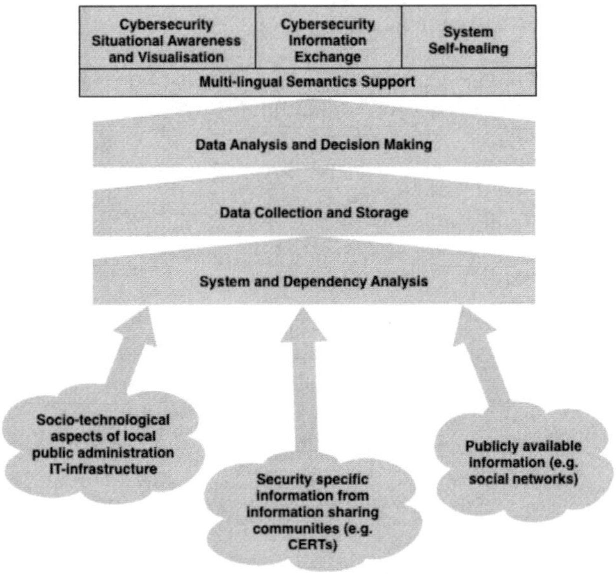

Figure 4. CS-AWARE overall concept

As can be seen in Figure 4, the main building blocks of the CS-AWARE solution are the system and dependency analysis, data collection and data analysis to achieve the project's goals of cybersecurity situational awareness, cybersecurity information exchange and system self-healing. The proposed solution aims at improving automated situational awareness in small- to medium-sized IT infrastructures, however it is expected that the same principals would also apply to large organizations or critical infrastructures. The system and dependency analysis presented in the previous section is an integral part of two project phases. Besides the actual system and dependency analysis, which will be conducted according to the methodology presented in Section III (Steps 1-4 of the SSM as well as PROTOS-MATINE/GraphingWiki related aspects), it will provide the main input for the self-healing component, based on steps 5-7 of the SSM.

The core idea of the CS-AWARE project is to automate the cybersecurity effort of organizations as much as possible, and provide an on-line situational awareness tool that aims to base its recommendations on a holistic view of an organization's IT systems and dependencies, but also on the cybersecurity situation in general (for example by observing the risk and threat landscape). The end users of the CS-AWARE solution are expected to be the people responsible for cybersecurity in an organization, such as the chief security officer (CSO), or system administrators. CS-AWARE is a decision support system that will allow its users to detect cybersecurity incidents quickly and identify the affected systems, since the key assets and security relevant dependencies have been identified during system and dependency analysis. Countermeasures can be initiated by the people responsible for cybersecurity in a timely manner. Besides manual countermeasures, CS-AWARE includes a self-healing component that is closely tied to the system and dependency analysis. The later steps of the SSM (especially steps 5-7) are concerned with defining solutions to the problems identified during analysis. In CS-AWARE one focus point will be to identify and develop possible countermeasures to cybersecurity threats and define policies and procedures that can be invoked if such a threat materializes. Those policies and procedures will be utilized by the self-healing component and can be configured to be invoked automatically if a threat materializes. This will allow the system, depending on the scenario, to prevent or mitigate the damage and/or recover from the incident.

The intelligent and fully automated part of the CS-AWARE project are the *data collection and storage* and *the analysis and decision making* components. Based on the system and dependency analysis results, the base measurements from internal and external sources are observed and when relevant data points are collected, pre-processed and stored. The data analysis component is capable of detecting suspicious behaviour like threat and attack patterns in the data sets it receives and will classify and rank them accordingly, as an input to the decision support in the situational awareness and visualization component. The accuracy of the decision making component will depend on the cooperation and collaboration efforts and the quality of data that is provided by information sharing authorities. It is envisaged that threat detection can achieve highly accurate unsupervised results once cybersecurity information exchange is an established concept and can provide accurate information relating to cybersecurity threats and attack patterns.

The *cybersecurity situational awareness and visualization* component is the user interface to the CS-AWARE solution. It will visualize the security relevant aspects of an organizations socio-technological systems, based on the dependency graph received during system and dependency analysis. State changes triggered by the decision making component will cause a visualization of the affected components and its dependencies. Possible countermeasures will be suggested and self-healing procedures can be configured and invoked, where relevant.

The *cybersecurity information exchange* is the connection point to the cybersecurity information sharing authorities, for example NIS competent authorities like national or EU CERTs. While cybersecurity information sharing is currently still in its infancy, it is seen as one of the major building blocks to a safer cyberspace in future. The CS-AWARE solution will on the one hand, benefit from the information provided by those authorities and on the other hand, provide information about newly detected and unmatched incidents (like threat or attack patterns). It is assumed that with more and more tools that provide capabilities for organizations to participate in security related information sharing, the benefit of sharing information for the common good will become evident and encourage organizations to engage in cybersecurity related information sharing. Cybersecurity information exchange would in that case become one of the most important information sources for cybersecurity awareness and threat detection.

In order to deal with the expected language barriers and usability concerns in the context of European local public administrations, the main focus of the CS-AWARE project, *multi-lingual semantics support* will be part of this project's solution. Where relevant, security related information coming from within the end user organizations, or information from external information sources, will be automatically translated to benefit from the information of different cultural contexts.

The project includes two pilot scenarios in the LPA context: the municipalities of Larissa (Greece) and Rome (Italy). This set-up will allow us to develop tailored system and dependency analysis procedures for the LPA context. The project will commence with workshops in both municipalities. A representative cross section of the LPA's staffs will be formed in each LPA and will use SSM in a workshop setting, where the LPA's staff, facilitated by the project team can help create a detailed understanding of the problem domain and the system dependency analysis, together with security experts, legal experts and CERT representatives.

V. Discussion

In the past years, we have seen a rapid growth in connectivity in all organizational contexts. For example, in critical infrastructures or the industry (Industrial IoT, Industry 4.0), the advances in the Internet of things allows devices in all levels of the organizational structure to be connected to the Internet - something that was not possible before. In administrations, more and more privacy related information about citizens is handled digitally, with interfaces to many different tools, accessed by many different devices and device classes. This trend makes the complex task of ensuring cybersecurity for those organizations even more complex, and the trend is continuing.

One major aspect of this situation is that each complex system is different. Not only are the systems of different industries/governmental institutions not comparable, but even the systems of different organizations within the same industry or government may have fundamentally different set-ups and needs related to cybersecurity. When looking for technological solutions to improve cybersecurity in this situation, there is no one-size-fits all solution that can be purchased and installed to provide out of the box protection. Especially when looking for solutions that enable cybersecurity collaboration and cooperation, some sort of abstraction layer is required to connect the individual systems of an organization with a common understanding about the security requirements and cybersecurity protection strategies. To achieve this abstraction level we see no way around an individual and methodical analysis of the complex environment in which an organization is operating, in order to determine which assets require protection and how they relate to the risk and threat landscape and protection strategies as laid out, for example, by NIS relevant authorities like national and EU CERTs. Tool support can build upon the abstraction layer introduced by this methodical analysis.

Some of the authors have very significant, broad and practical experience of systems thinking and the application and use of the Soft Systems Methodology to real-world problem domains. This experience has been acquired in a wide range of industrial and commercial and non-commercial settings, with widely differing organisational structures and technical, social and cultural constraints. The power of the method is that it captures and enables the expression of the tacit knowledge of the "actors" in the problem domain - the people who work with and within the system or systems under investigation. It is the expression and application of this tacit knowledge to the analysis and design process, that distinguishes the method from other analytical tools. The approach that was presented in this paper is ideally suited for situations where complex environments need to be analysed but a complete and optimal analysis is not feasible. Soft systems analysis is excellent for quickly and flexibly defining problems and any associated relevant factors for specific situations, such as providing cybersecurity and all the socio-technological aspects that relate to the cybersecurity of a complex system. Especially in the dynamic cybersecurity context, where situations (e.g., threat and risk landscape) change rapidly, it is necessary to complement the problem definitions that are mainly gathered in user workshops, with more dynamic and highly topical information from other sources. We think that we have found an ideal solution with GraphingWiki, which was specifically designed to collect and graphically present related information from different sources.

We are highly confident that the proposed analysis methodology will fulfil the analysis requirements of complex organizational systems in the context of cybersecurity, and to build the basis and required abstraction level for cybersecurity tools that build on it. In CS-AWARE we see the system analysis as the enabling factor for a highly automated cybersecurity solution. Built on a common understanding of the cybersecurity requirements, CS-AWARE will shift cybersecurity from a purely organizational problem to a cooperative and collaborative problem. At the same time, solutions to specific threats that are developed on the collaborative level (for example, through NIS competent authorities), can be more easily integrated on the organizational level based on the analysis results.

We will be using the pilot use cases in CS-AWARE to validate our approach in the LPA context, in combination with the technological capabilities of the CS-AWARE solution. Besides providing analysis for the case studies which are part of the project, we will develop procedures and policies for the system and dependency analysis tailored to the LPA context. The goal is to develop a quasi-standard in order to ensure that comparable results can be achieved, while at the same time, reducing the level of expertise required to conduct such an analysis. Once we have more relevant results within the project, we expect to do the same outside the LPA context. We expect that application areas like critical infrastructures, large organizations or SMEs can benefit in the same way from a soft systems based analysis in the context of cybersecurity, and we intend to tailor and apply the presented analysis methodology to those contexts.

VI. Summary and Outlook

In this paper, we have presented a system and dependency analysis methodology for complex systems based on soft systems thinking within the context of cybersecurity. The target for the analysis are organizations that rely on complex systems and procedures for their operation, like critical infrastructures, large organizations/SMEs or public institutions. The analysis methodology is focused on providing a holistic socio-technological view of the analysed system, based on the combination and visualization of different relevant information sources. Since one of the greatest sources of information about a system is coming from its users, workshops where users from all organizational levels and with different backgrounds work together to define the problem situation are a central aspect of this methodology. We have argued that each organizational set-up is different which makes generalized cybersecurity solutions difficult. We have shown that the presented system and dependency analysis methodology can be seen as an abstraction layer that allows to apply generalized cybersecurity solutions on top of it. As an example, we have presented the EU H2020 project CS-AWARE that utilizes the presented system and dependency methodology as a central part of its cybersecurity solution. The goal of CS-AWARE is to develop an automated cybersecurity situational awareness and decision support solution relying on cooperative and collaborative approaches, as laid out by the NIS directive.

As a next step, we will validate the presented analysis method in the context of LPAs, within the CS-AWARE piloting efforts in the municipalities of Larissa (Greece) and Rome (Italy). Besides providing the case dependent analysis required for the CS-AWARE solution, we intend to develop quasi-standardized policies and procedures for the LPA context to ensure repeatable and comparable analysis results for future cases. In a next step we intend to apply the methodology to cases outside the LPA context like, for example, critical infrastructures.

Acknowledgements

We would like to thank the EU H2020 project CS-AWARE ("A cybersecurity situational awareness and information sharing solution for local public administrations based on advanced big data analysis", project number 740723) and the Austrian national KIRAS project CERBERUS ("Cross Sectoral Risk Management for Object Protection of Critical Infrastructures", project number 854766) for supporting this work. The Biomimetics and Intelligent Systems Group (BISG) would like to acknowledge the support of Infotech Oulu.

References

[1] European Commission, "Proposal for a directive of the european parliament and of the council concerning measures to ensure a high common level of network and information security across the union," COM(2013) 48 final, 2013.

[2] European Commission and High Representative of the European Union for Foreign Affairs and Security Policy, "Cybersecurity strategy of the european union: An open, safe and secure cyberspace," JOIN(2013) 1 final, 2013.

[3] ENISA, "National cyber security strategies in the world." [Online]. Available: https://www.enisa.europa.eu/topics/national-cyber-security-strategies/ncss-map (Accessed 8/2017).

[4] ISO/IEC 27000:2016, "Information technology — security techniques — information security management systems — overview and vocabulary," ISO/IEC, Standard, 2016.

[5] ISO/IEC 29100:2011, "Information technology — security techniques — privacy framework," ISO/IEC, Standard, 2011.

[6] CEN, CENELEC and ETSI, "Focus Group on Cybersecurity (CSCG)." [Online]. Available: http://www.cencenelec.eu/standards/sectors/defencesecurityprivacy/security/pages/cybersecurity.aspx (Accessed 8/2017).

[7] P. B. Checkland, *Systems Thinking, Systems Practice.* John Wiley & Sons Ltd. 1981, 1998.

[8] P. B. Checkland and J. Scholes, *Systems Thinking, Systems Practice.* John Wiley & Sons Ltd., 1991.

[9] T. Maqsood, A. D. Finegan, and D. H. T. Walker, "Five case studies applying soft systems methodology to knowledge management," in *7th Annual Conference on Systems Engineering Research*, 2009, p. 18.

[10] C. H. Antunes, L. Dias, G. Dantas, J. Mathias, and L. Zamboni, "An application of soft systems methodology in the evaluation of policies and incentive actions to promote technological innovations in the electricity sector," *Energy Procedia*, vol. 106, pp. 258 – 278, 2016.

[11] J. Eronen and M. Laakso, "A case for protocol dependency," in *First IEEE International Workshop on Critical Infrastructure Protection (IWCIP'05)*, Nov 2005, p. 9.

[12] J. Eronen and J. Röning, "Graphingwiki – a semantic wiki extension for visualising and inferring protocol dependency," in *First Workshop on Semantic Wikis – From Wiki To Semantics*, 2006.

[13] J. Eronen et al., "Software vulnerability vs. critical infrastructure – a case study of antivirus software," *International Journal on Advances in Security*, vol. 2, no. 1, pp. 72–89, 2009.

[14] P. Pietikainen, K. Karjalainen, J. Roning, and J. Eronen, "Socio-technical security assessment of a voip system," in *2010 Fourth International Conference on Emerging Security Information, Systems and Technologies*, July 2010, pp. 141–147.

[15] T. Schaberreiter, K. Kittilä, K. Halunen, J. Röning, and D. Khadraoui, *Risk Assessment in Critical Infrastructure Security Modelling Based on Dependency Analysis*. Berlin, Heidelberg: Springer Berlin Heidelberg, 2013, pp. 213–217.

[16] G. Backfried et al., "Open source intelligence in disaster management," in *2012 European Intelligence and Security Informatics Conference*, Aug 2012, pp. 254–258.

Stochastic Dependencies Between Critical Infrastructures

Sandra König
Austrian Institute of Technology GmbH
Digital Safety & Security Department
Wien, Austria
Email: sandra.koenig@ait.ac.at

Stefan Rass
Universität Klagenfurt
Institute of Applied Informatics, System Security Group
Klagenfurt, Austria
Email: stefan.rass@aau.at

***Abstract*—Critical infrastructures (CIs) are characterized by their high importance for the welfare of a society and failure of such an infrastructure has a significant impact on our everyday life. However, a problem in one critical infrastructure also affects other infrastructures, e.g., if electricity is only partly available this also affects hospitals. The effects of even a partial failure of a provider on a critical infrastructures are hard to predict unless strict assumptions are made. The damage depends, among other things, on the availability of substitutes, but also on external influences such as weather, temporary demand or load peaks, etc., which is why we propose a stochastic model where the state of an infrastructure is a random variable. Each infrastructure changes its state depending on what the other CIs do, based on a probabilistic change transition regime. This allows to model complex interdependencies, whose underlying dynamics may be stochastic or deterministic yet partly unknown. The model of the entire CI thus consists of several Markov chains, which retains simplicity for implementation in a software such as R, and flexibility to capture various forms of mutual influence between CIs. We illustrate this by giving a small example. The main contribution of this work is a model that partly unifies three different models of risk propagation (Bayesian networks, percolation and system dynamics) under a single simulation/percolation framework.**

***Index Terms*—critical infrastructure; stochastic dependencies; Markov chain; risk propagation**

I. Introduction

Critical infrastructures (CIs) are typically supply networks satisfying the basic needs of society, such as power, water, food, health care, transportation, etc. Besides this high dependency of the society on CIs, there are also mutual dependencies among these CIs, such as hospitals depend on electricity, water, food supply and working transportation lines. A main characteristic of a CI is that a failure with a CI does not only affect the CI itself, but has a huge impact on the dependent CIs, as well as on society. This has manifested in the last years as, for example, the disruption of electric power in California in 2001 [1] affected several other critical infrastructures, the major power outage in Italy [2], which lasted for about 12 hours, resulted in a financial damage of over 1 billion euros or the most recent hacking of the Ukrainian power grid caused a power outage of several hours [3]. In general, such dependencies between CIs can be either *continuous*, as it is the case of electricity where a stable supply is required, or *instantaneous*, for example, if the CI's support is just required in an emergency situation (e.g., police, fire brigade, or similar). In this work, we consider structures that mutually and *continuously* depend on input from several providers, such as water or electricity (see [4][5], for a more detailed discussion). The case of an instantaneous dependency will be revisited briefly later on.

Reduced or even missing supply from a critical provider may cause significant problems for an infrastructure. The actual damage depends on the degree of failure of the provider, but is also influenced by many other factors such as availability of substitutes (see [6] for work related to water supply). Since the consequences of a reduced support are not always exactly predictable, we introduce a stochastic model that describes how a critical infrastructure depends on other infrastructures whose input is needed for smooth operation. This abstract model can be applied to any type of infrastructure, as long as the dependencies from other infrastructures are known and can be classified qualitatively in terms of "how severe" a provider's outage is on a finite scale (say, from 1 to 5. See [7] for a discussion of this requirement in light of compliance, auditing and monitoring). The model thus speaks about different "degrees of failure", where the particular meaning of such a "degree" is up to the specific characteristics of the CI (e.g., status 3 may mean different things or problems for a water provider than for a hospital). In particular, not every failure yields to a complete blackout of the infrastructure of interest. On the other hand, the model is not too complex by considering only dependencies between two infrastructures at a time and by grouping infrastructures into different classes with different characteristics.

Paper Outline

The remainder of this article is organized as follows: after a recap of the current research situation in Section II, Section III introduces our model for dependencies between critical infrastructures. Section IV describes how such a model may be used to simulate how the states of a critical infrastructures change and Section V shows a small example. Finally, we provide concluding remarks in Section VI.

II. Related Work

Several models have been developed for dependencies among critical infrastructures. In [8], a framework for addressing infrastructure interdependencies is presented that describes five different classes of critical infrastructure interdependencies (including also dependencies of information and communication technologies). Recent models consider random failure and stochastic dependencies. For example, a multi-graph model is used to analyze random failures and their effects on critical infrastructures in [9]. Other models look explicitly at interdependencies of higher order to identify and assess the effect of failures not only for direct "consumers" but also for subsequent infrastructures in the dependency chain [10][11]. Such cascading effects have been investigated in [12] by means of an Input-output Inoperability Model (IIM) that is based on financial data. Further, Hierarchical Holographic Modeling (HHM) [13] has been used to describe the diverse nature of CI networks and analyze failures therein. More complex models are based on Bayesian networks [14] as, for example, the Hierarchical Coordinated Bayes Model (HCBM) [15] or other approaches (cf. [16] and references therein). Our work is also related to various approaches by simulation and co-simulation [17][18][19][20][21]. Typically, these are applicable when the analyst is much more informed about the infrastructure in question, since the simulation depicts the internal dynamics (even up to the level of concrete network packets to be exchanged). Our perspective is much more high-level and assumes the absence of these details up to only categorical valuations of interdependencies (cf. [4][22][23][24] for more comprehensive overviews).

III. Random Dependencies of a Critical Infrastructure

Dependencies between CIs are conveniently described by a simple directed graph. The nodes represent the CIs and a directed edge from CI 1 to CI 2 indicates that CI 2 depends on input from CI 1. Such a visualization helps to get an overview of dependencies in a larger area (e.g., in a geographical region or an entire country) but it is not suitable to get a deeper understanding of how these dependencies influence the functionality of the CIs. For this sake, the model needs to describe both the critical infrastructures as well as the dependencies between them in more detail. At the same time, it is infeasible to describe every possible impact of every dependency since such a model grows exponentially (in the number of parameters). As a trade-off, we propose the following solution on middle ground.

A CI is described as a node that can be in one of k different *states* representing its functionality where state 1 represents the situation where everything works smoothly, ranging up to state k that means total failure, with intermediate states corresponding to different levels of restricted service provisioning. Each CI continuously depends on input from different *providers* that may not always work correctly themselves. Even a partial failure of one provider may change the CIs state. For example, if there is not enough electricity most infrastructures are affected in some way and may no longer work properly. This situation is captured by describing each CI as a 'big' node with two types of internal nodes: k *status nodes* indicate the state of the CI itself while $n_i \cdot k$ *input nodes* represent all possible states of the n_i input nodes (provider).

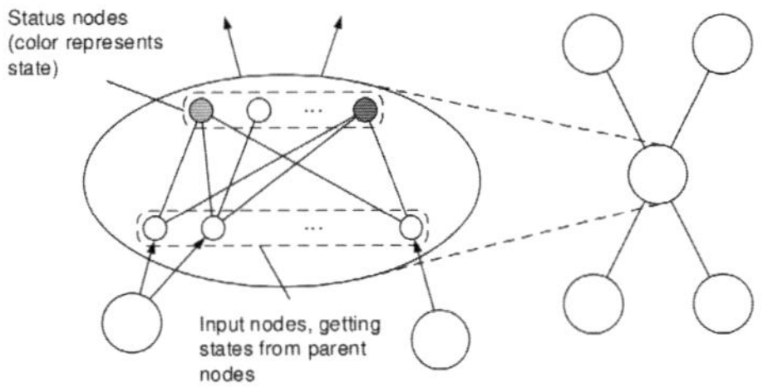

Fig. 1. Model of the inner structure of a critical infrastructure

This idea can be visualized, as shown in Figure 1, by representing each of the k states of the CI by a node with a color representing the degree of damage (cf. the top set of nodes in Figure 1). Each of the n_i provider may again be in one of the same k states and we represent all these different configurations by $n_i \cdot k$ nodes below the status nodes. Note that this modeling allows a node to be in several states simultaneously. The state communicated to the next node is, according to the maximum principle, the most severe among the given states (i.e., a system is only as secure as its weakest element). In practice, a node may indeed encounter multiple problems of different severity at the same time; nonetheless, the degree of trouble in which a CI is, is surely determined by the most severe of its current issues. Moreover, the model straightforwardly generalizes to several states in different respects, say, if a number $d > 1$ of distinct security goals are in question. For instance, a node could maintain a status regarding confidentiality, and another status regarding availability. In this context, imagine an electricity provider who has experienced a data leakage where customer data has been stolen. This is a confidentiality breach, but the power supply is still up and running, so there is no availability issue. In that case, we can make the internal graph d-partite, with d output layers, each corresponding to its own security goal. The status reported to subsequent nodes is then the worst status per security goal (and not the overall worst case status over all nodes, since this would not make sense for obvious reasons; just reconsidering the availability vs. confidentiality example from before).

As consequences of (partial) failure of a provider are not always predictable and depend on many factors that cannot be controlled (in particular they depend on other suppliers themselves), we apply a stochastic model to describe the influence an CI has on another. More explicitly, this means that the current state of one provider yields a specific state of the critical infrastructure only with a certain probability. In other words, any edges in Figure 1 transmits a problem with a specific probability. We assume that every node in the lower row (representing one state of one provider) has the potential to change the state of the CI. Technically speaking, we describe changes between the states of the CIs as a Markov chain, that is, every state of a provider influences the state of the infrastructure it provides input for. This includes the situation where the state does not change as well as the situation that the condition gets better since one of the providers recovered. A more detailed analysis of such situations is postponed to future work.

A. The Model

Let us take a look on a critical infrastructure v that provides input to another infrastructure u. The state of u changes depending on the states of its provider v but these changes are by no means predictable. Thus, we describe the state by a random variable S that is multinomial distributed, which we denote by MN($\vec{p}$), i.e., the j-th component p_j of $\vec{p}$ gives the probability that S takes on the value j. These likelihoods depend on the current state i of the input node, i.e., if u works properly it is not likely that the dependent node v faces serious problems. Thus, we describe these transitions by a stochastic matrix. However, the transition probability is also influenced by the type of connection between the two nodes. For that purpose, we classify all edges and define a transition probability matrix for each of the defined classes that represents its characteristics. Thus, if a node v is in state i and the connection to u is of class c, the state of u follows a multinomial distribution NM($\vec{p}_{i,c}$) with a probability vector $\vec{p}_{i,c}$. In the graphical model of Figure 1, the possible transitions and likelihoods are reflected in the bipartite graph, and the transition matrix is the *biadjacency* matrix of that bipartite graph.

B. Relation to Other Models

The model used here can be seen as a generalization of the stochastic error spreading model in [25] in the sense that the (real-valued) transition probabilities between different components are replaced by transition matrices that describe the influence for each level of failure. More precisely, we can replace the transition probability p_i for an edge of type i by a stochastic matrix $\vec{P}_i$ that describes the transition probabilities for each degree of failure for both the dependent and the depending node. As described in [26], these probabilities can be estimated by expert opinions (e.g., by taking the median of all scores assigned by experts) or other stochastic models, such as described in [27].

Moreover, some simple forms of Bayesian networks also appear as special cases of this model: let in be a node over which a parent reports its status, and let $v_1, \ldots, v_k$ be the status nodes of the CI. The weight that the model assigns to the edge $in \to v_i$ is the conditional probability $\Pr(v_i|in)$. This is just what a Bayesian network [28] would describe/require in the same modeling. The difference to general Bayesian networks lies in the difficulty to express joint distributions in this form, since an output state is conditionally dependent on several input nodes, but not jointly conditionally so.

Finally, by making the edge weights for the model binary, we can model deterministic dependencies to some extent: for example, if the outage of a parent node causes the outage of the given CI, then the respective internal edges in the bipartite inner model graph get assigned the weight 1. This will cause the simulated chain to go to the worst status node for sure when its parent has an outage. Again, not all kinds of dynamics can be expressed like this, for the same reasons as with the general Bayesian networks.

The limitations imposed here save us from the exponential complexity that Bayesian networks induce for their specification (as we would require a conditional probability on all subsets of parent nodes; and there are exponentially many of them). For deterministic dynamics, there are endless possibilities to describe what can happen using rules; a sufficiently flexible way of representing such dynamics is, indeed, offered by Bayesian networks, but this comes with the same complexity issues as mentioned before. In light of this, the limitations are a trade-off between model flexibility and computational feasibility of its specification.

IV. SIMULATION OF STOCHASTIC DEPENDENCIES

The stochastic dependency model between critical infrastructures can straightforwardly be implemented in a software such as R. This simulation starts with an incident happening at some node, which subsequently (and indirectly) triggers descendant CIs to change their status according to the likelihoods in their inner bipartite graphs. The simulation thus reveals how far an incident will propagate (within the runtime of the simulation), and can thus be used to estimate the effect a problem in one component has on a specific critical infrastructure or generally on other components. Additionally, it allows an empirical estimation of the number of components that are in a critical state (i.e., reach the highest status k).

More explicitly, we model the network of infrastructures as a graph with n vertices $v \in V$ that represent the infrastructures and edges $e \in E$ representing the connections between them. A usual difficulty in specifying such probabilistic models is the issue of where to get the conditional probabilities from. To mitigate this practical obstacle, we let the weighting be discrete and according to edge classes, meaning that each edge (representing an inner or mutual dependency) is assigned to one class c out of the set $\{1, 2, \ldots, C\}$ of candidate classes, in which each class represents a different levels of importance of a CI for its successor CI (provider-consumer dependency). Each edge $v \to u$ is then associated with a representative number for its class c that acts the probability used for the simulation. This allows the model parameterization to be done upfront and independent of the concrete CI, and eases matters of model parameterization in absence of empirical data to estimate conditional probabilities. Depending on this class c the state i of v influences the state of u through a multinomial distribution MN($p_{i,c}$). That is, the j-th component of the vector $p_{i,c}$ gives the probability that u will be in state j in this situation. In pseudo-code, an algorithm that simulates T timesteps looks as shown in Figure 2.

The result of this simulation is a network of connected critical infrastructures where each CI is in a specific state. For visualization, we can use color codes, ranging from green to indicate a working state to red, alerting about a critical

```
t ← 0
while t < T
  for each node v, set N(v) = {u ∈ V : (v,u) ∈ E}
    for each neighboring node u ∈ N(v)
      let c be the class of v → u,
      let i be the current state of node v,
      draw the status of u from MN(p_{i,c})
      t ← t + 1.
    endfor
  endfor
endwhile
```

Fig. 2. Simulation Algorithm

condition. Numerically, the results of the simulation can be summarized as a table that lists how many components are on average in any of the possible states.

V. An Illustrative Example

Let a subnetwork of a CI consist of a hospital that depends on a water provider, an electricity provider as well as transportation infrastructures (roads). The dependencies between the different components in the network are classified as either "minor", "normal" or "critical" depending on how important the service provisioning is for the CI. In this small example, we classified input from the electricity provider as "normal" (as we assume existence of an emergency power system), input from a water provider as "critical" (substitution by bottled water is usually just possible for a limited period of time) and the transport connection as "minor", since even if roads are temporarily congested or blocked, aerial transportation remains possible for critical patients.

Arbitrary transition matrices were chosen depending on the class of the connection. Here, we consider 5 possible states for each node, where 1 represents the situation where everything works smoothly, while 5 stands for serious problems including total failure. In a practical application, these values need to be estimated by experts familiar with the infrastructure's operation (possibly aided by other simulation methods accounting for the internal system dynamics). For the specification of a dependency on the chosen scale from 1 to 5, we specify a matrix $T_{minor/normal/critical} = (t_{ij})_{i,j=1}^{5}$, in which the ij-th entry corresponds to the conditional likelihood $t_{ij} := \Pr(\text{CI gets into state } j \mid \text{provider is in state } i)$. For the example, let

$$T_{minor} = \begin{pmatrix} 0.6 & 0.2 & 0.2 & 0.0 & 0.0 \\ 0.5 & 0.2 & 0.2 & 0.1 & 0.0 \\ 0.4 & 0.2 & 0.2 & 0.2 & 0.0 \\ 0.3 & 0.2 & 0.2 & 0.2 & 0.1 \\ 0.3 & 0.2 & 0.2 & 0.2 & 0.1 \end{pmatrix},$$

$$T_{normal} = \begin{pmatrix} 0.4 & 0.2 & 0.2 & 0.2 & 0.0 \\ 0.4 & 0.2 & 0.1 & 0.3 & 0.0 \\ 0.3 & 0.2 & 0.2 & 0.2 & 0.1 \\ 0.2 & 0.2 & 0.2 & 0.3 & 0.1 \\ 0.2 & 0.2 & 0.1 & 0.3 & 0.2 \end{pmatrix}$$

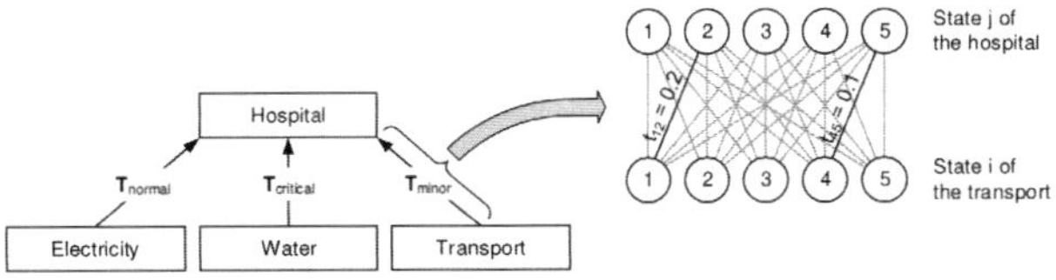

Fig. 3. Example Instance

and

$$T_{critical} = \begin{pmatrix} 0.3 & 0.2 & 0.2 & 0.2 & 0.1 \\ 0.2 & 0.2 & 0.2 & 0.2 & 0.2 \\ 0.0 & 0.2 & 0.2 & 0.3 & 0.3 \\ 0.0 & 0.1 & 0.2 & 0.3 & 0.4 \\ 0.0 & 0.0 & 0.0 & 0.2 & 0.8. \end{pmatrix}.$$

Figure 3 (left side) displays the dependencies graphically, with arrows annotated according to the criticality of the dependency. The right part of Figure 3 shows how the inner model of Figure 1 corresponds to a dependency, and is instantiated according to the matrices above. For example, if a provider classified as "minor" is in state 4 (i.e., it has rather serious problems) this will yield to a state 5 of the critical infrastructure that depends on it with a likelihood of 0.1.

Initially, we assume that all components operate smoothly and are in state 1 except for the water provider that is in state 2 facing some (temporary) problems. This scenario yielded to a critical state for the hospital in 16 out of 100 cases. Note that in this example, this critical state can only be caused by the state of the water provider since a CI of normal or even minor importance will never cause a critical level while bing in state 1 (i.e., both entries in the transition matrices are zero).

In Table I we show the average number of nodes (CIs) that are in each of the 5 possible states. This information is especially useful in larger networks to get an overview on the impact of a problem in one critical infrastructure on the entire network of CIs.

TABLE I. AVERAGE NUMBER OF AFFECTED NODES DUE TO INCREASED LEVEL OF CRITICALITY

Criticality	1	2	3	4	5
Nodes	2.05	1.15	0.31	0.33	0.16

VI. Conclusion and Future Work

In this work, we introduced a model for dependencies between critical infrastructures that assumes random effects of failures. In particular, the extent to which a problem in one infrastructure influences another one depends on how serious the problem is (represented by the state of this infrastructure) and by the nature of the connection between them (described by the connection's classification). The effect on another infrastructure is again described through several states that indicate the severity. However, the effect itself is random due to the impossibility of precise prediction. While this model captures many important aspects of such dependencies it is still quite simple and can straightforwardly be implemented. We have sketched the implementation in pseudo code and applied the simulation to a small example.

Extensions to the model along future work are possible in various ways. In the form presented, the model assumes an independent influence of all providers to a specific CI. Dependencies with an inner interplay of two providers cannot be described in the given model. For example, two providers being mutually substitutes for one another, a dependency of a CI on the total input of several providers (irrespectively of the individual supplies). Taking these into account seems to involve more complex stochastic dependency models (e.g., copulas [29]) to describe distributions conditional on several variables. At the same time, this also brings the model complexity closer to exponential in the number of the CIs, with Bayesian networks being located at the end of the spectrum along this generalization. A "middle ground model" is thus an interesting goal to strive for, starting from our work presented here.

ACKNOWLEDGMENT

This work was done in the context of the project "Cross Sectoral Risk Management for Object Protection of Critical Infrastructures (CERBERUS)", supported by the Austrian Research Promotion Agency under grant no. 854766.

REFERENCES

[1] S. Fletcher, "Electric power interruptions curtail California oil and gas production," *Oil Gas Journal*, 2001.

[2] M. Schmidthaler and J. Reichl, "Economic Valuation of Electricity Supply Security: Ad-hoc Cost Assessment Tool for Power Outages," *ELECTRA*, no. 276, pp. 10–15, 2014.

[3] J. Condliffe, "Ukraine's Power Grid Gets Hacked Again, a Worrying Sign for Infrastructure Attacks," 2016, URL: https://www.technologyreview.com/s/603262/ukraines-power-grid-gets-hacked-again-a-worrying-sign-for-infrastructure-attacks/ [accessed: 2017-07-26].

[4] R. Setola, V. Rosato, E. Kyriakides, and E. Rome, Eds., *Managing the Complexity of Critical Infrastructures: A Modelling and Simulation Approach*, ser. Studies in Systems, Decision and Control. Cham and s.l.: Springer International Publishing, 2016, vol. 90.

[5] R. Klein, E. Rome, C. Beyel, R. Linnemann, W. Reinhardt, and A. Usov, "Information modelling and simulation in large interdependent critical infrastructures in irriis," in *Critical Information Infrastructure Security: Third International Workshop, CRITIS 2008, Rome, Italy, October13-15, 2008. Revised Papers*, R. Setola and S. Geretshuber, Eds. Berlin, Heidelberg: Springer Berlin Heidelberg, 2009, pp. 36–47.

[6] E. Luiijf, M. Ali, and A. Zielstra, "Assessing and improving scada security in the dutch drinking water sector," *International Journal of Critical Infrastructure Protection*, vol. 4, no. 3-4, pp. 124–134, 2011.

[7] A. Abou El Kalam and Y. Deswarte, "Critical infrastructures security modeling, enforcement and runtime checking," in *Critical Information Infrastructure Security: Third International Workshop, CRITIS 2008, Rome, Italy, October13-15, 2008. Revised Papers*, R. Setola and S. Geretshuber, Eds. Berlin, Heidelberg: Springer Berlin Heidelberg, 2009, pp. 95–108.

[8] S. Rinaldi, J. Peerenboom, and T. Kelly, "Identifying, Understanding, and Analyzing Critical Infrastructure Interdependencies," *IEEE Control Systems Magazine*, pp. 11–25, 2001.

[9] N. K. Svendsen and S. D. Wolthusen, "Analysis and Statistical Properties of Critical Infrastructure Interdependency Multiflow Models," in *2007 IEEE SMC Information Assurance and Security Workshop*, June 2007, pp. 247–254.

[10] M. Theoharidou, P. Kotzanikolaou, and D. Gritzalis, "Risk assessment methodology for interdependent critical infrastructures," *International Journal of Risk Assessment and Management*, vol. 15, no. 2-3, pp. 128–148, 2011, [accessed: 2017-08-15]. [Online]. Available: http://www.inderscienceonline.com/doi/abs/10.1504/IJRAM.2011.042113

[11] P. Kotzanikolaou, M. Theoharidou, and D. Gritzalis, "Assessing n-order dependencies between critical infrastructures," *International Journal of Critical Infrastructures*, vol. 9, no. 1-2, pp. 93–110, 2013, URL: http://www.inderscienceonline.com/doi/abs/10.1504/IJCIS.2013.051606 [accessed: 2017-08-01].

[12] R. Setola, S. De Porcellinis, and M. Sforna, "Critical Infrastructure Dependency Assessment Using the Input-Output Inoperability Model," *International Journal of Critical Infrastructure Protection (IJCIP)*, vol. 2, pp. 170–178, 2009.

[13] Y. Y. Haimes, "Hierarchical Holographic Modeling," *IEEE Transactions on Systems, Man, and Cybernetics*, vol. 11, no. 9, pp. 606–617, 1981.

[14] M. I. Jordan, Ed., *Learning in graphical models*. Dordrecht, The Netherlands: Kluwer Academic Publishers, 1999.

[15] Y. Haimes, J. Santos, K. Crowther, M. Henry, C. Lian, and Z. Yan, "Risk Analysis in Interdependent Infrastructures," in *Critical Infrastructure Protection*, ser. IFIP International Federation for Information Processing. Springer, Boston, MA, 2007, pp. 297–310.

[16] T. Schaberreiter, S. Varrette, P. Bouvry, J. Röning, and D. Khadraoui, *Dependency Analysis for Critical Infrastructure Security Modelling: A Case Study within the Grid'5000 Project*. Berlin, Heidelberg: Springer Berlin Heidelberg, 2013, pp. 269–287.

[17] R. Caire, J. Sanchez, and N. Hadjsaid, "Vulnerability analysis of coupled heterogeneous critical infrastructures: A Co-simulation approach with a testbed validation," in *IEEE PES ISGT Europe 2013*. IEEE, 2013, pp. 1–5.

[18] R. Jaromin, B. Mullins, J. Butts, and J. Lopez, "Design and Implementation of Industrial Control System Emulators," in *Critical Infrastructure Protection VII*, ser. IFIP Advances in Information and Communication Technology, J. Butts and S. Shenoi, Eds. Berlin, Heidelberg: Springer Berlin Heidelberg, 2013, vol. 417, pp. 35–46.

[19] H. Lin, S. Sambamoorthy, S. Shukla, J. Thorp, and L. Mili, "Power system and communication network co-simulation for smart grid applications," in *ISGT 2011*. IEEE, 2011, pp. 1–6.

[20] M. Faschang, F. Kupzog, R. Mosshammer, and A. Einfalt, "Rapid control prototyping platform for networked smart grid systems," in *Proceedings IECON 2013 - 39th Annual Conference of the IEEE Industrial Electronics Society*. Vienna, Austria: IEEE, 2013, pp. 8172–8176.

[21] M. Findrik, P. Smith, J. H. Kazmi, M. Faschang, and F. Kupzog, "Towards secure and resilient networked power distribution grids: Process and tool adoption," in *Smart Grid Communications (SmartGridComm), 2016 IEEE International Conference on*. Sidney, Australia: IEEE Publishing, 2016, pp. 435 – 440.

[22] J. Butts, *Critical Infrastructure Protection VII: 7th IFIP WG 11. 10 International Conference, ICCIP 2013, Washington, DC, USA, March 18-20, 2013, Revised Selected Papers*, ser. IFIP Advances in Information and Communication Technology. Berlin/Heidelberg: Springer Berlin Heidelberg, 2013, vol. v.417, URL: http://ebookcentral.proquest.com/lib/gbv/detail.action?docID=3091963 [accessed: 2017-07-31].

[23] S. M. Rinaldi, "Modeling and simulating critical infrastructures and their interdependencies," in *37th Annual Hawaii International Conference on System Sciences, 2004. Proceedings of the*. IEEE, 2004, pp. 1–8.

[24] E. Wiseman, "Critical Infrastructure Protection and Resilience Literature Survey: Modeling and Simulation," URL: http://www.dtic.mil/get-tr-doc/pdf?AD=AD1003598 [accessed: 2017-07-31].

[25] S. König, S. Schauer, and S. Rass, *A Stochastic Framework for Prediction of Malware Spreading in Heterogeneous Networks*. Cham: Springer, 2016, pp. 67–81.

[26] S. König, S. Rass, S. Schauer, and A. Beck, "Risk Propagation Analysis and Visualization using Percolation Theory," *International Journal of Advanced Computer Science and Applications (IJACSA)*, vol. 7, no. 1, pp. 694–701, 2016.

[27] L. Carin, G. Cybenko, and J. Hughes, "Cybersecurity Strategies: The QuERIES Methodology," *Computer*, vol. 41, no. 8, pp. 20–26, 2008.

[28] T. Koski and J. M. Noble, *Bayesian Networks*, ser. Wiley Series in Probability and Statistics. Wiley, 2009.

[29] R. B. Nelsen, *An Introduction To Copulas*, ser. Lecture Notes in Statistics 139. Springer, 1999.

Assessing Security Protection for Sensitive Data

George O.M. Yee
Aptusinnova Inc. and Carleton University
Ottawa, Canada
email: george@aptusinnova.com, gmyee@sce.carleton.ca

Abstract—**The growth of the Internet has unfortunately been accompanied by an increasing number of attacks against an organization's computing infrastructure, leading to the theft of sensitive data. In response to such incursions, the organization installs security measures (e.g., intrusion detection system) for protecting its sensitive data. However, this installation is often done haphazardly, without any objective guidance regarding how many vulnerabilities must be secured in order to achieve a targeted level of protection that would be deemed acceptable. This work derives estimates of the levels of protection based on the number of vulnerabilities to attack that have been secured. The paper then shows how an organization can calculate these estimates, and use them to adjust the number of security measures installed, until a certain target level of protection is achieved subject to certain constraints. An application example is included.**

Keywords-assessment; security; protection; sensitive data; vulnerability.

I. INTRODUCTION

Recent attacks against computing infrastructure, resulting in the theft of sensitive data, have grabbed the headlines, and have devastated the victim organizations. The losses have not only been financial (e.g., theft of credit card information), but more importantly the damage to the organization's reputation. Consider the following data breaches that happened in 2016 [1]:

- February, 2016, University of Central Florida: Data breach affected approximately 63,000 current and former students, faculty, and staff, with the theft of information including social security numbers, first and last names, and student/employee ID numbers.
- February, 2016, U.S. Department of Justice: Hackers released data on 10,000 Department of Homeland Security employees one day, and the next day released data on 20,000 FBI employees. Stolen information included names, titles, phone numbers, and email addresses.
- March, 2016, Premier Healthcare: Theft of a laptop containing sensitive data pertaining to more than 200,000 patients, including names, dates of birth, and possibly social security numbers or financial information.
- March, 2016, Verizon Enterprise Solutions: Hackers stole information for about 1.5 million customers; the information was found for sale in an underground cybercrime forum by cyber security journalist Brain Krebs.
- September, 2016, Yahoo!: The company announced that a hacker had stolen information from 500 million accounts in 2014. The hacker, believed to be working for a foreign government, stole email addresses, passwords, full user names, dates of birth, telephone numbers, and in some cases, security questions and answers.

This is only a sampling, as there were many more breaches in 2016, and in fact, no year can be said to have been breach-free.

To protect themselves from attacks, such as the ones described above, organizations determine their vulnerabilities to attack, and then secure the vulnerabilities with security measures. Common measures include firewalls, intrusion detection systems, two-factor authentication, encryption, and training for employees on identifying and resisting social engineering. However, today's organizations install security measures without any way of calculating the overall level of protection that will result. They proceed based on recommendations from consultants or in reaction to attacks that have been observed. And in many cases, they are forced to stop this deployment once their security budget runs out. It would be far better if an organization can follow a top-down approach, by setting a target level of protection and then install security measures to achieve the target. The target would be set according to the expected threat situation, the nature of the business, the sensitivity of information kept, and an estimated financial budget. Before this can be done, it would be useful to have quantitative estimates of the level of protection based on the number of vulnerabilities secured. This work derives such estimates and shows how to apply them to not only set a protection target, but also how security measures can be installed to achieve the target.

The objectives of this work are i) derive estimates of the resultant protection level obtained by an organization through the installation of security measures to secure vulnerabilities, ii) show how these estimates can be calculated, iii) show how the estimates can be applied in a top-down and objective quantified approach to secure an organization, and finally iv) illustrate ii) and iii) using an example.

The rest of this paper is organized as follows. Section II discusses the nature of sensitive data and derives the estimates. Section III explains how the estimates are calculated and applied in a top-down quantified approach to secure an organization. Section IV presents an application example. Section V discusses related work. Finally, Section VI gives conclusions and future research.

II. ESTIMATING SECURITY PROTECTION LEVELS

Before deriving estimates of security protection levels, it is useful to examine the nature of sensitive data.

A. Sensitive Data

We all have some sense of what is meant by sensitive data: first and foremost it is data that must be safeguarded from falling into the wrong hands, the consequence of which would be damaging to an individual or an organization. For an individual, sensitive data usually means private information. The nature of private information will not be explored here but the reader is encouraged to consult [2]. For an organization, sensitive data may encompass private information, but may additionally include information that may compromise the competitiveness of a company if divulged, such as trade secrets or proprietary algorithms and secret formulas. For this work, sensitive data is defined as follows:

DEFINITION 1: *Sensitive data* is information that must be protected from unauthorized access in order to safeguard the privacy of an individual or the operational well being of an organization.

This work considers losses arising from sensitive data or sensitive information being in the possession of unintended malicious parties or entities. This covers theft and any unintended exposure of sensitive information such as accidental leakage or posting. Per Definition 1, "sensitive data" and "sensitive information" are used interchangeably in this work. Some researchers make a distinction between these terms but the popular usage calls for no distinction.

A. Attacks on Organizations

Attacks carried out against sensitive information residing with organizations may be categorized as "outside attacks" and "inside attacks". We define these as follows.

DEFINITION 2: An *attack* is any action carried out against sensitive information held by an organization that, if successful, results in that information being in the hands of the attacker. An *outside attack* (A_o) is an attack that is carried out by an outsider of the organization (i.e., the attacker is not associated with the organization in a way that gives her special access privileges to sensitive data, e.g., a regular member of the public). An *inside attack* (A_i) is an attack that is carried out by an insider of the organization (i.e., someone who has special access privileges to sensitive data by virtue of her association with the organization, e.g., employee).

DEFINITION 3: A *vulnerability* of an organization is any weakness in the organization's infrastructure, platform, or business processes that can be targeted by an attack. A *secured-vulnerability* was originally a vulnerability that has had protective security measures put in place so that it is no longer a vulnerability. For example, a vulnerability is private information stored in the clear. This becomes a secured vulnerability if the private information is encrypted.

Outside attacks target a range of security vulnerabilities, from software systems that can be breached to access the sensitive information to simple theft of laptops and other devices used to store sensitive information. An example of an outside attack is the use of a Trojan horse planted inside the organization's computer system to steal sensitive information.

Inside attacks arise from the attacker making use of her privileged position (e.g., as an employee) to cause a loss of sensitive data. In this case, the attack is often difficult to detect, since it would appear as part of the normal duties of the insider attacker. An example of an inside attack is where a disgruntled employee secretly posts the organization's sensitive information on the Internet to try to harm the organization. An inside attack can also be unintentional (e.g., an employee casually providing client names for a survey).

Both outside and inside attacks target the organization's vulnerabilities. Vulnerabilities that invite outside attacks include the use of badly provisioned firewalls, the failure to encrypt data, and simple carelessness (e.g., leaving a laptop containing sensitive information in a car). Vulnerabilities that attract inside attacks include a) poor business processes that lack mechanisms to track which data is used where, used for what purpose, and accessed by whom, b) poor working conditions that give rise to employees feeling unfairly treated by management which can lead to employees seeking revenge, and c) poor education and enforcement of company policies regarding the proper care and handling of sensitive information (e.g., the above survey example).

We have so far used the expressions "level of protection" and "protection level" informally relying on their everyday meaning. We now formalize this meaning in terms of vulnerabilities, introducing the idea of "security protection level".

DEFINITION 4: An organization's security protection level (SPL) is the degree of security protection from attacks that results from the organization having secured q vulnerabilities, leaving p vulnerabilities unsecured, where the organization has a total of $p+q$ vulnerabilities. Each pair of values (p, q) corresponds to a different SPL.

B. Deriving the Estimates

Intuitively, for the same organization, SPL A is more capable of protecting from sensitive information loss than SPL B if A is composed of more secured vulnerabilities than B, where all vulnerabilities have roughly the same level of loss risk. This is the idea behind the derivation below.

We seek the capability C of an organization's SPL to protect sensitive data. Suppose that an organization's SPL has p vulnerabilities and q secured-vulnerabilities, where no distinction is made between outside and inside attacks. The number of original vulnerabilities before any vulnerabilities were secured is $p+q$. Let $P(e)$ represent the probability of event e. For convenience, "data" is understood to be "sensitive data". We have

$$C = P(no\ data\ losses) = 1-P(data\ losses) \quad (1)$$

Since a data loss is the result of a successful attack on a vulnerability,

$$P(data\ losses) \approx p/(p+q) \quad (2)$$

where we have applied the additive rule for the union of probabilities of attacks on the p vulnerabilities, assuming that 2 or more attacks do not occur simultaneously. This is a fair assumption confirmed by experience. Substituting (2) into (1) and adjusting for a possible zero denominator gives

$$C \approx 1-[p/(p+q)] = q/(p+q) \quad if\ p+q > 0 \quad (3)$$
$$= 1 \quad if\ p+q = 0 \quad (4)$$

Since C is a probability, its value is between 0 and 1, attaining 0 if the organization has no secured vulnerabilities ($q=0$, (3)) and 1 if either all of its vulnerabilities are secured ($p=0$, (3)) or if the organization has no vulnerabilities ($p+q=0$, (4)). Since an organization having no vulnerabilities is highly improbable, (4) is unlikely to apply.

The above derivation can be done within each of the categories of outside attacks and inside attacks (we did not distinguish between outside and inside attacks above). Let C_o, C_i represent the capabilities of an organization's SPL to protect sensitive information from outside attacks and inside attacks, respectively. Let p_o, p_i represent the number of vulnerabilities to outside attacks and inside attacks, respectively. Let q_o, q_i represent the number of secured vulnerabilities to outside attacks and inside attacks, respectively. Then, repeating the above derivation for outside attacks and inside attacks gives

$$C_o \approx q_o/(p_o+q_o) \quad if\ p_o+q_o > 0 \quad (5)$$
$$\approx 1 \quad if\ p_o+q_o = 0 \quad (6)$$
$$C_i \approx q_i/(p_i+q_i) \quad if\ p_i+q_i > 0 \quad (7)$$
$$\approx 1 \quad if\ p_i+q_i = 0 \quad (8)$$

As above, C_o (C_i) have values between 0 and 1, attaining 0 if the organization has no secured vulnerabilities to outside (inside) attacks ((5) and (7)) and 1 if either all of the vulnerabilities are secured ((5) and (7)) or if the organization has no vulnerabilities ((6) and (8)). Since an organization having no vulnerabilities to outside and inside attacks is highly improbable, (6) and (8) are unlikely to apply.

The estimates of data protection capability are now assigned as follows for a given SPL. Let E be an estimate of data protection capability, where no distinction is made between outside and inside attacks. Let E_o be an estimate of data protection capability against outside attacks. Let E_i be an estimate of data protection capability against inside attacks. Then for the SPL,

$$E = q/(p+q) \quad if\ p+q > 0 \quad (9)$$
$$= 1 \quad if\ p+q = 0 \quad (10)$$
$$E_o = q_o/(p_o+q_o) \quad if\ p_o+q_o > 0 \quad (11)$$
$$= 1 \quad if\ p_o+q_o = 0 \quad (12)$$
$$E_i = q_i/(p_i+q_i) \quad if\ p_i+q_i > 0 \quad (13)$$
$$= 1 \quad if\ p_i+q_i = 0 \quad (14)$$

E has the advantage of providing a single number for ease of comparison between different SPLs within an organization. A threshold T for E may be pre-determined such that for E above T, the security measures installed by the organization to secure vulnerabilities against both outside and inside attacks (corresponding to a SPL) are deemed adequate. For a given SPL, E_o *and* E_i have the advantage of focusing in separately on where an organization stands in terms of its security measures against outside and inside attacks. Thresholds T_o and T_i may be pre-determined for E_o and E_i respectively, such that for both estimates above their respective thresholds, the corresponding installed security measures against outside and inside attacks are deemed adequate. If this is the case, we call the corresponding SPL an *adequate SPL*. In practice, E_o and E_i may be expressed as percentages that define a region in a 100 x 100 plane in which an organization's capability to protect data is adequate (acceptable), as represented by the shaded region in Figure 1. Each point in this shaded region corresponds to an adequate SPL. An organization strives to have the "best"

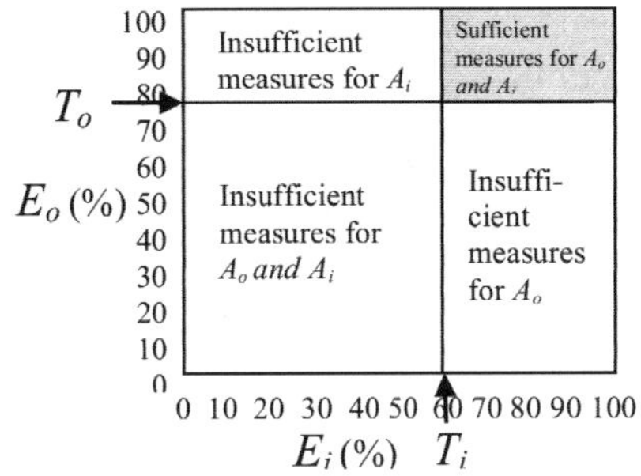

Figure 1. Sufficiency of Security Measures Against Outside Attacks (A_o) and Inside Attacks (A_i)

adequate SPL (one which has highest number of security measures possible against both outside and inside attacks) as allowed by its financial budget for adding security measures (see Section III).

III. APPLYING THE ESTIMATES TO OBTAIN A SPL

This section shows how an organization may use the estimates to establish a "best" adequate SDL as permitted by its financial budget. The description below separates outside attacks from inside attacks since organizations would need to account for them separately.

A. Determining the Vulnerabilities

For outside attacks, we recommend a threat analysis of security vulnerabilities in the organization's systems that could allow outside attacks to occur. The threat analysis can be carried out by a project team consisting of a security analyst, a privacy analyst, and a project leader acting as a facilitator. In addition to having expertise on privacy and security, the analysts must also be very familiar with the organization's systems. Threat analysis or threat modeling is a method for systematically assessing and documenting the security risks associated with a system (Salter et al. [3]).

Threat modeling involves understanding the adversary's goals in attacking the system based on the system's assets of interest. It is predicated on that fact that an adversary cannot attack a system without a way of supplying it with data or otherwise accessing it. In addition, an adversary will only attack a system if it has some assets of interest. The method of threat analysis given in [3] or any other method of threat analysis will yield $N_o = p_o + q_o$, which is the total number of vulnerabilities to outside attacks. We will not take up room to provide further details on threat analysis here.

For inside attacks, we recommend that the above project team carry out a special insider threat analysis, to identify vulnerabilities to inside attacks and identify measures to secure these vulnerabilities. The team would accomplish this by brainstorming answers to the questions in Table 1, or other questions from experience, identifying the vulnerabilities and measures to secure the vulnerabilities in the process. In Table 1, questions 1 to 6 address motivational or environmental vulnerabilities, which may also be "secured" by applying mitigating measures. Questions 7 and 8 address security vulnerabilities. In identifying vulnerabilities to inside attack, the project team may weigh the vulnerabilities in terms of how likely they are to lead to attacks, and eliminate the unlikely ones. The weighing process may consider such factors as risk to the attacker that she could be caught as well as her motivation for the attack. The value of $N_i = p_i + q_i$ would be determined at the end of this process.

B. *Determining the Thresholds T_o and T_i*

The values of T_o and T_i should be determined by the same threat analysis team mentioned above. The values would depend on the following:

- The potential value of the sensitive data – the more valuable the data is to a thief, a malicious entity, or a competitor, the higher the thresholds should be.
- The damages to the organization that would result, if the sensitive data were compromised – of course, the higher the damages, the higher the thresholds.
- The current and likely future attack climate – consider the volume of attacks and the nature of the victims, say over the last 6 months; if the organization's sector or industry has sustained a large number of recent attacks, then these thresholds need to be higher.
- Consider also potential attacks by nation states as a result of the political climate; attacks by individual hacktivist groups such as Anonymous or WikiLeaks may also warrant attention.

In general, an organization would like to be as secure as possible and establish a "best" adequate SPL. Therefore, values above 80% would not be uncommon. However, whatever the thresholds, the organization must find them acceptable after considering the above factors. It must also be kept in mind that the higher the thresholds, the higher will be the financial costs of implementing the security measures.

TABLE 1. QUESTIONNAIRE TO IDENTIFY VULNERABILITIES TO INSIDE ATTACK

	Question	Rationale
1.	Is the sensitive information of high value to outside agencies or a competitor?	The higher the value, the more an inside attacker will be tempted to steal and sell the information.
2.	Does the organization have an employee assistance program that includes counselling and help with financial difficulties?	Such a program may eliminate some financial motivation for an inside attack.
3.	Does the organization have an ombudsman or other impartial agent to assist employees with their grievances?	Such an impartial agent may eliminate or reduce the motivation to seek revenge by committing an inside attack.
4.	Does the organization have a history of perceived injustices to employees?	If the answer is 'yes', employees may be motivated by revenge to commit an inside attack.
5.	Does the organization conduct a stringent back-ground and reliability check on a candidate for employ-ment prior to hiring the candidate?	While a background and reliability check is not guaranteed to weed out potential inside attackers, it should eliminate those with criminal pasts.
6.	Does the organization require candidates for employment to disclose any potential conflicts of interest they may have with respect to their new employment and any outside interests prior to hire? Does the organization require ongoing disclosure of conflicts of interest after hire?	Eliminating conflicts of interest should reduce related motivations for malicious inside attacks. For example, an inside attacker may secretly compromise private information in favour of an outside interest, believing that the com-promise is undetected.
7.	What are some possible ways for an insider to gain access to sensitive informa-tion she should not be accessing? How to secure?	This question will identify security weaknesses.
8.	What are some possible ways for an insider to trans-mit sensitive information outside the organization undetected? How to secure?	This question will identify additional security weaknesses.

C. *Applying the Estimates for a "Best" Adequate SPL*

We now have values for the following: $N_o = p_o + q_o$, $N_i = p_i + q_i$ (Section IIIA), and T_o, T_i (Section IIIB). Rewriting (11) and (13) and using the ceiling function to avoid fractional numbers of secured vulnerabilities gives:

$q_o = \lceil N_oE_o \rceil$ where $T_o \leq E_o \leq 1$ (15)
$q_i = \lceil N_iE_i \rceil$ where $T_i \leq E_i \leq 1$ (16)

Equations (15) and (16) give all possible values of q_o and q_i such that the associated E_o and E_i (with $p_o = N_o - q_o$ and $p_i = N_i - q_i$) fall within the shaded region of Figure 1. In other words, these equations give all possible values of q_o and q_i for adequate SPLs. The ceiling function biases the security level upward by taking the number of secured vulnerabilities to the next higher integer where applicable, which should be fine since more security should be better than less security. The quantities $q_o = \lceil N_oT_o \rceil$ and $q_i = \lceil N_iT_i \rceil$ from (15) and (16), termed respectively the threshold q_o and the threshold q_i, will be useful below.

To obtain a "best" adequate SPL from among the adequate SPLs generated by (15) and (16), the organization applies the constraint that the total cost of implementing the $(q_o + q_i)$ security measures from (15) and (16) must be less than or equal to the financial budget for security measures. The organization separately prioritizes its outside attack and inside attack vulnerabilities, and then selects them for securing in order of high priority to low priority, until both the financial budget is exhausted and the number of secured vulnerabilities are at least as great as the threshold q_o and the threshold q_i. In this way, the organization determines the q_o and q_i, as well as the p_o and p_i (which are just $N_o - q_o$ and $N_i - q_i$ respectively) that define its "best" adequate SPL. This procedure may be precisely described as follows. Let $u_1, u_2, \ldots u_{No}$ and $v_1, v_2, \ldots v_{Ni}$ be the organization's prioritized outside attack and inside attack vulnerabilities, respectively, such that u_1 has higher (or equal) priority than u_2, u_2 has higher (or equal) priority than u_3, and so on. Similarly, v_1 has higher (or equal) priority than v_2, v_2 has higher (or equal) priority than v_3, and so on. Let B_o and B_i represent the budgets for securing against outside and inside attacks, respectively. Let C_o and C_i be the costs of securing the vulnerabilities to outside and inside attacks respectively. Let k be a counter variable. Then the pseudo code shown in Figure 2 describes the procedure for obtaining a "best" adequate SPL. Running this pseudo code will produce the following: a) q_o and q_i, defining the "best" adequate SPL, or b) one or two "insufficient budget" messages, in which case the organization has to increase the corresponding budgets and re-run the procedure. Only result a) would be acceptable.

Prioritizing the vulnerabilities may be based on four aspects of an attack, namely "risk", "access", "cost", and the resulting damages from the attack, where "risk" is risk to the safety of the attacker, "access" is the ease with which the attacker can access the system under attack, "cost" is the monetary cost to the attacker to mount the attack, and resulting damages is self evident. A full explanation of this prioritization procedure is given in Yee [2].

IV. APPLICATION EXAMPLE

Alice Inc., an online seller of goods (e.g., Amazon.com), has an objective to secure its vulnerabilities to outside and inside attacks and to establish a "best" adequate SPL using the approach in this work. The company hired a security consulting firm to perform threat analyses of its systems, resulting in a report of vulnerabilities found that could be targeted by outside and inside attackers. The report also provides values for the number of vulnerabilities as $N_o = 10$ and $N_i = 8$, and includes prioritizations of outside and inside vulnerabilities. For each type of vulnerability (i.e., outside or inside) the prioritizations identified which vulnerability required securing first, which one second, and so on, in declining order of urgency. Based on the consultant's recommendations, as well as its own internal deliberations, Alice Inc. assigned the following values:

```
Begin;
  C_o = 0; C_i = 0; k = 0;
  While k ≤ N_o and C_o ≤ B_o;
    k = k + 1;
    C_o = C_o + cost of securing u_k;
  EndWhile;
  If (k ≥ threshold q_o) q_o = k;
  Else Print "q_o unavailable -insufficient budget";
  k = 0;
  While k ≤ N_i and C_i ≤ B_i;
    k = k + 1;
    C_i = C_i + cost of securing v_k;
  EndWhile;
  If (k ≥ threshold q_i) q_i = k;
  Else Print "q_i unavailable – insufficient budget";
End;
```

Figure 2. Procedure for obtaining a "best" adequate SPL.

$$T_o = 0.80,\ T_i = 0.90,\ B_o = \$100{,}000,\ B_i = \$150{,}000$$

Therefore

$$\text{threshold } q_o = \lceil N_oT_o \rceil = \lceil 10 \text{ x } 0.80 \rceil = 8$$
$$\text{threshold } q_i = \lceil N_iT_i \rceil = \lceil 8 \text{ x } 0.85 \rceil = 7$$

meaning that at least 8 vulnerabilities to outside attacks and 7 vulnerabilities to inside attacks must be secured in order to have a "best" adequate SPL. Table 2 identifies the costs of securing the prioritized vulnerabilities where vulnerability 1 is the most urgent, vulnerability 2 is next urgent, and so on.

TABLE 2. COSTS OF SECURING OUTSIDE AND INSIDE VULNERABILITIES

u_k	Cost of Securing	v_k	Cost of Securing
1	\$20,000	1	\$40,000
2	\$15,000	2	\$40,000
3	\$10,000	3	\$30,000
4	\$10,000	4	\$20,000
5	\$8,000	5	\$10,000
6	\$7,000	6	\$5,000
7	\$5,000	7	\$5,000
8	\$5,000	8	\$5,000
9	\$3,000		
10	\$2,000		

As in Section III, outside and inside vulnerabilities are denoted as u_k and v_k respectively. Running the pseudo code in Figure 2 yields $C_o = \$85{,}000$ at $q_o = 10$ and $C_i =$

\$150,000 at $q_i = 7$. The budget for securing outside vulnerabilities was more than enough to secure all outside vulnerabilities. The budget for securing inside vulnerabilities was only enough to secure 7 inside vulnerabilities. Given the existing budgets, Alice Inc.'s "best" adequate SPL is realized with $q_o = 10, p_o = 0$ *and* $q_i = 7, p_i = 1$. Any additional security measure against inside attacks would require an increase in the budget.

V. RELATED WORK

Related work found in the literature includes risk and threat analysis applied to various domains as well as research on vulnerabilities. No other work was found that is similar to this work.

In terms of risk analysis, Jing et al. [4] present an approach that uses machine learning to continuously and automatically assess privacy risks incurred by users of mobile applications. Aditya et al. [5] catalog privacy threats introduced by new, sophisticated mobile devices and applications. Their work emphasizes how these new threats are fundamentally different and inherently more dangerous than prior systems, and present a new protocol for secure communications between mobile devices.

In terms of threat analysis, Schaad and Borozdin [6] present an approach for automated threat analysis of software architecture diagrams. Their work shows that automated threat analysis is feasible. Shi et al. [7] describe a hybrid static-dynamic approach for mobile security threat analysis, where the dynamic part executes the program in a limited way by following the critical path identified in the static part. Sanzgiri and Dasgupta [8] summarize and classify insider threat detection techniques based on the detection strategies used. Sokolowski and Banks [9] describe the implementation of an agent-based simulation model designed to capture insider threat behavior, given a set of assumptions governing agent behavior that pre-disposes an agent to becoming a threat.

With regard to vulnerabilities, Gawron et al. [10] investigate the detection of vulnerabilities in computer systems and computer networks. They use a logical representation of preconditions and postconditions of vulnerabilities, with the aim of providing security advisories and enhanced diagnostics for the system. Spanos et al. [11] look at ways to improve the open standard to score and rank vulnerabilities, known as the Common Vulnerability Scoring System (CVSS). They propose a new vulnerability scoring system called the Weighted Impact Vulnerability Scoring System (WIVSS) that incorporates the different impact of vulnerability characteristics. In addition, the MITRE Corporation maintains the Common Vulnerability and Exposures (CVE) list of vulnerabilities and exposures [12], standardized to facilitate information sharing.

VI. CONCLUSIONS AND FUTURE RESEARCH

Organizations need to protect their sensitive data from outside and inside attacks against their computer systems that store the data. This protection is achieved by adding security measures to secure vulnerabilities to attack. However, organizations have been implementing security measures without any way of setting security protection level targets, or knowing how an added security measure contributes to the protection target. Organizations also did not have a way of selecting which security measures to implement in order to stay within the financial budget. This work proposes a quantitative approach to estimate, set, and achieve safe security protection levels in terms of securing outside and inside vulnerabilities. In addition, the work proposes a procedure for selecting which security measures to implement in order to achieve targeted protection levels within the allowable financial budget.

Future research includes investigating other formulations of security protection levels, such as incorporating the effectiveness of security measures, as well as improving the methods for threat analysis and prioritization. In addition, it would be interesting to explore how this work complements existing work in the standardization community.

REFERENCES

[1] Identity Force, "The Biggest Data Breaches in 2016," retrieved: July, 2017, https://www.identityforce.com/blog/2016-data-breaches

[2] G. Yee, "Visualization and Prioritization of Privacy Risks in Software Systems," International Journal on Advances in Security, issn 1942-2636, vol. 10, no. 1&2, pp. 14-25, 2017, http://www.iariajournals.org/security/

[3] C. Salter, O. Saydjari, B. Schneier, and J. Wallner, "Towards a Secure System Engineering Methodology," Proc. New Security Paradigms Workshop, pp. 2-10, 1998.

[4] Y. Jing, G.-J. Ahn, Z. Zhao, and H. Hu, "RiskMon: Continuous and Automated Risk Assessment of Mobile Applications," Proc. 4th ACM Conference on Data and Application Security and Privacy (CODASPY '14), pp. 99-110, 2014.

[5] P. Aditya, B. Bhattacharjee, P. Druschel, V. Erdélyi, and M. Lentz, "Brave New World: Privacy Risks for Mobile Users," Proc. ACM MobiCom Workshop on Security and Privacy in Mobile Environments (SPME '14), pp. 7-12, 2014.

[6] A. Schaad and M. Borozdin, "TAM2: Automated Threat Analysis," Proc. 27th Annual ACM Symposium on Applied Computing (SAC '12), pp. 1103-1108, 2012.

[7] Y. Shi, W. You, K. Qian, P. Bhattacharya, and Y. Qian, "A Hybrid Analysis for Mobile Security Threat Detection," Proc. IEEE Annual Ubiquitous Computing, Electronics & Mobile Communication Conference (UEMCON), pp. 1-7, 2016.

[8] A. Sanzgiri and D. Dasgupta, "Classification of Insider Threat Detection Techniques," Proc. 11th Annual Cyber and Information Security Research Conference (CISRC '16), article no. 25, pp. 1-4, 2016.

[9] J. Sokolowski and C. Banks, "An Agent-Based Approach to Modeling Insider Threat," Proc. Symposium on Agent-Directed Simulation (ADS '15), pp. 36-41, 2015.

[10] M. Gawron, A. Amirkhanyan, F. Cheng, and C. Meinel, "Automatic Vulnerability Detection for Weakness Visualization and Advisory Creation," Proc. 8th International Conference on Security of Information and Networks (SIN '15), pp. 229-236, 2015.

[11] G. Spanos, A. Sioziou, and L. Angelis, "WIVSS: A New Methodology for Scoring Information System Vulnerabilities," Proc. 17th Panhellenic Conference on Informatics, pp. 83-90, 2013.

[12] MITRE, "Common Vulnerabilities and Exposures", retrieved: July, 2017, https://cve.mitre.org/

RMDM – A Conceptual ICT Risk-Meta-Data-Model

Applied to COBIT for Risk as underlying Risk Model

Martin Latzenhofer [1 2]
[1] Center for Digital Safety & Security
Austrian Institute of Technology
Vienna, Austria
email: martin.latzenhofer@ait.ac.at

Gerald Quirchmayr [2]
[2] Multimedia Information Systems Research Group
Faculty of Computer Science, University of Vienna
Vienna, Austria
email: gerald.quirchmayr@univie.ac.at

***Abstract*— The aim of this article is to introduce an approach that integrates the different models and methods currently applied for risk management in information and communication technologies (ICT). These different risk management approaches are usually bound to the organization where they are applied, thus staying quite specific for a given setting. Consequently, there is no possibility to compare or reuse risk management structures because they are individual solutions. In order to establish a common basis for working with different underlying risk models, a metamodeling approach from the area of Disaster Recovery is used. A first concept for a data model described in Unified Modeling Language (UML) is presented and its core components addressing the whole risk management lifecycle are described. This contribution describes a comprehensive mapping of information artefacts – in this case obtained from the COBIT for Risk framework – which are then lifted to the meta-level of the proposed ICT risk-meta-data-model in order to be able to work with them in a consolidated way. Through this mapping process, all information artefacts are extracted, consolidated and harmonized to minimize the number of relevant objects. It has turned out that both the list of consolidated objects and the derived describing attributes can in general be incorporated into the proposed ICT risk-meta-data-model (RMDM), i.e., the essential information for working with the COBIT for Risk model can be stored in the proposed ICT risk-meta-data-model. The results of the mapping show that it is worth examining a data-structure-oriented approach in order to develop both a model and a data structure for further framework-independent processing.**

Keywords-information and communication technology risk management; ICT risk-meta-data-model; COBIT for Risk; metamodeling; data model; UML.

I. INTRODUCTION

In literature and in practice, many different risk management approaches and models can be found for the area of information and communication technology (ICT) systems. Even within the field of ICT, these approaches and models are tailored quite narrowly to specific areas and are typically restricted to one single organization. Therefore, the information on risk management is usually not comparable and transferrable between different organizations. This means that the risk model, the established risk management method, the concrete process implementation, the required input data and the resulting outcome have to be adapted to the current requirements of an organization every time the risk management process is set up. This often leads to high efforts for an organization or a company because they have to initialize and re-establish the risk management frameworks and related processes each time. It is evident that these parameters result in a smaller degree of reusability of a given risk management process and less comparability of the information obtained from it.

When interpreting this problem as a pure ICT issue, an explicit ICT solution is required. This leads to the main research question of this paper, i.e., whether it is possible to develop a common risk management model, which is flexible enough to be applicable in different fields of the ICT area as well as among different organizations. To achieve that, it is crucial to define a suitable level of modeling. Therefore, the goal of the introduced approach is to design a meta-model for ICT risk management. By integrating different existing ICT risk management models, which are suitable for various fields of application into a meta-model, a generic data structure that focuses on common aspects of these models can be developed. This umbrella model simply obtains data from the underlying specialized models that have been defined by different frameworks. The approach introduced in this article postulates a superordinate meta-model for ICT risk management and represents it as a data model, expressed a UML class diagram. Considering the application of ICT risk management in practice, the state-of-the-art frameworks are well-established in the daily business of organizations. Consequently, it is not realistic to replace them by a new, universally valid model. The ICT risk-meta-data-model approach introduced here firstly establishes a common data base of risk information gathered by different risk management frameworks, secondly makes data retrieved from different sources comparable, and thirdly verifies its practical applicability by describing real-life use cases, shown as an instantiation of the ICT risk-meta-data-model.

The main goal is to specify the meta-model as a substantial data model. Using such a precise data model, the meta-model is directly applicable to real-life scenarios and enables the implementation of a dedicated ICT application or data structure. The data model is directly applicable for ICT tasks, provides a concrete ICT data structure where risk information can be stored, and is a fundamental (data) basis for ICT risk management applications.

This paper is divided into five main sections. Following this introduction, Section II discusses those processes of

COBIT for Risk, which are relevant for risk management in detail, describes the fundamentals of the metamodeling approach, and concludes with discussing related work. In Section III, the conceptual data model RMDM, described in Unified Modeling Language (UML) is introduced. Section IV discusses the mapping of the information artefacts, input and output components of COBIT for Risk – the core of the derived risk model – and the objects of the proposed ICT risk-meta-data-model (RMDM). The objective of Section IV is to apply the postulated meta-model by modelling an instance of a concrete risk model. The concluding Section V outlines the results and proposes further research that is needed to refine the ICT risk-meta-data-model (RMDM).

II. FUNDAMENTALS

A. *COBIT for Risk*

Typically, organizations have a continuous need to manage the risks in their business environment. Such a need due to extrinsical factors is often motivated by legal requirements. Organizations have to ensure compliance with regulations, especially relating to finance and public accounting. Therefore, the responsible person implements risk management – in this case limited to the ICT area – by doing research and building upon already existing risk management structures. Special risk management frameworks that are applicable to ICT, e.g., International Organization for Standardization (ISO) 31000 [1], National Institute of Standards and Technology (NIST) Special Publication (SP) 800-30/-37/-39 [2] [3] [4], Committee of Sponsoring Organizations of the Treadway Commission (COSO) Enterprise Risk Management (ERM) [5], Management of Risk [6] or COBIT for Risk [7], have proven to be effective within one single organization. These frameworks set up a baseline in an organization when it comes to implementing risk management structures. This usually generates isolated solutions. The different risk management frameworks are characterized by relatively similar objects and terms but very different artefacts, which cannot be related, compared, or summarized. One important issue is to harmonize the semantic differences between the various risk management frameworks, and even within one single framework.

COBIT for Risk [7] is a special publication edited by Information Systems Audit and Control Association (ISACA, since 2008 the acronym itself is used as a brand name) [8] and is entirely based on Control Objectives for Information and Related Technology (COBIT, since version 5 only the acronym itself is used as a brand name) 5.0 [9], a framework for governance and management of Enterprise ICT, especially for the interaction between ICT and classic business objectives. COBIT for Risk is a comprehensive guide for risk professionals. It elaborates the driving aspects for risk management in COBIT – principles and enablers – and extends the framework with risk scenarios. Furthermore, it provides suggestions for appropriate response measures using a combination of enablers. It has – similar to ISO 31000 [1] – a two-tier approach: the risk management perspective puts the high-level principles into practice and the risk function view seeks to identify relevant COBIT processes, which support the risk management, as depicted in Figure 1. In this figure, the two core risk processes are shown in light blue, the other twelve key supporting processes are colored in dark red.

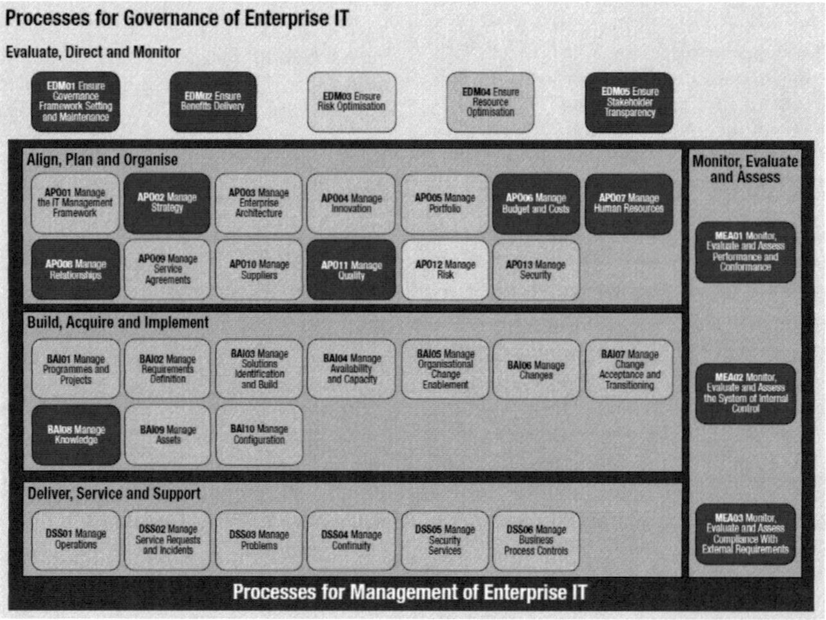

Figure 1. Supporting COBIT processes for the risk function [7, p. 35]

The COBIT for Risk framework was chosen as a the first candidate for the intended mapping because of its good balance between general applicability for risk management topics and very specific statements in form of concrete control objectives for risk management. It definitely provides much more topic-oriented reference-points than standard COBIT. The framework is clearly structured and its description is not too narrative. A highly narrative framework might increase the effort for identifying class objects. In summary, all these characteristics were considered to be good prerequisites for the practical mapping work. Other frameworks, e.g., ISO 31000 [1], might be too generic in order to derive substantial class objects to a sufficient extent or, e.g., NIST [2] [3] [4], is too text-heavy for an efficient proof of concept. Consequently, all the other frameworks are rather suitable for verifying the ICT risk-meta-data-model in a more advanced state of development.

B. Metamodeling Approach

The semantic meaning of a risk model must be transferred to the meta-level. A formal, scientific approach to build a consistent umbrella is missing. The meta-modeling process helps to create a common basis for standardization. The instantiation procedure of the meta-model down to the distinct risk management framework provides rules for transferring data from a concrete model up to the meta-model, and is in that way working as a normalization process. The first advantage of representing the risk-meta-model as data model is the immanent design of a structured data management based on a semantic model. It must be verified whether the general concepts can be divided from content-specific aspects in such a way that the interaction between meta- and model-level still remains efficient. The data model works as a structure model and holds static information. The risk management process and corresponding workflows change this data dynamically, providing a data model for the whole risk management life cycle. However, this article focuses on the verification of the basic content and on whether the data model can process the information. In addition, the meta-model approach for standardizing risk management information can be implicitly verified by setting up the data model, at least for those risk models which have been analyzed earlier. Certainly, it is no evidence for its comprehensiveness that all existing risk models still fit in the proposed meta-model. In fact, some models might be unsuitable for mapping. However, re-performing the transformation process for a specific number of widely accepted risk frameworks ensures that the meta-model is sufficiently applicable for risk management tasks in organizations.

In the context of a metamodeling hierarchy according to Karagiannis and Kühn [10] (cf., Figure 2.), the ICT risk-meta-data-model is situated on Level 2 – Metamodel, described by the Metamodeling Language UML. The selected risk management framework, e.g., COBIT for Risk [7], corresponds to Model on Level 1. It is described by means of the published framework, here in a semi-narrative way. The underlying Original itself can in fact be referred to as Level 0, and represents the organization's risk management structure facing a concrete risk situation. On the top of the hierarchy, the Meta²-Model on Level 3 defines the structural elements of the general UML class diagram. The Meta²-Modeling Language can be understood as the modeling language UML used to describe the ICT risk-meta-data-model.

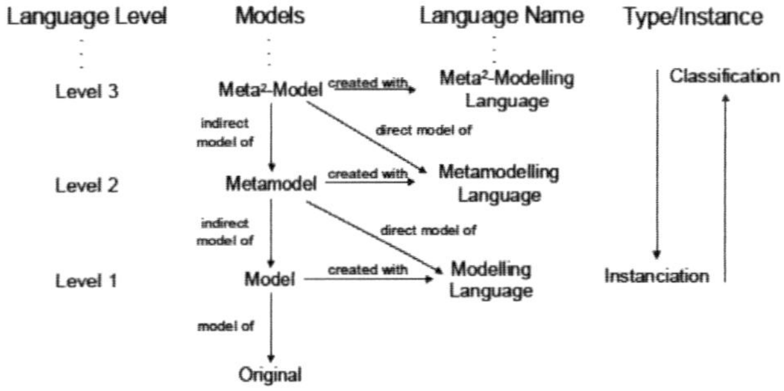

Figure 2. Metamodeling hierarchy [10]

C. Related Work

The approach introduced in this article is inspired by similar work in the field of disaster recovery [11] [12], which introduced a meta-model integrating data from different natural disaster scenarios. Othman and Beydoun have implemented a data model in order to store data relevant to disaster recovery and have conducted a proof of concept for two natural disaster incidents of recent history, the Christchurch earthquake and Fukushima nuclear incident [12]. In this article, their approach is shifted into the ICT risk management domain while verifying whether it is a sustainable method for risk management.

The conceptual ICT risk-meta-data-model was first introduced as a draft proposal at DACH Security 2016, Klagenfurt, Austria [13]. The present paper now provides a first comprehensive application of the mapping between the concrete risk model – here provided by COBIT for Risk – and the ICT risk-meta- data-model.

III. ICT RISK-META-DATA-MODEL (RMDM)

A. General Requirements

One of the main objectives of the conceptual ICT risk-meta-data-model is to record key information of any underlying risk model in a way that it can be compared, consolidated, merged and subsequently analyzed from an abstract meta-perspective. This approach ensures that risk management models that have already been implemented in organizations in practice continue to be used, at least the most commonly applied frameworks. Furthermore, this abstraction step reduces the information risk managers work with to the really essential requirements needed to establish the risk management framework and to perform the risk management process. This transformation from the risk model to the more abstract and general meta-level must follow specific rules and definitely causes some information loss. To succeed it is necessary to strike a viable balance between the appropriate level of detail of the information content – by selecting only the key data, combining it semantically correct and transferring it to the meta-level – and the complexity level of the risk-meta-data-model. The authors assume that an adequate level of abstraction is reached when three to four structurally different risk models can be consistently represented as instances of the ICT risk-meta-data-model. This iterative refinement of the risk-meta-data-model through the analysis of different underlying risk models enhances its sustainability and robustness for practical application. The major advantage of formulating the ICT risk-meta-data-model as an ICT data model is that this allows organizations and companies to apply it in practice. By depicting the meta-model as unified modelling language (UML) classes diagram the modeler can immediately generate the corresponding data structure, implementing a demonstrator, which can serve as a proof of concept. Consequently, the ICT risk-meta-data-model itself constitutes an ICT application that can be applied in practice. In other words, the ICT problem to merge data from different risk models requires an ICT solution, which can immediately be applied by IT means.

The first draft of the ICT risk-meta-data-model was developed based on literature research on different risk management frameworks, which all propagate distinct risk models but use the same or similar terms. The literature research also indicated that there is a need to reflect on the exact meaning of the used terms, even if they seem to be identical. A feasible mapping of the concepts used in different risk models is a prerequisite for successfully raising the key information of the risk model up to the meta-level. This requires the definition of consistent concepts on the meta-level in order to prevent overlapping of concepts and resulting misinterpretations. However, it depends on the specific framework whether the risk model can be derived directly from the publications. ISO 31000 [1], for example, is formulated in a generic way, thus leaving room for interpretation. COBIT for Risk [7], does in contrast provide very specific control objectives for the key and supporting processes on a more detailed level. This characteristic was the main reason for selecting COBIT for Risk for the first mapping of a risk model to the ICT risk-meta-data-model. The conceptual model aims at reflecting both the fundamental framework establishment and the operative risk management process that covers the risk management lifecycle. This dual perspective is a key feature of many frameworks and easily visible in, e.g., ISO 31000 [1], NIST [2] [3] [4], or even COBIT for Risk [7]. A core aspect was to identify appropriate objects, which represent the focus points within the risk management structure. These objects are further described by dedicated attributes, which are the variables for storing the relevant risk management information. These attributes can be changed, modified, extended, and adapted by specific methods. By setting up this data structure it is possible to transfer all relevant risk management data from the origin model up to the ICT risk-meta-data-model. A very first draft of the modelling was already introduced in [13]. This article included a first draft of the ICT risk-meta-data-model and a possible approach for a proof of concept by applying COBIT for Risk as the underlying risk model. The first version of the ICT risk-meta-data-model was the result of a creative process. This process followed the life cycle of risk management: starting with the identification of risk factors, followed by the analysis of the resulting risk by linking it to the current challenges that the organization has to cope with, and finally the evaluation of the risk. Furthermore, the data-model may represent the monitoring of established treatment activities. As a consequence, the data model fulfills the essential requirements of the risk management process as suggested in [1]. The next step is to perform a precise mapping of information artefacts propagated by COBIT for Risk [7] as described in Section IV.

B. *Main Components*

Figure 3 shows the status quo of the advanced ICT risk-meta-data-model (RMDM) after the mapping. Classes or relationships written in italics are represented in the UML diagram. On an abstract level, all classes are derived from class *Organisation* and further divided in *Input*, *Process*, *Output* and *Actor*. The class *Actor* represents all actors and the responsibilities taken over by organizational entities, persons or roles, e.g., by the risk manager. This construction with generalization relationships both introduces an additional inherent structure of the data model and applies generalization and inheritance of attributes by superior classes in order to cope with the rising complexity. However, especially the class *Process* should also be able to summarize all important processes, policies, standards and guidelines that form the operational environment. It is not only an abstract data structure, but rather a hybrid class.

The operative part of the conceptual model and the linked classes can be divided into three virtual parts, which are not explicitly included in the UML diagram in Figure 3. In the first phase, the conceptual model shows the causal chain from the single risk factors to the identified risk, which is in fact a prerequisite for performing an operational risk management process. The causal chain starts on the left side with a pure *Hazard,* which *threatens* a particular *Vulnerability*, resulting in the associated class *Threat*. Hence, the *Threat* explicitly *affects* an *Asset* of the organization, leading to one main risk factor *Impact*, which is also designed as an associated class. The *Threat has* also some *Probability* to materialize, which is the second main risk factor. Typically, the *Risk* can be characterized by its essential components *Impact* and *Probability*, which are often shown in a risk matrix and here designed as composition of both risk factors. However, the *Risk* reflects only the identified risks and does not yet link to a detailed assessment, which the organization is required to do as a next step. The second phase of the risk management process involves the assessment of the previously identified raw risks and linking them with the given influencing factors and framework conditions. Accordingly, the class *Risk* is a composition for *AssessedRisk*. This class records all necessary evaluations of the risks.

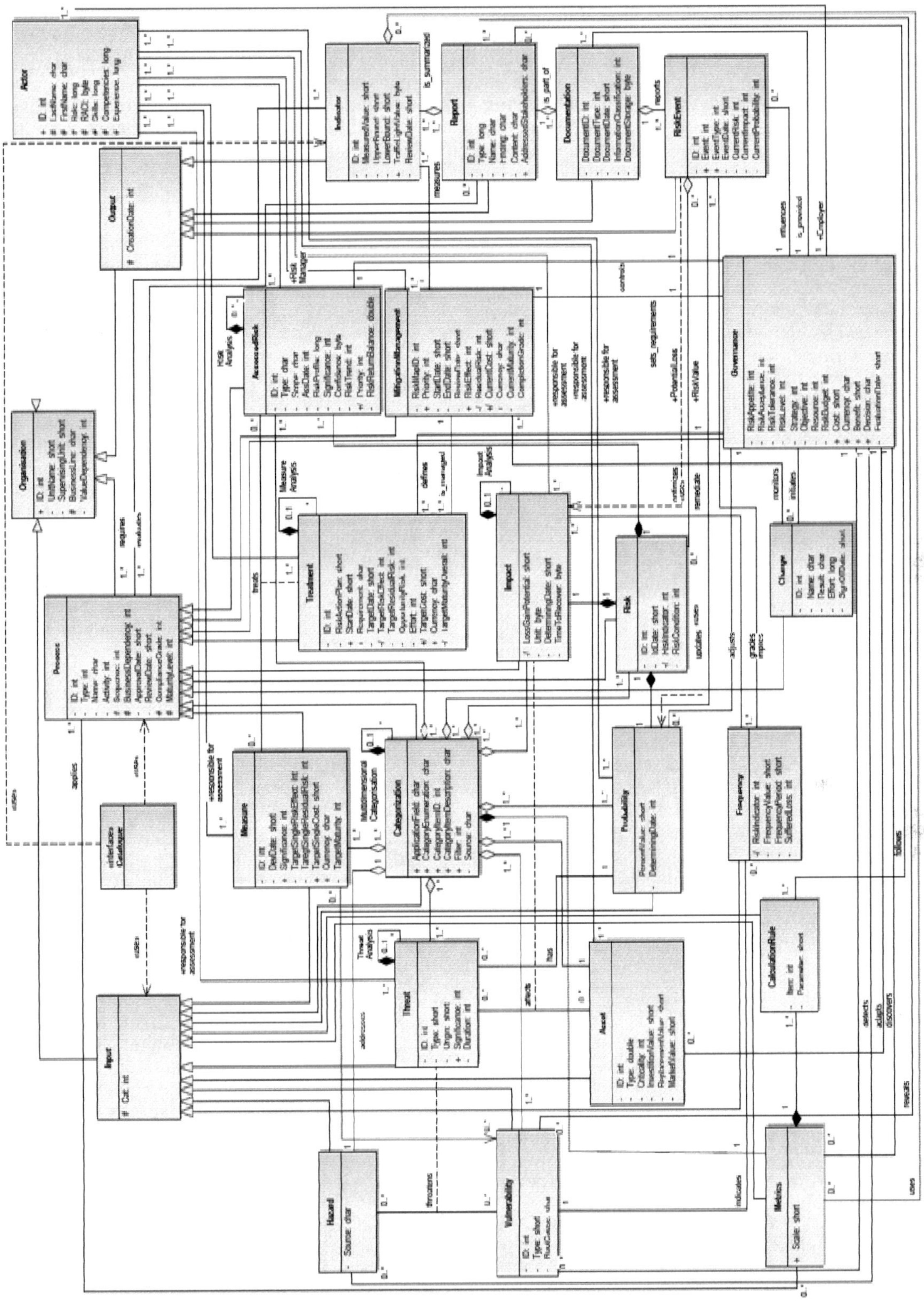

Figure 3. Conceptual ICT risk-meta-data-model (RMDM) described as UML class diagram

A *Measure* treats *AssessedRisk*, but there is no indication whether these measures are really applied in this stage. This is indicated by the associated class *Treatment*. In this way, a gradual filter starting from *Risk*, via *Measure* to *Treatment* can be applied. This filter allows focusing only on those risks, which should be actively addressed in the risk management process and further reduces the complexity of the model to the high-risk areas according to the individual risk level. Consequently, all the selected *Treatments* are managed by *Mitigation Management* during their whole lifecycle. Thus, this class represents the core structure for performing the risk management process within the defined risk management framework over time. The third part of the ICT risk-meta-data-model addresses the management's governance and its supporting elements, e.g., key output, risk events, or metrics. The class *Governance* establishes requirements for the class *MitigationManagement* and subsumes all the influencing factors to set up the appropriate risk environment. It holds management information about finance, strategy, objectives, risk appetite and tolerance etc. It is supported by ongoing *Changes*, which subsume all ancillary activities that support risk management activities, i.e., projects, changes. The class *Categorization* addresses all forms of structuring, e.g., categories, graduations, risk scales, and cluster definitions in the context of risk management efforts, and provides additional structure, while leaving enough leeway for individual metrics.

It is also possible to integrate external catalogues, frameworks, and regulations into the risk management model through the interface class *Catalogue*. *Documentation* in any form, especially *Reports* or (Key Risk) *Indicators,* has specifying classes, which are implemented as aggregations from the generic structure (*Documentation*) to more quantifiable information (*Indicator*). *Documentation* covers all documents that are relevant for governance decisions and thus creates an information repository. *Metrics* with specified *CalculationRules* stores all kinds of calculation bases, e.g., for Balanced Scorecard, Key Risk Indicators, or Process Performance. This ICT risk-meta-data-model also includes an important feedback loop. The class *RiskEvent* ensures the remediation of risk information based on new findings due to incidents based on real-life incidents. In combination with the class *Frequency,* the quantification of already suffered risk events enables the adjustment of the underlying risk factors, thus increasing the accuracy of further assessments. Intended self-referencing relationships for the classes *Categorization*, *Threat*, *Impact*, *AssessedRisk*, and *Treatment* enable further substantial analysis, e.g., multidimensional assessments of cascading effects if needed.

IV. MAPPING

A. Method

The critical success factor for the proper functioning of the meta-modeling idea is the coherent transformation of the information of the selected risk model up to the meta-model while at the same time sufficiently reducing the information content. This transformation is in fact a mapping of all the relevant pieces of information that is necessary for performing risk management with the selected risk model. The risk model COBIT for Risk was selected as the first proof of concept for the metamodeling approach. It provides an appropriate degree of concreteness in order to verify the draft concept that was first introduced in [13].

In a first step, both risk management core processes Evaluate, Direct and Monitor (EDM) 03 "Ensure Risk Optimisation" – the setup of the risk management environment in the organization – and Align, Plan and Organise (APO12) "Manage Risk" – the risk management process as discussed above – were analyzed. All information artefacts mentioned as input or output objects and in the description of the risk specific activities were extracted to a list. These have a different degree of concreteness, which was also assessed. This step was repeated for each of the other twelve supporting processes, which are marked in dark red in Figure 1. This finally resulted in a list of 1619 identified information artefacts, but this list included duplicates, synonyms, and different notations of the same objects, cf. Figure 4. In a second step, all these entries were consolidated in order to even out differences and reduce the amount of information artefacts for further analysis. All entries were transformed into a consolidated object, in fact performing a form of abstraction. This transformation resulted in a list of 26 objects, which corresponds to the column 'synonym' in Figure 4. The purpose of these objects was to set up a data store, leading to a UML class at the end of this process. This abstraction process was conducted as iterative working step because the consolidated object list initiated continuous improvement actions in order to get a coherent list for the subsequent steps. Once the list of consolidated objects had been verified, the consolidated object list was mapped to the classes in the UML diagram. In a third step, the class attributes were revised so that the essential data for risk management fit properly into the appropriate classes.

Process	Source	Artefact	Level of Detail	Synonym
APO012.01	1	analysis method	medium	Process
APO012.01	1.1	analysis model	low	Process
APO012.01	1.4	assessment of risk attribute	medium	Assessment
APO012.01	2.2	audit	medium	Actor
APO012.01	2.2	business source	low	Catalogue
APO012.01	2.2	CIO office	medium	Actor
APO012.01	1	classification method	medium	Category
APO012.01	1.1	classification model	high	Category
APO012.01	4.1	collected data	medium	Catalogue
APO012.01	1	collection method	medium	Process
APO012.01	1.1	collection model	low	Process
APO012.01	2.3	competition within industry	low	Metrics
APO012.01	2.3	competitor alignment	low	Metrics
APO012.01	2.2	compliance	medium	Requirement
APO012.01	4.1	contributing factor	high	Risk Factor
APO012.01	4.3	contributing factor	high	Risk Factor
APO012.01	3.1	data collection model	low	Process
APO012.01	1.4	data for incentive setting (risk-aware culture)	low	CorporateGovernance
APO012.01	2	data on enterprise's operating environment	medium	Catalogue

Figure 4. Excerpt of the list of information artefacts [own research]

B. Results

The mapping process showed that it is generally possible to transform the essential risk management data from COBIT for Risk up to the meta-level. Small amendments to the draft version of the ICT risk-meta-data-model were necessary after completing the mapping process, e.g., the introduction of the new class *Changes*, which reflects all current change management activities in the considered organization. The transformation is highly dependent on how concrete the specification of the risk model and its components is. If the risk model leaves too much room for interpretation inconsistencies may appear in the instantiation of the ICT meta-data-risk-model itself. This means that activities without inputs or outputs should be scrutinized. Almost all inputs, outputs and standard COBIT 5 activities specified in the twelve risk supporting processes were unsuitable for the mapping. Thus, certain problems are expected when using ISO 31000 as base risk model because of its highly generic approach. This means that not every risk management framework may be suitable for the mapping due to the different levels of detail of the different frameworks. Furthermore, the framework must provide storage of all kind of documentation that supports the functioning of the management system. Currently, the meta-model includes the dedicated class *Documentation* for this issue. It was originally intended only for risk management documentation, but it has a broader scope, providing a repository for all documentation produced by the applied management system.

The presented work extends the proof of concept that was outlined in [13] to all affected risk management processes of the COBIT for Risk framework. Some small adjustments of the first draft of the ICT risk-meta-data-model were made, but no fundamental changes of the inherent structure of the classes or relationships were necessary. This shows that the ICT risk-meta-data-model is able to represent and store the necessary information for applying the COBIT for Risk framework in principle.

C. Further Research

Further research is still needed to verify the transformation process with two or three other risk management frameworks. This verification should definitely be done for ISO 31000 [1], despite the above-mentioned difficulties to be expected The suitability of ISO 31000 should be verified because of its outstanding importance as a widely accepted standard. The NIST publications [2] [3] [4] and COSO ERM in its new published version [5] also provide the more detailed content that is necessary for the mapping and are thus good candidates. If it is possible to map their information requirements in the same way as it has been done for COBIT for Risk, the ICT risk-meta-data-model can be applied at least for these four risk management frameworks, in this way providing an adequately sustainable meta-model solution. If the mapping has been applied several times and the attributes are almost stable (except for a refinement of the definite data types and the visibility properties), the methods can be refined next. The methods of a class should be able to support the complete lifecycle of the concerning attributes. The third area in which refinements are needed is the relationships. It must be verified whether a direct data exchange between the different objects is needed or transitive relationships achieve the same result. Once these three research questions have been solved, the ICT risk-meta-data-model can be implemented as a first demonstrator, thereby starting the technical verification process. Analyzing these research questions is an ongoing process in order to verify the applicability and utility of the ICT risk-meta-data-model.

The fundamental idea of aggregating risk management data that is stored in different risk models and can be effectively applied when different risk information, e.g. from different companies or organization units that still apply different risk models, need to be migrated. This might be necessary when different companies merge or Comparisons across industry sectors are needed. This means that the final evidence for the added value of the ICT risk-meta-data-model can be provided when different risk models have been analysed. The upcoming research on applying the ICT risk-meta-data-model to a second risk model will further strengthen this evidence.

V. CONCLUSION

This article shows the basic instantiation of a specific risk model – in this case the risk model of COBIT for Risk – by means of the conceptual ICT risk-meta-data-model. The objective of the research design is to introduce an ICT risk-meta-data-model for ICT, and to embed it in the context of different established risk models that are commonly applied in the ICT area. The approach of designing a consistent superstructure in form of a meta-model with no need for replacement of the already established ICT risk management models is based on the principle of an ex-post adjustment. Additionally, it provides a data-oriented and more formalized way of overcoming the current organizational and model-related restrictions. The meta-model addresses the whole risk management lifecycle as recommended in [1], from identification, analysis, evaluation to treatment. It reflects both the risk management context and the monitoring and communication requirements for the process. The three main components and the conceptual background of the involved objects are discussed. The findings can be summarized as follows:

- An instantiation of the ICT risk-meta-data-model is generally possible and is a promising possibility to overcome the current situation in ICT, where many different risk models and methods are applied.
- The critical success factor is the coherent transformation of the information of the selected risk model up to the meta-model, while at the same time sufficiently reducing the information content. All essential data of the risk model have an equivalent reference in the superstructure.
- It is crucial to repeat the mapping with other appropriate ICT risk models in order to strengthen the ICT risk-meta-data-model. Moreover, this will reconfirm the general applicability of the meta-data-model and will increase its utility due to having several different risk models mapped to a meta-level.
- The methods and relationships of the objects in the ICT risk-meta-data-model need to be refined before a practical demonstrator can be implemented that can be fed with risk management use cases.

Results show that transferring the general information artefacts specified by COBIT for Risk into the classes of the meta-model is feasible and promising. The future refinement effort will iteratively improve the ICT risk-meta-data-model in order to further develop and evaluate it and strengthen its applicability for ICT risk management.

REFERENCES

[1] International Organization for Standardization (ISO), Ed., *ISO 31000:2009 Risk management - Principles and guidelines*. ISO, Geneva, Switzerland, 2009.

[2] National Institute of Standards and Technology (NIST), U.S. Department of Commerce, Joint Task Force Transformation Initiative Information Security, Ed., "NIST 800-30: Guide for Conducting Risk Assessments." Computer Security Division, Information Technology Laboratory, National Institute of Standards and Technology, Gaithersburg, MD 20899-8930, USA, Sep-2012 [Online]. Available: http://csrc.nist.gov/publications/nistpubs/800-30/sp800-30.pdf

[3] National Institute of Standards and Technology (NIST), U.S. Department of Commerce, Joint Task Force Transformation Initiative Information Security, Ed., "NIST 800-37: Guide for Applying the Risk Management Framework to Federal Information Systems: A Security Life Cycle Approach." Computer Security Division, Information Technology Laboratory, National Institute of Standards and Technology, Gaithersburg, MD 20899-8930, USA, Feb-2010 [Online]. Available: http://nvlpubs.nist.gov /nistpubs/SpecialPublications/NIST.SP.800-37r1.pdf

[4] National Institute of Standards and Technology (NIST), U.S. Department of Commerce, Joint Task Force Transformation Initiative Information Security, Ed., "NIST 800-39: Managing Information Security Risk - Organization, Mission, and Information System View." Computer Security Division, Information Technology Laboratory, National Institute of Standards and Technology, Gaithersburg, MD 20899-8930, USA, Mar-2011 [Online]. Available: http://csrc.nist.gov/publications/nistpubs/800-39/SP800-39-final.pdf

[5] Committee of Sponsoring Organizations of the Treadway Commission (COSO) and Price Waterhouse Cooper (PwC), "Enterprise Risk Management - Aligning Risk with Strategy and Performance (Public Exposure Draft)." Jun-2016.

[6] The Stationary Office (TSO), Ed., "Management of Risk: Guidance for Practitioners." 2010.

[7] Information Systems Audit and Control Association (ISACA), Ed., "COBIT 5 for Risk." Information Systems Audit and Control Association, Rolling Meadows, IL 60008 USA, 2013 [Online]. Available: http://www.isaca.org/ COBIT/Pages/Risk-product-page.aspx

[8] Information Systems Audit and Control Association (ISACA), "ISACA." [Online]. Available: https://www. isaca.org/Pages/default.aspx. [Accessed: 31-Mar-2016]

[9] Information Systems Audit and Control Association (ISACA), Ed., "COBIT 5: A Business Framework for the Governance and Management of Enterprise IT." Information Systems Audit and Control Association, Rolling Meadows, IL 60008 USA, 2012 [Online]. Available: http://www.isaca.org/cobit/Pages/CobitFrame work.aspx

[10] D. Karagiannis and H. Kühn, "Metamodelling Platforms," in *E-Commerce and Web Technologies*, vol. 2455, K. Bauknecht, Am. Tjoa, and G. Quirchmayr, Eds. Springer Berlin Heidelberg, 2002, p. 182 [Online]. Available: http://dx.doi.org/10.1007/3-540-45705-4_19

[11] S. H. Othman and G. Beydoun, "Metamodelling approach to support disaster management knowledge sharing," presented at the 21st Australasian Conference on Information Systems (ACIS), Atlanta, GA, USA, 2010, pp. 1–10 [Online]. Available: http://ro.uow.edu.au/cgi/view content.cgi?article=10789&context=infopapers

[12] S. H. Othman and G. Beydoun, "Model-driven disaster management," *Inf. Manage.*, vol. 50 (2013), no. Elsevier, pp. 218–228, Apr. 2013.

[13] M. Latzenhofer, "Ein Meta-Risiko-Datenmodell für IKT," in *Bestandsaufnahme, Konzepte, Anwendungen, Perspektiven*, Klagenfurt, pp. 161–173.

Recommendations for Risk Analysis in Higher Education Institutions

Lidia Prudente Tixteco, María del Carmen Prudente Tixteco, Gabriel Sánchez Pérez, Linda Karina Toscano Medina, José de Jesús Vázquez Gómez, Arturo de la Cruz Tellez
Instituto Politécnico Nacional
Sección de Estudios de Posgrado e Investigación ESIME Culhuacan
Santa Ana 1000, San Francisco Culhuacán, Coyoacán, D. F., México
email: lprudente@ipn.mx, mprudentet0900@alumno.ipn.mx, gasanchezp@ipn.mx, ltoscano@ipn.mx, jjvago@gmail.com, adelacruzt@ipn.mx

Abstract— **Computer attacks do not only happen in large companies or organizations. Educational Institutions have also started to become aware of computer threats to which their information assets are exposed. Among these institutions, universities, higher education and research centers are the most at risk, because they handle information regarding scientific and technological research and/or developments, personal data of their staff and students, academic records, and many others. A risk analysis is one step to start an information security strategy. It allows assessing the risk of information assets in order to know their security status, and helps to define a security controls implementation plan to avoid threats that exploit some vulnerability that could cause serious damage to an asset or infrastructure of *Higher Education Institutions* (*HEIs*). This paper presents some recommendations to perform a risk analysis in *HEIs* to identify threats and helps to reduce the risk of their information assets.**

Keywords-risk analysis; higher education institutions; information systems.

I. INTRODUCTION

Large companies or organizations are not the only ones concerned about their information assets security. Educational institutions are also becoming aware of the risk of incorporating information systems into their daily processes which makes them vulnerable to threats. Under these circumstances, implementing an information security strategy is required to help handle potential threats and reduce the risk of the information assets of the educational institutions.

Information Systems (*IS*) are used to contribute in education field, but they introduce more risks to educational processes. Information Technologies (*IT*) support *IS* and they could have some vulnerabilities that may compromise confidentiality, integrity and availability of the systems and their information. In 2014, the Organization of American States (*OAS*) and Symantec Corporation published the Cyber Security Latin America and Caribbean Report [1], which shows the extent of the cyber security incidents reported to the Mexican Federal Police against different entities. The report shows that 31% government institutions, 26% private sector institutions, 39% academic organizations and 4% other entities were affected.

Information security constitutes an important element for Higher Education Institutions (*HEIs*). Due to the use of Information Technologies (*IT*), the number of information security incidents in academic environment has increased, and these institutions need to implement a good information security management to protect their information assets. However, this can be difficult to accomplish [2].

A risk analysis is an objective and efficient way to start an information security strategy design, which allows to assess the risk of information systems. It helps to identify the security level of the critical assets and determines a security control implementation plan in order to reduce threats probability and attacks that can cause major damages to an organization [8].

In *HEIs*, it is unwise to implement controls or safeguards just because they seem to be the right thing to do or because other entities or organizations are doing so. Each organization is unique, and the levels of exposure are different. By conducting a proper risk analysis, the controls or safeguards will address specific needs of the institution.

This article presents a set of recommendations to perform a risk analysis to help *HEIs* and their staff to start an information security strategy in the institution.

This paper is organized as follows. Section II presents the state of the art. Section III presents an explanation of education information systems. Section IV describes the risk analysis functionality. Section V describes the development of this research. Section VI presents the results of this research and Section VII conclusion and future work.

II. STATE OF THE ART

Because *IT* provides opportunities to improve educational services' quality, *HEIs* have increased the use of *IT* to support their processes. Chen [4] mentions that the benefits of *IT* in education environment have attracted researchers attention. The document emphasizes that people, especially in the field of education, often ignore the risk in their processes, assets and *IS*. The risk in the education field should not be ignored and must be considered an important role to promote the development of innovative, protected and managed processes.

On the other hand, Sari [2] states that if an information system within an organization, including *HEIs*, is not safe or well protected, it will be a risk. Lack of control and prevention of data loss caused by disasters or security incidents, as well as inadequate recovery after disasters, will prevent institutions to continue their business.

Information security should not only be based on technological security tools, but should also be backed up by a good understanding of people in universities, about what processes or assets must be protected, and how to provide the right solution. It means that *HEIs* need a good information security management since they have potential security threats. Also, the document mentions internal and external factors that can influence the implementation of an *Information Security Management System* (*ISM*S) in an organization, which is necessary to protect its information.

An *ISMS* is constructed by some formal and informal controlling process as well as a technique that is applied to overcome any security risk. Its basic form could contain four phases, such as: identifying threats that could attack information sources, defining risks that could result from threats, determining information security policy, and implementing solutions to control and overcome the risk [2].

Furthermore, Azmi [5] states that data leak issues are due to a rapid growth of computer technologies that have resulted in an increase of vulnerabilities in systems. Many institutions, specifically educational institutions, have large amounts of personal data and they need to implement higher levels of security in their systems to stop any attempts of unauthorized users trying to access critical data intentionally. If adequate measures are not considered, records belonging to staff as well as students can be manipulated and used by unauthorized people. Finally, Azmi emphasizes that a risk analysis has to be done to understand the security level of an educational institution.

All of the above references consider implementing security strategies to protect against different risks in processes, assets and information systems of educational institution, but they do not mention how. This paper presents recommendations for performing an easy risk analysis in *HEIs* to identify threats and risk of their information assets.

III. Education Information Systems

HEIs are usually organizations where people receive education, conduct research, exchange knowledge. However, *HEIs* and their affiliated organizations, have a sufficient amount of official, confidential, and restricted data, which must be protected. Loss or disclosure of confidential information could result in property damage, financial and damage to their reputation, among others.

A wide range of processes, assets and information can be protected in *HEIs* such as: customer data, intellectual property, legal and financial records and correspondence.

There are certain areas that are in need of protection, such as [6]:

- Educational and research (tests, examinations, research and development information, intellectual development, information about students, research projects, etc.)
- Human Resources (data on staff and students, personal data, reports, etc.)
- Legal (internal documentation, contracts, confidential information about employees, even after termination of their employment, etc.)
- Financial and economic (procurement documentation, financial information, etc.)
- *IT* (databases, their infrastructure, *IT* management information, logins and passwords, copyright of *IT* developments, etc.).

Information is a critical resource in the operation and management of modern organizations. This is also true for *HEIs*. Availability of relevant information is vital for effective performance of managerial functions such as: planning, organizing, leading, and control. Today, *IS* are the link to connect all the components of organizations and universities and their departments, to provide better operation and survival in a competitive environment.

An education information system is a computer system, which collects, transmits, processes, and stores data within an educational institution, specifically *HEIs*. It is designed to support operations, management, and decision-making functions of the *HEIs*, as shown in Figure 1.

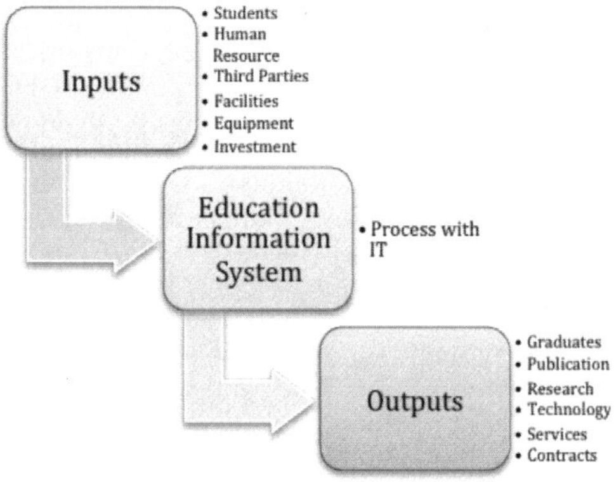

Figure 1. Educational Information System

Because of the growing use of information and its evolving nature, reforms at or within *HEIs* have an increased responsibility to ensure that they have robust policies in place to ensure confidentiality, integrity, and availability of their information. There are different factors that force *HEIs* to develop a security strategy to protect their *IT* assets that support their processes, such as [3]:

- New technologies, like mobile devices, wireless computing, virtual learning environment and portal software, digital libraries, etc. offer new possibilities for teaching, learning and research;
- University authorities, staff and users require a higher quality in their services specifically *IT* knowledge and systems;
- As *IT* and information systems continue to become deeply embedded in many activities and processes of *HEIs*, there is greater need to develop sophisticated models and make initial *IT* investments in infrastructure which would ensure that *IS* are robust and flexible to cope with changing requirements;

- The growing complexity of *IS*, their information technologies and inter-relationships increases difficulty for management to ensure that investments in security controls are aligned to institutional objectives.

IV. Risk Analysis

The objective of risk management is to reduce risk to an acceptable level. An information security risk analysis is a technique to identify and assess threats that may jeopardize an organization's processes and information assets. This technique also helps define security controls to reduce the probability of these threats from occurring.

Risk assessment is the estimate of threats that could exploit vulnerabilities that may cause harm to an asset, resulting in implementation of controls and safeguards to prevent identified risks from ever occurring and recovery plans if a risk becomes a reality in spite of all efforts, this process is known as risk mitigation [7].

The rapid development of *IT* and how to ensure and reduce potential risks of information systems, has been the focus of many organizations and academic areas. Risk assessment is an effective way to solve this problem. However, there are some issues in risk assessment process, such as evaluation indicators, that are difficult to be quantified because risk values are difficult to be defined in *HEIs*.

Once a risk analysis has been conducted, it will be necessary to conduct a risk assessment to determine what threats exist that could avoid achieving institutional mission of *HEIs*. These threats must be prioritized and possible safeguards and controls must be selected. To be effective, a cost-benefit analysis is necessary to determine which controls will help mitigate the risk to an acceptable level for the institution. Another important factor to consider in this process is the impact of regulatory compliance issues.

In conducting the risk assessment, consideration should be given to the advantages and disadvantages of quantitative and qualitative assessments. The main advantage of the qualitative style of risk assessment is that it prioritizes the risks and identifies areas for immediate action and improvement. The disadvantage of qualitative risk assessment is that it does not provide specific quantifiable measurements of the magnitude of the impacts, therefore making a cost-benefit analysis of recommended controls more difficult.

The major advantage of quantitative risk assessment is that it provides an impact magnitude measurement, which can be used in the cost-benefit analysis of recommended controls. The disadvantage is that, depending on the numerical ranges used to express the measurement, the meaning of the quantitative risk assessment may be unclear, requiring the results to be interpreted in a qualitative manner [7].

On the other hand, risk management is an essential part of an *ISMS* that requires measuring and assessing risks as well as reviewing and re-evaluating risks at a later stage to ensure that an effective information security strategy has implemented. Without being well informed about the risks an organization cannot achieve effective security management.

An *ISMS* is a systematic approach to managing sensitive organization information so that it remains secure. It includes people, processes and *IT* systems by applying a risk management process. There are different frameworks to implement an *ISMS* as ISO 27001, which is an international standard. It can help small, medium and large organizations in any sector to keep their information assets secure.

A. Risk Analysis of MAAGTICSI

In Mexico there is a mandatory guidelines for information and the management of communication technologies assets as well as their security, called *MAAGTICSI* (Manual Administrativo de Aplicación General en las materias de Tecnologías de Información y Comunicaciones y de la Seguridad de la Información, Administrative Manual of General Application in Information and Communication Technologies and Information Security). It is aimed at large public agencies and requires many resources for its implementation. *MAAGTICSI* includes a framework to implement an *ISMS* and perform a risk analysis taking reference from international standards and best practices of information security as ISO 27001, ITIL and COBiT.

The framework has a process called Information Security Management (*ASI*, Administración de Seguridad de la Información) that includes a methodology to perform a risk analysis. The objective of this analysis is to identify, classify and prioritize the risks to evaluate its impact on institutional processes and services to obtain risk analysis matrix.

Some activities that *HEIs* could implement to perform a risk analysis to start an information security management are [9]:

1) Establish risk management policy
2) Integrate risk analysis team
3) Identify critical processes
4) Identify information assets and person in charge
5) Identify vulnerabilities
6) Identify threats
7) Conduct identification and evaluation of risk scenarios
8) Develop cost-benefit analysis of security controls

In the case of educational institutions they often do not have sufficient and specialized human resources to carry out all the tasks of an *ISMS* or risk analysis to meet their particular needs, and therefore require other strategies to help them secure the critical assets that support their processes and comply with applicable regulations as *MAAGTICSI*.

V. Development

The following sentences describe some steps to perform a risk analysis in *HEIs* with some recommendations to help the staff in charge of carrying out the activities according to requirements of the institution.

1) Determine critical processes of *HEIs*. One of the most important activities in risk analysis is to determine critical processes to which the analysis will focus. In *HEIs*, critical processes are significant processes linked to this type of organization that allow them to achieve their institutional mission.

There are different processes associated with their operation and daily activities of *HEIs*, such as: student enrolment, staff assignment, student assessment, online education, scholarship assignment, research, academic planning, website, financial management, infrastructure management, collaboration agreements, among others.

Recommendation: Senior managers and staff in charge of information security management must establish a procedure to determine critical processes and take into account mainly those that support the institutional mission in the *HEIs*, and identify them with a unique number. For example, Table I shows the identification of a process that belongs to Maestría en Ingeniería en Seguridad y Tecnologías de la Información (*MISTI*) in the Sección de Estudios de Posgrado e Investigación of ESIME Unidad Culhuacan and was assigned a consecutive number as '01'.

TABLE I. PROCESS IDENTIFICATION.

Process Identification ("Process ID")		
[Acronym of Unit or Agency]	***[Area]***	***[Consecutive number]***
SEPICUL	MISTI	01
SEPICUL-MISTI-01		

2) Identify information assets in *HEIs*. Today, most of processes mentioned above have information systems and assets (which are information resources), in their activities e.g., hardware, software, communications, information, facilities and offices, image and reputation, people. It is necessary to establish an ISMS for all of them to guarantee their confidentiality, integrity and availability.

Some assets related to processes in *HEIs* are shown in Table II:

TABLE II. ASSETS IN HEIS.

Assets in HEIs		
Facilities	File servers	Personal records of employees and students
Administrative offices	Websites	Electronic files
Laboratories	Databases	Physical files
Site	Developed computer applications	Email accounts
Network infrastructure	Desktop computers	Research
Web servers	Personal computers	Collaboration agreements
Database servers	Specialized equipment	Contracts
Mail servers	Report cards	Financial statements

Recommendation: Once the assets belonging to critical processes have been identified, it is necessary to assign them an identifier, also describing them briefly, as well as register their managers, then, if it is possible to know their criticality within one or several processes in the institution to continue with the risk analysis, as is shown in Figure 2.

Process ID	Asset ID	Information Asset	Description	Clasification (critical/non-critical)	Responsible public servant
SEPICUL-MISTI-01	MISTI1-001	Site	Place where storage and services servers, and network devices are hosted	Critical	Network Administrator

Figure 2. Asset register

3) Establish an objective and scope of risk analysis.

Recommendation: It is recommended to propose an objective and scope taking into account critical process and information assets, and resources available to perform activities (human, material and time).

For example:

- Objective: To make necessary calculations to establish relative value of risk for each scenario, according to activities of the selected risk analysis methodology.
- Scope: The scope of evaluation is to establish risk values for risk scenarios associated with information assets of *MISTI* critical processes.

4) Make a list of possible threat scenarios in *HEIs* taking into account provided scenarios by *MAAGTICSI* and selecting only those that could apply to the scope and size of *HEIs*.

Recommendation: Reviewing the environment of *HEIs* to select threats and threat agents that may affect them, some examples, as shown in Figure 3.

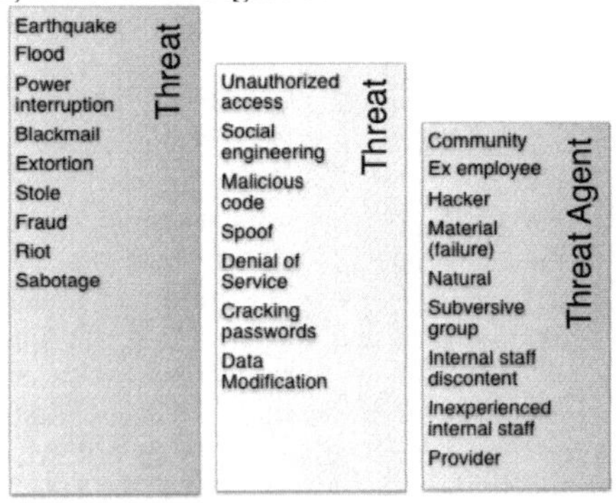

Figure 3. Threat scenarios

An example of a threat scenario is shown in Table III, which was assigned an identifier to recognize it during the process.

TABLE III. THREAT SCENARIO

Threat ID	Threat	Threat Agent
1032	Denial of service	Discontented internal staff (intentional)

5) Choose one of two suggested procedures to assess risk scenarios:

a) Use traditional method with high, medium and low scale to determine probability of occurrence of a threat and impact to institution to assess risk.

b) Apply a more objective evaluation method to determine the value of probability and impact. For probability additional factors associated to five different scales with representative values from 0.1 to 0.9 are included, as:

- Existence of threat agent from the perspective of a particular information asset (exist)
- Interest of threat agent to attack information asset (want)
- Ability of threat agent to attack the information asset (can), and
- Vulnerability of information asset

The impact considers aspects as: human, material, financial, operational and image with five scales also with representative values from 2 to 10.

Recommendation: If *HEIs* have few resources it is recommended to apply first method. The second method is recommended for staff with experience to facilitate the evaluation, as it becomes a complicated procedure.

6) Choose a form of risk treatment: avoid, prevent, mitigate, finance or assume threat scenarios.

Once the risk value of each threat scenario for each evaluated information asset is obtained, *MAAGTICSI* orders that all threat scenarios with a risk greater than 1.8 should be treated, a situation that for many institutions, especially *HEIs*, it will not be possible to accomplish when implementation of an information security strategy is in its initial stage and has generally limited resources.

Recommendation: In order to compensate for this issue, it is proposed to use another strategy that, instead of being based on threat scenarios, obtains an average risk value of information asset that allows it to know its risk level and considers a minimum risk value of 6 to set priorities for the care of information assets.

The risk matrix proposed by *MAAGTICSI*, shown in Figure 4, can be taken as a reference to indicate the risk value of assets.

Probability of de Ocurrence						
0.9	Almost sure	1.8	3.6	6.4	7.2	9
0.7	High	1.4	2.8	4.2	5.6	7
0.5	Medium	1	2	3	4	5
0.3	Low	0.6	1.2	1.8	2.4	3
0.1	Almost impossible	0.2	0.4	0.6	0.8	1
		Insignificant	Significant	Serious	Critical	Disastrous
		2	4	6	8	10
				IMPACT		

Figure 4. Risk Matrix (MAAGTICSI)

7) Perform a cost-benefit analysis, since not all risk scenarios will be possible to attend immediately.

Recommendation: It is proposed to use another representation form to help this task. For example, the risk matrix presented in Figure 5, which helps to make a decision when reflecting risk level of information assets and their required attention level.

8) Select security controls that will be applied to most critical information assets in *HEIs* to reduce their risk level.

Recommendation: The staff may take as base reference list of security controls in Annex A of ISO 27001.

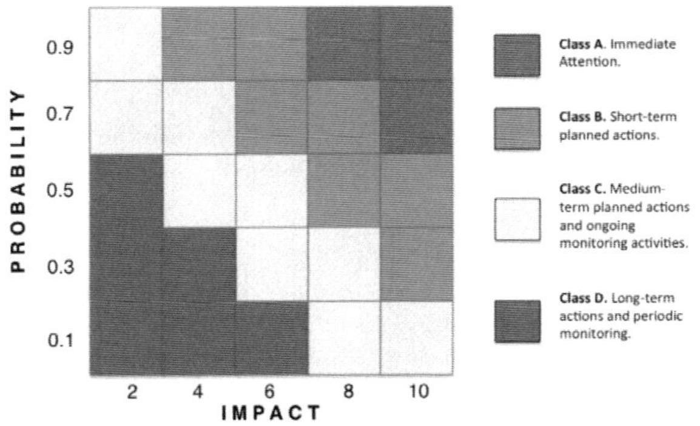

Figure 5. Proposed Risk Analysis Matrix

The general description made above shows some steps that information security management staff may perform a risk analysis in *HEIs*, to know their risk level of their information assets that support their critical processes.

VI. RESULTS

After following risk analysis procedure, steps and recommendations presented and applied to an HEI. The cost-benefit analysis was easy to perform with help of proposed risk matrix, as shown in Figure 6.

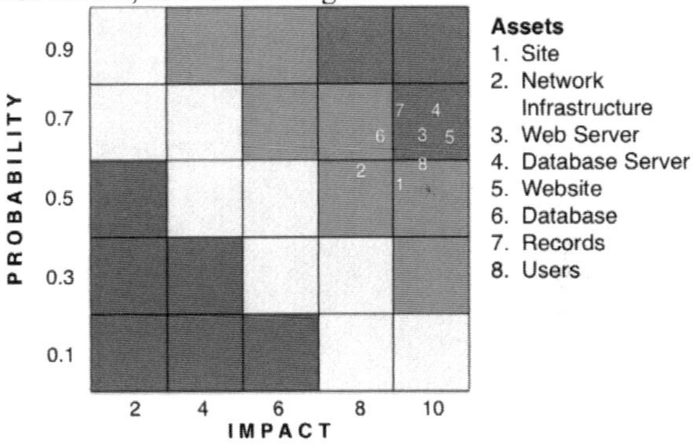

Figure 6. Result Risk Analysis Matrix

The previous matrix allowed us to make better decisions to determine risk treatment and to appropriately select safety controls to be applied when recognizing critical assets of HEI. For example, in this case, the assets that need to be attended to immediately are database server records, website and web server.

VII. CONCLUSION AND FUTURE WORK

With the shown recommendations, *HEIs* may perform an easy procedure to their risk analysis based on *MAAGTICSI* that could help them start generating a security strategy to protect their processes, information assets and data that manage through *IS* and *IT*, as well as, reduce the risk level by security controls selection to attend timely needs of the institution according its special requirements.

As future work, we propose to develop a framework to establish *ISMS* for *HEIs* and analyse institutions of other educational levels with procedures and recommendations presented.

ACKNOWLEDGMENT

We thank the Instituto Politécnico Nacional for the support granted during the development of this research.

REFERENCES

[1] OAS y Symantec Corporation, "Cyber Security Latin America and Caribbean Report," Organization of American States and Symantec Corporation, Multidimensional Security Organization of American States and Government Affairs and Global Cybersecurity Policies, 2014.

[2] P. K. Sari, N. Nurshabrina, and Candiwan, "Factor analysis on information security management in higher education institutions," *2016 4th International Conference on Cyber and IT Service Management*, Bandung, 2016, pp. 1-5.

[3] A. Adamov, M. Erguvan, and D. Ş. Durmaz, "Towards good governance through implementation of University Management Information System: Qafqaz university's Experience," *2010 4th International Conference on Application of Information and Communication Technologies*, Tashkent, 2010, pp. 1-7.

[4] Y. Chen, "Risk management of education information," *2011 IEEE International Symposium on IT in Medicine and Education*, Cuangzhou, 2011, pp. 170-173.

[5] I. M. A. G. Azmi, Q. M. Ashraf, S. Zulhuda, and M. B. Daud, "Critical data leak analysis in educational environment," *2016 4th International Conference on Cyber and IT Service Management*, Bandung, 2016, pp. 1-6.

[6] A. Boranbayev, M. Mazhitov, and Z. Kakhanov, "Implementation of Security Systems for Prevention of Loss of Information at Organizations of Higher Education," *2015 12th International Conference on Information Technology - New Generations*, Las Vegas, NV, 2015, pp. 802-804.

[7] T. R. Peltier, "Information Risk Analysis," (2ª ed.), USA: Auerbach Publications, 2005.

[8] Á. Gómez Vieites, and C. Suárez Rey, "Information Systems - Practical tools for business management," (4ª ed.), México: Alfaomega, 2012.

[9] Secretariat of Public Function, "Administrative Manual of General Application in Information and Communication Technologies and Information Security," Secretariat of Public Function. México: Official Journal of the Federation, 2014.

Extending Vehicle Attack Surface Through Smart Devices

Rudolf Hackenberg,
Nils Weiss, Sebastian Renner

University of Applied Sciences Regensburg, Germany
Email: rudolf.hackenberg@othr.de
{nils2.weiss, sebastian1.renner}@othr.de

Enrico Pozzobon

University of Padua, Italy
Email: enrico.pozzobon.1@studenti.unipd.it

Abstract—**Modern cars include more and more features that first emerged from the consumer electronics industry. Technologies like Bluetooth and Internet-connected services found their way into the vehicle industry. The secure implementation of these functions presents a great challenge for the manufacturers because products originating from the consumer industry can often not be easily transferred to the safety-sensitive traffic environment due to security concerns. However, common automotive interfaces like the diagnostics port are now also used to implement new services into the car. With dongles designed to read out certain vehicle data and transfer it to the Internet via the cellular network, the owner can access information about gas consumption or vehicle location through a mobile phone app, even when he is away from the car. This paper wants to emphasize new threats that appear due to the ongoing interconnection in modern cars by discussing the security of the diagnostics interface in combination with the use of an Internet-connected dongle. Potential attack vectors, as well as proof-of-concept exploits will be shown and the implications of security breaches on the safe state of the vehicle will be investigated.**

Keywords– On-Board-Diagnostics; Cellular Network; Automotive Security.

I. Introduction

The term "On-Board-Diagnostics (OBD)-II-dongle" refers to a group of aftermarket devices that can be connected through the OBD-II interface to upgrade the functionality of new and old cars, and can be installed by a customer without any technical knowledge [1]. These dongles are usually available at a low price and promise interesting features, like connecting the vehicle to a smartphone through the Internet and letting the owner monitor certain in-vehicle data like fuel consumption on different tracks and the Global Positioning System (GPS) data points to determine the cars's position over time. The OBD-II devices are available for every vehicle that implements an OBD-II diagnostic port, which applies to almost every vehicle which is participating in common traffic these days.

Even if the relatively easy improvement of cars' features through plugging in an OBD-II-dongle sounds tempting, the devices can bring along particular risks and alter the security of a vehicle in the long run. OBD-II-dongles use the same protocols as repair shop tester software to read data from the car's bus systems. [2] After reading the device conditions, the data is sent to a backend server on the Internet, which acts as a database for the frontend application that interfaces the user. If the device uses weak security measures, potential vulnerabilities in the dongle's firmware can open an insecure gateway to the electronic infrastructure of the whole car [3]. In further sections, this possible attack surface shall be described and a possible exploit will be introduced.

In Section II, related work to this paper will be shown; Section III will give a short overview over relevant automotive diagnostic protocols, while Section IV will explain discovered vulnerabilites of OBD-II-dongles, that have been investigated. Section V will cover security threats that can follow from installing an OBD-II-dongle, before Section VI will conclude the results of this paper and give a short outlook to possible future work in this field.

II. Related Work

Investigating security vulnerabilities and introducing possible attacks is already being researched for a couple of years. Especially exploiting weak in-vehicle protocols like Control Area Network (CAN) is a pretty well-known topic [4]. Also, attacks using a pirate Base Transceiver Station (BTS) in cellular networks have already been introduced by Paget in 2010 [5]. The possibility to perform an over-the-air attack on a specific telematics dongle, has been shown by Szijj et al. in 2015 [6]. More recent work, especially including targeting the standard OBD-II-interface through wireless signals, has been conducted by Zhang et al. in 2016 [7]. This research team also proposed an attack on OBD-II-dongles, but – unlike this article – their investigation was focused on controlling an OBD-II-dongle through a paired phone's Bluetooth connection. Besides attacks on dongles and the cellular network, additionally, ways to exploit a repair shop tester, including the diagnostic protocols that are also mentioned in this article, have been published [8]. This paper will cover parts of the different research areas mentioned above and propose a way to analyze and exploit OBD-II-dongles and the interface's diagnostic protocols wirelessly, without the use of supplementary devices like smartphones.

III. Automotive Diagnostics Protocols

After the first efforts to implement and unify a diagnosis interface in passenger vehicles more than 20 years ago, some standards regarding the hardware interface and the used protocols have been developed. Even though early perceptions of the capabilities of a diagnostic interface focused on the possibility of gathering information on the cars' emissions only, with the ongoing progress in car manufacturing a lot more functionality was realized through the OBD-II-connector. Therefore, also the protocols that handle the diagnostic communication evolved over time and are nowadays used for transferring complex data structures, for example during reprogramming an Electronic Control Unit (ECU). The following two subsections will introduce two important standards in the environment of automotive diagnostics.

A. Diagnostics on Control Area Networks

The ISO-15765-2 standard introduces the network and transport layer services of the Diagnostics over CAN protocol [9]. It describes the way data of different size can be transmitted in a reliable way. Besides the transferring of single frames – which are usually limited to a maximum length of 8 bytes in the CAN protocol – it especially specifies the handling of larger payloads. The standard, often also referred to the name ISO-TP, shows a dictate to enable the transmission of messages with a payload up to 4096 bytes. This rise of capacity is achieved by introducing a rule set for segmenting the data into multiple frames and implementing a specific frame type to indicate that a message is being segmented, the *Segmented Frame*.

B. Unified Diagnostic Services

The previously described ISO-TP standard is widely used for the transmission of data on the CAN bus and the Unified Diagnostic Service (UDS) protocol (also called ISO-14229) makes use of it [10]. The UDS protocol describes regulations to enable a standardized communication between a diagnostics tester and all ECUs present in the bus topology of a car. It implements a request/response message model on the ISO/OSI session layer and above. The model prescribes that every request has to be answered with a positive or negative frame according to the standard. Basically, a common request consists of a source and destination address, a service id that uniquely identifies the request and some request-specific parameters. To indicate if the request was successful, only the first byte of the response has to be examined. In the positive case, it has to contain the value of the service id added to *0x40*, if the response is negative the message starts with *0x7F*.

Besides the structure of the messages, the UDS protocol also describes a great amount of standard services. Some of them can be used to read out specific data from an ECU (*ReadDataByIdentifier*), but there also exist services that are designed to write certain bytes in the ECU's storage (*WriteDataByIdentifier*). Furthermore, routines to control specific functions inside the car are also defined by the standard. For example, the routine *ECUReset* sends a reboot request to the ECU with the address given in the destination address parameter. So, an individual that gains access to the OBD-II-interface under any circumstance can craft all standard messages by gathering information through reading the publicly available UDS-Standard. With this knowledge for example a reset of any ECU is possible. Another remarkable command is in charge of the control of the communication on the shared CAN-Bus (*CommunicationControl*). This command can completely turn of the reception and transmission functions of an ECU. This feature is usually used during the flash procedure of the ECU via the CAN-Bus. The whole traffic on the bus, except the traffic between a repair shop tester and the ECU which has to be flashed, gets disabled to speed up the flashing time by providing the full bus bandwidth. An attacker can easily shut down the communication of an ECU through this command.

IV. OBD-II DONGLE SECURITY

Multiple Internet-connected OBD-II-dongles have been tested for security vulnerabilities that could be exploited by an attacker to wirelessly inject malicious CAN frames into a vehicle over the OBD-II connector.

While the backend infrastructure and the user web interface for each of these dongles is made by the company responsible for the distribution of these dongles, the hardware and firmware are outsourced to different Original Equipment Manufactorers (OEMs). Local distributors do not have access to the source code of the firmware, and are unable to asses the security of their product. Due to inability to communicate with the OEMs, a blackbox security analysis has been conducted.

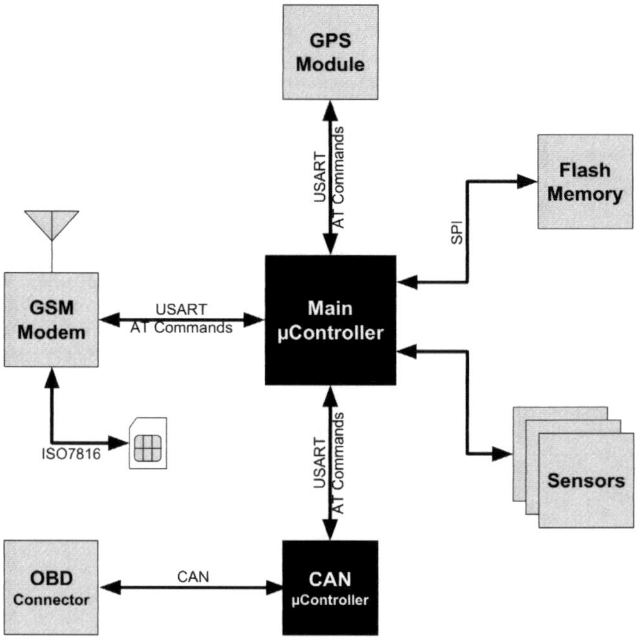

Figure 1. Example block diagram of dongle hardware

Figure 1 shows the general block diagram of the hardware found in the examined dongles. A primary microcontroller is responsible for power management, event logging, and firmware flashing. A secondary microcontroller communicates with the car via CAN bus and other protocols. A Global System for Mobile Communications (GSM) modem provides Internet connectivity and a GPS receiver allows for location tracking. Other sensors, like microphones, accelerometers and gyroscopes are also present in some of the examined hardware.

A. GSM Vulnerabilities

The cellular modem is the prime attack entry point for an attacker. These devices must be able to establish an Internet connection over long stretches of roads that might not be covered with 3G (or newer) cellular technology, which offers a good security model. Because of this, automotive Internet-connected hardware must support 2G cellular connectivity (GSM with General Packet Radio Service (GPRS)/Enhanced Data Rates for GSM Evolution (EDGE) Internet) which supports cryptographic authentication only of the Mobile Station (MS) and not the BTS.

Since the connection between the MS and the BTS is vulnerable to a Man-in-the-Middle (MITM) attack in GPRS and EDGE, authentication of the server must be done at the application layer by the MS. All the analyzed OBD-II-dongles fail to implement proper cryptographic authentication at the application layer, possibly because of insufficient resources on the embedded microcontroller used or disregard for security from the developers.

In our tests, both OsmoNITB and YateBTS were used to setup a pirate BTS and successfully hijack the connection from a dongle as Paget already demonstrated [5]. This allowed for the protocol to be reverse-engineered, which made it possible to write a pirate backend server to further exploit the dongle.

In some cases, the backend server would reject the hijacked connection, detecting that the dongle was not connected using the legitimate Access Point Name (APN) (the dongle provider would operate an APN themselves). In these situations, it is still possible to analyze the protocol either by probing the Universal Asynchronous Receiver Transmitter (UART) line to the GSM modem with a logic analyzer and decoding the Attention Commands (AT) and Point-to-Point-Protocol (PPP) frames coming from the microcontroller, or connecting the pirate BTS to the Internet using the Subscriber Identity module (SIM) card from another dongle of the same distributor.

It is notable that strong cryptographic authentication could have been achieved using a standard Hash Message Authentication Code (HMAC) with a different key for each dongle, which has low enough complexity to be implemented on the low power hardware used.

B. Over-the-Air Updates

All examined dongles support Over-the-Air (OTA) updates to replace the microcontroller firmware, fix bugs and add features. These updates are usually initialized by a command received from the backend server to which the dongle reacts by downloading a firmware image over Hypertext Printing Protocol (HTTP) from a simple web server. The downloaded binary is flashed either in place by the running firmware, or by a static bootloader which can't be updated and has the ability to revert the flashing process if something goes wrong.

Naturally, since no cryptographic authentication is implemented at the application layer, it is trivial to provide a customized firmware after the OTA update is triggered using the pirate backend server.

Some dongles try to verify the integrity of the downloaded binary by putting checksums and length fields in various positions inside the firmware. In order to pass this verification, a reverse-engineering of the firmware software has been performed.

Different techniques were used for different dongles in order to obtain the firmware for reverse-engineering it. When it was possible to manually trigger an OTA update, simply sniffing the connection as described earlier was sufficient to extract the unencrypted firmware out of the Transmission Control Protocol (TCP) stream, or to obtain the HTTP Uniform Resource Locator (URL) from which it was possible to download different firmware versions.

In all dongles, the downloaded firmware is cached before the actual flashing on a non-volatile memory outside the main microcontroller. These memory chips work using the Serial Peripherial Interface (SPI) protocol, the same used by Secure Digital Memory Cards (SD-Cards), which made it easy to read the content and find recently flashed firmwares and older rollback versions to use in case of boot failure.

In some dongles, an obstacle for the reverse-engineering was created by the presence of a static bootloader that handled the flashing procedure. This bootloader resides in a distinct location in the internal flash of the microcontroller, and can't be replaced via an OTA update. This means that it was not possible to intercept it as described before. Moreover, debug interfaces like Joint Test Action Group (JTAG) and Single Wire Debug (SWD) were disabled on these dongles. However, the bootloader could be dumped by getting the dongle to execute a small piece of custom assembly code (8 bytes) that used the original serial output routine. This exploit payload was small enough to be fitted in the known firmware without changing the length and only a checksum needed to be changed. The exploit simply calls the write function in the standard C library to dump the flash page containing the bootloader over an UART line.

C. Attack Procedures

Once the reverse-engineering of the software, protocols and hardware schematics was completed, a wide array of attacks became possible. The first step for all attacks was hijacking the victim's GPRS connection. This can usually be done by simply transmitting the pirate BTS signal with higher power than the legitimate BTS. Sometimes, jamming the legitimate BTS signal is also required (for example for devices supporting 3G connectivity).

After a temporary hijack of the Internet connection of the victim's dongle was achieved, a rogue Domain Name Service (DNS) server was used to trick the dongle into connecting to the pirate backend server. Now the pirate backend server could spoof the commands required to change the dongle configuration.

The dongles configuration includes the Internet Protocol (IP)-address of the backend server, which could be changed to the attacker's server IP-address. At this point, even when the GSM hijacking was interrupted, the dongle would still try to connect to the attacker's server.

The attacker's backend server could be used to trigger OTA updates which allow the attacker to flash exploited firmwares on both microcontrollers. This means the attacker had full access to the microcontroller responsible for interaction with the car, and could send any desired command on all the interfaces supported by the victim's dongle.

V. Security Threats

A. Surveillance

During the research on the investigated dongles, many possible ways to spy on an user were discovered. With the integrated sensors on the dongle, very accurate movement profiles can be created. An internal microphone of one investigated dongle could be used to eavesdrop on a driver.

B. Denial of Service

With the equipped CAN transceiver on the dongle, many sophisticated denial of service attacks on the car's internal network are possible. The simplest denial of service is a general or broadcasted *ECUReset* UDS command. This will reset all ECUs of the vehicle because the internal gateway distributes a broadcast command. With the possibility of modifying the dongle's firmware, ECU-targeted, conditional or persistent attacks are also possible. The Diagnostic communication over CAN (DoCAN) protocol with extended addressing allows an attacker to reset one specific ECU. It is possible to trigger a reset when certain conditions are met, for example if the accelerometer of the dongle is detecting high centrifugal forces. Also the reset of an airbag ECU based on the detection of brake force is possible. A persistent denial of service can be achieved with *CommunicationControl* commands or with setting ECUs in special modes, like the programming mode. An attacker can advice an ECU to be completely silent on the bus. Some of this mode changes are persistent. At least the erasure of some program parts on an ECU, which is usually performed from a repair shop tester during the flash procedure, leads to a persistent denial of service. A so-called smart device can increase the attack impact by specific conditions in dangerous situations of a car.

C. Distributed Denial of Service

Through persistent modification of a dongle's firmware, it is possible to hijack the communication and hide the MITM-attack for the dongle's operator. In this way, attackers can infect many dongles and start a distributed denial of service attack at a specific time. A distributed attack will create a much higher public visibility for such an attack, and can easily harm the image of a car manufacturer or a dongle operator. More advanced firmware modifications allow an attacker also to collect specific information about the host vehicle of an attacked dongle. It is possible to read out the Vehicle Identification Number (VIN), the vehicle manufacturer and even information about installed equipment. This allows extremely fine-grained attacks.

D. Malicious ECU reconfiguration

Usually car manufactures use the same ECU design for multiple car variants and sometimes even for different car models. For this reason, the firmware of an ECU has to be highly configurable. In this research, multiple ways to change the configuration of an ECU were discovered. For example, the functions for releasing airbags can be reconfigured. Such configurations can be done trough repair shop testers. Any authentication secrets can be extracted from the binary of the firmware, but also a security session hijack is possible. With a custom firmware on a GSM-OBD-II-dongle, the challenge can be caught and passed over GSM to a control server. There, a second software part can simulate a car and receive the proper response from an original repair shop tester. In this way, a dongle can get security access through a MITM-attack on a remote simulated repair shop tester connection.

E. Malicious ECU reprogramming

The signature processes of investigated ECUs did not show any weaknesses so far, but if an attacker is able to sign it's own firmware or bypass the verification process, he can also ship this firmware through an infected OBD-II-dongle. The dongle can independently flash this firmware to a specific ECU. Without any further work, an attacker is always able to downgrade a firmware to a previous and correctly signed version. Sometimes car manufacturers release new firmware versions because of security patches. By flashing an obsolete firmware, an attacker can reopen a fixed security vulnerability, which could be exploited in a second step.

VI. Conclusion and Future Work

While the vulnerabilities of the OBD-II-connector have been known for a long time, car manufacturers only had to worry about illicit modifications made by the car owners themselves, since access to the OBD-II-interface required for the attacker to be physically inside the car. More recently, a wide array of OBD-II-dongles appeared on the market, and many of them implement wireless connectivity with uncertain security. Zhang et al. demonstrated how Bluetooth OBD-II-dongles can be exploited by an attacker who has access to the victim's smartphone [7]. This paper showed how GSM-OBD-II-dongles are vulnerable to attacks from a relatively long range, and allow the attacker to obtain a persistent access to the OBD-II-connector over the Internet.

As more and more OBD-II-enabled devices are presented to the public, it is impossible to trust that all of them will maintain a good security architecture. Instead, it would be advisable that car manufacturers start treating the OBD-II-connector as a highly dangerous attack surface. It was shown that since the CAN bus interface on the OBD-II-connector is used by repair shops to make modifications to the car configuration, it is also possible for a remote attacker to realize the same operations through an insecure Internet-connected OBD-II-device. In a more secure car architecture, the OBD-II-connector would be used only for the standard diagnostic OBD-II PIDs, which shouldn't include operations critical for security and safety.

In the future, one approach to extend the work conducted could be trying to automate parts of a security investigation. Even if the results of the research on different OBD-II-dongles delivered new insights on the security of the interface, it would save time and the outcome would be more comparable, when some steps of the security analysis could be done automatically. Therefore, knowledge about previously discussed vulnerabilities has to be taken into account and specific test scenarios have to be created. In the end, a custom-built framework for performing penetrations tests on OBD-II-dongles will be the major goal. Also if certain parts – like the reverse-engineering of the device's hardware – need to be realized manually, a partly-automated tool to guide the security researcher regarding the execution of prearranged test cases could possibly improve the investigation process by saving time. By automating chosen test procedures and therefore uniforming the structure of their output, the test results will also be more standardized, which helps with interpreting and evaluating the accomplished findings.

Besides the attempt of automating the present investigation process of OBD-II-dongles, also applying and extending the discoveries already made to other in-vehicle systems, that are connected to the Internet, could be a valid proceeding. For example infotainment systems can implement a WiFi-Access-Point, to which passengers can connect to. Because these systems usually provide Internet access through their own GSM connection, they are possibly vulnerable to similar attacks based on a pirate BTS, like the one shown in this paper. Basically every connected device that is present in a modern car is worth analyzing in regards to security. As the number of such devices will grow and vehicles will get intra- and inter-networked, lots of different areas of research in this domain will need emphasized attention and could possibly be a follow-up for the presented investigations.

REFERENCES

[1] International Organization for Standardization, "ISO 15031-3: Road vehicles – Communication between vehicle and external equipment for emissions-related diagnostics – Part 3: Diagnostic connector and related electrical circuits: Specification and use," 2016. [Online]. Available: https://www.iso.org/standard/64636.html, visited 2017.07.13

[2] W. Yan, "A two-year survey on security challenges in automotive threat landscape," in 2015 International Conference on Connected Vehicles and Expo (ICCVE), Oct 2015, pp. 185–189.

[3] D. S. Fowler, M. Cheah, S. A. Shaikh, and J. Bryans, "Towards a testbed for automotive cybersecurity," in 2017 IEEE International Conference on Software Testing, Verification and Validation (ICST), March 2017, pp. 540–541.

[4] D. K. Nilsson and U. E. Larson, "Simulated attacks on can buses: Vehicle virus," in Proceedings of the Fifth IASTED International Conference on Communication Systems and Networks, ser. AsiaCSN '08, 2008, pp. 66–72.

[5] C. Paget, "Practical Cellphone Spying," DEFCON 18, 2010.

[6] A. Szijj, L. Buttyán, and Z. Szalay, "Hacking cars in the style of stuxnet," Oktober 2015. [Online]. Available: http://www.hit.bme.hu/ buttyan/publications/carhacking-Hacktivity-2015.pdf, visited 2017.07.13

[7] Y. Zhang, B. Ge, X. Li, B. Shi, and B. Li, "Controlling a car through obd injection," in 2016 IEEE 3rd International Conference on Cyber Security and Cloud Computing (CSCloud), June 2016, pp. 26–29.

[8] I. Foster, A. Prudhomme, K. Koscher, and S. Savage, "Fast and vulnerable: A story of telematic failures," in 9th USENIX Workshop on Offensive Technologies (WOOT 15), Washington, D.C., Aug. 2015.

[9] International Organization for Standardization, "ISO 15765-2:2016: Road vehicles – Diagnostic communication over Controller Area Network (DoCAN) – Part 2: Transport protocol and network layer services." [Online]. Available: https://www.iso.org/standard/66574.html, visited 2017.07.13

[10] ——, "ISO 14229-1: Road vehicles – Unified diagnostic services – Part 1: Specificatoin and requirements," 2013. [Online]. Available: https://www.iso.org/standard/55283.html, visited 2017.07.13

An Analysis of Automotive Security Based on a Reference Model for Automotive Cyber Systems

Jasmin Brückmann, Tobias Madl
Munich University of Applied Sciences
MuSe – Munich IT Security Research Group
Munich, Germany
email: madl@hm.edu, brueckma@hm.edu

Hans-Joachim Hof
Technical University of Ingolstadt
CARISSMA – Center of Automotive Research on Integrated Safety Systems and Measurement Area
Ingolstadt Research Group Applied IT Security
Ingolstadt, Germany
email: hof@thi.de

Abstract— **This paper presents an analysis of automotive security based on a reference model for Automotive Cyber Systems (ACS). In IT security, reference models are useful to conduct security analyses for either systems that do not exist yet, or for a number of existing systems that have similar properties. With Automotive Cyber Systems, both cases are present: some Original Equipment Manufacturers (OEMs) are already running Automotive Cyber Systems, whereas other OEMs only implemented partial Automotive Cyber Systems. The reference model presented in this paper is based on existing systems, as well as system architectures of research papers describing not yet existing applications of Automotive Cyber Systems. Hence, the reference model is of high relevance for future approaches on automotive security. The reference model was used to identify generic security requirements for automotive security in Automotive Cyber Systems. These security requirements are of high relevance for the design of upcoming Automotive Cyber Systems, as well as emerging applications like autonomous driving.**

Keywords- Automotive Security; Automotive Cyber System; Cyber-Phyiscal System;

I. INTRODUCTION

Digitalization is currently a big driver of the automotive industry. Unique features of new vehicles often are based on software, communication between vehicles, and connected automotive services. Forbs expects 152 million connected vehicles worldwide in 2020 [1]. The interconnection of vehicles with infrastructure, other vehicles, as well as a whole ecosystem of services will result in a so-called Automotive Cyber System. Current systems are limited, as the Original Equipment Manufacturers (OEMs) usually try to keep systems closed, offering only a very small set of services to drivers, limiting the potential of the ecosystem. However, startups in the automotive domain nowadays implement their services by using On-Board Diagnostics (OBD) dongles. An OBD dongle connects to the OBD II interface of a vehicle, as well as to a smartphone that provides Internet connectivity. By doing so, startups can access internal communication of vehicles via the Internet. Due to this strategy, OEMs are likely to open their platforms for third-party services to avoid dangerous fiddling with the OBD interface. With the increasing connectivity of vehicles, in combination with the importance of mandatory safety requirements and some serious hacks, e.g., [10], IT security became a priority for Automotive Cyber System. SAE 3160 is the first automotive safety standard that also addresses IT security. It is to be expected that more automotive security standards will be published in the near future.

This paper presents a reference model for Automotive Cyber Systems. Nowadays, in the observation of the authors, the automotive industry tends to favor partial security solutions over a holistic approach to IT security. The reference model aims on promoting a holistic approach to IT security in Automotive Cyber systems. The second part of the paper describes a security analysis based on the reference model. It results in a set of generic security requirements for Automotive Cyber Systems. These generic security requirements can be specialized for future systems in the automotive domain, hence support holistic approaches to IT security in Automotive Cyber Systems.

The rest of this paper is structured as follows: Section II discusses related work on reference architectures for Automotive Cyber Systems. Section III presents the reference model for Automotive Cyber Systems. Section IV presents the security analysis. Section V concludes the paper.

II. RELATED WORK

Most reference models in the automotive domain just model small parts of the whole systems. This is due to a very distinct "silo thinking" in the automotive industry in combination with the special structure of the automotive industry (many component suppliers that implement only small parts of the overall system). These reference models hinder a holistic approach to IT security. The reference architecture presented in this paper targets the whole Automotive Cyber System, including in-vehicle components, vehicle-to-vehicle communication, vehicle-to-infrastructure communication, as well as communication with an ecosystem of automotive services.

The works most similar to this paper are [2]-[4]. The models presented in these papers consider multiple parts of a full Automotive Cyber System. However, an analysis of these models showed that important components and data flows are missing. The reference architecture presented in this paper takes these components and data flows into consideration. Hence, it is more complete.

III. REFERENCE MODEL FOR AUTOMOTIVE CYBER SYSTEMS

The reference model for Automotive Cyber Systems was compiled from two sources: existing systems that implement parts of an Automotive Cyber System, and visions of future Automotive Cyber Systems collected from research papers and presentations on future products. Figure 1 gives an overview of the reference model.

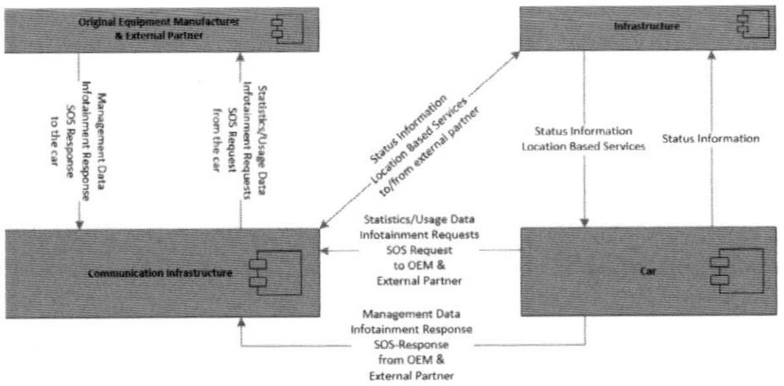

Figure 1. Overview of Automotive Cyber Systems (ACS) reference model.

The model consists of four components:

- OEM and external partners component
- Communication infrastructure component
- Infrastructure component
- Car component

The car communicates with nearby infrastructure and vehicles by Ad-hoc Long Term Evolution (Ad-hoc LTE) or WiFi. For long distance communication and access to other networks, the car component uses LTE or Universal Mobile Telecommunications System (UMTS). Both LTE and UMTS communication are represented by the communication infrastructure component in the reference model. The communication infrastructure component provides connectivity to the component OEM & external partners component. The OEM and other external partners offer automotive services. Components of the reference model are described in more detail in the following sections.

A. OEM and External Partners component

Figure 2 and Figure 3 show sub components and data flows of the OEM & External Partners component.

Subcomponent Management Services provide essential services for maintaining functionality and security of the car. Managed services include software updates over the air (SOTA) and firmware updates over the air (FOTA). Vehicles in Automotive Cyber Systems communicate a lot with other systems (vehicles, infrastructure, services). Hence, any vulnerability in a connected component is a potential danger for the vehicle. A timely provisioning of patches for vulnerabilities is considered a key success factor for security in Automotive Cyber Systems.

Advanced services become possible with the availability of statistics of vehicle usage and other mobility data. The Data Analysis Platform subcomponent is responsible for data collection, privacy-preserving data transformation, and data storage.

The OEM Services component offers additional services of the OEM. For example, an OEM could offer personalized reminder for service attendance. It could also provide information or sponsored offers from external partners. The car's driving assistance system (FAS - Fahrzeugassistenssysteme) and high autonomous driving (HAF - Hochauomatisiertes Fahren) systems get their information from OEM services, because these services have a better overview of the overall traffic situation.

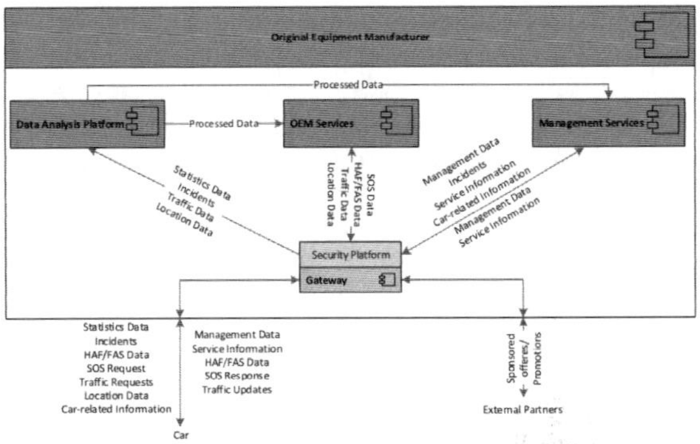

Figure 2. Subcomponents and their data flows at the OEM.

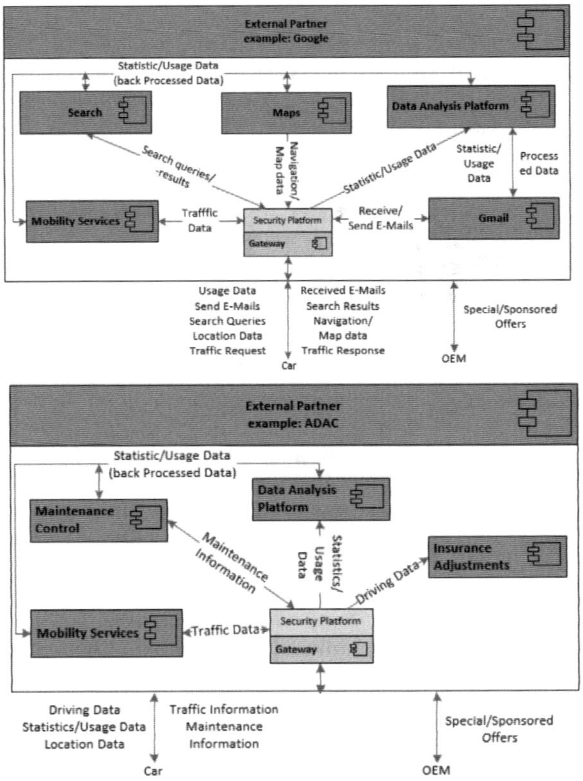

Figure 3. Subcomponent and data flows at two examples for external partners (Google and ADAC).

For the sake of this paper, Google and ADAC ("Allgemeiner Deutscher Automobil Club", association similar to the AAA in the US) were chosen as example of external partners. It is assumed that their subcomponents are prototypic for a wide range of other external partners. Subcomponents of external partners differ based on the services they are offering. Both institutions, ADAC and Google, offer mobility services, including information about the current traffic situation. Similar to the OEMs, external partners use a Data Analysis Platform component for data gathering, processing, and storage. The Security Platform component is similar to the Security Platform of the OEM. External partners may also offer some of their standard services adapted for automotive use. For example, Google may provide emails using their Gmail service, but emails are read to the user instead of a textual presentation. It should be noted that adaptations of standard IT services for automotive use might open new attack vectors for attackers.

ADAC offer extra subcomponents Maintenance Control and Insurance Adjustments. Among other things, the Maintenance Control subcomponent monitors the maintenance status of the car and informs the driver if the vehicle needs an inspection. The Insurance Adjustment subcomponent monitors the driving behavior and adjusts the insurance fee if the driver does not drive carefully (a so-called telematics tariff).

Figure 3 does not only show the subcomponents, but also the data flows of the OEM & external partners component. Most communication takes place between the OEM and the car. The data analysis platform receives statistics from the car, such as driving hours, hardware, or software incidents. Traffic and location data can be used for statistics, too. Once the collected data is processed, the OEM might improve its services and extends its product portfolio based on the data. The OEM Services receive traffic and emergency (SOS) requests and send the corresponding responses. For traffic requests and extended information they need the location data from the car. Additionally, they communicate with the HAF/FAS systems of the car, for example, to get advanced traffic information. This includes redirection because of current accidents or disruptions or automatic searching for a parking site. The Management Services component receives car related information to support the driver, for example, in case of incidents or hardware and software issues. Additionally, software and firmware updates are provided by the management services (called management data in Figure 3). Service information about the car and the OEM are also delivered by the management services.

Figure 3 also shows the data flows of external partners. The Google Search component receives search requests and answers with search results. For navigation purposes, maps and navigation instructions can be retrieved by the car from the Maps component. Gmail grants the passengers access to their mail accounts. The Mobility Services subcomponent is used to request a report on the current traffic situation. All components are sending statistics and usage data to the data analysis platform to be processed and used to improve offered services and to inspire new services. The Maintenance Control subcomponent monitors if the car should come to an inspection in the near future and informs the driver as needed. In order to analyze the driving behavior, the Insurance Adjustment subcomponent needs the driving data from the car. Both external partners are in contact with the OEM to share special or sponsored offers for the customers like bargains for.

B. *Communication Infrastructure component (external component)*

The Communication Infrastructure component handles long distance communication and access to other networks. Vehicles typically use LTE or UMTS. The communication infrastructure component provides connectivity to the component OEM & external partners component. It should be noted that the communication infrastructure is an external component.

C. *Infrastructure component*

The Infrastructure component includes the subcomponents Road-Side Units (RSUs) and Location Based Services (LBS) as can be seen in Figure 4.

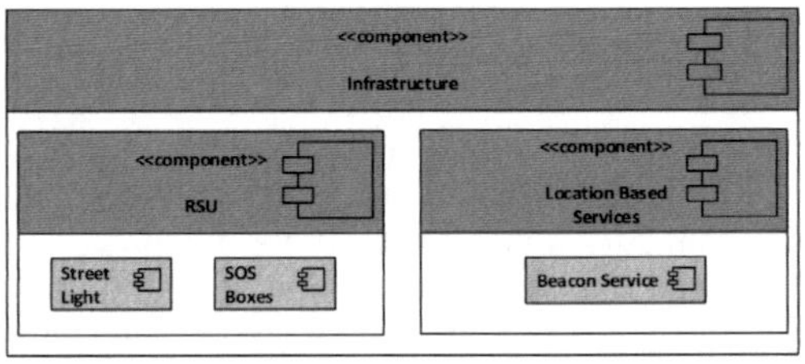

Figure 4. Subcomponents of Infrastructure component.

RSUs include traffic control devices like streetlights, road signs, or speed measurements.

LBS are services providing information that has been created, compiled, selected, or filtered taking into consideration the current locations of the users or those of other persons or mobile objects [11]. Local stores may provide LBS, for example, to promote current offers. An OEM may offer LBS to inform drivers about points of interest.

RSUs, as well as LBS communicate with the car using LTE, WiFi, or UMTS. Thereby, the RSU is directly talking with the cars Onboard Unit (OBU). The car and RSUs are exchanging status information, for example the current status of streetlights or the speed of the car. RSUs support emerging car applications like autonomous driving, as well as safety assistant systems. The Infrastructure component is communicating with the OEMs and external partners, too. It regularly sends status information about traffic or speed signs, receives commands to readjust the tempo limit, etc. Local stores or establishments provide LBS to the car. They may also send status information for big data analysis to the OEMs and external partners, or receive status information or additional offers.

D. *Car component*

The car has five subcomponents. The Infotainment Unit subcomponent, the Processing Unit subcomponents, the Communication System subcomponents, and the Sensor and

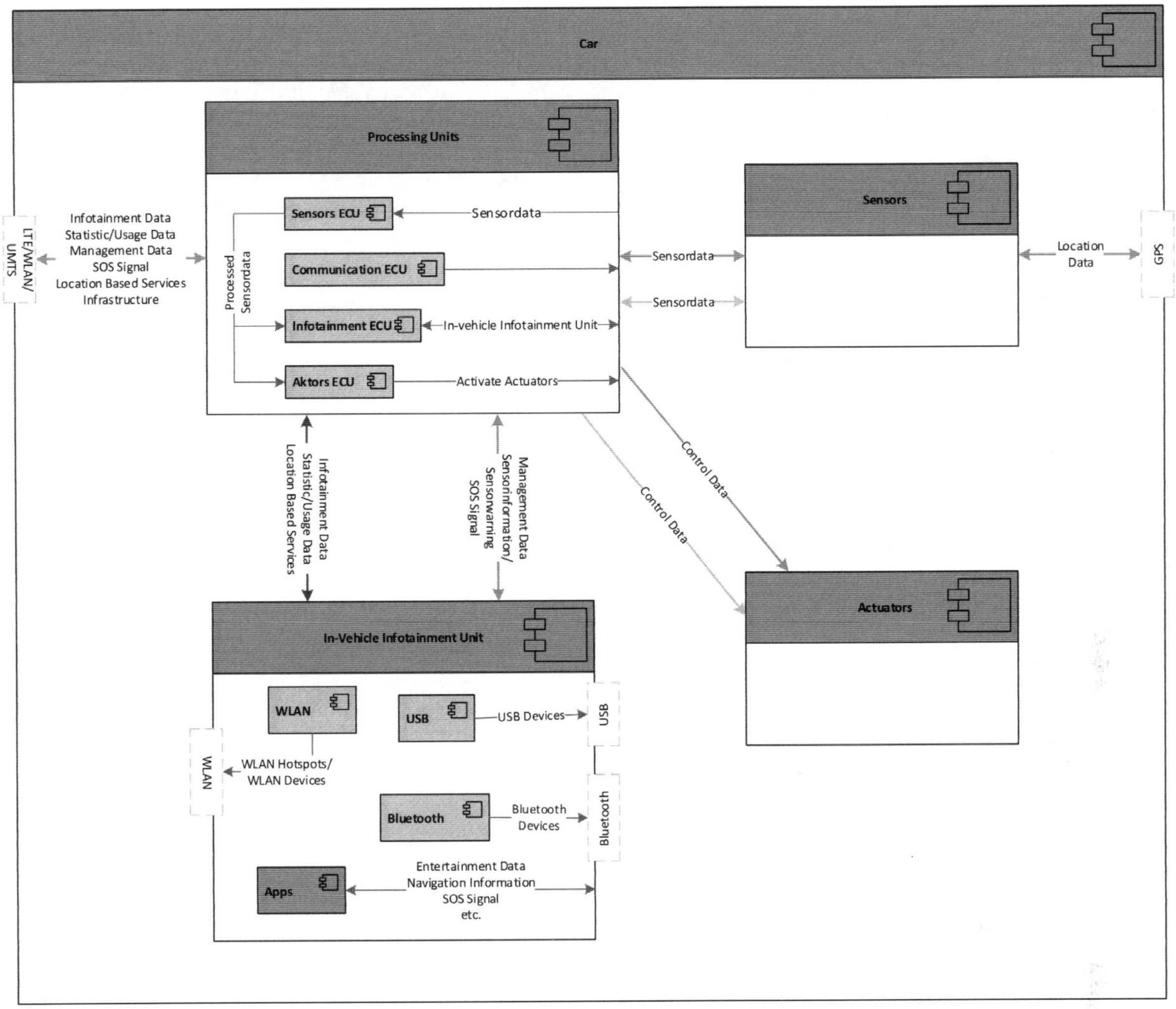

Figure 5. Subcomponent and data flows of the Car component.

Actor subcomponents. Figure 5 shows the subcomponents and the data flows between those subcomponents.

The Infotainment Unit subcomponent is the main interface for human interactions. It provides apps and services like telephone, mail, WWW, contacts, navigation, music, and emergency calls. It offers a wide range of short-range communication technologies that are suitable to connect to consumer devices. Supported communication standards typically include Bluetooth, WiFi, and USB.

Next, there are Processing Unit subcomponents. Normally, each subcomponent has at least one associated Electronic Control Unit (ECU) for processing incoming data and controlling resulting actions. These ECUs are distributed over the whole car and communicate with the respective unit to be controlled. An example would be a sensor ECU for receiving raw data from ultrasonic sensors and converting it to standardized data for further processing in the car. This data is then send to the central controlling ECU for processing.

The Communication System subcomponent supports various bus technologies for intra-vehicle communication. This system also provides interfaces for external communication (with OEM, external partners, or infrastructure). Inter-bus communication is possible via gateways. The Communication System also provides the well known OBD II interface that enables quick, easy and profound analysis of vehicles.

Other subcomponents include sensor and actuators. These are spread over the whole vehicle to provide various functionality. Sensors are used to gather data about the physical world (e.g., GPS position, open doors, park distance control, engine temperature, tire preassure, etc). Actuators are used to start actions, e.g., to start the windshield wipers.

IV. Security Analysis and Security Requirements for Automotive Cyber Systes

The security analysis presented in this paper is based on CORAS [9]. CORAS is customizable on any system and component and offers an own risk-modeling notation that is inspired by UML. Its adaptability allowed for an application of CORAS on the presented reference model, and allows integrating previous work on application-specific attacker models [5-8]. CORAS is used to identify risks for assets. CORAS consists of 8 steps.

In the first step, the scope of the analysis is defined. The scope of the analysis presented in this paper is an analysis of an Automotive Cyber System implementing the reference model presented in Section IV.

The second step involves an adjustment of the scope of the analysis by the customer of the analysis. This step was omitted, as there is no customer for this analysis.

The third step involves refining the target description using asset diagrams. The following assets were identified: "personal data" (personal data of driver and passengers), "critical systems" (systems ensuring safety of the car or safety of other critical systems), "integrity of the car" (car does not get harmed), "integrity of human" (humans do not get harmed), and "public trust" (trust in products of OEM and external partners). In step 4, the importance of the assets is rated (1=very important, 5= minor importance). The most important assets are "integrity of humans" and "personal data", see Figure 6 for the complete ranking. Strict laws for safety of humans, as well as very strict privacy laws of the European Union motivate this rating.

Asset	Importance	Type
Integrity of human	1	Indirect asset
Personal data	1	Direct asset
Critical data	2	Direct asset
Critical systems	2	Direct asset
Integrity of the car	2	Indirect asset
Public trust	3	Indirect asset

Figure 6. Asset rating.

In this step, a likelihood scale (see Figure 7), as well as consequences scales for each asset (see Figure 8 for the consequence scale of the asset "critical system") are defined. The likelihood scale is motivated by statistics about German car incidents in 2016.

Likelihood value	Description	Definition
Certain	more then twenty per year	$[200, \infty\rangle : 10y = [10, \infty\rangle : 1y$
Likely	ten to twenty times per year	$[100, 200\rangle : 10y = [10, 20\rangle : 1y$
Possible	five to nine times per year	$[50, 90\rangle : 10y = [5, 9\rangle : 1y$
Unlikely	Two to four times per year	$[20, 40\rangle : 10y = [2, 4\rangle : 1y$
Rare	Less than once per year	$[0, 10\rangle : 10y = [0, 1\rangle : 1y$

Figure 7. Likelihood scale.

Consequence value	Description
Catastrophic	Safety critical systems
Major	Most valuable core systems
Moderate	Valuable systems
Minor	Standard systems
Insignificant	Additional feature systems

Figure 8. Consequence scale for asset "critical systems".

In the next step, risks are identified using threat diagrams showing threat scenarios. The sixth step identifies consequences and likelihoods of the incidents that were identified in the prior step. In step seven, the risks are evaluated based on a risk matrix. The risk matrix uses likelihood and consequence of an incident to distinguish between acceptable risks and unacceptable risks. Figure 9 shows, as an example, the risks for the asset “personal data”, unacceptable risks are located in grey cells; acceptable risks are located in white cells. The risk matrix uses the shortcuts shown in Figure 10.

	Insgnificant	Minor	Moderate	Major	Catastrophic
Rare					
Unlikely			COI	CIU	COE, COI(1), COE(1)
Possible				CCS, CCT, COC	COC(1)
Likely			LDI	LUT	LUT(1)
Certain			VUS(1)		VUS

Figure 9. Risk evaluation matrix for asset "personal data".

Shortcut	Unwanted Incident
CIU	Compromised infotainment unit
CCS	Compromised communication system
UAC	Unauthorized access to car
SBS	Slow or broken system
VUS	Vulnerable system
CCT	Compromised confidentiality of transmitted data
COC	Compromised car
COE	Compromised oem or external partner
COI	Compromised infrastructure
LUT	Loss or unusability of transferred data
LDI	Loss of data/compromised integrity
UPB	Unpredictable behaviour
CSF	Complete service failure

Figure 10. Shortcuts for risks

The last step identifies risk treatment for unacceptable risks. To avoid unacceptable risks, the following generic security requirements were identified based on the presented reference model for Automotive Cyber Systems. Security requirements also include requirements for processes of the organizations running an Automotive Cyber System or automotive services:

Technical requirements:

- Trustworthy software sources: Software should only be downloaded from trustworthy sources. Authenticity of data sources must be ensured, as well as integrity protection of software during transit.
- Security Warning during software installation: Drivers should have the ability to avoid software installation in improper situations.
- Appropriate access control for all components and subcomponents of the Automotive Cyber System.
- Restriction of functional access for components.
- Authentication of all connecting devices and all communication partners.
- Integrity checks of incoming traffic.
- Encryption of all communications.
- Strict control of incoming and outgoing connections and traffic.
- Redundancy of important systems.

- Fail checks for important components.
- Fail safe states for important components.

Process requirements:

- Appropriate scope of training programs for employees.
- Use of secure software development life cycles throughout the development of all components of a Automotive Cyber System.
- Review of important changes and work.
- Careful selection for suppliers of software and hardware.

V. Conclusion And Future Work

The contribution of this paper is twofold: first, the paper provides a reference model for Automotive Cyber System that is more complete than previous models and takes into consideration upcoming applications like autonomous driving. The reference model is of great help for engineering new applications for Automotive Cyber Systems. The second contribution is a security analysis of Automotive Cyber Systems using the reference model as a basis. Output of the security analysis is a set of generic security requirements for automotive security in Automotive Cyber Systems. The generic security requirements are considered to be highly useful for the design of upcoming Automotive Cyber Systems, as well as emerging applications like autonomous driving. The use of the reference model allowed for a holistic approach to automotive security.

References

[1] N. McCarthy, "Connected Cars By The Numbers", Forbes Business, January 2015, https://www.forbes.com/sites/niallmccarthy/2015/01/27/connected-cars-by-the-numbers-infographic [last access August 1st, 2017].

[2] L. Zhang, "Modeling automotive cyber physical systems," in Distributed Computing and Applications to Business, Engineering & Sci- ence (DCABES), 2013 12th International Symposium on. IEEE, 2013, pp. 71–75.

[3] C. Ebert and I. N. Adler, "Automotive cyber-security" ATZextra, vol. 21, no. 2, 2016, pp.58–63.

[4] H. Abid, L. T. T. Phuong, J. Wang, S. Lee, and S. Qaisar, "V-cloud: vehicular cyber-physical systems and cloud computing," in Proceedings of the 4th International Symposium on Applied Sciences in Biomedical and Communication Technologies. ACM, 2011, p. 165.

[5] C. Ponikwar, H.-J. Hof, and L. Wischhof, "Towards a High-Level Security Model for Decision Making in Autonomous Driving", ACM Chapters Computer Science in Cars Symposium 2017 (CSCS 2017), Munich, Germany, July 2017, pp. 1-4.

[6] C. Ponikwar and H.-J. Hof, "Beyond the Dolev-Yao Model: Realistic Application-Specific Attacker Models for Applications Using Vehicular Communication", The Tenth International Conference on Emerging Security Information, Systems and Technologies (SECURWARE 2016), Nice, France, July 2016, pp. 4-9.

[7] M. Woerner and H.-J. Hof, "Realistic Attacker Model for Smart Cities", Applied Research Conference 2016, Poster, Augsburg, Germany, 2016.

[8] C. Ponikwar, H.-J. Hof, and L. Wischhof, „Towards a High-Level Security Model for Decision Making in Autonomous Driving", ACM Chapters Computer Science in Cars Symposium 2017 (CSCS 2017), Munich, Germany, July 2017, pp. 1-4.

[9] M. S. Lund, B. Solhaug, and K. Stølen, Model-driven risk analysis: the CORAS approach. Springer Science & Business Media, 2010.

[10] A. Greenback, „The jeep hackers are back to prove car hacking can get much worse", Wired, 08-Jan-2016. https://www.wired.com/2016/08/jeep-hackers-return-high-speed-steering-acceleration-hacks/. [last access: August 1st 2017].

[11] K. Axel, "Location-based services: fundamentals and operation," John Wiely & Sons, 2005.

Policy-Aware Provisioning Plan Generation for TOSCA-based Applications

Kálmán Képes, Uwe Breitenbücher, Markus Philipp Fischer,
Frank Leymann, and Michael Zimmermann

Institute of Architecture of Application Systems, University of Stuttgart,
70569 Stuttgart, Germany
Email: {kepes, breitenbuecher, fischer, leymann, zimmermann}@iaas.uni-stuttgart.de

Abstract—**A major challenge in enterprises today is the steadily increasing use of information technology and the required higher effort in terms of development, deployment, and operation of applications. Especially when different application deployment technologies are used, it becomes difficult to comply to non-functional security requirements. Business applications often have to fulfill a number of non-functional security requirements resulting in a complex issue if the technical expertise is insufficient. Therefore, the initial provisioning of applications can become challenging when non-functional requirements have to be fulfilled that arise from different domains and a heterogeneous IT landscape. In this paper, we present an approach and extend an existing deployment technology to consider the issue of security requirements during the provisioning of applications. The approach enables the specification of non-functional requirements for the automated deployment of applications in the cloud without the need for specific technical insight. We introduce a Policy-Aware Plan Generator for Policy-Aware Provisioning Plans that enables the implementation of reusable policy-aware deployment logic within a plug-in system that is not specific to a single application. The approach is based on the Topology and Orchestration Specification for Cloud Applications (TOSCA), a standard that allows the description of composite Cloud applications and their deployment. We prove the technical feasibility of our approach by extending our prototype of our previous work.**

Keywords–Cloud Computing; Application Provisioning; Security; Policies; Automation.

I. Introduction

A major challenge in enterprises today is the steadily increasing use of information technology (IT) due to the required higher effort in terms of development, deployment, and operation. Each new technology introduced to an enterprise's IT landscape also increases the complexity while the largest fraction of failures is beeing caused by manual operator errors [1]. These concerns have been addressed through outsourcing of IT to external providers, as well as through management automation of IT. Both of these aspects are enabled by Cloud Computing [2]. Due to a significant reduction of required technical knowledge, cloud services provide easy access to properties, such as elasticity and scalability [3].

Each IT solution has its functional and non-functional requirements that need to be addressed when using cloud services. Unfortunately, functional possibilities often outweigh the non-functional security issues that also have a need to be dealt with. Most cloud services are easy to use, but it is often difficult for users to extend and configure the cloud services to their particular needs, especially when non-functional aspects, such as security, have to be considered. Moreover, modern applications are often made up of complex and heterogeneous components that are hosted on cloud services or interact with them. Especially when different deployment technologies are used, it becomes difficult to comply to security requirements [4][5]. Such applications often have to fulfill a number of non-functional security requirements [6][7], which results in a complex provisioning challenge if the technical expertise is insufficient. Therefore, the initial automated provisioning of applications can become challenging when non-functional requirements have to be fulfilled that arise from many different domains and a heterogeneous IT landscape [8].

In this paper, we present a concept and extend an existing deployment technology to consider the issue of security requirements during the automated provisioning of applications. We present a *Policy-Aware Plan Generator* that enables generating executable *Policy-Aware Provisioning Plans* that respect policies that have to be fulfilled during the provisioning of an application. Our approach enables the implementation of reusable policy-aware deployment logic based on a plug-in system that is not specific to a single application. The approach is based on the *Topology and Orchestration Specification for Cloud Applications (TOSCA)*, a standard allowing the description of composite Cloud applications and their orchestration [9]. The extension to the existing technology [10] enables the fully automated deployment of Cloud applications while complying with security requirements defined as *Provisioning Policies*. Our approach enables the specification of non-functional requirements for the deployment of applications in the cloud without the need for specific technical insight other approaches require. Additionally, security experts of different domains are enabled to work collaboratively on a single model for applications. We validate our approach by a prototypical implementation based on the *OpenTOSCA Ecosystem* [11][12].

The remainder of this paper is structured as follows. In Section II, we explain the fundamental concepts of the TOSCA standard, which is used within our approach as a cloud application modeling language. Afterwards, we motivate our approach with a motivating scenario and introduce several exemplary Provisioning Policies in Section III. In Section IV, we describe our approach for generating executable Policy-Aware Provisioning Plans based on TOSCA. Section V presents a validation of the approach in the form of a prototypical implementation based on the OpenTOSCA Ecosystem. Section VI gives an overview of related work. Finally, we conclude this paper and give an outlook on future work in Section VII.

II. Topology and Orchestration Specification for Cloud Applications (TOSCA)

In this section, we introduce the TOSCA standard on which our approach and prototype are based. TOSCA enables to describe the automated deployment and management of applications in an interoperable and portable manner. In order to give a compact introduction to the OASIS standard, we only describe the fundamental concepts of TOSCA required to understand our presented approach. More details can be found in the TOSCA Specifications [9][13], the TOSCA Primer [14] and a more detailed overview is given by Binz et al. [15].

The structure of a TOSCA-modeled application is defined by a *Topology Template*, which is a multi-graph consisting of nodes and directed edges. The nodes within the Topology Template represent so called *Node Templates*. A Node Template represents software or infrastructure components of the modeled application, such as a hypervisor, a virtual machine, or an Apache HTTP Server. The edges connecting the nodes represent so called *Relationship Templates*, which specify the relations between Node Templates. Thus, the Relationship Templates are specifying the structure of a Topology Template. Examples for such relations are "hostedOn", "dependsOn", or "connectsTo". The semantics of the Node Templates and Relationship Templates are specified by *Node Types* and *Relationship Types*. These types are reusable classes that allow to define *Properties*, as well as *Management Operations* of a type of component or relationship. An "Apache HTTP Server" Node Type, for example, may specify Properties for the port number to be accessible and additionally define required credentials, such as username and password. The defined Management Operations of a Node Type are bundled in interfaces and enable the management of the component. For example, the "Apache HTTP Server" Node Type may define an operation "install" for installing the component itself and a "deployApplication" operation to deploy an application on the web server. A cloud provider or hypervisor Node Type typically defines Management Operations, such as "createVM" and "terminateVM" for creating and terminating virtual machines.

These Management Operations are implemented by so called *Implementation Artifacts (IAs)*. An Implementation Artifact itself can be implemented using various technologies. For instance, an Implementation Artifact can be a WAR-file providing a WSDL-based SOAP Web Service, a configuration management artifact executed by a tool, such as Ansible [16] or Chef [17], or just a simple shell script. Depending on the Implementation Artifact, they are processed in different ways: (i) IAs, such as shell scripts, are transfered to the application's target environment and executed there. (ii) IAs, such as WAR-files implementing a Web Service, are deployed and executed in the so called *TOSCA Runtime Environment* (See last paragraph). This kind of Implementation Artifact typically performs operations by using remote access to the components. (iii) Implementation Artifacts that are already running are just referred within the model, such as a hypervisor or cloud provider service and then are called directly with the help of adapters implemented within.

Besides Implementation Artifacts, TOSCA defines so called *Deployment Artifacts (DAs)*. Deployment Artifacts implement the business functionality of a Node Template. For example, a Deployment Artifact can be a WAR-file providing a Java application. Another example would be a PHP application where a ZIP file containing all the PHP files, images, and other required files implementing the application would be represented by the Deployment Artifact.

The automatic creation and termination of instances of a modeled Topology Template, as well as the automated management of the application is enabled by so-called *Management Plans*. A Management Plan specifies all tasks and their order for fulfilling a specific management functionality, such as provisioning a new instance of the application or to scale out a component of the application. A Management Plan that provisions a new instance of the application is called a *Provisioning Plan* in this paper. Management Plans invoke the Management Operations which are specified by the Node Types and implemented by the corresponding Implementation Artifacts of the topology. TOSCA does not specify how Management Plans should be implemented. However, the use of established workflow languages, such as the *Business Process Execution Language (BPEL)* [18] or the *Business Process Model and Notation (BPMN)* [19], is encouraged.

TOSCA also allows the specification of policies for expressing non-functional requirements. For example, a policy can define the security requirements of an application, e.g., that a component of the application must be protected from public access. Again, for reusability purposes, TOSCA allows the definition of *Policy Types*. A Policy Type, for example, defines the properties that have to be specified for a policy. However, the actual values of these properties are specified within *Policy Templates* attached to Node Templates for which the policy has to be fulfilled. A Policy Type can be also associated with a Node Type in order to describe the policies this component provides. Since TOSCA does not make any statement about policy languages, any language can be used to define them. We call policies that have to be fulfilled during the provisioning of the application *Provisioning Policies*.

In order to package Topology Templates, type definitions, Management Plans, Implementation Artifacts and Deployment Artifacts, as well as all required files for automating the provisioning and management of applications, the TOSCA Specification defines the so called *Cloud Service Archive (CSAR)*. A CSAR is a self-contained and portable packaging format for exchanging TOSCA-based applications.

Through the standardized meta-model and packaging format, CSARs can be processed and executed by any standard-compliant *TOSCA Runtime Environment*, thus, ensuring portability, as well as interoperability. However, since there are two approaches for provisioning an instance of a TOSCA-modeled application, there a two kinds of TOSCA Runtime Environments: (i) TOSCA Runtime Environments that support *declarative provisioning* and (ii) TOSCA Runtime Environments that allow *imperative provisioning* [10]. In declarative processing, the TOSCA Runtime Environment interprets the Topology Template to infer which Management Operations need to be executed in which order to provision the application, without the need for a Provisioning Plan. In imperative provisioning on the other side, the TOSCA Runtime Environment requires a Provisioning Plan provided by the CSAR to instantiate the application by invoking this plan. In this paper, we present a hybrid policy-aware deployment approach that interprets the declarative Topology Template and generates an imperative executable Policy-Aware Provisioning Plan.

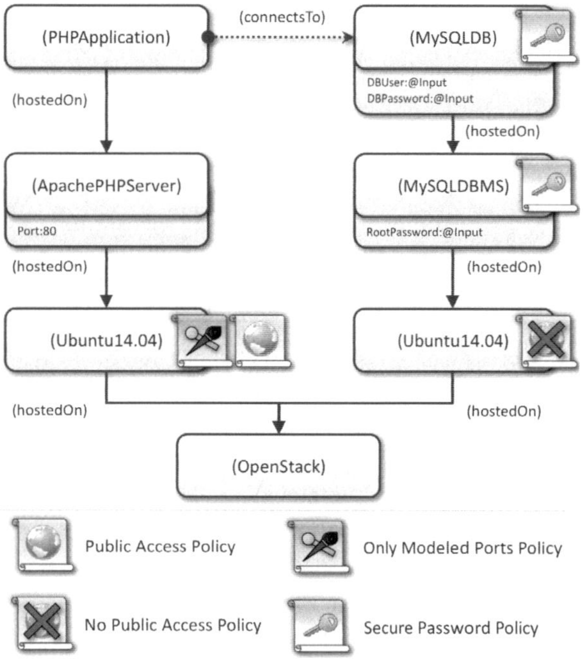

Figure 1. Our Motivating Scenario, where the backend needs to high security (right side), whereas the frontend needs to be publicly accessible.

III. Motivating Scenario

In this section, we describe a TOSCA-based motivating scenario that we will use throughout the paper to describe our approach. Our scenario is depicted in Figure 1 as a TOSCA Topology Template specifying a typical application to serve a website that is connected to a database system. The shown topology consists of a PHP web application with a MySQL database, additionally a set of Provisioning Policies are specified in the form of Policy Templates that must be enforced during provisioning. Components within the Topology Template are defined as TOSCA Node Templates (e.g., OpenStack, Ubuntu, Apache Web Server, PHP application, MySQL DBMS, and MySQL Database). These are connected through TOSCA Relationship Templates of the types "hostedOn" and "connectsTo" to either define that a component will be hosted on another component (e.g., MySQLDBMS is hosted on an Ubuntu 14.04 virtual machine) or to specify that a component is connected to another component (e.g., PHP application connects to its MySQL database by using the given password from the input of the DBPassword property). To instantiate an Ubuntu 14.04 virtual machine, the OpenStack Node Template exposes Management Operations, such as *createVM* which takes as parameters the specification of the virtual machine, e.g., RAM, CPUs, etc. Customizing the modeled application is restricted to setting credentials for the MySQL Database and its MySQL Database Management System at provisioning time. This is achieved by setting the value of the MySQL DB and MySQL DBMS Node Templates' Properties "DBUser", "DBPassword" and "RootPassword" to "@input". To model the desired non-functional security requirements, *Provisioning Policies* are attached to Node Templates of the Topology Template. In the following subsections, we describe the Provisioning Policies of our scenario in detail.

A. Public Access Policy

With the *Public Access Policy* a modeler specifies that the deployment system must ensure that the associated component is available and accessible from outside the cloud environment, hence open for the public internet. In our scenario, the website owner wants to make sure that the Ubuntu 14.04 virtual machine on the OpenStack cloud is accessible by the public. Therefore, the Public Access Policy is attached to the Ubuntu 14.04 virtual machine Node Template of the front-end Ubuntu virtual machine (Left side in Figure 1).

B. No Public Access Policy

While the Public Access Policy enforces accessibility from outside the cloud environment, the *No Public Access Policy* has the opposite goal. Its main purpose is to restrict access to the associated component by allowing to serve requests solely from within the cloud. For our scenario, the owner wants to be sure that his virtual machine that hosts sensitive data within the database is not directly accessible from the internet. Thus, he attaches the No Public Access Policy to the Ubuntu 14.04 virtual machine of the MySQL database management system to enforce restricted access (Right side in Figure 1).

C. Only Modeled Ports Policy

The intent of the *Only Modeled Ports Policy* is to restrict access to the associated component to the modeled ports. This allows the application owner to further secure his front-end, e.g., the Ubuntu 14.04 virtual machine hosting the PHP Application shall allow access to only explicitly modeled ports. To do so, the Only Modeled Ports Policy is attached on the Ubuntu 14.04 Node Template restricting access only to port 80, as the only installed component specifying a port within the topology is the Apache Server (Left side in Figure 1) that hosts the front-end PHP application.

D. Secure Password Policy

As the final policy within our scenario, the owner uses the *Secure Password Policy* that enforces the use of strong passwords for components. This increases the barrier for attackers of the application by preventing the usage of weak passwords at provisioning and runtime, e.g., when the PHP application component is connected to MySQL database. Thus, the application owner attaches Secure Password Policies on both, the MySQLDB and MySQLDBMS Node Templates (See right side at the top in Figure 1) running on the back-end Ubuntu virtual machine of the OpenStack cloud. As the passwords in the scenario are set at runtime (indicated by the Property value "@input") the system must ensure at runtime that the given data is compliant with the set policy.

With the attached Provisioning Policies Public Access and Only Modeled Ports the owner of our scenario is able to ensure that the front-end is available to the public and restricts access to only intended ports of the application running on the modeled Ubuntu virtual machine. To secure his backend, he is able to use the No Public Access and Secure Password Policy to restrict access from outside and to enforce the usage of strong passwords for the database running on the back-end Ubuntu virtual machine. In the following section, we will show how our deployment approach provisions this application while strictly enforcing the specified Provisioning Policies.

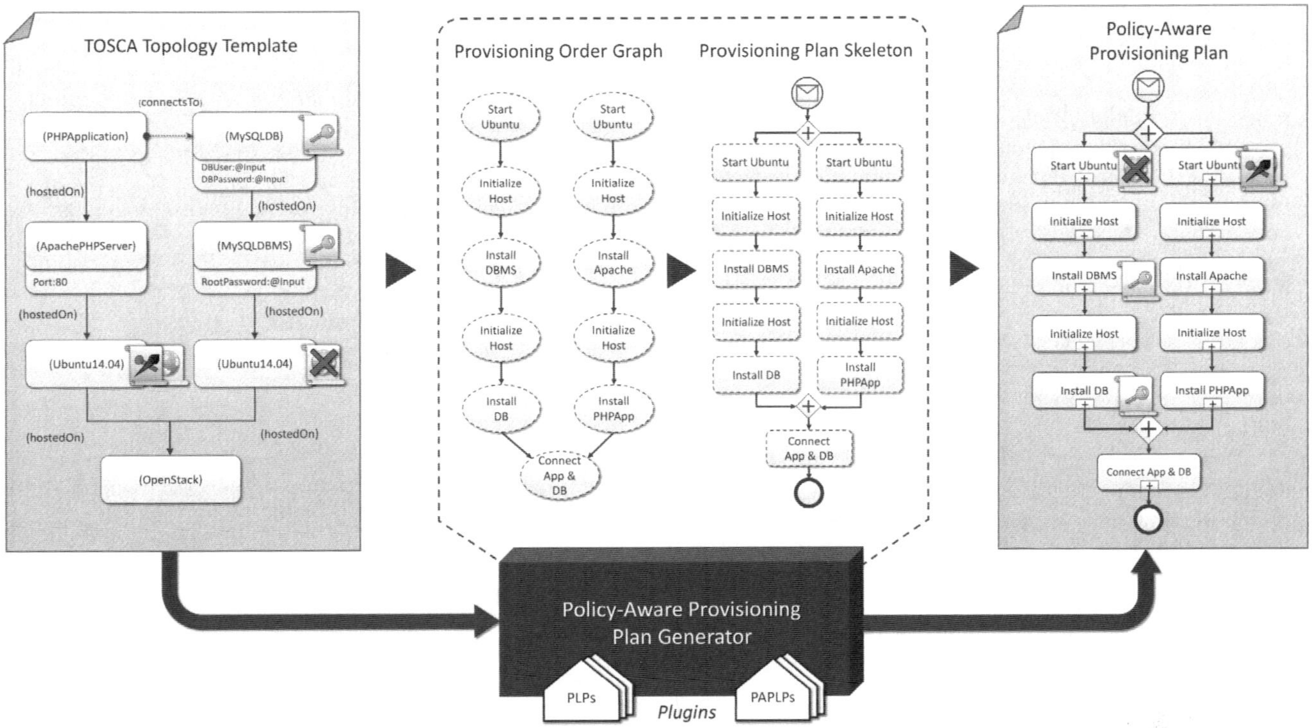

Figure 2. Overview of our approach for transforming a TOSCA Topology Template into a Policy-Aware Provisioning Plan.

IV. Policy-Aware Provisioning Plan Generation

In this section, we present our approach of provisioning applications while enforcing specified non-functional security requirements that are specified as policies attached to the deployment model. This section is structured as follows: In the first subsection, we detail out a *Role Model* for our approach. In the second subsection, we give an overview of our approach that entails transforming a TOSCA Topology Template into an executable Provisioning Plan that is able to provision the application while enforcing all specified Provisioning Policies. Afterwards, we describe all transformation phases in detail.

A. Role Model

Creating a TOSCA CSAR is taken care of by a *Cloud Service Creator* [9] by developing the Topology Template, the associated types, artifacts, and the policies to enforce. TOSCA enables reusing type definitions, so common Node-, Relationship- and Artifact Types can be reused without the need to create them from scratch. The final CSAR contains only the TOSCA Topology Template without a Provisioning Plan. This CSAR is then given to our *Policy-Aware Provisioning Plan Generator* that generates a *Policy-Aware Provisioning Plan* that also enforces the specified policies of the Topology Template during provisioning. Afterwards, the creator can inspect the generated Policy-Aware Provisioning Plan to customize the provisioning. Please note: the generated plan correctly enforces the policies, but additional tasks that cannot be modeled declaratively may be added to customize the execution if required. For example, a task for sending an e-Mail to the administrator can be added. However, the adaptation of the generated plan may also be forbidden in order to ensure that no policy-related tasks get influenced negatively. As the final step, the CSAR with the generated plan is sent to a *TOSCA-enabled Cloud Provider* hosting a *TOSCA Runtime Environment*, which is able to process and execute the generated Provisioning Plan contained in the CSAR.

B. Overview of the Plan Generation Phases

In this section, we describe an overview of how we generate a Policy-Aware Provisioning Plan for TOSCA Topology Templates. In the first phase, (i) a *Provisioning Order Graph (POG)* is generated. The POG only specifies the provisioning order of the Node and Relationship Templates for the given Topology Template. This graph is then (ii) translated into a *Provisioning Plan Skeleton (PPS)* in a particular plan language, for example, BPEL or BPMN. The PPS contains placeholder activities for the provisioning of all Node and Relationship Templates. These placeholder activities contain no provisioning logic and are following the provisioning order specified by the POG. Thus, each node and relation in the POG is translated into such a placeholder activity, the edges of the POG are translated into control flow constructs of the respective plan language. These two phases are the same as in our previous work [10], for which the goal was to generate Provisioning Plans. To enable policy-aware provisioning, we extend the last phase of our previous work in this paper as follows: In the last phase, the PPS is (iii) completed to an executable *Policy-Aware Provisioning Plan* where the placeholder activities of the skeleton are replaced by concrete Management Operation calls, which provisions the Node- and Relationship Templates while ensuring that all attached Policy Templates are fulfilled during execution. Figure 2 depicts this approach and in the following subsections, we will describe each phase in detail.

C. Provisioning Order Graph Generation Phase

In the first phase, we generate a *Provisioning Order Graph (POG)* that describes only the order in which the Node- and Relationship Templates have to be provisioned (see second graph from the left in Figure 2). In our scenario, we need to generate a POG that represents the deployment order of the front-end (i.e., Ubuntu 14.04 virtual machine, Apache PHP Server, PHP Application), the back-end (i.e., another Ubuntu 14.04 virtual machine, MySQL Database Management System, MySQL Database), and the connection of the two stacks (i.e., initializing the "connectsTo" Relationship Template). The POG consists of nodes for each Node and Relationship Template that represents the step of provisioning the respective component or relation. Edges between the nodes of the POG specify the order of the provisioning steps, i.e., the provisioning order of the Node Templates and Relationship Templates.

The calculation of the ordering is based on the semantics of the Relationship Templates' types: while a "hostedOn" Relationship Type expects that the target Node Template is provisioned before the source, the "connectsTo" Relationship Type forces the order of provisioning that both the source and target Node Templates must be provisioned before the connection can be initialized. The Relationship Types"hostedOn" and "connectsTo" are abstract types, i.e., concrete types derived from these abstract types inherit the semantic behavior. For our scenario, the POG would contain a series of nodes that represent the provisioning of the front- and back-end in parallel. For each Node Template that is the source of a "hostedOn" Relationship Template the abstract POG contains a node for the Node- and Relationship Template each. For example, in Figure 2 there is a node in the POG for each Node- and Relationship Template that must be started (e.g., virtual machines) or installed (e.g., Apache and MySQL DBSMS). After the provisioning of the front- and back-end stacks, the last Relationship Template of the type "connectsTo" is provisioned: To configure the PHP Application with the needed credentials for the database stack, an operation "connectTo" is invoked on PHP Application Node Template with the database credentials properties as parameters. More details on generating a Provisioning Order Graph can be read in [10]. Please note that the calculation of the provisioning order is independent of the specified Provisioning Policies.

D. Provisioning Plan Skeleton Transformation Phase

The second phase transforms the POG into a plan language-dependent *Provisioning Plan Skeleton (PPS)* that follows the provisioning order of the Node and Relationship Templates specified by the POG (third graph in Figure 2 from the left). These PPSs are implemented in a certain process modelling language, such as BPEL [18], BPMN [19], or BPMN4TOSCA [20][21]; but only entail empty *placeholders* for deployment activities and the general provisioning order. Therefore, each node in the POG is transformed into one placeholder while the provisioning order of the POG is translated into language-specific control flow constructs between these placeholders. Thus, the skeleton is not executable yet as the placeholders contain no provisioning logic. The Policy-Aware Plan Generator has different plug-ins for generating skeletons in different plan languages. For example, in BPEL these placeholders can be realized as empty `<scope>` activities.

procedure: *CompletePPS*(Topology Template t, Provisioning Plan Skeleton s)

```
 1: for (∀ Node- and Relationship Templates temp ∈ t) do
 2:   if (temp has attached Policy Set p ∧ p ≠ ∅) then
 3:     for (∀ Policy-Aware PLPs papl) do
 4:       if (papl can handle temp enforcing p) then
 5:         Replace Placeholder in s of temp with Executable Policy-Aware Provisioning Logic from papl
 6:       else if (No Policy-Aware PLP papl can handle temp with p) then
 7:         Abort completion of s
 8:       end if
 9:     end for
10:   else
11:     for (∀ PLPs plp) do
12:       if (plp can handle temp) then
13:         Replace Placeholder in s of temp with Executable Provisioning Logic from plp
14:       else if (No PLP plp can handle temp) then
15:         Abort completion of s
16:       end if
17:     end for
18:   end if
19: end for
```

Figure 3. Pseudocode for completing a Provisioning Plan Skeleton into an executable Policy-Aware Provisioning Plan.

E. Policy-Aware Provisioning Plan Completion Phase

In the third phase, the generated Provisioning Plan Skeleton is completed by adding the technical deployment activities into the placeholders. The Plan Generator provides a plugin system for *Provisioning Logic Providers (PLPs)*, which are responsible for filling the placeholders by executable technical provisioning logic. Each PLP is capable of providing the technical activities for the provisioning of one Node Type or Relationship Type to complete the skeleton into an executable form (See the graph on the right in Figure 2). We extend this original completion phase [10] by *Policy-Aware Provisioning Logic Providers (PAPLPs)*, which are capable of providing provisioning logic similarly to PLPs but additionally ensure that all policies attached to the Node or Relationship Template they support are enforced by the injected technical provisioning logic. An overview of this extended phase is outlined in Algorithm 3, which we now describe in detail.

As the input of the policy-aware completion phase the Topology Template t and its Provisioning Plan Skeleton (PPS) s is given (see Input before line 1 in Algorithm 3). The completion phase will begin to cycle through all Node- and Relationship Templates $temp$ (line 1) of the topology t, and checks whether $temp$ has a non-empty set of Provisioning Policies p attached (line 2). If this is the case, the algorithm starts to cycle through all available PAPLPs $papl$ (line 3) and checks whether there is one $papl$ that can provide executable activities to provision $temp$ while enforcing all attached Provisioning Policies p (line 4). A PAPLP is allowed to inspect the whole Topology Template t to decide whether it can provide provisioning logic for the given Node- or Relationship Template, respectively, while fulfilling the attached policies. For example, by traversing the topology t from a Node

Template $temp$ to find all port properties specified, which have to be set for enforcing the Only Modeled Ports Policy. If a $papl$ is found that is able to add technical activities for $temp$ ensuring that the attached policies p are enforced, the generator requests this $papl$ to inject the necessary activities to provision and enforce the policies into the corresponding placeholder in the PPS s (line 5). The injected activities typically invoke the Management Operations provided by the respective Node or Relationship Template and range from uploading files to executing scripts, etc. When there is no suitable $papl$ that can provide provisioning logic for a certain Node or Relationship Templates $temp$ while fulfilling all attached policies, (line 6), the system will abort the completion as it is not possible to provisioning the given topology t while enforcing all specified policies p (line 7).

While cycling through the Node and Relationship Templates and the algorithm detects that a $temp$ has no attached Policy Set p, it will start to cycle through the set of normal (non policy-aware) PLPs plp (line 11). Within the cycle it checks whether $temp$ can be provisioned by one of the PLPs plp (line 12), and if one plp is found it will be requested to replace the respective placeholder of $temp$ in s (line 13). When no plug-in plp is found (line 14), the algorithm aborts (line 15).

This algorithm forces the completion step to produce either Policy-Aware Provisioning Plans where policy enforcement is guaranteed or the generation will be aborted. Please note: We strictly separate the handling of Node and Relationship Templates that have attached policies from the ones that specify no policies. Thus, the algorithm does not try to find a PAPLP for a template that specifies no policies. The reason for this is that the injected provisioning logic should reflect exactly the deployment model and should not be more restrictive as required in terms of adding unrequested security stuff. However, the algorithm could be easily modified in line 11 to also check if there is a PAPLP $papl$ capable of providing (possibly unnecessarily secured) provisioning logic for a certain Node or Relationship Templates that does not specify any Provisioning Policy to be enforced.

After the step of completing the Provisioning Plan Skeleton into an executable Policy-Aware Provisioning Plan, all placeholder activities resembling the deployment graph of the original POG are replaced by language-dependent sets of executable provisioning activities whose execution provisions the respective Node- and Relationship Template while enforcing the attached Policy Templates. Finally, the Cloud Service Creator is able to review the generated plans and if needed, and may alter the technical activities to his needs. However, after modification of the generated activities, it cannot be guaranteed that the altered Policy-Aware Provisioning Plan correctly enforces the specified Provisioning Policies. Therefore, a manual adaptation is possible but should be considered carefully.

The presented algorithm is completely independent of any policy language used to specify Provisioning Policies: A PAPLP by itself decides if (i) it understands all attached policies of a Node or Relationship Template, respectively, and (ii) if it is able to provide appropriate provisioning logic. Thus, the presented algorithm is extensible to any policy language, by developing PAPLPs that are able to process elements of such a language and generate appropriate activities that enforce the specified policy.

V. VALIDATION

In this section, we describe a prototypical implementation of our approach to validate its practical feasibility. In the following two subsections, we describe how the Cloud Service Creator (See Subsection IV-A) can model the motivating scenario within the OpenTOSCA Ecosystem [11] using the TOSCA modeling tool *Winery* [12] and how the create can generate a Policy-Aware Provisioning Plan that provision the application while fulfilling all Provisioning Policies. Moreover, we explain how the *OpenTOSCA Container* [11] is able to execute these plans automatically to provision the application.

Modeling TOSCA Topology Templates and the generation of the Policy-Aware Management Plans is done solely within the Winery modeling tool. Winery is a Java-based web application that can be deployed on servers, such as Apache Tomcat (http://tomcat.apache.org). Users can define all their types, such as Node, Relationship, Artifact, and Policy Types inside the *Entity Modeler* and use them inside the *Topology Modeler* to graphically model the wanted Topology Template for their Service Template. By creating Node Templates from Node Types and connecting them by Relationship Templates of a certain Relationship Type, the user is able to specify a topology of the application. Afterwards, the modeler is able to configure the Topology Template by setting appropriate Properties on the Node- and Relationship Templates. To finally attach the required Provisioning Policies, Winery supports specifying Policy Templates from defined Policy Types. After modeling, the user can request the creation of a Policy-Aware Provisioning Plan for the Topology Template. Winery will then invoke the Policy-Aware Plan Generator to generate a BPEL Provisioning Plan, which is then packaged into the CSAR.

For the generation of Policy-Aware Provisioning Plans, we implemented our approach by extending the Plan Generator prototype that already is able to generate BPEL Provisioning Plans executable within the OpenTOSCA Ecosystems' TOSCA Runtime Environment *OpenTOSCA* (https://github.com/OpenTOSCA/container). The original implementation itself is written in Java and utilizes the OSGI-Framework as a plug-in system that enables adding additional provisioning logic as Provisioning Logic Providers (PLPs). For implementing our approach, we extended the plug-in system to allow the usage of Policy-Aware Provisioning Logic Providers (PAPLPs) and specified an according plugin interface. After creating the BPEL Provisioning Plan Skeleton, the additional policy plug-in layer is invoked to add its logic by processing attached Policy Templates while cycling through the Node- and Relationship Templates with the set of available PAPLPs as described in Section 2. Each of the PAPLPs is able to verify whether it can create activities that can enforce the given Policy Templates while provisioning the Node- or Relationship Templates. The implementation of the PAPLP plug-ins resulted in extended versions of the original PLP plug-ins [10].

The implementation for enforcing the Secure Password Policy resulted in a PAPLP plug-in for the MySQL Database and MySQL Database Management System Node Types. Each checks either the input of the BPEL plan at runtime or the specified passwords in the Node Template Properties, and stops execution of the plan when the given password data was not strong enough based on commonly accepted criteria. To enforce the No Public Access, Public Access, and Only Modeled Ports Provisioning Policies, we extended the PLP plug-in that already was able to provision an Ubuntu 14.04 virtual machine on an OpenStack cloud in two ways: The (i) first extension was made for the (No) Public Access Policy, which was implemented in a PAPLP plug-in that is additionally able to add activities to the BPEL Provisioning Plan Skeleton that configures the security group of a virtual machine to be either publicly available or not. The extension for the Only Modeled Ports Policy resulted in a (ii) second extension of the plug-in that enables it to additionally add activities that set a Unix Cron job to regularly re-set the ports modeled inside the application. The plug-in determines based on the hostedOn relations of the Topology Template which component is installed on the Ubuntu 14.04 Node Template attached with an attached Only Modeler Ports Policy Template, and while doing so, fetches the set ports or reads them at runtime and configures the activities in the BPEL Provisioning Plan Skeleton to set the Cron job on the Ubuntu 14.04 virtual machine after provisioning.

In summary, we implemented our scenario within the OpenTOSCA Ecosystem which already was extended by us to generate BPEL Provisioning Plans to be executed in the TOSCA Runtime Environment OpenTOSCA Container. In this paper, we further extended the prototype of the Plan Generator component to enable policy-aware provisioning by allowing to register Policy-Aware Provisioning Plugins that are able to generate provisioning activities for Node Templates of specific Node Types while enforcing the specified Policy Templates.

VI. Related Work

In this section, we present related work, which range from Management and Deployment Frameworks to Workflow and configuration management technologies that focus on enforcing policies at provisioning time.

Walraven et al. [22] present *PaaSHopper*, a Policy-Driven middleware for multi-PaaS environments. The main components of the approach enabling policy-awareness are the *Dispatcher* and the *Policy Engine*. While the Policy Engine retrieves data about the PaaS execution environment to monitor whether or not a policy is enforced, the Dispatcher uses the Policy Engine to decide based on the current context of the policies to which component a request is dispatched and, additionally, handles the deployment of components. To adapt the applications on changing policies at runtime, the PaaSHopper middleware is able to change deployment descriptors of the application components. The main difference to our approach is the ability to model policy-aware applications not only restricted to PaaS solutions and the ability to audit the generated plans whether the polices are enforced correctly at provisioning time as we explicity generate an executable Policy-Aware Provisioning Plan model.

The contributions of Ouyang et al. [23] integrate policies into workflows by using a *Policy Server* and a *Policy Repository*. The Policy Server acts as a service bus between the components and the workflow at runtime, similar to [22], but with the exception that the evaluation of actions to be taken is done in so-called *Decision Point Activities* of the workflow at runtime by interacting with the Policy Server. The difference to our approach is the use of a Policy Server, while our approach is based on provisioning logic injected by specific plugins to automatically generate a Policy-Aware Provisioning Plan.

Blehm et al. [24] present an approach to define policies on TOSCA Topology Templates similar to ours. The main difference between the two approaches is within the initial configuration and enforcement of the policies. While both phases of initial configuration and enforcement in the approach of Blehm et al. rely on special services packaged with the Policy Type definitions, our approach utilizes the Management Operations of the Node Templates itself and the policy-aware provisioning logic is injected by external plugins. An additional difference is that the approach of Blehm et al. requires manually developing the Provisioning Plan, while our approach supports automatically generating this plan.

In Keller et al. [25] the *CHAMPS* system to enable Change Management of IT systems and resources is presented. Similiarly to our approach Keller et al. generate so-called *Task Graphs* that specifies the abstract steps that have to be taken to serve a so-called *Request for Change* for the used IT systems and resources. These Task Graphs are then transformed into an executable plan as within our approach. CHAMPS also enables the specification of policies and SLAs, although the work gives no detail on how these are processed by their system.

Mietzner et al. [26] present the standards-based enterprise bus *ProBus* that is able to optimize resource and service selection based on policies. Clients are able to send invocation request with attached policies to ProBus, which then must be enforced by the service providers. Similar to our approach is the usage of processes to orchestrate provisioning services while enforcing the set policies, however, these processes are developed manually, a complex and error-prone task, and not generated as within our approach.

Jamkhedkar et al. [27] present a *Security on Demand* architecture which allows to provision and migrate virtual machines (VMs) with different security requirement levels for the servers they are running on. A user is able to request the provisioning of a VM along with a security policy that is processed by the so-called *Policy Validation Module*. The Policy Validation Module is connected to a *Trust Monitor* that monitors properties of the available servers the virtual machines are running on. Based on the properties collected, the Trust Monitor derives security capabilities, such as the isolation mechanism of the environment, for the hosting servers. These capabilities are matched by the Policy Validation Module to select an appropriate server to provision, or in case of changing server capabilities, migrate a VM. The main difference to our approach is the enforcement point of policies. While Jamkhedar et al. enforce security requirements on the level of hypervisors, our approach is generic and can support various types of components, e.g., also PaaS-based deployments.

Waizenegger et al. [28] present two approaches to implement security policy enforcement based on TOSCA. The two approaches are the *IA-Approach* and *P-Approach*. Within the IA-Approach the Implementation Artifacts implementing Node Type Management Operations are extended to enable policy enforcing capabilities by implementing the same operations but with additional policy enforcing steps. The P-Approach extends the Provisioning Plan of an application with policy enforcing activities similar to our approach, but with the difference that the plans determine the policies to enforce at runtime. Additional differences to our approach are the missing generation of plans and the need for extending Implementation Artifacts for each policy type to support.

VII. Conclusion and Future Work

In this paper, we presented an approach that enables users to model and provision composite Cloud applications with their set non-functional requirements specified as Provisioning Policies. The approach extends our previous work in which we showed how to provision applications by transforming an application model into an executable Provisioning Plan. To transform such an application model our approach (i) generates a Provisioning Order Graph (POG) that specifies the order of provisioning, afterwards, this is (ii) transformed into a language-dependent Provisioning Plan Skeleton that has placeholders with the same order to provisioning the application. As the last step (iii), the placeholders are replaced with provisioning activities to generate an Executable Provisioning Plan. The approach presented in this paper extends our previous work by replacing placeholders of the Provisioning Plan Skeleton with activities to provision applications while enforcing specified non-functional requirements. This extension eases the modeling of non-functional requirements, as the user only has to specify the Provisioning Policies for his application without the need of deep technical knowledge. We validated our approach by a prototypical implementation within the OpenTOSCA Ecosystem and by applying our approach to a scenario with the focus on non-functional security requirements. In future work, we plan to decouple the provisioning logic from the policy enforcement logic and extend the set of policy types applicable to scenarios, such as the Internet of Things.

Acknowledgment

This work is partially funded by the projects SePiA.Pro (01MD16013F) and SmartOrchestra (01MD16001F) of the BMWi program Smart Service World.

References

[1] D. Oppenheimer, A. Ganapathi, and D. A. Patterson, "Why do internet services fail, and what can be done about it?" in Proceedings of the 4th Conference on USENIX Symposium on Internet Technologies and Systems (USITS 2003). USENIX, Jun. 2003, pp. 1–16.

[2] F. Leymann, "Cloud Computing: The Next Revolution in IT," in Proceedings of the 52th Photogrammetric Week. Wichmann Verlag, Sep. 2009, pp. 3–12.

[3] M. Armbrust, A. Fox, R. Griffith, A. D. Joseph, R. Katz et al., "Above the Clouds: A Berkeley View of Cloud Computing," University of California, Berkeley, Tech. Rep., 2009.

[4] U. Breitenbücher, T. Binz, O. Kopp, F. Leymann, and M. Wieland, "Policy-Aware Provisioning of Cloud Applications," in Proceedings of the Seventh International Conference on Emerging Security Information, Systems and Technologies (SECURWARE 2013). Xpert Publishing Services, Aug. 2013, pp. 86–95.

[5] U. Breitenbücher, T. Binz, C. Fehling, O. Kopp, F. Leymann et al., "Policy-Aware Provisioning and Management of Cloud Applications," International Journal On Advances in Security, vol. 7, no. 1&2, 2014.

[6] S. Subashini and V. Kavitha, "A survey on security issues in service delivery models of cloud computing," Journal of network and computer applications, vol. 34, no. 1, 2011, pp. 1–11.

[7] C. A. Ardagna, R. Asal, E. Damiani, and Q. H. Vu, "From Security to Assurance in the Cloud: A Survey," ACM Computing Surveys (CSUR), vol. 48, no. 1, 2015, p. 2.

[8] W. Han and C. Lei, "A survey on policy languages in network and security management," Computer Networks, vol. 56, no. 1, 2012, pp. 477–489.

[9] OASIS, Topology and Orchestration Specification for Cloud Applications (TOSCA) Version 1.0, Organization for the Advancement of Structured Information Standards (OASIS), 2013.

[10] U. Breitenbücher, T. Binz, K. Képes, O. Kopp, F. Leymann et al., "Combining Declarative and Imperative Cloud Application Provisioning based on TOSCA," in International Conference on Cloud Engineering (IC2E 2014). IEEE, Mar. 2014, pp. 87–96.

[11] T. Binz, U. Breitenbücher, F. Haupt, O. Kopp, F. Leymann et al., "OpenTOSCA - A Runtime for TOSCA-based Cloud Applications," in Proceedings of the 11th International Conference on Service-Oriented Computing (ICSOC 2013). Springer, Dec. 2013, pp. 692–695.

[12] O. Kopp, T. Binz, U. Breitenbücher, and F. Leymann, "Winery – A Modeling Tool for TOSCA-based Cloud Applications," in Proceedings of the 11th International Conference on Service-Oriented Computing (ICSOC 2013). Springer, Dec. 2013, pp. 700–704.

[13] OASIS, TOSCA Simple Profile in YAML Version 1.0, Organization for the Advancement of Structured Information Standards (OASIS), 2015.

[14] ——, Topology and Orchestration Specification for Cloud Applications (TOSCA) Primer Version 1.0, Organization for the Advancement of Structured Information Standards (OASIS), 2013.

[15] T. Binz, U. Breitenbücher, O. Kopp, and F. Leymann, TOSCA: Portable Automated Deployment and Management of Cloud Applications, ser. Advanced Web Services. Springer, Jan. 2014, pp. 527–549.

[16] M. Mohaan and R. Raithatha, Learning Ansible. Packt Publishing, Nov. 2014.

[17] M. Taylor and S. Vargo, Learning Chef: A Guide to Configuration Management and Automation. O'Reilly, Nov. 2014.

[18] OASIS, Web Services Business Process Execution Language (WS-BPEL) Version 2.0, Organization for the Advancement of Structured Information Standards (OASIS), 2007.

[19] OMG, Business Process Model and Notation (BPMN) Version 2.0, Object Management Group (OMG), 2011.

[20] O. Kopp, T. Binz, U. Breitenbücher, and F. Leymann, "BPMN4TOSCA: A Domain-Specific Language to Model Management Plans for Composite Applications," in Proceedings of the 4th International Workshop on the Business Process Model and Notation (BPMN 2012). Springer, Sep. 2012, pp. 38–52.

[21] O. Kopp, T. Binz, U. Breitenbücher, F. Leymann, and T. Michelbach, "A Domain-Specific Modeling Tool to Model Management Plans for Composite Applications," in Proceedings of the 7th Central European Workshop on Services and their Composition, ZEUS 2015. CEUR Workshop Proceedings, May 2015, pp. 51–54.

[22] S. Walraven, D. Van Landuyt, A. Rafique, B. Lagaisse, and W. Joosen, "PaaSHopper: Policy-driven middleware for multi-PaaS environments," Journal of Internet Services and Applications, vol. 6, no. 1, 2015, p. 2.

[23] S. Ouyang, "Integrate Policy based Management and Process based Management–A New Approach for Workflow Management System," in Computer Supported Cooperative Work in Design, 2006. CSCWD'06. 10th International Conference on, IEEE. IEEE, 2006, pp. 1–6.

[24] A. Blehm, V. Kalach, A. Kicherer, G. Murawski, T. Waizenegger et al., "Policy-framework-eine methode zur umsetzung von sicherheits-policies im cloud-computing." in 44. Jahrestagung der Gesellschaft fr Informatik. GI, 2014, pp. 277–288.

[25] A. Keller, J. L. Hellerstein, J. L. Wolf, K.-L. Wu, and V. Krishnan, "The CHAMPS System: Change Management with Planning and Scheduling," in Proceedings of the 10th Network Operations and Management Symposium (NOMS 2004). IEEE, Apr. 2004, pp. 395–408.

[26] R. Mietzner, T. Van Lessen, A. Wiese, M. Wieland, D. Karastoyanova et al., "Virtualizing services and resources with probus: The ws-policy-aware service and resource bus," in Web Services, 2009. ICWS 2009. IEEE International Conference on, IEEE. IEEE, 2009, pp. 617–624.

[27] P. Jamkhedkar, J. Szefer, D. Perez-Botero, T. Zhang, G. Triolo et al., "A framework for realizing security on demand in cloud computing," in Cloud Computing Technology and Science (CloudCom), 2013 IEEE 5th International Conference on, vol. 1, IEEE. IEEE, 2013, pp. 371–378.

[28] T. Waizenegger et al., "Policy4TOSCA: A Policy-Aware Cloud Service Provisioning Approach to Enable Secure Cloud Computing," in On the Move to Meaningful Internet Systems: OTM 2013 Conferences. Springer, Sep. 2013, pp. 360–376.

Towards an Approach for Automatically Checking Compliance Rules in Deployment Models

Markus Philipp Fischer, Uwe Breitenbücher, Kálmán Képes, and Frank Leymann

Institute of Architecture of Application Systems, University of Stuttgart, 70569 Stuttgart, Germany
Email: {fischer, breitenbuecher, kepes, leymann}@iaas.uni-stuttgart.de

***Abstract*—An enterprise's information technology environment is often composed of various complex and heterogeneous systems and is subject to many requirements, regulations, and laws. This leads to the issue that technical experts should also have a firm knowledge about a company's compliance requirements on information technology. This paper presents an approach to ensure compliance of application deployment models during their design time. We introduce a concept that is able to locate compliance relevant areas in deployment models while also specifying how these areas have to be modeled to fulfill the compliance requirements.**

Keywords*–*Cloud Computing; Compliance; Security; Policies;

I. INTRODUCTION

An enterprise's information technology (IT) is subject to many regulations and laws, such as the German *Federal Data Protection Act* [1] or the ISO 27018 standard [2], which is especially concerned with data protection for cloud services (i.e. the privacy of personal data). Modern applications are often composed of various different and heterogeneous systems and form complex composite applications [3]. To avoid failures that are most often caused by human operators [4], there are efforts to automate the deployment and provisioning of applications [5] while also considering non-functional security requirements [6]–[10]. These approaches are implemented in various *deployment technologies* that consume *deployment models* to automatically deploy the described application. These models typically describe the structure of the deployment and the desired configuration, for example that an Java-based web application shall be hosted on an Apache Tomcat that has to be installed on a new virtual machine of a certain type. Unfortunately, companies are subject to a variety of requirements, therefore, it is difficult to ensure that modelers of deployment models are aware of all requirements that must be considered in these models to follow the company's compliance. Moreover, even modelers that are aware of compliance aspects can make mistakes that lead to deployments that are not conformant to the compliance regulations of the company. However, violations of compliance, in turn, can quickly result in serious consequences for the company's business.

In this paper, we present our work in progress about automating compliance ensurance for deployment models based on the *Topology and Orchestration Specification for Cloud Applications (TOSCA)* [11], a standard that allows the description of Cloud applications and their deployment. We introduce a concept for specifying *Deployment Compliance Rules for TOSCA models* that enable compliance experts to define reusable rules that can be used to ensure the compliance of deployment models. The approach enables the automation of compliance checking for deployment models during their design time. As a work in progress, the concept is not yet detailed completely and not implemented but will be integrated into the open source TOSCA modeling tool *Eclipse Winery* [12].

The remainder of this short paper is structured as follows: Section II describes the motivation and presents the concepts of TOSCA. Section III introduces the concept for our approach, followed by Section IV, which introduces selected works that are related. Finally, Section V draws a conclusion on the work in progress and gives an outlook on future work.

II. MOTIVATION

In this section, we describe a scenario to motivate our concept. The described scenario will be used throughout the paper to describe our approach. We also present the fundamentals of TOSCA, the basis of our prototype, in which the presented concept will be realized. Everything needed to understand our approach is described in this section, however, we refer interested readers to the TOSCA Specification [11], the TOSCA Primer [13], and the TOSCA Simple Profile [14] to provide more detailed information about the OASIS standard. TOSCA is a technology-agnostic approach that can be used to orchestrate other deployment technologies, such as *Chef* or Cloud provider APIs. Therefore, it is a suitable basis for a technology-independent compliance checking approach.

The basic structure of an application modeled in TOSCA consists of a *Topology Template*, which is a directed multigraph. The nodes of the graph represent software or infrastructure components such as a virtual machine, an Apache PHP Server, or an operating system. These components are represented in TOSCA as *Node Templates*. Node Templates can be connected via directed edges that describe the relationship between two adjacent nodes, such as a "hostedOn" or a "connectsTo" relationship. These edges are called *Relationship Templates*. *Node Types* and *Relationship Types* provide the semantics for nodes and edges in the Topology Template. Both are reusable classes that also allow the definition of properties, such as username and password for a virtual machine or a server. Figure 1 depicts our motivation scenario. The scenario consists of a PHP Application that is connected to a MySQL database. In this example, the PHP Application could be a website where users can register themselves with their personal data to receive regular newsletters from the company. The MySQL database is modeled as a Node Template with, for example, a property that semantically defines the type of data that is stored in the database. Both the application stack on the left side (PHP App, Apache PHP Server, Ubuntu 14.04 VM) and the application stack on the right (MySQL DB,

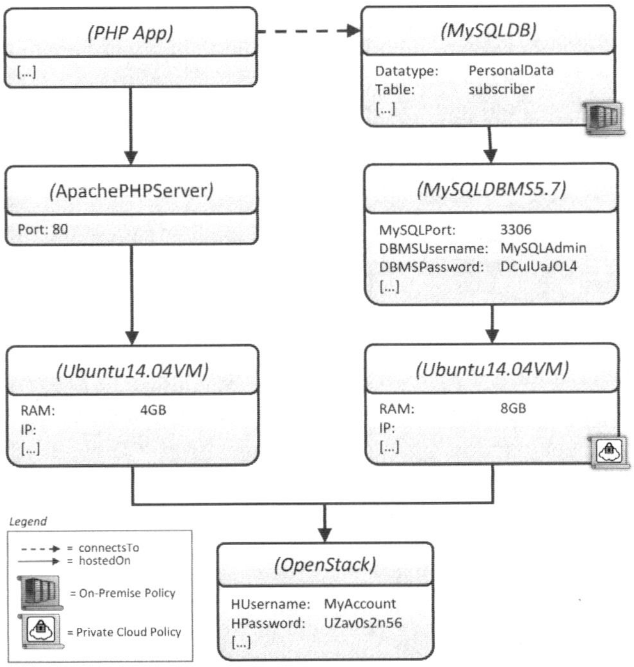

Figure 1. Motivating Scenario with two stacks modeled using the visual TOSCA notation *Vino4TOSCA* [15].

MySQL DBMS 5.7, Ubuntu 14.04 VM) are hosted on a Node Template of Node Type "OpenStack". The Relationship Type "hostedOn" means that the component where the Relationship Template originates, is installed on the target component, while "connectsTo" specifies that the PHP application connects to the MySQL database to store data [13]. The property *Datatype* with value "PersonalData", set in the MySQL database, indicates that the data stored in the database is personal data. If a company using this scenario is located in Germany, it falls under the German Federal Data Protection Act [1], which requires that the data is stored securely and access of third parties to the data is prevented. Another requirement is the adherence to the ISO 27018 standard [2], which is used to certify companies in the area of privacy of personal data in clouds. In our scenario, the company tries to enforce strict data security rules to avoid losing any personal data, to avoid coming in conflict with any law, and also they place importance to discretion. Thus, when personal data is involved, the company's compliance requirement is that it is to be ensured that the data is hosted *On Premise* and in a *Private Cloud*. Deployment models such as depicted in Figure 1 can be automatically executed with TOSCA Runtime Environments, such as OpenTOSCA [5]. Additionally, TOSCA not only allows the specification of application topologies and their orchestration but also enables modeling non-functional requirements using policies, e.g., concerning security or quality of service (QoS). For reusability, TOSCA provides *Policy Types*, which are classes of policies that can also have properties. The actual values of the properties are specified within the *Policy Templates* (*Policy Definitions* in the Simple Profile [14]). A Policy Template is associated with a Policy Type that can be associated with a set of Node Templates the policy can be applied to. The TOSCA Specification does not require a specific format for the policies, so any language is usable. Example policies used in our approach are the *On-Premise Policy* and the *Private Cloud Policy*. The On-Premise Policy is intended to restrict the deployment of components to pre-defined locations that are "On-Premise". This means that the associated components have to be hosted physically on infrastructure that is on the site of a company. This is often practiced with applications that process sensitive data, for example in international customs. With a Private Cloud Policy, a modeler can enforce that any Node Template the Policy is applied to, is hosted in a company-internal data center. This policy is related to the Cloud Computing Pattern *"Private Cloud"* by Fehling et al. [16]. Thus, policies are an instrument to address non-functional concerns such as security and quality of service requirements. However, the knowledge about compliance requirements is often held by compliance experts. Therefore, modelers can be unaware of the requirements, leading to non-compliant applications. It is desired that application models, which are ready to be provisioned, are compliant to the company's requirements. Therefore, each model has to be checked for compliance by experts, which is a time-consuming and error-prone task when done manually, especially for large and complex models. Thus, the issue of compliance checking for deployment models should be automated. In this paper, we present an approach for compliance checking in deployment models on the basis of the TOSCA standard.

III. Towards an Approach for Automatically Checking Compliance Rules in Deployment Models

This section introduces our concept for automated compliance checking of deployment models. We introduce *Deployment Compliance Rules* that can be modeled by compliance experts, which enable to automatically ensure that a certain compliance requirement is satisfied by a deployment model. Deployment Compliance Rules allow compliance experts to model allowed deployment structures, which are compliant to a company's compliance requirements, such as enforcing non-functional security requirements on customer data. Figure 2 shows an example of such a rule. A Deployment Compliance

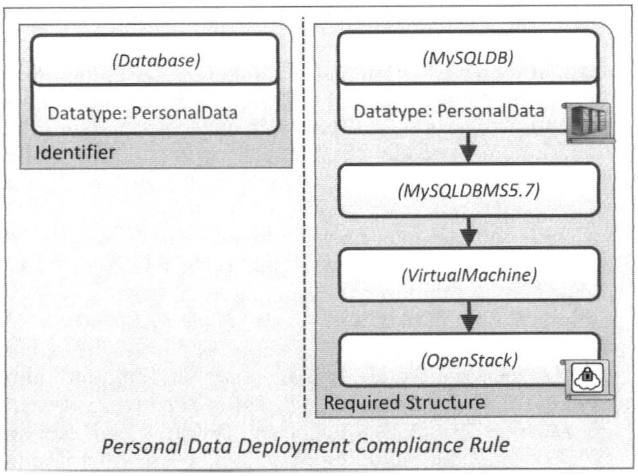

Figure 2. Example for a Compliance Rule.

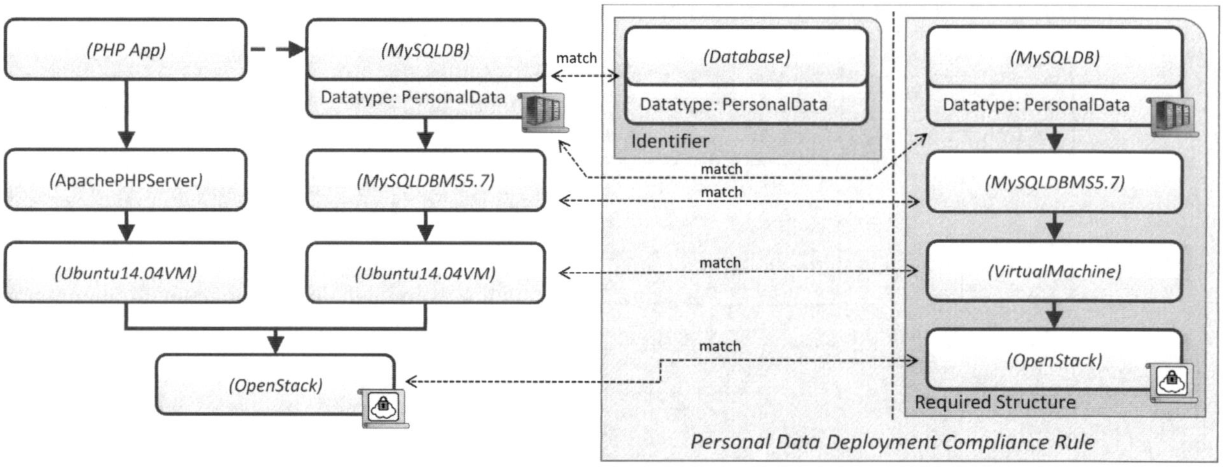

Figure 3. This figure shows how the Identifier and Required Structure of the Personal Data Deployment Compliance Rule is matched to the motivation scenario.

Rule consists of two directed, typed, and attributed multi-graphs, one being the *Identifier* graph (see left-hand side in Figure 2), the other being the *Required Structure* graph (see right-hand side in Figure 2). The basic idea is to use the Identifier to find compliance-relevant areas in the deployment model and to compare them to the defined Required Structure, which defines allowed structures for this Identifier. To find relevant areas and to compare them to the Required Structure, we reduce the problem to a *subgraph matching problem* [17]. The Identifier is used to define compliance-relevant areas of a deployment model as abstract as possible. TOSCA enables this by allowing to specify Node Types that are abstract. Each Node Type inherits the properties of Node Types it is derived from. We explain this matching concept on the basis of the *Personal Data Deployment Compliance Rule* scenario shown in Figure 2. The intention of this rule is to ensure that all databases of applications that store personal data have to be deployed on the local OpenStack of the company. Therefore, the Identifier graph depicted in Figure 2 on the left-hand side consists of a single abstract "Database" Node Template with the property "Datatype" and value "PersonalData". With this construct we ensure that all Node Templates that are derived from the "Database" Node Template are matched to this Identifier. The goal is to identify all areas of the deployment model where the Deployment Compliance Rule has to be applied. The Required Structure graph is used to define the proper structure and semantics of the area of the deployment model the Identifier matches, i.e., how the Deployment Compliance Rule must be fulfilled. In Figure 2 on the right side, the Required Structure specifies that all matching databases storing personal data must follow the structure of a "MySQLDB" NodeTemplate that is connected via "hostedOn" Relationship Templates to "MySQLDBMS5.7", "VirtualMachine", and "OpenStack" Node Templates. Similar to the "Database" Node Template in the Identifier graph, the "VirtualMachine" Node Template is abstract and, thus, allows any kind of virtual machines to be used as operating system for the database. The Policy Templates "Private Cloud' and "On-Premise" are attached to the Node Templates of the Required Structure to specify that the matched parts of the deployment model must be hosted on a private cloud and on premise.

A. Algorithm Sketch

Figure 3 shows the basic idea of the approach. The deployment model is tested for each defined Deployment Compliance Rule separately. In the following, we describe the algorithm for one exemplary rule namely the *Personal Data Deployment Compliance Rule* introduced in the previous section. The first step is to identify all areas where the rule has to be applied, i.e., all areas of the model that match the Identifier of the rule. In Figure 3, the Identifier consists of a single "Database" Node Template that has "PersonalData" as a "Datatype" property. Via subgraph isomorphism the Identifier can be matched to the "MySQLDB" Node Template, which has the same property. The match is indicated by the dashed double arrow between the Identifier and the deployment model. In a second step the Identifier's match has to be checked against the Required Structure. The deployment model is searched for subgraphs that contain the identified subgraph as well as the Required Structure. In Figure 3, the Required Structure consists of a "MySQLDB" Node Template with an "On-Premise" Policy attached and the specified Property and value. The "MySQLDB" Node Template has to be hosted on a Node Template of the specific type "MySQLDBMS5.7", which has to be hosted on a Node Template derived from the abstract Node Template "VirtualMachine". The last Node Template in the Required Structure is an "OpenStack" Node Template that has a "Private Cloud" Policy attached. As indicated by the dashed double arrows in Figure 3 there is a subgraph that matches to the Required Structure. Because the "MySQLDB" Node Template matched to the Identifier is also a part of the subgraph matched to the Required Structure, the Deployment Compliance Rule is fulfilled. The subgraph isomorphism problem is an NP-complete problem, therefore, its execution time has to be discussed. The Deployment Compliance Rule example shown in Figure 2 is defined by two graphs that have to be matched to the overall deployment model and represents a typical use case for the Deployment Compliance Rules defined in this paper. As the two graphs are very small graphs the execution time should be reasonable. However, if the rules become larger, the execution time will also increase. Therefore, the approach is suited for Compliance Rules of a small size to check the compliance of deployment models.

IV. Related Work

In this section, we present works that are related to our approach for compliance checking during design time. Martens et al. [18] propose a Reference Model that allows to capture several aspects of risk and compliance management in Cloud Computing. They use the Unified Modeling Language (UML) as modeling language and define their model as class diagrams. The model provides four different prospectives on risk and compliance management as they separate it by concerns. They provide constructs to characterize a Cloud computing service that also includes concepts such as *private cloud* or the location of a data center. The reference model also provides language constructs to associate a service with business processes, service level agreements, key performance indicators, risk factors, and compliance regulations. Schleicher et al. [19] introduce *Compliance Domains* to model data-restrictions in Cloud environments. Their focus is on the compliant execution of business processes in Cloud environments. Their approach allows to define certain areas of business processes, expressed in the Business Process Model and Notation (BPMN) [20], as Compliance Domains to be annotated by compliance experts with service level agreements and compliance rules, which are written in XPath and are intended to validate, if the data that is entering a Compliance Domain fulfills the compliance requirements. Schleicher et al. use a blood donation process as an example, where the name of a donor is not allowed to be associated with the donation within a certain Compliance Domain. The validation of a modeled business process is done during the design time of the process and the modeler is notified if any rules have been violated, to be corrected. The approach's method is similar to ours since compliance experts are required to specify the rules for compliance checking. They also introduce an algorithm that identifies Compliance Domains in existing business processes based on compliance rules and data flow in the processes. The method is similar to ours with the exception that we integrate locating compliance relevant areas in our Deployment Compliance Rules.

V. Conclusion

In this paper, we presented our work in progress to prevent modelers of deployment models from bothering with compliance requirements. We introduced Deployment Compliance Rules that can validate a deployment model during the design time. We separated the concerns of technical expertise and knowledge of a company's compliance requirements. Compliance experts are enabled to create such rules that can identify compliance relevant areas in deployment models while also providing the modeler with allowed structures that fulfill compliance requirements. In future work, we focus on the implementation and integration of the approach into the TOSCA modeling tool Winery [12] and also provide experimentation results on the execution time with various sizes of deployment models and Deployment Compliance Rules.

Acknowledgement

This work was partially funded by the German Research Foundation (DFG) project ADDCompliance and the BMWi project SmartOrchestra (01MD16001F).

References

[1] Federal data protection act. [Online]. Available: https://www.gesetze-im-internet.de/englisch_bdsg/ [Accessed: 2017-07-17]

[2] ISO/IEC 27018:2014 Code of practice for protection of personally identifiable information (PII) in public clouds acting as PII processors, International Organization for Standardization Std., 2014.

[3] U. Breitenbücher, T. Binz, O. Kopp, F. Leymann, and J. Wettinger, "Integrated Cloud Application Provisioning: Interconnecting Service-Centric and Script-Centric Management Technologies," in On the Move to Meaningful Internet Systems: OTM 2013 Conferences (CoopIS 2013). Springer, Sep. 2013, pp. 130–148.

[4] D. Oppenheimer, A. Ganapathi, and D. A. Patterson, "Why do internet services fail, and what can be done about it?" in Proceedings of the 4th Conference on USENIX Symposium on Internet Technologies and Systems (USITS 2003). USENIX, Jun. 2003, pp. 1–1.

[5] T. Binz et al., "OpenTOSCA - A Runtime for TOSCA-based Cloud Applications," in Proceedings of the 11th International Conference on Service-Oriented Computing (ICSOC 2013). Springer, Dec. 2013, pp. 692–695.

[6] U. Breitenbücher, T. Binz, O. Kopp, F. Leymann, and M. Wieland, "Policy-Aware Provisioning of Cloud Applications," in Proceedings of the Seventh International Conference on Emerging Security Information, Systems and Technologies (SECURWARE 2013). Xpert Publishing Services, Aug. 2013, pp. 86–95.

[7] U. Breitenbücher et al., "Policy-Aware Provisioning and Management of Cloud Applications," International Journal On Advances in Security, vol. 7, no. 1&2, 2014, pp. 15–36.

[8] T. Waizenegger et al., "Policy4TOSCA: A Policy-Aware Cloud Service Provisioning Approach to Enable Secure Cloud Computing," in On the Move to Meaningful Internet Systems: OTM 2013 Conferences. Springer, Sep. 2013, pp. 360–376.

[9] T. Waizenegger, M. Wieland, Tobias, U. Breitenbücher, and F. Leymann, "Towards a Policy-Framework for the Deployment and Management of Cloud Services," in SECURWARE 2013, The Seventh International Conference on Emerging Security Information, Systems and Technologies. IARIA, August 2013, pp. 14–18.

[10] C. A. Ardagna, R. Asal, E. Damiani, and Q. H. Vu, "From Security to Assurance in the Cloud: A Survey," ACM Computing Surveys (CSUR), vol. 48, no. 1, 2015, p. 2.

[11] OASIS, Topology and Orchestration Specification for Cloud Applications (TOSCA) Version 1.0, Organization for the Advancement of Structured Information Standards (OASIS), 2013.

[12] O. Kopp, T. Binz, U. Breitenbücher, and F. Leymann, "Winery – A Modeling Tool for TOSCA-based Cloud Applications," in Proceedings of the 11th International Conference on Service-Oriented Computing (ICSOC 2013). Springer, Dec. 2013, pp. 700–704.

[13] OASIS, Topology and Orchestration Specification for Cloud Applications (TOSCA) Primer Version 1.0, Organization for the Advancement of Structured Information Standards (OASIS), 2013.

[14] OASIS, TOSCA Simple Profile in YAML Version 1.0, Organization for the Advancement of Structured Information Standards (OASIS), 2015.

[15] U. Breitenbücher, T. Binz, O. Kopp, F. Leymann, and D. Schumm, "Vino4TOSCA: A Visual Notation for Application Topologies based on TOSCA," in On the Move to Meaningful Internet Systems: OTM 2012 (CoopIS 2012). Springer, Sep. 2012, pp. 416–424.

[16] C. Fehling, F. Leymann, R. Retter, W. Schupeck, and P. Arbitter, Cloud Computing Patterns: Fundamentals to Design, Build, and Manage Cloud Applications. Springer, 2014.

[17] B. Gallagher, "Matching structure and semantics: A survey on graph-based pattern matching," AAAI FS, vol. 6, 2006, pp. 45–53.

[18] B. Martens and F. Teuteberg, "Risk and compliance management for cloud computing services: Designing a reference model," Risk, vol. 8, 2011, pp. 5–2011.

[19] D. Schleicher et al., "Compliance domains: A means to model data-restrictions in cloud environments," in Enterprise Distributed Object Computing Conference (EDOC), 2011 15th IEEE International. IEEE, 2011, pp. 257–266.

[20] OMG, Business Process Model and Notation (BPMN) Version 2.0, Object Management Group (OMG), 2011.

Investigating SLA Confidentiality Requirements: A Holistic Perspective for the Government Agencies

Yudhistira Nugraha*†, Andrew Martin*

*Centre for Doctoral Training in Cyber Security
Department of Computer Science, University of Oxford, Oxford, UK
†Directorate of Information Security, Ministry of ICT, Jakarta, Indonesia

Email: {yudhistira.nugraha, andrew.martin}@cs.ox.ac.uk

Abstract—**Many governments consider the use of remote computing, communications and storage services provided by external service providers to process, store or transmit sensitive government data to increase scalability and decrease costs of maintaining services. The use of assurance approaches based on service level agreement (SLAs) is becoming increasingly important in procuring a wide range of such services from external service providers. However, such existing SLAs are not well-suited to a dynamic cyber threat environment because SLA security requirements (considering data confidentiality) have not been deeply studied by the academic computer security community. Such an understanding of the real needs of government is essential to the formulation of security-related SLAs. This paper seeks to provide such insights, by investigating 35 government participants using Indonesia as case study via a grounded adaptive Delphi study. We found that undeveloped SLA confidentiality requirements can illuminate other administrations to include government's security requirements and security capabilities of the service providers in SLAs when using such external services. Based on our findings, we make recommendations to the government agencies, service providers and researchers for improvement to existing SLA definition and future lines of research.**

Keywords–Security, Trust, Assurance, Confidentiality Requirements, Service Level Agreement (SLA), Service Provision

I. INTRODUCTION

In recent decades, many government agencies (`GAs`) generate, collect, store and share far more sensitive data than private organisations within and with external agencies. In fact, there is evidence that `GAs` increasingly rely on external service providers (`SPs`) to operate a wide range of remote computing, communications and storage services (e.g. cloud-based services) on behalf of the government. The relationships with external `SPs` are usually established through service level agreements (SLAs), which are binding agreements between `GAs` and external `SPs`. Such SLAs are mainly focused on the system availability and performance aspects, but overlook data confidentiality and integrity in SLAs.

Several attempts have been made to express security properties in SLAs, such as *Secure Provisioning of Cloud Services based on SLA Management* (SPECS) [1], the *Multi-Cloud Secure Applications* (MUSA) [2], SLA-Ready [3] and SLALOM [4]. However, these frameworks are not widely used in a government context, especially for procuring such remote computing, communications and storage services from external `SPs`. Yet there has been no detailed investigation of the government SLA confidentiality requirements that can be used in the formulation of security-related SLAs. Although some researchers have carried out extensive research on the development of security-related SLAs [5]–[10], no single study exists that has a clear direction for an understanding of government SLA confidentiality requirements. This indicates a need to understand various SLA confidentiality requirements that exist among the `GAs` when using such remote services offered by external `SPs`.

To increase the consideration of confidentiality and security requirements in SLA definition, it is necessary that external `SPs` should understand government SLA confidentiality requirements, as well as what types of government assets to protect and what types of risks to mitigate. However, the formulation of SLA confidentiality requirements has not been deeply studied by academic computer security community. We seek to fill the gap by understanding government's perspective about SLA confidentiality requirements, which are targeted at participants who are employed by or have experience working with government agencies using Indonesia as a case study.

To this end, we develop a grounded understanding of SLA confidentiality requirements for service provision using a grounded adaptive Delphi study [11]. Following accepted a Delphi study for qualitative study to elicit the views of government participants, we conducted a grounded Delphi study by asking 35 participants via group discussions and individual sessions [11] [12] and conducting a grounded theory analysis [13]–[15] of the Delphi study data to categorise the extracted statements.

Based on our preliminary findings, there are undeveloped government SLA confidentiality requirements, which might arise from the fact that our participants were influenced by existing security standards. However, our study can be used to guide the creation of trustworthy SLA capabilities a means of incorporating confidentiality requirements and capabilities in the formulation of security-related SLAs.

The remainder of this paper is structured as follows: In Section 2, we provide a background of this study. Section 3 presents the research methodology. Section 4 reports key findings. Section 5 discusses the implications of our findings, followed by the limitations of the study. We conclude this paper in Section 6.

II. BACKGROUND

Some governments have taken steps to reduce the level of cybersecurity risk, especially for government procurement of external computing, communications and storage products and services supplied by SPs or suppliers. We provide context for our study by looking at other governments' security requirements, such as the UK, the US and China.

The UK government has introduced cybersecurity requirements, called 'Cyber Essentials, which is intended for external SPs or suppliers that handle sensitive government data and personal information [16]. There are five technical security controls required for basic security requirements against common types of cyberattacks in such a government organisation. The cybersecurity requirements are *boundary firewalls, Internet gateways, secure configurations, access control mechanisms, malware protection systems, and patch management tools.* As a consequence, these minimum security requirements must be addressed by suppliers or contractors seeking to conduct business with the UK government.

Additionally, the Cyber Essentials is a continuous effort by the UK government to address cybersecurity risk, following the success of the 10 Steps of Cybersecurity guidance, which is designed for organisations as an effective means to protect information assets from cyber threats or attacks [17]. The security requirements are *risk management, secure configuration, network security, managing user privileges, user education and awareness, incident management, malware prevention, monitoring, removable media controls and home and mobile working.* The present requirements are significant for establishing the effectiveness of basic security controls against cyber threats.

Similarly, any potential and existing providers or contractors working with the U.S. Federal agencies are required to meet cybersecurity requirements described in NIST SP800-171 [18]. The standard consists of 14 security requirements, which are adapted from FIPS 200 and NIST SP800-53. Those requirements are *access control*, *awareness and training*, *audit and accountability*, *configuration management*, *identification and authentication*, *incident response*, *maintenance*, *media protection*, *personnel security*, *physical protection*, *risk assessment*, *security assessment*, *system and communication protection* and *system and information integrity* [19]. The derived security requirements are intended for use by federal agencies and for protecting the confidentiality of any information that law, regulation or policy requires to have security controls [18]. However, the NIST standard does not deal with information integrity or availability and aim to clarify specific security requirements applied to SPs or contractor who process or store sensitive government data on their information system services [18].

Furthermore, the NIST SP 800-171 standard is intended for suppliers or contractors that want to use internal cloud-based services as part of its internal enterprise network systems to process, store or transmit data when performing under the government contract requirements (e.g. DoD contract). However, it does not apply when suppliers or contractors intend to use external computing, communications and storage services provided by other external providers to store, process or transmit any sensitive data for the contract. Such suppliers or contractors need to apply security controls and independent assessments from the Federal Risk and Authorisation Management Program (FedRAMP) [20] when acquiring a variety of cloud-based services from other external providers, which are required to comply with security requirements contained within DFARS (Defense Federal Acquisition Regulation Supplement) 252.204-7012. The security requirements are as follows: cyber incident reporting, malicious software, media preservation and protection, access to additional information and equipment necessary for forensic analysis, and cyber incident damage assessment [21].

Likewise, the government of China has also proposed cybersecurity requirements for external suppliers that provide hardware and software to the banking industries in China. Those proposed security requirements include *source code disclosure*, *local presence*, *intellectual property rights*, *local encryption technology*, *regulatory backdoor* and *risk assessment* [22]. For example, the government approval is required for all products containing encryption technology of which cryptographic algorithms and encryption keys are required to disclose to the government. It is somewhat surprising that the government does not allow the import of foreign encryption technologies. The regulation does not give detailed guidance on the scope of this national security examination and how it will be implemented [22].

Overall lack of security considerations, especially data confidentiality and integrity in SLAs has remained as an open issue for many years. Research continues about the best approach for incorporating security capabilities into the formulation of security-related SLAs. Many governments to date have tended to focus on the use of certification schemes to evaluate security controls to ensure the controls are effective against identified risks [23]. Whereas, an assurance technique based on SLAs has only been applied to regulate service availability and quality of service (QoS). So far, no research has been found about understanding SLA confidentiality requirements in service provisioning.

III. THE STUDY

This paper investigates government SLA confidentiality requirements by means of 35 participants based in Indonesia using a grounded adaptive Delphi study [11]. We use Indonesia as a case study because according to Article 12 of Indonesian Government Regulation on the Operation of Electronic Systems and Transactions Number 82 of 2012, electronic system operators including SPs have obligations to ensure agreements on minimum service level and information security when providing such external service provision to GAs.

A. Ethical Consideration

Approval to conduct this study was obtained from the central university research ethics committee, University of Oxford. Research consent from participants was obtained after email communications. The participants were told the objective of the study, and asked for their involvement in the study. Our participants were voluntary and anonymous and they had the right to drop out in any round.

B. Recruitment

We recruited our participants for the Delphi study via our existing connections to the government employees including government consultants, usually via verbal or email communications with the participants, followed by an email containing an official invitation letter from the government ministry who looks after information assurance and security in Indonesia. In communication with the participants, we stressed a desire for balance in terms of participants' technical expertise and their involvement in policy-making process to achieve meaningful results and keep the failure rate as low as possible [12].

Before the study began, we gave participants a clear understanding of the problem statements along with the initial research questions to all invited participants before they agreed to participate in our series of data collection activities. Finally, we engaged with 35 of 45 invited participants. Most group discussions and individual sessions were conducted in-person, although some were conducted via Skype.

For this study, we limited our participants to those who were directly employed by or have experience working with Indonesian government. This focus allowed us to explore the problem of preserving the confidentiality of sensitive data across GAs. Our government participants came from a diverse work experience and technical backgrounds, such as cyber defence experts, malware experts, cryptography experts, pentesters, and information security management experts. Also, 12 participants hold a PhD degree in information technology-related topics and most participants hold security certifications. To maintain anonymity, we refer to the participants using labels P1 to P35, respecting the participant's identification. We will provide a summary of the participants, but the information given will be anonymised[1]

C. Delphi Study Procedure

We collected data primarily through a three-round Delphi study with 35 participants. We use some features of Delphi, such as group responses with group discussions for eliciting collective views and individual sessions with semi-structured interviews for collecting individual views where participants may not wish to elaborate in a group discussion. Unlike other Delphi studies [24], [25], this study used focus groups and interviews instead of questionnaires as the instrument for data collection because the questionnaires are impractical for the purpose of eliciting genuine views or thoughts from elite participants, such as senior government officials.

1) Round 1: Kick-Off Meeting: We conducted a kickoff meeting with government employees from the Indonesian Directorate of Information Security who looks after information security and assurance across all government agencies in Indonesia. This round was intended to gather comments and recommendations regarding the Delphi questions and other material. This stage was also important to refine the Delphi questions for the next round of Delphi.

2) Round 2: Brainstorming Phase: The second step was the brainstorming phase with exploratory group discussions with government participants. We conducted a series of group discussions to adapt the work schedules of government participants when participating in group discussions. Each panel discussed the problem of preserving the confidentiality of sensitive data across government agencies. Furthermore, we asked participants to explore Article 12 of the Government Regulation Number 82 of 2012. Also, we asked the participants how to incorporate confidentiality requirements and capabilities specified into SLAs according to reasonable risks.

[1]Participants information, https://goo.gl/w0Y4Sz, (Accessed March 2017).

For this round, we engaged with 18 of the 45 invited participants in three group discussions to explore a rich understanding of participants' experiences and beliefs, as well as to generate information on collective views [26] in which the optimum size for a focus group is 6 to 11 participants [26]. However, in practice, focus groups can work successfully with from three to fourteen participants [27]. For this study, the focus group varies from three participants to six participants to provide control over the period from securing participant work schedules to participating group discussions.

3) Round 3: Enrichment and Generalisation Phase: We conducted individual sessions using semi-structured interviews to elicit detailed information from government participants based on the results of the previous round. We sent the initial results of the first round in the form of Delphi questions and asked again 45 invited participants to take part in this study. In this round, we engaged with 32 government participants and recorded each individual interview in an audio format after receiving the participant's consent. Each individual interview took between 20-120 minutes. Interviews were later transcribed and coded. We then sent each transcription to the corresponding participants and asked for feedback and corrections, which we did not receive any.

D. Data Analysis

We applied the grounded theory analysis [13]–[15] to examine the Delphi study data, and to categorise and generalise the extracted statements. We conducted initial coding of a group discussion transcript from the brainstorming phase to identify general codes. Further, we analysed the interview transcripts from the enrichment and generalisation phase, using initial coding, intermediate coding and advanced coding [28].

The initial coding aims to identify topic of interest 'key-point coding' of which the researcher extracted useful sentences or statements and applied codes against the Delphi study data. In intermediate coding, we began to select categories from amongst topics of interest and found relationships among the initial codes (e.g. the most frequent or important codes) [15]. In advance coding, once categories were identified, we established the relationship between the categories to integrate them into a cohesive theory.

To illustrate the grounded theory process, we provide an example as follows. One participant commented that the greater threat to GAs mostly come from internal sources, such as an insider threat. We coded it as "collaborator", as described in Table II. Our Delphi study data were coded only by the main researcher due to confidentiality reasons. Thus, this was the rationale behind our decision to use the main researcher as the only coder. However, the main researcher discussed his findings with another researcher to receive feedback.

IV. Results

We organise our results into three themes: (1) *government asset*, (2) *risk perception* and (3) *SLA confidentiality requirements*. These findings reveal opportunities for improving the consideration of security requirements in SLA definition.

A. Government Asset

We began by looking from the perspective of what types of government assets to protect by identifying government data. Several statements have been made by participants related to government assets-based data classification. However, we noticed that the classification of sensitive government data has not been clearly defined. Therefore, we highlight the notion of government assets where applicable, as shown in Table I.

TABLE I. GOVERNMENT ASSET

Category	Government Data
Human Asset	Senior Government Officials Knowledge Others
Information Asset	Citizen Data Medical Record Financial Transaction Law Enforcement Data Diplomatic Information Personal representative deed Personally identifiable information National economic resilience Natural wealth/resources
Physical Asset	National defense and security systems Critical National Infrastructure Communication Servicea and Devices

1) Human Asset: Our participants agreed that human assets (e.g. employees, senior government officials) are part of intangible assets that the government has. Although the Public Information Disclosure Act No 14 of 2008 does exist, our participants typically reported that most GAs face a challenge of classifying sensitive human assets and non-sensitive human assets. Therefore, we placed emphasis on opinions from government participants regarding the concepts of sensitive human assets, such as the following:

> "*...In relation to human assets, if the person is a senior government official who performs such activities, the person itself is a national asset that needs to be protected...*" (P8).

2) Information Asset: Many public organisations routinely collect, create or process sensitive data. Our participants expressed concern in response to protecting information assets data that may not be appropriate for public release. For example, P2 indicated the following:

> "*...In government sectors, it looks "gray", for example, one has uploaded the entire local government meetings including their internal meetings to Youtube, with the aim to build trust to the public. However, all information related to strategic meetings should be protected...*"(P2).

3) Physical Asset: Although it used to be that security objectives were focused in protecting physical assets, such as communication channels, systems and devices, our participants considered the importance of protecting physical assets containing sensitive government data. Securing information assets is critical and may be more than important than protecting physical assets. For example, P1 pointed out the following:

> "*...such electronic information requires physical facilities like data centre, network, systems and devices. It is also necessary to ensure safety and effective physical protection for the facilities...*"(P12).

Our participants indicated that there is an absence of government security classifications that apply to the GAs, which generate, process, collect, store or transmit sensitive data in order to conduct government activities and to deliver public services. In response to this, the government should classify government data so that everyone who works with the GAs knows how best to protect sensitive data.

B. Risk Perception

We carefully examined specific risks that our participants are attempting to counter. Several statements have been made by participants related to risks that need to be mitigated. We noticed consensus was obtained regarding a specific risk and highlight the notions of threat models where applicable, as shown in Table II.

TABLE II. RISK PERCEPTION

Category	Threat/Attack
Collaborator	Insider (Employee) Insider (Former employee) Insider (Contractor) Malicious actions (Service provider)
Exfiltration	Connect-Transmit (Device) Outbound (Traffic) Extract (Content/Key) Brute-force (Key)
Observation	Discovery (State actor) Scan (Metadata/Traffic) Intercept (Device/Content/Traffic)
Insertion	Inject (Malware/Trojan/Backdoor/Scripts) Install (Ransomware/Rootkit)
Manipulation	Manipulate-Phishing (People/Content) Impersonate (People/System/Traffic)

1) Collaborator: Our participants discussed this threat as the main security concern, which allows a person to cooperate traitorously with an adversary. Therefore, our participants paid much attention to mitigating this threat (e.g. insider threats). For example, one participant highlighted that government data leakage is mainly caused by an insider who is a closely related person with senior government officials, as follows:

> "*...the issue about government data theft normally does not occur while data is transmitted, but when data was processed or created. For example, an insider can disclose and share the sensitive data obtained with an adversary...*" (P22).

2) Exfiltration: Our participants were concerned with the unauthorised transfer of sensitive data through various means. For example, one participant indicated the following:

> "*...Now the fact that threats and attacks can actually come from inside. For example, our observation discovered botnets keep sending out data...*" (P13).

3) Observation: Our participants discussed the importance of preventing pervasive surveillance, as this threat allows the adversary to closely observe or monitor targets. One participant indicated this type of threat, as follows:

"*...we are aware that when we are talking with our interlocutor, there must be other people listening without knowing them...*"(P4).

4) Insertion: Our participants reported that an adversary could place or insert malicious software (malware) on the targeted government's information systems through various methods, as indicated in the following statement:

"*...they embed code on the opposing side in any way to divulge the sensitive government data...*" (P1).

5) Manipulation: Our participants reported that the action of manipulating information systems is an effective way to obtain sensitive data from targets (e.g. people). This allows the adversary to pretend to be another person with the aim of obtaining sensitive government data from the target. For example, P3 pointed out the following statement.

"*...For threats to military information and sensitive government data, in general the threats were in the form of impersonation. Besides the impersonation, they can also do phishing...*" (P3).

Overall, our participants were clear about the perceived shortcomings of the existing knowledge to be used to understand the characteristics of threats. In so doing, it is of paramount importance to enforce SLA confidentiality requirements according to perceived threats for government assets-based data classification in security-related SLAs.

C. SLA Confidentiality Requirements

The statements from our participants confirmed that most government SLA confidentiality requirements are derived from a very high level of abstraction, such as laws, policies, regulations and standards. However, we noticed that the concepts of government SLA confidentiality requirements have not been clearly defined in the context of security-related SLAs. Thus, we highlight the government SLA confidentiality requirements where applicable, as shown in Table III.

1) Skills and Reputation: Our participants reported relatively strong support for inadequate awareness and training for employees, as described the following statement:

"*...at the simplest level, we still have problems due to lack of awareness of employees, so we need to mitigate such risk...*" (P2).

2) Zero Access to Data: Our participants reported that access control must be in place to ensure that all sensitive government data are limited to authorised users, as follows:

"*...Who gets access to the information systems? Trusted person must need approval first before directly go into the system...*" (P15).

3) Personnel Security: Our participants expressed concern about people as a point of security failure, as follows.

"*...Security screening should be there. Access restriction is based on a need-to-know basis...*" (P6).

TABLE III. SLA CONFIDENTIALITY REQUIREMENTS

Category	**Need**
`Skills and Reputation`	Awareness Training Certification IT Audit and Assurance Penetration Testing
`Zero Access to Data`	Separate duties Control and Limit Connections Privilege Access Control
`Personnel Security`	Implement Screening Identify behaviours Develop Security Culture Non-disclosure agreement (NDA)
`Physical Security`	Physical Access (e.g. Access Card, Keys) Audit logs of physical access CCTV (closed-circuit television) Alarm systsm (sensor)
`Media Protection`	Employ cryptography to protect media Access Control Policy
`Metadata Protection`	Metadata Standard Metadata retention
`Malware Protection`	Employ anti-malware Limit use of external devices
`Communications Protection`	Encryption Secure channels (e.g. VPN Tunnel) Use code in communications
`Data Protection`	Data Localisation IT Audit and Assurance
`Isolation`	Firewall Whitelist Block access to known file transfer Air-gapping
`Authentication`	Multifactor authentication

4) Physical Security: Our participants pointed out that physical security is one of the key security requirements. For example, one participant mentioned physical security measures as described in the following statement:

"*...it seems to me security controls should be integrated with physical elements, such as a room, doors and locks that need to be installed...*" (P32).

5) Media Protection: Our participants typically reported that it is important to prohibit the use of portable storage devices when such personal devices belong to government employees or contractors, as described in the following statement:

"*...data storage device should not be brought from outside, everyone who enters, does not allow to bring flash disks, and other media storage...*" (P1).

6) Metadata Protection: Our participants also expressed concerns about metadata protection related to sensitive government data that is processed, stored or transmitted in information system services provided by `SPs`, as follows:

"*...we should have a metadata standard for the benefit of the government, so that all are used unique, in preventing no data is revealed...*" (P4).

7) Malware Protection: Our participants expressed concern about malware. It is acknowledged that malware can come into our information systems from all types of sources, for instance:

> "*Malware including Ransomware mostly comes from email and web phishing*" (P15).

8) Communications Protection: Our participants reported that network communications are important to be controlled and secure against threats, as follows:

> "*...we need to think government secure networks are created with a single entrance point, so if there is a leak, we can know from which point...*"(P1).

9) Data Protection: Our participants expressed concerns about how to protect sensitive government data (the secrecy, integrity and availability of sensitive data). As data resides in many places, one participant expressed in the following case:

> "*...government requirements should not allow sensitive government data to store in other countries without additional security capabilities taken, such as a strong password...*" (P3).

10) Isolation: Our participants expressed concerns about isolation of communications and information systems to prevent unauthorised disclosure of data, as such the following:

> "*...It is clear that different treatments are required, such as a layer of insulation (e.g., VPN layers). So later, all sensitive data that really matter are protected and isolated using those layers...*" (P8).

11) Authentication: Our participants explicitly mentioned using authentication to access such services, as follows:

> "*...It is important to allow who is entitled to access the data. But authentication is required to enter the systems...*" (P8).

It is clear that our participants revealed undeveloped government SLA confidentiality requirements. The preference for the requirements was evident even though there would be room for improvement to better define such SLAs.

V. DISCUSSION

We discuss the implications of our findings for GAs, SPs, and researchers. We consider the following take-aways to be the most important one from our findings.

A. Implications

1) Implications for Government Agencies: Based on our findings, we give two recommendations to GAs. First, know your assets. Our study suggests that different assets have different risks associated with it. The SPs seem to neglect to consider appropriate security controls for protecting the value of government assets, while the GAs do not provide high-level security requirements up-front. In either case, GAs should understand what types of confidentiality requirements that need to be defined in SLAs according to acceptable risks that might affect government asset value. Second, understanding the risks to government assets. We found that specific threats are typically scattered across different participants. However, some conclusions were drawn from the findings concerning risk perception. Thus, GAs should identify which perceived threats are mitigated best by security capabilities (e.g. security controls) provided by external SPs.

2) Implications for Service Providers: It is acknowledged that many GAs commonly make decisions to preserve the confidentiality of government data by applying specific security capabilities through technical, physical and human elements. In this case, the GAs heavily rely on certification schemes such as ISO 27001, which is not sufficient to address specific perceived and emerging threats [23]. Our study shows that the derived findings provide basic insights into defining confidentiality requirements in SLAs. Thus, the SPs can determine and negotiate appropriate security capabilities, which demonstrate compliance with the government's security requirements. In the context of formulation of security-related SLAs, the level of trust between the GAs and external SPs can be determined by using confidentiality capabilities according to specific perceived threats for government assets-based data classification.

3) Implications for Researchers: Finally, our findings can provide a rich foundation for incorporating the interplay of perceived threats, security requirements and capabilities specified in SLAs according to government assets. However, we acknowledge that it is difficult to require explicit assumptions about confidentiality requirements and capabilities regarding perceived threats for government assets. Often, there is the risk of liability and compensation with the particular level of security expressed in SLAs. These questions sketch many avenues for future work.

B. Limitations

As with any research methodology, our choice of research methods has limitations.

1) Construct Validity: It is important to measure whether these findings can be correctly reflected by means of Delphi study. First, group discussions and individual feedback obviously rely on the statements of the participants. Insights and views from the participants are subjective and may not properly reflect the actual situations. However, we engaged with experienced participants from different expertise to gain a broader spectrum of viewpoints. While subjectivity is difficult to eliminate in a qualitative study, we limit its effects by basing our findings exclusively on multiple statements from a series of iterative data collection activities using group discussions and individual sessions. Further, the nature of our Delphi study allowed us to react to participants' statements, and to further clarify, whenever needed. Second, there are possible misperceptions associated with the interpretation of the statements by the main researcher. The coding process was performed manually and by only one researcher, which potentially a biased to the interpretation of the data. To mitigate this threat, we asked feedback from the participants.

2) Internal Validity: Since our study is of exploratory nature, our preliminary findings are determined mainly by the Delphi study data we have obtained from 35 selected government participants through a purposeful sampling strategy. We selected participants across Indonesian government employees including participants with a wide variety of insights and opinions as it is expected from the nature of Delphi study. This study is completely recorded that provides full traceability of findings back to the original statements from our participants.

3) External Validity: The applicability of our findings has to be established carefully. The main limit to the generalizability of our findings from the fact that we only engaged with 35 participants from one country. Although our findings may be applicable only to the domain and context being studied [15], the results of this study can illuminate other governments to include security capabilities of the service providers in SLAs when procuring such external computing, communications and storage services. We could increase confidence by involving more government participants in the country or from other countries may create a more rigorous findings. Bearing in mind that this study is of exploratory of nature and was not designed to be largely generalizable, but it aimed to understand what are the SLA confidentiality requirements needed from the government.

VI. CONCLUSION

It is acknowledged that, until now, security best practices and standards are often considered to be key elements of implementing and enforcing the most basic security requirements. However, government SLA confidentiality requirements have not been studied in depth by governments, providers, and researchers. To address this gap and inform ongoing and future work on external computing, communications and storage service provision, we conducted a grounded adaptive Delphi method with 35 government participants using Indonesia as a case study. Most importantly, we found that government SLA confidentiality requirements have seen limited demand for services provision in government contracts relating to external computing, communications and storage services supplied by external `SPs`. However, our findings provide insights to increase the consideration of confidentiality and security requirements in SLA definition. These findings suggest that there is a need for an approach to incorporate security capabilities specified in security-related SLAs to enhance the level of trust in service provision, such as cloud-based services between `GAs` and external `SPs`. We take an important step towards such an empirically grounded trustworthy SLA capabilities for incorporating security requirements and capabilities into security-related SLAs according to perceived risks for government assets-based data classification.

VII. ACKNOWLEDGMENT

This work was supported in part by the Indonesian Ministry of Communications and Information Technology under the Directorate of Information Security, and the Indonesia Endowment Fund for Education Scholarship (LPDP).

REFERENCES

[1] M. Rak, N. Suri, J. Luna, D. Petcu, V. Casola, and U. Villano, "Security as a service using an sla-based approach via specs," in Proceedings of the 5th IEEE International Conference on Cloud Computing Technology and Science, vol. 2, 2013, pp. 1–6.

[2] E. Rios, E. Iturbe, L. Orue-Echevarria, M. Rak, V. Casola et al., "Towards self-protective multi-cloud applications: Musa–a holistic framework to support the security-intelligent lifecycle management of multi-cloud applications," 2015.

[3] "SLAReady," 2015, URL: http://www.sla-ready.eu/consortium [accessed: 2017-07-15].

[4] "SLALOM Project," 2015, URL: http://slalom-project.eu/ [accessed: 2017-07-15].

[5] R. R. Henning, "Security service level agreements: Quantifiable security for the enterprise?" in Proceedings of the 1999 Workshop on New Security Paradigms (NSPW), 2000, pp. 54–60.

[6] K. Bernsmed, M. G. Jaatun, P. H. Meland, and A. Undheim, "Security slas for federated cloud services," in 6th International Conference on Availability, Reliability and Security, Aug 2011, pp. 202–209.

[7] M. G. Jaatun, K. Bernsmed, and A. Undheim, Security SLAs – An Idea Whose Time Has Come? Springer, 2012, pp. 123–130.

[8] A. Guesmi and P. Clemente, "Access control and security properties requirements specification for clouds' seclas," in 5th IEEE International Conference on Cloud Computing Technology and Science, vol. 1, Dec 2013, pp. 723–729.

[9] J. Luna, A. Taha, R. Trapero, and N. Suri, "Quantitative reasoning about cloud security using service level agreements," IEEE Transactions on Cloud Computing, vol. PP, no. 99, 2017, pp. 1–1.

[10] T. Takahashi, J. Kannisto, J. Harju, S. Heikkinen, B. Silverajan, M. Helenius, and S. Matsuo, "Tailored security: Building nonrepudiable security service-level agreements," IEEE Vehicular Technology Magazine, vol. 8, no. 3, Sept 2013, pp. 54–62.

[11] Y. Nugraha and A. Martin, Investigating Security Capabilities in Service Level Agreements as Trust-Enhancing Instruments. Cham: Springer International Publishing, 2017, pp. 57–75.

[12] Y. Nugraha, I. Brown, and A. S. Sastrosubroto, "An adaptive wideband delphi method to study state cyber-defence requirements," IEEE Transactions on Emerging Topics in Computing, vol. 4, no. 1, 2016, pp. 47–59.

[13] S. E. McGregor, P. Charters, T. Holliday, and F. Roesner, "Investigating the computer security practices and needs of journalists," in 24th USENIX Security Symposium, Washington, D.C., 2015, pp. 399–414.

[14] S. Egelman, S. Jain, R. S. Portnoff, K. Liao, S. Consolvo, and D. Wagner, "Are you ready to lock?" in 21st ACM Conference on Computer and Communications Security, 2014, pp. 750–761.

[15] K. Charmaz, Constructing grounded theory. Sage, 2014.

[16] "Procurement policy note-use of cyber essentials scheme certification," 2016, URL: https://www.gov.uk/government/collections/procurement-policy-notes [accessed: 2017-07-15].

[17] "National Cyber Security Centre: 10 Steps to Cyber Security," 2016, URL: https://www.ncsc.gov.uk/guidance/10-steps-cyber-security [accessed: 2017-07-15].

[18] "DoD Amends its DFARS Safeguarding and Cyber Incident Reporting Requirements with a Second Interim Rule," 2016, URL: http://www.hlregulation.com/2016/01/07/dod-amends-its-dfars-safeguarding-and-cyber-incident-reporting-requirements-with-a-second-interim-rule/ [accessed: 2017-07-15].

[19] R. Ross, P. VISCUSO, G. GUISSANIE, K. DEMPSEY, and M. RIDDLE, "Protecting controlled unclassified information in nonfederal information systems and organizations," NIST Special Publication, vol. 800, 2015, p. 171.

[20] "Federal risk and authorization management program," 2016, URL: https://www.fedramp.gov/resources/documents-2016/ [accessed: 2017-07-15].

[21] E. P. Roberson, "Adequate cybersecurity: Flexibility and balance for a proposed standard of care and liability for government contractors," Fed. Cir. BJ, vol. 25, 2015, p. 641.

[22] "China introduces new cybersecurity for rules for banking procurement," 2015, URL: http://knowledge.freshfields.com [accessed: 2017-07-15].

[23] R. Böhme, Security Audits Revisited. Berlin, Heidelberg: Springer Berlin Heidelberg, 2012, pp. 129–147.

[24] T. Päivärinta, S. Pekkola, and C. E. Moe, "Grounding theory from delphi studies," in International Conference on Information Systems, vol. 3. Association for Information Systems, 2011, pp. 2022–2035.

[25] K. Howard, "Educating cultural heritage information professionals for australia's galleries, libraries, archives and museums: A grounded delphi study," Ph.D. dissertation, Queensland University of Technology, 2015.

[26] M. C. Harrell and M. A. Bradley, "Data collection methods. semi-structured interviews and focus groups," RAND National Defense Research Institute Santa Monica-CA, Tech. Rep., 2009.

[27] P. Gill, K. Stewart, E. Treasure, and B. Chadwick, "Methods of data collection in qualitative research: interviews and focus groups," British dental journal, vol. 204, no. 6, 2008, pp. 291–295.

[28] M. Birks and J. Mills, Grounded theory: A practical guide. Sage, 2015.

Large-Scale Analysis of Domain Blacklists

Tran Phuong Thao*, Tokunbo Makanju†, Jumpei Urakawa‡, Akira Yamada§, Kosuke Murakami¶, Ayumu Kubota‖
KDDI Research, Inc., Japan
2-1-15 Ohara, Fujimino-shi, Saitama, Japan 356-8502
Email: {th-tran*, to-makanju†, ju-urakawa‡, ai-yamada§, ko-murakami¶, kubota‖}@kddi-research.jp

***Abstract*—Malicious content has grown along with the explosion of the Internet. Therefore, many organizations construct and maintain blacklists to help web users protect their computers. There are many kinds of blacklists in which domain blacklists are the most popular one. Existing empirical analyses on domain blacklists have several limitations such as using only outdated blacklists, omitting important blacklists, or focusing only on simple aspects of blacklists. In this paper, we analyze the top 14 blacklists including popular and updated blacklists like *Safe Browsing* from Google and *urlblacklist.com*. We are the first to filter out the old entries in the blacklists using an enormous dataset of user browsing history. Besides the analysis on the intersections and the registered information from Whois (such as top-level domain, domain age and country), we also build two classification models for web content categories (i.e., education, business, etc.) and malicious categories (i.e., landing and distribution) using machine learning. Our work found some important results. First, the blacklists *Safe Browsing version 3 and 4* are being separately deployed and have independent databases with diverse entries although they belong to the same organization. Second, the blacklist *dsi.ut_capitole.fr* is almost a subset of the blacklist *urlblacklist.com* with 98% entries. Third, largest portion of entries in the blacklists are created in 2000 with 6.08%, and from United States with 24.28%. Fourth, *Safe Browsing version 4* can detect younger domains compared with the others. Fifth, *Tech & Computing* is the dominant web content category in all the blacklists, and the blacklists in each group (i.e., small public blacklists, large public blacklists, private blacklists) have higher correlation in web content as opposed to blacklists in other groups. Finally, the number of landing domains are larger than that of distribution domains at least 75% in large public blacklists and at least 60% in other blacklists.**

***Keywords*—Web Security; Large-Scale Analysis; Empirical Analysis; Blacklist; Malicious Domain.**

I. INTRODUCTION

The Internet has become very important to our daily life, and thus, the content of the Web has been growing exponentially. According to a research by VeriSign, Inc. [1], the number of domains is already approximately 12 million as of March 31, 2016. Along with that is a huge amount of malicious domains. Just in 2015, the number of unique pieces of malware discovered is more than 430 million, up 36 percent from the year before [2]. Therefore, nowadays there are many competitive services constructed to detect malicious domains. Each service has its own method, which is often not disclosed and always said to be the best service by its authors. Furthermore, each service also has different definition (ground truth) of the term "malicious". For example, a blacklist A defines a domain D to be malicious if D satisfies a condition set AM while another blacklist B defines D to be malicious if D satisfies a condition set BM which is a subset, superset or completely different from AM. All of these have brought into **a question: how to measure and compare these services**. Many blacklists are freely available on the Internet (called *public blacklists*). However, some vendors do not want to publish their databases and only provide querying services via APIs or portal applications (called *private blacklists*). Our goal in this paper is to perform a large-scale analysis on popular blacklists including both public and private blacklists. We can then indicate the quality of the blacklists in some specific categories. This research can help the users to determine which blacklists should they choose for some conditions, and also can help the blacklist providers assess and improve their blacklists and methods.

A. Related Work

Sheng et al. [3] analyzed phishing blacklists, which are just subset of malicious blacklists that we are focusing on. A malicious domain's purpose includes all kinds of attacks: spamming, phishing, randomware, etc. Kuhrer et al. [4] analyzed malicious blacklists but only focused on constructing a blacklist parser to deal with varied-and-unstructured blacklist formats rather than researching the blacklists themselves. This is because some blacklists solely include domain names, URLs, or IP address. Other blacklists contain more information, such as timestamps or even source, type, and description for each entry. Therefore, their analysis results have poor information that only contains the entries' registration history in each blacklist, the intersection of every blacklist pair, and the top 10 domains in most of the blacklists. Kuhrer et al. [5] then analyzed blacklists via three measures: (i) identifying parked domains (additional domains hosted on the same account and displaying the same website as primary domain) and sinkhole servers (hosting malicious domains controlled by security organizations), (ii) the blacklist completeness by finding the coverage between each blacklist with an existing set of 300,000 malware samples, and (iii) the domains created by Domain Generation Algorithm. However, 300,000 entries in the second measure are not enough to assess the "completeness" because some large blacklists can contain millions of entries. Furthermore, the ground truth or definition of their malware samples may be different from that of other blacklists, and thus it is unfair when using them to confirm the completeness of other blacklists. The first and third measures are different for our analysis. Vasek et al. [6] only analyzed Malware Domain Blacklist (malwaredomains.com) which is just one of the blacklists in our analysis. Several other papers also performed empirical analysis but are different from our analysis which focuses on domain blacklists, e.g., [7] analyzed IP blacklists, [8] analyzed email spam detection through network characteristics in a stand-alone enterprise, [9] analyzed spam traffic with a very specific network, [10] analyzed detections of malicious web pages caused by drive-by-download attack, not blacklist analysis, [11] analyzed whitelist of acceptable advertisements.

B. Our Work

In this paper, we do not aim to figure out the ground truth or definition of "malicious", or the factors affecting malicious domain detection in each blacklist. Instead, we attempt to quantitatively measure and compare the blacklists based on six important aspects: blacklist intersections, top-level domains (TLDs), domain ages, countries, web content categories and malicious categories. To the best of our knowledge, we are the first to achieve the followings:

- We deal with top 14 popular blacklists in which there are two special private blacklists given by Google that are Safe Browsing version 3 and 4 (called GSBv3 and GSBv4). These newest versions are being deployed and used parallelly and independently, and have never been analyzed before. In [4], the old version GSBv2 was analyzed in 2011, which was 6 years ago.
- By designing 6 measures in our analsysis, we not only consider the coverage (intersection) as in previous works, but also compare the blacklists based on Whois (TLDs, countries, domain ages), web content categories using IAB [12] which are an industry standard taxonomy for content categorization (e.g., education, government, etc.), and malicious categories (landing and distribution).
- Our analysis is not straightforward, and not just simple statistics. For the measures of web content categories and malicious categories, we construct two supervised machine learning models using text mining, and a combination of text mining with some specific HTML tags to classify the entries in the blacklists, respectively.
- Last but not least, we filter out the active entries in the blacklists instead of old and useless entries as previous works by finding the coverage between each blacklist with a big live dataset.

Roadmap. The rest of this paper is organized as follows. The methodology of our analysis is presented in Section II. The empirical results are given in Section III. The discussion is described in Section IV. Finally, the conclusion is drawn in Section V.

II. METHODOLOGY

In this section, we introduce our chosen blacklists, how we pre-processed them, and our analysis design.

A. Blacklists

In this paper, we analyze 14 popular blacklists as described in Table I. Since they have different numbers of entries which can effect the fairness, we categorize them into 3 groups: (I) small public blacklists which have smaller than 1,000,000 unique entries, (II) large public blacklists which have equal or larger than 1,000,000 unique entries, and (III) private blacklists. In the group (III), we consider separately GSBv3 and GSBv4 although they both belong to the same vendor. This is because they are being deployed and used independently. Furthermore, according to our analysis, they have different API and even database.

TABLE I: 14 POPULAR BLACKLISTS.

No	Group	Abbr.	Blacklists	#Domains
1	(I)	MA	malwaredomains.com	17,294
2		NE	networksec.org	263
3		PH	phishtank.com	9,711
4		RA	ransomwaretracker.abuse.ch	1,380
5		ZE	zeustracker.abuse.ch	382
6		MAL	malwaredomainlist.com	1,338
7		MV	winhelp2002.mvps.org	218,248
8		HO	hosts-file.net	5,974
9	(II)	ME	mesd.k12.or.us	1,266,334
10		SH	shallalist.de	1,570,944
11		UR	urlblacklist.com	2,919,199
12		UT	dsi.ut_capitole.fr	1,346,788
13	(III)	GSBv3	Safe Browsing version 3	Unknown
14		GSBv4	Safe Browsing version 4	Unknown

In Table I, the last column indicates the number of unique domains in each blacklist. All the 14 blacklists were downloaded (in case of public blacklists) or queried (in case of private blacklists) on the same date 2017/02/28. Since the blacklists may contain old entries that attackers no longer use, we extract only active entries by finding the intersection between each blacklist with a real-world web access log that we call AL. AL has 3,991,599,424 records from 5 proxy servers, 9,091,980 raw domains with 80,464,378 corresponding URLs accessed by 659,283 users. The intersections between AL and each blacklist are given in Table II. The number of unique domains in the union of 14 blacklists is 50,519. Instead of the complete blacklists, we use these intersections in our analysis.

TABLE II: ACTIVE MALICIOUS DOMAINS IN 14 BLACKLISTS (INTERSECTIONS WITH AL).

No	Group	Intersection	Abbr.	#Domains	Percentage
1	(I)	AL ∩ MA	AMA	77	0.44%
2		AL ∩ NE	ANE	2	0.76%
3		AL ∩ PH	APH	367	3.78%
4		AL ∩ RA	ARA	3	0.22%
5		AL ∩ ZE	AZE	21	5.50%
6		AL ∩ MAL	AMAL	98	7.32%
7		AL ∩ MV	AMV	2,176	1.00%
8		AL ∩ HO	AHO	5,060	84.70%
9	(II)	AL ∩ ME	AME	19,812	1.56%
10		AL ∩ SH	ASH	32,248	2.05%
11		AL ∩ UR	AUR	33,674	1.15%
12		AL ∩ UT	AUT	24,020	1.78%
13	(III)	AL ∩ GSBv3	AGSBv3	189	unknown
14		AL ∩ GSBv4	AGSBv4	639	unknown

The final column indicates the number of filtered samples over that of original samples in Table I.

B. Analysis Design

In this section, we describe the design of our analysis with the following 6 measures.

1) Measure 1 (Blacklist Intersections): For every blacklist pair with the web access log AL, we find the intersection

TABLE III: OVERLAPPING OF EVERY BLACKLIST PAIR.

Intersection ∩	AMA	ANE	APH	ARA	AZE	AMAL	AMV	AHO	AME	ASH	AUR	AUT	AGSBv3	AGSBv4
AMA		2	7	0	0	0	0	35	77	1	13	1	1	4
ANE			0	0	0	0	0	1	2	0	2	0	0	2
APH				0	6	14	42	175	15	104	100	51	1	1
ARA					0	0	0	3	0	2	1	0	0	0
AZE						2	1	18	2	6	6	1	0	0
AMAL							21	67	6	30	36	6	0	0
AMV								1,241	262	1,152	948	626	0	0
AHO									754	2,070	1,733	1,179	3	5
AME										11,736	19,494	19,598	7	28
ASH											19,495	14,769	4	19
AUR												23,583	7	29
AUT													7	25
AGSBv3														170

of their domains. In total we found $\binom{14}{2} = 91$ intersection sets. Via the number of domains in each intersection, we can indicate certain correlation between the blacklists.

2) Measure 2 (Top-Level Domains (TLDs)): To evaluate this measure, we extract the final string after the dot in each domain name. For example, the TLD of the domain *kddi.com* is *com*, the TLD of the domain *yahoo.co.jp* is *jp*. There are two types of TLD:

- Original TLDs: which consist of *com*, *org*, *net*, *int*, *edu*, *gov*, *mil* and *arpa*.
- Country-code TLDs: which consist of the TLDs of each country or region. For example, *jp* (Japan), *us* (United States), *eu* (European Union), etc.

3) Measure 3 (Domain Ages) and Measure 4 (Countries): To evaluate these measures, we firstly extract the Whois information of each domain in all the intersections between the blacklists and the web access log AL as described in Table II. Whois is the registered information of the domains such as creation date, expiration date, organization, address, registrar server, etc. For the measure 3, we extract creation year (from the creation date) and for the measure 4, we extract the country. Note that, although the measure 2 (TLD) includes country-code TLDs, it does not always show correct countries. For example, the TLD of *jp* not only contains domains from Japan, but also another countries such as United States with a non-small portion. This is why we consider the measure 2 (TLD) and measure 4 (country), separately.

4) Measure 5 (Web Content Categories): This measure aims to classify the blacklisted domains into semantic web content categories, such as education, advertisement, government, etc. Although there are several tools (e.g., i-Filter [13], SimilarWeb [14]) which can be used to categorize a domain into semantic content categories, their coverages are low and they cannot label our entire dataset (this will be explained later). Therefore, to evaluate this measure, we construct our own classification model using supervised machine learning with the help of one of the tools for data labelling. Concretely, we first collect 20,000 URLs and label their semantic contents using i-Filter [13]. However, i-Filter cannot label all the samples but only 14,492 samples (72.46%) into 69 categories. Since the number of categories is quite large for the number of classes in our model, we thus generalize these 69 categories into 17 categories using the standardized category set called IAB [12]. We then extract HTML documents of the 14,492 samples and use *text mining* with Term Frequency-Inverse Document Frequency (TF-IDF) as the feature for the training process. We executed nine different supervised machine learning algorithms: Support Vector Machine (including C-based and Linear-based), Naive Bayes (including Multinomial-based and Bernoulli-based), Nearest Neighbors (including Centroid-based, KNeighbors-based and Radius-based), Decision Tree, and Stochastic Gradient Descent. We assessed the algorithms using k-fold cross validation by setting $k = 10$. We pick up the best algorithm which has highest accuracy and lowest false positive rate. Thereafter, we extract HTML documents of 50,519 domains in our blacklists. Note that, given a domain, we extract the main URL of the domains by adding prefix *http://www* to the domain. For example: the main url of *google.com* is *http://www.google.com*. We use the model computed by the chosen best learning algorithm to classify the 50,519 domains in the blacklists.

5) Measure 6 (Malicious Categories): There are two types of malicious categories. The first type is about the behaviours of attackers such as phishing, spamming or abusing, etc. This type has already been considered in many previous works. The second type is about the behaviours of the domains/URLs themselves such as *landing* and *distribution*, which are very important properties to understand the attacks but have not been widely considered before. Landing domains are what the web users are often attracted to access, and contain some malicious codes (usually Javascript) which can redirect the users (victims) to another malicious domains called distribution domains. Distribution domains are what the victims are redirected to unconsciously, and really install malwares into the victims' computers. To the best of our knowledge, currently there is a unique tool which can be used to classify a malicious domain into landing or distribution, which is GSBv4. GSBv4 not only is a blacklist (i.e., can detect whether a domain is malicious or benign) but also can classify a malicious domain into landing or distribution category. However, its classification rate is too low (this will be explained later); furthermore, it can only classify the domains belonging to its blacklist without being able to classify domains in other blacklists. This is why we construct our own classification model using supervised machine learning and only use GSBv4 for data labelling. Concretely, we first randomly collect 31,507 malicious URLs and label them using GSBv4. We then only have 5,772 samples (18.31%), which can be labelled by GSBv4 (4,124 landings and 1,648 distributions). After that, we extracted HTML documents of the labelled 5,772 samples to use in the training process. For feature selection, at first, adapting the idea of [15], we extracted and counted the following special HTML elements in each type:

- Type 1: 8 HTML tags, which are used very often in landing domains including: *<script>*, *<iframe>*, *<form>*, *<frame>*, *<object>*, *<embed>*, *<href>*, and *<link>*. This is because these tags allow to place URLs inside, and thus have potential for the redirection which is a specific characteristic of landing domains.
- Type 2: 3 elements which are commonly used in distribution domains including *swf*, *jar* and *pdf*. This is because these elements are mostly potential exploitable contents that distribution domains install into victim's computers.

However, our implementation showed that the accuracy of this method is very low (less than 71% using the 9 learning algorithms and 10-fold cross validation). Therefore, we then combine the 2 methods: the above HTML elements (in which the count of all tags in each type is used as one feature) along with text mining on entire HTML documents (in which the TF-IDF of each unique word is used as one feature). As a result, fortunately, we can get 98.07% in accuracy with merely 2.22% in false positive rate. Finally, we use the model of our combining method to classify 50,519 entries in the blacklists.

III. Empirical Results

In our implementation, we use two machines: a computer Intel(R) core i7, RAM 16.0 GB, 64-bit Windows 10; and a MacBook Pro Intel Core i5 processor, 2.7 GHz, 16 GB of RAM, OS X EI Capitan version 10.11.6. Since we do not consider the execution time, it does not matter that the two machines have different configurations. They are just used to speed up our evaluation modules which can be executed parallelly and independently. We execute the 6 measures using Python 2.7.11 programming language with *pandas* library to deal with big data. Furthermore, we use *python-whois* library for Whois extraction of measure 3 and 4. We also use *scikit-learn* library for text mining and *BeautifulSoup* library for HTML extraction of measure 5 and 6.

A. Measure 1: Blacklist Intersections

In Table III, we present the intersections of every blacklist pair. From this table, we can see certain correlations between every blacklist pair. For example, *UT and UR have highest correlation* compared with the others since the intersection AUT ∩ AUR contains largest number of domains (23,583 domains which is 70.03% of AUR and 98.18% of AUT). Furthermore, the table also indicates that the size of the values in this table is *not only dependent on the size of each original blacklist*. For example, ASH = 32,248 and AUR = 33,674 but ASH ∩ AUR = 19,495 which is smaller than AUT ∩ AUR = 23,583 even though AUT = 24,020 which is smaller than ASH.

B. Measure 2: TLDs

From 50,519 unique domains in all the blacklists, we found 253 different TLDs in totals in which the top 10 dominant TLDs *for all the blacklists* are given in Table IV. We then found top 5 dominant TLDs *for each blacklist* as given in Table V. The third column is the number of distinct TLDs in each blacklist. The fourth until the eighth columns are the top 5 TLDs in descending order. Similar to the measure 1, the number of unique TLDs (the 3rd column) is *not always dependant on the number of entries* in each blacklist. For example, the blacklist HO belongs to the group I (small public blacklists) and AHO has only 5,060 entries but the number of TLDs is 145; meanwhile, the ME belongs to the group II (large public blacklists) and AME has 19,812 entries which is almost 4× larger than that of AHO, but its number of TLDs is only 113.

TABLE IV: TOP 10 DOMINANT TLDs IN ALL BLACKLISTS.

No	TLD	#Domains	Percentage
1	com	32,691	64.71 %
2	jp	4,277	8.47 %
3	net	3,458	6.84 %
4	org	1,856	3.67 %
5	de	726	1.44 %
6	de	683	1.35 %
7	au	428	0.85 %
8	edu	375	0.74 %
9	tv	366	0.72 %
10	info	310	0.61 %

TABLE V: TOP 5 DOMINANT TLDs IN EACH BLACKLIST

No	Blacklist	#Distinct TLDs	1st	2nd	3rd	4th	5th
1	AMA	25	com	jp	pl	net	org
2	ANE	2	com	pl			
3	APH	68	com	net	org	ru	pl
4	ARA	3	to	org	cab		
5	AZE	9	net	com	ua	ru	jp
6	AMAL	22	com	net	it	jp	ru
7	AMV	79	com	net	de	ru	org
8	AHO	145	com	net	org	jp	de
9	AME	113	com	net	org	tv	jp
10	ASH	197	com	jp	net	org	de
11	AUR	180	com	net	org	jp	uk
12	AUT	137	com	net	org	jp	tv
13	AGSBv3	34	com	org	jp	net	cn
14	AGSBv4	61	com	net	top	org	biz

C. Measure 3: Domain Ages

Considering the union of all 14 blacklists, there are *34 distinct creation years* (from 1984 to 2017) as given in Figure 1. We can observe that the number of detected malicious domains created *after 1993 increases remarkably* compared to the years before 1993, and *drops down from 2016* (just 1 year before the date that we started our analysis). This indicates that most of the blacklists can *detect the new (young) malicious domains created after 2015 with very low rate*. The top 10 dominant years with corresponding number of domains are given in Table VI. For each blacklist, we also found the top 5 dominant creation years as presented in Table VII. We can observe that the blacklists *MA and GSBv4 can detect younger domains* compared with the other blacklists. Meanwhile, the blacklists *MAL and MV can detect very old domains*.

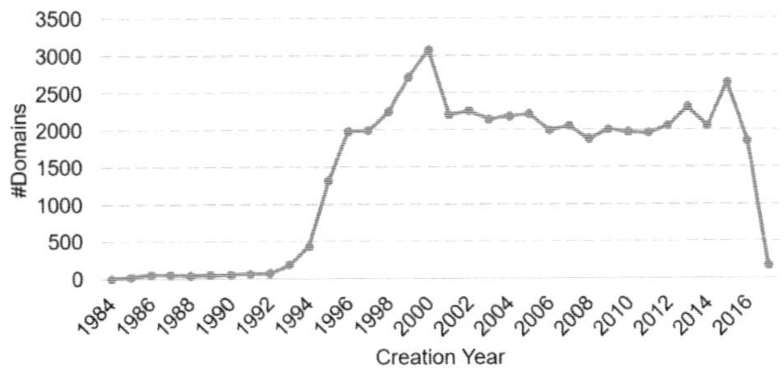

Figure 1: Distribution of Domain Ages (Creation Year).

TABLE VI: TOP 10 DOMINANT CREATION YEARS IN ALL BLACKLISTS.

No	Year	#Domains	Percentage
1	2000	3,073	6.08 %
2	1999	2,707	5.36 %
3	2015	2,633	5.21 %
4	2013	2,302	4.56 %
5	2002	2,249	4.45 %
6	1998	2,239	4.43 %
7	2005	2,209	4.37 %
8	2001	2,205	4.36 %
9	2004	2,181	4.32 %
10	2003	2,141	4.24 %

TABLE VII: TOP 5 DOMINANT CREATION YEARS IN EACH BLACKLIST.

No	Blacklist	#Distinct Years	1st	2nd	3rd	4th	5th
1	AMA	16	2016	2015	2014	2013	2012
2	ANE	2	2012	2006			
3	APH	27	2011	2009	2010	1999	2004
4	ARA	3	2014	2013	2008		
5	AZE	12	2007	2004	2001	2008	2006
6	AMAL	25	1999	1997	1998	1996	2005
7	AMV	32	1998	1999	1995	1996	2000
8	AHO	32	2005	2007	2016	1999	2012
9	AME	29	2015	2013	2012	2014	2011
10	ASH	33	2000	1999	2002	2001	1998
11	AUR	33	2015	2013	1999	2000	2007
12	AUT	33	2015	2013	2012	2014	2007
13	AGSBv3	21	2016	2012	2009	2013	2011
14	AGSBv4	21	2016	2015	2014	2012	2013

D. Measure 4: Countries

From the union of 14 blacklists, which contains 50,519 domains, we found 173 distinct registered countries. Note that, some domains are registered under one or multiple countries. That is, the registrator's addresses consist of one or multiple countries. For this reason, we consider each different country even in the same domain instead of just randomly choosing one of the countries for each domain when the domain has multiple countries. The top 10 dominant countries throughout the union of 14 blacklists are given in Table VIII. Besides the union of all the blacklists, we also found top 5 dominant countries in each blacklist as presented in Table IX. The third column is the number of distinct countries in each blacklist. The fourth until eighth columns are the top 5 dominant countries described in descending order. From this table, we can observe that ME and UT have highest correlation because their numbers of distinct countries are almost equal, and the order of their dominant countries from the fourth to the eighth column is exactly same.

TABLE VIII: TOP 10 DOMINANT COUNTRIES IN ALL BLACKLISTS.

No	Country	#Domains	Percentage
1	US	12,267	24.28 %
2	JP	7,959	15.75 %
3	CY	3,988	7.89 %
4	PA	3,207	6.35 %
5	RU	1,194	2.36 %
6	AU	1,172	2.32 %
7	FR	1,072	2.12 %
8	DE	1,072	2.12 %
9	CA	994	1.97 %
10	GB	983	1.95 %

TABLE IX: TOP 5 DOMINANT COUNTRIES IN EACH BLACKLIST.

No	Blacklist	#Distinct Countries	1st	2nd	3rd	4th	5th
1	AMA	28	JP	US	CN	CA	FR
2	ANE	2	PL	CN			
3	APH	54	US	RU	AU	DE	BR
4	ARA	3	TO	DE	CA		
5	AZE	11	US	UA	RU	JP	NU
6	AMAL	28	US	IT	RU	JP	KR
7	AMV	81	US	DE	CA	FR	PA
8	AHO	104	US	JP	PA	CN	DE
9	AME	125	US	CY	PA	JP	RU
10	ASH	153	US	JP	CY	PA	DE
11	AUR	152	US	CY	JP	PA	RU
12	AUT	126	US	CY	PA	JP	RU
13	AGSBv3	39	US	JP	CN	RU	PL
14	AGSBv4	58	US	CN	JP	PL	DJ

E. Measure 5: Web Content Categories

After labelling 14,492 samples by i-Filter and IAB as mentioned in Section II-B4, we got 17 categories as described in Table X. Note that, the order of the numbers of samples in these categories does not indicate that of the domains in the blacklists. Even the numbers of samples in the categories are varied, for example, the number of samples of *Tech & Comp.* is double that of *Business* in the training dataset, it does not mean that *Tech & Comp.* always has higher order than *Business* in the applied dataset. We used the 14,492 labelled samples for our training dataset and inputted them to the supervised algorithms. We obtained the accuracy and false positive rate for each algorithm as given in Figure 2. We found that Decision Tree gives the best accuracy (99.58%) and lowest false positive rate (0.04%). We thus choose it to classify the domains in our blacklists. For the union of all the blacklists which consists of 50,519 domains, the web content categories with the corresponding number of domains are given in Table XI. We observe that the top 3 dominant categories are *Technology and Computing*, *Business*, and *Non-Standard content* (such as *Pornography*, *Violence*, or *Incentivized*). For each blacklist, the top 5 dominant categories with corresponding number of domains are presented in Table XII. We found that all the blacklists belonging to the group II (large public blacklists including ME, SH, UR, and UT), have higher correlation in web content categories rather than the other blacklists since the number of distinct categories and the order of dominant categories are exactly the same. Furthermore, MV and HO which belong to the group I (small public blacklists) and GSBv3 which belongs to the group III (private blacklists) also have the same order of dominant categories.

TABLE X: 17 CATEGORIES IN TRAINING DATASET

No	Category	#Samples	No	Category	#Samples
1	Art & Entert.	65	10	Personal Finance	103
2	Automotive	29	11	Real Estate	18
3	Business	4,622	12	Tech & Comp.	7,632
4	Careers	17	13	Society	137
5	Education	15	14	Hobby & Interest	503
6	Shopping	604	15	Non-Standard	490
7	Food & Drink	37	16	News	117
8	Science	8	17	Sports	8
9	Travel	87			

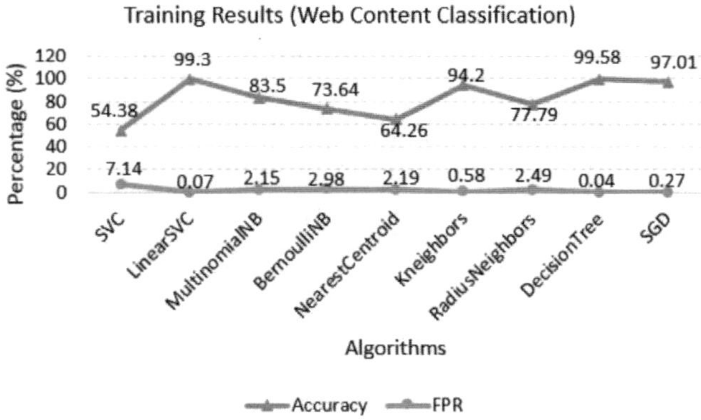

Figure 2: Accuracy and False Positive Rate of Each Algorithm

TABLE XI: WEB CONTENT CATEGORIES IN ALL BLACKLISTS.

Due to space limitation, we use first three characters in each category as the abbreviation in the 3rd column.

No	Category	Abbr.	#Domain	Percentage
1	Tech & Computing	Tec	13,987	27.69 %
2	Business	Bus	10,259	20.31 %
3	Non-Standard	Non	10,032	19.86 %
4	Shopping	Sho	6,179	12.23 %
5	Hobby and Interest	Hob	2,678	5.30 %
6	Travel	Tra	1,708	3.38 %
7	Education	Edu	994	1.97 %
8	Arts & Entertainment	Art	933	1.85 %
9	Food & Drink	Foo	816	1.62 %
10	Careers	Car	674	1.33 %
11	News	New	628	1.24 %
12	Personal Finance	Per	570	1.13 %
13	Automotive	Aut	446	0.88 %
14	Sports	Spo	231	0.46 %
15	Science	Sci	230	0.46 %
16	Society	Soc	78	0.15 %
17	Real Estate	Rea	76	0.15 %

F. Measure 6: Malicious Categories

Unlike the measure 5 which has 17 labels, this measure only has 2 labels: landing (4,124 samples) and distribution (1,648 samples). We train the dataset using the 9 algorithms and got the results as depicted in Figure 3. Decision Tree gives

TABLE XII: TOP 5 WEB CONTENT CATEGORIES IN EACH BLACKLIST.

No	Blacklist	#Distinct Categories	1st	2nd	3rd	4th	5th
1	AMA	11	Bus	Tec	Non	Sho	Art
2	ANE	1	Bus				
3	APH	16	Tec	Bus	Non	Sho	Hob
4	ARA	3	Sho	Bus	Tec		
5	AZE	5	Tec	Bus	Sho	Hob	Art
6	AMAL	12	Bus	Tec	Non	Sho	Tra
7	AMV	17	Bus	Tec	Non	Sho	Hob
8	AHO	17	Bus	Tec	Non	Sho	Hob
9	AME	17	Tec	Non	Bus	Sho	Hob
10	ASH	17	Tec	Non	Bus	Sho	Hob
11	AUR	17	Tec	Non	Bus	Sho	Hob
12	AUT	17	Tec	Non	Bus	Sho	Hob
13	AGSBv3	14	Bus	Tec	Non	Sho	Hob
14	AGSBv4	15	Bus	Tec	Non	Hob	Sho

the best result with 98.07% accuracy and merely 2.22% false positive rate. Therefore, Decision Tree is chosen to classify the entries in the blacklists and got the results as depicted in Table XIII. Most of the blacklists contains larger number of landing domains than number of distribution domains **at least 1.5 times**. This is reasonable because a distribution domain may have multiple corresponding landing domains that redirect users to the distribution domain. Concretely, we found that the landing domains occupy at least 60% of total distinct domains in each blacklist. Especially, in the group II (large public blacklists), the landing domains occupy even larger than 75% of total distinct domains in each blacklist.

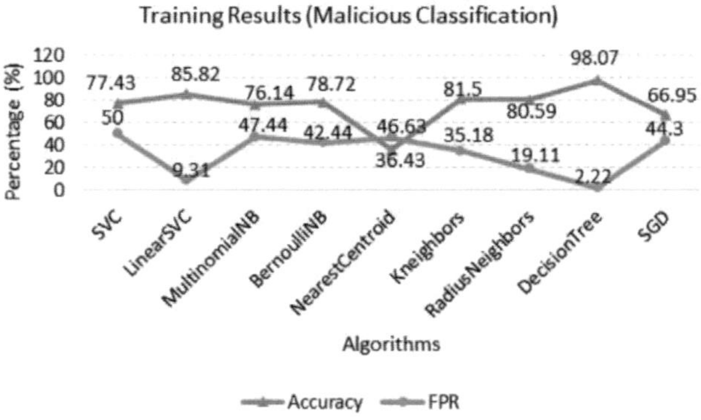

Figure 3: Accuracy and False Positive Rate of Each Algorithm

IV. DISCUSSION

In this section, we discuss several issues that can be addressed in future work.

Blacklist Extension. In this paper, we analyzed 14 popular blacklists. We are planning to analyze other private blacklists. The most prioritized candidate is VirusTotal (virustotal.com). VirusTotal checks domains/URLs by referring 40 other antivirus blacklists (however, all blacklists are not always used). VirusTotal also refers the feedbacks/comments from users. Besides the blacklists and user feedbacks, we currently do not know whether it has its own method to classify a domain/URL into malicious or benign. Furthermore, we plan to extend our

TABLE XIII: LANDING AND DISTRIBUTION IN THE BLACKLISTS.

No	Blacklist	#Distinct Domains	#Landings	#Distributions
0	Total	50,519	37,815 (74.85%)	12,704 (25.15%)
1	AMA	77	55 (71.43%)	22 (28.57%)
2	ANE	2	0 (00.00%)	2 (100.0%)
3	APH	367	234 (63.76%)	133 (36.24%)
4	ARA	3	3 (100.0%)	0 (00.00%)
5	AZE	21	14 (66.67%)	7 (33.33%)
6	AMAL	98	62 (63.27%)	36 (36.73%)
7	AMV	2,176	1,474 (67.74%)	702 (32.26%)
8	AHO	5,060	3,423 (67.65%)	1,637 (32.35%)
9	AME	19,812	15,232 (76.88%)	4,580 (23.12%)
10	ASH	32,248	24,408 (75.69%)	7,840 (24.31%)
11	AUR	33,674	25,508 (75.75%)	8,166 (24.25%)
12	AUT	24,020	18,411 (76.65%)	5,609 (23.35%)
13	AGSBv3	189	134 (70.90%)	55 (29.10%)
14	AGSBv4	639	389 (60.88%)	250 (39.12%)

analysis from domain blacklists to IP, URL and DNS blacklists. Two prioritized candidates are MXTools or also known as Spamhaus (mxtools.com) and Mxtoolbox (mxtoolbox.com), which provide large number of IP entries.

Analysis Extension. We plan to extend our current six measures to another measure about the registration time of malicious domains in each blacklist. In other words, this is the response time of each blacklist to a malicious domain. For example, when a domain D becomes malicious on 2017/05/01, blacklist A lists D in its dataset on 2017/05/02 but blacklist B lists D in its dataset on 2017/05/03; and thus, A is better than B. The challenge is that, not all blacklists provide this information. A naive method is to download each blacklist periodically to check whether specific malicious domains appear in each blacklist. For example, [16] analyzed the blacklist update frequency by monitoring download site. This method requires high communication costs and also cannot deal with private blacklists which do not allow to directly download blacklists. Therefore, better solutions should be investigated to analyze registration time of malicious domains in blacklists. Another interesting analysis is *how to decide whether a domain is malicious based on some blacklists when each blacklist has its own ground truth*. A naive method is based on *majority rule*. That is, if a domain is detected by larger than 50% number of blacklists, it can be determined as a malicious domain. Another better method is based on the weight of malicious domain in each blacklist. For example, a blacklist A weights a malicious domain D at 80% while another blacklist B weights it at 30%; then we can weight D at 55%, which is the average weight. Similar to the above analysis about registration time, the challenge is that almost all blacklists do not provide the information about malicious weighting. Therefore, finding how to weight domains in each blacklist is a promising approach to label a domain into malicious or benign.

V. CONCLUSION

In this paper, we analyze 14 popular blacklists including 8 small public blacklists, 4 large public blacklists and 2 private blacklists by Google. We designed 6 important measures including blacklist intersections, TLDs, domain ages, countries, web content categories and malicious categories. Especially, we construct our two models using machine learning to analyze the last 2 measures. We finally found several important results: Google is developing GSBv3 and GSBv4 independently; the large public blacklist *urlblacklist.com* contains 98% entries in the blacklist *dsi.ut_capitole.fr*; most of domains in all the blacklists are created in 2000 with 6.08%, and from United States with 24.28%; GSBv4 can detect younger domains compared with other blacklists; (v) *Tech & Computing* is the dominant web content category, and the blacklists in each group have higher correlation in web content than the blacklists in other groups; and (vi) the number of landing domains is larger than that of distribution domains at least 75% in group II (large public blacklists) and at least 60% in other groups.

ACKNOWLEDGEMENT

This research was carried out as part of WarpDrive: Web-based Attack Response with Practical and Deployable Research InitiatiVE, a Commissioned Research of the National Institute of Information and Communications Technology (NICT), JAPAN.

REFERENCES

[1] VeriSign, Inc., "Internet Grows to 326.4 Million Domain Names in the First Quarter of 2016". Available: https://investor.verisign.com/releaseDetail.cfm?releaseid=980215. Retrieved: 2016/07/19.

[2] Symantec, Inc. "Internet Security Threat Report". Available: https://www.symantec.com/content/dam/symantec/docs/reports/istr-21-2016-en.pdf.

[3] S. Sheng, B. Wardman, G. Warner, L. F. Cranor, and J. Hong, "An Empirical Analysis of Phishing Blacklists", *6th Conference on Email and Anti-Spam (CEAS)*, 2009.

[4] M. Kuhrer and T. Holz, "An Empirical Analysis of Malware Blacklists", *Praxis der Informationsverarbeitung und Kommunikation*, vol. 35, no. 1, p. 11, 2012.

[5] M. Kuhrer, C. Rossow, and T. Holz, "Paint it Black: Evaluating the Effectiveness of Malware Blacklists", *17th Symposium on Research in Attacks, Intrusions and Defenses (RAID)*, pp. 1-21, 2014.

[6] M. Vasek and T. Moore, "Empirical analysis of factors affecting malware URL detection", *eCrime Researchers Summit (eCRS'13)*, pp. 1-8, 2013.

[7] C. J. Dietrich, and C. Rossow, "Empirical research of IP blacklists", *Securing Electronic Business Processes (ISSE'08)*, pp. 163-171, 2008.

[8] T. Ouyang, S. Ray, M. Allman, and M. Rabinovich, "A large-scale empirical analysis of email spam detection through network characteristics in a stand-alone enterprise", *Journal of Computer and Telecommunications Networking*, vol. 59, pp. 101-121, 2014.

[9] J. Jung and E. Sit, "An empirical study of spam traffic and the use of DNS black lists", *4th ACM SIGCOMM conference on Internet measurement (IMC'04)*, pp. 370-375, 2004.

[10] D. Canali, M. Cova, G. Vigna, and C. Kruegel, " Prophiler: a fast filter for the large-scale detection of malicious web pages", *20th Conference on World wide web (WWW'11)*, pp. 197-206, 2011.

[11] R. J. Walls, E. D. Kilmer, N. Lageman, and P. D. McDaniel, "Measuring the Impact and Perception of Acceptable Advertisements", *Internet Measurement Conference (IMC'15)*, pp. 107-120, 2015.

[12] List of IAB Categories. Available: https://www.iab.com/guidelines/iab-quality-assurance-guidelines-qag-taxonomy/. Retrieved: 2015/09/01.

[13] Digital Arts. Available: http://www.daj.jp/en/

[14] SimilarWeb. Available: https://developer.similarweb.com/

[15] G. Wang, J. W. Stokes, C. Herley, and D. Felstead, "Detecting Malicious Landing Pages in Malware Distribution Networks", *43rd IEEE/IFIP Conf. on Dependable Systems and Networks (DSN'13)*, pp. 1-11, 2013.

[16] Y. Takeshi et al., "Analysis of Blacklist Update Frequency for Countering Malware Attacks on Websites", *IEICE Transactions on Communications*, vol. E97-B, no. 1, pp. 76-86, 2014.

Hugin: A Scalable Hybrid Android Malware Detection System

Dominik Teubert, Johannes Krude, Samuel Schüppen, Ulrike Meyer
Department of Computer Science
RWTH Aachen University
Aachen, Germany
Email: {teubert,krude,schueppen,meyer}@itsec.rwth.aachen.de

Abstract—**Mobile operating systems are a prime target of today's malware authors and cyber criminals. In particular, Google's Android suffers from an ever increasing number of malware attacks in the form of malicious apps. These typically originate from poorly policed third-party app stores that fail to vet the apps prior to publication. In this paper, we present *Hugin*, a machine learning-based app vetting system that uses features derived from dynamic, as well as static analysis and thus falls into the scarcely studied class of hybrid approaches. *Hugin* is unique with respect to using IPC/RPC monitoring as source for dynamically extracted features. Furthermore, *Hugin* uses a short (and yet effective) feature vector that leads to a high efficiency in training as well as classification. Our evaluation shows that *Hugin* achieves a detection accuracy of up to 99.74% on an up-to-date data set consisting of more than 14,000 malware samples and thus, is easily capable of competing with other current systems.**

Keywords–mobile malware detection; app vetting; machine-learning.

I. Introduction

Smartphones are omnipresent in our society. According to a recent study, 72% of the adults in the U.S. and 60% in Europe own a smartphone [1]. Google's Android is particularly popular with a leading market share of 86.2% [2] at the time of writing. Similar to its competitors, Android does not only provide an operating system, but a complete eco-system for app development and distribution. Unlike platforms, such as Apples's iOS, Android does not restrict users to the official app store. This lead to the emergence of a number of third-party app stores, gaining popularity especially in world regions such as Russia and Asia. These alternative markets are not as tightly regulated as the official Google Play store and are therefore often used for malware distribution. It is estimated that up to 3-7% of the available apps in Asian app stores are malware, compared to only 0.1% malicious apps in Google's official Play store [3]. Google recently warned that the chance of installing a potentially malicious app is ten times larger outside the official store [4]. In Russia, up to 8.3% of the apps installed from outside Google's Play store are potentially harmful [5].

The operators of the official app stores fight malware with different approaches. Google introduced the Bouncer [4] [6], a semi-automated approach that utilizes mainly dynamic analysis for malware detection. Apple even performs a manual review of the apps submitted to their app store. Although third-party app stores have an equally strong interest in keeping their market places free of malware, the numbers above show that many of them are poorly policed. Large enterprises that have a mobile device management (MDM) solution in place create an additional barrier to keep their devices safe. Mobile devices under MDM are often restricted to company operated app stores that have a particularly high security standard but a limited amount of apps to choose from. However, there is no established procedure how to vet apps before they are published in such a store for the first time. This demonstrates the importance of scalable automated mobile malware detection for third-party app store operators and large companies alike.

This gap is filled by malware detection systems that are based on machine learning and therefore are able to detect yet unknown threats. Existing approaches use various types of features derived from static analysis (e. g., [7]–[10]), dynamic analysis (e. g., [11] [12]), or even both (e. g., [13]). However, while inter process communication has previously been used to analyze the malicious behavior of a specific app [14]–[16], none of the prior malware detection system uses higher level Inter Process Communication (IPC)/Remote Procedure Calls (RPC) (monitoring as source for dynamically extracted features. In this paper, we introduce *Hugin*, a novel malware detection system based on a hybrid of static and dynamic features. Hugin is unique with respect to using IPC/RPC as feature source and has a very good detection capability comparable to the best already existing mobile malware detection systems. In particular, *Hugin* has the following properties:

Hybrid Detection: *Hugin* uses as feature vector containing features derived by static as well as features derived by dynamic analysis. We evaluate the static and the dynamic part of the feature vector separately and show that *Hugin* benefits from the hybrid approach in terms of detection accuracy.

IPC-based Features: Although IPC is heavily used on Android, to the best of our knowledge, *Hugin* is the first approach using higher level IPC/RPC calls as a source for dynamic features in the context of an Android malware detection system.

Reliable Features: Android malware detection that relies on static features derived from disassembled or decompiled code often suffers from degraded detection performance due to obfuscation. In contrast, *Hugin* relies mainly on static features derived from parts of the APK that are hard to obfuscate.

Compact Feature Vector: *Hugin* makes use of a comparatively low number of (static and dynamic) features selected by feature engineering. This short and thus compact feature vector allows for efficient training ($< 32\ s$) and classification ($< 3\ ms$).

Strong Detection Performance: *Hugin* shows an excellent detection rate of about 99% (with a false-positive rate well below 1%) on the well established Drebin data set (covering the time period from 2008–2012) and even better accuracy on the more recent, newly generated *Hugin* data set.

The remainder of this paper is structured as follows: The most closely related work is summarized in Section II. A system overview on *Hugin* with details on the feature extraction and the training and classification is given in Section III. We present the results of our evaluation of *Hugin* in Section IV. We conclude in Section V.

II. Related Work

In the following section, we summarize the most relevant mobile malware detection approaches from related work. We focus on those approaches that are similar to *Hugin* in the sense that they use either static or dynamic analysis to extract features and machine learning techniques for detection or classification. Note that a systematic comparison of detection results between the proposed systems is only possible for systems that made their data sets publicly available (such as Drebin [8]) or base their evaluation on such data sets (such as Droidsieve [10] and DroidScribe [12]).

1) Detection based on static analysis: Many approaches from the field of machine learning aided mobile malware detection use features that are derived from static analysis. For unobfuscated malware, static features are typically easy and computationally inexpensive to extract from APK files and therefore allow for fast and scalable solutions. Additionally, many static features are well established and understood (e. g., Android permissions). One of the earlier approaches of static mobile malware detection was proposed by Peng et al. [7]. The authors used probabilistic generative models such as Naive Bayes to rank Android apps according to their asscociated risk for the user. For training these models, Peng et al. relied mainly on the requested permissions. With DroidSIFT [9] Zhang et al. proposed a system that extracts API dependency graphs to reconstruct Android app semantics. Graph similarity metrics are then used to obtain a classification decision and thus to distinguish benign from malicious apps. Following this procedure DroidSIFT achieves a detection rate of 93% on a malware set of 2200 samples. Drebin [8] provides a static detection method that extracts features such as permissions, filtered intents, API calls, and URLs. For classification Drebin also uses SVMs, but constructs the vector space in such a way that the system can present explanations for the detection decision to the user. Furthermore, its lightweight nature allows for detection on the end-user device. The authors of Drebin provide a public data set consisting of 5560 malicious apps, which is also used to evaluate *Hugin*. On this data set, Drebin achieves a detection rate of up to 94% based on 545,000 features. One of the most recent approaches that was proposed in this area is DroidSieve [10]. DroidSieve aims for classifying obfuscated as well as unobfuscated Android malware solely with the help of static features. Obfuscation-invariant features as well as artifacts indicating obfuscation are used to enable the system to also classify obfuscated samples correctly. The elaborated feature engineering results in a promising accuracy of up to 99.64% on the Drebin data set using 22,584 features. Using feature selection as an additional step, DroidSieve reduces the number of features to 859 with a slight drop in accuracy (99.57%).

2) Detection based on dynamic analysis: The landscape of related approaches that derive features from dynamic analysis is smaller. This is mainly due to high demands of dynamic analysis regarding the setup of the emulation environment and the hardware requirements when performing analysis at scale. Note that there are also various systems such as Droidscope [14], AppsPlayground [15], and Copperdroid [16] that assist dynamic analysis of mobile malware, but do not aim for automated detection. Among the first systems that used dynamic features is Crowdroid [11]. Burgueara et al. used system call invocations counts as features and subsequently performed clustering using the k-means algorithm. The correct label for each cluster (benign or malicious) is determined using a crowdsourcing-based approach, assuming that a large enough user base will reveal the significantly smaller malicious cluster. Most recently Dash et al. proposed DroidScribe [12], a system that focuses on classifying Android malware samples into families. DroidScribe exclusively uses run-time behavior such as system call traces, file/network access, and Binder communication to construct dynamic features. Using different flavors of SVMs the system achieves a classification accuracy of up to 94%.

3) Detection based on hybrid analysis: Hybrid mobile malware detection, i. e., the combination of static and dynamic features for later classification, is even less comprehensively studied. The only closely related approach to *Hugin* is Marvin [13]. Lindorfer et al. extract a pile of 450,000 static and dynamic features and use SVMs as well as linear classifier to calculate a malice score for each app. Their best configuration achieves a convincing detection rate of 98.24% at a low false-positive rate. Marvin also uses feature selection as additional step in its training procedure, ending up with 27,808 highest ranked features (and a strong emphasis on the dynamic features). In contrast to the fetch-all feature extraction of Marvin, *Hugin* uses feature engineering and ends up with far less features (about 2,000) at a comparable accuracy. Furthermore, while Marvin relies on traditional dynamic features such as file/network operations and data leakage, *Hugin* incorporates IPC/RPC-based features for the first time in the field of Android malware detection.

III. System Overview

Since *Hugin* is a machine learning-based approach, it operates in two phases: the training phase and the classification phase. The training phase takes labeled data sets of benign and malicious apps as input and results in a trained model. The classification phase represents the actual operational mode: apps that are submitted to an app store are processed and a binary decision on basis of the pre-trained model is made. Depending on the outcome further actions can be necessary, e.g. the rejection of the app. To detect Android malware, *Hugin* analyzes each app to get a comprehensive representation of its behavior. While many proposed approaches focus either on static or dynamic analysis *Hugin* combines both techniques to soften the limitations of either of these lines of work. Figure 1 shows an overview of *Hugin*'s detection approach and its different stages. The key aspects are:

Static feature extraction. Our approach uses static analysis to inspect each Android installation package. *Hugin* focuses on features that can be extracted reliably, even for many obfuscated malware samples.

Dynamic feature extraction. The dynamic analysis part of *Hugin* relies on monitoring the inter-process communication (IPC) of each sample at runtime. IPC is heavily used on Android and almost all potentially harmful functionality of apps has to pass this interface. Thus, a detailed profile of the

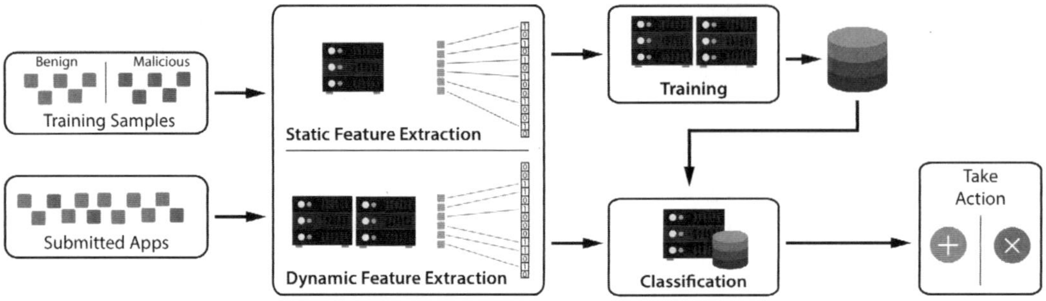

Figure 1. *Hugin* system overview.

runtime behavior of the analyzed apps is created and is used to derive features from it.

Training & Classification. For training and classification SVMs with different kernels are used. SVMs showed outstanding classification performance in a variety of application areas. The utilization of kernels provides a high degree of flexibility. Due to the comparably short length of our feature vector even computationally expensive kernels such as the Radial Basis Function (RBF) kernel can efficiently be used for classification.

A. Static Feature Extraction

Static analysis is frequently used for malware detection purposes and eases automation and scalability through its lightweight nature. However, static analysis also has several downsides. Properties that can be statically extracted can be differentiated into those which are particularly prone to obfuscation techniques and those which are reliably extractable in most cases. The higher the semantic level of information that is gained through static analysis, the higher the chance that this analysis can be hindered by malware. In particular, complex code recovery through disassembling or decompilation is often affected by obfuscation mechanisms. Detection approaches that rely solely on features derived from static analysis are therefore easy to circumvent by sophisticated malware. In contrast, *Hugin* confines itself to those static properties that can reliably be extracted from Android install packages (APK files) and uses these to derive features. On Android, the `Manifest` file is a particularly good source for static analysis, since it contains essential information about each app such as permissions, activities, services, broadcast receivers, and intent-filters. Furthermore, the `Manifest` is mandatory for the installation of new apps and has a pure declarative character, both usually preventing it from being obfuscated. *Hugin* therefore primarily relies on a comparatively small set of 1326 static features that originate from the `Manifest` file. Since the size of the feature vector is a crucial factor for training and classification efficiency, our approach supports efficient classification even with complex algorithms such as RBF-SVMs.

Specifically, we extract the following static features:

Permissions. Android makes use of permissions to separate apps according to their privileges. Permissions are therefore app-specific and are actively granted once by the user at installation time. Access to many sensitive system resources such as the location- or telephony-subsystem is controlled via permissions. Malware depends on using such resources to suceed and therefore usually requests many security-related permissions [17] [18].

Hardware components. In the case apps want to use hardware components such as the camera, the microphone, or the GPS this has to be declared in the `Manifest`. Many types of malware, in particular spyware, heavily depend on using such hardware features. The request of multiple sensitive hardware components can therefore be indicative for malicious behavior.

Intent-filters. Intents on Android allow apps to listen for different events that are propagated through the system. Malware often uses intents to trigger certain malicious actions, e. g., starting a background service after the `BOOT_COMPLETED` intent is received.

Activity count. The primary goal of malware is to execute its malicious payload. Most malware is therefore kept rather simple regarding its interface to the user. We represent this common property with the activity count, being 1 if the app has > 3 activities and 0 otherwise.

Service count. The service count follows the same logic. Malware frequently makes use of background services to perform malicious actions without the user's awareness. However, malware tends to put its malicious code into a single service, a high number of services is rather indicative for a complex benign app. We therefore add a 1 to the binary feature vector if the app has > 2 services and 0 otherwise.

Third-party libraries. The only features that are not directly derived from the `Manifest` are the utilized third-party libraries. For extraction, the `androguard` framework is used. Our assumption is that some third-party libraries can be particularly indicative for adware.

Automating the static analysis of APK files to extract the 1326 features does not pose a major challenge. There exist well established tools included in the Android SDK and from the open-source community that were used within *Hugin* (in particular `aapt` and `androguard`). For each analyzed app, a binary feature vector indicating the presence or absence of each feature is created. This static feature vector is later merged with the dynamic feature vector yielding a comprehensive vector for training and classification.

B. Dynamic Feature Extraction

Static analysis often does not suffice to detect sophisticated malware that uses code obfuscation or dynamic code loading. To reveal such hidden malicious behavior malware analysts often make use of dynamic analysis. Monitoring the runtime behavior of apps can provide additional insights that

TABLE I. EXAMPLES FOR EACH SET OF FEATURES.

Static features
Permissions (518 features)
`android.permission.INTERNET`
`android.permission.READ_SMS`
`android.permission.REBOOT`
Hardware components (104 features)
`android.hardware.MICROPHONE`
`android.hardware.LOCATION`
`android.hardware.CAMERA`
Intent-filters (638 features)
`android.intent.action.SERVICE_STATE`
`android.intent.action.BOOT_COMPLETED`
`android.intent.action.SCREEN_OFF`
Third-party libraries (62 features)
`com.google.android.maps`
`android.software.device_admin`
`sonymobile.enterprise.api_1`
Dynamic features
System services (195 features)
`android.os.IServiceManager`
`android.app.IAlarmManager`
`android.os.IPowerManager`
Remote Procedure Calls (516 features)
`sendText`
`getSubscriberId`
`startService`
Dynamic permissions (58 features)
`android.permission.RECEIVE_SMS`
`android.permission.WAKE_LOCK`
`android.permission.SEND_SMS`

might disclose potentially harmful actions, but does also raise a number of new challenges. In contrast to static analysis, dynamic analysis has very high demands regarding the analysis environment in terms of hardware, performance, and setup. As described below, *Hugin* meets these challenges and complements the static features with dynamic features derived from monitored IPC/RPC logs.

1) IPC on Android: The architecture of the Android operating system heavily relies on IPC/RPC mechanisms to provide a variety of functionality to apps. Namely, Android utilizes Binder for IPC, a reimplementation of a protocol dating back to OpenBinder [19]. Various important features of modern smartphones such as sending SMS, accessing the GPS location, and taking pictures are made accessible to developers via Binder and its RPC interface [20] [21]. Most aspects of the implementation details of Binder IPC are hidden from the Android developers using this RPC interface and corresponding Java APIs that built on it. However, whenever the funtionality of a (sensitive) Android system service is being used, the Binder interface has to be passed. Note that it is irrelevant if some functionality provided by a system service is used in the context of a Java-written app or using native code. The Binder is involved in both cases. Therefore, monitoring the IPC interface allows to create detailed profiles of the behavioral aspects of apps at run-time. For this reason, IPC monitoring was already used, e.g., in [14], [16] with the goal of supporting the analysis of the malicious behavior of a specific app. However, to the best of our knowledge, we are the first who use IPC/RPC calls on Android to derive features for an automated malware detection system.

2) Dynamic Analysis Environment: One challenge in dynamic malware analysis in general is that malware tries to detect that it runs in a sandbox. The same holds for malicious apps: malicious apps try to detect if they are running in an emulator and change their behavior if they do. Thus there is a complete line of research on how malware can detect that it is running in an emulator and how to make a malcious app believe that it runs on an actual device (e.g. [22] [23]). While this line of work is orthogonal to our work, we tried to incorporate some of these findings into the Android Virtual Devices (AVDs) used during our dynamic analysis. In particular, we used the list of properties that can be queried via the Android API to perform sandbox detection published in [22] to modify the AVDs. We also tried to mimic the actual usage of the emulated device by installing some common apps (e.g. signed-in Facebook and Twitter apps) and storing data such as some contacts in the phone book.

Besides considering sandbox detection, the stimulation of dynamically tested apps to increase code coverage is a much discussed topic. In recent years sophisticated stimulation approaches were proposed [24] [25]. *Hugin* incorporates some simpler heuristics to trigger typical malware behavior. In particular, we reboot the emulator to trigger the commonly used `BOOT_COMPLETED` intent-filter, send and receive SMS, perform a phone call, and modify time and date settings. Additionally, we make use of the `monkey`, an application exerciser included in the Android SDK that allows injecting random events for a specific duration. Each `monkey` phase runs for 180 sec in our test setup, the complete dynamic analysis of each app takes about 10 mins.

3) IPC Monitoring: To monitor IPC on Android we implemented *BTrace* (short for Binder Trace). *BTrace* is a modified Android Emulator to capture Android Binder inter-process communication events using virtual machine introspection. These captured events range from low-level Binder `ioctl`'s to high level remote procedure calls, intent broadcasts, content provider access and the dynamic evaluation of used permissions. *BTrace* produces both human-readable and machine-readable output, the former intended for manual inspection, the latter for automatic analysis. Although we used DroidScope [14] (that publicly provides only very basic hooking mechanisms) as a starting point, *BTrace* does not reuse anything from DroidScope with the exception of emulator system call hooks and emulator memory access routines. Unlike DroidScope, *BTrace* derives all monitored binder events from a kernel system call view. To evaluate binder remote procedure calls and higher level events, system call arguments and return values are used. The structures on how to interpret this data were extracted, in large parts automatically, from the Android source code. *BTrace* employs an automata describing the Android process creating and naming behavior. This automata is used to determine the point of time at which the name of an app may securely be read from user-space. Events are attributed to app-name by remembering the once read app-name for a process and the transitive hull of its child processes.

For different kinds of actions, *BTrace* dynamically analyses whether permissions are needed to perform these actions. Unfortunately, the Android permission specification does not exist in the form of a formal specification but only through an implementation spread across the Android Java and C++ source code. To evaluate dynamic permission usage, *BTrace* employs a permission specification obtained through executing PScout [26], a tool that performs static program analysis on the Android source code to generate the corresponding specification.

Specifically, we extract the following dynamic features:

Used system services. For each analyzed app we monitor which system services are used via the Binder interface during run-time. The combination of several sensitive system services can already be indicative for suspicious behavior.

Remote Procedure Calls. The specific method calls that are performed on each system service give even deeper insights into the run-time behavior. Since many system services provide a broad set of methods the actually used methods allow a better differentiation between benign and potentially harmful actions.

Dynamically used permissions. Using the permission specification obtained from PScout we are able to monitor the permissions that are actually used at run-time. The rationale behind this is that many benign apps statically request too many permissions that are not or only very rarely used. In contrast, aggressive malware will very likely use many of the statically requested permissions even in the limited timeframe of analysis.

C. Training & Classification

As described before, the app store vetting scenario *Hugin* aims for has exceptionally high demands regarding the detection capabilities of deployed systems. In particular, detection engines that guard an app store from unwanted software should be able to detect previously unknown threats. These requirements naturally suggest the application of machine learning and binary classification in particular. To this end, we utilized Support Vectors Machines (SVMs) [27] [28] for all evaluated classification tasks. Specifically, we implemented the classification part of *Hugin* using the efficient LIBSVM library [29].

SVMs are non-probabilistic binary classifiers which were successfully applied in a variety of application areas (e.g. in computational biology and chemistry [30]). Besides their strong classification performance [31], SVMs provide further interesting properties: flexibility through utilization of kernels [28], strong theoretic guarantees regarding the generalization performance [32], and the support of one-class classification through an extension [33]. Kernels are particularly interesting because they allow efficient non-linear classification. The "kernel trick" performs an implicit mapping from the input vector space into a (higher or even infinite-dimensional) feature vector space. Data points that are not linearly separable in the input vector space may be separable in this higher-dimensional vector space. *Hugin* was evaluated with the standard linear kernel and the Gaussian Radial Basis Function (RBF) kernel. In case of the RBF kernel the linear inner product $K(x, x') = x \cdot x'$ is replaced with $K(x, x') = \exp(\frac{-|x-x'|^2}{\gamma})$ within the dual representation of the SVM. Note that the RBF kernel is computationally much more expensive than the linear kernel.

TABLE II. TOP 10 FAMILIES OF THE EVALUATED DATA SETS.

Drebin data set			*Hugin* data set		
Id	**Family**	**# samples**	**Id**	**Family**	**# samples**
A	FakeInstaller	925	A	FakeInstaller	5724
B	DroidKungFu	667	D	Opfake	1078
C	Plankton	625	K	SmsSpy	735
D	Opfake	613	L	Dowgin	708
E	GingerMaster	339	M	RuSMS	438
F	BaseBridge	330	N	SmsStealer	274
G	Iconosys	152	O	FakeToken	261
H	Kmin	147	P	Lotoor	233
I	FakeDoc	132	F	BaseBridge	185
J	Geinimi	92	Q	Boxer	123

Here, *Hugin* profits from its comparatively short feature vector of over all 2095 binary features allowing efficient classification even for complex kernels.

IV. Evaluation

In this section, we present the results of our evaluation of the performance of *Hugin*. In particular, we detail the evaluation methodology and data sets used, present the detection performance of *Hugin* for the static part, the dynamic part and the hybrid feature vector, compare the performance to prior approaches as far as possible, and detail the training and classification efficiency of *Hugin*. Note that a systematic and sound comparison between systems with respect to their detection capabilities is only possible if the systems are evaluated on the same data sets. This is only possible for systems that published the data sets on which they evaluated themselves (such as Drebin [8]) or systems that in turn based their evaluation on such public data sets (such as Droidsieve [10] and DroidScribe [12]). We therefore compare the detection performance of *Hugin* on the Drebin data set to the performance of these systems on the same data set only.

A. Data Sets and Methodology

1) Data sets: We evaluate *Hugin* on two different malicious data sets, the Drebin dataset [8] containing 5560 malicious samples and a newly assembled dataset of 14,043 malicious samples referred to as *Hugin* dataset throughout the rest of this paper. To compare our approach to prior work, we used the Drebin data set [8], which covers the time period between August 2010 and October 2012. Note that we were able to extract features from 5317 samples only. The remaining 243 were either corrupted APK files and failed already in the static analysis or failed in the dynamic analysis because the could not be installed on the emulated device. Additionally, the more recent *Hugin* data set covers the time-period between January 2015 and September 2016. To compose this *Hugin* data set we used the VirusTotal intelligence search, querying the mentioned time period and requesting at least 35 AV matches to ensure the sample is indeed malware. Table II shows the top 10 families of the Drebin and the *Hugin* data set. While some families such as FakeInstaller and Opfake are still popular in the newer *Hugin* data set, others such as DroidKungFu and Plankton dropped out of this top-list. Last but not least, we composed a benign *Hugin*-b data set. To this end, we downloaded 14,068 popular apps from the official Google Play store, assuming that the fraction of potentially harmful apps in

TABLE III. SVM EVALUATION FOR THE DREBIN DATA SET.

Linear Kernel $C = 1$				RBF Kernel $\gamma = 0.03125, \nu = 0.03125$			
Features	**TPR**	**FPR**	**ACC**	**Features**	**TPR**	**FPR**	**ACC**
hybrid	97.21%	1.03%	98.49%	hybrid	97.57%	0.52%	98.95%
static	93.19%	1.39%	97.12%	static	95.81%	1.21%	97.97%
dynamic	93.56%	5.69%	94.11%	dynamic	88.60%	3.21%	94.54%

TABLE IV. SVM EVALUATION FOR *HUGIN* DATA SET.

Linear Kernel $C = 1$				RBF Kernel $\gamma = 0.03125, \nu = 0.0039062$			
Features	**TPR**	**FPR**	**ACC**	**Features**	**TPR**	**FPR**	**ACC**
hybrid	99.70%	0.54%	99.58%	hybrid	99.66%	0.19%	99.74%
static	99.14%	1.02%	99.06%	static	99.57%	0.48%	99.55%
dynamic	98.92%	5.14%	96.89%	dynamic	95.67%	3.32%	96.18%

TABLE V. DATASETS USED IN THE EVALUATION OF HUGIN.

Data set name	**Ground truth**	**# samples**
Drebin	malware	5,317
Hugin	malware	14,043
Hugin-b	benign	14,068

the most popular apps is particularly low. Note that the *Hugin*-b data set was used as the benign training set in all performed experiments due to the fact that the Drebin-b data set is not publicly available. Table V summarizes the sizes of all data sets used for evaluation.

2) Methodology: The detection performance of *Hugin* was measured by performing various experiments. In these experiments all relevant performance measures were calculated by splitting each data set into a training partition (66% of the samples) and a validation partition (33% of the samples). To this end, we applied repeated random subsampling and averaged our results over 10 runs. We used standard performance measures like the true-positive rate (TPR), the false-positive rate (FPR), and the accuracy (ACC) to assess the performance of *Hugin* and to be able to compare our approach to others. Additionally, we used Receiver Operating Characterstic (ROC) curves to visualize different parameter combinations [34]. In our first series of experiments, we evaluated *Hugin* against two malicious data sets, the publicly available Drebin data set and the newly assembled *Hugin* data set. For classification we tested SVMs with linear kernel and SVMs with RBF kernel. In case of the RBF kernel we performed a grid search to determine the kernel parameter γ and ν. We also evaluated the static feature vector, the dynamic feature vector, and the hybrid feature vector (concatenation of static and dynamic vector) separately.

B. Overall Detection Performance

Table III shows the results for the Drebin data set for the best kernel parameter determined through grid search. Overall, *Hugin* achieves an accuracy of just below 99% on the Drebin data set, with the RBF kernel showing superior TPR and FPR

TABLE VI. COMPARISON OF RELATED APPROACHES EVALUATING THE DREBIN DATA SET (STATING THE BEST MENTIONED CONFIGURATION).

Approach	**Features**	**Best ACC**	**# features**
Drebin [8]	static	~96.50%	~545,000
DroidSieve [12]	static	99.64%	~22,500
Hugin-static	static	97.97%	1326
Droidscribe [10]	dynamic	94.00%	254
Hugin-dynamic	dyanmic	94.54%	769
Hugin	hybrid	98.95%	2,095

compared to the linear kernel. Interestingly, in case of the RBF kernel considering only the static feature vector yields far better results than considering only the dynamic feature vector, while the results are more balanced for the linear kernel. However, in both cases the hybrid feature vector performs best, underpinning the assumed benefits of hybrid mobile malware detection. In case of the public Drebin data set we are able to directly compare *Hugin* to related approaches. While there are minor methodical differences between the detection approaches (e. g., regarding the fraction of the samples that are used for training and validation), the overall trend should be unaffected. Section IV-A2 shows *Hugin*'s excellent accuracy compared to the most closely related approaches that have evaluated the Drebin data set. Only the purely static DroidSieve [10] approach that is optimized for obfuscated malware achieves an even higher accuracy, but requires 16 times more features to achieve its best performance (see Section IV-A2). Note that *Hugin* is on par with the highly feature intensive Drebin and the Droidscribe approach when considering only the static or dynamic feature vector, respectively. The overall superiority of *Hugin* can therefore be attributed to the combination of both analysis techniques.

Table IV summarizes the detection results on the more up-to-date *Hugin* data set. Overall, the detection performance is even better than on the Drebin data set. Both the Linear-SVM and the RBF-SVM achieve an accuracy of over 99.5%, with the RBF-SVM performing best regarding the FPR. Evaluated

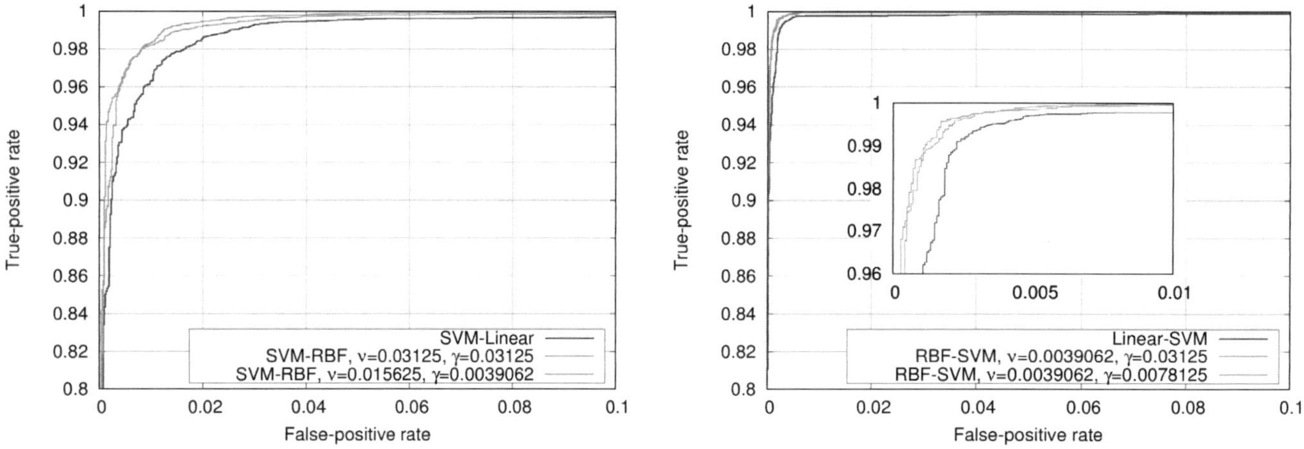

(a) ROC for Drebin data set.

(b) ROC for *Hugin* data set.

Figure 2. ROC curves for both data sets.

individually, we again observe that the dynamic feature vector performs worse than the static feature vector and that this effect is more pronounced for the RBF-SVM. However, it also becomes evident on the *Hugin* data set that the detection performance profits from the hybrid detection approach.

C. Detection Performance of Malware Families

The considerable better detection performance on the *Hugin* data set compared to the Drebin data set is also illustrated with the ROC curves in Figure 2. For both data sets the curves for the Linear-SVM and for the RBF-SVM parameter optimizing the ACC and TPR, respectively, are plotted. In addition to the better detection performance on the *Hugin* data set, the main finding is the consistently better performance of the RBF-SVM compared to the Linear-SVM on both data sets. We also assume that the considerably better performance on the *Hugin* data set can mainly be attributed to the benign data set used for training: Since it covers a similar time span as the malicious *Hugin* data set, it is easier for the classifier to distinguish these apps than on the considerably older Drebin data set (note that the Drebin-b data set is not publicly available). A lesson learned therefore is, that the benign and malicious training data set should always stem from a similar time period.

Figure 3 shows the detection rates of *Hugin* for the top 10 families of the Drebin and the *Hugin* data set. Compared to the Drebin approach, *Hugin* performs similar or better on the 10 most frequent malware families with an average detection rate of 99.35%. For the families E and F (GingerMaster and BaseBridge) that were particularly hard to detect for Drebin (detection rates of below 93%) our approach achieves significantly better detection rates of 99.41% and 96.86%, respectively. The authors of Drebin also reported a particular bad detection rate for the Gappusin family (not ranked top 10) and explained this result with the low number of extractable features. Interestingly, we can replicate this result when considering solely the static feature vector (51.44% TPR) or the dynamic feature vector (68.58% TPR). However, the hybrid feature vector achieves a compelling detection rate of 93.95%. This result once again indicates that the combination of static and dynamic features can help detecting mobile malware that is otherwise hard to detect. The top 10 families of the *Hugin* data set show even higher detection rates with an average of 99.51%. When considering only the dynamic feature vector we can observe a significantly higher average detection rate of 99.09% on the *Hugin* data set (compared to 96.89% on the Drebin data set). This phenomenon can easily be explained with age of the data sets: Since the Drebin data set is much older, the dynamic analysis can extract less features because, e. g., command and control server are put offline and therefore less behavior is shown during the analysis. Consistently, the gap in the average detection rate is smaller when using only the static feature vector for classification (99.10% on the *Hugin* data set, 97.74% on the Drebin data set). For the families that are included in both data sets (A, D, and F) the BaseBridge family (Id F) is particularly interesting. With a detection rate of below 93% in the original Drebin paper, BaseBridge is among the families that are most difficult to detect. *Hugin* achieves a detection rate of 96.86% for the BaseBridge samples in the Drebin data set and even 97.51% detection rate for the samples included in the *Hugin* data set, while the detection rate for the dynamic feature vector again increased notably on the newer data set. This leads us to conclude that the hybrid *Hugin* approach shows its strongest performance for most recent malware samples that emit a considerable amount of dynamic behavior the system can profit from.

D. Efficiency

The feature extraction part of *Hugin* consists of a dynamic as well as a static module. While the dynamic analysis of each app is quiet costly (8-10 minutes, see Section III), the actual extraction of the feature vector from the log data is negligible (52.37 ms per app, averaged over the Drebin data set). As expected the static feature extraction shows far better performance, with an average of only 55.39 ms for the entire analysis of each app.

The advantage of the short feature vector of *Hugin* (which is one of its strength) shows best in the training and classifi-

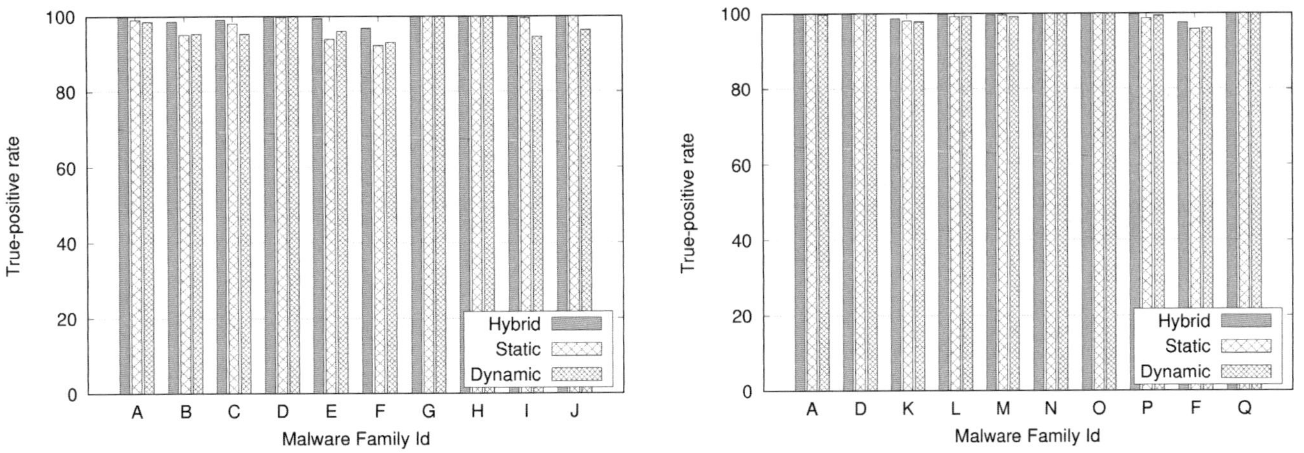

(a) Drebin data set. (b) Hugin data set.

Figure 3. Detection rates per malware family for the Linear-SVM.

cation performance. To get the most meaningful numbers, we measured the performance for the experiment with the highest number of feature vectors (training with the *Hugin* data set, i.e. about 28,000 feature vectors) and averaged over 10 runs. Using the RBF kernel the training of the SVM took 31.56 sec, while the classification of the 9559 apps in the validation set took 22.05 sec (i. e., 2.31 ms on average per app). The linear kernel shows even better performance. In this case the training took 24.78 sec and the classification 17.57 sec, i. e., only 1.84 ms per app.

Note that all numbers were measured on quiet dated desktop hardware (Intel i7-2600@3.40GHz) and therefore leave much room for improvements (either through more powerful hardware or through persistent use of parallelization).

V. Conclusion and Future Work

In this paper, we present *Hugin*, a hybrid and scalable Android malware detection system. We show how lightweight static analysis and complex dynamic analysis can be combined to create a comprehensive yet compact feature vector. *Hugin* achieves an accuracy of up to 99.74% on an up-to-date data set with far less features than related approaches. Our evaluation proves that the system profits significantly from the hybrid approach, both in terms of overall detection performance and in terms of detection performance for malware families that are particularly hard to detect. In particular, our dynamic feature extraction that relies on monitored interprocess communication proved to be a meaningful addition. Each of the individual components of *Hugin* is subject to continuous advances of the academic community, which could also improve *Hugin*. Static analysis could benefit from more elaborated feature engineering that allow better detection of obfuscated malware samples. Dynamic analysis could be enhanced by incorporating more complex stimulation techniques that increase code coverage. Furthermore, the post-processing of the results which can include report generation for analysts was not addressed so far and is another direction of future work.

Acknowledgments

We want to thank VirusTotal as well as the authors of Drebin for providing us with data sets to evaluate our approach. Additionally, we want to thank Madebyoliver from www.flaticons.com for his marvelous icon sets.

References

[1] J. Poushter, "Smartphone ownership and internet usage continues to climb in emerging economies," Online, 2016, URL: http://www.pewglobal.org/2016/02/22/smartphone-ownership-and-internet-usage-continues-to-climb-in-emerging-economies/ [retrieved: July, 2017].

[2] Gartner Inc., "Gartner says five of top 10 worldwide mobile phone vendors increased sales in second quarter of 2016," Online, Aug. 2016, URL: http://www.gartner.com/newsroom/id/3415117 [retrieved: July, 2017].

[3] F-Secure, "Mobile threat report," Online, 2014, URL: https://www.f-secure.com/documents/996508/1030743/Mobile_Threat_Report_Q1_2014.pdf [retrieved: July, 2017].

[4] Google Inc., "Android security 2015 year in review," Tech. Rep., 2016.

[5] ——, "Android security 2014 year in review," Tech. Rep., 2015.

[6] H. Lockheimer, "Android and security," online, 2012, URL: http://googlemobile.blogspot.de/2012/02/android-and-security.html [retrieved: July, 2017].

[7] H. Peng et al., "Using probabilistic generative models for ranking risks of android apps," in Proceedings of the 2012 ACM conference on Computer and communications security. ACM, 2012, pp. 241–252.

[8] D. Arp, M. Spreitzenbarth, M. Hubner, H. Gascon, and K. Rieck, "DREBIN: Effective and Explainable Detection of Android Malware in Your Pocket." in NDSS, 2014.

[9] M. Zhang, Y. Duan, H. Yin, and Z. Zhao, "Semantics-aware android malware classification using weighted contextual api dependency graphs," in Proceedings of ACM CCS, 2014, pp. 1105–1116.

[10] G. Suarez-Tangil et al., "Droidsieve: Fast and accurate classification of obfuscated android malware," in CODASPY. ACM, 2017, pp. 309–320.

[11] I. Burguera, U. Zurutuza, and S. Nadjm-Tehrani, "Crowdroid: behavior-based malware detection system for android," in Proceedings of the 1st ACM workshop on Security and privacy in smartphones and mobile devices. ACM, 2011, pp. 15–26.

[12] S. K. Dash et al., "Droidscribe: Classifying android malware based on runtime behavior," in IEEE Symposium on Security and Privacy Workshops. IEEE Computer Society, 2016, pp. 252–261.

[13] M. Lindorfer, M. Neugschwandtner, and C. Platzer, "Marvin: Efficient and comprehensive mobile app classification through static and dynamic analysis." in COMPSAC. IEEE Computer Society, 2015, pp. 422–433.

[14] L. K. Yan and H. Yin, "DroidScope: Seamlessly Reconstructing the OS and Dalvik Semantic Views for Dynamic Android Malware Analysis," in Presented as part of the 21st USENIX Security Symposium (USENIX Security 12). USENIX, 2012, pp. 569–584.

[15] V. Rastogi, Y. Chen, and W. Enck, "Appsplayground: automatic security analysis of smartphone applications," in Proceedings of the third ACM conference on Data and application security and privacy. ACM, 2013, pp. 209–220.

[16] K. Tam, S. J. Khan, A. Fattori, and L. Cavallaro, "Copperdroid: Automatic reconstruction of android malware behaviors." in NDSS, 2015.

[17] Y. Zhou and X. Jiang, "Dissecting Android Malware: Characterization and Evolution," in Proceedings of IEEE S&P. IEEE Computer Society, 2012.

[18] B. P. Sarma, N. Li, C. Gates, R. Potharaju, C. Nita-Rotaru, and I. Molloy, "Android permissions: a perspective combining risks and benefits," in Proceedings of the 17th ACM symposium on Access Control Models and Technologies. ACM, 2012, pp. 13–22.

[19] D. K. Hackborn, "Openbinder," online, 2005.

[20] K. Yaghmour, Embedded Android: Porting, Extending, and Customizing. O'Reilly Media, Inc., 2013.

[21] N. Elenkov, Android Security Internals: An In-Depth Guide to Android's Security Architecture. No Starch Press, 2014.

[22] T. Vidas and N. Christin, "Evading android runtime analysis via sandbox detection." in ASIA CCS. ACM, 2014, pp. 447–458.

[23] T. Petsas, G. Voyatzis, E. Athanasopoulos, M. Polychronakis, and S. Ioannidis, "Rage against the virtual machine: hindering dynamic analysis of android malware," in Proceedings of the Seventh European Workshop on System Security. ACM, 2014, p. 5.

[24] A. Gianazza, F. Maggi, A. Fattori, L. Cavallaro, and S. Zanero, "Puppetdroid: A user-centric ui exerciser for automatic dynamic analysis of similar android applications." CoRR, vol. abs/1402.4826, 2014.

[25] P. Carter, C. Mulliner, M. Lindorfer, W. Robertson, and E. Kirda, "CuriousDroid: Automated User Interface Interaction for Android Application Analysis Sandboxes," in Proceedings of the 20th International Conference on Financial Cryptography and Data Security (FC), 2016.

[26] K. W. Y. Au, Y. F. Zhou, Z. Huang, and D. Lie, "PScout: analyzing the Android permission specification," in ACM Conference on Computer and Communications Security. ACM, 2012, pp. 217–228.

[27] C. Cortes and V. Vapnik, "Support-vector networks," Machine learning, vol. 20, no. 3, 1995, pp. 273–297.

[28] C. Bishop, Bishop Pattern Recognition and Machine Learning. Springer, New York, 2001, p. 325ff.

[29] C.-C. Chang and C.-J. Lin, "LIBSVM: A library for support vector machines," ACM Transactions on Intelligent Systems and Technology, vol. 2, 2011, pp. 27:1–27:27, software available at URL: http://www.csie.ntu.edu.tw/~cjlin/libsvm [retrieved: July, 2017].

[30] O. Ivanciuc, "Applications of support vector machines in chemistry," Reviews in computational chemistry, vol. 23, 2007, p. 291.

[31] M. Fernández-Delgado, E. Cernadas, S. Barro, and D. Amorim, "Do we need hundreds of classifiers to solve real world classification problems," J. Mach. Learn. Res, vol. 15, no. 1, 2014, pp. 3133–3181.

[32] V. Vapnik, The nature of statistical learning theory. Springer Science & Business Media, 2013.

[33] B. Schölkopf, R. C. Williamson, A. J. Smola, J. Shawe-Taylor, and J. C. Platt, "Support vector method for novelty detection." NIPS, vol. 12, 1999, pp. 582–588.

[34] D. M. W. Powers, "Evaluation: From Precision, Recall and F-Measure to ROC, Informedness, Markedness & Correlation," Journal of Machine Learning Technologies, vol. 2, no. 1, 2011.

Towards Protected Firmware Verification in Low-power Devices

Yong-Hyuk Moon and Jeong-Nyeo Kim
Hyper-connected Communication Research Laboratory
Electronics and Telecommunication Research Institute (ETRI)
Daejeon, Republic of Korea
email: {yhmoon, jnkim}@etri.re.kr

Abstract—**It is barely conceivable to ensure the security state of a device without a trusted computing base. However, a hardware security module is not provided in most low-power devices. This paper presents a new design approach, which can securely verify a current state of firmware at a booting time utilizing untrusted components. We discuss a Memory Protection Unit (MPU) enabled memory access control to ensure that memory regions of a bootloader are not accidentally compromised from unintended access. Further extensions of the suggested approach are also addressed for achieving the enhanced security confirmation.**

Keywords-firmware verification; memory protection; device security.

I. Introduction

Secure booting is a fundamental security technique of computing devices and recently become a mandatory option for protection of computing tasks and resources. However, most Microcontroller Units (MCUs) of low-power devices do not contain a hardware security module functioning as a Trusted Computing Base (TCB). The commodity MCUs may not provide sufficient chip-level protection. It is difficult to validate if a device is correctly programmed as intended. Further, devices are highly vulnerable to a simple piece of exploits since run-time verification of code and data is performed on the uncertain assumption that a verification process may be trustable.

To tackle this limitation, we discuss a feasible design approach, which can confirm a current security state of a device with the existing untrusted components. Our primary contributions can be summarized as two aspects: *i*) we first suggest how firmware verification can be performed by a custom bootloader; and *ii*) we then discuss an MPU-enabled memory protection scheme, which guarantees the reliability of firmware verification by controlling code and data access to the bootloader. In addition, the proposed design approach has been partially implemented and tested as a prototype software modules on devices working with Advanced RISC Machine (ARM) Cortex M3/M4 for checking its validation.

The remainder of this paper is organized as follows. Section II briefly reviews the conventional approaches for maintaining device security. We discuss a new design approach for firmware verification and bootloader protection in Section III. Section IV provides further extensions on the proposed design. Finally, we conclude the paper in Section V.

II. Related Work

Recent lines of research related to device security are reviewed and their issues are discussed in this section.

A. Secure Booting

A built-in Read Only Memory (ROM) is a minimal requirement for designing and implementing secure booting at small-footprint devices. Once some ROMs of MCUs are masked during manufacturing, further modifications are not allowed for bootloader protection [1]. Alternatively, a custom bootloader can be loaded from some blocks of flash memory. However, it is difficult to prevent an accidental erasure or modification of the bootloader and its related configurations and secure materials from unintended access. This directly implies that the genuine of firmware or operating system working at a device cannot be guaranteed.

B. Remote Attestation

To revalidate a programmed firmware at a device, software attestation schemes have been widely proposed [2]. One common assumption is that a remote verifier is trustable and secure communication is established between a prover and a verifier [3]. However, a prover's trustworthiness remains unclear and manipulated checksum functions may not be complicated enough against a guessing attack. Another limitation is that this approach tends to focus on verifying the integrity of working codes only [4]. Moreover, code verification is performed at a pre-defined interval of time in a verifier-driven manner. Therefore, attackers may have more chances to compromise devices.

C. Memory Protection

Sancus [5] is a memory access control scheme based on program counter, so that a new hardware implementation is required as an extension of MCUs. This approach also depends on a specifically modified C compiler and a TCB. Similarly, Smart [6] uses a special hardware-controlled memory for a secure key storage and allows that ROM-resident code only access to the keys. For execution-aware memory protection, TrustLite [7] uses an MPU built in a secure System on a Chip (SoC) and the on-chip memory is required to store MPU configurations. One critical drawback of this scheme is that authenticity and integrity of a secure loader cannot be verified at a booting time.

III. PROTECTED FIRMWARE VERIFICATION

We suggest one feasible design approach to security designers and system programmers for ensuring firmware protection without any hardware modifications.

A. *Memory Construction*

Figure 1 shows an example of memory layout, which is used in the proposed protected firmware verification. In this approach, we assume that the cryptographic computations, such as key derivation, firmware encryption, key wrapping, and signature creation can be completed prior to loading a custom bootloader and a firmware to a flash memory.

To construct such memory layout, two offline processes, such as *i*) encrypting a firmware and *ii*) signing a firmware are required as depicted in Figure 2. In the first phase, a symmetric key generator creates a Firmware Encryption Key (FEK) and we derive a Confidentiality Root Key (CRK) from a given Production Unique Key (PUK). We then encrypt an original firmware image with the FEK and using the derived CRK, we also wrap the FEK based on the Advanced Encryption Standard (AES) [8] for containing the integrity information of FEK. In the latter, an authenticity key generator creates a key pair and compute a firmware signature based on the Elliptical Curve Digital Signature Algorithm (ECDSA) [9]. Through the above steps, we have the encrypted firmware, AES-wrapped FEK, ECDSA public key, and firmware signature as security materials for firmware protection. Those data are finally allocated to flash memory regions.

B. *Bootloader Protection*

Immediately after power-on or reset, the booting code performs an initial system configuration by referring to its header. We assume that a Custom Bootloader (CBL) resides on some memory regions of flash and its code and security materials can be protected by setting lock bits at a flash register. However, locking the booting related memory blocks may not be a strong method of ensuring code and data isolation of the CBL. To mitigate this problem, we adopt a MPU-enabled memory access control to prevent unauthorized access to those memory regions during booting. Moreover, this approach can be applied in protecting code and data memory even after the firmware (i.e., kernel) loading. Due to this reason, the CBL then initializes a MPU according to a predefined policy to protect itself and its related data sections, which are colored in grey during booting sequences and firmware verification as illustrated in Figure 3.

When a Central Processing Unit (CPU) tries to execute a code (i.e., instruction pointer) or access read/write a memory region (e.g., stack), an MPU [10] can enforce these accesses to code and data memory with pre-configured settings. For example, the header, keys, signature, and flash registers can be only accessed by instructions defined in the CBL with a read permission. Moreover, addresses of currently fetched instructions by a CPU core are also checked for validating code regions. It is necessary to define what interrupt handlers can perform hardware processing for booting code; an MPU needs to know which addresses of Static Random Access Memory (SRAM) are allocated to the CBL. These considerations can be made as MPU rules.

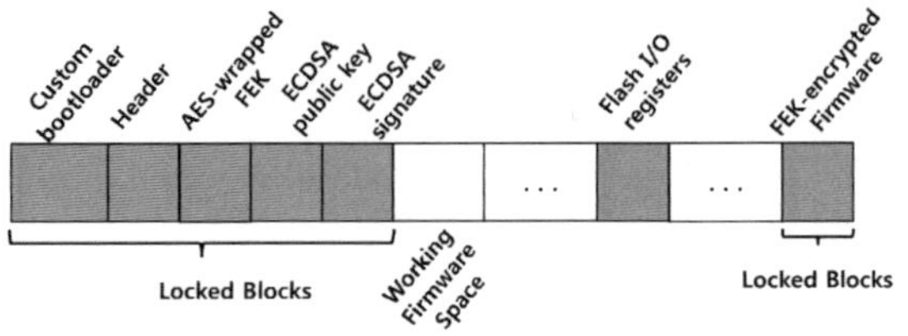

Figure 1. Memory construction for firmware verification

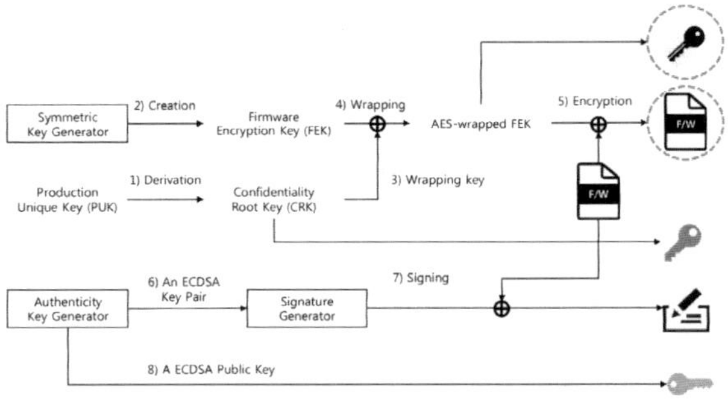

Figure 2. Generation of security materials

C. *Firmware Verification*

If it is confirmed that a CBL is not compromised and an MPU is activated as intended, a CBL can verify a firmware's security state in terms of confidentiality, authenticity, and integrity. The following phases describe how a CBL verifies a firmware only using a One-Time Programmable (OTP) memory under the monitoring of MPU as shown in Figure 3.

i) The CBL tries to obtain a CRK from an OTP memory. An illegal access to a CRK in the OTP memory violates the MPU rules, so that a memory fault can be detected by an MPU. After that the CBL unwraps a FEK based on the AES cryptographic algorithm with the CRK. If the FEK turns out to be available, the CBL can decrypt the protected firmware. The above process is effective to avert firmware cloning.

ii) The CBL calculates a digest value of firmware, which can be compared to the original one in an OTP memory for checking the integrity of decrypted firmware. Further, the firmware digest and an ECDSA public key are utilized to compute a new signature of the decrypted firmware according to the ECDSA. If the generated signature is equal to the contained one (see an ECDSA signature in Figure 1), the CBL accepts that the decrypted firmware is authentic. As a result, the CBL can copy the decrypted firmware to a particular memory space for a working firmware and delegates its control to the working firmware.

In the aforementioned phases, validation of CRK, FEK, and ECDSA public key can be confirmed by a simple hash comparison using an OTP memory. Moreover, the security state of updated firmware can be verified in the same way as above by adding a newly computed ECDSA signature of a new version of firmware into a differencing data package encoded by the VCDIFF standard [11].

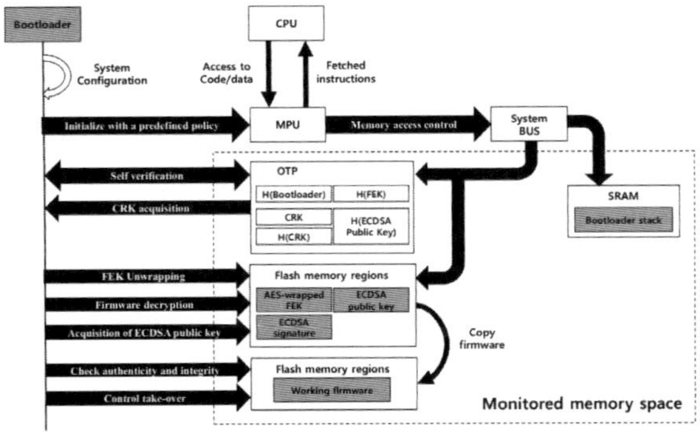

Figure 3. Firmware verification with MPU-enabled bootloader protection

IV. DESIGN EXTENSIONS

This section describes architectural extensions of the proposed protected firmware verification in the following three perspectives.

A. *Kernel Level Support*

Any privileged task can unexpectedly unlock the memory-mapped registers including flash, MPU, etc. Despite this weakness, some operating systems allow that every task is executed with a privileged mode only. For this reason, it is required that kernel separates user mode tasks from system modules and interrupt service routines (ISR). This required feature can be new to some operating systems but is effective to prevent user mode tasks from accessing privileged instructions. Besides, code and stack regions of each task, interrupt handler, and kernel modules must be monitored by an MPU and memory access violation must be handled as well in an appropriate manner. This MPU-enabled memory protection mechanism can guarantee that, a privileged/user task and an interrupt handler can be restricted from removing or modifying boot related memory regions, even after a firmware is loaded.

B. *Secure Memory Loader*

Booting codes can be built and activated in a dedicated mask ROM. In this case, we can replace the custom bootloader on flash with special codes, which is called a Secure Memory Loader (SML). One effective way to improve the execution reliability of security-sensitive codes for the protected firmware verification is to reduce the size of the CBL by excluding booting functionalities. If the SML can be precisely defined and limited, more secure and correct invocation of SML and cryptographic computations are within the realm of possibility. Removing or overwriting a SML is beyond the scope of this paper. However, an external verifier would be a better option rather than using an OTP memory for coping with this vulnerable situation.

C. *Trustworthy Remote Entity*

Custom bootloader's code and data can be attested by a remote verifier to provide an extension option for increased security confirmation if bootstrapping a device must be completed through a trusted server. Besides, a CRK can be received via an end-to-end encrypted network session between a device and a server but this alternative approach would cause more delays than using an OTP memory. After the firmware are loaded, if a memory access violation occurs against the MPU policy, a remote server can exclusively handle such system fault by taking some countermeasures such as remote wipe, network isolation, device recovery, and firmware update.

V. CONCLUSIONS

In this paper, we have suggested a new design approach for protected firmware verification with respect to memory construction, its cryptographic operations, and memory access control. Further extensions as discussed in Section IV will be addressed with respect to implementation and feasibility in our future work.

ACKNOWLEDGMENT

This work was supported by Institute for Information and communications Technology Promotion (IITP) grant funded by the Korea government (MSIT) [2015-0-00508, Development of Operating System Security Core Technology for the Smart Lightweight IoT Devices].

REFERENCES

[1] ATMEL, Application Note, "Atmel AT02333: Safe and Secure Bootloader Implementation for SAM3/4," June, 2013.

[2] Arvind Seshadri et al., "Pioneer: Verifying Code Integrity and Enforcing Untampered Code Execution on Legacy Systems," SOSP'05, pp. 1-16, October 23-26, 2005, United Kingdom.

[3] Y.-H. Moon and Y.-S. Jeon, "A Functional Relationship Based Attestation Scheme for Detecting Compromised Nodes in Large IoT Networks," CUTE'15, vol. 373, pp. 713-721, December 2015.

[4] N. Asokan et al., "SEDA: Scalable Embedded Device Attestation," CCS'15, pp. 964-975, October 12–16, 2015.

[5] J. Noorman et al., "Sancus: Low-cost Trustworthy Extensible Networked Devices with a Zero-software Trusted Computing Base," In USENIX Security Symposium. USENIX, pp. 479-494, 2013.

[6] E. Karim, F. Aurélien, P. Daniele, and T. Gene, "SMART: Secure and Minimal Architecture for (Establishing a Dynamic) Root of Trust,“ NDSS'12, February 5-8, USA.

[7] P. Koeberl, S. Schulz, A.-R. Sadeghi, and V. Varadharajan, "TrustLite: A Security Architecture for Tiny Embedded Devices," EuroSys'14, April 13-16, 2014.

[8] J. Schaad and R. Housley, "Advanced Encryption Standard (AES) Key Wrap Algorithm," Internet Engineering Task Force (IETF), Network Working Group, RFC 3394, September, 2002.

[9] National Institue of Standards and Technology (NIST), FIPS PUB 186-4, Digital Signature Standard (DSS), July 2013.

[10] ATMEL, Application Note, "Atmel AT02346: Using the MPU on Atmel Cortex-M3 / Cortex-M4 Based Microcontrollers," April, 2013.

[11] D. Korn, J. MacDonald, J. Mogul, and K. Vo, "The VCDIFF Generic Differencing and Compression Data Format," Internet Engineering Task Force (IETF), Network Working Group, RFC 3284, June 2002.

A System to Save the Internet from the Malicious Internet of Things at Home

Lukas Braun
Munich University of Applied Sciences
MuSe – Munich IT Security Research Group
Munich, Germany
email: lukas.braun@muse.bayern

Hans-Joachim Hof
Technical University of Ingolstadt
CARISSMA – Center of Automotive Research on Integrated Safety Systems and Measurement Area
Ingolstadt Research Group Applied IT Security Ingolstadt,Germany
email: hof@thi.de

Abstract— **Botnets are a big hassle for the Internet. A recent attack by the Mirai botnet showed how easy it is to exploit Internet of Things devices and use them for malicious activities, e.g., for sending spam or executing Distributed Denial of Service attacks. Hence, increasing protection of Internet of Things (IoT) devices as well as increasing protection against malicious Internet of Things devices is an important challenge. Many of the Internet of Things devices used in the Mirai botnet are located in smart homes (e.g., surveillance cameras). This paper presents a novel smart home security system that raises the bar for an attacker by separating different classes of Internet of Things devices in a smart home from each other, as well as separating other devices within the smart home network (e.g., desktop computers) from Internet of Things devices. Amongst other measures, the smart home security system enforces strict security policies on outgoing communication of Internet of Things devices. By doing so, the proposed smart home security system is able to limit the effect hacked Internet of Things devices in a smart home have on the Internet.**

Keywords- Secure Smart Home; Internet of Things security;

I. INTRODUCTION

In October 2016, a gigantic botnet, the Mirai botnet, was used for various attacks on the Internet. Amongst other things, the Mirai botnet attacked parts of core Internet services, resulting in outages or slow responses from popular websites like Twitter, Spotify, and Reddit [1]. A notable aspect of the Mirai network is that it maliciously uses a large number of IoT devices in smart homes, e.g., DVRs (Digital Video Recorders) and surveillance cameras. The high number of malicious IoT devices allows the Mirai botnet to achieve an attack load of 1.2 Tbps (Terabit per second). Such intensive traffic renders even advanced protection useless mechanisms or makes using them very expensive.

The IoT connects IoT devices with each other and with gateways, infrastructure, and backend services. IoT devices are things from the physical world that are equipped with sensors and/or actuators. As a whole, the IoT extends the cyberspace to the physical world by sensing and acting in the physical world via IoT devices. IoT devices are known for being vulnerable to attacks. A study conducted by HP in 2014 found serious security flaws in IoT devices, e.g., 70% of IoT devices did not encrypt communication to the Internet and local network and 60% of IoT devices raised security concerns with their user interface [2]. IoT devices may be used in different domains and for different applications, e.g., in manufacturing, commercial building automation and the like. This paper focuses on IoT devices used in smart homes by private users. IoT devices for private smart homes often have a low security level due to three reasons: Reason number one is a huge cost pressure on IoT device manufacturers by the market. In such a situation, security, as a non-functional requirement that results in no product feature, may be the number one requirement to be dropped to save money during development of IoT devices. The second reason is the user. Users of IoT devices in private smart homes are usually not well educated regarding IT security. Hence, a thorough security analysis and a rigorous hardening of IoT devices is not expected in this domain. Reason number three is the limited user interface of a typical private smart home IoT device. Security configuration by the user may not be intended because of the lack of a suitable user interface or management protocol. Taking into consideration the low security level of IoT devices in private smart homes, the powerful network connection of smart home, and the missing network based security controls, these IoT devices are valuable attack targets for botnet owners.

The rest of this paper is structured as follows. Section II presents the state of the art in smart home security as well as related work on this topic. Section III presents the reference architecture of the work presented in this paper. The section also states important security requirements the smart home security system presented in this paper must fulfill. Section IV gives an overview on the proposed smart home security system and presents selected aspects in more detail. Section V reports on the ongoing implementation of the prototype. Section VI concludes the paper.

II. STATE OF THE ART IN SMART HOME SECURITY AND RELATED WORK

In a typical private smart home network, mostly two different security methods are used: A firewall runs on the internet gateway (home router) to prevent attacks from the internet and some endpoints are secured using security controls like virus scanners and personal firewalls. However, endpoint security controls are typically only used on desktop computers. Other devices like smart TVs, surveillance cameras, or DVRs usually do not have security controls in place, albeit nowadays these devices are often based on traditional operating systems like Windows or Linux. A typical private smart home network does not implement security controls to monitor or restrict internal network traffic, or to separate devices from each other. Hence, one vulnerable device in a private smart home network may be enough for an attacker to spread malware throughout the network or to hack into other systems. In contrast, many companies are using network-based security controls to separate network traffic, e.g., based on the criticality of the traffic. However, this approach needs an in-depth network engineering that is likely not happening in home networks because the average smart home network owner neither has the necessary experience with secure network nor the willingness to pay for network engineering services. This paper presents a smart home security system that implements advanced network security controls and is suitable for private users. Users do not need special security training to use the smart home security system.

Many existing solutions for smart homes are focused on special aspects or special applications of smart home security, e.g., they focus on smart homes as part of the smart grid [7-10] These solutions are not suitable to protect the Internet from IoT devices in smart homes. Other publications like [13] focus on special network protocols used in current building automation systems, e.g., ZigBee. This paper assumes that IoT devices do not use special communication protocols, but rather are integrated using WiFi. The Universal Home Gateway presented in [11] is a similar approach to smart home security as presented in this paper. However, the approach of [11] is based more on services to be implemented on the home router than on having a smart network filtering available. The smart home security system presented in this paper is compatible with legacy IoT devices, allowing them to also participate in the network. Also, devices being aware of the proposed smart home security system do not need to provide code for services running on a home router as in [11]. They only need to provide a special kind of attribute certificate. Hence, the approach presented in this paper is more flexible.

III. Smart Home Reference Architecture and Smart Home Security Requirements

Figure 1 shows the smart home reference architecture used for the work presented in this paper. It is based on our previous work [3]. The smart home consists of several networks, e.g., a home automation network (e.g., based on Z-Wave, ZigBee, KNX, or any other proprietary home automation protocol), and a home network (based on WiFi or Ethernet). Gateways (GW) may interconnect these networks. The smart home security system presented in this paper is implemented in the home network (based on WiFi or Ethernet) as many recent IoT devices for smart homes support WiFi (at least via a gateway). A home router typically controls the home network. The home router also connects the home network to the Internet. The range of the home router may be extended by so called range extenders (not shown in Figure 1). The reference shows different classes of devices typically used in private smart homes (e.g., smartphones, tablets, home entertainment equipment, household appliances, etc.). These classes are essential for the design of the presented system and are presented in more detail in Section IV.A.

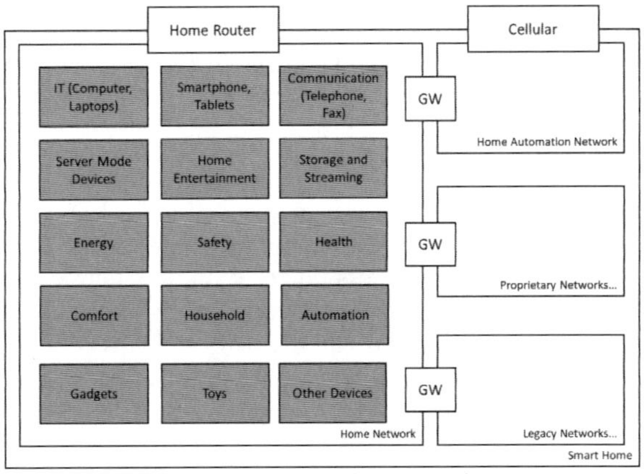

Figure 1. Smart Home Reference Architecture

The following security requirements are considered essential for security in a private smart home implementing the reference architecture:

- R1: IoT devices are only allowed to communicate with intended communication partners.
- R2: IoT devices are assigned to classes based on their application area and communication properties.
- R3: Communication between classes is only allowed based on well-defined security policies.

R1 ensures that IoT devices can only communicate with a known number of external partners. For example, a Sony smart TV may only be allowed to communicate with communication partners in the domain sony.com as well as streaming providers like Netflix. This drastically reduces the number of attackable systems if this IoT device gets hacked. R3 separates IoT devices of different device classes from each other. Together with R2, this enables the definition of generic rules for intra-home network communication. For example, a Playstation 3 in the home entertainment class may only get access to a media server in the storage and streaming class, but no access to devices in the smartphone class, whereas a smart phone from the smart phone class may be allowed to initiate communication with all other device classes for content streaming.

Non-security requirements include usability of the proposed system. Usability is very important in private smart homes as inexperienced users are considered the default users. The system follows the design guides presented in [4-6], especially design guidelines G1 (understandability, open for all users), G3 (no jumping through hoops), G4 (efficient use of user attention and memorization capabilities), G6 (security as default), and G7 (fearless system) are obeyed in design of the smart home security system. Compliance with these guidelines is achieved by automating as many tasks as possible, hence requiring as little user interaction as possible. If smart home IoT devices are aware of the proposed smart home security system, the only user interaction is a confirmation request for the addition of a new device. The rest of the configuration process is hidden from the user. This allows even users that are unexperienced in IT security or even IT to use the proposed smart home security system.

IV. Design of the Smart Home Security System

The home router is the central point for enforcement of security policies for the smart home security system. It enforces network security policies on a per-class and per-device basis. Security policies allow or forbid certain communication partners. They state allowed traffic patterns. Communication partners may, e.g., be described as a class (only intra-home network communication), a domain, a subdomain, or an IP address range. Wildcards may be used (but should be avoided if possible). See Section IV.B for details on the hierarchical ordering used in the definition of communication partners. Using this approach, total transparency is achieved, as all communication partners of IoT devices must be registered at the home router, and the home router can list all communication partners for each device to the user. For example, if an IoT device uses a third party IoT platform and sends data to this platform, it is necessary to state this in the security policy for this device; otherwise, no connection with the IoT platform is possible. Hence, a user buying a device from a German IoT company may learn that this device regularly communicates with servers in mainland China by inspecting the security policies on the home router. Transparency enables the customer to only buy IoT devices that satisfy their privacy needs (e.g., IoT devices that do only communicate with communication partners in Europe, where the General Data Protection Regulation applies).

The attacker model for the proposed smart home security architecture considers IoT devices to be trusted at integration time. Automated detection of malicious IoT device manufacturers is out of scope of this paper. A malicious IoT device manufacturer usually has full control over the IoT device and encrypted communication with the manufacturer is not suspicious (software updates may be an expected feature). Hence, there is not much possibility to detect or avoid such an attack.

A. Classification of Smart Home Devices

During the integration into the network the device get a class assigned and relevant security policies are retrieved. Available classes are described in more detail in Table 1. They are based on currently existing IoT devices in typical smart home use cases.

TABLE I. DEVICE CLASSES

Class	**Example / Description**	**Challenge / properties**
IT	Classical IT devices like computers or laptops	Typical devices in this class are multipurpose, hence it is not possible to describe typical traffic patterns or have a full description of communication partners. As there are typically already many security controls installed (virus scanner, personal firewall, ...), devices in this class are allowed to make generous use of wildcards when stating security policies. However, existing filter lists for websites and the like may be used.
Smartphones, Tablets	Smartphone, tablet	Similar to class "IT". Additional, these devices are often used for remote control of IoT devices or for convenient access to IoT device interfaces. In contrast to devices in the class "IT", smartphones and tablets usually do not offer services to other devices (e.g., no SSH server or media server running on smartphones).
Communication	IP-telephone, fax	Protocols in use are limited to typical protocols for voice-over-IP-communication.
Server Mode Devices	Devices that open a server (e.g., IP-Cameras)	Devices offering services to other devices in the network/Internet. Typically open ports to the Internet.
Home Entertainment	Game console, HiFi system, Smart TV	Typically communicate with entertainment companies (e.g., provider of online games). May be the source of considerable amount of traffic.
Storage and Streaming	Smart TV, NAS	Communicate with streaming services or cloud storage. May causes considerable amount of traffic
Energy	Heater, air condition	Important devices, since they have an influence on well-being of users. Usually do not generate much traffic. May communicate with energy provider (smart grid) or other energy-related services in the Internet.
Safety	Smoke detector, door	Critical devices, since they have an influence on human safety. Usually only communicate in the local network.
Health	Smart toothbrush, smart glucose meter	Class may include some critical devices, since they have an influence on human safety. Only have limited communication to the Internet
Comfort	Bed mattress, massage chair	Rather unimportant devices, no Internet communication.
Household	Fridge, washing machine	Important for everyday life, little Internet communication (e.g., for smart grid purpose to supervise/ control energy usage)
Automation	Devices for automation like "Homee"	Must communicate with a lot of different devices, but limited to communication in the home network.
Gadgets	All kind of gadgets like alarm clock, weather sta-	Difficult to describe the traffic, because many devices with different tasks belong to this class. However, these devices often

	tion	have very limited Internet communication (e.g., only with a weather service).
Toys	Teddy bears, remote controlled car	Rather unimportant devices, usually only with limited Internet communication. No communication with other classes necessary.
Other Devices	Other devices	Difficult to describe the traffic, because many devices with different tasks belong to this class. This class should have strict security policies.

Gateways between legacy/proprietary networks may exist. Gateways are typically used to integrate legacy/proprietary networks into the smart home WiFi network. The smart home security system on the router can not operate inside legacy or proprietary networks, but it can affect the traffic which goes inside and outside the network and passes the router. Gateways get assigned the class that best describes the devices in the legacy/proprietary network.

B. Hierarchical Ordering

The approach presented in this paper asks for the most precise possible description of data traffic and communication partners to be useful. If the description of data traffic is too general, the smart home security system cannot effectively restrict the communication or it erroneously allows traffic. If the description of traffic is too strict, it becomes too complex or would increase the false alarm rate (especially false negatives). As already mentioned, it is hard to describe the set of allowed communication partners for each device. Therefore, a hierarchical ordering is helpful. This ordering enables making decisions on a more abstract level. That means it is possible to state that a device cannot communicate with a device of a special class (e.g., a special toy is not allowed to communicate with household devices, or even that toys can't communicate with health devices at all). The smart home security system uses six hierarchical levels, shown in Table 2.

TABLE II. HIERARCHICAL ORDERING IN A SMART HOME

Level	Name	Description	Categorization	Configured by
6.	**Environment**	Environment	Network	System
5.	**Subnet**	Subnet		
4.	**Class**	Class of device	Classification	
3.	**Type**	Type of device		
2.	**Union**	Union of devices	Device	Manufacturer
1.	**Device**	Single Device		

This ordering allows defining security policies on different levels, e.g.,

- for the whole home network (level 6),
- for a subnet (level 5),
- for different device classes (level 4), for the list of classes (see Table 1),
- types of devices (level 3) like Smart TV or Heater,
- a union of devices (level 2) that make it possible to set up rules for devices of the same manufacturer or same subsystem,
- and a single device itself (level 1).

The levels fall in one of three categories:

- Network (level 5 and 6),
- classes (level 3 and 4), and
- device (level 1 and 2).

Security policies for the levels "network" and "classes" are preconfigured on the home router. These rules originate from the company implementing the smart home security system for the home router and may be extended by third parties, or the owner of the home router.

The "Device" rules originate either from the device itself, from trusted third parties, from a profiling algorithm, or from the user. See Section IV.C for a more detailed description. Table 3 shows an example of the use of the hierarchical levels.

TABLE III. SMART HOME HIERARCHY EXAMPLE

<table>
<tr><td>6</td><td>Environment</td><td colspan="8">Smart Home</td><td>...</td></tr>
<tr><td>5</td><td>Subnet</td><td colspan="7">Subnet 1</td><td>...</td><td></td></tr>
<tr><td>4</td><td>Class</td><td colspan="6">Energy</td><td>...</td><td></td><td></td></tr>
<tr><td>3</td><td>Type</td><td colspan="5">Heater</td><td>...</td><td></td><td></td><td></td></tr>
<tr><td>2</td><td>Union</td><td colspan="2">Company 1</td><td colspan="2">Company 2</td><td>...</td><td></td><td></td><td></td><td></td></tr>
<tr><td>1</td><td>Device</td><td>Heater 1</td><td>Heater 2</td><td>Heater 3</td><td>...</td><td></td><td></td><td></td><td></td><td></td></tr>
</table>

Manufacturers of IoT devices are only allowed to influence security policies on the device levels "union" and "device", and a single device may only influence security policies regarding itself. Hence, a device may define communication from itself to another device, from itself to the network, from the network to itself, from the device to a class of devices and from a class of devices to the device.

Security policies from higher levels overrule security policies at lower levels. That means if a manufacturer of a toy wants to allow communication from the toy to a health device but the communication between toys and health devices is forbidden on the class level, the home router forbids this communication. Security polices should follow the security principle "least privilege". That means that the scope of the permissions of devices should be as limited as much as possible.

C. Integration Process

All relevant security processes take place when a device joins the network. In most home networks, the Dynamic Host Configuration Protocol (DHCP) [14] is used to dynamically assign IP addresses to devices and send additional configuration data. The smart home security system presented in this paper piggybacks on DHCP. The DHCP protocol is executed at every initiation of a device. An ideal sequence, without disturbances, is shown in Figure 2. The home router acts as DHCP-Server. This section gives an overview on different methods for device integration.

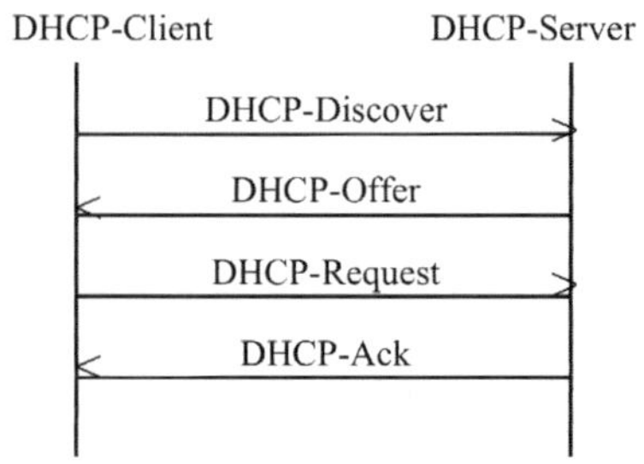

Figure 2. Typical DHCP sequence

1) Integration using Self-descriptions

The self-description approach requires the device's manufacturer to be aware of the system described in this paper. In a nutshell, the device provides a self-description of the intended communication partners of the device as well as a detailed description of traffic patterns produced by this device. Self-descriptions come in the form of attribute certificates and are signed by the device manufacturer. The integration of the device using self-description is nearly fully automatic. In fact, the user is only involved once to ask if a device should really get integrated into the network. This results in good usability of the integration process. The home router company may decide to allow for additional configuration using the home router administrative user interface (e.g., a web application running on the home router).

When a device sends a DHCP-Discovery, the home router takes notice of this device. In the DHCP-Offer, it starts the integration process. When a device gets connected to the home network, it transmits its identification data first, including a firmware version. The following situations can occur:

- A: Device known to home router, firmware version known to home router, signature of self-description valid
- B: Device known to home router, firmware version known to home router, signature of self-description invalid (e.g., signing key no longer valid)
- C: Device known to home router, firmware version not known to home router
- D: Device unknown to home router

In the case of situation A, the home router continues the DHCP protocol and integrates the device into the network. All security policies are enforced. In the case of situations B and C, the home router requests the self-description again. Only self-descriptions from the same manufacturer are accepted and only for the same type of device. The home router validates the possession of the private key associated with the self-description (attribute certificate) to make sure it has been issued for this device. By doing so, the home router ensures that a hacked device could not gain more communication privileges by reusing the self-description of another manufacturer or the self-description of the same manufacturer but for another kind of device. After the integration, all updated security policies are enforced. In the case of situation D, the home router also requests the self-description but self-descriptions of all manufacturers are accepted. As described above, the system presented in this paper assumes a device that is integrated in the smart home network for the first time is to be trusted ("leap of faith"). However, to avoid a hacked device using the self-description of a device from another manufacturer or another device class, the user is queried to confirm that a new device was added to the home network. In all cases, after a successful transmission of the self-descriptions, the allowed communication partners as well as the traffic characteristics are stored in the routers database together with the device identification, device credentials for secure IDs, and the firmware version. Security policies are updated according to the new information and all security policies get enforced.

2) Integration using the built-in scanner

It is very likely that the smart home security system presented in this paper will need an extended period of time to become adapted by all smart home device manufacturers (if ever). The scanner described in this section allows for support of legacy devices as well as support of devices by manufacturers that willingly decide not to support this system. The scanner profiles devices, identifies them, and acquires an appropriate description of allowed communication partners and communication characteristics from trusted third parties. Such trusted third parties are quite common in other security domains, e.g., web filtering or spam detection. If the system cannot obtain the necessary description of a device, manual integration by the user is necessary. The scanner is invoked during the DHCP-protocol if the home router does not receive any self-description of the device. In this case, the user is queried if there really is a new device in the network to prevent an attacker from hacking a device and then trying to trick the scanner to identify the hacked device as a different device than it is. If the user confirmed that there is a new device, the scanning process starts. The home router uses methods from penetration testing to identify characteristics of the device, e.g., it scans for open ports, grabs banners of available services, fingerprints TCP/IP communication, etc. All the resulting characteristics are uploaded to the trusted third party that compares those characteristics to its database of known IoT devices. The third party returns the security policy to apply. If the fingerprinting does not work, the user can select the device with the app via a given list or it would also be imaginable that he is scanning the product code from the packing of the device. If it is successful, the scanner tries to download the identification and communication data from an external data source (manufacturer or trusted third party).

3) Manual integration

The third option is the manual integration of the device by the user via a smartphone app. There are four different ways to do so. W1 is analogous to the scanners alternative, if the fingerprinting does not work. W3 and W4 do not need a traffic profile to integrate the device into the home network.

- W1: The user is asked to enter the type of device, manufacturer, and model. Alternatively, the user scans the product code from the packaging of the device. All associated data is retrieved from a trusted third party, which returns the security policy to apply.
- W2: The user downloads the identification data and communication data manually from the manufacturer's website or trusted third party and imports it.
- W3: The user enters only the type of device and accepts the generic security policy for this type (level 3 in the hierarchy model).
- W4: The user enters the allowed communication partners as well as communication characteristics by hand. It is highly recommended to avoid this approach, as it is error prone.

V. IMPLEMENTATION

The security system for smart homes is currently getting implemented on a standard home router (TP-Link TL-WR841ND) using a Linux distribution for home routers (OpenWRT version Chaos Calmer v15.05.1). The current implementation is a proof-of-concept subset of the security system described in this paper: it solely uses integration by self-description and a feature limited version of traffic descriptors (basically rules for packet-filter firewalls). User interaction uses the administration interface of the home router. Challenges for implementation of the complete security systems for smart homes include handling the complexity of the full syntax traffic descriptors, certificate handling, efficient handling of security policies in the hierarchical model, and reducing memory usage and performance overhead. A major challenge will be an efficient implementation of the scanner for the integration of legacy devices. The scanner will be part of future research, as it also requires more conceptual work.

VI. CONCLUSION

This paper presented a smart home security system with a special focus on IoT devices in smart homes. The smart home security system enforces security policies per class of IoT devices. Such security policy limits the communication of IoT devices to a predefined set of communication partners, and hence protects the Internet from hacked IoT devices. IoT devices from different classes are isolated such that a security incident in one class of devices cannot influence the other devices, thereby limiting the outbreak of an attack. If IoT devices support the smart home security system presented in this paper, only one user interaction is necessary during integration of new devices. There is also a process to integrate legacy devices that requires slightly more user interaction. The proposed security system offers full transparency of communication partners of IoT devices during their integration into the network. This transparency enables consumers to buy only IoT devices that satisfy their security and privacy needs (e.g., by buying only IoT devices communicating with communication partners in countries implementing the General Data Protection Regulation).

REFERENCES

[1] B.Krebs, "DDoS on Dyn Impacts Twitter, Spotify, Reddit", in: "Krebs on Security – In-depth security news and investigation", https://krebsonsecurity.com/2016/10/ddos-on-dyn-impacts-twitter-spotify-reddit/ , October 2016 [accessed 05/23/2017].

[2] Hewlett-Packard Development, "Internet of Things Resarch Study", September 2014.

[3] L. Braun and H.-J. Hof, "Smart Home Security", Poster, Applied Research Conference 2016, Augsburg, Germany, 2016.

[4] H.-J. Hof, "Towards Enhanced Usability of IT Security Mechanisms – How to Design Usable IT Security Mechanisms Using the Example of Email Encryption", International Journal On Advances in Security, volume 6, number 1&2, pp. 78-87 ISSN 1942-2636, 2013.

[5] H.-J. Hof, "User-Centric IT Security – How to Design Usable Security Mechanisms" , The Fifth International Conference on Advances in Human-oriented and Personalized Mechanisms, Technologies, and Services (CENTRIC 2012), pp. 7-12, November 2012.

[6] H.-J. Hof and G. Socher, "Security Design Patterns with Good Usability", 9th ACM Conference on Security and Privacy in Wireless and Mobile Networks (ACM WiSec 2016), Darmstadt, Germany, pp. 227-228, July 2016.

[7] S. Fries and H.-J. Hof, "Secure Remote Access to Home Energy Appliances" in: Lars Torsten Berger, Krzysztof Iniewski, "Smart Grid: Applications, Communications, and Security", John Wiley & Sons, Inc, pp. 443-454, ISBN: 978-1-118-00439-5, 2012.

[8] R. Falk, S. Fries, and H.-J. Hof, "ASIA: An Access Control, Session Invocation and Authorization Architecture for Home Energy Appliances in Smart Energy Grid Environments", in The First International Conference on Smart Grids, Green Communications and IT Energy-aware Technologies (ENERGY 2011), pp. 19-26, ISBN: 978-1-61208-136-6, Mai 2011.

[9] C. Müller, J. Schmutzler, C. Wietfeld, S. Fries, A. Heidenreich, and H.-J. Hof, "ICT Reference Architecture Design based on Requirements for Future Energy Grids", First International Conference on Smart Grid Communications (IEEE SmartGridComm 2010), pp. 315-320, ISBN: 978-1-4244-6510-1, Oktober 2010.

[10] N. Komninos, E. Philippou, and A. Pitsillides, "Survey in Smart Grid and Smart Home Security: Issues, Challenges, and Countermeasures", IEEE Communications Surveys&Tutorials, Vol. 16, No. 4, pp. 1933-1954, 4/2014.

[11] D. Pishva and K. Takeda, "Product-Based Security Model for Smart Home Appliances", IEEE A&E Systems Magazine, pp. 32-41, 10/2008.

[12] B. Schneier, "Lessons From the Dyn DDoS Attack", in "Schneier on Security", https://www.schneier.com/blog/archives/2016/11/lessons_from_th_5.html, November 2016 [accessed 05/23/2017].

[13] Y.Xu, Y. Jiang, C. Hu, L. He, and Y. Cao, "A balanced security protocol of Wireless Sensor Network for Smart Home", Proceedings of 2014 IEEE 12th International Conference on Signal Processing (ICSP), HangZhou, China, pp. 2324-2327, 2014.

[14] R. Droms, "Dynamic Host Configuration Protocol", RFC 2131, https://tools.ietf.org/html/rfc2131, March 1997 [accessed 08/31/2017].

Frictionless Authentication System: Security & Privacy Analysis and Potential Solutions

Mustafa A. Mustafa, Aysajan Abidin, and Enrique Argones Rúa

imec-COSIC KU Leuven
Kasteelpark Arenberg 10, B-3001 Leuven, Belgium
Email: {firstname.lastname}@esat.kuleuven.be

Abstract—**This paper proposes a frictionless authentication system, provides a comprehensive security analysis of and proposes potential solutions for this system. It first presents a system that allows users to authenticate to services in a frictionless manner, i.e., without the need to perform any particular authentication-related actions. Based on this system model, the paper analyses security problems and potential privacy threats imposed on users, leading to the specification of a set of security and privacy requirements. These requirements can be used as a guidance on designing secure and privacy-friendly frictionless authentication systems. The paper also sketches three potential solutions for such systems and highlights their advantages and disadvantages.**

Keywords–Frictionless authentication; Threat analysis; Security and privacy requirements; Threshold signature; Fuzzy extractors.

I. Introduction

The widespread adoption of mobile and wearable devices by users results in more personal information being stored or accessed using Personal Devices (PDs) such as smartphones. In addition to enhancing user experience, this also creates new opportunities for both users and Service Providers (SPs). However, this also brings with it new security and privacy challenges for both users and SPs [1]. Usually, these PDs and wearable devices, from now on named Dumb Devices (DDs), have limited computational and interaction capabilities. Nevertheless, users expect a frictionless user experience (making minimum effort) when using their PDs or DDs to access services or resources. Since these devices are small, light, and easy to carry, they are susceptible to loss and theft, and easier to break. And the use of context information (such as the user's current location, his typical behaviour, etc.), which can easily be accessed from these devices, also triggers privacy concerns. Taking into account the users' needs and the associated security and privacy risks of using such devices, the way users are authenticated and granted access to a wide range of on-line services and content becomes more challenging [2].

The current authentication systems [3]–[7] do not provide a satisfactory answer to address these (conflicting) needs: (i) users prefer a single password-less solution, (ii) wearable devices do not offer convenient authentication interface for passwords, (iii) strong biometric authentication solutions score low on usability, or are not suited for continuous authentication with minimal interaction with the user, (iv) certain risk-based techniques work well for desktop and laptops (e.g., device fingerprints), but fall short on mobile devices, and (v) smartphones and wearables are more prone to loss and theft. Thus, there is a clear need for solutions that are tailored towards the user, his devices, the context and sensitivity of his assets.

In this paper, we propose a Frictionless Authentication System (FAS) that allows users to authenticate themselves using their devices to third party SPs without intentionally performing any authentication-related specific actions. We also analyse the security and privacy implications of such systems and propose three potential solutions. The main contributions of this paper are three-fold.

- Firstly, it proposes a novel FAS that allows secure, privacy-friendly as well as frictionless user experience when a user authenticates to SPs.
- Secondly, it performs a threat analysis of and specifies a set of security and privacy requirements for the FAS.
- Thirdly, it proposes three potential high level solutions to achieve secure and privacy-friendly FAS.

The remainder of this paper is organised as follows: Section II discusses related work. Section III proposes a frictionless authentication system. Section IV analyses potential security threats and attacks to the proposed system. Section V specifies a set of security and privacy requirements. Section VI provides a high-level overview of three potential solutions for a secure and privacy-friendly FAS. Finally, Section VII concludes the paper.

II. Related Work

In contrast to conventional challenge-response protocols which use a single prover and verifier, collaborative authentication schemes use a challenge-response protocol with multiple collaborating provers and a single verifier. To mitigate the threat of PDs/DDs being stolen or lost as well as to support a dynamic set of devices as users may not always carry the same set, threshold-based cryptography is used. Threshold cryptography allows one to protect a key by sharing it amongst a number of devices in such a way that (i) only a subset of the shares with minimal size (a threshold $t + 1$) can use the key and (ii) having access to t or less shares does not leak any information about the key. Shamir [8] first introduced this concept of secret sharing, which was later extended to verifiable secret sharing by Feldman [9]. Pedersen [10] used this concept to construct the first Distributed Key Generation (DKG) protocol. Shoup [11] showed how to transform a standard signature scheme such as RSA into a threshold-based variant. In 2010, Simoens et al. [12] presented a new DKG protocol which allows devices not capable of securely storing secret shares to be incorporated into threshold signature schemes. Peeters et al. [13] proposed a threshold-based distance bounding protocol which also takes into account the

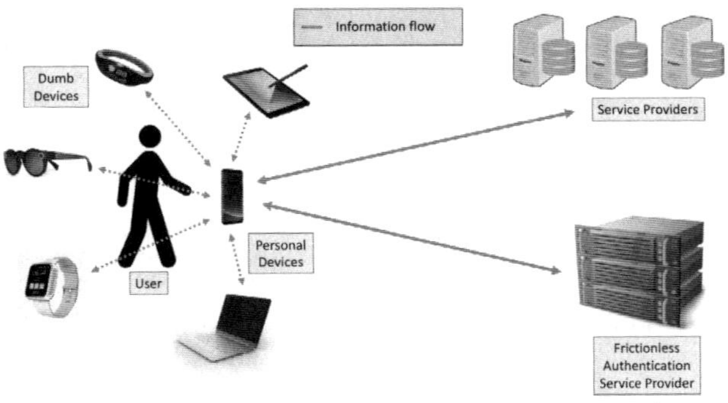

Figure 1. A system model of a FAS.

proximity of devices holding the share to the verifier. An overview of recent developments in continuous authentication schemes is given in [14].

III. Frictionless Authentication System

This section details the system model, functional requirements, and interactions amongst entities of a FAS.

A. A System Model

As shown in Figure 1, a system model of a FAS consists of the following entities. A *user* who wants to access various services provided by different *Service Providers (SPs)*. The user also carries or wears a number of personal or dumb devices which she uses to authenticate herself in a frictionless manner, i.e., without intentionally performing any specific authentication-related actions such as entering a password. *Personal Devices (PDs)* are owned by the user and have a secure storage where their owner's secret data such as (parts of) her private key can be stored. The user communicates with SPs via her PDs. *Dump Devices (DDs)* do not have secure storage. They can communicate with PDs, but not necessarily with the SPs. Usually, DDs are wearable which are not paired with the user, and have sensors. Each PD and DD may have one or more *sensors* integrated to measure different data such as location, gait, blood pressure and heart beats. *SPs* are the entities to which users want to authenticate in order to have access to data or services. Usually, this authentication is done by a user digitally signing a challenge sent by the SP. *Frictionless Authentication Service Provider (FASP)* is the SP that assists users in performing a frictionless authentication.

B. Functional Requirements

To be practical and adopted by users, any FAS should be: *frictionless* - the involvement of the user should be minimum while authenticating to various SPs; *adaptive* - the FASP should be able to tailor the multi-modal and -factor authentication scheme to user content data; *collaborative* - the authentication score (AuthScore), i.e., the score which determines how confident the FASP is that the user is who she is claiming to be, should be constructed based on data provided by multiple user's PDs and/or DDs; *flexible* - AuthScore should be constructable using various combinations of user's data collected by user's PDs/DDs; *robust & resilient* - a failure/lack of a single user device should not require any additional effort by the user; and *compatible* - a user should always be able to use conventional authentication methods if desired or needed.

C. Interactions among Entities

Next, we describe the potential message types and interactions among the entities within the FAS.

1) System setup: the FASP performs all the necessary initial steps in order to assist users experience frictionless authentication service. These steps include obtaining the necessary cryptographic keys and certificates.

2) User device setup/registration: the user obtains or generates a public/private key pair and a certificate for the public key. The entire (or part of the) private key is stored in her PDs.

3) User registration: a user provides the SPs with all the necessary information for the service registration such as user identity, public key and certificate.

4) Frictionless authentication: the user proves her identity to a SP without performing any intentional authentication-related actions. It consists of four steps. *Authentication request:* a user informs a SP that she wants to access data or service provided by the SP, or the SP informs the user that she will have to prove her identity. *Identity verification challenge:* the SP sends a challenge to the user to prove her identity. *User AuthScore calculation:* a user's data gathered by the user's PDs and/or DDs are forwarded (via a single user PD) to the FASP which uses these data to compute the AuthScore of the user. Such calculation could be performed on demand (when requested by the SP) or continuously. If the AuthScore is above a certain predefined threshold, the user's private key becomes available for use. Note that the AuthScore can be computed by the FASP on the cloud or locally on the user's PD. See Section IV-D for more details regarding the choice of where the AuthScore is calculated. *Identity verification response:* the user uses her private key to digitally sign the verification challenge and sends the result to the SP. *User identity verification and service access:* the SP checks the user response and if the verification response holds, it grants the user with access to the requested data or services.

IV. Threat Analysis

We describe the threat model and provide an analysis of the security and privacy threats to the proposed FAS.

A. Threat Model

Users are untrustworthy and malicious. A malicious user might try passively and/or actively to collect and alter the information stored and exchanged within the FAS, in an attempt to gain access to data or services which she does not have permission to access. *PDs are trustworthy (tamper-evident).* We assume that PDs are equipped with security mechanisms to provide access control and protection against data breaches and/or malware. *DDs are untrustworthy.* The data they measure and forward to the FASP might be corrupted. *The FASP is honest-but-curious.* It follows the protocol specification, but it might try to learn and extract unauthorised information about users. *SPs are untrustworthy or even malicious.* They may try to eavesdrop and collect information exchanged within the FAS. Their aim might be to gain access, collect and/or modify information exchanged within a FAS in an attempt to disrupt, and extract confidential information about users, competitors (other SPs) and the FASP itself.

B. Security Analysis

This section analyses the possible security threats to a FAS. The analysis is based on the STRIDE framework [15] which mainly covers security threats.

Spoofing: A malicious entity may attempt to get unauthorised access to services provided by a SP. Such spoofing attacks introduce trust related issues, and may have an economic impact to the SP, especially if the SP provides financial services. Hence, it is important to have thorough user registration procedures and strong mutual authentication.

Tampering with data: A malicious entity may attempt to modify the information stored and/or exchanged within the FAS such as manipulating (i) the data sent from the sensors of a user's devices, (ii) AuthScore and/or (3) user content data such as location. By stating inaccurate information, an adversary may attempt to lower the credibility of users, SPs and the FASP. Therefore, the integrity and authenticity of the data exchanged/stored should be guaranteed.

Information disclosure: A malicious entity may attempt to eavesdrop messages sent within the FAS. By eavesdropping messages one may attempt to retrieve information such as who, when, how often and which services access. Such information is considered as private. Hence, confidentiality of data must be guaranteed. Information disclosure also constitutes a privacy threat to users posing additional risks such as users' profiling.

Repudiation: Disputes may arise when users (do not) access services offered by the SP and claim the opposite. Hence, the non-repudiation of messages exchanged and actions performed by the FAS's entities must be guaranteed, using mechanisms to ensure that disputes are promptly resolved.

Denial-of-Service (DoS): DoS attacks aim to make the FAS inaccessible to specific or all users. An adversary may target a user's PDs/DDs or the FASP in an attempt to make the service unavailable to that specific user or all users, respectively.

Elevation of privilege: An adversary may attempt to gain elevated access to SP resources. For instance, a malicious user may attempt to elevate her privileges from accessing the basic available service to accessing premium service, by, for example, manipulating her AuthScore. Thus, to mitigate these attacks, authorization mechanisms that comply with the principle of least privilege should be deployed.

C. Privacy Analysis

This section analyses the possible privacy threats to a FAS. The analysis is based on the LINDDUN framework [16] which mainly covers privacy threats.

Linkability: An adversary may attempt to distinguish whether two or more Items of Interest (IOI) such as messages, actions and subjects are related to the same user. For instance, an adversary may try to correlate and deduce whether a user has accessed a particular service by a SP at a particular location. Hence, unlikability among IOIs should be guaranteed.

Identifiability: An adversary may attempt to correlate and identify a user from the types of messages exchanged and actions performed within the FAS. For instance, an adversary may try to identify a user by analysing the messages the user exchanges with the SPs. If a user has considerably more PDs/DDs, this may make her more identifiable. Thus, the anonymity and pseudonymity of users should be preserved.

Non-repudiation: In contrast to security, non-repudiation can be used against users' privacy. An adversary may attempt to collect evidence stored and exchanged within the FAS to deduce information about a user. It may deduce whether a user has accessed a particular service at a particular location. Thus, plausible deniability over non-repudiation should be provided.

Detectability: An adversary may try to distinguish the type of IOIs such as messages exchanged amongst FAS entities from a random noise. For instance, an adversary may attempt to identify when a user's PD communicates with a SP. Thus, user undetectability and unobservability should be guaranteed.

Information disclosure: An adversary may eavesdrop and passively collect information exchanged within the FAS aiming at profiling users. For instance, an adversary may attempt to learn the location and availability of a user. Moreover, the user's behaviour may be inferred by a systematic collection of the user's information [17]. For instance, if a SP and/or the FASP collect the data from the user's PDs/DDs and analyse these data, they may infer (i) the user's health related data by collecting their physiological information, (ii) users' activities by analysing the history of service access, and (iii) circles of trust by analysing with whom, when and how often they use the service. Profiling constitutes a high risk for users' privacy. Thus, the confidentiality of information should be guaranteed.

Content Unawareness: A misbehaving FASP may attempt to collect more user information than it is necessary aiming to use such information for unauthorised purposes such as advertisement. For instance, the FASP may only need to know whether a user is eligible to access a service without necessarily the need to identify the user nor the service. Hence, the content awareness of users should be guaranteed.

Policy and Consent Noncompliance: A misbehaving FASP may attempt to collect, store and process users' personal information in contrast to the principles (e.g., data minimisation) described in the European General Data Protection Regulation 2016/680 [18]. For instance, a misbehaving FASP may attempt to (i) collect sensitive information about users such their location, (ii) export users' information to data brokers for revenue without users' consent, and (iii) read users' contacts from their PDs. Thus, privacy policies and consent compliance should be guaranteed.

D. Local versus Cloud-based Frictionless Authentication

The AuthScore, as mentioned earlier, can be computed by the FASP either on the cloud or locally on a PD of a user. The choice will inevitably affect not only the performance of a FAS but also the risk of privacy breaches.

1) Cloud-based AuthScore Calculation: The cloud-based AuthScore calculation requires that all user data gathered by the sensors of the user's PDs/DDs are sent to the cloud where the FASP fuses them to compute the AuthScore of the user. Although outsourcing all the calculations to the cloud should allow the FASP to use more complex fusing algorithms, it also adds an additional risk to users' privacy. As some of these data will be highly user-specific, the confidentiality of these data should be protected. In other words, the communication channels between the user's PD and the FASP servers should be encrypted so that no external entity has access to these data. Also, user's privacy should also be protected from the FASP. Having access to these data may allow the FASP to extract sensitive information about the user, thus profiling users. Ideally, the FASP should not have access to the user data in the cleartext, but operate only with encrypted data. This could be achieved if the user data are encrypted with a cryptographic scheme that supports homomorphic properties such as the Paillier cryptosystem [19]. Moreover, the FASP should not be able to identify the SP to whom the user authenticates. Otherwise, the FASP would be able to track the user online over the different data/services the user accesses.

2) Locally AuthScore Calculation: In contrast to the cloud-based solution, calculating the AuthScore on the user's PD is more privacy-friendly as no user data leave the PD. However, on one hand, given that the computational resources of PDs are usually much lower than the ones of the cloud, the complexity of the fusion algorithm will be limited. On the other hand, as the user data is not sent to the FASP services, the fusing algorithm running on the user's PD could use much more fine-grained user data. Having access to such data should allow the FASP to use less complex fusion algorithms but yet achieve results comparable to the ones achieved with more complex fusion algorithms used in cloud-based AuthScore calculation.

V. SECURITY AND PRIVACY REQUIREMENTS

Based on the threat analysis, this section specifies a set of security and privacy requirements for the proposed FAS.

A. Security Requirements

To mitigate the aforementioned security threats, the following security requirements needs to be satisfied.

Entity Authentication assures to an entity that the identity of a second entity is the one that is claiming to be. It aims to mitigate spoofing attacks.

Integrity ensures that the information stored and exchanged within the FAS have not been altered. It aims to mitigate tampering with data attacks. Integrity is achieved with the use of hash functions, MACs and digital signatures.

Confidentiality ensures that only the intended entities are able to read the user data stored and transferred within the FAS. It aims to mitigate information disclosure attacks. Confidentiality can be achieved with the use of encryption schemes, e.g., symmetric, asymmetric and homomorphic encryption schemes.

Non-repudiation is achieved when an entity cannot deny her action or transaction. It aims to mitigate repudiation attacks (disputes). Non-repudiation can be achieved with the use of digital signatures, timestamps and audit trails.

Availability ensures that the resources of the FAS are available to legitimate users. It aims to mitigate DoS attacks. To safeguard availability, network tools such as firewalls, intrusion detection and prevention systems should be used.

Authorisation ensures that an entity has the correct access. It aims to mitigate elevation of privilege attacks. For authorisation, access control mechanisms, e.g., access control lists and role based access control, should be used, following the principle of least privilege for user accounts.

B. Privacy Requirements

To mitigate the specified privacy threats, the following privacy requirements need to be satisfied.

Unlinkability ensures that two or more IOIs such as messages and actions are not linked to the same user [20]. It aims to mitigate linkability attacks. Unlinkability can be achieved with the use of pseudonyms as in [21], anonymous credentials [22] and private information retrieval [23].

Anonymity ensures that messages exchanged and actions performed can not be correlated to a user's identity. It aims to mitigate identifiability attacks. Anonymity can be achieved using Mix-nets [24] and multi-party computation.

Pseudonymity ensures that a pseudonym is used instead of a user's real identity. As anonymity, it aims to mitigate identifiability attacks. It can be achieved by using unique and highly random data strings as pseudonyms.

Plausible deniability over non-repudiation ensures that an adversary cannot prove that a user has performed a specific action and operation. It aims to mitigate non-repudiation privacy threats. However, non-repudiation service should be provided when necessary such as when a user needs to be hold accountable for cheating and/or misbehaving, as in [25].

Undetectability and unobservability ensures that messages exchanged and actions performed by a user cannot be distinguished from others. It aims to mitigate detectability attacks, and can be achieved by using Mix-nets and dummy traffic [24].

Confidentiality is a privacy requirement too (see Sect. V-A).

Content Awareness aims to raise users' awareness by better informing them of the amount and nature of data they provide the FASP. It aims to mitigate the content unawareness threats, and can be achieved with the use of transparency enhancing technologies, e.g., privacy nudges [26] and dashboards [27].

Policy and consent compliance ensures the compliance of the FAS with legislations, e.g., the European General Data Protection Regulation 2016/680 [18]. It aims to mitigate the policy and consent non-compliance privacy threats, and can be achieved with the use of Data Protection Impact Assessments [28] and Privacy Impact Assessments [29] for the FAS.

VI. POTENTIAL SOLUTIONS

In this section, we propose three possible solutions for a FAS and analyse their pros and cons with respect to their security and privacy properties. The authentication is achieved using a digital signature, wherein the private key is held by the user (i.e., the user device) and the verifier (i.e., the SP) challenges the user to prove that she holds the private key by asking her to sign a challenge. However, the solutions differ from each other in the way the private key is handled.

A. CASE 1: using no Advanced Crypto

1) High-level Description: The first straightforward solution is to password protect the private key. However, this has the obvious drawback of frequent user interaction, as the user has to provide her password every time there is an authentication request. Similarly, protecting the private key using biometrics, e.g., the private key is generated from user biometrics or a local biometric verification is used to grant access to the private key, has the same drawback as the password protected solution. Nevertheless, the user should always be able to authenticate herself using passwords/biometrics. To make it frictionless, one can incorporate behaviometrics/contextual data such as gait, location, or other sensor data. In this case, access to the private key is granted if the behaviometric/contextual data collected from PDs and DDs provide sufficient authentication score; see Figure 2 for a high level description. As can be seen, this solution does not use any advanced cryptographic techniques.

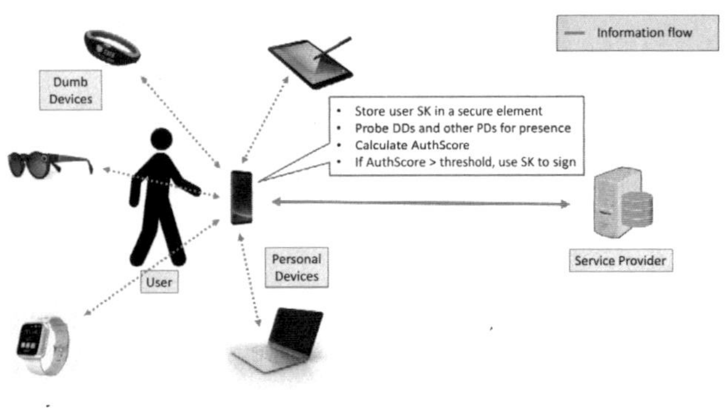

Figure 2. CASE 1: FAS using no advanced crypto.

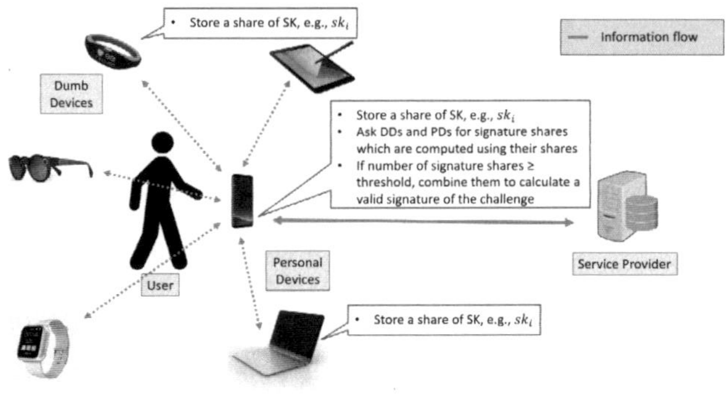

Figure 3. CASE 2: FAS using threshold signature.

2) Advantages: As this solution does not require implementation of any advanced cryptographic algorithms other than the already implemented digital signature algorithm, it is *easy to set-up and implement*. It also has a *simple access control mechanism* as it only requires device presence check and calculation of the AuthScore by matching sensor data.

3) Disadvantages: As the key is stored on a single device, this results in *a single point of failure*. Moreover, there are potentially *higher risks for privacy breach* depending on where the AuthScore is calculated based on the behaviometric/contextual data and whether these data are protected.

B. CASE 2: using Threshold Signature

1) High-level Description: The disadvantages of the previous solution can be addressed by using threshold cryptosystems, in particular, threshold signatures [11], as depicted in Figure 3. In this case, during the enrolment stage, the secret key (i.e., the private key) is shared among the user devices using a threshold secret sharing scheme, so each device stores only a share of the secret key. During the authentication stage, the devices jointly computes a signature on the authentication challenge. In particular, each device computes only one signature share and provides this share to the gateway device, e.g., the user's PD. A valid signature can be computed only if the number of signature shares provided is greater than or equal to a predefined threshold value.

2) Advantages: As the secret key is shared amongst the user devices and never stored as one piece on any user device, *no key is stored as whole*. Furthermore, the key is not even reconstructed. Only if a sufficiently large enough number of shares (more than the predefined threshold) are stolen, then the key can be reconstructed. Also, as the key is not stored in its entirety, this solution has *no single point of failure*.

3) Disadvantages: As threshold signatures are more involved than the traditional digital signatures, they may incur some *performance issues in practice*. In addition, even though the key is never stored as a whole, it can be reconstructed using sufficient number of shares. Therefore, *shares need to be protected*. This might be an issue especially for DDs as they usually do not have the capacity for secure storage, which brings us to our third solution described next.

C. CASE 3: using Threshold Signature and Fuzzy Extractors

1) High-level Description: In the previous solution, shares of the secret key are stored in users' DDs. As these DDs usually do not have secure storage, storing sensitive data on them (i) might be undesirable and (ii) can pose a threat to security of the FAS, in general. To overcome this limitation, one option is to use Fuzzy Extractors (FEs) to allow DDs to recover their shares of the secret key, thus avoiding the storage of sensitive data on DDs (see Figure 4). FEs use noisy data from a source and Helper Data (HD) to recover a fixed discrete representation. Using mechanisms such as the uncoupling procedure presented in [30], where the binary representation bound in the fuzzy commitment is independent of the fuzzy source, it is possible to make a FE to produce a given key, producing HD which does not disclose any information about the produced key. In our case, each DD uses a FE to obtain its corresponding key share, and the HD are stored in the user's PD. During the enrolment stage, a key share and the associated HD is generated for each DD. The key share is discarded, while the HD is stored in the PD. During the authentication stage, the PD provides the DDs with their corresponding HD. Then, DDs use the collected sensory data and the provided HD to recover the corresponding key share by using the FE. This generated key share is then used to jointly sign the challenge.

2) Advantages: The online generation of the key shares during the authentication stage means that *key shares are not stored* at different devices, thus the security threat associated to their storage simply disappears. In addition, *the stored HD is unlinked with the key shares*, thus avoiding information disclosure and improving the security of the system.

3) Disadvantages: This solution relies on the use of FE, where performance issues and the nature of the stored HD have to be taken into account when evaluating the risks. Although the HD is not linked to the produced key shares, *the stored HD is linked to the biometrics/behaviometrics of the user*, thus providing information about the user's biometric data, which could be used to link the user amongst services, or to obtain information useful for spoofing attacks. Therefore, the HD have to be protected and stored in a secure element in the PD. There might also be some *performance issues* as FEs differ from authentication methods based on fixed factors in the associated uncertainty in their outputs. They are subject to possible errors in genuine attempts (False Rejections) and impostor attempts (False Acceptances). In our case, several DDs will collaborate to generate a response, and $t + 1$ of them need to successfully recover their respective share. These considerations should be kept in mind, when generating the HD, to properly decide the working point for different FEs.

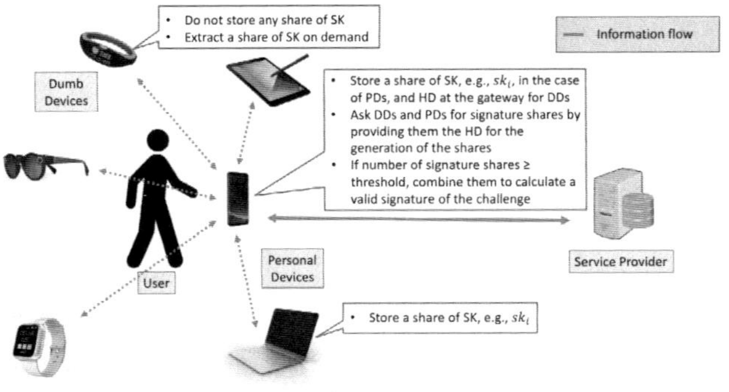

Figure 4. CASE 3: FAS using threshold signature and fuzzy extractors.

VII. Conclusions and Future Work

In this paper we have presented a comprehensive security and privacy analysis of a FAS, starting from a set of functional requirements. Three different approaches for a secure and privacy-friendly FAS have been analysed, integrating possession-based and behavioural authentication factors in a flexible authentication scheme based on threshold signatures. The main advantages and disadvantages of the different approaches have been analysed. Although all the three analysed solutions meet the main security and privacy requirements, we recommend the solution that combines threshold signature with fuzzy extractors, as no key material is stored at user devices. As future work, we will design a concrete protocol for a FAS that combines threshold signature with fuzzy extractors, and evaluate its performance in terms of computational complexity, communication costs, and authentication rates.

Acknowledgment

This work was supported by the Research Council KU Leuven: C16/15/058, the European Commission through the SECURITY programme under FP7-SEC-2013-1-607049 EKSISTENZ, imec through ICON DiskMan, and FWO through SBO SPITE S002417N.

References

[1] S. Sagiroglu and D. Sinanc, "Big data: A review," in Int. Conf. on Collaboration Technologies and Systems (CTS'13), 2013, pp. 42–47.

[2] T. Van hamme, V. Rimmer, D. Preuveneers, W. Joosen, M. A. Mustafa, A. Abidin, and E. Argones Rúa, "Frictionless authentication systems: Emerging trends, research challenges and opportunities," in the 11th International Conference on Emerging Security Information, Systems and Technologies (SECURWARE'17). IARIA, 2017.

[3] A. Bhargav-Spantzel, A. Squicciarini, and E. Bertino, "Privacy preserving multi-factor authentication with biometrics," in the 2nd ACM Workshop on Digital Identity Management (DIM'06), 2006, pp. 63–72.

[4] J. Bonneau, C. Herley, P. C. v. Oorschot, and F. Stajano, "The quest to replace passwords: A framework for comparative evaluation of web authentication schemes," in IEEE Symposium on Security and Privacy (SP'12), 2012, pp. 553–567.

[5] E. Grosse and M. Upadhyay, "Authentication at scale," IEEE Security Privacy, vol. 11, no. 1, Jan 2013, pp. 15–22.

[6] R. P. Guidorizzi, "Security: Active authentication," IT Professional, vol. 15, no. 4, July 2013, pp. 4–7.

[7] D. Preuveneers and W. Joosen, "SmartAuth: dynamic context fingerprinting for continuous user authentication," in the 30th ACM Symposium on Applied Computing (SAC'15), 2015, pp. 2185–2191.

[8] A. Shamir, "How to share a secret," Communications of the ACM, vol. 22, no. 11, 1979, pp. 612–613.

[9] P. Feldman, "A practical scheme for non-interactive verifiable secret sharing," in SFCS '87, ser. SFCS '87, 1987, pp. 427–438.

[10] T. P. Pedersen, "Non-interactive and information-theoretic secure verifiable secret sharing," in CRYPTO'91, ser. LNCS, vol. 576. Springer, 1992, pp. 129–140.

[11] V. Shoup, "Practical threshold signatures," in EUROCRYPT'00, ser. LNCS, vol. 1807. Springer, 2000, pp. 207–220.

[12] K. Simoens, R. Peeters, and B. Preneel, "Increased resilience in threshold cryptography: Sharing a secret with devices that cannot store shares," in International Conference on Pairing-Based Cryptography, ser. LNCS, vol. 6487. Springer, 2010, pp. 116–135.

[13] R. Peeters, D. Singelee, and B. Preneel, "Toward more secure and reliable access control," IEEE Pervasive Computing, vol. 11, no. 3, 2012, pp. 76–83.

[14] V. M. Patel, R. Chellappa, D. Chandra, and B. Barbello, "Continuous user authentication on mobile devices: Recent progress and remaining challenges," IEEE Signal Proc. Mag., vol. 33, no. 4, 2016, pp. 49–61.

[15] Microsoft. The STRIDE threat model. Accessed Aug, 2017. [Online]. Available: https://msdn.microsoft.com/en-us/library/ee823878(v=cs.20).aspx

[16] M. Deng, K. Wuyts, R. Scandariato, B. Preneel, and W. Joosen, "A privacy threat analysis framework: supporting the elicitation and fulfillment of privacy requirements," Requirements Engineering, vol. 16, no. 1, 2011, pp. 3–32.

[17] Uber. New App Features and Data Show How Uber Can Improve Safety on the Road. Accessed July, 2016. [Online]. Available: https://newsroom.uber.com/safety-on-the-road-july-2016/

[18] Regulation 2016/680 of the European Parliament and of the Council. Accessed Aug, 2017. [Online]. Available: http://eur-lex.europa.eu/legal-content/EN/TXT/?uri=uriserv:OJ.L_.2016.119.01.0089.01.ENG

[19] P. Paillier, "Public-key cryptosystems based on composite degree residuosity classes," in EUROCRYPT'99, ser. LNCS, vol. 1592. Springer, 1999, pp. 223–238.

[20] A. Pfitzmann and M. Hansen, "A terminology for talking about privacy by data minimization: Anonymity, unlinkability, undetectability, unobservability, pseudonymity, and identity management (v0.34). tech. rep." pp. 1–98, 2010.

[21] M. A. Mustafa, N. Zhang, G. Kalogridis, and Z. Fan, "Roaming electric vehicle charging and billing: An anonymous multi-user protocol," in IEEE Int. Conf. on Smart Grid Communications, 2014, pp. 939–945.

[22] J. Camenisch and A. Lysyanskaya, "Signature schemes and anonymous credentials from bilinear maps," in CRYPTO'04, ser. LNCS, vol. 3152. Springer, pp. 56–72.

[23] B. Chor, E. Kushilevitz, O. Goldreich, and M. Sudan, "Private information retrieval," Journal of the ACM, vol. 45, no. 6, 1998, pp. 965–981.

[24] D. L. Chaum, "Untraceable electronic mail, return addresses, and digital pseudonyms," Com. of the ACM, vol. 24, no. 2, 1981, pp. 84–90.

[25] I. Symeonidis, A. Aly, M. A. Mustafa, B. Mennink, S. Dhooghe, and B. Preneel, "Sepcar: A secure and privacy-enhancing protocol for car access provision," in the 22nd European Symposium on Research in Computer Security (ESORICS'17), ser. LNCS, vol. 10493. Springer, 2017, pp. 475–493.

[26] Y. Wang, P. G. Leon, K. Scott, X. Chen, A. Acquisti, and L. F. Cranor, "Privacy nudges for social media: an exploratory facebook study," in the 22nd Int. Conf. on World Wide Web (IW3C2'13), 2013, pp. 763–770.

[27] M. Nebel, J. Buchmann, A. Ronagel, F. Shirazi, H. Simo, and M. Waidner, "Personal information dashboard: Putting the individual back in control," Digital Enlightenment, 2013.

[28] E. Commission. Test phase of the Data Protection Impact Assessment (DPIA) Template for Smart Grid and Smart Metering Systems. Accessed Aug, 2017. [Online]. Available: http://ec.europa.eu/energy/en/test-phase-data-protection-impact-assessment-dpia-template-smart-grid-and-smart-metering-systems

[29] D. Wright and P. De Hert, Privacy impact assessment. Springer Science & Business Media, 2011, vol. 6.

[30] A. Abidin, E. Argones Rúa, and R. Peeters, "Uncoupling biometrics from templates for secure and privacy-preserving authentication," in the 22nd Symposium on Access Control Models and Technologies (SACMAT'17). ACM, 2017, pp. 21–29.

Frictionless Authentication Systems: Emerging Trends, Research Challenges and Opportunities

Tim Van hamme, Vera Rimmer, Davy Preuveneers, and Wouter Joosen

imec-DistriNet KU Leuven
Celestijnenlaan 200A, B-3001 Leuven, Belgium
Email: {firstname.lastname}@cs.kuleuven.be

Mustafa A. Mustafa, Aysajan Abidin, and Enrique Argones Rúa

imec-COSIC KU Leuven
Kasteelpark Arenberg 10, B-3001 Leuven, Belgium
Email: {firstname.lastname}@esat.kuleuven.be

Abstract—**Authentication and authorization are critical security layers to protect a wide range of online systems, services and content. However, the increased prevalence of wearable and mobile devices, the expectations of a frictionless experience and the diverse user environments will challenge the way users are authenticated. Consumers demand secure and privacy-aware access from any device, whenever and wherever they are, without any obstacles. This paper reviews emerging trends and challenges with frictionless authentication systems and identifies opportunities for further research related to the enrollment of users, the usability of authentication schemes, as well as security and privacy trade-offs of mobile and wearable continuous authentication systems.**

Keywords–Frictionless authentication; Behaviometrics; Security; Privacy; Usability.

I. INTRODUCTION

Nowadays, the ubiquitous nature of mobile and wearable devices has allowed users to access a multitude of new applications, services and content. More and more personal related information is stored on (or accessed via) personal devices such as smart phones, which enhances users' experience and convenience, and creates new opportunities for both, consumers and service providers. However, such access of multitude applications via personal devices also brings new challenges for service providers that must now secure access from a wide variety of devices [1]. Moreover, there is a continuous growth of mobile malware and other mobile security threats. Thus, it is important these mobile devices to be equipped with reliable means of authentication and authorization.

However, usually, these mobile and wearable devices have limited computational and interaction capabilities. Furthermore, because these devices are small, light, and easy to carry, there is also an associated risk in that they are susceptible to loss and theft, and easier to break. The use of context information (such as the user's current location, his typical behavior, etc.) may also trigger privacy concerns. Moreover, due to the increased prevalence of wearable and mobile applications, users nowadays expect a frictionless customer experience, making minimum effort. Taking into account these characteristics, the way users are authenticated and granted access to a wide range of online services and content becomes more challenging.

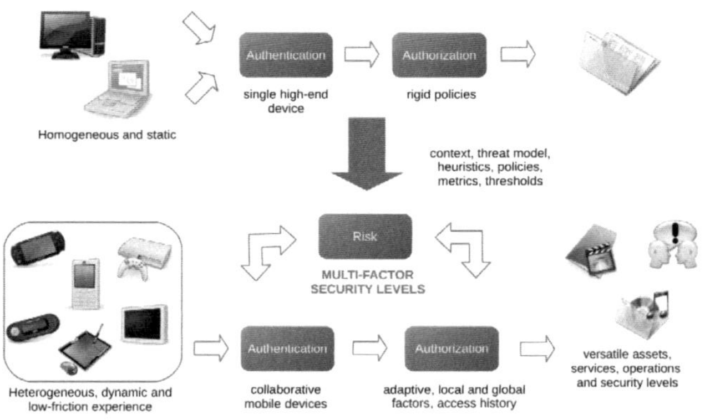

Figure 1. Collaborative, frictionless and adaptive mulfi-factor authentication with many mobile devices.

Ideally, users' devices will jointly and continuously operate in the background to establish the identity of the individual by continuously monitoring the context and detecting unusual deviations, as depicted in Figure 1. The advantage is that this will move the verification of the additional factors away from the user, making it transparent, and thereby greatly improving the convenience for the user, but posing important privacy challenges when sensitive context information is used, the addressing of which is an important aspect. The objective of pursuing a collaborative multi-device approach is that it can be less vulnerable against malicious users or unauthorized access after theft or loss of a device. Systems that support such user experience are called frictionless authentication systems [2].

In this paper we provide an overview of the emerging trends, research challenges and opportunities in such frictionless authentication systems that allow users to authenticate themselves using their devices to service providers without intentionally performing any specific authentication-related actions, such as entering a password.

The rest of this paper is structured as follows. In Section II, we review the current state of practice in mobile and multi-factor authentication, as well as risk-adaptive solutions. Emerging trends on collaborative and behavioral are highlighted in Section III. Section IV reviews challenges and opportunities for further research. We conclude the paper in Section V.

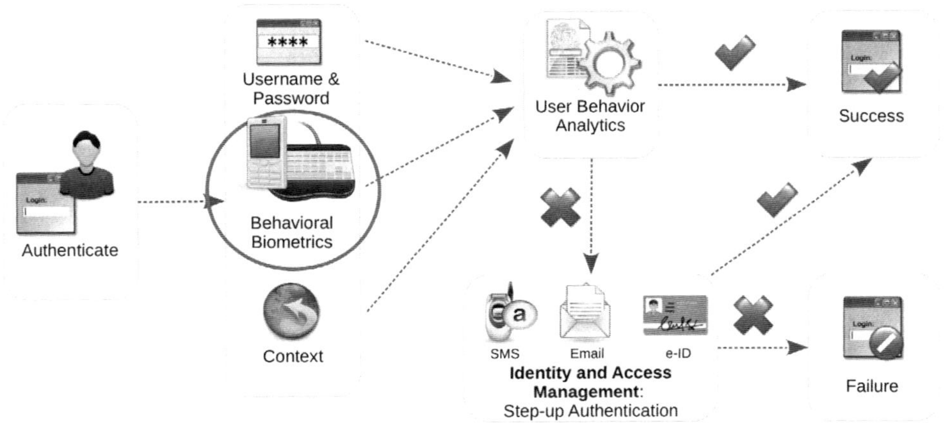

Figure 2. Risk-adaptive step-up authentication leveraging context and behaviometrics adopted within contemporary Identity and Access Management systems.

II. State-of-Practice in Authentication

Before highlighting emerging trends in frictionless authentication systems, we will briefly review current best practices and the state-of-the-art in multi-factor authentication.

A. Mobile and Multi-Factor Authentication

Weak passwords are a major cause of data and security breaches [3]. With dictionary attacks and optimized password cracking tools, users with simple or short (i.e., less than 8 characters) passwords are easy prey, especially if they use the same password for various services. Additionally, complex passwords are difficult to enter on mobile and wearable devices. This illustrates the generally acknowledged conception that passwords are problematic. Therefore, efforts are ongoing to replace password-based authentication with better alternatives [4]–[7]. With multi-factor authentication, users authenticate with a combination of authentication factors, i.e., knowledge, intrinsic (biometrics) and possession. Biometric factors like speaker recognition, fingerprints, iris or retina scans cannot be forgotten, but may require expensive equipment to implement. Furthermore, such solutions require storing biometric templates, which can also be compromised and which are often cumbersome to revoke.

An interesting alternative to multi-factor mobile authentication is the Pico, a concept introduced by Stajano [8]. The Pico is a dedicated hardware token to authenticate the user to a myriad of remote servers; it is designed to be very secure while remaining quasi-effortless for users. The authentication process is based on the use of public-key cryptography and certificates, making common attacks on passwords (such as sniffing, phishing, guessing, and social engineering) impossible. Although being an interesting proposal, an actual implementation is currently lacking.

Leveraging on these recent initiatives, dynamic, multi-factor, collaborative and context-based authentication could further improve the current state-of-the-art on mobile authentication, finding an optimal balance between cost, user-convenience and security and privacy. Early work in this direction was presented in [9] in which the authors presented SmartAuth, a scalable context-aware authentication framework built on top of OpenAM, a state-of-practice Identity and Access Management (IAM) suite (see Figure 2). It uses adaptive and dynamic context fingerprinting based on Hoeffding trees [10] to continuously ascertain the authenticity of a user's identity.

However, existing solutions that exploit context information often depend on a single device. Especially for mobile devices, a simple device or browser fingerprint is hardly unique and can easily be intercepted and spoofed by an attacker [11].

B. Risk-based Access Control and Enabling Technologies

Authentication is a basic building block of practically all business models. As mobile devices and wearables continue to proliferate and become part of the user's expanded computing environment - fundamentally changing the way people access services and content - there is an associated security risk in that these devices are susceptible to loss and theft because they are small, light, and easy to carry.

The latest trend in access control models is Risk-Adaptive Access Control (RAdAC) where access decisions depend on dynamic risk assessments. There is a large body of knowledge on this topic in the scientific literature [12]–[19], and risk-based authentication and access controls are being adopted in contemporary identity and access management solutions, such as SecureAuth IdP 8.0, RSA SecurID Risk-Based Authentication, CA Technologies and ForgeRock's OpenAM 14. Contextual information (device fingerprints, user location, time zone, IP address, time of day and other parameters) is used to evaluate the risk of users attempting to access a resource, but the approach is often based on weighted score functions or meaningless user-defined risk thresholds.

III. Emerging Trends

In this section we provide an overview of the emerging trends in collaborative authentication and behaviometrics.

A. Collaborative Authentication

Authentication means solely based on possession factors bear the risk that the unique possession factor could be lost or stolen, hence compromising the security of the authentication system. Combining these schemes with other authentication factors, such as passwords or PINs, could improve the security, but at the cost of user-friendliness. Furthermore, one still needs to take into account the typical attacks on knowledge-based authentication factors, such as PIN guessing or phishing attacks. An interesting alternative are collaborative authentication schemes, where multiple devices jointly authenticate to a remote server or within a device-to-device setting. To limit the cost, the combination of wearables and the user's smartphone would be preferred. Such collaborative authentication schemes overcome the security problems of using a single possession factor during the authentication process as an adversary would have to steal multiple wearables to successfully impersonate a user, while still offering user-friendliness. Moreover, by using wearables the user is carrying anyhow, one avoids the need of employing external hardware authentication tokens, which could be quite costly.

The concept of collaborative authentication is to transform a challenge-response protocol with a single prover and verifier, to a challenge-response protocol with multiple collaborating provers and a single verifier. To mitigate the threat of wearables being stolen or lost, and the fact that the set of wearables is dynamic (the user is not always carrying the same set of wearables), threshold-based cryptography is used. The aim of threshold cryptography is to protect a key by sharing it amongst a number of entities in such a way that only a subset of minimal size, namely a threshold $t+1$, can use the key. No information about the key can be learnt from t or less shares. Shamir [20] was the first to introduce this concept of secret sharing. Feldman [21] extended this concept by introducing verifiable secret sharing. Pedersen [22] then used this idea to construct the first Distributed Key Generation (DKG) protocol. Shoup [23] showed how signature schemes such as RSA could be transformed into a threshold-based variant.

To increase the resilience in a threshold-based authentication scheme, the number of devices included in the threshold scheme should be maximized. Therefore, Simoens et al. [24] presented a new DKG protocol and demonstrated how this allows wearables not capable of securely storing secret shares to be incorporated. Peeters et al. [25] used this idea to propose a threshold-based distance bounding protocol. A gap that remains to be filled is a threshold-based mobile authentication scheme, where the secret keying material is distributed among a set of personal wearables. For recent developments in continuous authentication, we refer the reader to [26].

B. *Behaviometrics*

A recent trend in the area of continuous authentication is the use of behaviometrics. DARPA hosted the Active Authentication program [27] in which various kinds of behavioral biometrics, i.e., metrics that measure human behavior to recognize or verify the identity of a person, are investigated. Several studies have investigated the application of using behaviometrics in order to provide an authentication method that is (a) *continuous*, during an entire user session, and (b) *non-intrusive*, since the normal user interaction with the system is analyzed. It has been demonstrated that a user identity can be recognized and verified by means of several behaviometrics, such as keystroke dynamics, mouse movements (together with display resolution) [28], gait analysis [29], CPU and RAM usage [30], accelerometer [31] and battery fingerprints of mobile devices [32], stylometry [33], web browsing behavior [34], etc.

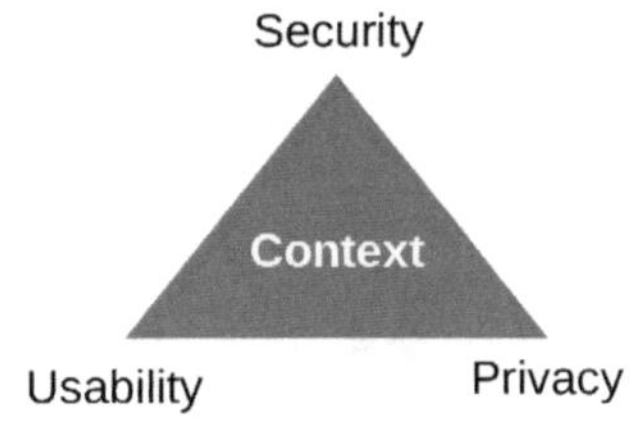

Figure 3. Security, privacy and usability trade-offs in frictionless authentication.

An overview of techniques can be found in these works [35]–[37] and survey [38]. A key challenge will be to investigate which combination of behaviometrics will deliver a sufficient low number of false positives (mistakenly granted access = security concern) and false negatives (mistakenly denied access = user experience concern) such that the risk is acceptable given the circumstances.

IV. CHALLENGES AND OPPORTUNITIES

A frictionless authentication system is a complex system, involving multiple devices and sensors that interact with each other. This complexity makes such systems also a very flexible kind of authentication system. Nonetheless, several challenges and research opportunities remain. Authentication systems are usually characterized by the following interacting dimensions (see Figure 3):

- *Security*, which refers to how difficult it is for an impostor to be falsely authenticated.
- *Usability*, which describes how easy and convenient it is for genuine users to be authenticated.
- *Privacy*, which describes how any private information about the user being used are securely stored and/or processed by the system.

Security and usability are usually a trade-off in most authentication systems. For instance, False Acceptance and False Rejection Rates (FAR and FRR, respectively) are usually depicted in a ROC curve in biometric systems, and the lower the FAR is the higher the FRR is, where FAR is related to security, and FRR is related to usability. Hence, authentication systems are characterized by a specific security-usability trade-off. Regarding privacy, it can be also related to the security and usability of an authentication system. For instance, biometric systems based on protected templates, with a superior privacy protection when compared to their unprotected counterparts, usually provide an inferior set of working points regarding usability and security. In addition, the disclosure of a biometric template can lead to a security problem, unless appropriate revocation mechanisms are incorporated.

Active authentication systems involve multiple devices and sensors that interact with each other. This complexity also makes a frictionless authentication system a very flexible and powerful kind of system, which can be dynamically adapted to different usage scenarios, security-usability trade-offs, and overcome situations in which other types of authentication mechanisms would normally fail. In what follows, we expose different challenges and opportunities related to these three dimensions, *security*, *usability* and *privacy*, and specific to frictionless authentication systems

A. Security

Regarding security, active authentication systems based on multiple behaviometrics and/or biometrics can provide increased security, since they are intrinsically multi-factor, and each employed behavioural modality makes them more difficult to spoof. However, the authentication decision will be based on the outcome of the classification and/or clustering algorithms. Such algorithms are usually not 100% accurate [38], and in some cases the templates must be retrained by discarding old data to account for changes in the user's behaviour. This creates an opportunity for an attacker to impersonate a legitimate user by manipulating input data to compromise the learning process (i.e., a poisoning attack).

A specific security concern in continuous authentication systems is related to the enrollment. The enrollment phase establishes the identity of the subject within the authentication systems. Typically, this is based on credentials or certificates. However, with behavioral and context-dependent authentication, the enrollment phase becomes far more challenging, especially when using a collaborative authentication relying on multiple mobile and wearable devices. In the case of other biometrics, this can be done by ensuring the identity of the user during the enrollment phase by other means. However, since the enrollment in behaviometrics is done in an uncontrolled environment, the enrollment can also pose a threat to security, since it may be easier to inject artificial data to the system. Furthermore, behavioral authentication systems relying on machine learning methods require a time-consuming training step on an individual basis before they become effective.

B. Usability

Regarding usability, the frictionless nature of continuous authentication makes these systems one of the most convenient and easy to use modalities, since the user does not even need to learn how to use the authentication system, and the authentication process is transparent, potentially providing a smooth user experience. Furthermore, the availability of different sensors and modalities opens the opportunity to provide a very flexible authentication mechanism, where the system can implement different security/usability trade-offs for controlling the access to different functionalities or services. However, this also poses a challenge regarding the design of template protection techniques, since this flexibility may increase significantly the complexity of the system.

C. Privacy

Another key challenge with frictionless authentication systems is addressing the privacy concerns which arise when user behaviour analytics on sensitive data is used to continuously authenticate against online services. *Honest but curious* service providers can use the keystrokes – collected for behavioral authentication purposes – to reconstruct the original text typed by the users. In addition, accelerometer data could be used by the same kind of adversary to reconstruct the whole history of a user's location. Furthermore, continuous authentication can also use physiological biometric measurements, whose implications regarding privacy are well known. Hence, employing the adequate biometric template protection mechanisms and appropriately imposing data minimality principles in the system design is even more important in continuous authentication.

V. Conclusions

There is a continuous quest for stronger authentication systems that at the same time offer a frictionless experience towards users of mobile and wearable devices. Context and behavioral information are nowadays being adopted in the enterprise marketplace as part of an adaptive authentication strategy that better serves the needs of the mobile consumer in diverse situational circumstances. However, irrespective of the technological advances to have multiple mobile and wearable devices collaborate to authenticate a user, the adoption of frictionless authentication will only be successful when the right balance between usability, security and privacy can be found that meets the demands of a diverse set of users.

Acknowledgements

This work was partially supported by the Research Council KU Leuven: C16/15/058. In addition, it was also funded by FWO through SBO SPITE S002417N and imec through ICON DiskMan. DiskMan is a project realized in collaboration with imec. Project partners are Sony, IS4U and Televic Conference, with project support from VLAIO (Flanders Innovation and Entrepreneurship).

References

[1] S. Sagiroglu and D. Sinanc, "Big data: A review," in International Conference on Collaboration Technologies and Systems (CTS 2013), May 2013, pp. 42–47.

[2] M. A. Mustafa, A. Abidin, and E. Argones Rúa, "Frictionless authentication system: Security & privacy analysis and potential solutions," in the 11-th International Conference on Emerging Security Information, Systems and Technologies (SECURWARE 2017). IARIA, 2017.

[3] M. Jakobsson and M. Dhiman, The Benefits of Understanding Passwords. New York, NY: Springer New York, 2013, pp. 5–24.

[4] A. Bhargav-Spantzel, A. Squicciarini, and E. Bertino, "Privacy preserving multi-factor authentication with biometrics," in Proceedings of the Second ACM Workshop on Digital Identity Management, ser. DIM '06. New York, NY, USA: ACM, 2006, pp. 63–72.

[5] J. Bonneau, C. Herley, P. C. v. Oorschot, and F. Stajano, "The quest to replace passwords: A framework for comparative evaluation of web authentication schemes," in Proceedings of the IEEE Symposium on Security and Privacy, ser. SP '12. Washington, DC, USA: IEEE Computer Society, 2012, pp. 553–567.

[6] E. Grosse and M. Upadhyay, "Authentication at scale," IEEE Security Privacy, vol. 11, no. 1, Jan 2013, pp. 15–22.

[7] R. P. Guidorizzi, "Security: Active authentication," IT Professional, vol. 15, no. 4, July 2013, pp. 4–7.

[8] F. Stajano, Pico: No More Passwords! Berlin, Heidelberg: Springer Berlin Heidelberg, 2011, pp. 49–81.

[9] D. Preuveneers and W. Joosen, "Smartauth: Dynamic context fingerprinting for continuous user authentication," in Proceedings of the 30th Annual ACM Symposium on Applied Computing, ser. SAC '15. New York, NY, USA: ACM, 2015, pp. 2185–2191.

[10] P. Domingos and G. Hulten, "Mining high-speed data streams," in Proceedings of the Sixth ACM SIGKDD International Conference on Knowledge Discovery and Data Mining, ser. KDD '00, 2000, pp. 71–80.

[11] J. Spooren, D. Preuveneers, and W. Joosen, "Mobile device fingerprinting considered harmful for risk-based authentication," in Proceedings of the Eighth European Workshop on System Security, ser. EuroSec '15. New York, NY, USA: ACM, 2015, pp. 1–6.

[12] J. Li, Y. Bai, and N. Zaman, "A fuzzy modeling approach for risk-based access control in ehealth cloud," in 12th IEEE International Conference on Trust, Security and Privacy in Computing and Communications, July 2013, pp. 17–23.

[13] I. Molloy, L. Dickens, C. Morisset, P.-C. Cheng, J. Lobo, and A. Russo, "Risk-based security decisions under uncertainty," in Proceedings of the Second ACM Conference on Data and Application Security and Privacy, ser. CODASPY '12. New York, NY, USA: ACM, 2012, pp. 157–168.

[14] R. A. Shaikh, K. Adi, and L. Logrippo, "Dynamic risk-based decision methods for access control systems," Computers and Security, vol. 31, no. 4, 2012, pp. 447 – 464.

[15] Q. Ni, E. Bertino, and J. Lobo, "Risk-based access control systems built on fuzzy inferences," in Proceedings of the 5th ACM Symposium on Information, Computer and Communications Security, ser. ASIACCS '10. New York, NY, USA: ACM, 2010, pp. 250–260.

[16] D. R. d. Santos, C. M. Westphall, and C. B. Westphall, "A dynamic risk-based access control architecture for cloud computing," in 2014 IEEE Network Operations and Management Symposium (NOMS), May 2014, pp. 1–9.

[17] "An adaptive risk management and access control framework to mitigate insider threats," Computers and Security, vol. 39, 2013, pp. 237 – 254. [Online]. Available: http://www.sciencedirect.com/science/article/pii/S0167404813001119

[18] H. Khambhammettu, S. Boulares, K. Adi, and L. Logrippo, "A framework for risk assessment in access control systems," Computers & Security, vol. 39, 2013, pp. 86 – 103.

[19] S. Kandala, R. Sandhu, and V. Bhamidipati, "An attribute based framework for risk-adaptive access control models," in 6th International Conference on Availability, Reliability and Security, Aug 2011, pp. 236–241.

[20] A. Shamir, "How to share a secret," Communications of the ACM, vol. 22, no. 11, 1979, pp. 612–613.

[21] P. Feldman, "A practical scheme for non-interactive verifiable secret sharing," in SFCS '87, ser. SFCS '87, 1987, pp. 427–438.

[22] T. P. Pedersen, "Non-interactive and information-theoretic secure verifiable secret sharing," in CRYPTO'91, ser. LNCS, vol. 576. Springer, 1992, p. 129140.

[23] V. Shoup, "Practical threshold signatures," in Advances in Cryptology–EUROCRYPT 2000. Springer, 2000, pp. 207–220.

[24] K. Simoens, R. Peeters, and B. Preneel, "Increased resilience in threshold cryptography: Sharing a secret with devices that cannot store shares," in International Conference on Pairing-Based Cryptography, ser. LNCS, vol. 6487. Springer, 2010, pp. 116–135.

[25] R. Peeters, D. Singelee, and B. Preneel, "Toward more secure and reliable access control," IEEE Pervasive Computing, vol. 11, no. 3, 2012, pp. 76–83.

[26] V. M. Patel, R. Chellappa, D. Chandra, and B. Barbello, "Continuous user authentication on mobile devices: Recent progress and remaining challenges," IEEE Signal Processing Magazine, vol. 33, no. 4, 2016, pp. 49–61.

[27] R. P. Guidorizzi, "Security: active authentication," IT Professional, vol. 15, no. 4, 2013, pp. 4–7.

[28] P. X. de Oliveira, V. Channarayappa, E. O'Donnel, B. Sinha, A. Vadakkencherry, T. Londhe, U. Gatkal, N. Bakelman, J. V. Monaco, and C. C. Tappert, "Mouse movement biometric system," Proc. CSIS Research Day, 2013.

[29] T. V. hamme, D. Preuveneers, and W. Joosen, "Improving resilience of behaviometric based continuous authentication with multiple accelerometers," in Data and Applications Security and Privacy XXXI - 31st Annual IFIP WG 11.3 Conference, DBSec 2017, Philadelphia, PA, USA, July 19-21, 2017, Proceedings, 2017, pp. 473–485.

[30] I. Deutschmann, P. Nordström, and L. Nilsson, "Continuous authentication using behavioral biometrics," IT Professional, vol. 15, no. 4, 2013, pp. 12–15.

[31] T. van Goethem, W. Scheepers, D. Preuveneers, and W. Joosen, "Accelerometer-based device fingerprinting for multi-factor mobile authentication," in Engineering Secure Software and Systems - 8th International Symposium, ESSoS 2016, London, UK, April 6-8, 2016. Proceedings, 2016, pp. 106–121.

[32] J. Spooren, D. Preuveneers, and W. Joosen, "Leveraging battery usage from mobile devices for active authentication," Mobile Information Systems, vol. 2017, 2017, pp. 1 367 064:1–1 367 064:14.

[33] K. Calix, M. Connors, D. Levy, H. Manzar, G. MCabe, and S. Westcott, "Stylometry for e-mail author identification and authentication," Proceedings of CSIS Research Day, Pace University, 2008, pp. 1048–1054.

[34] M. Abramson and D. W. Aha, "User authentication from web browsing behavior," DTIC Document, Tech. Rep., 2013.

[35] M. Karnan, M. Akila, and N. Krishnaraj, "Biometric personal authentication using keystroke dynamics: A review," Applied Soft Computing, vol. 11, no. 2, 2011, pp. 1565 – 1573.

[36] I. Deutschmann, P. Nordstrm, and L. Nilsson, "Continuous authentication using behavioral biometrics," IT Professional, vol. 15, no. 4, July 2013, pp. 12–15.

[37] H. Saevanee, N. L. Clarke, and S. M. Furnell, Multi-modal Behavioural Biometric Authentication for Mobile Devices. Berlin, Heidelberg: Springer Berlin Heidelberg, 2012, pp. 465–474.

[38] L. Wang, Behavioral Biometrics for Human Identification: Intelligent Applications. IGI Global, 2009.

International Academy, Research,
and Industry Association (IARIA)
412 Derby Way
Wilmington, DE 19810

ISBN 978-1-5108-5136-8

CURRAN ASSOCIATES INC.
proceedings.com